H · O · L · T

PHYSICAL SCIENCE

TEACHER'S EDITION

WILLIAM L. RAMSEY
LUCRETIA A. GABRIEL
JAMES F. McGUIRK
CLIFFORD R. PHILLIPS
FRANK M. WATENPAUGH

HOLT, RINEHART AND WINSTON, PUBLISHERS
New York · Toronto · Mexico City · London · Sydney · Tokyo

THE AUTHORS

WILLIAM L. RAMSEY
Former Head of the Science Department
Helix High School
La Mesa, California

CLIFFORD R. PHILLIPS
Former Head of the Science Department
Monte Vista High School
Spring Valley, California

LUCRETIA A. GABRIEL
Science Consultant
Guilderland Central Schools
Guilderland, New York

FRANK M. WATENPAUGH
Former Chairman, Science Department
Helix High School
La Mesa, California

JAMES F. McGUIRK
Head of the Science Department
South High Community School
Worcester, Massachusetts

EDITORIAL DEVELOPMENT: Karen Kennedy Gotimer, Lorraine Smith-Phelan
PRODUCT MANAGER: Tom Rooney
FIELD ADVISORY BOARD: Max Callahan, Robert Davis, James Dellisanti, Debbie Deruy, Jim Donatelli, John Eskew, Joseph Hammond, Dave Miller, Robert Moore, Stuart Natof, Barbara Orloff, George Rybak, Marion Stewart, L. Jean Slankard
MARKETING RESEARCH: Erica S. Felman
EDITORIAL PROCESSING: Margaret M. Byrne, Pamela K. Caugherty
ART AND DESIGN: Carol Steinberg, Amy Newberg
PRODUCTION: Judy Baller, Nina R. West, Sandra Moore
PHOTO RESOURCES: Linda Sykes, Anita Dickhuth

Picture Credits appear on page 564.
Cover photograph by NASA

About the Cover:
Astronaut Bruce McCandless flies the MMU (manned maneuvering unit) during the February 1984 flight of the orbiter *Challenger.* The image of a human being floating free in space illustrates the scientific curiosity that leads men and women out of the laboratory and into new and often hostile environments in search of knowledge about the universe. This photograph also illustrates the close relationship between science and technology.

Printed in the United States of America

ISBN: 0-03-001928-1

56789 039 987654321

CONTENTS

INTRODUCTION

Rationale

HOLT PHYSICAL SCIENCE consists of an introductory chapter (Chapter 1: What Is Science?) followed by 20 chapters organized into six units. The first three units deal with the study of physics. The last three units are concerned with chemistry. Each unit consists of three or four chapters. Chapter Goals at the beginning of each chapter define the learning objectives for that chapter. The chapters are divided into sections, which also have their own objectives that are tested at the end of each section. The consistent section format is beneficial in the following ways:

(1) It encourages student independence and frees the teacher to aid slower students.
(2) It can easily be adapted for various methods of teaching.
(3) It increases success and enjoyment for students of all ability levels.
(4) It provides optional Investigations and Skill-Building Activities that can be used in a variety of ways. If the facilities are available, a laboratory-oriented course can be built around these features.

The authors and editors have devoted particular attention to the readability of HOLT PHYSICAL SCIENCE. The manuscript was tested by the Fry and Dale-Chall reading formulas. In addition, and perhaps more importantly, the text is written in an interesting and lucid style that students will find easy to read.

Components

The optional components that accompany HOLT PHYSICAL SCIENCE include:

- Annotated Teacher's Edition of the student text.
- Teacher's Resource Book containing Review Exercises, Skills Exercises, Enrichment Exercises, Laboratories, Text Blackline Masters, Extension Blackline Masters, Overhead Transparency Masters, and Tests.
- Pupil's Edition of Exercises and Investigations containing the Review, Skills, and Enrichment Exercises and Laboratories in consumable form.
- Teacher's Edition of Exercises and Investigations.
- Test Masters containing Chapter, Midterm, and Final Tests in the form of duplicating masters.

Field Testing

The HOLT PHYSICAL SCIENCE program first appeared in 1978. It has been tested in schools around the country. These schools represent a range of locations from urban to rural. For the present edition, comments and suggestions from classroom teachers presently using the program, as well as from teachers who reviewed the manuscript, have been incorporated. Content-area specialists also reviewed the manuscript.

How to Use the Annotated Teacher's Edition

The annotated Teacher's Edition for HOLT PHYSICAL SCIENCE contains the following information:

- Introduction: The rationale and components of the program are described. Reduced pages of the student text are reproduced, highlighting features.
- Teaching Strategies: This section contains a chart listing suggested components to use in

a one-module (30-minute class period), two-module (55- to 60-minute class period), or three-module (90-minute class period) course.

- Safety in the Science Classroom: This section provides useful and practical information on the very important topic of safety in science. Guidelines are given for safety in the classroom, in the laboratory, and on field trips. References, safety equipment suppliers, and audiovisual aids are also listed.
- The Exceptional Student in the Science Class: Suggestions are offered for the effective instruction of exceptional students in the regular classroom.
- Writing a Science Research Report: This section includes specific suggestions and guidelines that students should follow when writing (1) a library research report or (2) a laboratory report.
- Basic Science Skills: This section is designed to help teachers in the development of students' reading and writing skills. These skills are essential to the study of science as well as other subject areas. A description of the skills covered is provided. Math skills, which are particularly important in the study of physical science, are also included.
- Materials List: The materials necessary to do the Investigations and Skill-Building Activities are listed along with quantities needed and the sections in which they are used. A list of equipment and materials suppliers is also provided.
- Teacher Commentary: The chapter-by-chapter commentary includes an easy reference chart that lists section numbers and titles, approximate time needed, basic science skills covered, a pacing guide, and a list of audiovisual, print, and computer materials. The commentary itself consists of a Chapter Overview, section background and motivation, hints for performing Investigations and Skill-Building Activities and answers to questions, suggestions for special features, and answers to Chapter Review Questions.
- Teacher Annotations: In addition to the commentary, marginal annotations for the teacher are found throughout this Teacher's Edition. The annotations are divided into the following categories:

  Answers to text questions: Provide answers to questions asked within the body of the text.

  Word study: Emphasizes the importance of prefixes, suffixes, and roots in science words.

  Reinforcement: Suggests different ways to present content for the benefit of students who may be slow learners.

  Enrichment: Provides additional facts and information for advanced students.

  Skills: Identifies particular skills covered in the text.

  Suggestion: Provides tips to help the teacher clarify the concepts for the students.

TEXT FEATURES

CHAPTER 11

All of the electronics for a simple computer can be put on one silicon chip. This chip is called a microprocessor. Microprocessors are used in many different kinds of electronic machines.

USING ELECTRICITY

CHAPTER OPENER PHOTOGRAPH Each chapter begins with an exciting full-page photograph and descriptive caption. These high-interest photos immediately focus students' attention on the subject of the chapter.

CHAPTER GOALS A list of Chapter Goals clearly tells the students what they will learn in the chapter. These goals are tested in the Chapter Review at the end of the chapter.

SECTION FORMAT Each chapter is divided into several self-contained sections. The first section begins immediately following the Chapter Goals. The easy to follow format helps promote individualized study.

OBJECTIVES Each section starts with a list of section objectives, which tells the students what they will learn in that section. These performance objectives are an aid to individualized study and reduce the need for teacher direction.

MOTIVATION A short, intriguing motivational paragraph introduces the concept developed in the section.

MARGINAL DEFINITIONS New science words are defined in the text margin to aid student comprehension and to help build a working scientific vocabulary. These words are also printed in boldface type in the text, where they are introduced and used in context.

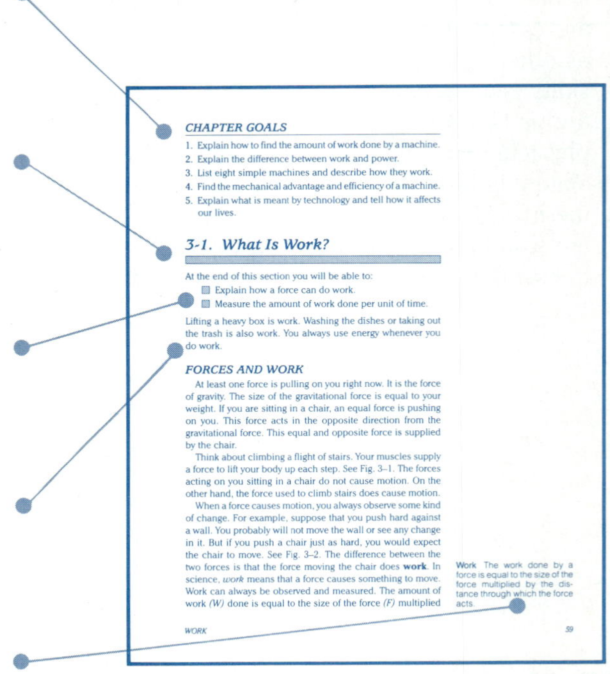

CHAPTER GOALS

1. Explain how to find the amount of work done by a machine.
2. Explain the difference between work and power.
3. List eight simple machines and describe how they work.
4. Find the mechanical advantage and efficiency of a machine.
5. Explain what is meant by technology and tell how it affects our lives.

3-1. What Is Work?

At the end of this section you will be able to:

- Explain how a force can do work.
- Measure the amount of work done per unit of time.

Lifting a heavy box is work. Washing the dishes or taking out the trash is also work. You always use energy whenever you do work.

FORCES AND WORK

At least one force is pulling on you right now. It is the force of gravity. The size of the gravitational force is equal to your weight. If you are sitting in a chair, an equal force is pushing on you. This force acts in the opposite direction from the gravitational force. This equal and opposite force is supplied by the chair.

Think about climbing a flight of stairs. Your muscles supply a force to lift your body up each step. See Fig. 3–1. The forces acting on you sitting in a chair do not cause motion. On the other hand, the force used to climb stairs does cause motion.

When a force causes motion, you always observe some kind of change. For example, suppose that you push hard against a wall. You probably will not move the wall or see any change in it. But if you push a chair just as hard, you would expect the chair to move. See Fig. 3–2. The difference between the two forces is that the force moving the chair does **work**. In science, *work* means that a force causes something to move. Work can always be observed and measured. The amount of work *(W)* done is equal to the size of the force *(F)* multiplied

Work The work done by a force is equal to the size of the force multiplied by the distance through which the force acts.

WORK 59

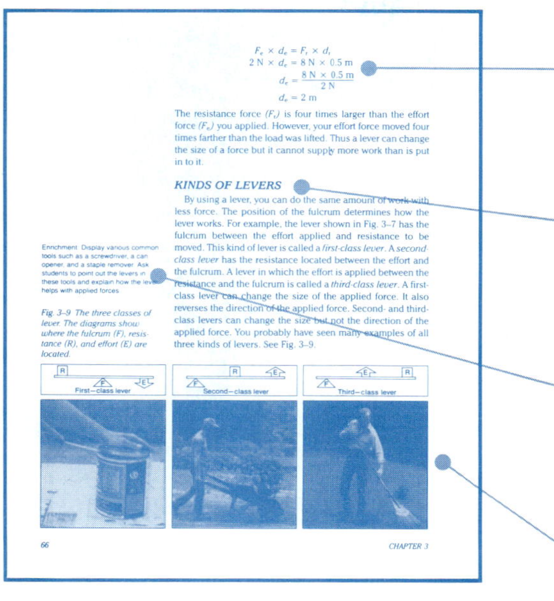

$$F_e \times d_e = F_r \times d_r$$
$$2\text{ N} \times d_e = 8\text{ N} \times 0.5\text{ m}$$
$$d_e = \frac{8\text{ N} \times 0.5\text{ m}}{2\text{ N}}$$
$$d_e = 2\text{ m}$$

The resistance force (F_r) is four times larger than the effort force (F_e) you applied. However, your effort force moved four times farther than the load was lifted. Thus a lever can change the size of a force but it cannot supply more work than is put in to it.

KINDS OF LEVERS

By using a lever, you can do the same amount of work with less force. The position of the fulcrum determines how the lever works. For example, the lever shown in Fig. 3–7 has the fulcrum between the effort applied and resistance to be moved. This kind of lever is called a *first-class lever*. A *second-class lever* has the resistance located between the effort and the fulcrum. A lever in which the effort is applied between the resistance and the fulcrum is called a *third-class lever*. A first-class lever can change the size of the applied force. It also reverses the direction of the applied force. Second- and third-class levers can change the size but not the direction of the applied force. You probably have seen many examples of all three kinds of levers. See Fig. 3–9.

Enrichment: Display various common tools such as a screwdriver, a can opener, and a staple remover. Ask students to point out the levers in these tools and explain how the lever helps with applied forces.

Fig. 3–9 The three classes of lever. The diagrams show where the fulcrum (F), resistance (R), and effort (E) are located.

66 CHAPTER 3

MATH DEVELOPMENT Easy to follow sample problems are worked out in the text to help students develop math skills and to reinforce concepts.

SUBHEADS Concise subheads appear throughout the section. They can serve as a quick reference or study guide to help students review the section.

TEACHER ANNOTATIONS Throughout the text, helpful annotations provide answers to questions, highlight skills development, and give teachers useful and interesting suggestions for enhancing concept development.

DIAGRAMS AND PHOTOS Illustrations that are attractive as well as functional aid in concept development and reinforce the main ideas of the section.

Appliance	Typical Wattage
Color television	300 W
Hair dryer	1,000 W (1 kW)
Refrigerator	400 W
Toaster	750 W
Range/oven	3,000 W (3 kW)
Vacuum cleaner	500 W

Table 11–2

Enrichment: Have students calculate the hourly cost of operating various electrical appliances.

Most electric appliances have labels attached, telling how many watts of electricity they use. See Fig. 11–13. Table 11–2 shows the typical wattage of some common appliances. At $0.12 per kilowatt hour, how much would it cost to run each appliance for two hours? In order to find the cost of operating an appliance, first multiply its wattage times the number of hours it is used. This gives you the number of watt hours. Then divide this result by 1,000 to find the number of kilowatt hours. Multiply the number of kilowatt hours by the amount the electric company charges per kilowatt hour. For example, if electricity costs $0.12 per kilowatt hour, a 300-W television set operating for five hours would cost:

$$300\text{ W} \times 5\text{ h} = 1{,}500\text{ Wh}$$
$$\frac{1{,}500\text{ W h}}{1{,}000\text{ W/kW}} = 1.5\text{ kWh}$$
$$1.5\text{ kWh} \times \$0.12/\text{kWh} = \$0.18$$

SUMMARY

Electricity is one of the most commonly used forms of energy. It is useful mainly because it can be changed into other forms of energy so easily. Electricity can also be sent over long distances. It is supplied in a home by several low-voltage circuits connected to the power lines. Each circuit must be protected from overloads.

QUESTIONS

Use complete sentences to write your answers.

1. A transformer is needed in the electric power system to your house. Explain why this is so.
2. Discuss the reason why parallel circuits are used in the wiring of your home.
3. Electric circuits in your home have safety devices to protect them. What are these devices called? What do they do? Where are these devices in your home?
4. Where is the electric meter in your home located? What does it measure?
5. In your own words, state at least five safety rules you should follow in using electricity in your home.

1 The electricity is delivered at a dangerously high voltage on the power poles. A transformer is needed to lower the voltage to that used in your home. (110 volts is most common.)
2 Parallel circuits are used in homes so that an overload on one circuit won't cause a blackout. They also give a constant voltage that wouldn't be available if series wiring were used.
3 The safety devices are called circuit breakers (or fuses). They keep the wiring from overloading and becoming hot. Students should know where fuses or circuit breakers are located.
4 Locations will vary. The electric meter measures the number of kilowatt hours of electric energy delivered to the home.
5 (1) Do not touch electrical appliances while in water. (2) Do not touch electrical appliances while also touching a metal pipe. (3) Do not touch wires on power poles. (4) Do not put metal objects into electrical outlets. (5) Do not use appliances with worn electric cords. (6) Never overload an electrical outlet by plugging several appliances into it.

274 CHAPTER 11

TABLES AND GRAPHS Information is often presented in the form of visually appealing charts and graphs.

SUMMARY A brief paragraph at the end of the section reviews the main ideas of the section and reinforces concept development.

QUESTIONS Several end-of-section questions provide a self-test of the section objectives and encourage students to practice their writing skills.

INVESTIGATIONS Most sections are followed by an optional laboratory Investigation, which emphasizes the development of good lab techniques and safety procedures. The easy to follow format facilitates the writing of lab reports.

INVESTIGATION

See teacher's commentary for teaching tips, safety, and answers to questions.

MEASURING GRAVITATIONAL ACCELERATION

PURPOSE: You will find a value for the acceleration caused by gravity by using the period of a pendulum.

MATERIALS:
string, 1.5 m long
eraser or rubber stopper
watch with second hand
metric ruler

0.5m

Fig. 2–25

PROCEDURE:
A. Set up a pendulum. See Fig. 2–25.
B. Copy the following table.

Trial	Length (l)	Time (t)	Swings	Period (T)

C. Pull the eraser 10 cm to one side and release it.
D. Count the number of complete swings the eraser makes in 60 seconds. Record.
E. Find the period (T) of your pendulum. This is the number of seconds needed to complete one swing:

$$T = \frac{60 \text{ seconds}}{\text{number of swings}}$$

Record.
F. Repeat steps C through E at least three times. Find the average period of your pendulum.
G. Find the value of the gravitational acceleration (g). Use the following formula:

$$g = 4\pi^2 l/T^2$$

In this formula, π = 3.14, l = length of pendulum, T = period of pendulum.

CONCLUSIONS:
1. What is the acceleration caused by gravity in your classroom?
2. Suppose you did this experiment on top of a high mountain. Would the value of g be different? Explain.

54 CHAPTER 2

SKILL-BUILDING ACTIVITY These Activities follow the same format as the Investigations while focusing on basic science skills such as measuring, observing, classifying, hypothesizing, comparing and contrasting, and finding cause and effect.

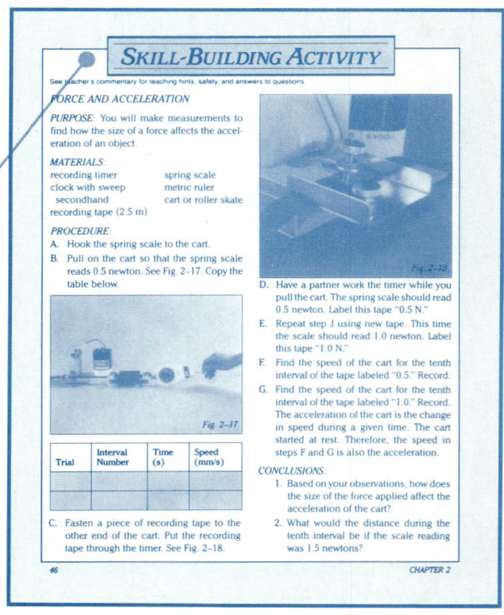

SKILL-BUILDING ACTIVITY

See teacher's commentary for teaching hints, safety, and answers to questions.

FORCE AND ACCELERATION

PURPOSE: You will make measurements to find how the size of a force affects the acceleration of an object.

MATERIALS:
recording timer
clock with sweep secondhand
recording tape (2.5 m)
spring scale
metric ruler
cart or roller skate

PROCEDURE:
A. Hook the spring scale to the cart.
B. Pull on the cart so that the spring scale reads 0.5 newton. See Fig. 2–17. Copy the table below.

Fig. 2–17

Trial	Interval Number	Time (s)	Speed (mm/s)

C. Fasten a piece of recording tape to the other end of the cart. Put the recording tape through the timer. See Fig. 2–18.

Fig. 2–18

D. Have a partner work the timer while you pull the cart. The spring scale should read 0.5 newton. Label this tape "0.5 N."
E. Repeat step J using new tape. This time the scale should read 1.0 newton. Label this tape "1.0 N."
F. Find the speed of the cart for the tenth interval of the tape labeled "0.5." Record.
G. Find the speed of the cart for the tenth interval of the tape labeled "1.0." Record. The acceleration of the cart is the change in speed during a given time. The cart started at rest. Therefore, the speed in steps F and G is also the acceleration.

CONCLUSIONS:
1. Based on your observations, how does the size of the force applied affect the acceleration of the cart?
2. What would the distance during the tenth interval be if the scale reading was 1.5 newtons?

46 CHAPTER 2

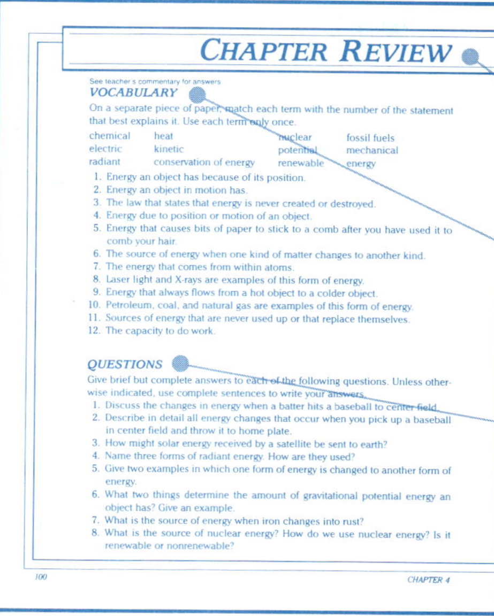

CHAPTER REVIEW

See teacher's commentary for answers

VOCABULARY

On a separate piece of paper, match each term with the number of the statement that best explains it. Use each term only once.

chemical	heat	nuclear	fossil fuels
electric	kinetic	potential	mechanical
radiant	conservation of energy	renewable	energy

1. Energy an object has because of its position.
2. Energy an object in motion has.
3. The law that states that energy is never created or destroyed.
4. Energy due to position or motion of an object.
5. Energy that causes bits of paper to stick to a comb after you have used it to comb your hair.
6. The source of energy when one kind of matter changes to another kind.
7. The energy that comes from within atoms.
8. Laser light and X-rays are examples of this form of energy.
9. Energy that always flows from a hot object to a colder object.
10. Petroleum, coal, and natural gas are examples of this form of energy.
11. Sources of energy that are never used up or that replace themselves.
12. The capacity to do work.

QUESTIONS

Give brief but complete answers to each of the following questions. Unless otherwise indicated, use complete sentences to write your answers.

1. Discuss the changes in energy when a batter hits a baseball to center field.
2. Describe in detail all energy changes that occur when you pick up a baseball in center field and throw it to home plate.
3. How might solar energy received by a satellite be sent to earth?
4. Name three forms of radiant energy. How are they used?
5. Give two examples in which one form of energy is changed to another form of energy.
6. What two things determine the amount of gravitational potential energy an object has? Give an example.
7. What is the source of energy when iron changes into rust?
8. What is the source of nuclear energy? How do we use nuclear energy? Is it renewable or nonrenewable?

100 CHAPTER 4

CHAPTER REVIEW The two-page Chapter Review tests student recall of the chapter concepts in several ways.

VOCABULARY Students are asked to match the science words introduced in the chapter with their definitions or to use them in context.

QUESTIONS The Chapter Goals are tested by a series of problems or essay questions that also give students a chance to practice their writing skills.

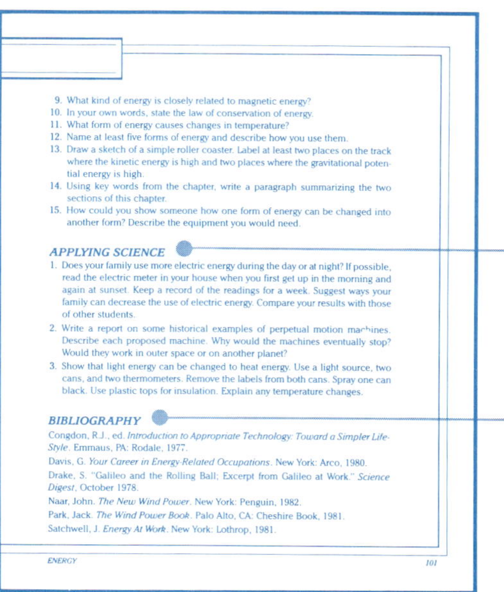

9. What kind of energy is closely related to magnetic energy?
10. In your own words, state the law of conservation of energy.
11. What form of energy causes changes in temperature?
12. Name at least five forms of energy and describe how you use them.
13. Draw a sketch of a simple roller coaster. Label at least two places on the track where the kinetic energy is high and two places where the gravitational potential energy is high.
14. Using key words from the chapter, write a paragraph summarizing the two sections of this chapter.
15. How could you show someone how one form of energy can be changed into another form? Describe the equipment you would need.

APPLYING SCIENCE

1. Does your family use more electric energy during the day or at night? If possible, read the electric meter in your house when you first get up in the morning and again at sunset. Keep a record of the readings for a week. Suggest ways your family can decrease the use of electric energy. Compare your results with those of other students.
2. Write a report on some historical examples of perpetual motion machines. Describe each proposed machine. Why would the machines eventually stop? Would they work in outer space or on another planet?
3. Show that light energy can be changed to heat energy. Use a light source, two cans, and two thermometers. Remove the labels from both cans. Spray one can black. Use plastic tops for insulation. Explain any temperature changes.

BIBLIOGRAPHY

Congdon, R.J., ed. *Introduction to Appropriate Technology: Toward a Simpler Life-Style*. Emmaus, PA: Rodale, 1977.

Davis, G. *Your Career in Energy-Related Occupations*. New York: Arco, 1980.

Drake, S. "Galileo and the Rolling Ball; Excerpt from Galileo at Work." *Science Digest*, October 1978.

Naar, John. *The New Wind Power*. New York: Penguin, 1982.

Park, Jack. *The Wind Power Book*. Palo Alto, CA: Cheshire Book, 1981.

Satchwell, J. *Energy At Work*. New York: Lothrop, 1981.

ENERGY 101

APPLYING SCIENCE Students are given an opportunity to explore beyond the scope of the chapter development. Applying Science may involve experiments that can be done at home, consumer-related problems, library research, or written reports.

BIBLIOGRAPHY A list of relevant books and magazine articles is provided to encourage further student reading on topics of interest.

TEXT FEATURES

CONTINUED

SPECIAL FEATURES Three categories of special features are found throughout the text. They are Careers in Science, Technology, and ¡Compute!

CAREERS IN SCIENCE These one-page features highlight an interesting assortment of possible careers in physical, earth, and life science.

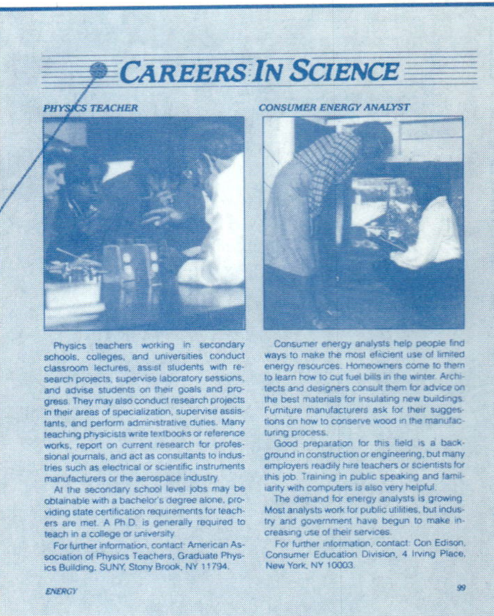

CAREERS IN SCIENCE

PHYSICS TEACHER

Physics teachers working in secondary schools, colleges, and universities conduct classroom lectures, assist students with research projects, supervise laboratory sessions, and advise students on their goals and progress. They may also conduct research projects in their areas of specialization, supervise assistants, and perform administrative duties. Many teaching physicists write textbooks or reference works, report on current research for professional journals, and act as consultants to industries such as electrical or scientific instruments manufacturers or the aerospace industry.

At the secondary school level jobs may be obtainable with a bachelor's degree alone, providing state certification requirements for teachers are met. A Ph.D. is generally required to teach in a college or university.

For further information, contact: American Association of Physics Teachers, Graduate Physics Building, SUNY, Stony Brook, NY 11794.

CONSUMER ENERGY ANALYST

Consumer energy analysts help people find ways to make the most efficient use of limited energy resources. Homeowners come to them to learn how to cut fuel bills in the winter. Architects and designers consult them for advice on the best materials for insulating new buildings. Furniture manufacturers ask for their suggestions on how to conserve wood in the manufacturing process.

Good preparation for this field is a background in construction or engineering, but many employers readily hire teachers or scientists for this job. Training in public speaking and familiarity with computers is also very helpful.

The demand for energy analysts is growing. Most analysts work for public utilities, but industry and government have begun to make increasing use of their services.

For further information, contact: Con Edison, Consumer Education Division, 4 Irving Place, New York, NY 10003.

ENERGY 99

TECHNOLOGY The Technology features focus on new and exciting research topics and on technological applications of basic science.

TECHNOLOGY

COMPUTER GRAPHICS

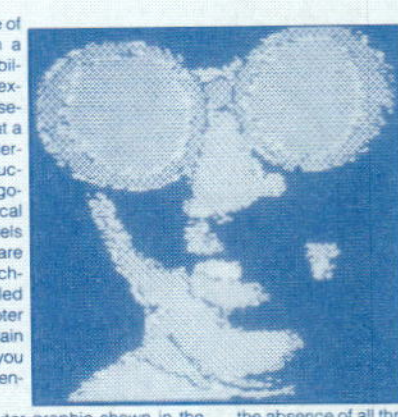

The art and science of creating images with a computer lies in the ability to translate form, texture, and color into a series of instructions that a computer can understand. These instructions are called algorithms or mathematical models. These models and others like them are explained in the Technology Feature called "Digitization" in Chapter 12. Here we will explain the nature of what you see in a computer-generated picture.

Look at the computer graphic shown in the photo. Notice the squarish and jagged edges of the image. Most graphics programs currently in use contain pictures with squared or jagged edges. They do not produce smooth, rounded images because of the method by which the video screen produces its image. The screen is made up of picture elements called "pixels." These are rows and columns of squares similar to the boxes in a crossword puzzle. Just as the directions for the crossword tell what letter goes into each box, so the instructions for the computer tell what color goes into each pixel. The picture, or computer graphic, is made by filling in all the boxes on the screen. The number of pixels on a screen determines how round or square the graphic will be. The greater the number of pixels on the screen, the more realistic the picture is. This same principle applies to different kinds of print. Look at a picture in this book, then look at a picture on the front page of a newspaper. The book picture is clearer, the objects are more defined. To find out why, look at each again with a magnifying glass. There are more dots and fewer spaces in the book. The newspaper picture is printed with 60 dots of ink per square inch. But the textbook picture is printed with 120 dots of ink per square inch.

To add color to an image, the computer mixes what is called a palette from the three primary colors with red, blue, and green sources of light. Black is, of course, the absence of all three. The palette is stored as information in the memory of the computer.

Computer graphics are being used for a number of purposes, video games being only one of them. Advertising is currently the heaviest user of computer graphics and may continue to be for some time. They are also used to produce charts, graphs, and illustrated tables and simulations in business, medicine, the military, and education. They are used by the military for what are called "simulations." (A simulation is a model or game that resembles the actual thing very closely.) Science fiction and fantasy films are also making heavy use of this technology as well. With computer graphics they can create worlds that would be very expensive (or impossible) to actually manufacture or engineer.

What will the future bring? Suppose a computer could produce a perfect picture of you standing either next to the President of the United States or at the scene of a crime. Then could we still say seeing is believing?

COLOR 227

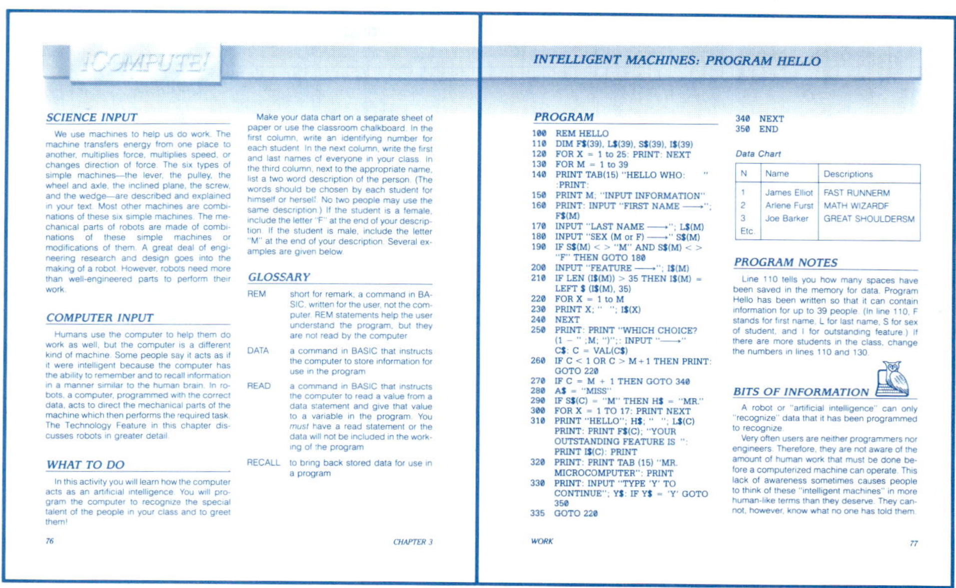

¡COMPUTE!

SCIENCE INPUT

We use machines to help us do work. The machine transfers energy from one place to another, multiplies force, multiplies speed, or changes direction of force. The six types of simple machines—the lever, the pulley, the wheel and axle, the inclined plane, the screw, and the wedge—are described and explained in your text. Most other machines are combinations of these six simple machines. The mechanical parts of robots are made of combinations of these simple machines or modifications of them. A great deal of engineering research and design goes into the making of a robot. However, robots need more than well-engineered parts to perform their work.

COMPUTER INPUT

Humans use the computer to help them do work as well, but the computer is a different kind of machine. Some people say it acts as if it were intelligent because the computer has the ability to remember and to recall information in a manner similar to the human brain. In robots, a computer, programmed with the correct data, acts to direct the mechanical parts of the machine which then performs the required task. The Technology Feature in this chapter discusses robots in greater detail.

WHAT TO DO

In this activity you will learn how the computer acts as an artificial intelligence. You will program the computer to recognize the special talent of the people in your class and to greet them!

Make your data chart on a separate sheet of paper or use the classroom chalkboard. In the first column, write an identifying number for each student. In the next column, write the first and last names of everyone in your class. In the third column, next to the appropriate name, list a two word description of the person. (The words should be chosen by each student for himself or herself. No two people may use the same description.) If the student is a female, include the letter "F" at the end of your description. If the student is male, include the letter "M" at the end of your description. Several examples are given below.

GLOSSARY

REM — short for remark; a command in BASIC, written for the user, not the computer. REM statements help the user understand the program, but they are not read by the computer.

DATA — a command in BASIC that instructs the computer to store information for use in the program.

READ — a command in BASIC that instructs the computer to read a value from a data statement and give that value to a variable in the program. You *must* have a read statement or the data will not be included in the working of the program.

RECALL — to bring back stored data for use in a program.

76 CHAPTER 3

INTELLIGENT MACHINES: PROGRAM HELLO

PROGRAM

```
100  REM HELLO
110  DIM F$(39), L$(39), S$(39), I$(39)
120  FOR X = 1 to 25: PRINT: NEXT
130  FOR M = 1 to 39
140  PRINT TAB(15) "HELLO WHO:     "
     :PRINT:
150  PRINT M; "INPUT INFORMATION"
160  PRINT: INPUT "FIRST NAME ——→";
     F$(M)
170  INPUT "LAST NAME ——→"; L$(M)
180  INPUT "SEX (M or F) ——→" S$(M)
190  IF S$(M) < > "M" AND S$(M) < >
     "F" THEN GOTO 180
200  INPUT "FEATURE ——→"; I$(M)
210  IF LEN (I$(M)) > 35 THEN I$(M) =
     LEFT $ (I$(M), 35)
220  FOR X = 1 to M
230  PRINT X; "  "; I$(X)
240  NEXT
250  PRINT: PRINT "WHICH CHOICE?
     (1 - " ;M; ")";: INPUT "——→"
     C$: C = VAL(C$)
260  IF C < 1 OR C > M+1 THEN PRINT:
     GOTO 220
270  IF C = M + 1 THEN GOTO 340
280  A$ = "MISS"
290  IF S$(C) = "M" THEN H$ = "MR."
300  FOR X = 1 TO 17: PRINT NEXT
310  PRINT "HELLO"; H$; "  "; L$(C)
     PRINT: PRINT F$(C); "YOUR
     OUTSTANDING FEATURE IS  ":
     PRINT I$(C): PRINT
320  PRINT: PRINT TAB (15) "MR.
     MICROCOMPUTER": PRINT
330  PRINT: INPUT "TYPE 'Y' TO
     CONTINUE"; Y$: IF Y$ = 'Y' GOTO
     350
335  GOTO 220
340  NEXT
350  END
```

Data Chart

N	Name	Descriptions
1	James Elliot	FAST RUNNERM
2	Arlene Furst	MATH WIZARDF
3	Joe Barker	GREAT SHOULDERSM
Etc.		

PROGRAM NOTES

Line 110 tells you how many spaces have been saved in the memory for data. Program Hello has been written so that it can contain information for up to 39 people. (In line 110, F stands for first name, L for last name, S for sex of student, and I for outstanding feature.) If there are more students in the class, change the numbers in lines 110 and 130.

BITS OF INFORMATION

A robot or "artificial intelligence" can only "recognize" data that it has been programmed to recognize.

Very often users are neither programmers nor engineers. Therefore, they are not aware of the amount of human work that must be done before a computerized machine can operate. This lack of awareness sometimes causes people to think of these "intelligent machines" in more human-like terms than they deserve. They cannot, however, know what no one has told them.

WORK 77

¡COMPUTE! These highly motivating two-page features encourage students to explore the use of computers in life, earth, and physical science.

TEACHING STRATEGIES

HOLT PHYSICAL SCIENCE is intended to be used as a one-year course in physical science. However, the flexibility of its design allows it to be used as part of a survey course in conjunction with HOLT LIFE SCIENCE and HOLT EARTH SCIENCE.

When used alone, the HOLT PHYSICAL SCIENCE program can be adapted to class periods of approximately 30, 60, or 90 minutes. The table below recommends which components of the program to use for a 30-minute class period (1 module), a 55- to 60-minute class period (2 modules), or a 90-minute class period (3 modules).

It should also be noted that, following Chapter 1, the units of HOLT PHYSICAL SCIENCE can be taught in any order without discontinuity. However, it is recommended that the sequence of units and chapters appearing in the text be followed.

PART OF COURSE	1 MODULE	2 MODULES	3 MODULES
Text	All sections except the Investigations	All sections	All sections
Skill-Building Activities	Most	All	All
Investigations	As time allows	As many as equipment permits	All
Chapter Review Questions	All	All	All
Applying Science	As time allows	All	All with some discussion
Demonstrations	Occasional use	As suggested	Maximum effort with discussion
Exercises and Investigations	Occasional use	Regular use (not every day)	Daily use

SAFETY IN THE SCIENCE CLASSROOM

Students have a right to learn how to think scientifically and solve problems through the active use of scientific processes. Students should have ample opportunities to engage in scientific work through laboratory and other "hands-on" activities. However, unless safety precautions are taken to protect the students and others during the performance of certain science activities, science programs could eventually be considered too dangerous to be included as part of our school curricula.

The responsibility for safety and the enforcement of safety regulations and laws in the science classroom and laboratory are those of the principal, teacher, and student—each assuming his or her share. This means that proper attitudes toward safety should be developed from the outset. The information contained in this section is designed to aid in accomplishing this end. This information is not intended to be all-inclusive, but it is designed to alert teachers to potential hazards, to provide suggestions for averting potential dangers, and to list resources for obtaining additional information.

It is imperative that teachers pass along the proper attitude toward safety to their students. To aid in student understanding of the seriousness of safety in the science classroom, students may be required to read, understand, and sign a student safety contract, such as the one that follows, after they have been instructed in safety procedures.

Student Safety Contract

I will:

- Follow all instructions given by the teacher
- Read directions thoroughly before starting an activity
- Protect eyes, face, hands, and body while conducting an activity
- Know the location of first-aid and firefighting equipment
- Conduct myself in a responsible manner at all times in a laboratory situation.

I, ______________________, have read and agree to abide by the safety regulations as set forth above and also any additional printed instructions provided by the teacher and/or district. I further agree to follow all other written and verbal instructions given in class.

Date ____________

____

Signature

In HOLT PHYSICAL SCIENCE, students are reminded of safety procedures throughout the text, by the use of the word CAUTION followed by specific safety instructions.

School Safety Audit

It is recommended that at the beginning of the school year, and throughout the year as the need arises, a safety audit of classroom and laboratory facilities be conducted by the teacher. A form could be used to indicate areas needing attention by maintenance staff or others. As conditions are corrected, a notation could be made on the form, which should be kept on file for future reference.

Storing Chemicals

It is not advisable to store large amounts of potentially hazardous chemicals over long periods of time. In order to help avoid this, every effort has been made in the materials list of HOLT PHYSICAL SCIENCE to indicate the minimum amount of each substance needed to perform the activities. After having ordered the necessary chemicals, it is a good idea to compile an alphabetical list of all chemicals on hand in your school laboratory. Include the amount of each and the date it was obtained. Additions to and deletions from this list should be made whenever necessary. Contact your regional EPA solid waste office for information on proper disposal of surplus or dangerous chemicals. See page T15. To aid in identification of chemicals, a standard labeling system should be used.

Incident/Accident Report

In the science classroom, as well as in any other class, any accident, hazardous incident, or potentially hazardous incident should be officially recorded and reported as soon as possible. A standard report form can be used to facilitate the recording of such incidents and to insure that all necessary information is recorded.

Field Trips

When taking students on field trips to visit sewage treatment plants, power generating stations, and so on, it is advisable for the teacher to visit the area beforehand to note any possible hazards. These potential dangers should then be discussed with the students and rules for safe conduct should be established. Students should be advised of any special clothing to be worn, for example, low-heeled shoes with rubber soles that will prevent tripping on stairs or slipping on wet floors.

Adequate supervision by teachers and/or parents should be insured, and school policies for obtaining proper consent prior to the field trip should be followed.

While actually at the field trip location, it is imperative that students adhere to all necessary safety regulations required in any particular area, such as the wearing of hard hats, protective goggles, and so on.

Laboratory Safety Guidelines

The following is a list of some of the general guidelines that should be followed in the science laboratory at all times. Teachers should review these guidelines with their students and be sure that they are understood.

- All science laboratories should have and use the following safety items: fire extinguishers, first-aid kits, fire blankets, sand buckets, eyewash facilities, emergency shower facilities, approved safety goggles, laboratory aprons, gloves, tongs, respirators, wire gauze.
- Good housekeeping is essential for maintaining safe laboratory conditions.
- Confine long hair and loose clothing. Laboratory aprons should be worn.
- Never have students conduct experiments in the laboratory without supervision.
- Proper eye protection devices should be worn by all persons who are supervising or observing science activities that involve potential hazards to the eye.
- Make certain that all hot plates and open burners are turned off before leaving the laboratory.
- Every laboratory should have two unobstructed exits.
- There should be an annual, verified safety check of each laboratory.
- One teacher should not have to supervise more than twenty-four students engaged in laboratory activities at one time.
- Master cutoff valves or switches for gas, water, and electricity are advisable for laboratories.
- Emergency instructions of procedures for fires, explosions, chemical reactions, spillage, and first aid should be conspicuously posted near all storage areas.
- Always perform an experiment or demonstration prior to allowing students to do the ac-

tivity. Look for possible hazards. Alert students to potential dangers. Safety instructions should be given each time an experiment is begun.

- Horseplay or practical jokes of any kind are not to be tolerated.
- Never eat or drink in the laboratory or from laboratory equipment, such as beakers or flasks.
- Exercise great care in noting odors or fumes. Use a wafting motion of the hand.
- Never use mouth suction in filling pipettes with chemical reagents. (Use a suction bulb.)
- Never "force" glass tubing into rubber stoppers. Constant surveillance and supervision of student activities are essential.
- A positive attitude toward safety is imperative. Students should not be afraid to do experiments or to use reagents and equipment, but they should respect them as potential hazards.

Hazardous Waste Disposal

Contact your regional Environmental Protection Agency (EPA) office for information on proper disposal of surplus or dangerous chemicals or solid wastes.

Region 1
Solid Waste Program
John F. Kennedy Building
Boston, MA 02203
(617) 223-5775

Region 2
Solid Waste Section
26 Federal Plaza
New York, NY 10007
(212) 264-0503/4/5

Region 3
Solid Waste Program
Sixth and Walnut Streets
Philadelphia, PA 19106
(215) 597-0980

Region 4
Solid Waste Section
345 Courtland Street NE
Atlanta, GA 30308
(404) 881-3016

Region 5
Solid Waste Program
230 South Dearborn Street
Chicago, IL 60604
(312) 353-2197

Region 6
Solid Waste Section
First International Building
Dallas, TX 75270
(214) 767-2645

Region 7
Waste Management Section
324 East 11th Street
Kansas City, MO 64108
(816) 374-3307

Region 8
Solid Waste Section
1860 Lincoln Street
Denver, CO 80203
(303) 837-2221

Region 9
Solid Waste Program
215 Freemont Street
San Francisco, CA 94105
(415) 556-4606

Region 10
Solid Waste Program
1200 Sixth Avenue
Seattle, WA 98101
(206) 442-1260

THE EXCEPTIONAL STUDENT IN THE SCIENCE CLASS

PL 94-142

Mainstreaming has come to mean the integration of handicapped children into the mainstream of our society and into the educational mainstream wherever feasible. Some students with handicaps have always been mainstreamed. Their exceptionalities are not severe, or they are given the opportunities to achieve normal educational goals under conditions in which their exceptionalities are not thought to be handicapping. Others attend special education classes or receive related services that meet their educational needs.

Federal Law PL 94-142 requires all students with handicapping conditions to be identified, tested, and evaluated by the appropriate agencies or school services. (If you suspect that a student has a handicap never before identified, contact the school health department immediately.) The school service, in agreement with the student and his or her parents, selects the most appropriate and least environmentally restrictive educational plan. The plan can include total integration with related special services, such as speech therapy, or partial integration, with enrollment in selected courses for part of the day and enrollment in special education courses for the remainder.

Handicapping Conditions

Physical impairments include those of an orthopedic nature, visual impairments, blindness, and other health impairments.

Communicative handicaps are any of the following conditions that adversely affect a student's ability to effectively use language: hearing impairments, deafness, speech impairments, and specific learning disabilities. The term "specific learning disability" refers to a dysfunction in any one, or more, of the basic psychological processes involved in understanding or using language. Specific learning disabilities include the following: dyslexia, minimal brain injury, perceptual impairments, and developmental aphasia.

Mild mental retardation refers to slowed intellectual functioning.

Emotional disturbance refers to an emotional condition that hinders a student's overall functioning.

Instructional Management Systems

Be aware of the educational plan selected for each handicapped student in the science class. If a student is partially integrated and returns to the special education teacher or resource teacher for supportive and additional instruction, the resource teacher should write an Individualized Educational Plan (IEP) with input from the course instructors.

Strategies

Management strategies are necessary for optimal student achievement and are individualized depending on the degree of the exceptionality.

Regardless of the system selected, the student is maintained as a full-fledged member of the class and is expected to participate in all activities and assignments.

Careers for Persons with Handicapping Conditions

As educational opportunities for handicapped persons have increased, so have opportunities for employment. The Rehabilitation Act of 1973, Public Law 93-112, Section 504, provides for the nondiscrimination of qualified handicapped individuals for employment opportunities in any program receiving federal financial assistance.

Gifted Children

In considering the position of exceptional children in the regular classroom, teachers should not neglect gifted or talented children. These children can often experience frustration if they are not presented with a sufficiently challenging program. In the Pacing Guide for each chapter of HOLT PHYSICAL SCIENCE, suggestions are offered for additional projects, activities, etc., which will help to enrich the course work for your gifted students. These students are identified in the Guide as "Above Average." The section Applying Science at the end of each chapter provides many opportunities for above average students to do independent research, write reports, perform optional activities, etc. Many of the Investigations and Laboratories have optional parts that would be suitable for above average students.

Bibliography

The following books may be helpful in planning a classroom strategy to deal with gifted students. All are available from The Council for Exceptional Children, 1920 Association Drive, Reston, Virginia 22091.

- E. Coston Frederick, *Teaching Content Through Reading: A Human Experience,* Charles C. Thomas Pub., 2600 South First St., Springfield, Illinois. 1984.
- Thinking and Learning Skills: *Volume I: Relating Instruction to Research Volume II: Research and Open Questions* edited by: Judith H. Segal, Susan F. Chipman and Robert Glaser; Lawrence Erlbaum Associates, Inc., 365 Broadway, Hillsdale, New Jersey. 1985.
- Thaiss, Christopher, "Language Across the Curriculum," ERIC/RCS Digest, Urbana, Illinois,: ERIC/NCTE, 1984.
- Alfred F. Collete and Eugene L. Chiappetta, *Science Instruction in the Middle and Secondary School,* C.V. Mosby Co., St. Louis, Missouri.
- Bill Gearheart and Mel H. Weishahn, *The Exceptional Child in the Regular Classroom,* C.V. Mosby Co., St. Louis, 1983.
- A. Harry Passaw, ed. *The Gifted and the Talented: Their Education and Development,* Chicago; University of Chicago Press, 1979.
- Mary M. Dupuis and Eunice N. Askov, *Content Area Reading: An Individualized Approach,* Englewood Cliffs, NJ. 1982.

BASIC SCIENCE SKILLS

This section of the Teacher's Edition is designed to help teachers develop in their students the reading, writing, and math skills essential to the study of science.

Science teachers often feel that they do not have time to teach reading and writing skills if they are to cover the science material in the curriculum. Actually, they already spend a great deal of time helping their students develop these skills. The materials in this section will help you to organize, develop, and reinforce these skills as you teach physical science.

Reading and Writing in Science

PREPARATION: Science teachers, as well as teachers in other content areas, have become concerned about "reading level." There are two major methods of determining the reading level of a text. One method makes use of graded word lists, while the other uses a readability scale based on average sentence length and total number of syllables. In order to be used in a wide variety of circumstances, these methods must of necessity be mechanical. As a result, nonsense or gibberish can have a low "reading level" when tested by these methods. Coherent expository writing can have a high reading level. Yet this material may actually be more readable (that is, understandable) to students than short, choppy sentences which test at a lower reading level. The final test of "readability" is whether or not students can read and comprehend the text material.

DIAGNOSIS: One method of determining whether a student understands the text material is the Cloze test. The results of this test can help you determine whether the student can work independently, whether he or she requires instruction, or whether, even with prior instruction, the student will have reading difficulties.

To make your own Cloze test, select a 250-word passage from the material you would like to assign. This material must be new to the students. Leave the first sentence complete. Starting with the second sentence, leave a uniform blank for every fifth word. Continue to delete every fifth word until there are 50 blanks. Give this passage to your students. Tell them to fill in each blank with the word that makes the most sense. Score 2 points for each exact original word. Do not count synonyms at this time since it takes more time and requires subjective judgment. If a student scores below 43%, score 2 points for each synonym or appropriate new word. Some students may even use better words than in the original. The level of the material for students can be graded as follows:

58 to 100% correct: The student can study the material independently.

44 to 57% correct: The student needs instruction.

0 to 45% correct: The student will experience frustration.

SAMPLE CLOZE TEST: The following short sample from Chapter 2 page 40 will give you some idea of what a Cloze test looks like.

Great discoveries in science are often made when someone asks the right question. Scientists always ask questions. ________ Newton, the question usually________about motion was, "Why ________objects move?" Experiments seemed ________show that a push________pull was needed to ________motion. Any push or________ is called a **force**. ________saw that an object ________no force acting on________did not move.

However, ______ saw the problem differently. ______ asked the question, "Why ______ objects *stop* moving?"

Newton ______ that moving objects are ______ stopped by a force. ______ call this force **friction.** ______ is caused by two ______ rubbing together. For example, ______ is a force between ______ shoes and the floor. ______ there were no friction, ______ would have trouble walking. ______ Fig. 2-9. Have ______ ever slipped on a ______ floor? Smooth surfaces reduce ______.

Wheels can also reduce ______ amount of friction. Have ______ ever fallen at a ______ skating rink? Friction can ______ be reduced by using ______ slippery substance like oil. ______ is why we put ______ on the moving parts ______ machines. We can only ______ friction. We cannot get ______ of it altogether. There ______ always some friction present. ______ would moving objects behave ______ friction?

Math Skills

Since mathematics is the language of science, it is important that students be as fluent in mathematics as they are in technical vocabulary. Students using HOLT PHYSICAL SCIENCE will learn to apply basic math skills as they learn scientific concepts. You may wish to review these basic skills before assigning problems. See the Appendix for a brief math reinforcement. Math skills are stressed throughout the text where appropriate. For example, concepts such as speed and acceleration are developed using sample worked-out math problems. Questions at the end of sections or chapters often include math problems.

Skill Development

Many of the following basic science skills are essential to the successful reading and understanding of science materials. Students will have the opportunity to practice these skills throughout HOLT PHYSICAL SCIENCE. Teacher annotations identify places where these skills appear in the text.

USING THE TEXTBOOK: Very early in the course, it is a good idea to review the parts of the text and their uses. Students must be familiar with the table of contents, Glossary, and Index, and know how to use them to find information.

FOLLOWING DIRECTIONS: The importance of following directions cannot be stressed too much in a science class. At times, even the safety of the experimenter is at stake if proper procedures and techniques are not followed. Develop several exercises for the students to show them the importance of following directions.

READING AND CONSTRUCTING GRAPHS AND TABLES: Very often in science, information can be most easily depicted or summarized in the form of a graph or table. HOLT PHYSICAL SCIENCE makes use of these tools in its presentation of material to the students. It is important that students know how to interpret graphs and tables in order to obtain as much information from them as possible. Students should also know how to arrange data in the form of graphs and tables. Sample data tables are provided for this purpose in many of the Investigations and Skill-Building Activities.

READING ILLUSTRATIONS: The many photographs and diagrams in the text are designed to help the students understand the concepts better or to help them follow a sequence of steps or directions more easily.

CAUSE AND EFFECT: Scientists are constantly relating cause and effect in their research and experiments. Students should be able to do the same in their reading and investigations. They will learn facts faster if they look for cause and effect relationships between them.

COMPARE AND CONTRAST: Scientists use the reading skills of comparing and contrasting in their work. In analyzing the results of experiments, they look for similarities and differences. These may provide the key to a discovery. By looking for similarities and differences in their reading and laboratory work, students will find it easier to remember facts, to relate them to one another, and to apply them to new situations.

SEQUENCING: Sequencing is an important part of science. The continuity of many scientific theories, concepts, and experiments relies on sequencing. Being able to follow a logical order is a valuable skill that will help students perform investigations and recognize concepts. Sequencing will help students predict the outcome of investigations and apply concepts logically to new situations.

CLASSIFICATION: We all use classification in our everyday lives. For example, we use a classification system to find books in a library. Science systematizes knowledge so that it can be studied. Physical science is the study of nonliving things. The enormous size of this area of study makes it necessary to have classification systems. Huge topics, such as matter, must be broken down into manageable concepts, such as mixtures, compounds, and solutions. By grouping or classifying topics, students can grasp a great deal of information easily.

SCIENCE VOCABULARY: Many new words are introduced to students for the first time in a science class. In HOLT PHYSICAL SCIENCE, important new terms are printed in boldface type and are defined in the margin. At the end of each chapter, a Vocabulary review tests students' recall of these terms. The Glossary contains an alphabetical listing of all the terms defined in the margins. Students may be confused by new meanings for familiar words, for example, pattern, property, current, and bond. It is a good idea to preteach these familiar words in the context of new content. Suggest that students search for the meaning of a new word in the material surrounding it. In the case of long words, show them how to break them down into smaller ones. The *Word study* teacher annotations will help you to break words down into roots, prefixes, and suffixes.

PROBLEM SOLVING: Problem solving can be defined as thinking of ways to combine observations with facts to find a solution. Scientists use the scientific method to solve problems. Students should be encouraged to use the scientific method to solve problems in their everyday lives as well as in science. Students should realize that not every step of the scientific method is applicable to every problem. Knowing how to approach mathematical solutions is also a part of problem solving.

FINDING THE MAIN IDEA: Students may sometimes finish reading a paragraph without being able to identify the main idea of the paragraph. This inability to find the main idea can also prevent students from taking effective notes in class or writing a useful outline. Therefore, it is wise to spend some time teaching students how to find the main idea of a paragraph. The format of each section in HOLT PHYSICAL SCIENCE should help students to write a brief outline of the section for use as a study guide.

WRITING: Students must be able to read the text, understand the concepts, and use problem-solving skills to arrive at conclusions. In addition, they must be able to express those conclusions in writing. The problems students may encounter in writing may fall into one or more of the following categories: (1) difficulty in converting mental ideas into written expression; (2) inability to understand a specified task; (3) lack of organization; (4) lack of familiarity with writing conventions, sentence structure, correct usage, and correct spelling. In HOLT PHYSICAL SCIENCE, students are directed to respond to end-of-section and Chapter Review questions in complete sentences. In addition, the format of the Investigations and Skill-Building Activities facilitates the writing of student laboratory reports.

WRITING A SCIENCE RESEARCH REPORT

It is important that students are afforded an opportunity to express themselves in writing. Suggestions for library research are presented in the Applying Science section of the Chapter Review. Students are motivated when they select or volunteer to investigate a particular topic. Physical science offers many such opportunities. No experiment or research is really complete until the conditions and results of the experiment have been stated clearly and conclusions have been drawn from the results. The following guide will help students to research and organize a science report. The two types discussed are *The Library Research Report* and *The Laboratory Experiment.*

The Library Research Report

SELECTING A TOPIC:

- Students may select their own topics, subject to teacher approval; teachers may assign topics; or teachers may compile a list of possible topics and allow individual students to select from the list.
- Be certain that titles are specific.

INTRODUCTION:

- The topic should be stated clearly or defined.

SOURCES:

- Information can be compiled as homework and/or class time can be devoted to library research.
- Students should use a variety of sources, including various reference texts, magazines, and newspapers. The use of low-readability texts should be permitted where necessary for student comprehension.
- Librarians and English teachers can be of help regarding the use of the card catalog, *Reader's Guide to Periodical Literature,* microfilm, and so on.
- Encourage students to write letters to specific sources for pertinent information.
- Require a minimum of sources for each report, for example, no less than five.

COMPILING INFORMATION:

- Select one source at a time.
- At the top of a sheet of paper, or on an index card, record all the information necessary for the bibliography.*
- Note page numbers of material used for the report.
- Whenever possible, students should take notes without copying directly from books. Direct quotes should be surrounded by quotation marks and be followed by exact page numbers. This procedure is crucial for accurate footnoting.
- Information from each source should be recorded on a separate sheet of paper or index card. If more than one is needed for a particular source, the pages or cards should be stapled together.

WRITING THE ROUGH DRAFT

- Students are now ready to construct a working outline of their reports. You should ap-

* All students should learn how to record sources in a research report. There are several acceptable styles, but the students should be consistent in the style used. Information usually needed for books in a bibliography includes: Author's last and first names, title of book, city where it was published, name of publishing company, year of publication, and pages cited in report. See your school librarian for information regarding other bibliography entries, or use the style of the reading lists at the ends of chapters. Footnotes may be listed either at the end of the report or at the bottom of the page on which the footnoted material appears. Consult an advanced text or a scientific journal for styles. Your school librarian may also be able to help.

prove each outline before students begin writing their rough drafts. The outline should list the order of topics to be covered in a logical sequence. The teacher can help by giving a review of what an outline should look like.

- Students should follow the approved outline in writing a first draft.
- Information in quotes should now be marked by number, and their sources credited in footnotes. In addition to direct quotes, footnotes should be used when stating someone's opinion or reporting important statistics.

COMPONENTS OF THE FINISHED REPORT

- Title page
- Introduction
- Outline
- Body of report
- Student's conclusions
- Footnotes
- Bibliography

The Laboratory Experiment

SELECTING A TOPIC

- Students can select scientific topics; teachers can assign topics to students; teachers can compile a list of possible topics and allow individual students to select topics from the list.
- Be certain that titles are specific.

INTRODUCTION

The student will clearly state a specific question and a hypothesis.

COMPILING INFORMATION

- The student should research available scientific information regarding the selected area of experimentation.
- The teacher should indicate what portion of the report should be devoted to gathering pertinent information through library research.
- An outline of an experimental design should next be made. The teacher can review this to be certain that the proposed experiment will answer the question proposed in the introduction, and that the experiment is both practical and safe.

MATERIALS AND PROCEDURES

- List all materials used.
- Explain procedures used in laboratory experiments. List chemicals and equipment used; describe apparatus; tell how the experiment was set up and under what conditions it was carried out. Stress the importance of using control experiments and testing only one variable at a time.
- Stress that the procedures section should contain enough information so that another person would be able to repeat the procedure.

RECORD OBSERVATIONS MADE AND DATA COLLECTED

- Include all observations made during the experiment.
- For clarity, data may be presented in the form of charts, graphs, tables, or diagrams.

DRAW CONCLUSIONS

Based on the data and observations recorded above, the student should be able to draw conclusions. Do they agree with the original hypothesis? If not, why?

COMPONENTS OF THE FINISHED LABORATORY REPORT

- Title page
- Introduction
- Library research
- Hypothesis
- Materials and procedures
- Observations and data collected
- Conclusions
- Footnotes
- Bibliography

MATERIALS

MATERIAL	NUMBER NEEDED FOR 30 STUDENTS	SECTION IN WHICH USED
Acid, hydrochloric, 0.1M	1 L	20–3
Aluminum foil	1 roll	7–1, 10–1, 12–1, 16–3, 20–2
Ammeter, 0–1 amp	10	11–1
Ammonia (household)	0.5 L	20–2
Ammonium chloride and manganese dioxide paste		16–2
Anvil (heavy metal plate)	2	16–3
Bag, plastic sandwich	15	13–3
Baking powder	1 can	13–1
Balance, 0–300 grams	10	14–2
Balloon	20	7–1, 7–2
Battery, 1.5 V	30	10–2, 10–3, 11–1, 11–2, 12–3, 16–3, 17–2
Beaker, 250 mL	30	5–3, 14–1, 17–2, 18–4
Beaker, 400 mL	15	7–2, 19–3
Beaker, 500 mL	15	9–2
Book	15	3–1
Box, with lid	15	15–1, 21–2
Bread, white	2 slices	18–1
Bulb, flashlight No. 48, with socket	30	10–2, 10–3, 11–2, 12–3, 16–2, 16–3, 17–2
Bulb, 60 watt, with socket	15	5–2, 8–2, 9–1
Burner, Bunsen	15	1–2, 5–3, 13–1, 14–1, 17–2, 18–1, 18–4
Cabbage leaf, purple	2 large leaves	20–2
Can of water for burned matches	10	Whenever matches are used
Carbon (battery rod)	5	16–3
Cardboard, cover for beaker	15	9–2
Card, index	15	8–2, 8–3
Cards, "element," set of 9	30	16–1
Cart, dynamics (or skate)	10	2–2, 3–3
Chalk	5 sticks	4–1, 10–1, 10–2, 12–1
Clay	2 kg	15–2

MATERIAL	NUMBER NEEDED FOR 30 STUDENTS	SECTION IN WHICH USED
Clock, wall, with sweep second hand	1	1–3, 2–1, 2–2, 2–3, 5–3, 6–2
Cloth, black, 15 × 15 cm	10	8–1
Cloth, white, 15 × 15 cm	10	8–1
Coiled spring (2 cm diam., 2 m long)	10	6–2
Coloring, food, dark	5 small bottles	5–1
Compass, magnetic	15	12–3
Copper (bare wire)	1 small spool	16–3
Cubes (100/set), one side marked	10 sets	21–2
Cup, small paper	15	5–1, 6–2, 13–2, 19–1
Dropper, medicine	15	6–2, 20–1, 20–3
Eraser (or other light object)	15	1–3, 2–3, 10–2, 12–1
Gelatin, unflavored	1 box	18–4
Glass, window, 3 × 3 cm	15	8–3
Goggles	30	Investigations and Skill-Building Activities
Grating, diffraction, inexpensive, mounted	15	9–1
Hammer	5	16–3
Hydrogen chloride soln.	250 mL	20–2
Hydrogen peroxide	0.5 L	14–2, 19–2
Hypo (sodium thiosulfate)	0.5 kg	19–3
Ice cube	15	5–1, 13–2
Ink, black	1 bottle	9–2
Lead, wire	0.5 kg	16–3
Lemon juice	250 mL	20–2
Lens, double convex 5–10 cm focal length (reading glass)	15	8–3, 13–2
Magnesium sulfate (epsom salt)	1 small bottle	20–1
Magnet, bar, alnico	20	12–1, 12–2, 12–3
Manganese dioxide	10 spoons	14–2, 19–2
Marble, 1.2 cm	15	2–1
Matches, safety	15 boxes	1–2, 5–3, 13–1, 14–1, 14–2, 17–2, 18–1, 18–4
Meat, hamburger	0.25 kg	19–2
Meter stick	15	6–2, 7–1, 7–2, 8–2
Mirror, concave	10	8–2

MATERIAL	NUMBER NEEDED FOR 30 STUDENTS	SECTION IN WHICH USED
Mirror, plane	10	8–2
Molecular model kit, hydrocarbon	10	18–2, 18–3
MSG	1 small box	18–4
Nail, 16D, finishing	15	12–1, 12–2
Needle, steel	15	12–2
Oil, vegetable	0.5 L	18–4
Pan, pie (or round dish)	15	6–2
Paper	1 ream	ALL
Paper, filter	15 strips	9–2
Paper, graph	15	21–2
Paper, litmus, blue	30	20–2
Paper, litmus, red	30	20–2
Paper clip	30	10–2, 12–2, 12–3, 13–2, 15–2
Paraffin	0.5 kg	13–1
Pencil	30	ALL
Pencil, marking	5	20–2
Penny, copper	15	16–2
Phenolphthalein soln.	50 mL	20–3
Pin, steel	1	7–1
Plaster of paris	0.5 kg	19–1
Plastic, (broken spoon or ruler)	10 pieces	10–2, 12–1
Prism, glass	3	9–1
Pulley, single	10	3–3
Rack, test-tube	15	18–4, 19–2, 20–2, 20–3
Resistor, 5 ohms	20	11–1
Ring stand, with ring	15	5–3, 9–2, 18–4
Rod, metal, 50 cm	2	7–1, 7–2
Rod, stirring	15	5–3, 19–3
Rubber band, No. 16	10	7–1, 7–2
Ruler, metric, 30 cm, with groove	30	1–3, 2–1, 2–2, 2–3, 3–1, 3–2, 4–1, 5–2, 7–2, 8–3, 10–1
Salt, rock	0.5 kg	13–3
Salt, table	0.5 kg	13–3, 14–1, 17–2, 18–1, 19–2, 20–2
Sand	0.5 kg	14–1
Sandpaper (or steelwool)	2 sheets	16–2
Scale, spring, 500 g	15	2–2, 3–1, 3–3, 4–1
Sinker, lead (heavy wt)	15	1–3, 2–3
Slinky, 7.5 cm diam., double length	10	6–1

MATERIAL	NUMBER NEEDED FOR 30 STUDENTS	SECTION IN WHICH USED
Soda, baking	0.5 kg	17–2, 20–2
Soda, washing	0.5 kg	19–3
Sodium carbonate soln.	250 mL	20–1
Sodium chloride soln.	250 mL	20–2
Sodium hydroxide soln.	100 mL	20–3
Sodium tetraborate soln.	0.5 kg	20–1
Spoon, plastic	15	13–1, 16–2, 19–1, 19–3, 20–2
Staple	15	10–2, 12–1
Starch	0.5 kg	18–4
String	1 spool	1–3, 2–3, 3–1, 3–3, 7–1, 7–2
Sugar	0.5 kg	13–1, 17–2, 18–1, 18–4, 20–2
Sulfur	0.5 kg	16–3
Tape, masking	1 roll	20–2
Tape, recording timer	10 rolls	2–2
Tape, transparent	1 roll	9–2, 10–1, 12–2
Test tube, 13 × 100 mm	75	10–2, 12–1, 13–1, 14–1, 17–1, 18–1, 18–4, 19–2, 20–2, 20–3
Test tube, 18 × 150 mm	30	7–2
Test-tube holder	15	13–1, 14–1, 17–2, 18–1
Thermometer, −10°C to 110°C	15	5–3, 8–1, 19–3
Thread, nylon	1 spool	10–1, 12–2
Timer, recording	10	2–2
Toothpick, wood	1 box	14–2
Tube, glass	15	13–2
Tuning fork, 256 cps	3	7–1
Vinegar, white	0.5 L	20–2
Vitamin C, powdered	1 small bottle	20–2
Voltmeter, 0–3 volts	10	11–1
Watch, stop	10	4–1
Water, distilled	4 L	20–2
Water, hot	3 L	5–1
Water, tap	5 L	5–3, 6–2, 7–1, 7–2, 9–2, 13–2, 17–2, 18–4, 19–1, 19–3
Waxed paper	1 roll	10–1, 20–1
Wire, stranded, insulated, 30 cm, with clips	60	10–2, 10–3, 11–1, 11–2, 12–3, 16–2, 16–3, 17–2

MATERIAL	NUMBER NEEDED FOR 30 STUDENTS	SECTION IN WHICH USED
Wire, stranded, insulated, 1.5 m	15	12–3
Wire gauze square	15	5–3
Wood, 2.5 × 5 × 25 cm	15	1–2, 7–2
Wood, 50 × 15 cm	15	3–3, 4–1
Wood, tongue depressor	15	10–2, 12–1
Zinc, 2 × 2 cm	15	16–2

SOURCES OF EQUIPMENT AND SUPPLIES

Scientific Supply Companies

CSG Scientific Inc.
2600 S. Kostner Avenue
Chicago, IL 60623

Edmund Scientific Co.
ECO2 Edscorp Building
Barrington, NJ 08007

Fisher Scientific Co.
203 Fisher Building
Pittsburgh, PA 15219

Klinger Educational
Products Corp.
83–47 Parsons Blvd.
Jamaica, NY 11432

La Pine Scientific Co.
6001 S. Knox Avenue
Chicago, IL 60629

Sargent-Welch Scientific Co.
7300 N. Linder Avenue
P.O. Box 1026
Dept. T
Skokie, IL 60077

Scientific International Inc.
P.O. Box 1590
Bloomfield, NJ 07003

Audiovisual Supply Companies

AIMS Media
626 Justin Avenue
Glendale, CA 91201

American Educational Films, Inc.
Box 8188
Nashville, TN 37207

Allied Chemical Corporation
Columbia Rd. and Park Avenue
Morristown, NJ 07960

Brooklyn Union Gas Company
Public Relations and Advertising
195 Montague Street
Brooklyn, NY 11201

Bureau of Mines
Motion Pictures
4800 Forbes Avenue
Pittsburgh, PA 15213

Carousel Films, Inc.
241 East 34th Street
New York, NY 10016

Coronet
65 East South Water Street
Chicago, IL 60601

Current Affairs
Box 426
Ridgefield, CT 06877

Dow Chemical Company
Audio Visual Department
2030 Dow Center
Midland, MI 48640

Educational Dimensions Corp.
Box 126
Stamford, CT 06904

Encyclopaedia Britannica
425 North Michigan Avenue
Chicago, IL 60611

Filmstrip House
6633 West Howard Street
Niles, IL 60648

GTE Sylvania
Sylvania Lighting Ctr.
Danvers, MA 01923

Guidance Associates, Inc.
Box 3000
Communications Park
Mount Kisco, NY 10549

Houghton Mifflin Co.
One Beacon Street
Boston, MA 02108

Hubbard Science
2855 Shermer Road
Northbrook, IL 60002

McGraw-Hill Films
1221 Avenue of the Americas
New York, NY 10020

Mobil Oil Company
150 East 42nd Street
New York, NY 10017

Modern Talking Picture Service, Inc.
5000 Park Street N.
St. Petersburg, FL 33709

Moody Institute of Science
12000 East Washington Avenue
Whittier, CA 90606

National Bureau of Standards
Kaithersburg, MD 20899

National Geographic Society
17 and M Streets NW
Washington, DC 20036

National Science Foundation
1860 G Street NW
Washington, DC 20550

New York Times Education Division
229 West 43rd Street
New York, NY 10036

Pathescope Educational Media, Inc.
Box 6000
Communications Park
Mount Kisco, NY 10549

Prentice-Hall Media, Inc.
150 White Plains Road
Tarrytown, NY 10591

Society for Visual Education, Inc.
1345 Diversey Parkway
Chicago, IL 60614

Time-Life Films
1100 Avenue of the Americas
New York, NY 10036

Universal Pay TV
100 Universal City Plaza
Universal City, CA 91608

Notes

1. When ordering film loops, specify Kodak or Technicolor.
2. In almost all cases, preview is possible at no charge.
3. Addresses of U.S. Government agencies can be found in your local telephone book.

CHAPTER 1 WHAT IS SCIENCE?

SECTION/ TIME NEEDED	MATERIALS (30 STUDENTS)	BASIC SCIENCE SKILLS	PACING GUIDE
1–1. A Scientific Problem (1–2 periods)	15 medicine droppers pH papers tap water distilled water vinegar lemon juice milk 75 test tubes	Problem Solving (p. 3) Reading Illustrations (p. 2)	Mainstreaming: Be sure that provisions are made for disabled students with wheelchairs or other devices to move about. Slow Learners: For visual impact, show some common products with metric labels.
1–2. Science Is Curiosity (1–2 periods)	Skill-Building Activity I 15 Bunsen burners matches containers of water for burned matches Skill-Building Activity II 15 m string 15 light weights 15 heavy weights 15 metric rulers wall clock	Observing (p. 15) Using Laboratory Equipment (p. 14)	Above Average: Refer to Applying Science in the Chapter Review. A group could report on the history of measurement.
1–3. Measuring (1–2 periods)	Skill-Building Activity I 15 graduated cylinders water 10 m string solid objects small square objects Skill-Building Activity II metric ruler triple beam balance several objects	Measuring (p. 23) Using Laboratory Equipment (p. 24) Sequencing (Teacher's Resource Book, p. 1–2)	

SUPPLEMENTAL MATERIALS

Audiovisual

L*I*G*H*T. Direct Cinema Limited. Color film (15 min).

Meters, Liters, and Grams. General Motors Corp. Color film (11 min).

Standards for Excellence (M323). Association Films, Inc. Color film (28.5 min).

The Metric Song. J.C. Penney Co. Sound filmstrip (10 min).

Observing and Describing (186002-9). McGraw Hill. Color film (12.5 min).

Measurements Are for a Purpose (5621RR). SVE. Color filmstrips.

Measuring Things. Coronet. Set of 6 color filmstrips on measuring (10 min each).
Using the Scientific Method (618). Coronet. Color or B/W filmstrips (11 min).

Print

Eber, D.H. *Genius at Work: Images of Alexander Graham Bell.* New York: Viking, 1982.
Mallow, J. *Science Anxiety: Fear of Science and How to Overcome It.* New York: Elsevier, 1981.
Shapiro, S.J. *Exploring Careers in Science.* New York: Richards Rosen Press, 1981.
Turk, A. and J. Turk. *Physical Science with Environmental and Practical Applications, 2nd ed.* New York: Holt, 1981.
Weber, R.L. *Pioneers of Science: Nobel Prize Winners in Physics.* Philadelphia: Heyden, 1980.

Computer

Connections. Krell Software Corp. APL II Series, COM 64; TRS-80 Models III, 4.
Discovering the Scientific Method: Snigs . . . Flirks . . . Blurgs. Focus Media, Inc. APL II Series; TRS-80 Models III, 4.

CHAPTER OVERVIEW

Chapter 1 deals with the way in which scientists ask questions, look for patterns in observations, develop a hypothesis, conduct experiments to test the hypothesis, and develop a theory. The International System of Units (SI), commonly called the metric system, is presented.

1–1. A SCIENTIFIC PROBLEM

BACKGROUND: Acid rain is the problem that is discussed in this section. What is acid rain? What problems has it caused? How are scientists trying to solve those problems? These questions are the topic of this section.

MOTIVATION: How can we test whether rain is acid or not? Simple tests are best. Set up three beakers. Put distilled water in one, sugar water in the second, and a small amount of sulfuric acid added to water in the third. Ask if students can see any difference in the liquids. Use blue litmus paper to test for an acid.

INVESTIGATION

Teaching Hint: pH paper must be used in this Investigation since students are asked to compare the levels of acidity.

Answers to Questions:

1. Lemon juice has the lowest pH.
2. Distilled water (perhaps tap water) has the highest pH and is the least acidic.

Conclusion:

1. Lemon juice would be the most harmful to fish since it has the lowest pH of the liquids tested.

Extension:

1. Answers will depend on samples.
2. If the pH in the answer to question 1 is greater than 4.5, the answer is yes. Otherwise, no.

1–2. SCIENCE IS CURIOSITY

BACKGROUND: The scientific method is a common-sense method of solving problems. Make sure students understand that there is nothing wrong with changing your hypothesis if you find it is in error.

SKILL-BUILDING ACTIVITY I

Safety: Be sure the students understand that lighting the match before turning on the gas, and holding it in the proper position, will avoid an accumulation of gas and a flare-up when the gas ignites.

Conclusions:

1. Light a match, hold the match near the top of the barrel, turn on the gas, adjust air and gas if necessary to produce a light blue cone in the flame. It is important that the match be lit and in the proper position before turning on the gas.
2. A properly lighted Bunsen burner will have a light blue cone inside the flame.

SKILL-BUILDING ACTIVITY II

Answers to Questions:

1. Answers may vary. Since this is a hypothesis, any answer can be accepted.
2. Answers will vary. Many students will not realize that the period of a pendulum does not depend on the mass of the bob. They will need to change their hypothesis.
3. The control was the original pendulum. The variable is the weight.

Extension:

1. Yes.
2. Answers will vary. Since students are about to test the hypothesis, any answer is satisfactory.
3. The control was the original pendulum. The variable is the length of the pendulum string.

Conclusions:

1. Changing the weight of the bob of a pendulum does not have any effect on the period.

2. Changing the length of the pendulum will change the period of the pendulum.

1–3. MEASURING

BACKGROUND: Students may be interested in the history of some common units of measurements. An inch is the length of three kernels of barleycorn placed end to end. A yard was defined as the distance from the king's nose to the tip of his finger.

MOTIVATION: Have students calculate their weight and height in metric units.

SKILL-BUILDING ACTIVITY I

Teaching Hint: Bolts, nuts, and pieces of metal rod are good reusable objects. The objects chosen should not float in water.

Conclusion:

1. The volume of the object can be found by putting it in a partially filled graduated cylinder and observing the change in volume readings.

Extension:

1. milliliters
2. cubic centimeters
3. Yes, within the limits of accuracy.

Conclusion:

1. Cubic centimeters and milliliters are basically the same measurement; a solid with a volume of 1 cm^3 displaces a volume of 1 mL of water.

SKILL-BUILDING ACTIVITY II

Answers to Questions:

1. Answers will vary.
2. Answers will vary. The measurements will probably be slightly different.
3. Results may vary because of differences in estimating or simple errors.

Conclusion:

1. Place the balance on a level surface, adjust the indicator and the riders to zero, adjust the balancing nuts if necessary, place the object on the balance, move the 100-g, 10-g, and 1-g riders until the pointer swings equally on both sides of the zero mark. Add the readings on the three riders.

SPECIAL FEATURES

CAREERS: When discussing career choices with your students, point out the need to redefine skills constantly in the light of new technology.

TECHNOLOGY: These segments offer brief discussions of fairly technical research and technology. Students should be encouraged to explore various avenues of information to increase their understanding.

COMPUTER: COMPUTE! is not meant to teach computer programming. It is meant to show how the computer can be integrated with science education. These sections are also designed to provide a degree of computer literacy.

CHAPTER REVIEW

Vocabulary:

1. variable 2. data 3. scientific method 4. hypothesis 5. experiment 6. measurement 7. kilogram 8. meter 9. liter 10. observation 11. scientific theory 12. Celsius

Answers to Questions:

1. Scientists want to know why things are as they are. This curiosity, or desire to know, is a basic trait of a scientist, since science is a way of answering questions about nature.
2. Scientists are trying to find answers to questions about acid rain because it is not known whether acid rain is harmful to humans.
3. A scientist might try to solve a problem by following the steps of the scientific method: a. make observations and ask a question, b. gather additional data, c. form a hypothesis, d. construct one or more experiments to test the hypothesis, e. form conclusions based on the results of experiments.
4. A scientific theory may be changed if it is found to be in error in some way, or if a new theory better explains the observations.
5. Measurements are used for making many scientific observations because number values can be communicated easily and accurately.
6. Scientists in the United States use the metric system because the metric system is commonly used throughout the world.
7. A meter stick is a ruler one meter long that is used for measuring length. A graduated cylinder is a cylinder calibrated to show volume. It can be used to find the volume of a liquid or an irregular solid. A scale uses a stretched spring to determine mass. A balance measures mass by balancing one mass against another.
8. Two kilometers equals 2,000 meters, 50 cm equals 0.5 meters, 100 mm equals 0.1 meter.
9. A milliliter measures volume of a liquid and a cubic centimeter measures volume of a solid.
10. Making several measurements and finding the average of all the measurements causes the errors to balance and cancel each other.

CHAPTER 2 MOTION

SECTION/ TIME NEEDED	MATERIALS (30 STUDENTS)	BASIC SCIENCE SKILLS	PACING GUIDE
2–1. What Is Motion? (1–2 periods)	10 metric rulers 10 marbles wall clock	Problem Solving (pp. 33, 34, 36, 37) Compare and Contrast (p. 34) Reading Graphs (pp. 33, 35)	Above Average: See Applying Science at end of chapter. Slow Learners: Identify several examples of reference points.
2–2. Changing Motion (1–2 periods)	10 recording timers 25 m timer tape wall clock 10 spring scales 10 metric rulers 10 carts or roller skates	Measuring (p. 46) Predicting (p. 49)	Above Average: Have students weigh themselves and convert the weight to newtons. Slow Learners: Demonstrate examples of friction.
2–3. Gravity (1–2 periods)	25 m string 15 rubber stoppers wall clock 15 metric rulers	Compare and contrast (p. 50) Cause and Effect (Teacher's Resource Book, p. 2–3)	Above Average: Read some of Aristotle's writing on falling objects to the class.

SUPPLEMENTAL MATERIALS

Audiovisual

Einstein's Universe. Corinth Films. Color film (120 min).

Introduction to Basic Physical Science. Educational Dimensions Group. 4 color filmstrips.

Citizen Seat Belt (F-001459). National Highway Traffic Safety Administration. Color film (15 min).

About Our Missiles (SEP1796). Department of the Air Force. Color film (15 min).

Cars that Crash and Burn (N-407). Association Films, Inc. Color film (17 min).

Newton's Laws of Motion (482-1). SVE. Color film.

Zero-G (HQa-260A). National Aeronautics and Space Administration. Color film. (15 min).

How Airplanes Fly (11131). Modern Talking Pictures Service. Color film (18 min).

Print

Hecht, E. *Physics in Perspective.* Reading, MA: Addison-Wesley, 1980.

Lilley, S. *Discovering Relativity for Yourself.* New York: Cambridge University Press, 1981.

Taffel, A. *Physics: Its Methods and Meanings, 4th ed.* Boston: Allyn and Bacon, 1981.

Computer

Motion. J & S Software. APL II Series.

Motion. Micro Learningware. APL II.

CHAPTER OVERVIEW

All motion is relative. Sitting in the classroom, students may not realize that they are moving through space because they cannot see any reference points to confirm the motion. When an object's velocity changes, the object is accelerated. Acceleration is the result of forces. In this chapter, students are given the opportunity to experience the way in which forces affect the motion of an object.

2–1. WHAT IS MOTION?

BACKGROUND: Motion is defined in terms of distance and time. Motion is one of the most obvious events in nature. Students must learn how to recognize motion and also how to measure motion using appropriate units. Speed, velocity, acceleration, and terminal velocity are introduced by discussing human activities and other natural events.

MOTIVATION: Remind students that even as they sit at their desks they are moving since the earth is moving through space. The motion through space is not noticeable in short periods of time. The classroom is moving about 1,280 km/h because of the rotation of the earth. It is also moving around the sun at about 96,000 km/h. Do not get too involved with relative motion at this time.

INVESTIGATION

This simple investigation of motion involves distance, time, and speed. Floor space can be used if smooth, level table tops are not available. Dust, dirt, and other obstacles should be cleared away so that the marble has a clear path. Times of 2 and 3 seconds are used so that the distances covered are reasonable. The students' measurements of average speed should be nearly equal.

Skill: Recording data in a data table is a useful skill.

Safety: Be sure students pick up all the marbles from the floor. Stray marbles could cause falls.

Answers to Questions:

1. Answers will vary.
2. Answers will vary.
3. Answers will vary.
4. Answers will vary.
5. The speed should be less during the third second than during the first second.
6. The marble accelerated during the three-second interval.

Conclusions:

1. Measure the distance that an object moves in a known time. The distance divided by the time is the speed.
2. If there is a change in the speed of the object from one time period to the next, then you know the object is accelerating.

2–2. CHANGING MOTION

BACKGROUND: Changes in motion are the result of forces acting on an object. Starting, stopping, speeding up, slowing down, and changing direction all require forces. Newton's three laws of motion are discussed as they apply to changes in motion.

MOTIVATION: Motion seems to be a fundamental property of matter. It would be very difficult to explain why everything in nature is in motion. However, changes in motion are readily accounted for. Place a magnet on an overhead projector and roll a steel ball bearing slowly past it so that the ball changes direction. Ask students to account for all of the changes in motion, including the initial motion. A force is necessary in each case.

SKILL: Students can practice solving problems on Newton's second law.

SKILL-BUILDING ACTIVITY

Teaching Hints: Students will need to become familiar with the operation of the recording timer in order to do this activity. A skateboard or roller skate can be used in place of the dynamics cart in this activity. This activity can also be done by having the students tap a pencil at a regular rate of four times per second instead of using a recording timer. Run adding machine tape under an index card with a hole cut in it. Tape the card to the desk top and run the adding machine tape under it. The student taps a pencil lightly as the tape is pulled under the hole. It requires practice and concentration, but it works. The tenth interval referred to in this activity is counted from the point on the tape where the dots can just be distinguished from each other. You may wish to have the students use the twentieth interval if the dots are not far enough apart at the tenth.

Safety: Do not allow students to skate or ride skateboards in school.

Conclusions:

1. The larger the force, the larger the acceleration.
2. Answers will vary. The distance during the interval is directly proportional to the force applied. In this case, the distance at 1.5 N would be three times the distance at 0.5 N.

2–3. GRAVITY

BACKGROUND: Newton recognized the role of mass in determining the earth's pull on objects. Students should have little difficulty in understanding mass since it is an unchanging property of matter. Weight is the pull of the earth on the mass of an object. It is a force described by Newton's second law of motion ($F = ma$). The force needed to accelerate an object increases directly with the mass of the object. On earth the acceleration of gravity at the surface is 9.8 m/s^2. A 1-kg mass weighs 9.8 N. Force (weight) can be used to measure mass even though they are not the same.

MOTIVATION: Do heavy objects fall at the same rate as lighter objects? Describe Galileo's experiments. Students should recognize that for short distances, all fairly heavy objects seem to fall at the same speed. Do heavy objects hit the floor with the same force? Ask "Which would you rather not have fall from the table onto your foot, a book or a brick?" Make sure the answer is obvious. Students should be able to explain why they chose their answers. It takes a greater force to accelerate the heavy brick but the gravitational force on it is greater because it has a greater mass. It also takes a greater force (supplied by your foot) to stop it.

HINT: Ask, "What would a person weigh on the moon (0.165 × earth), Mercury (0.38 × earth), Mars (0.377 × earth), Jupiter (2.54 × earth), and Saturn (1.06 × earth)?" Discuss the athletic abilities on various planets. The height a person could jump (without a space suit) is the inverse of the person's weight. On the moon, this would be six times as high. On Jupiter (if there were a solid surface), it would be 0.39 times as high.

COMPUTER

Students should concentrate on the game-playing aspect of this program and on the mathematical calculations necessary for decision making, not on the program itself. After students have worked through several ¡COMPUTE! features, you may wish to review the program for points of computer information.

INVESTIGATION

Teaching Hints: This Investigation gives very good and predictable results. Students need to make careful measurements in order to get accurate results. The period of the pendulum is constant as long as the distance it is pulled to the side is small compared to the pendulum's length. For example, a pull of 20 cm for a 50-cm pendulum will give the same period as a 5-cm pull. The swings must be complete back-and-forth swings. Remind students that the length of a pendulum is the distance from the point of suspension to the middle of the bob.

Conclusions:

1. Answers will vary. A range of 900 to 1,060 cm/s^2 is reasonable. The more careful the students are with their measurements, the closer to 980 cm/s^2 their answers will be.
2. On a mountaintop, the value of g would be smaller because you are farther from the center of the earth.

CHAPTER REVIEW

Vocabulary:

1. gravity 2. friction 3. velocity 4. weight 5. acceleration 6. inertia 7. force 8. mass 9. motion 10. speed

Answers to Questions:

1. If you were sitting in a train at the depot and the train on the next track started moving, it would be difficult to tell whether your train or the other train was moving without seeing a stationary reference point.
2. Velocity includes both speed and direction of motion while speed is only the distance divided by the time. For example, a velocity might be 55 km/h east, where the speed is 55 km/h.
3. (a) When a bicycle coasts straight down a hill, only the speed changes. (b) When a bicycle turns a corner without changing its speed, the acceleration is only a change in direction.
4. At first the object is accelerated by 9.8 m/s^2 in its free fall. As it falls, it soon reaches its fastest speed, which is called its terminal speed.
5. acceleration = change in speed/change in time. 100 km/h/5 s = 20 km/h/s.
6. If there were no friction or other force acting on a body, it would continue to move in the same manner forever.
7. If you were in a moving car that stopped suddenly, your inertia would cause you to continue to move forward until a force, which should be supplied by your seat belt, stopped you.
8. A force of 9.8 N is required to lift a 1 kg mass. Therefore, 9.8 N/kg × 2.5 kg = 24.5 N.
9. It would cause the object to accelerate at 2 m/s^2.
10. The larger the masses, the greater the gravity force; the larger the distance the less the gravity force.
11. The attraction of the person for the earth is also 400 N.
12. (a) The gravitational force is 400 N.
    (b) The gravitational force is 25 N.
13. (a) The gravitational force is 200 N.
    (b) The gravitational force is 400 N.
14. If you weigh 534 N on earth, your weight on the moon would be 89 N. However, your mass (54.5 kg) would be the same on the moon as it is on earth.

CHAPTER 3 WORK

SECTION/ TIME NEEDED	MATERIALS (30 STUDENTS)	BASIC SCIENCE SKILLS	PACING GUIDE
3–1. What Is Work? (1–2 periods)	15 spring scales, 500 g 15 books 15 1–m pieces of string 15 metric rulers	Problem Solving (pp. 60, 61) Cause and Effect (p. 63)	Slow Learners: Draw electric meter readings on the board. Above Average: Work problems on the board and discuss.
3–2. Simple Machines (1–2 periods)	none	Problem Solving (p. 65 and Teacher's Resource Book, p. 3–3)	Slow Learners: Make a screw using a pencil and a piece of paper as in Fig. 3–16. Above Average: Draw levers on the board and discuss mechanical advantage.
3–3. Machines at Work (1–2 periods)	15 boards, 50 X 15 cm 15 spring scales, 500 g 15 dynamics carts 30 m string 15 single pulleys books	Problem Solving (p. 71) Cause and Effect (p. 78)	Slow Learners: Identify simple machines in an egg beater or other complex machine. Above Average: Work and discuss problems on ideal and actual mechanical advantage.

SUPPLEMENTAL MATERIALS

Audiovisual

Simple Machines: Inclined Planes and Levers, 3rd ed. EBEC. Color film (17 min).

Introduction to Basic Physical Science. Educational Dimensions. 4 color filmstrips with sound cassettes (20 min each).

U.S.A. Road to Energy. Association Films, Inc./Modern Talking Picture Service. Color film (29 min/13.5 min).

Up the Power Curve (0515). U.S. Department of Energy. Color film (10 min).

Man, Tools, and the Necessary Nuisance. Master Chemical Corp. Color film (24 min).

Print

D'Ignazio, F. *Working Robots*. New York: Lodestar Books, 1981.

Florman, S. *Blaming Technology: The Retreat from Responsibility.* New York: St. Martin's, 1981.

Klein, A. E. and C. L. Klein. *The Better Mouse Trap: A Miscellany of Gadgets, Labor-Saving Devices, and Inventions that Intrigue.* New York: Beaufort Books, 1982.

Pursell, C., Jr., ed. *Technology in America: A History of Individuals and Ideas.* Cambridge, MA: MIT Press, 1981.

Computer

Simple Machines—I. Micro-Ed., Inc. COM 64, Pet.

CHAPTER OVERVIEW

This chapter develops the concepts of energy and work. Work is shown to be a measurement of the amount of energy transferred. Power is defined as the rate at which work is done. Simple machines are introduced as a means of magnifying a force by increasing the distance through which the force acts.

3–1. WHAT IS WORK?

BACKGROUND: Students should be encouraged to begin using the terms "work," "energy," and "power" in their strict technical senses. The metric unit of energy, joules (J), should be used properly. Students should learn the amount of energy in one joule (0.1 kg lifted 1 meter equal to 0.98 J). Work is only done when there is motion in the direction of the force. Thus, standing still does not require work. Climbing stairs or pushing a pencil both require work. Power is the number of joules of energy used per second. It is measured in watts.

MOTIVATION: Discuss with the students the nature of the forces involved when you sit in a chair. Point out that the force of gravity is pulling you toward the center of the earth while the chair is pushing in the opposite direction with the same force.

INVESTIGATION

The objective is to emphasize the requirements that must be met in order for work to be done.

Teaching Hints: If the force is applied at an angle, only the component of the force in the direction of the motion does work. Students must pull the book parallel to the table top if all the force is to do work. In step G, the work to lift a book can be calculated as follows: A mass of about 1,000 grams requires a force of about 9.8 newtons. The height is about 0.40 to 0.70 meter. This gives a range of about 4 to about 7 joules of work.

Answers to Questions:

1. Students will probably find some difference in the amount of work when the speed is increased. This will most likely be the result of errors in measurement or pulling the book over different places on the table. Ideally, the amount of work will be the same because the friction forces do not depend on the speed.
2. Answers will vary. They will depend on the table surface, the book surface, the mass of the book, and whether or not the student can keep the speed constant.

Conclusions:

1. To find the amount of work needed to lift a book you must first determine the force needed to lift the book. Change the mass of the book to weight by multiplying by 9.8 newtons for each kilogram of mass. The weight of the book multiplied by the height (1.5 meters) will give you the work needed to lift it. To lift a 2.0-kg book 1.5 meters would require 2.0 kg $\times$ 9.8 N $\times$ 1.5 m = 29.4 J of work.
2. In order to do work, a force must act through a distance.

3–2. SIMPLE MACHINES

BACKGROUND: Explain what is meant by a simple machine (lever, inclined plane, hydraulic press). Describe how it can change the direction of a force, the magnitude of the force, or both. All simple machines can be classified as a modification of a lever, an inclined plane, or a hydraulic press.

MOTIVATION: The three classes of levers can be exhibited and demonstrated. The lever system in the human body should be pointed out. Arms, legs, and feet use fairly obvious levers. They are powerful levers under the right conditions. For example, a heavy weight can be lifted if the weight is placed on the middle of the forearm. An inclined plane can also be demonstrated as a way to lift an object using less force than is needed to lift it straight up.

3–3. MACHINES AT WORK

BACKGROUND: All complex machines are made from simple machines combined in different ways. The force a machine produces divided by the force put into the machine is called the machine's mechanical advantage.

MOTIVATION: Have at least one complex machine available for demonstration and discussion. An egg beater is a possibility although it is difficult to measure the input and output forces. The simple machines (levers and gears) are easily seen.

COMPUTER

You may wish to introduce your students to one of the many computer magazines directed toward young adults. Most sections of these magazines do not deal with programming. They generally contain articles about the uses of computers and about young adults who are involved in some aspect of computer electronics. These magazines can help to increase computer literacy, to encourage the students to identify themselves as potential computer users, and to communicate interesting information. Two such magazines are *ENTER* and *k POWER*. You can write to the following addresses for subscription information: *ENTER*, One Lincoln Plaza, New York, NY 10023, (212) 595–3456 and *k POWER*, 730 Broadway, New York, NY 10003, (212) 505–3580.

SKILL-BUILDING ACTIVITY

Teaching Hints: If spring scales calibrated in newtons are available, use them. It will save converting from grams to newtons. If laboratory carts are not easily available, you can have students bring skates from home, or they can use a book and pull it up the incline. If time permits, you may wish to have students calculate the amount of work needed to lift the cart from the table top to the height of the incline. Compare this with the work needed to lift it using a single movable pulley, and then with the work needed using the pulley and the incline together.

Answers to Questions:

1. Answers will vary from cart to cart.
2. This should be half of the answer to question 1.

Conclusions:

1. Using a pulley as shown, the force needed is half as much as without it.
2. An incline reduces the force needed to lift an object.
3. Using a pulley and an incline together reduces the force needed to lift an object more than using either by itself.
4. The effect of using a pulley and an incline together is equal to the effect of using a pulley alone times the effect of using an incline alone.

TECHNOLOGY

New journals and magazines emerge continually in this field. One example you might find interesting for reference is *Robotics Age: The Journal of Intelligent Machines*. It is published by Robotics Age, Inc., located in the Strand Building, 174 Concord Street, Peterborough, NH 03458, (603) 924–7136.

CHAPTER REVIEW

Vocabulary:

1. work 2. energy 3. power 4. watt 5. mechanical advantage 6. efficiency 7. technology 8. engineer 9. simple machine

Answers to Questions:

1. There must be a change in position, or motion must occur, for work to be done; $W = F \times d$.
2. Simple machines are useful because they produce the same work but require less force.
3. (1) lever: can move a heavy object by pushing down a short distance. (2) pulley: can lift a heavy object by applying a downward force. (3) gear wheel: can apply a large force on an axle using a smaller force. (4) hydraulic press: can apply a large force to a piston by applying a smaller force to a second piston. (5) inclined plane: can lift a heavy object by sliding it up a ramp. (6) screw: can apply a long inclined plane to do work over a short distance. (7) wedge: can split or separate two surfaces from one another with little force. (8) wheel and axle: can apply a large force on the axle by applying a smaller force to the wheel.
4. See Fig. 3–8 on page 65. Student drawings should show that the effort distance times the effort force is equal to the resistance distance times the resistance force.
5. effort distance × effort force = resistance distance × resistance force
   3.0 m × effort force = 0.30 m × 4,469 N effort force = 0.30 m/3.0 m × 4,469 N effort force = 446.9 N
6. (a) 2.5 J/4 J = 0.625 efficiency = 62.5% (b) 3.0 J/4 J = 0.75 efficiency = 75%
7. Technology is the application of science for useful purposes. Answers will vary but should include the fact that we use the products of technology in many different ways.
8. Sitting and reading a book does not require work in the technical sense because there is no force or motion. Walking to school requires a small force in the direction of motion (most of the force is vertical); therefore, a small amount of work is done. More work will be done if you have to climb a hill.
9. $W = F \times d$ = 446 N × 4 m = 1,784 Nm (joules)
10. The amount of energy gained is equal to the work done (1,784 joules).
11. It would take the person 1,000 × 10 seconds to do the same work that the machine does in 30 seconds, therefore the machine has a power rating of 10,000/30 = 333 compared to the person.
12. 373 watts × 1 h.p./746 watts = 0.500 h.p.
13. 1,250 watts × 6 h = 7,500 Wh = 7.5 kWh
    7.5 kilowatt hours × 10 cents/kilowatt hour = 75 cents.
14. See Fig. 3–9 on page 66 for drawings and examples.
15. mechanical advantage = effort distance/resistance distance = 2.0 m/0.10 m = 20

CHAPTER 4 ENERGY

SECTION/ TIME NEEDED	MATERIALS (30 STUDENTS)	BASIC SCIENCE SKILLS	PACING GUIDE
4–1. Energy Causes Motion (1–2 periods)	15 carts 15 boards, 50 cm × 15 cm 5 stopwatches 15 metric rulers 15 books 15 pieces of chalk 5 spring scales	Compare and Contrast (pp. 85, 86, 89) Measuring (p. 89)	Above Average: Students should turn in written reports and summaries. See Applying Science. Slow Learners: Draw a diagram of the Investigation and label the kinds of energy at various places.
4–2. Forms of Energy (1–2 periods)	none	Classifying (pp. 92–93 and Teacher's Resource Book, p. 4–3) Sequencing (Teacher's Resource Book, p. 4–3)	Above Average: Students might report on what is being done by your school district or local government to help conserve energy.

SUPPLEMENTAL MATERIALS

Audiovisual

Decision: Energy for the Future. Bullfrog Films, Inc. Color film (11 min).

Energy: New Sources, 2nd ed. Churchill Films. Color film (24 min).

Energy: How We Got Where We Are. Moody Institute of Science. Color film (20 min).

Introduction to Basic Physical Science. Educational Dimensions Group. 4 color filmstrips with sound cassettes (20 min each).

The Forms of Energy. Focus Media, Inc. 2 color filmstrips with sound cassettes (13-17 min each).

Energy. American Gas Association. Color film with sound (20 min).

Geothermal—Natures' Boiler (0519). U.S. Department of Energy. Color film (7.5 min).

One Turn of the Earth. Caterpillar Tractor Co. Color film (28 min).

Turning on Energy. American Gas Association. Color film (6.5 min).

Energy and Its Forms. Coronet. B/W film (11 min).

Conservation of Energy. MCA. B/W film (27 min).

Print

Bernstein, J. *Hans Bethe: Prophet of Energy.* New York: Basic, 1980.

DeVore, P.W. *Technology: An Introduction.* Worcester, MA: Davis, 1980.

Hobson, A. *Physics and Human Affairs.* New York: Wiley, 1982.

Hyde, M.O. *Energy: The New Look.* New York: McGraw-Hill, 1981.

Landsberg, H.H., ed. *Energy: The Next Twenty Years.* Cambridge, MA: Ballinger, 1979.

Wasserman, H. *Energy War: Reports from the Front.* Westport, CT: Lawrence Hill, 1979.

Williams, J.E. *Modern Physics.* New York: Holt, 1984.

Computer

Energy. J&S Software. APL II Series.

Atarilab Starter Set. Atari, Inc. Atari 800 XL; APL II: COM 64.

CHAPTER OVERVIEW

This chapter discusses the energy problem by presenting four questions: "What is energy?," "What kinds of energy are we using?," "What sources of energy are available?," and "What sources may become available in the future?" Until new or better ways of using renewable sources are found, we are likely to have energy shortages from time to time. Everyone should be aware of the problem since we are all part of the problem.

4–1. ENERGY CAUSES MOTION

BACKGROUND: Work and energy are closely related since work is a measure of energy use. Energy conservation and the law of conservation of energy are two different concepts. Energy conservation refers to the efficient use of the energy available. The law of conservation of energy states that energy can change from one form to another but cannot be created or destroyed.

MOTIVATION: Have students hold a book at arms' length for a short period of time with their eyes closed. Ask the students if they can imagine a stretched spring pulling the book down. A stretched spring stores energy just as a book held above the floor stores gravitational potential energy.

SKILL-BUILDING ACTIVITY

Teaching Hint: You may wish to have students calculate the potential energy lost by the cart. Use PE = mgh to find the potential energy. When the mass, (m) is in kilograms, g is 9.8 N/kg or 9.8 m/s^2, and h is the distance in meters from the top of the incline to the table top. Using these units, the potential energy will be in joules.

Answers to Questions:

1. Answers will vary.
2. Answers will vary. The cart should lose about the same amount of potential energy as the kinetic energy it had in question 1.
3. The kinetic energy will be slightly less than the potential energy because some of the energy will be lost due to friction.

Conclusion:

1. The potential energy of a cart at the top of an incline is changed to kinetic energy as the cart rolls down the incline. The kinetic energy is found using the formula KE = 0.5 mv^2. The kinetic energy will be in joules when the mass (m) is in kilograms and the speed (v) is measured in meters per second.

4–2. FORMS OF ENERGY

BACKGROUND: This section deals with the six forms of energy identified by scientists and the manner in which they may change from one form to another. Later chapters will include more details on all of these forms of energy. Renewable and nonrenewable energy sources are discussed. Future civilizations will need to make use of a combination of energy sources.

MOTIVATION: The concept that any change requires energy should be emphasized. Use an example of a recent change that has taken place at or near your school. The students should recognize that work was done to cause the change and that work results from the expenditure of energy.

CHAPTER REVIEW

Vocabulary:

1. potential 2. kinetic 3. conservation of energy 4. mechanical 5. electric 6. chemical 7. nuclear 8. radiant 9. heat 10. fossil fuels 11. renewable 12. energy

Answers to Questions:

1. Answers will vary. When the batter hits the ball, energy is transferred into kinetic energy in the bat. Part of this energy is transferred to the ball. The kinetic energy of the ball is changed to gravitational potential energy and then back to kinetic energy. The energy finally turns to heat as the ball hits the ground or is caught.
2. Picking up a baseball gives it potential energy. When you throw it, you give it kinetic energy. Part of that kinetic energy is changed to potential energy as the ball goes up in the air. As it falls, the ball gains back the kinetic energy by losing potential energy. The ball also loses a small amount of energy as heat due to air resistance.
3. Solar energy received by a satellite could be changed to microwaves and sent to earth. These microwaves could then be changed to electric energy.
4. Radio waves, visible light, and X-rays are forms of radiant energy. Radio waves are used for communication. We need visible light in order to see. X-rays are used in medicine.
5. Answers will vary.
6. Gravitational potential energy depends on the weight of an object and on how high the object is lifted. For example, a diver on a high board has more potential energy than the same diver on a low board.
7. When iron changes into rust, chemical energy is involved.

8. Nuclear energy comes from changes in the core or nuclei of atoms. We use nuclear energy to generate electricity. It can be thought of as a renewable source of energy.
9. Electric energy is closely related to magnetic energy.
10. Energy is never created or destroyed but is only changed from one form to another.
11. Heat energy causes changes in temperature.
12. Answers will vary. All students use heat, electromagnetic, chemical, electric, and mechanical energy daily. They should be able to describe how they use each form.
13. Drawings should show the high parts of the roller coaster labeled high potential energy and the low parts labeled high kinetic energy.
14. Answers will vary. Check for the use of the vocabulary words and complete sentences.
15. Answers will vary. A stretched spring stores potential energy. The spring can then be used to propel an object thus giving it kinetic energy.

CHAPTER 5 HEAT

SECTION/ TIME NEEDED	MATERIALS (30 STUDENTS)	BASIC SCIENCE SKILLS	PACING GUIDE
5–1. Heat Energy (1–2 periods)	30 small beakers 10 bottles dark food coloring 20 medicine droppers 10 ice cubes hot water	Predicting (p. 105) Observing (p. 108)	Above Average: Students can construct a model of Watt's steam engine.
5–2. Heat Transfer (1–2 periods)	none	Compare and Contrast (pp. 109–112) Observing and Predicting (Teacher's Resource Book, p. 5–2)	Slow Learners: Have students examine and compare different types of insulating materials.
5–3. Temperature and Heat (1–2 periods)	20 250-mL beakers 10 Bunsen burners 10 matches 10 ringstands with rings 10 wire gauze squares 10 thermometers 10 stirring rods water wall clock with sweep secondhand containers of water for burned matches	Compare and Contrast (pp. 118–120, 126) Problem Solving (p. 121)	Above Average: Students can calibrate a thermometer.

SUPPLEMENTAL MATERIALS

Audiovisual

Heat–Its Transmission and Control Through Insulation. Johns-Manville Sales Corporation. Color film (19 min).

The Solar Generation (0510). U.S. Department of Energy. Color film (21 min).

The Ultrasonic Thermometer. National Bureau of Standards. Color film (4 min).

The Ultimate Energy (0509). U.S. Department of Energy. Color film (28 min).

Fusion: The Ultimate Fire (532). U.S. Department of Energy. Color film (14.5 min).

Print

Taffel, A. *Physics: Its Methods and Meanings, 4th ed.* Boston: Allyn and Bacon, 1981.

Wilson, D. *The Colder, the Better,* New York: Atheneum, 1980.

Computer

Atarilab Starter Set. Atari, Inc. Atari 800 XL; APL II; COM 64.

Energy Series. Focus Media, Inc. APL II Series; TRS-80 Models III, 4; COM 64, Pet.

CHAPTER OVERVIEW

Heat is studied as a form of energy through its effects on matter. Mechanical energy (potential and kinetic) eventually becomes heat as a result of friction. This transformation completes the energy cycle since heat can also be changed into other forms of energy.

5–1. HEAT ENERGY

BACKGROUND: The old concept that heat is a fluid called phlogiston is discussed and discarded for lack of evidence. The idea that heat is a form of energy stored as particle motion is consistent with experiments showing that heat is transferred from one object to another. Count Rumford's cannon-boring experiment was a breakthrough in the concept of heat as a form of energy. It provided the incentive for Joule to discover the mechanical equivalent of heat.

MOTIVATION: Most people are familiar with the heat that is generated when they rub their hands together. Few have thought about where the heat comes from. Have the students rub their hands together briskly. Ask how many feel the heat. A class discussion should bring out that heat is considered a form of energy and that work produces waste energy in the form of heat. The molecules that make up your hands are agitated when you rub them together, thus transferring energy by molecular activity.

INVESTIGATION

Teaching Hints: A hot plate can be used to heat water for the class if Bunsen burners are not available. Any dark food coloring will work.

Answers to Questions:

1. The food coloring starts to spread out as soon as it hits the water. The drop sinks and spreads out.
2. Answers will vary. The food coloring will spread more rapidly in the hot water.
3. Hot.
4. Hot.

Conclusion:

1. In hot water the particles are moving faster than in cold water. Therefore, the food coloring will mix faster in the hot water.

5–2. HEAT TRANSFER

BACKGROUND: Heat is transferred by any of three methods. Conduction is the direct transfer of heat by contact. Convection transfers heat by fluid movement as a result of a change in density. It is used to heat many homes and schools. Heat energy can be transferred through a vacuum in the form of radiation. Radiation is different from conduction and convection, in which particles actually have to move in order to transfer heat energy. You may wish to mention the electromagnetic spectrum and the fact that all parts of the electromagnetic spectrum will transfer energy and cause heating.

MOTIVATION: Poll the students and list on the board the various ways in which their homes are heated.

HINT: A 60-watt light bulb can be used to illustrate the three forms of heat transfer.

CAUTION: Do not allow anyone to touch the bulb after 5 seconds. After the bulb has been lighted for 2 minutes or more, have a student hold a hand about 5 cm to the side of the bulb and then about 5 cm above the bulb. Have the student compare the heat transfer at these two positions. To the side the transfer is by radiation while above the transfer is by both radiation and convection. Therefore the heat felt above the bulb should be noticeably greater.

5–3. TEMPERATURE AND HEAT

BACKGROUND: The comparison of heat and temperature should be obvious when students correctly predict from the motivation that the heat energy in a pot full of hot tea would be more dangerous than that in a cup of tea even though they are both at the same temperature. The characteristics of liquid thermometers and solid metal thermometers are discussed. The Fahrenheit and Celsius temperature scales are discussed and compared. The calorie is introduced as a unit of heat energy and related to the kilocalories (Calories) used to measure the energy content of foods. The joule, which was previously introduced as an energy unit, is also used here to measure heat.

MOTIVATION: Discuss the need for measuring devices to measure temperature. Perform the following demonstration:

1. Have three Styrofoam cups available.
   (a) Put very cold water in cup A.
   (b) Put room-temperature water in cup B.
   (c) Put warm (50°C) water in cup C.
2. Have a student put one finger of one hand in cup A and one finger of the other hand in cup C.
3. Ask which cup contains the hotter water.
4. After about 1 minute, have the student quickly place both fingers in cup B.
5. Ask immediately whether this water is hot or cold.
   (a) The two fingers will give conflicting reports of the temperature.

(b) The finger that was in cup A (cold water) will feel warm while the finger that was in cup C (warm water) will feel cold.

COMPUTER

Using programs with built-in mathematical formulas might lead students to ask why they should bother to learn mathematical calculations at all. Stress the difference between being able to run a mathematical program and being able to assess the accuracy of the program. You might want to emphasize this aspect of computer literacy in terms of students' career opportunities and earning power.

SKILL-BUILDING ACTIVITY

Answers to Questions:

1. Answers will vary. The temperature change for beaker B will be less than for A.
2. The temperature change in beaker B was half that of A.
3. The amount of heat was the same for each beaker.
4. In beaker B the same amount of heat was being used to heat twice the amount of water.
5. To calculate the amount of heat energy you also need to know the amount of water in each of the beakers.

Conclusion:

1. Temperature is a measure of how hot an object is while heat refers to the amount of energy that is involved.

TECHNOLOGY

Low-temperature physics, as a specialty, is not well known. For further information, contact: Cryogenic Society of America, c/o Huget Advertising, 1033 South Blvd., Oak Park, IL 60302.

CHAPTER REVIEW

Vocabulary:

1. heat engine 2. radiation 3. conduction 4. specific heat capacity 5. convection 6. temperature 7. calorie

Answers to Questions:

1. Count Rumford's experiment was one of the first to show that heat is a form of energy. As long as work was done in boring the cannon, heat was produced.
2. Add a drop of food coloring to a cup of hot water and a cup of cold water at the same time. The coloring will spread more rapidly in the hot water.
3. When a solid is heated, the particles move faster.
4. An automobile engine is a heat engine. It burns fuel to produce hot gases inside the cylinders. The hot gases push the pistons. Much of the heat energy is wasted.
5. Conduction involves the transfer of heat energy between particles of matter within an object or between two objects by contact. An example is heat traveling through a frying pan. Convection is caused by the uneven heating of a gas or liquid. The change in density results in the transfer of heat. The heat from a fire going up a chimney is an example. Radiation is the transfer of heat energy by means of infrared rays. Heat from the sun is an example.
6. A frying pan on the stove receives heat by conduction. If you touch the hot pan, you will get burned since your skin receives heat from the hot metal by conduction.
7. Solar heating systems use the radiation from the sun as a source of heat. The radiation from the sun heats a liquid which stores the heat energy and transfers it when it is needed. Other types of solar energy converters may be described.
8. The temperature of an object measures how fast the particles of matter are moving in the object.
9. $5/9 \times (70°F - 32°F) = 21.1°C$.
10. Temperature is a measure of how hot an object is while heat is a measure of how much energy is in the object.
11. $5/9 \times (190°F - 32°F) = 5/9 \times 128°F = 71°C$.
12. Freezing water is 0 degrees on the Celsius scale and 32 degrees on the Fahrenheit scale. Boiling water is 100 degrees Celsius and 212 degrees Fahrenheit. The diagram should resemble Fig. 5-20.
13. It would require more heat to change the temperature of 100 grams of water by 5°C because Celsius degrees are larger than Fahrenheit degrees.
14. Put the thermometer into ice water and mark the level of the liquid on the glass. Put the thermometer in boiling water and mark the new level. Divide the distance between the two marks into 100 equal parts. Each part is 1 degree Celsius.
15. The amount of heat needed is the same:

$$\begin{aligned} H &= M \times \Delta T \\ &= 50g \times (30°C - 20°C) \\ &= 500 \text{ cal} \times 4.19 \text{ J/cal} \\ &= 2{,}095 \text{ J} \end{aligned}$$

$$\begin{aligned} H &= M \times \Delta T \\ &= 10g \times (70°C - 20°C) \\ &= 500 \text{ cal} \times 4.19 \text{ J/cal} \\ &= 2{,}095 \text{ J} \end{aligned}$$

CHAPTER 6 WAVE MOTION

SECTION/ TIME NEEDED	MATERIALS (30 STUDENTS)	BASIC SCIENCE SKILLS	PACING GUIDE
6–1. Waves (1–2 periods)	10 coiled springs pencils paper	Problem Solving (p. 138) Compare and Contrast (p. 139)	Slow Learners: Demonstrate properties of waves on a coiled spring. Above Average: Solve problems on the board.
6–2. Wave Interaction (1–2 periods)	10 coiled springs 10 meter sticks paper pencils clock 10 shallow round dishes 10 small beakers 10 medicine droppers water	Observing (p. 146) Compare and Contrast (Teacher's Resource Book, p. 6–3)	Above Average: Have students measure angles using a protractor. Slow Learners: Generate standing waves on a small diameter coiled spring.

SUPPLEMENTAL MATERIALS

Audiovisual

What Is a Wave? Focus Media, Inc. Color filmstrip with sound cassette (16 min).

Waves on Water. U.S. Army Engineer District, Los Angeles.

Progressive Waves: Transverse and Longitudinal (advanced). McGraw-Hill. B/W film (9 min).

Sound Waves and Stars: The Doppler Effect. Film Associates. Color film (12 min).

Print

Haber-Schaim, U., et al. *Physics, PSSC,* Lexington, MA: DC Heath & Co., 1981.

Williams, J.E. *Modern Physics.* New York: Holt, 1984.

CHAPTER OVERVIEW

This chapter deals with waves. Students are asked to study some of the features of waves and use them to understand how waves behave. The wave phenomena studied here apply to all waves and will be emphasized further in Chapters 7 and 8. A ripple tank would be a useful demonstration apparatus for this chapter as well as Chapters 7 and 8.

6–1. WAVES

BACKGROUND: The concept that waves are always the result of energy moving from one place to another is emphasized. The terms "transverse," "longitudinal," "frequency," "wavelength," "trough," "crest," "amplitude," and the unit "hertz" are introduced in this section.

MOTIVATION: Set up a ripple tank to show waves. An alternate method is to place a shallow dish of water on an overhead projector. Disturbances on the surface of the water will be projected on the screen as traveling waves. You may wish to point out that the bright lines on the screen are the result of the focusing effect of the wave crests on the light from the projector. Students will learn more about this effect in their study of light in Chapter 8.

INVESTIGATION

Teaching Hints: Coiled springs are available from most science supply houses. Some houses will only sell them along with a smaller coiled spring. The smaller coiled spring can be attached to the large one end-to-end to form a second medium. The change in speed that occurs as a wave enters the second medium is striking and will set the stage for Section 6-2 of this chapter. Caution students not to release the spring after it is stretched. It will get tangled and will need to be replaced. A second kind of reflection occurs if you attach a heavy nylon string to the end of the spring that is being held tightly. Hold on to the string to allow the end of the spring to move freely when a wave reflects from it. In this case, the wave does not reflect on the reverse side.

Answers to Questions:

1. Yes, the speed is nearly constant.
2. No, the wave remains the same shape but gets smaller.
3. The speeds of large waves and small waves are the same.
4. Stretching the spring causes the waves to travel faster.
5. Yes, the speed is constant.
6. Large and small waves travel at the same speed.

Conclusions:

1. You can make transverse waves by moving a coiled spring from side to side. You can make longitudinal waves by gathering several coils together and suddenly releasing them.
2. The speed of a wave in a coiled spring is greatest when the tension (stretch) of the spring is greatest. When a wave reflects from the stationary end of a coiled spring it returns on the opposite side from the original wave.

6–2. WAVE INTERACTIONS

BACKGROUND: This section deals with reflection, refraction, the Doppler effect, and standing waves. An example of each of these phenomena should be shown as you discuss the section with students. Use the new terms and have students use the new terms properly both orally and in writing.

MOTIVATION: Have students use their own experiences to describe the behavior of waves in different situations, for example, hitting a barrier (a wall and a post cause different effects) or approaching shore. Reflection and refraction can be shown by using a ripple tank. In-depth discussions are not necessary at this time except to introduce the terms connected with waves.

HINTS: The Doppler effect can be demonstrated with a ripple tank. Allow drops of water to fall at a regular rate (a medicine dropper connected by hose to a container of water) onto the surface of the ripple tank. Point out the circular waves that are generated. Then move the dropper at a constant speed above the ripple tank to produce the Doppler effect. Students should understand what is causing the Doppler effect. The Doppler effect can also be demonstrated by attaching a 1-m piece of rubber tubing to a whistle. Blow in the free end of the tubing while you swing the whistle around your head at the end of the tubing. The students will be able to hear the changing pitch as the whistle moves toward and away from them. The Doppler effect can also be demonstrated by swinging a vibrating tuning fork around your head on the end of a piece of heavy cord. Be sure the cord is securely attached to the tuning fork. Drill a hole in the handle to tie the cord through.

INVESTIGATION

Answers to Questions:

1. Answers will vary.
2. Answers will vary. The wavelength of the traveling waves should be twice the wavelength of the standing waves.
3. Answers will vary.

Conclusions:

1. Hold one end of a coiled spring. Stretch it out on the floor and have a second person hold the other end steady. Move the spring from side to side. Increase the frequency until you observe standing waves.
2. Find the frequency and measure the wavelength of the standing waves. The wavelength of the traveling waves will be twice that of the standing waves. You can then calculate the speed of the traveling waves.

SKILL-BUILDING ACTIVITY

Teaching Hint: If a ripple tank is available there are other demonstrations that can be done. An elliptical barrier and a point source will show the foci of the ellipse if a wave is generated at one focus. This also shows other properties of the ellipse. A circular wave reflecting from a straight barrier will show that the reflected wave seems to come from a point as far behind the barrier as the initial wave was in front of the barrier. Single concept Super-8 film cartridges showing ripple tank phenomena are available from science supply houses. They can be used to supplement the student Investigation.

Answers to Questions:

1. Waves are formed when a drop of water strikes the surface of the water.
2. A circular wave forms when a drop of water strikes the surface.
3. The wave is reflected from the side of the dish.
4. The wave remains circular after reflecting from the side of the dish.
5. The angles are equal.
6. Circular waves striking a circular barrier reflect in a circular shape since each tiny segment of the wave reflects straight back at the same angle as the angle at which the wave strikes the barrier.
7. At least two diagrams should be drawn, one to show a slightly curved wave approaching a slightly curved barrier with an arrow to show its direction, the other drawing to show the same shaped wave reflecting from the barrier.
8. Answers will vary.
9. Results may or may not confirm the hypothesis. The curvature of the wave is greater than the curvature of the side of the dish so that when the wave strikes and reflects at equal angles, a straight wave results.

Conclusion:

1. The angle at which a wave strikes a barrier is equal to the angle at which the wave reflects from the barrier.

CHAPTER REVIEW

Vocabulary:

1. amplitude 2. frequency 3. reflection 4. wave
5. refraction 6. hertz 7. Doppler effect 8. wavelength

Answers to Questions:

1. A wave is a disturbance caused by the movement of energy from one place to another. Drawings should look like Fig. 6–5.
2. A transverse wave is one in which the vibrations are at right angles to the direction of motion of the wave. A wave on a rope is an example of a transverse wave.
3. The properties of speed, frequency, and wavelength can be used to describe any wave.
4. Speed is the rate at which a wave travels through a material. Frequency is the number of waves generated each second. Wavelength is the distance from the crest (or trough) of one wave to the crest (or trough) of the next wave.
5. Reflection is the process in which a wave is thrown back after striking a barrier. Refraction is the process in which a wave changes direction because its speed changes. Both processes involve a change in direction.
6. In addition to a change in direction, there is a change in speed when a wave is refracted.
7. In the diagram the angle at which a wave strikes the barrier should be equal to the angle at which it is reflected.
8. Waves travel more slowly in shallow water.
9. The diagram should be similar to Fig. 6–13.
10. A longitudinal wave could be generated in a coiled spring by gathering in several coils and releasing them.
11. speed = frequency × wavelength
speed = 60 Hz × 5 m = 300 m/s
12. wavelength = speed/frequency
wavelength = 30 cm/s / 15 Hz = 2 cm
13. The Doppler effect can be observed when an automobile drives by while blowing its horn. The sound becomes lower when the car passes you.
14. As ocean waves approach shore they enter shallower water and are refracted so that they approach the shore head on.
15. (a) When a wave strikes a barrier it is reflected.
(b) When a wave enters shallow water it slows down and is refracted.

CHAPTER 7 SOUND

SECTION/ TIME NEEDED	MATERIALS (30 STUDENTS)	BASIC SCIENCE SKILLS	PACING GUIDE
7–1. Sound Waves (1–2 periods)	10 tuning forks 10 pieces aluminum foil 10 pieces of string 10 beakers 10 shoe boxes 10 balloons 10 meter sticks 10 metal rods 10 straight pins water	Observing (p. 159) Problem Solving (pp. 152, 155) Cause and Effect (Teacher's Resource Book, p. 7–3)	Slow Learners: Study sounds made by several different tuning forks. Solve several problems using the formulas on pages 152 and 155. Above Average: See item 2 of "Applying Science" at the end of the chapter.
7–2. Music and Noise (1–2 periods)	none	Compare and Contrast (p. 161) Classifying (pp. 163–166)	Slow Learners: Demonstrate and discuss how string, wind, and percussion instruments make sounds. Above Average: See items 1 and 3 of "Applying Science" at the end of the chapter.

SUPPLEMENTAL MATERIALS

Audiovisual

Sounds in the Sea (MN–10409). Department of the Navy. 16mm color film (28 min).

Approaching the Speed of Sound. Shell Film Library. 16mm color film (28 min).

Learning About Sound (2nd edition). EBEC. 16mm color film (16 min).

The Nature of Sound. Coronet. 16mm color film (13 min).

Noise Pollution. LCA. 16mm color film (18 min).

Sound Waves in Air. MLA. 16mm B/W film (36 min).

Light and Sound Energy (TD107). Millikan Publishing Co., St. Louis, MO. 20 color transparencies, 20 duplicating masters, teacher's guide.

Basic Physical Science, Sound. Learning Arts, Wichita, Kansas. Sound filmstrip.

Light and Sound (1226 CB). Educational Dimensions Group, Stamford, CT. 2 color filmstrips, 2 cassettes, teacher's guide.

Print

Hecht, E. *Physics in Perspective.* Reading, MA: Addison-Wesley, 1980.

Hobson, A. *Physics and Human Affairs.* New York: Wiley, 1982.

Taffel, A. *Physics: Its Methods and Meanings, 4th ed.* Boston: Allyn and Bacon, 1981.

Computer

Science-Sound. Right On Programs. APL II; COM 64, Pet.

Energy Series. Focus Media, Inc. APL II Series; TRS-80 Models III, 4; COM 64, Pet.

CHAPTER OVERVIEW

The nature of sound, how it is produced, and the manner in which we perceive it are the main subjects of this chapter. There is a strong emphasis on music and musical instruments. This practical side of sound allows you to extend the scope of the material presented into the music field as far as you wish.

7–1. SOUND WAVES

BACKGROUND: The students will be familiar with the transverse waves studied in Chapter 6. It is necessary to show the difference in sound waves by discussing the nature of longitudinal waves. Unlike some transverse waves, such as light, sound requires a medium in order to be transmitted. Humans no longer depend greatly on sound as a warning of danger. We have invented many ways to enjoy sound as music. If you or any of your students have any talent in this direction, use it to its advantage in this chapter.

MOTIVATION: You may wish to start a discussion concerning how important sound is to our lives and how we usually take hearing for granted. Pose the question "How would your life be different if you could not hear sound?"

We still need hearing to some extent to warn us of dangers. You could demonstrate this by making a sudden, loud, unexpected noise. Then discuss the students' basic reactions to the noise. Discuss the fact that these reactions were designed for defense and preservation. Recall that fireworks were invented and used by early civilizations to scare away evil spirits.

INVESTIGATION

This investigation is designed to sharpen the student's ability to make observations as well as to learn how sound is produced. The music teacher may have the only tuning fork available in your school. If this is the case, borrow it and demonstrate steps A, B, and C. Use student help and an overhead projector.

Answers to Questions:

1. Students may feel a vibration, hear a sound, or report nothing happened.
2. The ball bounces off the tuning fork.
3. The water splashes. The vibrations of the tuning fork cause the splashing.
4. It vibrates and gives off a sound.
5. It vibrates faster and the sound changes.
6. The neck of the balloon vibrates, giving off a sound.
7. Sound is given off by vibrating objects.
8. Yes.
9. Better through the metal rod.
10. Metal.

Conclusion:

1. Answers will vary. Students should indicate that a medium must vibrate in order to produce a sound and that sound travels at different speeds in different media.

7–2. MUSIC AND NOISE

BACKGROUND: Most people have little difficulty distinguishing between music and noise. Music is said to be pleasing to the ears. The mixture of sound waves that produces musical tunes depends on certain mathematical relationships of the frequencies of the sound waves involved. A musical scale has been developed by musicians in which the standard pitch is A above middle C, 440 cycles/s (440 Hz). Other musical scales are also in use, however. Physicists designate 427 cycles/s (427 Hz) as A above middle C. In either case, musical sounds are produced when certain mathematical relationships exist between the notes being blended. Electronic synthesizers use these principles to produce electronic tones which are mixed together to produce music.

MOTIVATION: There are many ways you could use musical instruments to prepare students to learn about music and noise. You may also wish to introduce the section by pointing out the difference between music and noise as follows:

1. Let the students become somewhat noisy.
2. Say in a low voice, "If you can hear what I am saying, raise your hand."
3. Call the class to attention and ask one of the students who raised his or her hand to tell why the others did not hear you. Point out that random sounds result in noise which is annoying and confusing to listen to.
4. Ask the students if 30 people, all making sounds at the same time, could produce sound that is pleasant rather than annoying. Many students will suggest a choir, glee club, orchestra, etc.

HINT: Have some of the following musical instruments available for students to examine: trumpet, clarinet, oboe, trombone, violin, drum, chimes. Include string, woodwind, brass, and percussion instruments. Your music department or individual students can help. There is more to the sounds produced by musical instruments than described in this section. Have students who play instruments tell the class more about how they work.

CHAPTER REVIEW

Vocabulary:

1. sound waves 2. pitch 3. ultrasonic 4. interference 5. resonance

Answers to Questions:

1. Answers will vary.
2. Air particles are alternately pushed closer together and then spread farther apart as the sound wave passes.
3. Sound usually moves faster through a solid material such as steel than it does through air.
4. Answers will vary. Any sound pleasing to the ear is music. Random, unpleasant sound is noise. Musical sounds are mathematically related while nonmusical sounds are not.
5. Sounds above 90 dB can cause hearing damage. Constant exposure to loud sounds can cause high blood pressure. Sounds above 160 dB can cause permanent hearing loss. Student experiences will vary.
6. An echo is the sound that is reflected from a barrier that does not absorb all of the sound energy.
7. The speed of sound is 331 m/s in air at 0°C and 348 m/s in air at 30°C.
8. $v = d \times t$ = 350 m/s × 15 s = 5,250 m (5.25 km)
9. speed = wavelength × frequency
   (a) at 20°C: 343 m/s = wavelength × 400 Hz
   wavelength = 343 m/s / 400 Hz
   wavelength = 0.858 m
   (b) at 30°C: 348 m/s = wavelength × 400 Hz
   wavelength = 348 m/s / 400 Hz
   wavelength = 0.870 m
10. In a wind instrument, an air column is made to vibrate, usually by blowing. In a stringed instrument, a string or wire is made to vibrate, usually by rubbing or plucking. In a percussion instrument, a stretched material is made to vibrate, usually by striking it.
11. The speed of sound in air increases by about 0.6 m/s for each 1°C increase in temperature.
12. The object to be cleaned is placed in a liquid. Ultrasonic waves are then sent through the liquid. The vibrations of the liquid particles caused by the ultrasonic waves scrub the object clean. Ultrasonic waves are also used in medicine and to find cracks or hidden flaws in objects.
13. A longitudinal wave is caused by back-and-forth motions of the particles of the medium through which the wave travels. In a transverse wave, the medium moves up and down, that is, at right angles to the direction of motion of the wave. Sound waves and waves in a spring are longitudinal. Waves in a rope are transverse waves.

CHAPTER 8 LIGHT

SECTION/ TIME NEEDED	MATERIALS (30 STUDENTS)	BASIC SCIENCE SKILLS	PACING GUIDE
8–1. The Electromagnetic Spectrum (1–2 periods)	10 pieces white cloth or paper 10 pieces black cloth or paper 30 thermometers 10 pieces each red, green, and blue cellophane ice cubes rubber bands glass plates clock	Compare and Contrast (pp. 173–174) Classifying (pp. 177–180) Cause and Effect (p. 181)	Above Average: See "Applying Science" at end of chapter. Slow Learners: Students could look at the home radio dial and report the lowest and highest frequencies on the dial. They could also locate their favorite radio station, then refer to the spectrum in Fig. 8–4 to identify its position.
8–2. Movement of Light (1–2 periods)	10 light bulbs 10 sockets 10 110–V outlets 10 concave mirrors 10 large white index cards 10 meter sticks 10 plane mirrors	Inferring (p. 183) Compare and Contrast (p. 185) Problem Solving (p. 186)	Above Average: Have students draw ray diagrams to illustrate the Skill-Building Activity. Slow Learners: Discuss the effects of curved mirrors used in an amusement park funhouse.
8–3. Lenses (1–2 periods)	10 pieces window glass 10 magnifying lenses 10 pieces white cardboard 10 sheets paper 10 rulers	Compare and Contrast (p. 191) Problem Solving (p. 194 and Teacher's Resource Book, p. 8–3) Inferring (Teacher's Resource Book, p. 8–3)	Above Average: Have students do the Investigation using a concave lens in place of the magnifying lens. They can find the focal length by using a ray diagram. Slow Learners: Let students examine eyeglasses, binoculars, and microscopes to see how the lenses are used.

SUPPLEMENTAL MATERIALS

Audiovisual

Where New Ideas Are Brought to Light. GTE-Sylvania. 16mm color film (12 min).
A Sea We Cannot Sense (0491). U.S. Department of Energy. 16mm color film (28 min).
Conquest of Light. Bell Telephone Laboratories. 16mm color film (10 min).
Lasers Unlimited. Bell Telephone Laboratories. 16mm color film (10.5 min).
Micro. Western Electric Company. 16mm color film (14 min).
Schlieren. Shell Film Library. 16mm color film (18 min).
Light (480–0515F). Science Software Systems, Inc., Los Angeles, CA. 5 filmstrips, includes The Story of Lenses and Physical Optics.
Energy Transmissions, Light and Sound (480–0535F). Science Software Systems, Inc., Los Angeles, CA. 6 filmstrips, including Geometric Optics (ray diagrams).
The Cosmos: The Study of the Universe. Educational Dimensions Group, Stamford, CT. 4-part videotape program, Part 2: Light and Space (20 min).

Print

Branley, F. *The Electromagnetic Spectrum: Key to the Universe.* New York: Crowell, 1979.
Johnson, B.J. *Optics and Optical Instruments.* New York: Dover.
Maycock, P.D. and E.N. Stirewalt. *Photovoltaics: Sunlight to Electricity in One Step.* Andover, MA: Brick House Publishing Co., 1981.
Minnaert, M. *The Nature of Light and Color in the Open Air.* New York: Dover.
Waldman, G. *Introduction to Light: The Physics of Light, Vision, and Color.* Englewood Cliffs, NJ: Prentice Hall, 1983.

Computer

Atarilab Light Module. Atari, Inc. Atari 800 XL.
Optics: Mirrors and Beams. HRM Software, APL II Series.

CHAPTER OVERVIEW

Although this chapter introduces light, the entire electromagnetic spectrum is also presented. Electromagnetic waves are compared and contrasted with wave forms studied previously.

8–1. THE ELECTROMAGNETIC SPECTRUM

BACKGROUND: Students are in almost constant contact with waves from all parts of the electromagnetic spectrum. While they may not be consciously aware of it, they use the visible portion of the spectrum continuously. At this level, it is not necessary to present the wave-particle nature of light in depth. The wave characteristics of light adequately explain all of the phenomena introduced here.

MOTIVATION: Since the emphasis in the chapter is on light as a wave phenomenon, the short experiment of viewing a light through a pinhole in an index card, described on page 173, could be done by the entire class and discussed.

HINT: The numbers involved in discussing the speed and frequency of light are necessarily large. Exponential notation must be used.

INVESTIGATION

Teaching Hint: Ideally, it is best to measure the heating effect of infrared waves from direct sunlight. If this is not possible, incandescent lamps could be used.

Answer to Question:

1. The dark cloth is warmer.

Conclusion:

1. Black surfaces absorb light, white surfaces reflect light. Sunlight consists of infrared waves which are heat waves. When absorbed, they heat up the material.

EXTENSION

Conclusions:

1. Answers will vary depending on the colors of cellophane used. In general, dark colors such as blue and red will absorb heat fastest.
2. Answers will vary. Light-colored clothing will keep you coolest.

8–2. MOVEMENT OF LIGHT

BACKGROUND: Light is nearly always described as moving in straight lines. As we see it on the macroscopic scale, this is the way light behaves. Using ray diagrams based on this straight-line motion, we can explain how light interacts with mirrors and lenses to produce images.

MOTIVATION: Students will probably have an instinctive feeling that light travels in straight lines. You may wish to extend the short experiment described on page 182 which is intended to show this. Discuss some common observations that show that light travels in straight lines. Ask what is meant by the term "line of sight."

SKILL-BUILDING ACTIVITY

Teaching Hint: Shaving or cosmetic mirrors could be brought from home. Many of them have a concave side as well as a plane side. If small laboratory mirrors are used, you may want to use a battery and a small light bulb in place of the 110-V bulb.

Answers to Questions:

1. Right side up
2. It gets larger.
3. Smaller.
4. Right side up
5. The image becomes blurry and then flips upside down.
6. Answers will vary depending on the mirror used.
7. It is twice the focal length.
8. No, it is upside down.

Conclusions:

1. Images in a concave mirror are larger than those formed by a plane mirror. They are upside down instead of right side up.
2. Measure the distance from the mirror to an image of the object formed by the mirror on a screen.

8–3. LENSES

BACKGROUND: We see by using convex lenses to focus light on the retinas of our eyes. In this section the students will learn that this kind of lens produces images that are upside down. Everything we see forms an upside-down image on the retinas of our eyes. The resulting signals are sent to the brain. They are interpreted by the brain to show the objects as right side up.

MOTIVATION: Most people at one time or another will need to use eyeglasses or magnifying lenses to help them see things more clearly. Have available as many devices as possible that use lenses.

INVESTIGATION

Teaching Hints: Some students may be able to bring magnifying lenses from home. They are sometimes called reading glasses or hand magnifiers. Glass squares are often found as a part of the equipment in chemistry laboratories and can be purchased from scientific supply houses. Plastic lenses are less expensive than glass and give a comparable image. Large magnifying glasses are ideal but they are more expensive.

Answers to Questions:

1. The print becomes smaller.
2. The print becomes larger.
3. Smaller.
4. Upside down.
5. It becomes blurred.
6. Answers will vary depending on the lens used.
7. The image is not as bright, but it does not change much.

Conclusions:

1. A piece of cardboard held at the focal length of the lens and on the opposite side of the lens from the object will show an image of the object.
2. The image is a real image. It can be projected on the index card.
3. Focus the image of a distant object on a piece of cardboard. The distance from the lens to the cardboard is the focal length of the lens.

TECHNOLOGY

If your school is equipped for conference calls, it would be interesting to arrange such a call for your class. Homebound students could be connected with the class or the class could call various experts to talk about their different areas of study.

COMPUTER

The concept of a looping mechanism within the computer is not an easy one for students to grasp. It is important to explain the relationship among the user's input, the computer software, and the resulting flow of electric impulses. Emphasize that the processes occurring within the computer are physical processes and therefore take up time and space.

CHAPTER REVIEW

Vocabulary:

1. electromagnetic spectrum 2. focal length 3. rays 4. convex lens 5. lens 6. concave lens 7. focal point 8. electromagnetic waves 9. convex mirror 10. focus 11. concave mirror

Answers to Questions:

1. Radio waves: used for communications; infrared

waves: important heat source; visible light waves: allow us to see; ultraviolet waves: used to kill germs; X-rays: used to photograph inside the body; gamma rays: used to fight cancer.

2. It shows that light spreads out like waves.
3. AM radio waves can be reflected by the ionosphere while the FM radio waves are not.
4. Your image in a plane mirror is smaller depending on your distance from the mirror. It is reversed with respect to right and left sides.
5. Lenses produce images by refraction, bending the rays as they pass through the lens, while mirrors produce images by reflection, changing the direction of the rays as they bounce off the surface of the mirror.
6. Convex lenses are used to correct farsighted vision since the person's eyes do not bend the light rays enough to see near things clearly. Concave lenses are used to correct nearsighted vision since the person's eyes bend the light rays too much.
7. Light can travel about 7.5 times around the earth in one second. This is about 1.08 billion kilometers per hour.
8. visible light:
   speed = wavelength × frequency
   3×10^8 m/s = wavelenght × 10^{14} Hz
   $\frac{3 \times 10^8 \text{ m/s}}{10^{14} \text{ Hz}}$ = wavelength
   3×10^6 m = wavelength
   radio waves:
   3×10^8 m/s = wavelength × 10^6 Hz
   $\frac{3 \times 10^8 \text{ m/s}}{10^6 \text{ Hz}}$ = wavelength
   3×10^2 (300) m = wavelength
9. Speed in air/speed in medium = index of refraction.
   1/0.75 = 1.33
10. (a) It is less than the index of refraction for real diamonds.
    (b) One half the speed of light in natural diamonds.
11. $\frac{d_o}{d_i} = \frac{s_o}{s_i}$

    $\frac{50 \text{ m}}{0.05 \text{ m}} = \frac{s_o}{0.025 \text{ m}}$

    $25 \text{ m} = s_o$

CHAPTER 9 COLOR

SECTION/ TIME NEEDED	MATERIALS (30 STUDENTS)	BASIC SCIENCE SKILLS	PACING GUIDE
9–1. Light and Color (1–2 periods)	10 glass prisms 10 diffraction gratings 1 or 2 straight filament lights with sockets	Compare and Contrast (pp. 212, 216) Cause and Effect (pp. 209, 210–211)	Above Average: Research color-blindness. Write a report on rods and cones and color vision. Mainstreaming: Visually handicapped students should work with partners in the Investigation.
9–2. Seeing Color (1–2 periods)	15 water soluble black felt-tip pens 15 strips of filter paper 15 400-mL beakers 15 cardboard covers for beakers transparent tape water 30 colored objects 3 slide projectors red, green, and blue filters to fit the projector	Predicting (p. 225 and Teacher's Resource Book, p. 9–2) Observing; Compare and Contrast (p. 226)	Above Average: Analyze pigment combinations for various colors.

SUPPLEMENTAL MATERIALS

Audiovisual

Introducing Sound, Light, and Color. National Geographic Society, Educational Services. 2 color filmstrips with sound cassettes (15 min each).

Where New Ideas Are Brought to Light. GTE—Sylvania. Color (12 min).

Conquest of Light. Bell Telephone Laboratories. Color (10 min).

Lasers Unlimited. Bell Telephone Laboratories. Color (10.5 min).

Schlieren. Shell Film Library. Color (18 min).

Print

Burroughs, W. *Lasers.* New York: Warwick, 1982.

Greenler, R. *Rainbows, Halos, and Glories.* New York: Cambridge University Press, 1980.

Purcell, J. *From Hand Ax to Laser: Man's Growing Mastery of Energy.* New York: Vanguard, 1982.

Waldman, G. *Introduction to Light: The Physics of Light, Vision, and Color.* Englewood Cliffs, NJ: Prentice Hall, 1983.

Computer

Reflections. HesWare. APL II Series, COM 64; IBM PC, PC Jr.

CHAPTER OVERVIEW

Students are familiar with the visible part of the electromagnetic spectrum. In this chapter they will study how white light can be broken down into its component colors by means of a prism. They will learn how laser light is produced. The difference between the primary colors of light and the primary colors of pigments is explained. Mixing the primary colors of light produces quite different results from mixing the primary colors of pigment. The interference of light waves to produce colors is explored and the method of printing four-color pictures is described.

9–1. LIGHT AND COLOR

BACKGROUND: Most mammals lack color vision. However, humans, apes, and monkeys have highly developed color vision. Many animals see very well by light of various wavelengths without discriminating between the wavelengths. Dogs, cats, and horses apparently lack the degree of discrimination necessary to see color.

MOTIVATION: Start a discussion by asking the students if they believe that dogs and cats see colors as we do. Most people are used to seeing things in color and do not realize that dogs and cats see little, if any, color.

HINT: If you have access to a low-power helium-neon (He-Ne) laser you can diverge the beam with a lens and allow students to try reading a book in the laser light. (Be sure the beam diverges to at least a 30-cm diameter beam.)

INVESTIGATION

Teaching Hints: Inexpensive diffraction gratings are available from Edmund Scientific Co. or Sargent-Welch Scientific Co. Gratings from inexpensive spectroscopes can also be used. Your local high school physics teacher might be able to lend you some gratings. A single showcase bulb with a straight filament can be used for the whole class to view. Place it in a socket so that the filament is vertical and above the heads of the students. The spectrum as viewed through a prism is a little more difficult to see than with the diffraction grating.

Answers to Questions:

1. Violet, blue, green, yellow, orange, and red. (Other colors may be listed. The order may be reversed.)
2. Yes, there is more than one spectrum to the right of the bulb.
3. The colors on the left are in reverse order from the colors on the right.
4. Violet, blue, green, yellow, orange, and red.

Conclusions:

1. A spectrum of the colors contained in white light can be displayed by looking at a light bulb through a diffraction grating or passing the light through a prism.
2. The spectrum produced by a diffraction grating is the same as that produced by a prism.

9–2. SEEING COLOR

BACKGROUND: Mixing light colors and mixing pigment colors is not the same. The light colors add together while the pigments subtract a part of the visible spectrum to produce the resulting color. Interference causes colors in soap bubbles and oil films on water. The reflected light rays from the top and bottom surfaces of the film interfere. The color depends on the thickness of the film. Since the film varies in thickness, the color varies.

MOTIVATION: A demonstration can be set up using the three primary light colors. Use filters that will isolate the red, green, and blue light needed to produce white (or near white). You can then use three projectors to show the combination of the three primary light colors.

HINTS: Have students look at a soap bubble carefully enough to see the color swirls. Tell them that they will learn more about why this happens later in this section. Have magnifying glasses available for students to look at the colored pictures in the text to see how the dots combine to form the full-color image. Students could do this at home.

SKILL-BUILDING ACTIVITY

Teaching Hints: Newspaper will work very well for this activity. Use the margin of the newspaper so that there will not be any print on it. The filter paper or newspaper should be cut into strips 1 cm wide by 15 cm long. Quart jars can be used instead of beakers. Be sure to try the ink that you want to use. Not all inks will work with water. Water-soluble ink is best. Avoid India ink. Some food coloring will also work well in this activity.

Answers to Questions:

1. Students should predict that all the primary colors are present in black ink.
2. As the water soaks into the paper, the colors present in the ink separate out.

3. All the primary pigment colors are present in black ink. Student hypotheses may or may not be correct.

Conclusion:

1. The pigments in ink can be separated by placing a dot of the ink on a piece of paper and soaking the end of the paper in water. The water rises in the paper and dissolves the ink, distributing the colors in bands along the paper.

INVESTIGATION

Teaching Hints: Try to have some objects that are nearly the color of the light to be used. You should try the objects ahead of time. Set up several projectors to facilitate student observations.

Answers to Questions:

1. Answers will vary.
2. Red.
3. Answers will vary.

Conclusion:

1. An object can only reflect certain colors, depending on its own color. If the light shining on the object contains one or more of the colors in the object, these colors will be reflected. If the color of the light shining on the object is not one of the colors in the object, the object will not reflect any light and it will appear black.

TECHNOLOGY

An interesting book in this field is *Computer Images: State of the Art,* by Joseph Deken. New York: Workman, 1983.

CHAPTER REVIEW

Vocabulary:

1. complementary colors 2. visible spectrum 3. prism 4. incandescent 5. interference colors 6. laser 7. primary light colors.

Answers to Questions:

1. When white light enters a prism, different colors are refracted by different amounts. When the light leaves the prism the same thing happens again and the result is a spectrum. The student diagrams should be similar to Fig. 9-2.
2. As sunlight passes through the atmosphere, blue light is scattered by the air and dust. It is this scattered light that we see as the blue color of the sky. Light from the sun passes through more air and dust at sunset than at noon. More blue is scattered out and we see the sun as red.
3. A mixture of many different wavelengths of sound is called noise. White light is a mixture of many wavelengths of light and therefore is similar to noise. Laser light is made up of one frequency and resembles a pure musical tone.
4. Incandescent sources produce light by heating, as in the filament of a light bulb. Neon light sources produce light by passing an electric current through a gas. Fluorescent lamps produce light when ultraviolet light causes the coating in the bulb to glow. A laser produces light similar to a neon light. Mirrors only allow high intensities of nearly identical light waves to escape.
5. In green light, the white would appear green; the red and blue would appear black. In red light, both the red and the white would appear red; the blue would appear black.
6. Stare at a red object for about a minute, then stare at a sheet of white paper. The color you will see is the complement of red.
7. The primary light colors are red, blue, and green. They add together to produce other colors of light. Paint colors absorb all but certain colors of light. The colors that are not absorbed by the paint are reflected.
8. A color TV screen is made up of lines that glow in the primary colors of red, blue, and green when they are struck by a beam of electrons. The proper combination of these colors produces the colored picture on the screen.
9. When light from the sun is passed through a prism, it is spread out into a spectrum of colors.
10. In passing into and out of a raindrop, red light is refracted least. This causes it to be the outer band of the rainbow.
11. The spectrum produced by a prism results from the colors being separated by refraction while in a soap film the colors are the result of reinforcement of different colors at different places in the film caused by interference.
12. Laser light is produced in a gas-filled tube. The tube has a mirror at each end, but one of the mirrors is only partially reflecting. When an electric current passes through the gas, the gas gains energy and produces light. The light bounces back and forth between the two mirrors. Finally, the gas gains so much energy that a beam of coherent light passes out through the partial mirror. Coherent light is made up of light waves that all have the same frequency.
13. A red sweater would appear black in green light. A green sweater would appear green in green light.
14. Student diagrams should be similar to Fig. 9–1 on page 208. The colors should be labeled red, orange, yellow, green, blue, and violet from top to bottom. Violet has the highest frequency. Red has the lowest frequency.

CHAPTER 10 ELECTRICITY

SECTION/ TIME NEEDED	MATERIALS (30 STUDENTS)	BASIC SCIENCE SKILLS	PACING GUIDE
10–1. Static Electricity (1–2 periods)	30 plastic rulers 15 pieces of wool or waxed paper 15 pieces of aluminum foil transparent tape nylon thread paper 5 chalk erasers	Observing (p. 242) Cause and Effect (p. 234) Sequencing (p. 240)	Above Average: Write a report on electrostatic pollution filters. Slow Learners: Show how a charged comb will pick up small pieces of paper. Above Average: Solve several Coulomb's law problems.
10–2. Electric Current (1–2 periods)	20 1.5-V batteries 30 insulated wires with clips 10 pieces of wood 10 staples 10 pencils 10 3-V light bulbs with sockets 10 paper clips 10 pieces of glass 10 pieces of chalk 10 rubber erasers	Classifying (pp. 248, 250) Compare and Contrast (p. 249) Hypothesizing, Predicting, and Compare and Contrast (Teacher's Resource Book, p. 10–3)	Slow Learners: Compare conductors of electricity with conductors and insulators of heat. Slow Learners: Show examples of commonly used models, for example, architect's blueprints, home floor plans, model ships and planes, and so forth.
10–3. Electric Circuits (1–2 periods)	20 1.5-V batteries with holders 30 3-V light bulbs 30 sockets 40 insulated wires	Cause and Effect (p. 258) Compare and Contrast (p. 251)	Above Average: Draw several electric circuits on the board and have students set them up. Also see Applying Science, page 261.

SUPPLEMENTAL MATERIALS

Audiovisual

Micro. Western Electric Company. Color film (14 min).

Story of the Modern Storage Battery (62005). Association Films. Color film (17 min).

Print

Goldberg, J. *Fundamentals of Electricity.* Englewood Cliffs, NJ: Prentice-Hall, 1981.

Williams, J. I. *Modern Physics.* Holt, 1984.

Computer

Electricity. J & S Software. APL II Series.

CHAPTER OVERVIEW

Students are familiar with electric charge from their own experiences. This chapter extends the students' understanding of electricity by the study of electric charges, how charges react to each other, how an electric field affects charged objects, and how an electric current is produced.

10–1. STATIC ELECTRICITY

BACKGROUND: In order for students to understand the bonding of atoms it is necessary for them to have an understanding of electric forces as well as gravitational and magnetic forces. These forces play an important role in holding matter together and keeping things the size they are.

MOTIVATION: Vinyl plastic takes on a negative charge when rubbed with wool (and many other materials) while acetate takes on a positive charge when rubbed with cotton (or many other materials). Hang a strip of vinyl and a strip of acetate near each other where the class can see them. Rub the vinyl with wool and the acetate with cotton. Rub another piece of vinyl with wool and bring it near the hanging vinyl strip. They will repel each other. Bring the vinyl near the hanging acetate strip. They will attract each other. Rub another acetate strip with cotton and bring it near each hanging strip. Rub a piece of wood with wool and bring it near the hanging strips. This will introduce the students to the concepts of positive, negative, and neutral. (The wood is neutral since it loses its charge through your hand very quickly.)

HINTS: Kits containing vinyl, acetate, wool, and cotton pieces that work well in the study of static electricity are available from science supply houses. If you have a Van de Graaff generator available, you can perform several demonstrations.

INVESTIGATION

Teaching Hints: Vinyl rubbed with wool gives a good charge. Acetate rubbed with cotton also gives a good charge. On very humid days it may be difficult to get a satisfactory charge on the rulers.

Answers to Questions:

1. Yes.
2. It repels the rulers.
3. No.
4. Yes.
5. The rulers attract each other.
6. The ball is attracted.
7. The ball moves farther from its rest position.
8. The force on the ball is greater when the ruler is closer.
9. Yes, reducing the charge reduces the force.

Conclusions:

1. Answers will vary. For example, "To charge a plastic object, rub it with a piece of cloth."
2. Answers will vary. For example, "If the charge on two objects increases, the force will increase. If the distance increases, the force will decrease."

10–2. ELECTRIC CURRENT

BACKGROUND: The concept of the electron is introduced as a scientific model that explains some of the behavior of electricity. The scientific model is expanded to include the proton which then enables all the usual electrical phenomena to be explained.

MOTIVATION: Explain that scientists use models to describe objects or phenomena that they cannot see directly. Such is the model of the atom. Place two or three familiar objects (paper clip, rubber eraser, chalk eraser, pencil, marble) in a shoe box. Seal the box with tape. Give the box to a student and ask how many objects are in the box. What shapes are the objects? What size are the objects? Are there any hard objects, round objects, or flat objects? List the student's "observations" on the board. Take the lid off the box to show the objects inside.

SKILL-BUILDING ACTIVITY

Teaching Hint: When the students are finished, check to be sure that they did not leave the battery short-circuited by means of the wires. The wires can get very hot and the batteries will not last long if they are short-circuited.

Answers to Questions:

1. If the object tested is a conductor, it will allow an electric current to flow and the bulb will light.
2. If the object tested is an insulator, it will not allow an electric current to flow and the bulb will not light.

Conclusions:

1. Answers will vary. Students should name three insulators and three conductors.
2. Students should draw a diagram similar to Fig. 10–21 and state that by placing material between the clips of the apparatus a material can be classified as an insulator or conductor.
3. The wires used in the activity are surrounded by an insulator in order to keep the electrons from

escaping when an electric current flows through the wire.
4. Electric wires are made of a metal because metals are good conductors of electricity.

10–3. ELECTRIC CIRCUITS

BACKGROUND: A complete electric circuit is necessary for a current to flow. The comparison with water flowing through pipes is used to explain this.

MOTIVATION: Set up a couple of simple electric circuits (complete and incomplete) containing a battery, a switch, a light bulb, and visible wiring. Also draw the circuits on an overhead transparency. Using the transparency, discuss what will happen when the switch is closed. Then test the hypothesis. The role of each part of the circuit can be discussed. DC circuits using two 1.5-volt batteries and flashlight bulbs are safest.

INVESTIGATION

Teaching Hint: If enough ammeters are available, they can be used to measure the current rather than using the brightness of the bulbs, as called for in the Investigation.

Answers to Questions:

1. The bulb lights.
2. Yes.
3. Greater.
4. The brightness is very nearly the same.
5. The current is the same.
6. Answers will vary.
7. Answers will vary. The correct answer is that the bulbs are dimmer.
8. The current through each bulb is the same as for one battery and one bulb.

Conclusions:

1. The more batteries you connect in series to a given number of bulbs, the greater the amount of current that will flow. The more bulbs you connect in series to a given number of batteries, the less the current in the circuit.
2. Two bulbs wired in parallel to a battery will each have the same amount of current flow through them as with one battery and one bulb. (This means that the battery must provide twice as much current to the circuit.)

CHAPTER REVIEW

Vocabulary:

1. positive charge 2. neutral 3. electric field 4. scientific model 5. electron 6. proton 7. electric current 8. insulator 9. electric circuit 10. alternating current 11. series circuit 12. parallel circuit 13. direct current 14. conductor 15. negative charge 16. electric force

Answers to Questions:

1. Franklin showed that clouds can have an electric charge and that lightning is a form of electricity. He also suggested a method for naming electric charges.
2. Two objects will attract each other if you give one of them a positive charge and one of them a negative charge.
3. A scientific model can explain how an object becomes charged by the movement of electrons.
4. Combing your hair, walking across a rug, or stroking a cat are examples of energy of motion being converted into electric energy. (Other examples are acceptable.)
5. An electric current is the motion of electrons.
6. If the number of electrons equals the number of protons the object is neutral. If the number of electrons is greater than the number of protons the object is negative. If the number of electrons is less than the number of protons the object is positive.
7. Insulators are: plastic ruler, rubber rod, glass window, cover on electric wire, and plastic spoon. Conductors are: copper wire, aluminum pan, iron skillet, and silver ring.
8. If clouds are negatively charged, electrons jump from the clouds to the lightning rod and thus to the ground. If the clouds are positive, the electrons come from the ground to the lightning rod and then jump to the clouds.
9. If you touch a current-carrying wire while you also touch a water pipe, you may become part of an electric circuit and receive a deadly shock.
10. In an alternating current, the electrons move back and forth while in a direct current the electrons move in only one direction.
11. Using a parallel circuit allows you to turn one branch on or off without affecting the other branches.
12. Small charges are picked up at the bottom of a belt that travels up to a pulley which is inside a hollow metal dome. The charges are transferred to the dome. The belt travels back to a pulley at the bottom and continues the transfer of charge.
13. Power companies use the same frequency (60 Hz) so that they can connect into each others' networks and help each other in case of a power shortage.

CHAPTER 11 USING ELECTRICITY

SECTION/ TIME NEEDED	MATERIALS (30 STUDENTS)	BASIC SCIENCE SKILLS	PACING GUIDE
11–1. Measuring Electricity (1–2 periods)	10 ammeters (0–1 A) 10 voltmeters (0–3 V) 60 wires with clips 20 resistances (5 ohms) 20 1.5-V batteries	Measuring and Problem Solving (p. 267 and Teacher's Resource Book, p. 11–2) Cause and Effect (pp. 265, 266)	Slow Learner: Demonstrate the use of a voltmeter and an ammeter. Above Average: See Applying Science, page 291.
11–2. Electric Power (1–2 periods)	20 flashlight bulbs and sockets 40 wires with clips 20 1.5-V batteries and holders	Cause and Effect (p. 271) Problem Solving (p. 274)	Above Average: Demonstrate how a transformer works.
11–3. Electronic Devices (1–2 periods)	pencils paper	Predicting and Problem Solving (p. 286) Sequencing (p. 284)	Above Average: Demonstrate a computer. Slow Learner: Show how an electronic device such as a calculator speeds up numerical computations.

SUPPLEMENTAL MATERIALS

Audiovisual

Electricity and Magnetism. National Geographic Society. Color filmstrip with sound (14 min).

Sandia Microelectronics. Sandia Laboratories. Color film (17 min).

Superhighways for Power. Tennessee Valley Authority. Color film (25 min).

To Build a Dam. Chelan County Public Utility District, No. 1. Color film (27 min).

The Quiet Revolution. National Rural Electricity Cooperative Association. Color film (27 min).

Magnetism and Electricity. SVE (EME-1620). 12 transparencies.

Print

Awad, E.M. *Introduction to Computers.* Englewood Cliffs, NJ: Prentice-Hall, 1983.

D'Ignazio, F. *Small Computers: Exploring Their Technology and Future.* New York: Watts, 1981.

Laver, M. *Computers and Social Change.* New York: Cambridge University Press, 1980.

Maycock, P.D. and E.N. Stirewalt. *Photovoltaics: Sunlight to Electricity in One Step.* Andover, MA: Brickhouse Publishing Co., 1981.

Stern, N. and R.A. Stern. *Computers in Society.* Englewood Cliffs, NJ: Prentice-Hall, 1983.

Computer

Power Grid. HRM Software. APL II Series; TRS-80 Models III, 4.

Science Package I. Micro Learningware. TRS-80 Models III, 4.

CHAPTER OVERVIEW

This chapter deals with electric currents and the interrelation of current, voltage, and resistance and their measurement. Electric power and electronic devices are discussed in some detail. The safe use of electricity in the home is studied and several rules of safety are stressed.

11–1. MEASURING ELECTRICITY

BACKGROUND: The analogy between water flowing through pipes and an electric circuit is expanded to compare water pressure with voltage, water flow with electric current, and size of the pipes with resistance. The details of how the characteristics of an electric circuit are measured are explained. Ohm's law ($V = I \times R$) is discussed and examples are given.

MOTIVATION: Electric energy is becoming more expensive. Students need to realize that the most efficient use of electric energy depends on the characteristics of the circuits in which it is used. The characteristics are measured in units of volts, amperes, and ohms. Students should be able to use these terms. The relationship among the characteristics is based on an understanding of circuits and how they are used.

SKILL-BUILDING ACTIVITY

Teaching Hints: Use large No. 6 dry cells if they are available; they will last longer. Meters with different limits than those in the materials list can be used. Try them to be sure they will not be overloaded. Keep checking to see that students disconnect the batteries after reading the meters. The batteries will last longer if they are not left connected.

Answer to Question:

1. For two equal resistances in series, the voltage across each resistance is the same.

Conclusions:

1. The greater the voltage, the greater the current.
2. The greater the resistance in a series circuit, the less the current that will flow.
3. Ohm's law is $V = I \times R$ or $R = V/I$. In each case the resistance is 5 ohms.

11–2. ELECTRIC POWER

BACKGROUND: Electricity is used as an energy source worldwide. Most day-to-day energy requirements are supplied by electric energy. This section describes the reasons why electricity supplies so much of our energy needs and points out the kind of circuits utilized in the home. Alternating current allows electricity to be transported over great distances. It is important to know how transformers, parallel circuits, circuit breakers (or fuses), and kilowatt-hour meters are used in order to understand how this energy is supplied to homes.

MOTIVATION: Demonstrate parallel circuits as used in the home. Have the students find the burned-out bulb in a series circuit, for example, a set of Christmas tree lights.

HINT: Discuss the list of safety hints given in this section. Add any others you wish. Students need to know how to use electricity properly. They should not be afraid of it but should treat it with proper respect. Have all students make a list of possible safety hazards in their homes.

INVESTIGATION

Teaching Hint: Use No. 6 dry cells if you have them. They will work better to supply the current in a parallel circuit. You may need to show students how to hook them up.

Answers to Questions:

1. The bulbs are somewhat dimmer when two are in series.
2. Unscrewing one of the bulbs causes the other bulb to go out.
3. Three bulbs in series glow more dimly than one or two.
4. Unscrewing a bulb in a parallel circuit does not affect the other bulb. (A brightening of the second bulb may occur. If so, it is because the batteries are weak and cannot supply enough current to the two bulbs in parallel.)

Conclusion:

1. Parallel wiring is used so that the various lights and appliances do not all need to be turned on in order to use one of them, as is the case in a series circuit.

11–3. ELECTRONIC DEVICES

BACKGROUND: Telephones, video games, television sets, calculators, computers, and radios are some electronic devices with which students are familiar. An understanding of how these devices work can make them even more useful.

MOTIVATION: Divide the class into two groups. Have one group work out several arithmetic problems using pencil and paper. Have the other group use calculators. See which group finishes first.

INVESTIGATION

Teaching Hint: You may prefer to give the students a cost per kilowatt-hour from your own electric bill. A cost of about \$0.10/kWh could be used, but a current local rate would be better.

Conclusions:

1. Answers will vary. The estimate the student makes will differ from the actual cost and will probably be too low.
2. Answers will vary. The difference is probably caused by underestimating the amount of electricity used by automatic devices such as the refrigerator and heating system.

TECHNOLOGY

If students are not convinced of the pervasive influence of computer electronics, you might suggest the following research exercise. Have students bring daily newspapers to class every day for one week. Have them read through their papers page by page, looking for references to computers, microchips, wafers, silicon, and digital systems. Have them cut out any articles they find and paste them in their notebooks. After one week, compare and discuss the articles.

COMPUTER

Students may be more familiar with the idea of a flow chart than they think. Many board games, such as Monopoly, incorporate steps that are in the form of a flow chart and can be thought of as programs. Throughout the game, players pick cards that represent "input." The players are often required to make decisions presented in an "if-then" format. "If" you own a certain property, for example, "then" certain options are open to you. Players are also instructed to "goto" another spot on the board and follow the instructions there. You should be able to present many other analogies between the steps in a board game and the steps in a flow chart.

CHAPTER REVIEW

Vocabulary:

1. volt 2. ampere 3. resistance 4. ohm 5. transformer 6. fuse 7. circuit breaker 8. kilowatt hour 9. electronic device

Answers to Questions:

1. Automobiles have voltmeters or indicator lights to tell the driver the condition of the battery or electrical system.
2. The resistance in an electric circuit limits the amount of current that flows.
3. 240 A, 1.5 Ω, 110 V.
4. Some of the reasons that electricity is used in so many different ways are: It is easily changed to other forms of energy. It can be sent long distances through wires. It is easy to connect wires where you want the electricity. Other answers are also acceptable.
5. In a string of lights that are in parallel, only the bad lights go out. In a series, all the lights go out. The same thing is true in a building. If one of the appliances in a parallel circuit goes out, the others will still work.
6. Home wiring always has fuses or circuit breakers to protect it from an overload.
7. Answers will vary. Computers are very fast. They do routine chores. They are very accurate and seldom make mistakes.
8. Any circuit similar to Fig. 11–5 should be accepted. It must have only one resistance and one ammeter.
9. 546 kWh × \$0.12/kWh = \$65.52.
10. The picture and sound are sent from the station to your home by means of electromagnetic waves. The waves are received at your home by an antenna. They are changed to electric signals and carried by wires to your television set.
11. Your voice changes the resistance of the telephone you speak into. The change of resistance changes the amount of current that flows. The changing current at the receiving end of the line changes the strength of an electromagnet which vibrates a metal disk to reproduce your voice.
12. First change 240 watts to kilowatts: 240 W/1,000W per kW = 0.24 kW. At \$0.12 per kilowatt hour, 0.24 kW × ? h × \$0.12/kWh = \$1.00

$$\frac{\$1.00}{0.24\text{ kW} \times \$0.12/\text{kWh}} = 34\text{ h}$$

CHAPTER 12 MAGNETISM

SECTION/ TIME NEEDED	MATERIALS (30 STUDENTS)	BASIC SCIENCE SKILLS	PACING GUIDE
12–1. Magnets (1–2 periods)	30 bar magnets plastic wrap various magnetic and nonmagnetic objects	Compare and Contrast (pp. 293–294) Observing (p. 298 and Teacher's Resource Book, p. 12–13)	Above Average: Determine which of two iron bars is a magnet.
12–2. Earth As a Magnet (1–2 periods)	15 bar magnets 15 steel needles 15 50-cm lengths of nylon thread transparent tape 15 paper clips	Inferring (p. 301) Sequencing (p. 303)	Slow Learners: Locate the geographic and magnetic poles on a map or globe. Compare magnetic fields to other fields, such as gravitational and electric. Above Average: What is the latest theory of the cause of the earth's magnetic field?
12–3. Electromagnetism (1–2 periods)	10 nails (16d finishing) 10 1.5-m pieces of stranded wire 20 1.5-V batteries 20 wire connectors 10 light bulbs and sockets 10 paper clips 10 compasses 10 bar magnets pencils	Cause and Effect (p. 314) Sequencing (p. 307)	Above Average: Construct an electric motor. Slow Learners: Visit the local power company.

SUPPLEMENTAL MATERIALS

Audiovisual

Magnetic Effects in Space (HQ-260F). NASA. Color (14 min).

Magnetism in Space (HQ-260E). NASA. Color (19.5 min).

Superconducting Magnets (358). U.S. Department of Energy. Color (12.5 min).

The Earth: Its Magnetic Field. Coronet. Color (14 min).

Electromagnetic Induction (advanced). Coronet. Color (13 min).

Exploring Electromagnetic Energy. Film Associates. Color (9 min).

How To Produce Electric Current with Magnets (elementary). EBF (10 min).

Magnetism and Electricity. SVE. (EME-1620). 12 transparencies.

Print

Hecht, E. *Physics in Perspective.* Reading, MA: Addison-Wesley, 1980.

Taffel, A. *Physics: Its Methods and Meanings, 4th ed.* Boston: Allyn and Bacon, 1981.

Hobson, A. *Physics and Human Affairs.* New York: Wiley, 1982.

Williams, J.E. *Modern Physics.* New York: Holt, 1984.

Computer

Magnetism. J & S Software. APL II, IIe.

CHAPTER OVERVIEW

Magnetism is closely related to electric currents. Do not try to convince students that permanent magnets, such as the ones used in the Investigations, are caused by electric currents. If you wish, you can explain to them that the electrical nature of the particles that make up matter is responsible for the magnetic properties of iron and steel. The relationship between magnetism and electricity is demonstrated in the Investigation.

12–1. MAGNETS

BACKGROUND: The lodestone, a form of iron oxide, has been known for its magnetic properties for centuries. Its ability to attract iron and to align itself so that one end always points toward the north while the other end points south was attributed to some mysterious property that it contained. Lodestone means "leading stone." Lodestones were originally abundant in Magnesia, an ancient town in Asia Minor, from which the term "magnet" derives.

MOTIVATION: Do the following demonstration: Place a bar magnet on an overhead projector. Place a piece of plastic, the size of the lighted area of the projector, over the magnet. Sprinkle iron filings over the plastic and magnet. The filings will align themselves in the magnetic field of the magnet, showing its shape and where the field is strongest.

HINTS: Use two ring magnets on an overhead projector to show attraction and repulsion. Students are not as likely to be acquainted with ring magnets. You may need to explain their magnetic fields. Small magnets can be used with a sheet of iron to make a magnetic dart board.

INVESTIGATION

Answers to Questions:

1. Answers will vary. The magnets may attract or repel each other.
2. The answer will be the opposite of question 1.
3. The ends of the magnet behave differently.
4. Plastic does not affect the magnets.

Conclusion:

1. Answers will vary. For example, "The objects made of iron or steel were attracted by the magnet."

12–2. EARTH AS A MAGNET

BACKGROUND: The fact that a magnet, suspended so that it swings freely, always lines up with one pole pointing north indicates that the earth behaves like a magnet. These facts were known prior to an understanding of magnetic principles. An explanation of why the north magnetic pole and the south magnetic pole have not been renamed is discussed in this section.

MOTIVATION: Steel objects that remain in the same position in the earth's magnetic field for a long time may become magnetized. For example, the steel frames on students' chairs may be magnetized. Also iron rails and fences often are magnetized. Students could use a compass to test various iron or steel objects for magnetism. Remember that the only true test for magnetism is repulsion. Have students slowly bring the compass near various locations on the steel frame. When they find a place that repels the magnet, they can be sure that the frame is magnetized.

INVESTIGATION

Safety: Caution the students to be careful when handling the steel needles.

Teaching Hint: If the magnetized needle is pushed through a cork carefully, it is possible to float the cork and needle in a container of water to make a compass.

Answers to Questions:

1. The point of the needle points north.
2. The point of the needle is a north pole.
3. The needle may point in the same direction, but it probably will not. Twisting the thread will cause it to change direction.
4. Yes.
5. Rubbing the needle, from eye to point, with the

north pole of a magnet will make the point of the needle into a south pole. The eye of the needle will point north.

Conclusion:

1. A compass can be made by rubbing a needle with a magnet, then hanging the needle by a thread. Magnetic materials near the needle will affect the direction in which it points.

12–3. ELECTROMAGNETISM

BACKGROUND: This section discusses whether or not a magnetic field can produce electricity. Joseph Henry in the United States, and Michael Faraday in England, discovered electromagnetic induction. A discussion of how electric current is produced by magnets leads to descriptions of the generator and alternator. The role of the transformer in transmission of electric current is also discussed.

MOTIVATION: If you have, or can borrow, a hand-cranked generator that can light a 7.5-watt bulb, it would be interesting to have a student crank it for one minute and then calculate what it would cost to generate enough electricity to run a home. Estimate $2 per hour. Using leg power, students could probably generate about 100 watts for several hours. It takes about 1 kilowatt to run a house, which would cost $20 per hour. Students will soon realize why energy is such a bargain even at today's rates. The same approach could also be used to calculate what a student's efforts to generate electricity are worth at $0.12/kWh.

COMPUTER

For the sake of the game, assume that the program allows for magnetic variation. There is a copymaster in the Teacher's Resource Book on which students can plot their compass choices and the computer's responses (p. 12–5).

SKILL-BUILDING ACTIVITY

Teaching Hints: Different nails will be needed for each class since they will hold some of the magnetism from the previous class and mislead the students. The light bulb in the circuit will make the batteries last longer but the magnetic effects are reduced. The stronger the magnets, the more convincing this Activity will be. Also, the greater the number of turns in the coil, the greater the effect will be. Remind students to tap the compass to make sure the needle is free to turn.

Answers to Questions:

1. No, the nail does not attract the paper clip.
2. The bulb lights.
3. Yes, the nail attracts the paper clip.
4. Answers will vary. The nail head will either attract or repel the south pole of the compass.
5. Answers will be the opposite of the answer to question 4.
6. The reaction of the compass to the point of the nail will be the opposite of its reaction to the head of the nail.
7. When the magnet is pulled out of the coil, the compass needle moves. Yes.

Conclusions:

1. Wrap the wire around the nail in coils and connect the ends of the wire to the battery. This will cause the nail to be magnetized.
2. Wrap the wire into a coil and join the ends of the wire together. When a magnet is moved in the coil, a current is generated.

TECHNOLOGY

Digitization and digital systems are basic to a great deal of modern technology. Take the class on a field trip to a local electronics retail outlet. If possible, ask a knowledgeable salesperson to explain the equipment to your students. Have the students write a report on what they learned.

CHAPTER REVIEW

Vocabulary:

1. magnetic poles 2. electromagnetic induction 3. transformer 4. magnetic variation 5. electric motor 6. magnetic field 7. aurora 8. electromagnet 9. generator

Answers to Questions:

1. Two north magnetic poles or two south magnetic poles will repel each other. A north pole and a south pole will attract each other. Two positive electric charges or two negative electric charges will repel each other. A positive charge and a negative charge will attract each other.
2. If a magnet is cut in half and then in half again, each part will be a magnet with its own north and south poles.
3. A compass does not point true north because it points to the earth's magnetic poles, which are not located at the geographic poles. This error is called magnetic variation.
4. An electromagnet can be made stronger or weaker by increasing or decreasing the electric current. An electromagnet can be turned off. The

poles of an electromagnet can be changed by reversing the current.

5. When a wire is moved in an electric field an electric current is generated. This is called electromagnetic induction.
6. In a motor, electricity produces the magnetism to turn the motor. In a generator, the movement of a wire through a magnetic field causes an electric current to flow.
7. In a magnetized piece of iron, the small magnets that make up the iron are aligned in the same direction so that there is a north and a south pole. In an unmagnetized piece of iron the small magnets are arranged in a random fashion so that there is no definite pole.
8. The north pole of a magnet is the pole that points north. The south pole is the pole that points south. In a bar magnet, the north and south poles are located at opposite ends of the magnet.
9. A simple compass can be made by suspending a bar magnet from a string so that it is free to turn or by placing a bar magnet on a cork floating in a glass dish of water. In both cases, the magnet will line up in a north-south direction.
10. An electric current moving in a wire produces a magnetic field around the wire. This field can be detected by a compass. Likewise, when a wire is moved in a magnetic field, an electric current is generated in the wire. This can be shown by attaching a coil of wire to a light bulb. When a magnet is thrust into the coil, an electric current flows in the wire and the bulb lights.
11. As charged particles from the sun reach the earth they interact with the earth's magnetic field. The reaction of the particles with the atmosphere causes the auroras.
12. An electric motor consists of two magnets. One is held fixed and the other is an electromagnet that turns. The poles of the magnets attract through half of a turn. Then the electromagnet reverses its poles causing the other half turn. Then it reverses again.
13. A transformer consists of two coils of wire wrapped around an iron core. A current sent through one coil induces a current in the other coil. If the output has twice the number of turns of wire as the input, the output voltage will be twice that of the input but the current will be half as large.

CHAPTER 13 THE STRUCTURE OF MATTER

SECTION/ TIME NEEDED	MATERIALS (30 STUDENTS)	BASIC SCIENCE SKILLS	PACING GUIDE
13–1. Matter (1–2 periods)	60 heat-resistant test tubes 0.5 kg sugar 15 test-tube holders 15 Bunsen burners matches 8 containers of water 0.1 kg paraffin 15 microscope slides 0.5 kg baking soda water 0.5 L vinegar	Compare and Contrast (pp. 323–324) Observing, Compare and Contrast (p. 327)	Slow Learners: Try the experiment described on page 322 at home.
13–2. Gases (1–2 periods)	15 small beakers 15 small-diameter glass tubes 15 ice cubes water	Predicting (p. 331) Cause and Effect (pp. 331–332)	Above Average: See Applying Science at the end of the chapter. Slow Learners: Demonstrate the compression of air with a pump.
13–3. Solids and Liquids (1–2 periods)	0.5 kg table salt 15 plastic sandwich bags 15 small magnifying lenses 0.5 kg rock salt pencils	Observing (p. 344 and Teacher's Resource Book, p. 13–2)	Slow Learners: Demonstrate that the same volume of water will fill containers of various shapes.

SUPPLEMENTAL MATERIALS

Audiovisual

Introduction to Physical Science. Educational Dimensions Group. Set of 4 color filmstrips with sound cassettes (20 min each).

Introduction to the Atom. National Geographic Society, Educational Services. Color filmstrip with sound cassette (15 min).

The Behavior of Matter. Encyclopedia Britannica Educational Corp. Color film (15 min).

Chemicals: A Fact of Life (10971). Modern Talking Picture Service. Color film (27 min).

Chemistry and Man (31999). Modern Talking Picture Service. Color film (28 min).

Chemical and Physical Change (641721). McGraw-Hill. Color film loop.

Atoms and Molecules (427-22). SVE. Color filmstrip.

Print

Metcalfe, H.C. *Modern Chemistry.* New York: Holt, 1982.
Rayner-Canham, G., et al. *Foundations of Chemistry.* Reading, MA: Addison-Wesley, 1983.

Computer

Matter. J & S Software, APL II Series.
Chemistry: Series I. Focus Media, Inc. APL II Series; TRS-80 Models III, 4; COM 64, Pet.

CHAPTER OVERVIEW

Beginning with the macroscopic and proceeding to the molecular, the students are introduced to the molecular and atomic structure of matter. The kinetic molecular theory is introduced as a means of explaining how matter can change from solid to liquid to gas and back again without any change in its substance.

13–1. MATTER

BACKGROUND: Matter is introduced from the macroscopic viewpoint. This is the way one usually sees matter. The molecular nature of matter comes into view upon closer inspection. Physical changes are the result of the rearrangement of the particular kinds of molecules. Chemical changes, unlike physical changes, cause a change to occur within the molecules.

MOTIVATION: The introductory paragraph of this section gives an excellent example of the approach to the study of matter, starting with the macroscopic and proceeding to the molecular. The students may discuss what they would expect to see if a piece of chalk were continuously broken down into smaller and smaller pieces.

INVESTIGATION

Teaching Hints: You will probably need new test tubes and microscope slides for each class. They are not easily cleaned. Tin can lids can be used in place of microscope slides and test tubes if you wish.

Answers to Questions:

1. It melts.
2. No.
3. It darkens and turns black.
4. No.
5. Heating sugar causes a chemical change.
6. No.
7. Yes.
8. Melting and hardening wax are physical changes.
9. There was a physical change in the test tube with water, and a chemical change in the test tube with vinegar. The water dissolved the baking soda but the vinegar caused a gas to be released by the baking soda.
10. Yes. The difference in the reactions with water and vinegar is quite different.

Conclusion:

1. A physical change is usually reversible while a chemical change results in a new product, such as a gas, being formed.

13–2. GASES

BACKGROUND: The kinetic molecular theory explains how a given substance can change from a solid to a liquid to a gas merely by a change in temperature. The theory is particularly useful in explaining why gases behave the way they do.

It is necessary to introduce all three phases of matter before going into detail on any one. Students may need to be told that not all substances can exist in all three phases. (Some substances decompose when heated.)

MOTIVATION: Use a bicycle pump to demonstrate the compressibility of air. Pinch off the delivery tube while a student presses down rapidly on the pump handle. Discuss why gases can be compressed in this manner while liquids and solids cannot.

INVESTIGATION

Teaching Hint: Students may confuse melting ice with water dripping from inside the tube.

Answers to Questions:

1. The water rises slightly above the water level in the beaker.
2. Yes.
3. Heating the air in the tube causes the air to expand and force the water out of the tube.
4. The drop goes back into the tube.
5. Yes.
6. Warming the air causes it to expand.

Conclusion:

1. When trapped air is cooled, it contracts and the drop of water goes back into the tube. When the air is heated, it expands and the drop of water is forced out of the tube.

13–3. SOLIDS AND LIQUIDS

BACKGROUND: Solids and liquids are condensed phases of matter. Solids are composed of an orderly arrangement of molecules, atoms, or ions. Liquids are composed of atoms, molecules, or ions that are not in an orderly arrangement. Some solids, such as glass and plastic, are like liquids in that their molecules are not in an orderly arrangement. The orderly arrangement of crystals results in equal bonds, and thus a sharp melting point. Glass and similar solids have many bonds of different strengths, resulting in a softening through a temperature range rather than a sharp melting point.

MOTIVATION: Large crystals of zinc can usually be seen on the surface of galvanized steel. Pass a piece of galvanized steel and a hand magnifier to several students. Ask the students to describe the appearance of the surface. Most solid substances are arrangements of crystals.

COMPUTER

You will need some advance planning time in order to run this program since the data consist of temperature and barometric readings for 14 days. Students can collect local readings or they may record 14 days of readings from a national newspaper.

INVESTIGATION

Teaching Hints: Low-power microscopes can be used in place of hand magnifiers. Have students observe noncubic crystals also. Sugar and alum are readily available examples.

Answers to Questions:

1. Yes.
2. Some are rectangular.
3. Yes.
4. Yes.
5. Yes.
6. Yes.
7. Yes.
8. Yes.
9. Yes.
10. Yes.
11. Answers will vary.

Conclusion:

1. The salt crystals appear as tiny cubes. They have flat surfaces that meet at 90° angles.

CHAPTER REVIEW

Vocabulary:

1. molecule 2. physical change 3. physical property 4. chemical change 5. chemical property 6. kinetic theory of matter 7. absolute zero 8. Kelvin temperature scale 9. crystal 10. melting point 11. heat of fusion 12. boiling point 13. heat of vaporization 14. pressure

Answers to Questions:

1. Boiling and freezing (or melting) are physical changes. They are called physical changes because they do not change the molecules of the substance.
2. The three phases of matter are solid, liquid, and gas. The molecules of a substance do not change as they go from one phase into another. However, the speed of the molecules is greater at higher temperatures.
3. First, the particles of a gas are moving very fast and have large distances between them. Second, gases can be compressed. Third, the temperature of a gas determines how fast its particles are moving.
4. All motion stops at 0° Kelvin, which equals −273° Celsius.
5. A crystal is a piece of solid matter with a regular shape. Examples are ice, diamonds, rock candy, and salt. (Other examples are acceptable.)
6. As water freezes, the molecules move more slowly. The molecules move faster as water boils, but there is no change in the molecules themselves.
7. These are both physical changes. Melted chocolate has the same taste and color as before it was melted. Water can be frozen and melted repeatedly without changing it.
8. Raising the temperature by 91° will increase the volume by 91/273 or 1/3. The new volume will therefore be 4/3 of its original volume. The new volume = 4/3 × 300 mL = 400 mL.
9. 80 cal/g × 5 × 40 g = 16,000 cal
   4.18 J/cal × 16,000 cal = 66,880 joules
10. 540 cal/g × 150 g = 81,000 calories
    4.18 J/cal × 81,000 cal = 338,580 J
11. Glass and some plastics are examples of solids that are not crystals.
12. Sublimation is the process by which a solid changes into a gas without first becoming a liquid. For example, moth balls usually do not melt but change directly into a gas.
13. As water is heated, the water molecules gain enough energy to leave the liquid water and escape as a gas.
14. In the solid phase, the molecules are like people sitting in rows in a theater. In the liquid phase, the molecules are like people leaving their seats and walking in the aisles. In the gas phase, the molecules are like people leaving the theater and walking away from each other.

CHAPTER 14 THE PROPERTIES OF MATTER

SECTION/ TIME NEEDED	MATERIALS (30 STUDENTS)	BASIC SCIENCE SKILLS	PACING GUIDE
14–1. Mixtures, Compounds, and Solutions (1–2 periods)	400 mL sand 400 mL salt 30 beakers 4 L distilled water 30 test tubes and test-tube holders 15 Bunsen burners matches containers of water	Compare and Contrast (p. 353) Observing (p. 355)	Slow Learners: Observe a piece of granite and try to identify several of its component minerals. Above Average: Try to separate sand and sugar by dissolving in water and evaporating.
14–2. Elements and Atoms (1–2 periods)	15 test tubes 0.5 L hydrogen peroxide 10 balances 100 g manganese dioxide matches 30 wooden toothpicks 15 one-hole rubber stoppers containers of water	Compare and Contrast (p. 358 and Teacher's Resource Book, p. 14–2) Problem Solving (p. 358) Inferring (Teacher's Resource Book, p. 14–2)	Above Average: See Applying Science on page 363.

SUPPLEMENTAL MATERIALS

Audiovisual

Chemistry: Elements, Compounds and Mixtures, 2nd ed. Coronet Films & Video. Color film (20 min).

Explaining Matter: Chemical Change, 2nd ed. EBEC. Color film (13 min).

Calcium Chloride—The Dust Fighter. Dow Chemical Company. Color film (15 min).

Symbol B, Number 5: Boron and the Borates. Bureau of Mines. Color film (28 min).

Tungsten. Bureau of Mines. Color film (18.5 min).

Elements, Compounds and Mixtures (493-2). SVE. Color filmstrip.

Periodic Chart of the Elements. Merck and Company.

International Atomic Weights Chart and Periodic Chart of the Elements. Allied Chemical Corporation. Atomic Weights Chart.

Print

Brady, J.E, and J.R. Holum. *Fundamentals of Chemistry.* New York: Wiley, 1981.

Metcalfe, H.C. *Modern Chemistry.* New York: Holt, 1982.

Computer

Physical Science Keyword. Focus Media, Inc. APL II Series; TRS-80 Models III, 4.

Matter. J & S Software. APL Series, 14 programs.

CHAPTER OVERVIEW

Compounds and elements are seen as manifestations of molecules and atoms, respectively. Most materials appear to be composed of a number of pure substances. Materials that can be separated by physical means are called mixtures. Materials that cannot be separated by physical means are called compounds. Some compounds are made up of ions while other, more complex, compounds are made up of both ions and molecules.

14–1. MIXTURES, COMPOUNDS, AND SOLUTIONS

BACKGROUND: The general characteristics and some examples of mixtures, compounds, and solutions are given. The components of mixtures and solutions can be separated by physical means. Solutions are described as a special case of mixtures. Compounds cannot be separated into simpler parts by physical means.

MOTIVATION: A handful of dry soil would be an excellent focal point for a discussion designed to investigate the kinds of matter. Allow students to inspect the soil. Place some of the soil on an overhead projector to show the class the different kinds of material found in a soil sample.

SKILL-BUILDING ACTIVITY

Teaching Hint: Tin can lids can be used in place of test tubes. A couple of drops of solution on the lid is all that is needed. Microscope slides held by clothespins can also be used if they are heated very slowly.

Safety: Be careful of sharp edges on microscope slides or tin can lids. Caution students about the heated test tubes, slides, or lids. Caution students to be careful when lighting and using Bunsen burners. Dispose of used matches in a container of water.

Answers to Questions:

1. A mixture.
2. Cloudy (possibly clear).
3. Answers will vary. When molecules of salt go into solution, they leave the crystal and occupy the spaces between the water molecules.
4. The water boils and evaporates.
5. The solution boils and the liquid evaporates, leaving behind a solid white substance.
6. Yes.

Conclusion:

1. Answers will vary. Add water to the mixture and dissolve one of the materials. Then boil away the water, leaving behind the dissolved material.

14–2. ELEMENTS AND ATOMS

BACKGROUND: Water is used as the example of a compound which, when broken down by chemical means, produces the elements hydrogen and oxygen. Atoms are identified as the parts that make up molecules of matter.

MOTIVATION: The ideas of chemical change, compounds, and elements could be introduced by demonstrating a chemical change. Heat a small sample of sugar slowly in a test tube. Draw the students' attention to the water that collects around the cool top part of the test tube. An overhead projector could be used to insure that all students will see. Note that when you continue to heat the sugar it will melt, turn to caramel, and then char. Point out that the final products, carbon and water, are completely different from sugar. The simplest way, at this point, to show the formula for sugar is $C(H_2O)$. While not complete, it will make the point more easily.

INVESTIGATION

Teaching Hints: Baby food jars with holes punched in the lids can be used in place of test tubes and stoppers. You should make the holes in the lids yourself. Manganese dioxide can be obtained from old dry cells. CAUTION: Do not use alkaline batteries. Cut the dry cell open and save the black paste for use when manganese dioxide is needed.

Safety: Remind the students to dispose of burned matches in a container of water. Be sure that these containers are available. Coffee cans filled with water work very well. Demonstrate the correct procedure for wafting the fumes in order to smell them. Wave your hand over the material in order to draw some of the fumes toward you.

Answers to Questions:

1. Hydrogen peroxide looks like water and does not have an odor.
2. The gas does not have a color nor an odor.
3. When the bubble breaks the toothpick flares up.
4. Answers will vary.
5. Oxygen does not burn.
6. Yes, oxygen is coming from the hole.

Conclusion:

1. Answers will vary. For example, "Mixing manganese dioxide with hydrogen peroxide will generate oxygen. Test for oxygen by using a glowing toothpick. It will flare up if oxygen is present."

CHAPTER REVIEW

Vocabulary:

1. solution 2. mixture 3. concentrated 4. atom
5. compound 6. solute 7. solvent 8. element
9. saturated 10. dilute 11. solubility

Answers to Questions:

1. Sand is usually a mixture. Sand usually has dark grains among the light grains, indicating two kinds of materials. Examples of mixtures will vary.
2. A compound contains only one kind of molecule. A compound is a substance that cannot be broken down into simpler parts by a physical change. Examples of compounds will vary.
3. A solute is the substance being dissolved in a solvent to form a solution. Examples of a solute are salt and sugar. Examples of a solvent are water and alcohol.
4. Raising the temperature, stirring, and increasing the surface area will all increase the rate at which a substance dissolves.
5. A concentrated solution contains a large amount of solute while a saturated solution contains all the solute that the solvent can hold. A dilute solution contains only a small amount of solute.
6. A mixture can be separated by physical means while a compound cannot.
7. Add a small amount of sulfuric acid to water and send an electric current through the water. The water will be separated into hydrogen gas and oxygen gas.
8. An element is the simplest form of matter. The smallest particle of an element is called an atom. Each element is made up of only one kind of atom.
9. The three elements which are found in greatest amount in the human body are oxygen, carbon, and hydrogen.
10. There are seven elements that are common in the earth's crust as well as in the human body. They are oxygen, iron, calcium, sodium, potassium, magnesium, and hydrogen.
11. 0.89×150 g $=$ 133.5 g of oxygen in 150 grams of water. 0.11×150 g $=$ 16.5 g of hydrogen in 150 grams of water.
12. A crushed aspirin tablet dissolves faster in water than a whole aspirin tablet because crushing increases the surface area, which speeds up the rate of dissolving.
13. When sugar dissolves in water, the sugar molecules leave the solid sugar and mix with the water molecules.
14. Place the same amount of water in two beakers. Add sugar to one beaker and salt to the other. Continue adding sugar and salt until no more will dissolve in the water. A larger amount of sugar than salt will dissolve in the same amount of water.
15. (a) A mixture of water and alcohol is an example of a liquid solution. (b) The mixture of gases in the air is an example of a gaseous solution. (c) Steel is an example of a solid solution.

CHAPTER 15 ATOMS

SECTION/ TIME NEEDED	MATERIALS (30 STUDENTS)	BASIC SCIENCE SKILLS	PACING GUIDE
15–1. Atomic Particles (1–2 periods)	30 sealed boxes, each containing 1 object pencils paper	Compare and Contrast (pp. 365, 367) Inferring (p. 369)	Above Average: Write a report on the development of atomic theory from Democritus to Dalton to Thomson.
15–2. Atomic Structure (1–2 periods)	30 clay balls with hidden objects 30 paper clips paper pencils	Inferring (p. 379)	Above Average: Research quantum and wave mechanics. Slow Learners: Do the wire fence experiment described on page 371.
15–3. Atomic Mass (1–2 periods)	none	Problem Solving (p. 381) Classifying and Inferring (Teacher's Resource Book, p. 15–3)	Slow Learners: Make models of atoms using Styrofoam balls. Pins with different colored heads could represent protons and neutrons.

SUPPLEMENTAL MATERIALS

Audiovisual

An Added Sense: The Detection of Nuclear Radiation (0486). U.S. Department of Energy. Color film (24 min).

"A" Is for Atom (0001). U.S. Department of Energy. Color film (15 min).

The Mass of Atoms (0202). U.S. Department of Energy. Color film (47 min).

Atomic and Molecular Weights (493-4). SVE. Color filmstrip.

Structure of the Atom (from the Chemistry series, 619005-6). McGraw-Hill, filmstrip, color and B/W.

Print

Brady, J.E., and J.R. Holum. *Fundamentals of Chemistry.* New York: Wiley, 1981.

Holum, J.R. *Elements of General and Biological Chemistry, 6th ed.* New York: Wiley, 1983.

Metcalfe, H.C. *Modern Chemistry.* New York: Holt, 1982.

Rayner-Canham, G., et al. *Foundations of Chemistry.* Reading, MA: Addison-Wesley, 1983.

Computer

Science Package II. Micro Learningware. TRS-80 Models III, 4.

Chemistry: Series I. Focus Media, Inc. APL II Series; TRS-80 Models III, 4; COM 64; Pet.

Molecules and Atoms: Exploring the Essence of Matter. Science Management Corp. APL IIe, IIc; IBM PC, PC Jr.

Structure of Matter. Classroom Consortia Media, Inc. IBM PC, PC Jr.

CHAPTER OVERVIEW

The study of atoms, atomic structure, and atomic particles requires the use of scientific models. Students can examine scientific models in the Investigations. The scientific model of an atom is introduced as a mental picture of what an actual atom might look like. The reason for choosing a particular model of an atom is considered. The roles played by various parts of an atom in determining its characteristics are studied.

15–1. ATOMIC PARTICLES

BACKGROUND: This section introduces the concept of the atom as a scientific model. J.J. Thomson was the first to suggest that atoms have electric charges. Early concepts of the atom did not involve any notion of positive or negative electricity. In 1898, Thomson suggested that atoms were composed of equal quantities of positive and negative electricity. Thomson envisioned the atom as being made up of negative charges embedded in a sphere of positive electricity, like raisins in a cake.

MOTIVATION: J.J. Thomson used his atomic model to explain the results of many experiments with beams of electric charges in vacuum chambers.

Review electric charge by showing that two different charges can be produced by rubbing strips of vinyl and acetate plastic hanging by threads. These opposite charges then attract each other just as electrons and protons attract each other in atoms. The electrostatic investigations of Chapter 10 can be related to material in this chapter.

INVESTIGATION

Teaching Hints: Keep the objects simple. Shoe boxes are excellent, but smaller boxes with lids can also be used and may be easier to store. Number the boxes and keep a record of the box numbers and the contents. Student answers will vary depending on the objects used. Use objects with different shapes as well as different materials, for example, a glass marble, an iron nail, a rubber eraser, and so forth. If magnets are available, students can use them to determine if the objects are made of steel or iron, which would be attracted by the magnet. If small magnets are put inside some of the boxes students can detect them with unmagnetized paper clips or a compass.

Answer to Question:

1. Answers will vary. For example, the question "Is the object a magnet?" can be tested with a magnetic compass.

Conclusion:

1. Answers will vary. By performing various tests, it is possible to get some ideas about the size, shape, texture, etc., of a hidden object. From these observations about the object, one can develop a mental image of the object. This is what is called a model of the object.

15–2. ATOMIC STRUCTURE

BACKGROUND: Some unusual properties are assigned to the atom in order to explain its makeup and behavior. The electron level approach is used with the understanding that the real nature of the arrangement and behavior of the electrons is more complicated.

Niels Bohr improved the Rutherford model of the atom. Bohr explained how an electron of a hydrogen atom could gain energy in discrete packets. The energy gained allows the electron to move to a position farther from the nucleus. The movement from one energy level to another either absorbs energy or gives off energy as electromagnetic radiation. The more recent theory involving quantum and wave mechanics would complicate the mental model too much for students at this level.

MOTIVATION: The introductory paragraph at the beginning of the section could be used as a point of discussion. The Bohr model of the atom is presented and can be used to reinforce the fact that an atom is mostly empty space.

SKILL-BUILDING ACTIVITY

Teaching Hints: In step C, sketches will vary depending on the objects and the students' ability to draw. Use modeling clay to make spheres 2 to 3 cm in diameter. Each sphere should contain a small hard object. Steel ball bearings work well. Glass marbles work also. Use standard paper clips, straightened out except for one loop.

Answers to Questions:

1. It contains a hard object.
2. Answers will vary.
3. Answers will vary.
4. Answers will vary.
5. Answers will vary.
6. Answers will vary. The sketch should show the position and shape of the hidden object.

Conclusion:

1. Gathering information by probing or other physical means (weighing, for instance) allows one to infer the structure of an object.

15–3. *ATOMIC MASS*

BACKGROUND: This section describes the nature of the atomic nucleus. The nuclear mass is measured in atomic mass units to avoid using extremely small metric units. Most of the mass of an atom is concentrated in the nucleus. The mass of the electron is so small (1/1,840 u) that it can be ignored when calculating atomic mass. The mass of the atom depends on the number of protons and neutrons. Isotopes account for the fact that atoms of the same element can have different masses. An isotope of an atom has the same number of protons, but a different number of neutrons. Almost all elements have several isotopes.

MOTIVATION: The idea that atoms of the same element can differ in mass is used to explain properties of atoms that are not related to their chemistry. For example, the action of ionized neon when it passes through a magnetic field is not related to the chemistry of neon atoms. Ionized neon atoms travel in two groups. Each group of neon atoms follows three distinct curving paths. The two groups correspond to the Ne^{+} and Ne^{2+} charged ions. The three paths or subgroups correspond to Ne-19, Ne-20, and Ne-21. The heaviest atom (Ne-21) follows a path that is curved least by the magnetic field.

An analog of this behavior could be discussed by using a hypothetical situation: Suppose a pitcher were to throw three baseballs for you to hit. All the balls are the same size. One ball is a standard ball, one is five times heavier, and one is ten times heavier. If you hit each ball with the same force, how would their paths to center field differ? The lightest ball would travel farthest. The heaviest ball would move slowest and cover the least distance. The other ball would fall between the two.

TECHNOLOGY

For a comprehensive layperson's view of the world of high-energy physics, see *The Dancing Wu Li Masters: An Overview of the New Physics,* by Gary Zukav, New York: Bantam, 1979.

CHAPTER REVIEW

Vocabulary:

1. energy level 2. atomic particles 3. nucleus 4. atomic number 5. symbol 6. isotope 7. atomic mass unit 8. mass number 9. atomic mass

Answers to Questions:

1. Electron: mass = 1/1,836 u, negative charge. Proton: mass = 1 u, positive charge. Neutron: mass = 1 u, no charge.
2. Scientists use scientific models to study things they cannot see directly. Atoms are too small to be seen, thus scientists use models to study them.
3. A wire fence is mostly empty space just like an atom. Ernest Rutherford's experiment showed that an atom has a small positively charged nucleus surrounded by empty space.
4. In each case the atomic number, the number of protons, and the number of electrons is the same. (a) Hydrogen: 1. (b) Helium: 2. (c) Carbon: 6. (d) Neon: 10. (e) Aluminum: 13.
5. In a solar system, the planets follow certain orbits around the central sun. In Bohr's atomic model, electrons can follow various orbits within a certain energy level.
6. The first level can hold 2 electrons, the second level can hold 8 electrons, and the third level can hold 8 electrons.
7. The atomic number of an atom is the same as the number of protons and the number of electrons. Aluminum therefore has 13 protons and 13 electrons.
8. The mass of an atom is determined by the number of protons and neutrons in the nucleus. It is usually expressed in atomic mass units (u).
9. Atoms of an element can have different mass numbers if the number of neutrons differs from atom to atom. For example, hydrogen has atoms with atomic mass numbers of 1, 2, and 3.
10. See table below.
11. The atomic mass of an element is the average value of the mass numbers of the atoms of the element as they occur in nature. The mass number is the sum of protons and neutrons in the nucleus.

ELEMENT	ATOMIC NUMBER	MASS NUMBER	NUMBER OF PROTONS	NUMBER OF NEUTRONS	NUMBER OF ELECTRONS
Lithium	3	7	*3*	4	*3*
Boron	*5*	*11*	5	6	*5*
Carbon	5	*11*	*6*	6	*6*
Neon	*10*	20	*10*	10	*10*

CHAPTER 16 FAMILIES OF ATOMS

SECTION/ TIME NEEDED	MATERIALS (30 STUDENTS)	BASIC SCIENCE SKILLS	PACING GUIDE
16–1. Atoms and Energy (1–2 periods)	30 sets element cards (Teacher's Resource Book, p. 16–5) paper pencils	Cause and Effect (pp. 389–390) Compare and Contrast (p. 391) Classifying (p. 396)	Above Average: Students might report on the development of high-energy machines used to study atomic structure. Slow Learners: Make a graph similar to Fig. 16–6 to help students understand this important concept.
16–2. Atoms and Chemical Activity (1–2 periods)	15 copper pennies 15 pieces of zinc, 2 cm square ammonium chloride-manganese dioxide paste 15 plastic spatulas 15 flashlight bulbs 30 wire leads with clips 30 pieces of sandpaper or steel wool	Classifying (pp. 400–401) Sequencing (p. 403) Predicting (p. 408) Compare and Contrast (Teacher's Resource Book, p. 16–2)	Above Average: Students might report on the history of lighter-than-air aircraft. Slow Learners: Draw diagrams to show how an atom can become stable by gaining or losing electrons.
16–3. Metals and Nonmetals (1–2 periods)	15 pieces each of carbon, copper, lead, sulfur, and aluminum 5 hammers 5 anvils 15 light bulbs and sockets 15 batteries 30 wires with clips	Compare and Contrast (p. 414) Classifying (p. 416)	Slow Learners: Have students point out the location of the metals and nonmetals on the periodic chart.

SUPPLEMENTAL MATERIALS

Audiovisual

The Laser Beam, 2nd ed. Handel Film Corp. Color film (20 min).

Electricity Produced by Chemical Action (GC726). Scott. Color film loop.

Electricity Produced by Chemical Action (GC727). Scott. Color film loop.

Atoms, Molecules, and Ions (493-B). SVE. Color filmstrip.

The Periodic System (493-8) SVE. Color filmstrip.

The Halogens (403-10). SVE. Color filmstrip.

Chemistry Series (set of 2, Ionization, Periodic Table, 619005-6). McGraw-Hill. Color and B/W filmstrip.

Symbols, Formulas, and Equations (493-3). SVE. Color filmstrip.

Hydrogen, Oxygen, and Water (493-5). SVE. Color filmstrip.

Print

Brady, J.E., and J.R. Holum. *Fundamentals of Chemistry.* New York: Wiley, 1981.
Holum, J.R. *Elements of General and Biological Chemistry, 6th ed.* New York: Wiley, 1983.
Metcalfe, H.C. *Modern Chemistry.* New York: Holt, 1982.
Rayner-Canham, G., et al. *Foundations of Chemistry.* Reading, MA: Addison-Wesley, 1983.

Computer

Families of Atoms. J & S Software. APL II Series.

CHAPTER OVERVIEW

The chemical activity of an element is directly related to the number of electrons in the outer energy level of its atoms. Evidence for determining the electron structure of an atom is provided by its emission spectrum and ionization. A few kinds of atoms, known as noble gases, have a stable arrangement of electrons and, as a result, resist chemical action. All atoms tend to fall into families. The members of a given chemical family are found in a vertical column of the periodic chart. They have certain physical and chemical similarities. Elements tend to be metals or nonmetals according to their properties. A few elements fail to meet all the tests for metals, but have many characteristics of metals. They are called metalloids.

16–1. ATOMS AND ENERGY

BACKGROUND: Atoms are stable in elements but may, under certain conditions, absorb energy and emit electromagnetic radiation. The electron's role is described. The ultimate result, if sufficient energy is absorbed, is ionization. Some atoms hold their electrons more tightly than others. The method of bombarding atoms with electrons in order to determine how tightly an atom holds its electrons is discussed.

The colored bands of light given off by gas discharge tubes such as mercury fluorescent tubes, neon lights, etc., are readily explained using the model in which electrons absorb energy in certain definite amounts called quanta. The energy is released in discrete amounts which produce certain colors of light. Each kind of atom has a number of energy levels which electrons can occupy. There is an energy difference between the energy levels. The loss of energy as an electron falls back toward the lowest energy ground state is exactly equal to the energy of the light emitted.

Sufficient energy can cause one or more electrons to completely escape the attraction of the nucleus. The atom then is left with a positive charge. The noble gases are covered prior to discussion of chemical activity and other elements in order to develop the concept that the stable electron arrangement is a characteristic that all elements tend to attain.

The electron arrangement of the first 20 elements is not difficult to show. The third energy level begins to fill with more electrons in the elements after calcium. This level will hold 18 electrons before the fourth level begins to fill with its 8 electrons. It is probably not wise to go into this concept at this time. The outer level always tends to fill with 8 electrons. Helium is the exception to this rule. The electrons in the outer level determine the chemistry of most elements.

MOTIVATION: Demonstrate the ionization of air. Point out that the results will be explained in the section. The following demonstration should be performed without mentioning ionization: A small wad of aluminum foil suspended on a thread will be repelled when charged by a plastic ruler rubbed with wool. While the sphere is being repelled by the plastic ruler, hold a lighted match so that the air between the sphere and the ruler is heated. The repulsion will be quickly diminished by the ionization of the air caused by the lighted match. The heated air loses electrons, allowing the negative charges to leak rapidly off the ruler and sphere.

INVESTIGATION

Answers to Questions:

1. There are three families.
2. The three families are the alkali metals, the halogens, and the noble gases.
3. Alkali metals: lithium, sodium, potassium.
   Halogens: fluorine, chlorine, bromine.
   Noble gases: helium, argon, neon.

Conclusions:

1. Each member of a family has the same number of electrons in its outer energy level.
2. The elements in the noble gas family are stable.

Teaching Hint: Copymasters for the cards used in this Investigation can be found in the Teacher's Resource Book (pp. 16–5 to 16–15).

16–2. ATOMS AND CHEMICAL ACTIVITY

BACKGROUND: Chemical activity is explained on the basis of an atom's tendency to attain a stable electron configuration. Certain electron arrangements in atoms are stable, making those atoms inert. Atoms with similar electron configurations have similar chemical properties.

The analogy of human or animal families can be used to introduce the periodic chart. The alkali and halogen families are singled out for discussion. Students will recognize that arranging elements into families is a logical method of dealing with a great amount of chemical information.

MOTIVATION: Write the electron arrangements of hydrogen and oxygen on the board. Show how, by sharing electrons, two hydrogen atoms and one oxygen atom can attain the electron arrangements of the noble gases. Tell students that this accounts for the stability of the water molecule.

Chemical elements are classified into families because in that way a great deal of information about all the members of a family can be gained by studying one element of the family. This type of classification can be related to everyday examples. Have students discuss the use of fasteners such as paper clips, metal screws, wood screws, nails, etc. Note the similarities and differences between the fasteners. Show the students an unusual fastener such as a hot pin, a roofing nail, an aluminum nail, etc. Have students identify it and describe its probable use. Point out that early chemists used this classification technique, which is the basis for this section.

INVESTIGATION

Teaching Hints: The black paste will stain hands and clothing. Warn students to wash immediately with soap and water in order to remove it. Other combinations of metals could be tested by those students who finish early.

Answers to Questions:

1. The bulb is used to detect an electric current.
2. The bulb lights.
3. This indicates that a current is flowing.
4. No.

Conclusions:

1. The different metals are needed to make a voltaic cell. One metal loses electrons while the other gains electrons, causing a current to flow.
2. Answers will vary. Check for complete sentences and be sure the drawing is labeled correctly.

16–3. METALS AND NONMETALS

BACKGROUND: This section discusses the ways in which metals are alike and how they differ from nonmetals. The value placed on metals through the ages is based on some very important properties of metals. The properties of metals are related to their atomic structure. Some elements, known as metalloids, have both metallic and nonmetallic properties, forming a link between the metals and nonmetals.

You may wish to extend the discussion of alloys to include some of those used in local industry. (Alloys are very important in the use of metals.) The metals have many characteristics in common but nonmetals are all different from one another.

MOTIVATION: A display of various metals and nonmetals could be used to start the section. A discussion could be centered around an example of a metal, such as a lead sinker, and a nonmetal, such as a piece of sulfur. Point out that these elements are similar only in that each is made up of only one kind of atom. Discuss such differences as color (scratch the surface of the lead to show that it has a shiny, silver color), malleability (hit each with a hammer, but be careful of flying sulfur), melting point (sulfur can be melted by the heat of a match), and conductivity (a simple conductivity tester used earlier will work).

INVESTIGATION

Teaching Hints: You may wish to do this Investigation as a demonstration and have the students record their observations. A hammer and heavy piece of metal (anvil) are needed for the malleability test. Copper wire can be used for the element copper. Wire solder is a convenient form of lead although it is usually an alloy containing 40 percent tin. Carbon can be obtained from the center electrodes of old zinc-carbon dry cells. Aluminum foil can be used for aluminum. Sulfur is available from science supply houses. A light bulb, battery, and wires can be used to test for conductivity.

Conclusions:

1. Lead, copper, and aluminum are metals.
2. Carbon and sulfur are nonmetals.

TECHNOLOGY

The types of satellite put into orbit, and their uses, will increase dramatically in the near future. For continual updates you can write to NOAA/Satellite Data, Services Division, Room 100, World Weather Building, Washington, DC 20233. The telephone number is (301) 763-8111.

CHAPTER REVIEW

Vocabulary:

1. halogens 2. ion 3. alkali metals 4. corrosion 5. chemical family 6. alloy 7. inert 8. metalloid 9. periodic chart 10. excited electron 11. stable electron arrangement 12. chemical activity 13. noble gases

Answers to Questions:

1. When an electron has gained enough energy to move farther from the nucleus, the electron is excited. It has stored, or potential, energy which is released as electromagnetic energy when the electron returns to its original position.
2. When an excited electron in an atom moves back closer to the nucleus, energy is released in the form of light.
3. A dark-line spectrum is a complete spectrum with certain lines missing. It is formed when white light is passed through a cool gas. The gas absorbs certain spectral lines, which appear as dark lines in the spectrum.
4. A positive ion is an atom that has lost one or more electrons. A negative ion is one that has gained one or more electrons.
5. Helium is almost always the gas of choice in balloons. It is much safer than hydrogen because it doesn't burn.
6. The number of electrons in the outer energy level of an atom determines its chemical activity.
7. Lithium - Li, sodium - Na, potassium - K, rubidium - Rb, cesium - Cs, francium - Fr. These elements make up a family of elements called the alkali metals.
8. The alkali metals and the halogens have atomic numbers that differ from a stable number by one. The alkali metals have atomic numbers that are one more than a stable number and the halogens have numbers that are one less than a stable number.
9. Metals conduct electricity, can be hammered into different shapes and rolled into thin sheets, and are shiny. Nonmetals have none of these physical properties.
10. Metalloids have some characteristics of both metals and nonmetals.
11. Metalloids are used to make semiconductors. Radios, television sets, and other solid-state electronic devices use semiconductors.
12. Neon signs produce light when an electric current passes through neon gas.
13. The alkali metals are in the far left column of the periodic chart while the halogens are one column to the left of the far right column. The inert or noble gases are in the far right column.
14. The metallic bond is the result of electrons being free to move between neighboring atoms. This freedom makes it easy for metals to conduct electricity and allows metals to bend without breaking.

CHAPTER 17 ATOMIC BONDS

SECTION/ TIME NEEDED	MATERIALS (30 STUDENTS)	BASIC SCIENCE SKILLS	PACING GUIDE
17–1. Bonding of Atoms (1–2 periods)	none	Compare and Contrast (pp. 422–423)	Slow Learners: Draw electron dot models on the chalkboard.
17–2. Kinds of Chemical Bonds (1–2 periods)	15 250-mL beakers distilled water 0.5 kg baking soda 45 test tubes matches 15 test-tube holders 15 Bunsen burners 0.5 kg salt 45 wires and clips 30 1.5-V batteries 0.5 kg sugar 15 flashlight bulbs and sockets 30 goggles 15 containers of water for burned matches	Predicting (pp. 427–429) Compare and Contrast (p. 430 and Teacher's Resource Book, p. 17–2) Cause and Effect (Teacher's Resource Book, p. 17–2)	Above Average: See Applying Science at end of chapter.
17–3. Chemical Formulas (1–2 periods)	none	Following Directions (pp. 432–433)	Slow Learners: Practice writing chemical formulas.

SUPPLEMENTAL MATERIALS

Audiovisual

Electron Arrangements and Chemical Bonds (9080). Encyclopaedia Britannica. Color filmstrip.

Ionic and Covalent Bonds. Encyclopaedia Britannica. Color filmstrip.

The Structure of the Ionic Crystal (S-80708). Encyclopaedia Britannica. Color film loop.

The Structure of a Covalent Molecule (CCl_4) (S-80710). Encyclopaedia Britannica. Color film loop.

Print

Brady, J.E., and J.R. Holum. *Fundamentals of Chemistry.* New York: Wiley, 1981.

Holum, J.R. *Elements of General and Biological Chemistry, 6th ed.* New York: Wiley, 1983.

Metcalfe, H.C. *Modern Chemistry.* New York: Holt, 1982.

Rayner-Canham, G., et al. *Foundations of Chemistry.* Reading, MA: Addison-Wesley, 1983.

Computer

Chemistry: Series I. Focus Media, Inc. APL II Series; TRS-80 Models III, 4; COM 64, Pet.

Molecules and Atoms: Exploring the Essence of Matter. Science Management Corp. APL IIe, IIc; IBM PC, PC Jr.

Structure of Matter. Classroom Consortia Media. Inc. IBM PC, PC Jr.

CHAPTER OVERVIEW

The chemical bonding between atoms results from the tendency of atoms to gain or lose electrons in order to become stable. Oxidation number is introduced as an aid to determining whether atoms will gain, lose, or share electrons during bonding. The formation of covalent or ionic bonds can be predicted by knowing the number of valence electrons of the atoms involved. Once students know the number of atoms bonded, they can write a formula for the compound formed. Simple chemical equations are written and balanced.

17–1. BONDING OF ATOMS

BACKGROUND: The nature of the chemical bond is explained by describing the tendency of an individual hydrogen atom to gain or lose an electron to reach a stable number of electrons. The number of valence electrons is easily shown through electron dot models. The nature of the chemical bond is a critical concept upon which following chapters are based. Stress that oxidation number and electron dot models are aids intended to help students understand bonding.

MOTIVATION: Discuss John Dalton's model of atomic bonds showing atoms held together by various kinds and numbers of hooks and barbs. Have the students look at a picture of a diamond. Ask the students if they can explain the hardness of a diamond in terms of Dalton's concept of bonding. (The more hooks and barbs, the stronger the bond.) Tell students that the only difference between Dalton's theory and the modern theory is in the description of the "hooks" and "barbs." Explain that the modern theory of atomic bonding says that the simultaneous attraction of a pair of electrons to two different nuclei provides the "hooks" that hold the carbon atoms in a diamond together.

17–2. KINDS OF CHEMICAL BONDS

BACKGROUND: Students are already aware that atoms tend to gain or lose electrons in order to become stable and should easily accept the two types of bonds described here. Introduce covalent bonding first. Present ionic bonding as an extreme form of covalent bonding. The covalent bond of the oxygen atom is described using electron dot models to show how a pair of electrons is shared between oxygen atoms. The ionic bond in sodium chloride is used as an example of how electrons are transferred from one atom to another.

The electron dot model presents a clearer picture of the covalent bond. Atoms that must gain electrons in order to attain a stable electron configuration can do so by sharing electrons. Ionic bonds, which result when an atom loses electrons in order to attain a stable electron configuration, are formed because of the attraction between a positive ion and a negative ion.

MOTIVATION: Use a Petri dish and an overhead projector to do the following demonstration: Place 0.5 cm of water in the Petri dish. Place a small piece of sodium (the size of a pea) in the water. The sodium reacts vigorously with the water. Sufficient heat is produced to melt the sodium into a ball. Hydrogen gas is released by this reaction. The ball of sodium moves rapidly over the water on a cushion of hydrogen gas. CAUTION: The resulting solution of sodium hydroxide is quite caustic. Dispose of the sodium hydroxide solution down the drain carefully, with plenty of water.

SKILL-BUILDING ACTIVITY

Teaching Hint: Sensitive ammeters can be used but there is the danger of the electrodes touching while they are in the solution. This would cause a large current to flow and could damage the meter.

Answers to Questions:

1. Sugar.
2. Sugar.
3. No.
4. Yes.
5. Yes.
6. Yes.

Conclusions:

1. Ionic.
2. Substances with covalent bonds melt at a much lower temperature than those with ionic bonds. Heating a substance while using salt as a control will help identify ionic bonded molecules. Also, ionic bonded substances will conduct an electric current when dissolved in water. Covalently bonded substances will not.

17–3. CHEMICAL FORMULAS

BACKGROUND: The positive oxidation numbers and negative oxidation numbers in a compound must be balanced. The "crisscross" technique described on page 432 will give students a method for predicting the chemical formulas when two elements combine.

MOTIVATION: Demonstrate the crisscross method of writing chemical formulas. An understanding of this method will make students' work in future chapters much easier. Compare the crisscross method with the electron dot method as a means of determining chemical formulas.

CHAPTER REVIEW

Vocabulary:

1. chemical bond 2. electron dot model 3. oxidation number 4. valence electrons 5. radical 6. covalent bond 7. ionic bond 8. diatomic molecule 9. chemical formula

Answers to Questions:

1. Hydrogen atoms need only one electron each to fill an energy level. Two hydrogen atoms bond by sharing their electrons to fill the levels.
2. Neon atoms do not bond with other atoms because their outer energy levels are filled. Hydrogen atoms will bond with many other types of atoms as well as with other hydrogen atoms in order to fill their energy levels.
3. F:F
4. The outer (valence) electrons determine how atoms form bonds. Atoms form bonds in order to fill their outer energy levels.
5. Covalent bonding involves the sharing of electrons by atoms while ionic bonding results from the actual exchange of electrons between atoms.
6. The oxidation numbers are: aluminum 3+, calcium 2+, magnesium 2+, and sodium 1+. Because sulfur has an oxidation number of 2−, three atoms of sulfur combine with two atoms of aluminum; one atom of calcium combines with one atom of sulfur; one atom of magnesium combines with one atom of sulfur; and two atoms of sodium combine with one atom of sulfur to form compounds.
7. Since the oxidation number of hydrogen is 1+ and two hydrogen atoms are used, the oxidation number of the sulfate radical must be 2−.
8. A silicon atom, like a carbon atom, has a half-filled outer energy level. Thus, it may either gain four electrons or lose four electrons, giving it an oxidation number of either 4+ or 4−, depending on the atom with which it combines.
9. See table below.

OXIDATION NUMBER →		1−	2−	3−	1−	2−
↓	ELEMENT → ↓	F	S	N	OH	CO_3
1+	Na	NaF	Na_2S	Na_3N	NaOH	Na_2CO_3
2+	Be	BeF_2	BeS	Be_3N_2	$Be(OH)_2$	$BeCO_3$
3+	B	BF_3	B_2S_3	BN	$B(OH)_3$	$B_2(CO_3)_3$

CHAPTER 18 ORGANIC CHEMISTRY

SECTION/ TIME NEEDED	MATERIALS (30 STUDENTS)	BASIC SCIENCE SKILLS	PACING GUIDE
18–1. Carbon and Its Compounds (1–2 periods)	30 goggles 45 test tubes 15 test-tube holders 15 test-tube racks 15 Bunsen burners samples of white bread, sugar, and salt matches cans of water for burned matches	Compare and Contrast (p. 440) Inferring (p. 443)	Above Average: Use a biology text to find the effect of CO in the blood.
18–2. Hydrocarbons (1–2 periods)	15 hydrocarbon molecular model kits	Classifying (pp. 444, 448–450)	Above Average: See Applying Science at the end of the chapter.
18–3. Substituted Hydrocarbons (1–2 periods)	15 hydrocarbon molecular model kits	Compare and Contrast (p. 458)	Slow Learners: Make substituted hydrocarbon molecular models for display.
18–4. Molecules Needed for Life (1–2 periods)	samples of sugar, starch, MSG, gelatin, and vegetable oil water 75 test tubes 15 test-tube holders 15 test-tube racks 15 Bunsen burners 30 goggles 15 beakers matches 15 ring stands 15 cans of water for burned matches	Classifying (pp. 459–460) Inferring (p. 468) Recording Data (Teacher's Resource Book, p. 18–2)	Above Average: Find names and structures for the amino acids in the human body.

SUPPLEMENTAL MATERIALS

Audiovisual

Oil. Shell Film Library. Color film (28 min).
Refining Processes. Shell Film Library. Color film (20 min).
Rubber by Design. Shell Film Library. Color film (27 min).
Carbon and Its Compounds. Coronet. Color film (16 min).
Fill 'er Up. E.I. duPont de Nemours and Company. Color film (12 min).
The "Alfol" Alcohols. Continental Oil Co. Color film (29 min).
Refinery at Work. Humble Oil Company. Color film.
Flowing Solids. Humble Oil Company. Color film (15 min).
The Carbon Compounds. Society for Visual Education (Singer). Filmstrip.
Organic Chemistry (67121). Denoyer-Geppert. Filmstrip.
Additional Polymerization (S81443). EBF. Super 8mm film loop.
Nomenclature—Organic Chemistry (003-42). Eyegate House. Transparencies.

Print

Bailey, P.S., Jr., and C.A. Bailey. *Organic Chemistry: A Brief Survey of Concepts and Applications, 2nd ed.* Boston: Allyn and Bacon, 1981.
Holum, J.R. *Elements of General and Biological Chemistry, 6th ed.* New York: Wiley, 1983.
Metcalfe, H.C. *Modern Chemistry.* New York: Holt, 1982.
Scott, R.M. *Introduction to Organic and Biological Chemistry.* New York: Harper & Row, 1980.
Widom, J.M., and S.J. Edelstein. *Chemistry: An Introduction to General, Organic, and Biological Chemistry.* San Francisco: Freeman, 1981.

Computer

Carbon Chemistry. J & S Software. APL II Series.

CHAPTER OVERVIEW

This chapter begins with a description of familiar materials composed of carbon compounds. The uniqueness of the carbon atom in forming a huge number of compounds is presented. The study of organic compounds centers around the hydrocarbons.

18–1. CARBON AND ITS COMPOUNDS

BACKGROUND: The study of carbon compounds and carbon chemistry began as the study of living things. The word "organic" means "coming from life." Organic compounds can now be made in the chemistry laboratory.

MOTIVATION: Display a number of substances that contain carbon, for example, paper, pencils, wood, coal, etc. Ask the students questions such as: How do these substances differ? Where do they come from? How are they made? What do they all have in common? Why is the study of carbon compounds called organic chemistry? What does "organic" mean?

INVESTIGATION

Teaching Hints: A tin can lid to hold the three samples can be placed on a ring stand and heated instead of using test tubes. Be sure that students understand their observations in this Investigation. Bread and sugar, which are carbon compounds, will burn when heated. The carbon remains as a black residue. The test tubes may be hard to clean. Clean test tubes will be needed for each class.

Answers to Questions:

1. The bread turned brown or black.
2. The sugar melted and turned brown or black.
3. Nothing happened to the salt.

Conclusion:

1. Bread and sugar contain carbon, salt does not. Both bread and sugar burned to leave a black residue of carbon.

18–2. HYDROCARBONS

BACKGROUND: Hydrocarbons are presented as the basis of all organic compounds. The discussion begins with methane and progresses through the alkane series to show that a large number of hydrocarbons exists. The existence of isomers and the ability of hydrocarbons to form double bonds, triple bonds, and ring structures account for the great number of different hydrocarbons.

MOTIVATION: Discuss the composition of gasoline, since it is probably the most well-known mixture of hydrocarbons. Gasoline is mainly a mixture of hexanes (C_6H_{14}), heptanes (C_7H_{16}), and octanes (C_8H_{18}).

INVESTIGATION

Conclusions:

1. One.
2. Four.
3. Propane, butane, and pentane.
4. Propane, one isomer; butane, two isomers; pentane, three isomers.
5. The bonding positions in a carbon atom are equally spaced around the atom.

18–3. SUBSTITUTED HYDROCARBONS

BACKGROUND: The need to classify a large number of organic compounds is discussed. Most organic compounds can be thought of as hydrocarbon derivatives. Halogen compounds, alcohols, organic acids, esters, and amino acids are discussed. The IUPAC has designed a system of nomenclature in which all organic compounds are named as though they were derived from hydrocarbons.

MOTIVATION: Freon is the common name given to the chlorine and fluorine derivatives of methane and ethane. Freon-22 is the common refrigerant whose formula is $ClCHF_2$. Freon-13 has the formula $ClCF_3$ and is a gas which was once commonly used as a propellant in spray cans.

INVESTIGATION

Answers to Questions:

1. Methanol.
2. One.
3. Two.
4. Two.
5. Three.

Conclusions:

1. A substituted hydrocarbon molecule is one in which an atom or radical has replaced one or more of the hydrogen atoms.
2. An isomer is a molecule with the same formula but a different arrangement of the atoms.
3. Answers will vary. The alcohol molecules constructed in this Investigation are similar in that they consist of a chain of carbon atoms with an OH group attached to one of the carbons.

18–4. MOLECULES NEEDED FOR LIFE

BACKGROUND: Living things require a constant supply of certain kinds of organic compounds. Certain classes of foods are important in our diets.

MOTIVATION: Display an empty breakfast cereal box which lists the ingredients and their nutritional values. Have a student read the list while you copy it on the board. Ask students why each ingredient is necessary for life.

COMPUTER

This game will be both more challenging and more fun if you divide the class into at least two teams.

INVESTIGATION

Conclusions:

1. Sugar and MSG.
2. Starch and gelatin.
3. An amino acid is more soluble than a protein.
4. Proteins are broken down in the body into the soluble amino acids from which they are made. The amino acids can then combine to form the particular proteins that are needed by the body.

CHAPTER REVIEW

Vocabulary:

1. alkenes 2. isomers 3. amino acid 4. structural formula 5. fats 6. carbohydrates 7. alcohol 8. hydrocarbon 9. organic acid 10. proteins 11. alkynes 12. ester 13. aromatics 14. double bond 15. polymer 16. alkanes 17. organic chemistry

Answers to Questions:

1. An organic compound is one which contains carbon. Methane, alcohol, freon, and acetic acid are examples.
2. Student diagrams should be similar to Fig. 18–1. An atom of carbon-12 has six electrons, six protons, and six neutrons.
3. Hydrocarbon molecules are composed of hydrogen atoms and carbon atoms and nothing else.
4. These hydrocarbons are all burned as a source of heat.
5. Alcohols can be identified by the OH group, organic acids by the COOH group, and amino acids by the NH_2 and COOH groups in the molecule.
6. Glucose and fructose are simple sugars found in fruits. Sucrose is a double ring sugar formed from glucose and fructose rings. Starch is a long polymer made up of glucose molecules. They are all carbohydrates.
7. Your body breaks down the starch into simple sugars which combine with oxygen to release energy.
8. Saturated fats have only a single bond between carbons and are found in meats and milk products. Unsaturated fats have at least one double bond and are found in fats from plants.

9. Diamond and graphite are both composed of carbon atoms and nothing else. The carbon atoms in diamond are bound equally to four other carbon atoms, while in graphite one of the bonds is weaker.

10.

```
   H  H  H  H  H
   |  |  |  |  |
H—C—C—C—C—C—H
   |  |  |  |  |
   H  H  H  H  H
```

```
   H  H  H  H
   |  |  |  |
H—C—C—C—C—H
   |  |  |  |
   H  H  |  H
         |
      H—C—H
         |
         H
```

```
      H
      |
   H—C—H
      |
   H  |  H
   |  |  |
H—C—C—C—H
   |  |  |
   H  |  H
      |
   H—C—H
      |
      H
```

11. Propanol contains three carbon atoms and butanol contains four carbon atoms.

```
   H  H  H
   |  |  |
H—C—C—C—OH
   |  |  |
   H  H  H
```

```
   H  H  H  H
   |  |  |  |
H—C—C—C—C—OH
   |  |  |  |
   H  H  H  H
```

12.

```
   H     H
     \ /
   H  N  O
   |  |  ||
H—C—C—C—OH     or     H—N—C—C—C—OH
   |  |                    |  |  |  ||
   H  H                    H  H  H  O   (above)
```

```
        H  H  H  O
        |  |  |  ||
     H—N—C—C—C—OH
           |  |
           H  H
```

13. Polyethylene is a polymer made of a long chain of ethylene molecules. It is used to make many plastic products such as trash bags.

CHAPTER 19 CHEMICAL REACTIONS

SECTION/ TIME NEEDED	MATERIALS (30 STUDENTS)	BASIC SCIENCE SKILLS	PACING GUIDE
19–1. Types of Reactions (1–2 periods)	10 paper cups 0.5 kg plaster of paris 10 stirring rods 30 goggles water	Classifying (pp. 479–480) Observing (p. 481) Problem Solving (Teacher's Resource Book, p. 19–3)	Above Average: Balance equations showing single and double replacement reactions.
19–2. Speed of Reactions (1–2 periods)	60 test tubes 15 test-tube racks 0.5 L hydrogen peroxide small amount of hamburger meat 0.5 kg salt manganese dioxide	Cause and Effect (pp. 483–485, 487)	Above Average: Report on automobile catalytic converters.
19–3. Endothermic and Exothermic Reactions (1–2 periods)	30 400-mL beakers 15 thermometers 0.5 kg washing soda 0.5 kg hypo 15 stirring rods water	Compare and Contrast (p. 489 and Teacher's Resource Book, p. 19–3) Observing (p. 494) Problem Solving (See Teacher's Resource Book, p. 19–3)	Above Average: Report on fractional distillation using a diagram.

SUPPLEMENTAL MATERIALS

Audiovisual

Chemical Reactions: The Quest for Synthetic Fuels. Science Screen Report, Inc. Color film (12 min).

Chemical Reactions. Focus Media, Inc. 2 color filmstrips with sound cassettes (13-18 min each).

The Electrolysis of Brine (30603). Modern Talking Picture Service. Color film (18 min).

Refining Process. Shell Film Library. Color film (20 min).

Refinery (4879). Modern Talking Picture Service. (14 min).

Liquid Natural Gas. American Gas Association. Color film (15 min).

Crisis in Energy. Brooklyn Union Gas Company. Color film (23 min).

Chemical Reactions (10800). Encyclopaedia Britannica. Color filmstrip.

Print

Brady, J.E. and J.R. Holum. *Fundamentals of Chemistry.* New York: Wiley, 1981.

Holum, J.R. *Elements of General and Biological Chemistry, 6th ed.* New York: Wiley, 1983.

Metcalfe, H.C. *Modern Chemistry.* New York: Holt, 1982.

Computer

Chemistry—Stoichiometry. Encyclopaedia Britannica Corp. APL II Series.

Chemistry Lab. Tandy/Radio Shack. TRS-80 Models I, III.

Writing Chemical Formulas. Microcomputers Workshops Courseware. APL II Series.

CHAPTER OVERVIEW

Simple chemical equations can be written to illustrate chemical reactions. The effects of concentration, temperature, surface area, and catalysts on the rate of chemical reactions are described. Exothermic and endothermic reactions are discussed and related to the growing concern about the importance of fuels.

19–1. TYPES OF REACTIONS

BACKGROUND: The burning of charcoal in a grill is introduced as an example of a chemical reaction. Chemical equations are explained as a means of describing chemical reactions. The importance of the law of conservation of matter in writing and balancing equations is emphasized. Students should understand the mechanics of writing equations as a result of the previous discussion of bonding.

MOTIVATION: Introduce this section by demonstrating several chemical reactions. Begin with a burning reaction, such as a lit match. Point out that you know a reaction is occurring because heat and light are given off and new substances are produced. Relate this reaction to the burning of charcoal in which more heat but less light is produced.

HINT: Produce hydrogen in a 13 × 100 mm test tube using a piece of zinc and hydrochloric or sulfuric acid. Use this demonstration to illustrate the synthesis reaction between hydrogen and oxygen to produce water.

INVESTIGATION

Answer to Question:

1. Yes, it gets warm.
   Step D: $(CaSO_4)_2 \cdot H_2O + 3H_2O \longrightarrow 2CaSO_4$
   $2H_2O$ + heat

Conclusion:

1. When a chemical reaction takes place, heat may be produced, causing a change in temperature.

Extension:

1. Heat and light were given off.
2. No mass was gained or lost in this chemical reaction.

19–2. SPEED OF REACTIONS

BACKGROUND: The collision theory is used to describe conditions required for a chemical reaction to take place. The speed of chemical reactions is influenced by concentration, temperature, surface area, and the presence of a catalyst. The kinetic molecular theory of chemical interaction should be used as much as possible. Collisions must be energetic enough to cause chemical interaction.

The equation $2H_2 + O_2 \longrightarrow 2H_2O$ only gives the overall picture of the reaction. A two-body collision between an H_2 molecule and an O_2 molecule begins a sequence of steps resulting in the production of a water molecule.

MOTIVATION: Discuss how fast chemical reactions may occur. Mention some of the examples given in Chapter 17 and any others you choose. Explain to students how fast reactions may be slowed down and slow reactions speeded up, thus allowing us to utilize many more reactions than we otherwise could.

INVESTIGATION

Teaching Hints: Hydrogen peroxide, in a 3% solution, is available at grocery and drug stores. Hydrogen peroxide is not particularly hazardous, but as with any chemical, do not allow any to be taken internally. Hydrogen peroxide changes into water and oxygen continuously but at a very slow rate. Heat will speed up the change but not make it rapid enough to see.

Answers to Questions:

1. No.
2. The rate was fastest in the tube with manganese dioxide.

Conclusions:

1. Meat and manganese dioxide are catalysts.
2. Manganese dioxide.

19–3. ENDOTHERMIC AND EXOTHERMIC REACTIONS

BACKGROUND: Endothermic and exothermic reactions are explained as a result of the role of energy in chemical reactions. Substances that are used as sources of chemical energy are identified as fuels. Solid, liquid, and gaseous fuels are discussed.

The main idea of this section is the way in which chemical energy can be released through chemical reactions. A car parked on a hill is a good analogy for exothermic reactions. Endothermic reactions are the reverse of exothermic reactions. Endothermic reactions are thus like pushing a car up a hill. Exothermic reactions are important as sources of energy. The energy stored in fuels is the result of endothermic reactions carried on by formerly living plants and animals.

MOTIVATION: One method of telling that a chemical reaction has taken place is a change in temperature. Demonstrate the following reaction: Place about 2 mL of water in a test tube. Have a student observe the liquid in the tube and note its temperature by touching the test tube. Add a medicine dropper full of concentrated sulfuric acid or a pellet of sodium hydroxide to the test tube. (CAUTION: Use extreme care when handling these substances.) Shake the tube carefully to mix the ingredients. Ask the students if they see any evidence of a reaction. (None will be visible.) Let the students touch the test tube and observe the rise in temperature. (CAUTION: It may get very hot.) Discuss the following reaction:

$$H_2SO_4 + H_2O \longrightarrow H_3O^+ + HSO_4^-$$

Tell the students that this is an example of an exothermic reaction. Other evidence of reactions are a color change, formation of a precipitate, or formation of a gas.

SKILL-BUILDING ACTIVITY

Teaching Hints: Adding concentrated sulfuric acid to water results in an exothermic reaction. A medicine dropper full of acid added to 2 or 3 mL of water in a test tube will illustrate this kind of reaction. Do not allow students to do this. You can do it as a demonstration. A pellet of sodium hydroxide added to 2 or 3 mL of water in a test tube works also. Do not allow students to do this. You can do it as a demonstration. Students will not see anything but will be able to feel the released heat through the test tube. Heat packs used in sports cause exothermic reactions. Ice packs used in sports cause endothermic reactions.

Answers to Questions:

1. Endothermic.
2. Exothermic.

Conclusions:

1. An exothermic reaction is one in which heat is released, resulting in a rise in temperature, for example, when washing soda is added to water.
2. An endothermic reaction is one in which heat is absorbed, resulting in a decrease in temperature, for example, when hypo is added to water.

TECHNOLOGY

To date there have been five world conferences for the purpose of discussing research and development of hydrogen as an energy source. For information on the conference held in Toronto in 1984 write to The National Research Council of Canada, Ottawa, Ontario K1A OR6 Canada.

CHAPTER REVIEW

Vocabulary:

1. chemical reaction 2. endothermic reaction 3. catalyst 4. concentration 5. exothermic reaction 6. fuel 7. petroleum 8. collision theory 9. chemical equation

Answers to Questions:

1. $2H_2 + O_2 \longrightarrow 2H_2O$
2. Four atoms of aluminum react with three molecules of oxygen to form two aluminum oxide molecules.
3. The law of conservation of matter is shown in a chemical equation since the same number of each kind of atom appears on both sides of the equation.
4. Synthesis: $C + O_2 \longrightarrow CO_2$
   Decomposition: $2H_2O \longrightarrow 2H_2 + O_2$
   Single replacement: $Zn + 2HCl \longrightarrow H_2 + ZnCl_2$
   Double replacement: $AgNO_3 + NaCl \longrightarrow AgCl + NaNO_3$
5. Coefficient numbers must be written in front of the formulas, and subscript numbers after the elements are needed to make sure all atoms are accounted for.
6. Answers may vary. Examples are: granulated sugar dissolves faster than sugar cubes. Sawdust, coal dust, and flour can burn explosively because of the great surface area.
7. Chemical reactions occur more quickly at a higher temperature because the atoms and molecules move more rapidly and collide more often and with greater impact. Threshold energy is the amount of energy needed to start a chemical reaction.
8. The catalytic converter on an automobile causes the rapid conversion of pollutants to carbon dioxide and water.
9. In a chemical reaction, atoms move to a lower energy condition and release the excess energy in the form of heat.
10. $C + O_2 \longrightarrow CO_2 + \text{heat}$
    This is an exothermic reaction.
11. $H_2O + \text{energy} \longrightarrow 2H_2 + O_2$
    $6CO_2 + 6H_2O + \text{energy} \longrightarrow C_6H_{12}O_6 + O_2$
    These are called endothermic reactions. Heat is needed to break the bonds holding together the original substance.
12. Fossil fuels are in solid (coal), liquid (oil), and gaseous (methane) forms. Since there is a limited supply of fossil fuels, we may someday use them up. Solar, wind, geothermal, nuclear, and tidal energies may be used in the future.

CHAPTER 20 ACIDS, BASES, AND SALTS

SECTION/ TIME NEEDED	MATERIALS (30 STUDENTS)	BASIC SCIENCE SKILLS	PACING GUIDE
20–1. Water (1–2 periods)	15 sets of solutions A, B, C, and D 15 unknown solutions 15 medicine droppers waxed paper	Cause and Effect (pp. 500, 502–503) Observing (p. 506)	Slow Learners: Plan a field trip to a local sewage treatment plant. Above Average: Have students report on local efforts to fight water pollution.
20–2. Acids and Bases (1–2 periods)	90 test tubes 15 test-tube racks 0.5 kg baking soda 2 purple cabbage leaves aluminum foil 0.5 L NaCl solution 0.5 L HCl solution 30 goggles SKILL-BUILDING ACTIVITY distilled water vitamin C, powdered lemon juice 0.5 L household ammonia 0.5 kg sugar 15 plastic spoons red and blue litmus paper 0.5 L vinegar 0.5 kg salt 0.5 kg baking soda 15 medicine droppers	Compare and Contrast (pp. 508–509) Classifying (p. 510) Classifying (p. 513)	Slow Learners: Stress the operational, rather than the theoretical, definitions of an acid. Use pH Hydrion paper to measure the pH of several substances. Above Average: Demonstrate the experiment described on page 507.
20–3. Salts (1–2 periods)	phenolphthalein HCl solution acid samples NaOH solution 15 medicine droppers 15 test tubes 15 test-tube holders 30 goggles	Cause and Effect (p. 514) Classifying (Teacher's Resource Book, p. 20–2)	Above Average: Students might report on the reactions of salt in the body.

SUPPLEMENTAL MATERIALS

Audiovisual

Chemistry: Acids, Bases, and Salts, 2nd ed. Coronet Films and Video. Color film (23 min).
Chemistry: Solutions (Ionic and Molecular), 2nd ed. Coronet Films and Video. Color film (23 min).
Piping the Problem Liquids. Dow Chemical Company. Color film (22 min).
Handling Dangerous Chemicals—Acids. Centron Corporation. Color (8 min).
Handling Dangerous Chemicals—Bases. Centron Corporation. Color (8 min).
From Brimstone to Bread. Freeport Sulfur Co. Color film (28 min).
A Grain of Salt. Modern Talking Picture Service. Color film (28 min).
Salt of the Earth. Swank Motion Pictures, Inc. Color film (20 min).
Acids, Bases, and Salts (493-7). Society for Visual Education (Singer). Filmstrip.
Ionization of Acids, Bases, and Salts (003-27). Eyegate House. Transparencies.

Print

Metcalfe, H.C. *Modern Chemistry.* New York: Holt, 1982.
Holum, J.R. *Elements of General and Biological Chemistry, 6th ed.* New York: Wiley, 1983.
Goldin, A. *Water: Too Much, Too Little, Too Polluted?* San Diego, CA: Harcourt Brace Jovanovich, 1983.

Computer

Chemistry—Acids and Bases. Encyclopaedia Britannica Corp. APL II Series.
Chemistry: Series I. Focus Media, Inc. APL II Series; TRS-80 Models III, 4; COM 64, Pet.

CHAPTER OVERVIEW

A discussion of the structure of the water molecule, emphasizing its polarity, precedes the introduction of electrolytes and nonelectrolytes. Ion theory is used to explain why some solutions conduct electricity. When ions react chemically, precipitates may be formed. A table of solubilities is used to predict when precipitates may be expected to form.

20–1. WATER

BACKGROUND: The unusual properties of water are attributed to the shape of the water molecule, which results in the electric dipole. The ability of water to dissolve almost everything is related to the problem of water pollution.

MOTIVATION: Have students draw pictures or take photographs of local water pollution. Discuss the problem.

INVESTIGATION

Teaching Hint: The unknown solutions given to the students in step E are the solutions A, B, C, and D coded in some fashion (for example, Z, Y, X, W). Solutions A, B, C, and D may be prepared as follows:

Solution A: Mix 1 tsp of the black paste inside a dry cell in a glass of distilled water. (CAUTION: Do not use an alkaline battery.) Allow the mixture to settle and use the clear liquid at the top.

Solution B: Mix 1 tsp of sodium carbonate (washing soda) in a glass of distilled water.

Solution C: Mix 1 tsp of magnesium sulfate (epsom salt) in a glass of distilled water.

Solution D: Mix 1 tsp of sodium tetraborate (borax) in a glass of distilled water.

Conclusions:

1. Answers will vary.
2. $Na_2CO_3 + MgSO_4 \rightarrow MgCO_3 + Na_2SO_4$
   $ZnCl_2 + Na_2CO_3 \rightarrow ZnCO_3 + 2NaCl$
   $Na_2B_4O_7 + ZnCl_2 \rightarrow ZnB_4O_7 + 2NaCl$

20–2. ACIDS AND BASES

BACKGROUND: The properties of acids are discussed. The theoretical definition of an acid is followed by some operational definitions. An operational definition can be tested in the laboratory. An example of an operational definition is the reaction of an acid with litmus.

INVESTIGATION

Safety: Use only 0.1M HCl. Students should never have access to higher strength acids.

Teaching Hints: To prepare 0.1M HCl pour 8.6 mL of concentrated HCl into 1 L of water. Remember, always add the acid to the water. This solution is still a strong irritant and must be handled with care. To prepare an NaCl solution dissolve 5.9 g of salt per liter of solution.

Conclusions:

1. HCl
2. H^+. There was no reaction in the tubes with NaCl. Therefore, neither Na^+ nor Cl^- could be responsible for the observed reactions.

SKILL-BUILDING ACTIVITY

Conclusions:

1. Ammonia and baking soda.
2. Lemon juice, vitamin C, and vinegar.
3. Distilled water, salt, and sugar.

20–3. SALTS

BACKGROUND: The neutralization reaction between an acid and a base results in the formation of heat, water, and a salt. The reaction of hydrogen ions from an acid with the hydroxide ions from a base to form water molecules is called neutralization.

MOTIVATION: Demonstrate the reaction between baking powder and water. Baking powder contains a base (sodium bicarbonate) and a weak acid. The acid reacts slowly with the sodium bicarbonate in the presence of water to produce a salt, water, and carbon dioxide.

INVESTIGATION

Teaching Hints: Some other acidic solutions are carbonated beverages, lemon juice, orange juice, and vinegar. The 0.1M solutions suggested for use in this Investigation should be handled with care. Any spills should be cleaned up immediately. To prepare the hydrochloric acid solution, add 8.6 mL of concentrated HCl to 1 liter of water. Always add the acid to the water. To prepare the sodium hydroxide solution, dissolve in water 4.0 g of NaOH pellets per liter of solution. (CAUTION: The NaOH pellets are caustic; do not touch them with your bare hands.) To prepare the phenolphthalein solution, dissolve 1 g phenolphthalein in 50 mL ethanol and add 50 mL of distilled water.

Safety: Caution students to use extreme care when handling acids and bases.

Answer to Question:

1. It remained pink.

Conclusions:

1. Add a couple of drops of indicator to the acid, then add a basic solution until the indicator shows that the end point has been reached.
2. If the indicator is phenolphthalein, the solution will turn pink at the end point.
3. $HCl + NaOH \longrightarrow H_2O + NaCl$

COMPUTER

This program essentially involves creating a database. Students may say that they could look up the information just as fast in a book. This may well be true with a database as small as the one in this program. However, with a database of hundreds or thousands of items, this would not be true. Databases are slowly becoming the equivalent of a nationwide library system. You might want to discuss this development with your students.

CHAPTER REVIEW

Vocabulary:

1. polar molecule 2. polluted 3. electrolyte 4. nonelectrolyte 5. precipitate 6. soluble 7. acid 8. indicator 9. base 10. neutral 11. neutralization 12. salt

Answers to Questions:

1. Only a small part of the world's water supply is available to support life. Pollution reduces that amount even more.
2. Some substances form ions in solution. Ions allow the solution to conduct electricity.
3. Ag^+ and Cl^-; Mg^{2+} and CO_3^{2-}.
4. ZnB_4O_7 and AgCl.
5. An acidic solution is one that has more H^+ ions present than does water. HCl and H_2SO_4 are acidic solutions.
6. Answers will vary. For example: An acid turns blue litmus paper red. When an acid is added to baking soda, a gas is produced.
7. A basic solution is one in which there are more OH^- ions than in water. NaOH and $Mg(OH)_2$ are basic solutions.
8. The pH scale uses the numbers from 0 to 14 to describe how acidic or how basic a solution is. Scientists use the pH scale to measure the strength of acids and bases.
9. When an acid and a base are mixed, water and a salt are produced. Equations will vary. For example, $HCl + NaOH \longrightarrow H_2O + NaCl$.
10. KOH, LiOH, and $Ca(OH)_2$ will form salts with HCl.
11. KCl, KBr, KF, $CaCl_2$, $CaBr_2$, CaF_2, LiCl, LiBr, LiF.
12. (1) Obtain a piece of red litmus paper and a piece of blue litmus paper. (2) Wet the litmus papers. (3) Place a small amount of the white solid on the red and the blue litmus papers. (4) Observe any color changes. If the litmus paper turns from red to blue, the solid is basic. If it turns from blue to red, the solid is acidic.
13. $ZnCl_2 + Na_2B_4O_7 \longrightarrow ZnB_4O_7 + 2Na^+ + 2Cl^-$

CHAPTER 21 THE NUCLEUS

SECTION/ TIME NEEDED	MATERIALS (30 STUDENTS)	BASIC SCIENCE SKILLS	PACING GUIDE
21–1. Radioactivity (1–2 periods)	none	Cause and Effect (p. 525) Compare and Contrast (pp. 526–527)	Slow Learners: Demonstrate a Geiger counter using a watch dial or other safe source of radiation.
21–2. Radioactive Atoms (1–2 periods)	10 sets of 100 marked cubes 10 boxes with lids 30 sheets of graph paper pencils paper	Measuring (pp. 532–533, 535) Problem Solving (Teacher's Resource Book, p. 21–3)	Above Average: Students might do research and report on the use of radioactive tracers in agriculture and medicine.
21–3. Fission and Fusion (1–2 periods)	none	Compare and Contrast (pp. 538–539)	Slow Learners: Plan a field trip to a local nuclear research facility.
21–4. Nuclear Energy (1–2 periods)	none	Compare and Contrast (pp. 543–544)	Above Average: Students might report on the status of nuclear fusion as a power source.

SUPPLEMENTAL MATERIALS

Audiovisual

Atomic Energy: Inside the Atom, 2nd ed. EBEC. Color film (14 min).

After Oil What? International Film Bureau, Inc. Color film (25 min).

Nuclear Energy. National Geographic Society, Educational Services. Color film (23 min).

Print

Holton, Gerald, et al. *Project Physics.* New York: Holt, 1981.

Romer, A. *The Restless Atom: The Awakening of Nuclear Physics.* New York: Dover, 1982.

Computer

Chemistry: Series I. Focus Media, Inc. APL II Series; TRS-80 Models III, 4; COM 64, Pet.

CHAPTER OVERVIEW

The study of atoms and molecules is completed with an investigation into the nature of the nucleus. The degree of stability of nuclei is related to their proton-neutron structure and the amount of binding energy present. Nuclei with insufficient binding energy are unstable, resulting in radioactivity. Natural radioactive decay produces alpha, beta, or gamma radiation. The radioactive elements can be used to help fight certain diseases or as tracers in the diagnosis of disease. Nuclear fission and fusion reactions are explained. Their roles in producing artificial atoms, and as possible energy sources for the future are discussed and compared.

21–1. RADIOACTIVITY

BACKGROUND: The number of protons and neutrons in its nucleus determines whether an atom is stable or unstable. The force that holds the nucleus together is described as the binding energy. Alpha, beta, and gamma decay processes are described as mechanisms by which unstable nuclei become more stable.

MOTIVATION: Display a wristwatch with a luminous dial that glows in the dark. These dials are usually alpha emitters. The alpha particles strike zinc sulfide, causing light to be produced. Ask students if the watch is radioactive. One reason why the word "radioactive" seems ominous is that it describes an invisible process. The radioactive sources used in watches and smoke alarms are regulated by law. The watch dial may register on a Geiger counter.

21–2. RADIOACTIVE ATOMS

BACKGROUND: The concept of half-life is related to methods of dating fossil plant and animal materials. Radioactive tracer techniques using radioactive isotopes are described. The decay of unstable nuclei through the process of radioactivity occurs at a unique rate for each type of nucleus. Radioactive isotopes are used to follow the paths of chemical reactions. Other radioactive isotopes are used to diagnose or treat human diseases. Radioactivity can be harmful since it can cause mutations in or kill living cells.

MOTIVATION: Demonstrate the concept of half-life using pennies or other coins, washers, or sugar cubes with one side marked. Explain that this demonstration serves as an analogy for the radioactive decay process.

SKILL-BUILDING ACTIVITY

Teaching Hint: You can have 1 cm wooden cubes made in the woodshop. You will need 100 cubes for each group. A few extra will be needed to replace lost cubes. Sugar cubes can be used but they leave granules of sugar to clean up after shaking them.

Answers to Questions:

1. In theory, there will be about 33 cubes remaining. Any prediction close to that should be accepted.
2. Answers willl vary. Not all students will be able to guess correctly.

Conclusions:

1. One-half decayed after about 3.8 shakes. Any value close to that should be accepted.
2. The half-life of the cubes is about 3.8 shakes.

21–3. FISSION AND FUSION

BACKGROUND: The nucleus becomes more stable through radioactive decay. The role of particle accelerators is discussed as related to radioactivity. The chain reaction is emphasized.

MOTIVATION: Have students bring a magazine or newspaper article that discusses uses of nuclear energy to class. Tell the class that Sections 21–3 and 21–4 contain information that will help them to interpret such news articles and make more informed judgments about them. Save the articles for Section 21–4.

21–4. NUCLEAR ENERGY

BACKGROUND: The growing worldwide demand for energy may make nuclear fission a promising source of energy. Nuclear fusion may eventually be used as a clean, efficient source of energy. You can use the analogy of breeding rabbits to explain the fission process. Controlled nuclear chain reactions take place in nuclear reactors.

MOTIVATION: Use the articles on nuclear energy that you collected in Section 21–3 after the students have read the section. Read several articles and discuss them in relation to the information in Sections 21–3 and 21–4.

TECHNOLOGY

Research on the properties of plasmas is going on in many countries. The concept of a plasma is an important one for the students to grasp because of the importance of plasmas in controlled nuclear fusion, which has the potential to become a major source of energy in the next century. An interesting way to introduce students to plasmas is by reading the article in OMNI magazine of October 1984. This article presents some interesting and graphic photographs of artistic displays using plasma.

COMPUTER

You and your students may want to use this program to double-check your own calculations of half-life.

CHAPTER REVIEW

Vocabulary:

1. chain reaction 2. beta decay 3. fusion 4. gamma rays 5. radioactive 6. alpha decay 7. half-life 8. fission 9. tracer 10. nuclear reactor 11. binding energy

Answers to Questions:

1. Some atoms are radioactive because they have unstable nuclei with too little binding energy. Those that have enough binding energy are stable.
2. Radium-226 undergoes alpha decay. Carbon-14 undergoes beta decay.
3. Alpha decay results in the release of a helium nucleus (alpha particle) from the nucleus of the decaying atom. Beta decay results when a neutron changes to a proton and an electron, which is ejected from the nucleus. Gamma decay results in electromagnetic waves being emitted from the nucleus of the decaying atom.
4. Three-fourths of the atoms will have decayed in 4,000 years.
5. Plants and animals take in radioactive atoms while they are alive. This stops when the plant or animal dies. The amount of radioactivity in a certain sample of the dead plant or animal, along with the known half-life of the radioactive atoms, makes it possible to determine how long the sample has been dead.
6. The fission of each U-235 atom releases energy. The energy comes from the binding energy that holds the U-235 nucleus together.
7. In nuclear fission, a large nucleus splits into smaller nuclei. In nuclear fusion, two small nuclei join to form a large nucleus.
8. Fusion reactions would produce little radioactive wastes to dispose of and use plentiful hydrogen fuel.
9. A fission reactor uses rods made of a material that absorbs neutrons to control the reaction.
10. Three problems arising from the use of nuclear energy are: (1) keeping radioactivity out of the environment; (2) disposing of radioactive wastes; (3) using up a limited supply of uranium.

H · O · L · T

PHYSICAL SCIENCE

WILLIAM L. RAMSEY
LUCRETIA A. GABRIEL
JAMES F. McGUIRK
CLIFFORD R. PHILLIPS
FRANK M. WATENPAUGH

HOLT, RINEHART AND WINSTON, PUBLISHERS
New York · Toronto · Mexico City · London · Sydney · Tokyo

THE AUTHORS

William L. Ramsey
Former Head of the Science Department
Helix High School
La Mesa, California

Lucretia A. Gabriel
Science Consultant
Guilderland Central Schools
Guilderland, New York

James F. McGuirk
Head of the Science Department
South High Community School
Worcester, Massachusetts

Clifford R. Phillips
Former Head of the Science Department
Monte Vista High School
Spring Valley, California

Frank M. Watenpaugh
Former Chairman, Science Department
Helix High School
La Mesa, California

About the Cover:

Astronaut Bruce McCandless flies the MMU (manned maneuvering unit) during the February 1984 flight of the orbiter *Challenger.* The image of a human being floating free in space illustrates the scientific curiosity that leads men and women out of the laboratory and into new and often hostile environments in search of knowledge about the universe. This photograph also illustrates the close relationship between science and technology.

Picture Credits appear on page 564.
Cover photograph by NASA

Art Credits:

Andre Acosta, Robin Brickman, Leslie Dunlap, Bob Frank, Network Graphics Inc., Bob Rich

Printed in the United States of America

ISBN 0-03-001927-3

56789 039 987654321

ACKNOWLEDGMENTS

Teacher Consultants

Constance Brandon
Norwood Junior High School
Norwood, Ohio

Rev. Mark M. Payne, O.S.B.
St. Benedict's Preparatory School
Newark, New Jersey

Gerald Slutzky
Hauppauge High School
Hauppauge, New York

Content Critics

David G. Haase
Department of Physics
North Carolina State University
Raleigh, North Carolina

Jack T. Yaxley
Chemistry teacher
South Plantation High School
Plantation, Florida

Safety Consultant

Franklin D. Kizer
Executive Secretary
Council of State Science Supervisors
Lancaster, Virginia

Readability Consultant

Jane Kita Cooke
Assistant Professor of Education
College of New Rochelle
New Rochelle, New York

Computer features written by

Anthony V. Sorrentino, D.Ed.
District Coordinator of Computer Instruction
Monroe-Woodbury School District, New York

Computer Consultant

Nicholas Paschenko, M. Ed.
Computer Coordinator
Englewood Cliffs School System
Englewood Cliffs, New Jersey

TO THE STUDENT

Science is like a tree. As scientists learn more about nature, the tree grows new branches. Two of the most important branches of the tree of science have grown from the study of energy and of matter. One branch is called physics. Physics is the study of energy. The second branch is called chemistry. Chemistry is the study of matter. These two main branches of science together make up the study of physical science.

HOLT PHYSICAL SCIENCE consists of 21 chapters organized into six units. In the first chapter, What Is Science?, you will learn about science and some of the tools scientists use to solve problems. The three units following Chapter 1 are concerned with physics, the study of energy. The last three units deal with chemistry, the study of matter. Each unit contains several chapters. Chapter Goals at the beginning of each chapter tell you what you will learn in that chapter. Each chapter is further divided into several sections that begin with a list of section objectives. You will find many interesting and helpful diagrams and photographs in each section. Science words that may be new to you are printed in boldface type. Their definitions are printed alongside in the page margin. Each section ends with a brief Summary of the important ideas developed in the section. Questions at the end of the section will help you to test if you have accomplished the objectives for that section. Most sections are followed by an Investigation or a Skill-Building Activity. These Investigations and Activities will help you to develop good laboratory techniques and to practice basic science skills. At the end of each chapter a Chapter Review made up of Vocabulary, Questions, Applying Science, and a Bibliography will help you to remember what you learned in that chapter and to explore some applications and extensions of that knowledge. Three features of special interest called Careers, Technology, and ¡Compute! are found throughout the book. The Career features will tell you about careers in physical science. The Technology features will tell you how technology affects our lives. ¡Compute! will show you how to use computers to learn about science.

Throughout HOLT PHYSICAL SCIENCE the use of problem-solving skills will be stressed. These skills included observing, classifying, sequencing, measuring, comparing and contrasting, finding cause and effect, recording data, predicting, hypothesizing, and inferring. These skills are important tools for scientists. More than that, they can be important tools for anyone. You will read about how scientists use these skills in Chapter 1, What Is Science? You can also use these skills both in your school work and in your daily life. Be sure that you learn to use these skills effectively.

In your study of physical science, you will learn many fascinating things about the natural world. However, the study of science can also involve many potential dangers. Science classrooms and laboratories contain equipment and chemicals that can be dangerous if they are not handled properly. You should always follow the directions and caution statements in your textbook when doing an activity or investigation. In addition, your teacher will explain to you the precautions and rules that must be followed to insure the safety of you and your classmates. Your responsibility is to follow these rules carefully and to demonstrate a positive attitude toward laboratory safety.

CONTENTS

Chapter 8: Light — 172

Chapter 9: Color — 206

UNIT 3: CURRENTS AND CIRCUITS — 230

Chapter 10: Electricity — 232

CHAPTER

1

The person in the photo is a scientist. This chapter introduces the study of physical science, and tells about scientists and some of the questions they try to answer. Science means curiosity.

WHAT IS SCIENCE?

CHAPTER GOALS

1. Give an example of how scientific problems are studied by scientists.
2. Define physical science and describe some of the things physical scientists do.
3. List the steps that scientists use to solve problems.
4. Explain why measurements are used in science and be able to use metric units of measurement.

1-1. A Scientific Problem

At the end of this section you will be able to:

- Explain what is meant by acid rain.
- Describe how scientists are trying to answer questions about acid rain.
- Name the two branches of physical science and give an example of each.

Suggestion: New science terms are defined for students in the margins and printed in boldface the first time they appear. Students should become familiar with these vocabulary terms and be able to use them in complete sentences.

Suppose you are caught outside in a sudden rainstorm. As the rain comes down, your eyes begin to sting. You notice that the rainwater has a sour taste. These raindrops are not pure water. The falling rain is more like white vinegar or lemon juice than pure water.

This kind of rain actually fell in 1978 during a storm in western Pennsylvania. It is called **acid rain.** What causes *acid rain?* Is acid rain harmful? Some physical scientists are trying to find answers to these questions.

Acid rain Rain containing acids formed from gases given off by power plants and industrial boilers. Acid rain has a pH below 5.6.

ACID RAIN

In 1959, a European scientist noticed that the fish in certain lakes were dying. He collected samples from the lakes. Then he carried out tests on the water. These tests showed what materials were in the water. The scientist found that the lake water contained materials that made the water an acid. Many kinds of materials will change pure water into an acid. Vinegar and lemon juice are examples of weak acids. Scientists use a scale of numbers called the **pH scale** to measure the strength

pH scale A scale, used to measure acidity, on which each number lower than the preceding number represents ten times the acidity. For example, a lake with a pH 5.0 is ten times as acidic as a lake of pH 6.0.

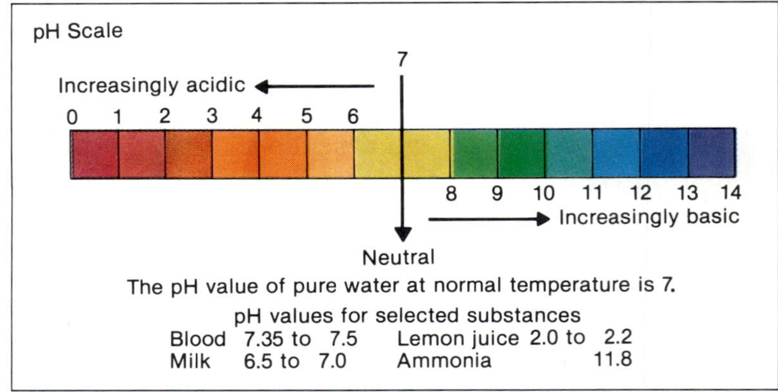

Fig. 1–1 The pH scale is used to determine whether a substance is an acid or a base. For example, a substance with a pH of 2 is strongly acidic.

Reinforcement: Use litmus paper or other acid-base indicators to show the acidity of some common materials such as vinegar and lemon juice. Acids and the pH scale are covered more fully in Chapter 20.

of acids. The *pH scale* is shown in Fig. 1–1. Pure water has a pH number of 7.0. Any pH number less than 7.0 describes an acid. The lower the number, the stronger the acid. Fish cannot live in water with a pH lower than about 4.5. See Fig. 1–2.

Fig. 1–2 This fish lived in a lake with a low pH. The fish died as a result of the acid level of the water.

Enrichment: The average annual pH of precipitation in the eastern United States is between 4.5 and 4. Rain with a pH of 1.5, more acidic than vinegar, has been recorded.

Scientists thought the acid in the European lakes might have come from rain and melting snow. They set up research stations in northern and western Europe. There they tested the pH of rain and snow. They found that acid rain was common. The rain was becoming more acidic each year. By the 1970's, acid rain had been found in the United States and Canada. The problem had become international. There was no clear answer to one question: What caused the almost pure water in rain and snow to become acidic?

A SCIENTIFIC QUESTION: WHAT CAUSES ACID RAIN?

Scientists studied the problem of acid rain. They thought that human activities might be the cause. Acid rain was not common in the past. This was found by measuring the pH of snow that fell a long time ago. Samples of ice were taken from deep within glaciers and ice sheets in Greenland. This ice came from snow that fell more than 180 years ago. The samples of ice had a pH greater than 6.0. In other words, it was not very acidic. This showed that acid rain was not common before the Industrial Revolution. Scientists thought that acid rain developed along with the industry that is now an important part of modern life.

A second piece of evidence came from the sampling stations in Europe and North America. They found that acid rain occurred most often in certain places. These places were always downwind from industrial areas. It seemed that three things were happening. First, something was given off into the air. Then it was carried by the wind. Finally, it mixed with clouds to produce acid rain and snow. Now scientists could begin to search for the cause of acid rain. They looked for something that is commonly produced by industry and is given off into the air.

Enrichment: In the United States the region of heaviest acid rain is in and downwind of the coal-using states of Ohio, Indiana, and Illinois.

Fig. 1–3 Smoke billowing from factory smokestacks was seen as a sign of progress during the Industrial Revolution. Today, however, people are aware that many materials in this smoke are harmful to plants, animals, and people.

Oxide A gas formed when an oxygen molecule combines with another material.

Reinforcement: Most students are familiar with carbon dioxide, which can be used as an example of oxides.

The scientists guessed that burning fuels might be the source of acid rain. When a fuel such as coal is burned, **oxides** are produced. *Oxides* are formed when oxygen joins with another material. For example, sulfur in coal produces sulfur oxides when the coal is burned. Nitrogen oxides are also released from burning coal. See Fig. 1–3. Sulfur oxides and nitrogen oxides combine with oxygen and water vapor in the air. They form sulfuric acid and nitric acid. These are the acids found in acid rain. Electric power plants that burn coal produce most of the sulfur oxides. Tall smokestacks at many of these power plants release the oxides high into the air. The oxides then are carried long distances by the wind. Thus, the acid rain can fall over a large region. See Fig. 1–4. Exhaust from automobiles is also a source of nitrogen oxides. Car exhaust is one of the causes of acid rain around large cities.

Fig. 1–4 As shown in the diagram, the fumes from these smokestacks can be carried to areas far away from the factory. Thus oxides from factories and power plants can cause acid rain even in places that have no local industry.

Fig. 1–5 (a) The scientist in this photo is testing the acidity of lake water. (b) Look closely and you will see the damage caused by acid rain on this statue.

Understanding the cause of acid rain is only the beginning. Many more questions must be answered. For example, scientists need to measure the pH of rain in many places over a long period of time. This will show if acid rain is becoming more common. Scientists now know that acid rain can harm some lakes. However, the other effects it may have are unknown. See Fig. 1–5. Will acid rain harm the soil and reduce the amount of crops grown on farm land? Does acid rain have a harmful effect on humans? Can acid rain produce harmful materials in our water supplies? All of these questions can only be answered by more research. This research is being done by many different scientists.

Enrichment: There is little evidence so far that a moderate level of acid rain harms crops. No one has been able to establish that acid rain is harmful to human health. There is concern that acidified water can cause increased corrosion of pipes and thus add heavy metals such as copper and lead to natural water supplies.

WHAT DO PHYSICAL SCIENTISTS DO?

Physical science includes the study of both matter and energy. The two main branches of physical science are *chemistry* and *physics*. Chemistry is the study of matter in all its forms. Physics is the study of energy and its changes. Both of these branches include special areas of study.

Word study: Chemistry from *chemikos* (Gr.), of or concerning juices or extracts. Physics from *physikos* (Gr.), of nature.

If you asked a scientist studying acid rain, "What do you do?" the reply might be, "I am a chemist. I am trying to find how much of the acid in acid rain comes from sulfur oxides." Another physical scientist measures the oxides given off from car exhausts. Both of these scientists are doing research in one of the areas that make up physical science. Other scientists study the stars or planets. Have you seen pictures of a distant planet taken from a spacecraft? You were seeing the results of the work of physical scientists. Some scientists helped design the cameras or the spacecraft. Others study the pictures to learn about other planets. See Fig. 1–6. As you study physical science, you will see how it is an important part of your life.

Fig. 1–6 The scientists in this photo, taken at the Jet Propulsion Laboratory in California, are studying photos of the planet Saturn sent back to earth by the Voyager spacecraft.

Reinforcement: Many students would benefit from writing a summary of the main ideas in the section, in their own words and using complete sentences. Doing an outline is another way of reviewing.

1. Acid rain is rain that contains acid as a result of industry putting waste products from the burning of fuels into the air. Automobile exhaust may be another cause.
2. Acid rain may affect the soil and thus plant growth. It also kills fish in acidified lakes.
3. Scientists are studying where acid rain occurs, its relation to human activities around the area, its possible causes, and ways to control it.
4. The two branches of physical science are chemistry and physics.

SUMMARY

Finding the cause of acid rain is an important scientific problem. More scientific research is needed to understand acid rain. The study of acid rain is only one of the many areas of physical science.

QUESTIONS

Use complete sentences to write your answers.

1. What is meant by acid rain? What might be some causes of acid rain?
2. Why is acid rain a problem?
3. How are scientists trying to study the problem of acid rain?
4. What are the two branches of physical science?

INVESTIGATION

See teacher's commentary for teaching hints, safety, and answers to questions.

TESTING THE ACIDITY OF SOME COMMON HOUSEHOLD LIQUIDS

PURPOSE: You will use pH paper to find the pH of several liquids and predict which of them would be harmful to fish.

MATERIALS:

medicine dropper
pH papers
5 test tubes
mossy zinc
samples of tap water, distilled water, milk, vinegar, lemon juice

PROCEDURE:

A. Label the test tubes A, B, C, D, and E.

B. Fill each test tube about half-full of one of the liquids. Put tap water in A, distilled water in B, vinegar in C, lemon juice in D, and milk in E. Write the name of each liquid on the label. See Fig. 1–7.

C. Copy the following table.

Test Tube	Liquid	pH
A	Tap water	
B	Distilled water	
C	Vinegar	
D	Lemon juice	
E	Milk	

D. Place a sheet of white paper on a flat surface. Spread five pH papers on the white paper. Label them A to E.

E. Place one drop of liquid A on pH paper A, liquid B on pH paper B, and so on. Be sure to clean the medicine dropper after testing each liquid.

F. Compare the results of your tests with the pH scale on the container. Record the pH of each liquid in your table.

1. Which liquid has the lowest pH?
2. Which liquid is the least acidic?

G. Place a small piece of mossy zinc in each test tube. Observe the reactions.

3. How do your observations relate to your answers to questions 1 and 2?

CONCLUSION:

1. Of the five liquids tested, which would be most harmful to fish? Explain.

EXTENSION:

A. Obtain a sample of water from a local pond or lake.

B. Test your water sample with pH paper.

1. What is the pH of your sample?
2. Do you think fish could live safely in this water? Explain.

Fig. 1–7

Suggestion: Before beginning this section, ask the students to prepare a list of the things that they think a scientist working on a problem such as acid rain does. Later, compare the items on the student lists with the steps in the scientific method given in the text.

1-2. Science Is Curiosity

At the end of this section, you will be able to:

- Explain the steps of the scientific method.
- Describe what is meant by a controlled experiment.
- Explain and give an example of a scientific theory.

Which person do you think is a scientist? What is the best way to describe a scientist? See Fig. 1–8.

Fig. 1–8 Most people think of a scientist as a person who works in a laboratory. But people like Dr. Sally Ride, the astronaut, are also scientists, even though they may work in places that are very far from a laboratory.

WHO IS A SCIENTIST?

You probably think of a scientist as a person who wears a white coat and works in a laboratory. However, scientists do not always look the same or work in laboratories. Scientists are people who are curious about nature. They ask questions and then try to find answers to those questions.

Suggestion: Students often "know" that objects are supposed to fall at the same speed regardless of differences in mass. Ask students to suggest experiments to prove that this is true.

Modern experimental science began about 400 years ago. An Italian named Galileo Galilei (1564–1642) performed experiments to test ideas about nature. Galileo tried to find basic rules that explain the way things happen in the natural world. Today we call Galileo's way of finding answers the **scientific method.** It is not a method that always gives the right answer to a problem. Rather, it is a way of thinking about nature. Galileo used the *scientific method* to study the motion of falling objects. See Fig. 1–9. He believed that scientific understanding of the natural world comes from **observations** and experiments. He refused to accept blindly the ideas about falling objects that people had believed for thousands of years.

Scientific method The set of skills used to solve problems in an orderly way.

Observation Any information that we gather by using our senses.

Modern scientists are using the scientific method to study the problem of acid rain. The first step is making *observations*.

Enrichment: Galileo said: "In questions of science the authority of a thousand is not worth the humble reasoning of a single individual."

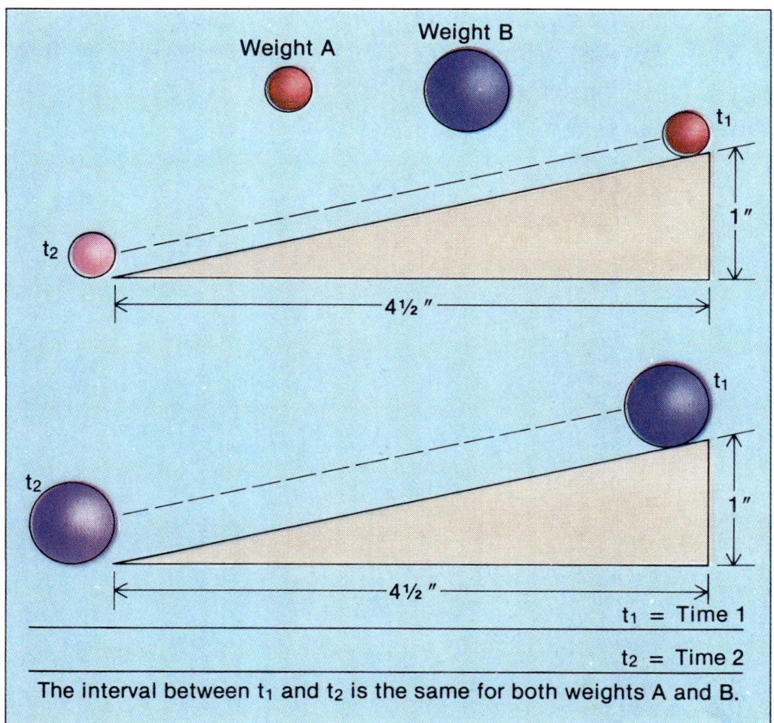

Fig. 1–9 Galileo used ramps as a way of studying falling objects. He showed that two heavy balls of different weights will roll down the same ramp in the same time.

THE SCIENTIFIC METHOD

Skills: The scientific method is an example of *sequencing* and is widely used in science.

A careful look at the scientific method shows that scientists usually follow several separate steps in carrying out scientific research. These steps are as follows:

1. Make observations and ask a question. All scientific research begins with a question. Scientists observed that the water in certain lakes was becoming acidic. This observation led to a question. Is the water draining into the lakes from rain and snow the source of the acid?

Word study: Data is plural of *datum* (L.), given. It is now common to use data as both singular and plural.

2. Gather data related to the question. The existence of acid rain can be shown by testing the pH of rain and snow. This must be done as often and in as many places as possible. These observations are called **data.** Scientists collected many pieces of *data.* They found that acid rain happens most often in certain places. They then went on to the next step.

Data Recorded observations.

Word study: Hypothesis from *hypotithenai* (Gr.), to suppose.

3. State an explanatory hypothesis. Scientists tried to explain why acid rain is more common in some places than in others. They guessed that acid rain is caused by oxides released by burning fuels. This guess is called a **hypothesis.** A *hypothesis* must be tested to see if it is correct.

Hypothesis A statement that explains a group of related observations.

4. Perform experiments in order to test the hypothesis. In an **experiment**, scientists control the conditions to test their hypothesis. For example, scientists believe that acid rain may damage plants. This hypothesis can be tested by *experiments*

Experiment An activity designed to test a hypothesis.

Fig. 1–10 This photo shows the results of an experiment to test the effects of acid rain on young trees. At a certain pH level, seedlings were damaged, as shown by the brown plants.

that expose plants to acid rain. See Fig. 1–10. Scientists can control the level of acid to which the plants are exposed. Then they can decide if the levels of acid rain observed can damage certain plants.

5. Form conclusions based on the results of experiments. Experiments showed that the pH of acid rain determines how it affects crops. Acid rain with a high pH actually makes some crops grow better. But very strong acid rain with a low pH can harm the ability of the soil to support plant growth. Thus, the hypothesis that acid rain is harmful to plants depends on the exact pH of the acid rain.

Suggestion: Most scientific experiments are no different from the way people use common sense to try to solve ordinary problems. A discussion of the way the students solve everyday problems will probably show many similarities to the methods used by scientists to test a hypothesis.

CONTROLLED EXPERIMENTS

Scientific results are based on observations. These observations can be shared by all scientists.

Most scientific problems are studied by many scientists working together. Often they are in different parts of the world. For example, scientists in Europe, the United States, and Canada are all studying acid rain. It is important for all scientists to share the results of their research.

Scientists do not accept their results until they have tested them many times. A scientist may do a *controlled experiment* to test a hypothesis. Look again at Fig. 1–10. The scientists wondered what effect different levels of acid rain had on plants. They set up an experiment to find out. Two groups of plants were used. In both groups, all of the conditions were carefully controlled. The scientists used the same types of plants. The plants were grown in the same soil. They were exposed to the same amount of light. Only one condition was changed. In one group, the pH of the water used was normal. This is called the *control group.* In the other group, the pH was changed. The pH level was the **variable** being tested. The scientists observed the growth of both groups of plants. They compared the results in the group with the changing *variable* to the results in the control group. They could then see what effect the pH level had on the plant growth.

Variable Any factor in an experiment that affects the results of the experiment.

Scientists accurately describe the conditions of their experiments. Then other scientists can repeat the experiment. If the results are not the same, the hypothesis may have to be changed or discarded.

SCIENTIFIC THEORIES

Scientific theory A general statement based on hypotheses that have been tested many times.

The basis of the scientific method is experimenting. Scientists do not believe any hypothesis to be correct until it has been tested by experiment. A hypothesis that has been found to be correct many times is called a **scientific theory.** A *scientific theory* must be tested thoroughly by experiment before it is accepted as part of the body of scientific knowledge. Any theory can be replaced by a new one that better explains the observations. For example, until about 300 years ago, scientists accepted the theory that the earth was the center of the solar system. The sun and planets were thought to move around the earth. Then Nicolaus Copernicus (1473–1543) proposed a new theory. See Fig. 1–11. His theory said that the sun was the center of the solar system. The earth and other planets went around the sun. In time, scientists found that Copernicus' theory was a simpler explanation for their observations of the planets. The old theory was replaced. Modern scientific theories can also be changed at any time.

Fig. 1–11 (a) The top diagram shows what Ptolemy, who lived around A.D. 150, thought the universe looked like. He thought that everything moved around the earth. (b) Copernicus proposed that the sun, not the earth, is in the center (bottom).

Some scientific theories have been tested many times and always found to be correct. After a theory has passed many tests, it is called a *scientific law.* Laws, or parts of them, can also be changed as a result of new tests.

The steps of the scientific method cannot be applied in the same way to all the branches of science. For example, astronomers who study distant stars cannot perform direct experiments on them. However, astronomy is a science because it is based on direct observations. Any hypothesis can be compared with these observations to test its accuracy.

SUMMARY

Reinforcement: Have students write their own summary using their own words and complete sentences.

A set of problem-solving skills used by scientists is often called the scientific method. Scientists test their ideas by experimenting. The scientific method has resulted in theories and laws that explain some parts of nature. Fig. 1–12 shows how the steps of the scientific method can be used to solve a problem.

Fig. 1–12 Scientists use the steps of the scientific method in their research.

1. (a) Observations lead to a question. (b) Additional data are gathered. (c) A hypothesis is formed. (d) Experiments are constructed to test the hypothesis. (e) The hypothesis is accepted, changed, or discarded.
2. Comparing an experiment with the control shows the scientist if the experiment was correctly designed. Using only one variable simplifies the interpretation of the results.
3. A scientific theory is a hypothesis that has been tested many times and found to be correct in each case.
4. A theory can be changed when the evidence warrants it. The theory that the earth is the center of the universe was changed when the evidence showed the sun to be the center of the solar system with the earth moving around it.

QUESTIONS

Use complete sentences to write your answers.

1. Briefly describe the steps that scientists usually follow in scientific research.
2. What is the purpose of a controlled experiment?
3. What is a scientific theory?
4. Can a theory ever be changed? Give one example.

SKILL-BUILDING ACTIVITY

See teacher's commentary for teaching hints, safety, and answers to questions.

USING A LABORATORY BURNER

PURPOSE: You will learn to light and adjust a laboratory burner.

MATERIALS:

Bunsen burner   matches
container of water

PROCEDURE:

A. Fig. 1–13 shows the parts of a Bunsen burner. You probably will use this type of burner often in your laboratory experiments. It is important that you know how to use it safely. Study the diagram to see where the gas and air enter, where the air and gas mix, and where the lighted match should be held.

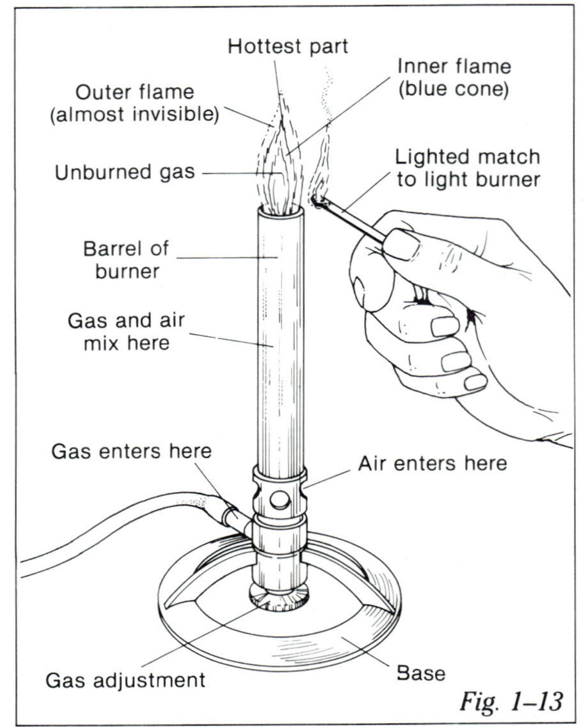

Fig. 1–13

B. To light the burner, bring a lighted match up the side to the top of the barrel. Now turn on the gas. If the match blows out, turn off the gas until you have a lighted match in position again. CAUTION: Discard burned matches in a container of water.

C. Fig. 1–13 also shows what the flame should look like. If the flame is large or bright yellow, too much gas is entering. Use the air adjustment to allow more air to enter.

D. To make a smaller flame, turn the gas partly off. Use the valve on the burner or the main gas valve.

E. If there is a gap between the flame and the top of the barrel, decrease the amount of air entering at the base. Use the air adjustment.

F. If the flame seems to be burning inside the barrel, turn off the gas. Decrease the amount of air and light the burner again. CAUTION: The barrel may be hot.

G. When the burner is properly lighted, you will see a light blue cone in the center of the flame. If the flame is yellow or too large, adjust the burner as described in steps B through D.

CONCLUSIONS:

1. List the steps, in order, to light a laboratory burner.
2. Describe the flame of a properly lighted burner.
3. Describe how to adjust the flame of a Bunsen burner.

OBSERVING THE PERIOD OF A PENDULUM

PURPOSE: You will make a hypothesis about the period of a pendulum and then test that hypothesis.

MATERIALS:

string, 1 m long
weight, light
weight, heavy
clock with second hand
metric ruler

PROCEDURE:

A. Set up a pendulum 50 cm long. Use the lighter of the two weights. See Fig. 1–14.

B. Copy the table below in your notebook. Record the length of your pendulum.

Trial	Length (cm)	Swings (number)	Time (s)	Period (s)
1				
2				
3				

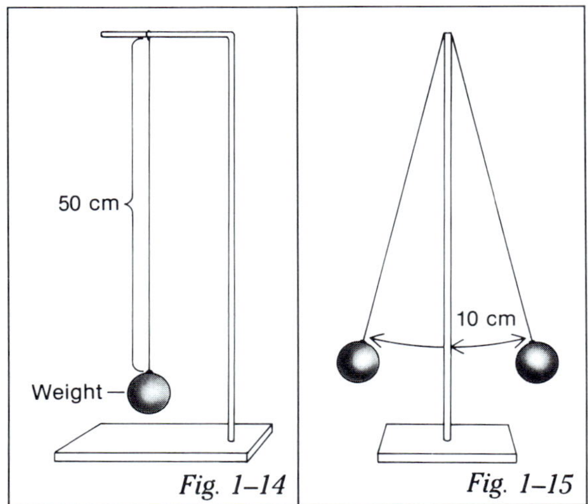

Fig. 1–14 Fig. 1–15

C. Pull the weight about 10 cm to one side and release it. See Fig. 1–15.

D. Measure the time that it takes for the pendulum to complete 50 complete back-and-forth swings. Record this in the table.

E. Find the period of the pendulum by dividing the time by 50 swings. Record the period in your table.

F. Repeat steps C, D, and E three times.

G. Now answer the following question. This will be your hypothesis.

1. Will the period change when the weight is increased?

H. Repeat steps A through E with the heavier weight. Record the results in your data table.

2. Was your hypothesis correct?
3. What was the control in this experiment? What was the variable?

EXTENSION:

A. Shorten the pendulum to 25 cm.

1. Will the period of the pendulum change if you change the length?

B. Repeat steps B through F above.

2. Was your hypothesis correct?
3. What was the control in this experiment? What was the variable?

CONCLUSION:

1. In your own words, describe how changing the weight of a pendulum affects the period of the pendulum.
2. In your own words, describe how changing the length of a pendulum affects the period of the pendulum.

1-3. Measuring

At the end of this section you will be able to:

- Explain why many scientific observations are made in the form of measurements.
- Use metric units to measure length, volume, mass, and temperature.
- Explain how to use instruments to make measurements of length, volume, and mass.

Which of the figures in Fig. 1–16 is tallest? Use a ruler to check your answer. Could you have made an accurate observation of the height of each figure without measuring it?

Fig. 1–16 This diagram is an example of an optical illusion. The figures shown are really all the same height. Measure them yourself.

SCIENTIFIC MEASUREMENTS

Many of the data that form the basis of scientific thinking are **measurements.** When you measure something, you compare it to a standard. *Measurements* make up a large part of scientific observations. This is because numbers can be communicated easily and accurately. For example, suppose you tell someone that the distance to the next city is "a long way." The person will have only a very general idea of the distance. If you say that the city is 161 miles away, the person has a good idea of the distance. See Fig. 1–17.

Measurement An observation made by comparing something to a standard.

Fig. 1–17 Mission control says to take a left at Mars and keep going until we get there.

In most parts of the world, people use the *metric system* in their daily lives. Scientists make measurements in the *International System of Units,* generally called *SI.* The letters SI come from the French *le Système International.* SI units are almost the same as units in the metric system.

Enrichment: The SI system was defined and given official status in 1960 by the General Conference of Weights and Measures, an international agency. It replaced the older metric systems, although the terms "SI" and "metric" are now commonly used as if they describe the same system of measurement.

THE ADVANTAGE OF THE METRIC SYSTEM

Scientists use the metric system because it is the same all over the world. They can share their observations easily with other scientists. You should always use the metric system when making measurements in science. It is an easy system to use because it is a *decimal* system. This means that the units are related to each other by multiplying or dividing by ten. This is not true for the system we commonly use. For example, a foot is divided into 12 inches. A yard is equal to three feet. There are 5,280 feet in a mile. You must remember all of these numbers to change inches to feet, feet to yards, or yards to miles. A system in which all units are related by factors of ten is much easier to use.

Reinforcement: Conventional or English equivalents to quantities expressed in SI units are not used in this book in order to encourage students to think using only SI units.

Reinforcement: A review of basic math skills using decimals is given in the Appendix.

You can change measurements in the metric system easily because it is a decimal system like dollars and cents. There are 100 cents in a dollar. If you have 176 cents, you have $1.76. Notice that only the position of the decimal point changes.

USING THE METRIC SYSTEM

Meter (m) The basic unit of length or distance in the metric system.

Reinforcement: A summary of metric units and SI metric prefixes is given in the Appendix.

1. Measuring length or distance. You will measure length and distance in **meters** (m) or parts of a *meter.* You are between one and two meters (1 to 2 m) tall. Doorknobs are usually about one meter from the floor. You can change a metric unit into a smaller unit by dividing by ten. For example, one-tenth of a meter is called a *decimeter* (**des**-uh-meet-ur). The prefix *deci* tells you that one decimeter (1 dm) is equal to one-tenth of one meter (0.1 m). Dividing a meter into 100 equal parts gives *centimeters* (**sent**-uh-meet-urz). One centimeter (1 cm) equals 1/100 of a meter. The prefix *centi* means 1/100 (0.01). Shorter lengths can be measured in *millimeters.* One millimeter (1 mm) is 1/1,000 of a meter. The prefix *milli* means 1/1,000 (0.001).

Lengths or distances longer than one meter are measured by multiplying by ten. A *decameter* (1 dkm) is equal to ten meters. A *hectometer* (1 hm) is 100 meters. A *kilometer* (1 km) is 1,000 meters. Table 1–1 shows the common metric prefixes and their meanings.

Suggestion: Have students bring in labels of various household products (detergents, soft drinks, etc.) whose ingredients are listed in metric units.

Prefix	Meaning	Example
milli (m)	1/1,000 (0.001)	millimeter (mm)
centi (c)	1/100 (0.01)	centimeter (cm)
deci (d)	1/10 (0.1)	decimeter (dm)
		meter (m)
deca (dk)	10 ×	decameter (dkm)
hecto (h)	100 ×	hectometer (hm)
kilo (k)	1,000 ×	kilometer (km)

Table 1–1

Kilogram (kg) The basic unit of mass in the metric system.

2. Measuring mass. Mass is the amount of matter in an object. Normally, mass is measured in the same way as weight. The terms "mass" and "weight" are often used as if they have the same meaning. In Chapter 2, you will see why this is not true. The basic metric unit of mass is the **kilogram** (kg). The most commonly used smaller unit of mass in the metric system is the *gram* (g). One gram (1 g) is equal to 1/1,000 of a *kilogram* (0.001 g). The mass of a paper clip is about one gram.

Liter (L) A commonly used unit of volume in the metric system.

3. Measuring volume. Volume is the amount of a liquid or the space taken up by a solid. The commonly used volume unit in the metric system is the **liter** (L). Soft drinks are often

sold in 1-*liter* (1-L) bottles. Smaller volumes are usually measured in *milliliters* (mL). One milliliter (1 mL) is equal to 1/1,000 liter (0.001 L). The volume of a cube that is 1 cm on each side is the same as 1 mL. The volume is 1 cm × 1 cm × 1 cm = 1 cm^3. Thus one cubic centimeter (1 cm^3) is the same as 1 mL. The basic unit of volume in the SI system is the cubic centimeter.

Enrichment: $X \times X = X^2$
$X \times X \times X = X^3$
Also, $cm \times cm = cm^2$
$cm \times cm \times cm = cm^3$
These are convenient ways of writing area and volume units.

4. Measuring temperature. Scientific measurements of temperature use the **Celsius** temperature scale. The *Celsius* (C) scale is not an official part of the metric system. However, scientists use the Celsius scale because it is now used most often all over the world. The basic unit of temperature in the SI system is the Kelvin. The Celsius scale is the same as the Kelvin scale, but with a different zero point. You are probably more familiar with the Fahrenheit temperature scale. A comparison of the Celsius, Kelvin, and Fahrenheit scales is shown in Fig. 1–18.

Celsius (C) The most common temperature scale used in science.

Enrichment: The origin of the Kelvin temperature scale is described in Chapter 13.

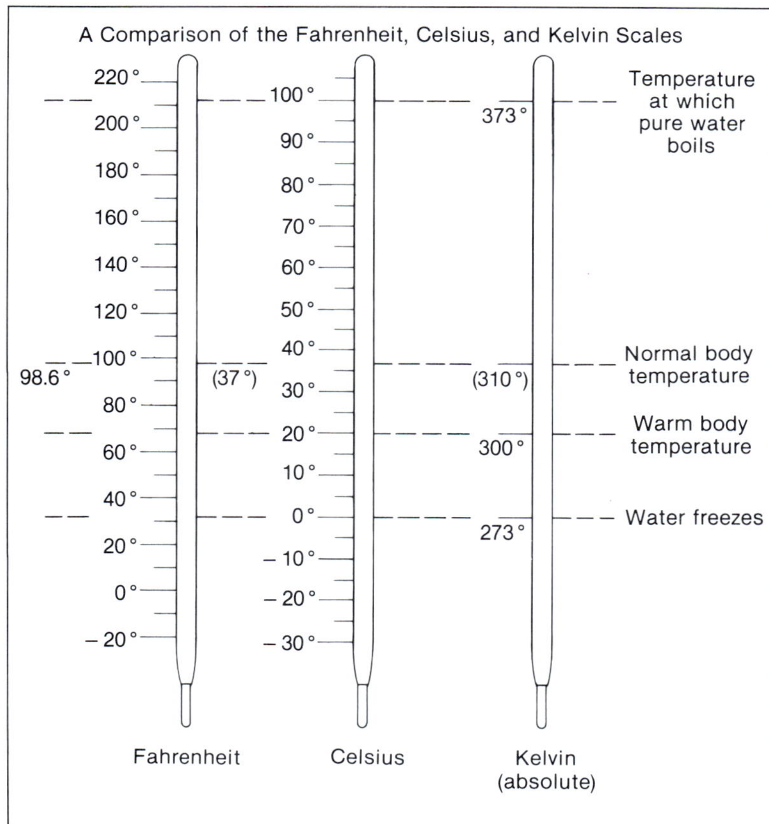

Fig. 1–18 The Fahrenheit, Celsius, and Kelvin temperature scales. This diagram also shows you how to convert temperatures from one scale to another.

MAKING MEASUREMENTS

All measurements are made by using some kind of instrument. You will learn to use various kinds of instruments to make measurements in metric units. One of the simplest is the *metric ruler.* A metric ruler one meter in length is called a meter stick. Almost all metric rulers are marked off in centimeters. These are further divided into ten smaller units. Thus the smallest division on most metric rulers is 1 mm (0.001 m). See Fig. 1–19.

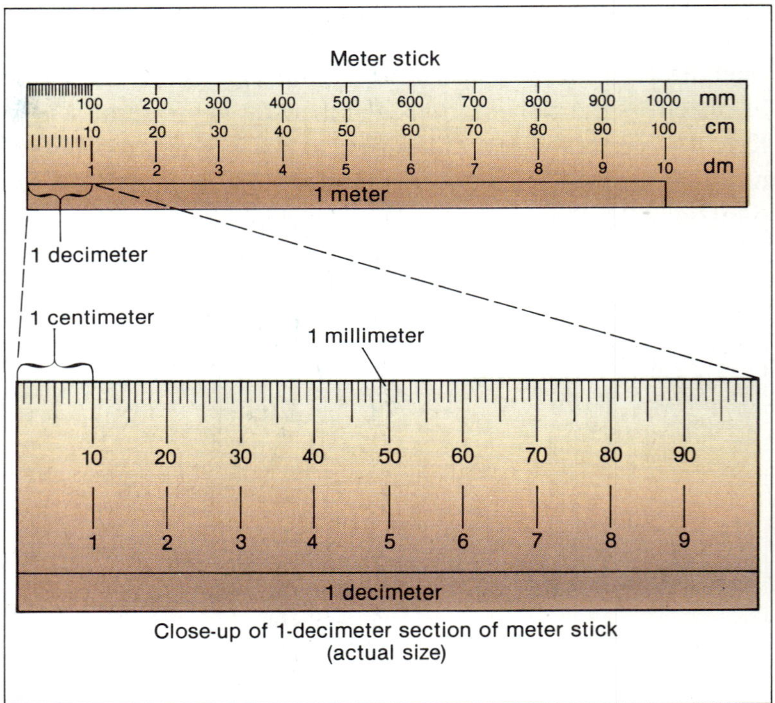

Fig. 1–19 This diagram shows the divisions on a meter stick in decimeters, centimeters, and millimeters.

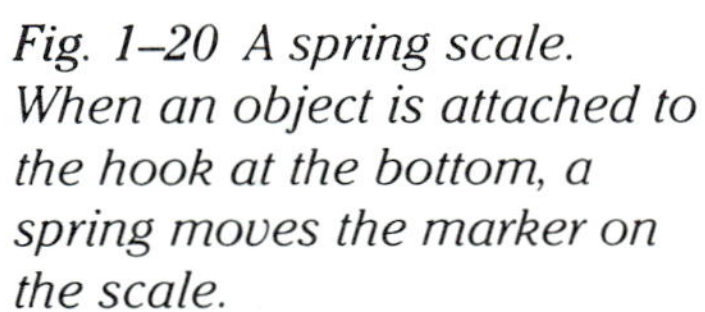

Fig. 1–20 A spring scale. When an object is attached to the hook at the bottom, a spring moves the marker on the scale.

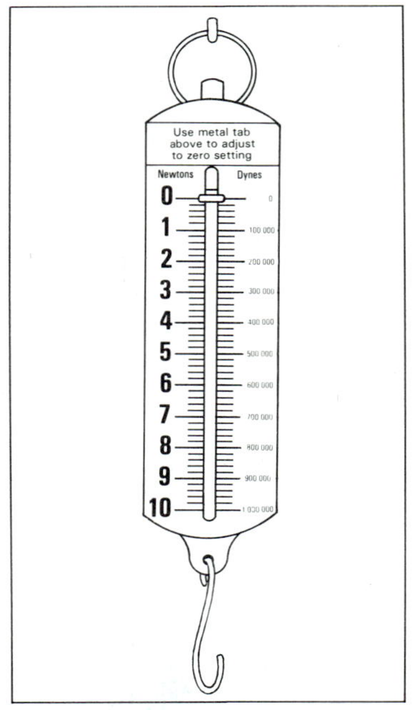

Mass can be measured in different ways. A common instrument used to measure mass is a *spring scale.* The spring is stretched by the mass being measured. See Fig. 1–20. Your bathroom scale is probably a spring scale. In laboratories, mass is most often measured by using a *balance.* In one kind of balance, an object is placed on a flat pan. *Riders* are moved along the scales until the pointer moves equally on both sides of the pointer scale. The mass indicated by the riders exactly balances the mass of the object on the pan. The position of each rider is read from its scale. The sum of the riders is the mass of the object.

Volume is usually measured by using a graduated cylinder. See Fig. 1–21 (a). The volume of a liquid is measured by pouring it into the cylinder. The liquid surface must be level with your eyes. It is usually curved. The bottom of the curve is called the *meniscus.* The volume is measured by reading the mark on the cylinder closest to the meniscus. See Fig. 1–21 (b). The meniscus probably will not fall exactly on a mark. You must *estimate* which mark is closest to the meniscus. You will need to make similar estimates of the closest mark on rulers and on the scales of other measuring instruments.

Word study: Meniscus from *meniskos* (Gr.), moon or crescent.

You can also measure the volume of a solid object using a graduated cylinder. If you lower the object into water, the water level will rise. The change in the water level is equal to the volume of the object. See Fig. 1–21 (c). The initial volume (v_i) is 30 mL. The final volume (v_f) is 50 mL. Therefore, the volume of the stopper is $v = v_f - v_i = 50$ mL $- 30$ mL $= 20$ mL or 20 cm^3.

ERRORS IN MEASUREMENT

Measurements made with any instrument are subject to error. Errors are always present in measurements no matter how careful you are. For example, suppose that you want to

Fig. 1–21 (a) A graduated cylinder is used to measure volume. (b) Read the mark on the cylinder closest to the meniscus. (c) The difference in the water level tells you the volume of the object.

Empty graduated cylinder

250
230
210
190
170
150
130
110
90
70
50
30
10

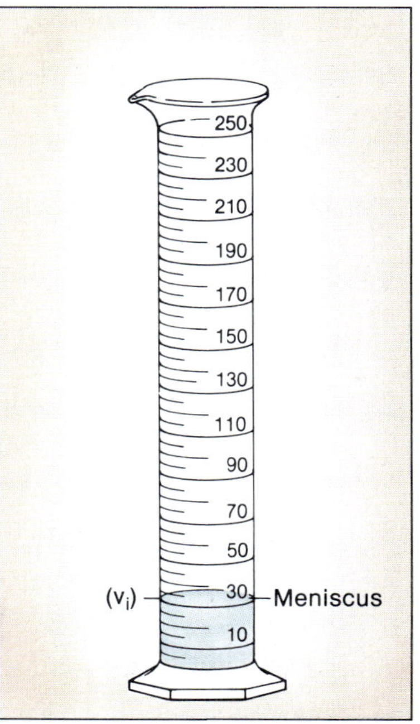

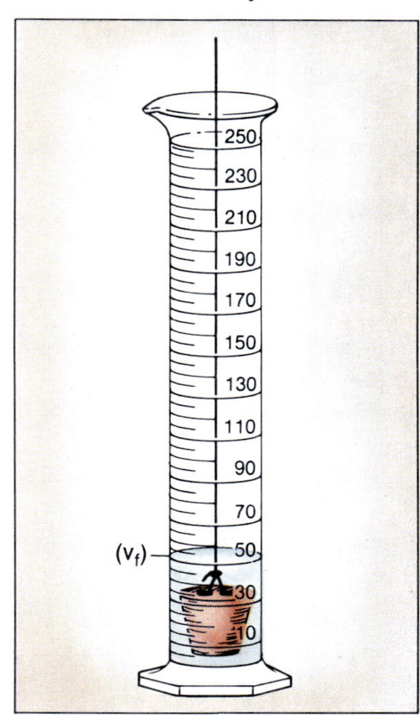

Enrichment: Scientists commonly use significant figures to express the precision of a measurement. Significant figures are all the certain digits plus the next uncertain one.

measure the thickness of one page in this book. You have only a metric ruler. You could count 100 pages. Then measure the total thickness of the 100 pages. Find the thickness of one page by dividing the total thickness by 100. Does the answer contain some error? Remember that when you measured the total thickness, you probably estimated the closest mark on the ruler. This will introduce some error into your final answer. Measuring a different group of 100 pages will probably give a slightly different answer. This also shows that each measurement contains some error.

You can reduce the error by making the same measurement many times. Then take the *average* of all the results as the final answer. Some of the measurements were probably a little too large. Others were too small. Averaging many measurements tends to make these errors cancel each other. However, there is no way to reduce errors to zero. Scientists try to keep errors as small as possible.

1. Observations are made in the form of measurements in science because number values can be communicated easily and accurately.
2. 1/10 m = 1dm, 1/100 m = 1 cm, 1/1000 m = 1 mm, 1000 m = 1 km. 1/10 L = 1 dL, 1/100 L = 1 cL, 1/1000 L = 1 mL. 1/10 g = 1 dg, 1/100 g = 1 cg, 1/1000 g = 1 mg, 1000 g = 1 kg.
3. In the laboratory temperatures are usually measured in degrees Celsius.
4. The instruments used to measure mass are a spring scale and a balance. A spring scale uses the stretch of a spring by the mass being measured. A balance uses a known mass to balance the mass being measured.
5. The instrument used to measure volume is called a graduated cylinder. The cylinder has been marked with volume indications.
6. Making the same measurement several times and averaging them is one way to help reduce errors. This is in addition to just being careful.

SUMMARY

Scientific observations are often made in the form of measurements. The metric system is used in science. It is also the system of measurement most commonly used throughout the world. Measurements of length, mass, and volume are made by using instruments. Measurements always contain some error.

QUESTIONS

Use complete sentences to write your answers.

1. Why are many scientific observations made in the form of measurements?
2. Name the units of measurement that mean 1/10, 1/100, and 1,000 meters; 1/10, 1/100, and 1/1,000 liters; 1/10, 1/100, and 1,000 grams.
3. In what units do scientists usually measure temperature?
4. Name two instruments used to measure mass. How do they differ?
5. Describe an instrument used to measure volume.
6. How can you help reduce errors in measurements?

SKILL-BUILDING ACTIVITY

See teacher's commentary for teaching hints, safety, and answers to questions.

MEASURING THE VOLUME OF A SOLID OBJECT

PURPOSE: You will use a graduated cylinder to find the volume of a solid object.

MATERIALS:

graduated cylinder
water
string
various solid objects

PROCEDURE:

A. Fill the graduated cylinder with water to the 30-mL mark. This is the initial volume (v_i).

B. Copy the following table in your notebook.

Object	(v_i) (mL)	(v_f) (mL)	$v_f - v_i$

C. Tie an object such as a rubber stopper to the end of the string.

D. Lower the stopper into the cylinder.

E. Observe the difference in the water level in the cylinder to the nearest 0.5 mL. Record this number as the final volume (v_f) in your table.

F. Find the volume of the object as follows:

$$\text{volume} = v_f - v_i$$

Record the volume in the table.

G. Repeat steps A through F using several different objects.

CONCLUSION:

1. In your own words, describe how to find the volume of a solid using a graduated cylinder.

EXTENSION: You will find the volume of a regular solid object using two different methods and compare the results.

MATERIALS:

graduated cylinder
water
string
metric ruler
small square object

PROCEDURE:

A. Find the volume of the object using the procedure described in the first part of this activity. Record.

   1. What units did you use to measure this volume?

B. Using the metric ruler, measure the length, width, and height of the object to the nearest 0.5 cm.

C. Find the volume of the object as follows:

$$\text{volume} = \text{length} \times \text{width} \times \text{height}$$

Record.

   2. What units did you use to record this volume?
   3. Are your results the same using the two methods?

CONCLUSION:

1. Why can the volume of a solid be expressed in either milliliters or cubic centimeters?

SKILL-BUILDING ACTIVITY

See teacher's commentary for teaching hints, safety, and answers to questions.

USING A BALANCE TO MEASURE MASS

PURPOSE: You will learn how to use a standard laboratory balance to measure mass. Your balance may differ slightly from the one described in this activity but it will be basically the same.

MATERIALS:

triple beam balance
several solid objects
pencil
paper

PROCEDURE:

A. Check the balance with no mass on it. Be sure the balance is on a level surface. If there is a level indicator, adjust the balance until the indicator shows it is level. Move all the riders to zero. See Fig. 1–22. If the pointer on the right-hand end of the beam does not swing equally on both sides of the zero mark on the scale, adjust the balancing nuts until it does. The balance should always be swinging slightly when being used. Your teacher will be able to help you if you have trouble.

B. Place your pencil on the balance. Move the 100 g rider until the pointer goes below the zero mark. Then move the rider back one notch.

C. Repeat step B using the 10 g rider.

D. Move the 1 g rider until the pointer swings equally on both sides of the zero mark. The mass of the pencil is the sum of the readings of the riders.

   1. What is the mass of your pencil?

E. Repeat steps B through D to find the mass of several other objects.

F. Have a partner find the masses of the same objects you used in step E.

   2. How do your measurements of mass compare with your partner's?

   3. What reasons can you give for the differences between your results and your partner's results?

CONCLUSIONS:

1. Briefly state how you can find the mass of an object by using a balance.

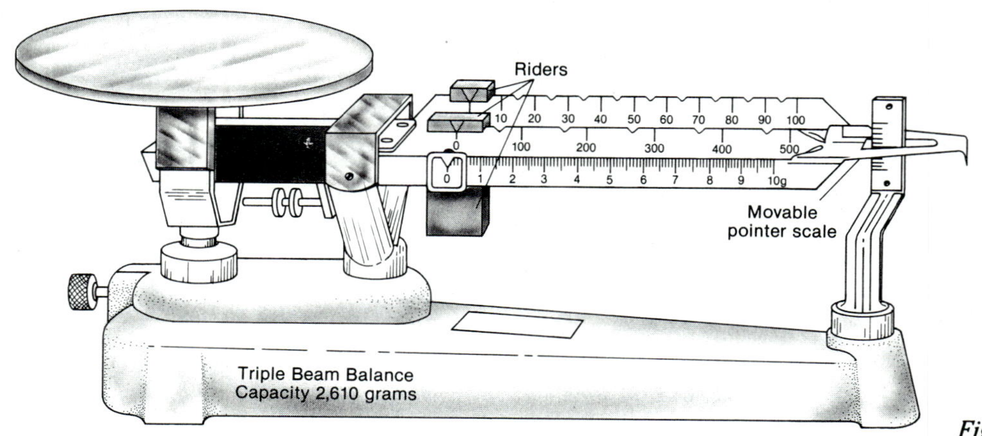

Fig. 1–22

TECHNOLOGY

INTRODUCTION

Welcome to the future, a world created by scientific research and development. More than knowledge of facts that have already been discovered, science is an activity for asking and answering questions and seeking new knowledge. Science is the foundation upon which new technology is built. In the Special Features section of your textbook we have tried to describe current research and technological developments which have actually extended the subject matter of science or changed the nature of what you must learn in order to live and work in modern society. The Special Features sections go beyond the textbook material to encourage you to explore, on your own, events in the scientific world, events which are constantly changing and which often raise more questions than they answer.

The thrill of a scientific discovery is often linked to a way of solving a real problem. That might involve finding a new source of fuel, or mapping the universe, or building a tiny supercomputer! In the Technology Features you will read about research in all these areas. You will also read about research projects which could not even exist without current technology. For example, for many years physicists had thought there were tiny particles of matter, smaller than atoms. Only in recent scientific history, however, have there been machines that could prove that some of these particles actually existed. By studying these small particles, physicists hope to answer very basic questions about the nature of matter. Problems in both medical science and astrophysics have begun to be solved because of technology that allows us to lower the temperature of certain materials to hundreds of degrees below freezing. This has made possible a form of surgery that is almost bloodless and a satellite that can operate under conditions of great heat. And because of the development of miniature lasers, it is now possible to send several hundred telephone messages through a cable of glass no thicker than spaghetti.

Computers, too, have changed our lives. Some of the technology features will help you to understand how computers work. In addition, COMPUTE! is a section which will help you to learn science through computers and to learn more about computers by applying information in your text to the programs.

As our ideas about the universe have changed with the discovery of new knowledge, new career opportunities have also been developed. Some of the careers you will read about in the Special Features did not even exist twenty years ago. In many cases, this means learning skills that are different from those that people had to learn even a short ten years ago.

All these changes require strong and continuing efforts toward understanding. Be patient with yourself; this is only the beginning of a long journey we hope you will enjoy.

CHAPTER REVIEW

See teacher's commentary for answers.

VOCABULARY

On a separate piece of paper, match the number of the sentence with the term that best completes it. Use each term only once.

Celsius	experiment	liter	data
scientific method	hypothesis	measurement	variable
observation	kilogram	meter	scientific theory

1. A(n) ______ is any factor in an experiment that affects the results of the experiment.
2. Recorded observations are called ______.
3. The ______ is the set of skills that can be used to solve problems in an orderly way.
4. A(n) ______ is a statement that explains a group of related observations.
5. The test of a hypothesis under controlled conditions describes a(n) ______.
6. A(n) ______ is an observation that is compared to a standard.
7. In the metric system, the ______ is the basic unit of mass.
8. The ______ is the basic unit of length in the metric system.
9. A commonly used unit of volume in the metric system is the ______.
10. Any information that we gather by using our senses is called a(n) ______.
11. A general statement that is based on hypotheses that have been tested many times is called a(n) ______.
12. The commonly used temperature scale in science is the ______ scale.

QUESTIONS

Give brief but complete answers to each of the following questions. Unless otherwise indicated, use complete sentences to write your answers.

1. Discuss why curiosity is an important characteristic of a scientist.
2. Why is the problem of acid rain being studied by scientists?
3. When scientists try to solve problems, what steps are they most likely to take?
4. What might be two reasons for changing a scientific theory?
5. Why are measurements used for making many scientific observations?
6. Give one reason why scientists in the United States use the metric system of measurement rather than some other system.

7. Describe a meter stick, a graduated cylinder, a spring scale, and a balance. Tell how you would use each one as part of an experiment.
8. Change each of the following measurements to meters: 2 km, 50 cm, 100 mm.
9. Explain the difference between a milliliter and a cubic centimeter as a unit of volume.
10. In measuring, why should several measurements be made and the average taken?

APPLYING SCIENCE

1. Write to the National Bureau of Standards, Washington, D.C. 20234, for information on how standard units are determined.
2. Report to the class on the conversion to the metric system in the United States. You may want to find out what is being done in your own state. Write to the National Bureau of Standards, Washington, D.C. 20234 or to the American National Metric Council, 1625 Massachusetts Ave., N.W., Washington, D.C. 20036.
3. Make a survey of your home and list places where metric measurements are used.
4. Write a short paper on the history of one type of measurement. For example, you might choose length. Use your school library or public library for reference material.
5. Choose one area of physical science. Write a report on an interesting career in that area.

BIBLIOGRAPHY

Beller, J. *So You Want To Do a Science Project!* New York: Arco, 1982.

Harpur, P. *The Timetable of Technology*. New York: Hearst, 1982.

"Metrics Ahead, How You Can Cope." *Science Digest,* February 1977.

Norris, J. *Metrics and Me*. Indianapolis: Youth Publications, Saturday Evening Post, 1976.

Shapiro, S. *Exploring Careers in Science*. New York: Richards Rosen Press, 1981.

"Through Metrics." *Science World.* May 1976.

UNIT 1

MOTION AND ENERGY

CHAPTER
2

This is not a photograph. The image was made by a computer graphic technique called ray tracing. Even the blur of the moving balls was created by the computer program.

MOTION

CHAPTER GOALS

1. Define motion, and explain how to find average speed, velocity, and acceleration.
2. State and explain Newton's three laws of motion.
3. Explain the difference between mass and weight.
4. State and explain Newton's law of gravitation.

2-1. What Is Motion?

At the end of this section you will be able to:

- ☐ Explain how you know when an object is in motion.
- ☐ Define speed, velocity, and acceleration.
- ☐ Find the average speed of a moving object.

The world around you is full of motion. Leaves fall from trees. Cars and trucks move along city streets. People walk from place to place. Maybe you walked to school today. You see movement everywhere. But what exactly is motion?

Enrichment: The velocity of the earth's surface at the equator, caused by the earth's rotation on its axis, is $\frac{\text{circumference}}{\text{time for 1 rotation}} = \frac{40{,}000 \text{ km}}{24 \text{ h}} =$ 1,670 km/h (approximately 1,000 mi/h).

OBSERVING MOTION

What do you mean when you say something is moving? First, you always compare a moving object with an object that appears to stay in place. The object that stays in place is called a *reference point*. When an object changes its position compared to a reference point, it is in **motion.** For example, you are in a car driving along a highway. The street lights along the road seem to move past your car. See Fig. 2–1. Actually, the lights are standing still. Your car is in *motion*. You are moving past the lights. The lights are reference points.

Motion A change in position of an object when compared to a reference point.

Look at Fig. 2–2. What reference points do you see in these pictures? Compare the two pictures. You can see that the balloon has moved past the trees. Now look at the time between the two pictures. The time is 20 seconds. During that time, the balloon moved a distance of 100 meters. Every moving object covers a certain distance in a certain period of time. The distance it moves divided by the time equals the **speed.** The formula for finding the *speed* of a moving object is speed (v) equals distance (d) divided by time (t), or: $v = d/t$.

Skill: *Compare and contrast* the photos in Fig. 2–2. This skill should be developed throughout this course.

Speed The distance covered by a moving object per unit of time.

Fig. 2–1 As shown in these two diagrams, the lamppost appears to move past the car windows. Actually, the lamppost is a stationary reference point. The car is moving.

Fig. 2–2 The balloon has moved past the edge of the trees between the top photo and the bottom photo. The time between the two photos was 20 seconds.

In the example shown in Fig. 2–2, you can find the speed of the balloon as follows:

$$v = \frac{d}{t} = \frac{100 \text{ m}}{20 \text{ s}} = 5 \text{ m/s}$$

The speed is written as 5 m/s, or 5 meters per second. This means that the balloon covers 5 meters each second. After 20 seconds, it has moved a distance of 100 meters.

The speed of your car would be measured in kilometers per hour (km/h). If you traveled 135 kilometers in 1.5 hours, your speed would be:

$$v = \frac{d}{t} = \frac{135 \text{ km}}{1.5 \text{ h}} = 90 \text{ km/h}$$

AVERAGE SPEED

Let's look again at your car trip. You traveled 135 kilometers in 1.5 hours. So your speed was 90 km/h. But suppose you were stuck in traffic for the first half hour. Or maybe you stopped along the way to look at the view. In other words, you did not move at a constant speed of 90 km/h for the entire trip. Since the speed of a car usually is *not* constant during a trip, the **average speed** is generally given. *Average speed* is equal to the total distance traveled divided by the time. For example, the average speed for your trip of 135 kilometers that lasted 1.5 hours is 135 km/1.5 h = 90 km/h. The formula $v = d/t$ always gives the average speed. See Fig. 2–3. What would be the average speed for a trip of 97.5 kilometers lasting 1.5 hours? What is the average speed of a marble that rolls 45 centimeters in five seconds?*

* $v_1 = d/t = 97.5 \text{ km}/1.5 \text{ h} = 65 \text{ km/h}$
$v_2 = 45 \text{ cm}/5 \text{ s} = 9 \text{ cm/s}$

Average speed The total distance traveled divided by the total time.

Fig. 2–3 The graph on the left shows that the car is moving at a constant speed. In the graph on the right, the speed is changing.

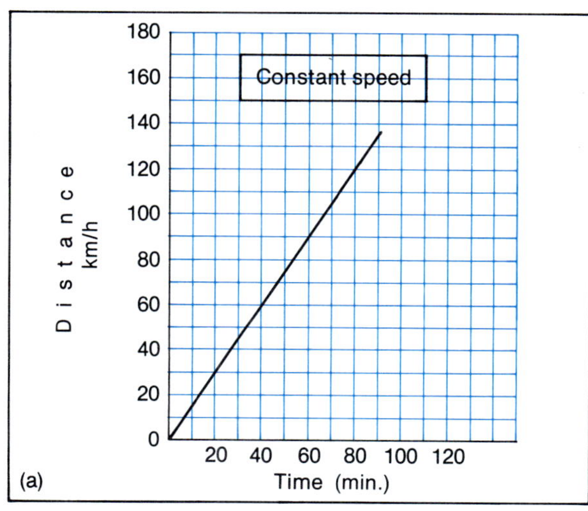

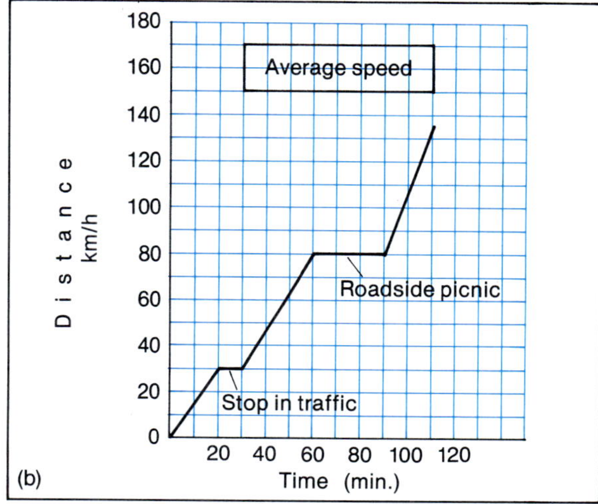

If you know the average speed and the time, you can find the distance. The formula is distance equals speed multiplied by time:

$$d = v \times t$$

For example, a running horse moved at an average speed of 5 m/s for 20 seconds. The distance covered in that time was:

$$d = v \times t = 5 \text{ m/s} \times 20 \text{ s} = 100 \text{ m}$$

How far will you travel in two hours if your average speed is 75 km/h?*

* $d = v \times t$
$= 75 \text{ km/h} \times 2 \text{ h}$
$= 150 \text{ km}$

If you know the distance traveled and the average speed, you can find the time. Simply divide the distance by the speed:

$$t = \frac{d}{v}$$

For example, suppose you travel 150 kilometers at an average speed of 50 km/h. Use the following formula:

$$t = \frac{d}{v} = \frac{150 \text{ km}}{50 \text{ km/h}} = 3 \text{ h}$$

Your trip would take three hours.

VELOCITY

Suppose you want to drive to your aunt's house. She lives 70 kilometers away. You want to be there in an hour. Can you just get in your car and drive at an average speed of 70 km/h for one hour? No. First you have to point your car in the right *direction*. You have to drive toward your aunt's house, not away from it.

In a moving car, you are going at a certain speed. At the same time, you are moving in a certain direction. Any moving object moves in some direction as well as at a certain speed. For example, a car travels west at a speed of 70 km/h. Scientists use the term **velocity** to express both speed and direction of a moving object. A car moving 70 km/h west has a different *velocity* from one going 70 km/h east. See Fig. 2–4.

Velocity The speed and direction of a moving object.

Word study: Velocity from *velocitas* (L.), quick.

People often use the words "speed" and "velocity" as if they have the same meaning. They do not. You can talk about speed without mentioning direction. However, in science you include both speed and direction when talking about velocity.

Fig. 2–4 Velocity takes into account both speed and direction. In this diagram, both cars are moving at the same speed. However, since their directions are different, their velocities are different.

ACCELERATION

Most moving objects do not move at a constant speed. For example, think of riding a bicycle. Going uphill, your speed is slower than when you are on level ground. Then your speed increases as you go downhill. This kind of motion is called **acceleration.** If the speed of a moving object changes, its motion is accelerated. See Fig. 2–5.

The word *acceleration* is commonly used to mean an increase in speed. However, to a scientist, acceleration is any change in the velocity of a moving object. Remember that velocity includes both speed *and* direction. Therefore, a scientist would say that when a bicycle slows down, or turns a corner, it is accelerating. Acceleration is a change in speed, direction, or both.

Acceleration A change in the velocity (speed or direction) of a moving object.
Word study: Acceleration from *acceleratus* (L.), swift.

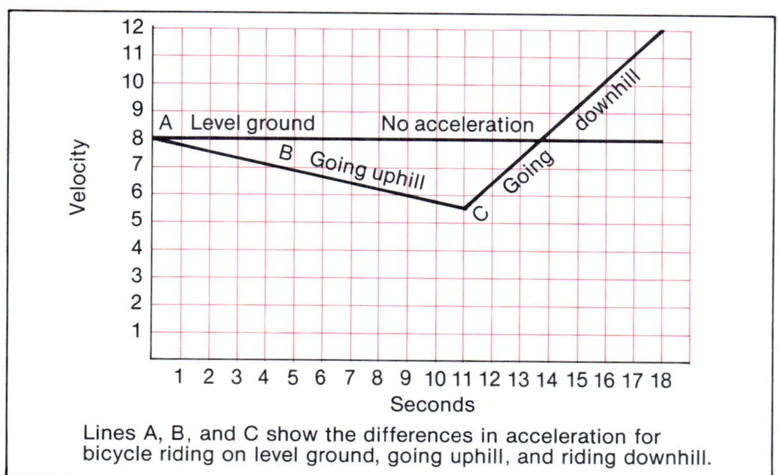

Lines A, B, and C show the differences in acceleration for bicycle riding on level ground, going uphill, and riding downhill.

Fig. 2–5 This graph shows accelerated motion since the speed is changing.

Suggestion: Show the class a stroboscopic photo of an accelerating object and point out the evidence for acceleration.

To find the acceleration (a), you must first find the change in speed. A change is indicated by using the Greek letter *delta* (Δ). The change in speed (Δv) is found by subtracting the initial speed (v_i) from the final speed (v_f): $\Delta v = v_f - v_i$

Acceleration (a) equals the change in speed (Δv) divided by the time (t):

$$a = \frac{v_f - v_i}{t} = \frac{\Delta v}{t}$$

Suggestion: Ask students to describe the motion of a car that has zero acceleration. They should say that the car is moving at a constant speed. If they think zero acceleration means that the car is not moving, they have confused velocity or speed with acceleration.

For example, suppose a car stops at a red light. When the light turns green, the car begins to move. It reaches a speed of 36 km/h in 12 seconds. The initial speed is 0 km/h. The final speed is 36 km/h. The time taken for the change in speed is 12 seconds. The acceleration is:

$$a = \frac{v_f - v_i}{t} = \frac{36 \text{ km/h} - 0 \text{ km/h}}{12 \text{ s}} = 3 \text{ km/h·s}$$

This means that the speed of the car increased by 3 km/h each second. The acceleration is read as three kilometers per hour per second.

If a car is going 60 km/h and increases speed to 80 km/h in five seconds, its acceleration is:

$$a = \frac{v_f - v_i}{t} = \frac{80 \text{ km/h} - 60 \text{ km/h}}{5 \text{ s}} = \frac{20 \text{ km/h}}{5 \text{ s}} = 4 \text{ km/h·s}$$

Fig. 2–6 A parachute slows down a skydiver. The upward force of air resistance on the parachute works against the downward force of gravity.

A falling object is a good example of accelerated motion. A freely falling object accelerates at 9.8 m/s·s or 9.8 m/s^2. This means that the speed of the object increases by 9.8 m/s each second. See Fig. 2–6.

Actually, a falling object will accelerate at 9.8 m/s^2 only if it falls in a vacuum. An object falling through the air will accelerate only for a definite time. The resistance of the air stops the acceleration once a certain speed is reached. The greatest speed reached by an object falling through air is called its *terminal speed.* For example, if you jump from an airplane, you will reach a maximum terminal speed of only about 190 km/h before you open your parachute. All objects falling through the air reach a certain terminal speed.

SUMMARY

You can tell that an object is moving by comparing it to a reference point. Motion is described by speed, velocity, and acceleration. When a moving object changes its speed or direction, it is accelerating.

QUESTIONS

Use complete sentences to write your answers.

1. Describe a bicycle ride from your home to school. Use each of the following terms: reference point, speed, velocity, acceleration.
2. Complete the following table:

Distance	Time	Average Speed
10 km	2 h	(a)
(b)	3 h	40 km/h
40 km	(c)	30 km/h

3. You are walking at a speed of 5 km/h. How far will you walk in 3.5 hours?
4. A runner reaches a speed of 40 km/h in five seconds. What is the acceleration?
5. Why does an object falling through air reach a certain terminal speed?

1. Answers will vary. Look for complete sentences and correct usage of the terms reference point, speed, velocity, and acceleration.
2. (a) 5 km/h (b) 120 km (c) 1.33 h
3. You would travel 5 km/h × 3.5 h = 17.5 km.
4. $a = v/t = 40$ km/h ÷ 5 s = 8 km/h·s.
5. Air friction causes all objects falling through air to reach a terminal velocity.

INVESTIGATION

See teacher's commentary for teaching hints, safety, and answers to questions.

SPEED AND ACCELERATION

PURPOSE: You will measure the speed and acceleration of a marble.

MATERIALS:

metric ruler (30 cm)
marble
clock with second hand

PROCEDURE:

A. Use a table top or level floor about 1.5 meters long.

B. Using a ruler, make an incline about 30 centimeters long. Raise it about 1.5 centimeters at one end. See Fig. 2–7.

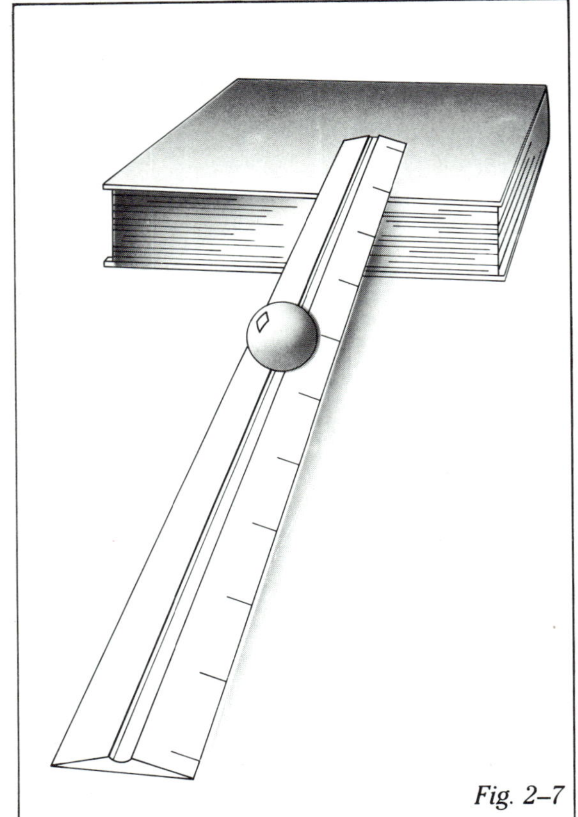

Fig. 2–7

C. Roll a marble down the incline.

D. Measure how far the marble rolls from the bottom of the incline in two seconds. Record your observations in a table like the one below.

Trial	Time (s)	Distance (cm)
1		
2		
3		

E. Repeat steps C and D at least three times. Record all measurements.

1. What is the average distance the marble rolled in two seconds?
2. What is the marble's average speed?

F. Using the same setup, find the distance the marble rolls in three seconds. Make several measurements. Record.

3. How far did the marble roll during the third second?
4. What was its average speed during the third second?
5. Compare the speed during the third second with the speed during the first two seconds.
6. Did the marble accelerate during the three-second trials?

CONCLUSIONS:

1. How can you measure the speed of a moving object?
2. How can you find out if the motion of an object is accelerating?

2-2. Changing Motion

At the end of this section you will be able to:

- ☐ Describe how forces affect moving objects.
- ☐ Explain and give examples of Newton's three laws of motion.
- ☐ Find the size of a force in newtons.

A Greek philosopher called Aristotle (384–322 B.C.) said that a moving object would stop moving unless it was pushed or pulled. Do you think this is true?

Aristotle's ideas were generally thought to be correct. Then one of the greatest scientific thinkers of all time stated the basic natural laws that explain how objects move. The scientist was Isaac Newton (1642–1727). See Fig. 2–8.

Fig. 2–8 In addition to his famous three laws of motion, Isaac Newton also studied the force of gravity and the nature of light.

Word study: Force from *fortis* (L.), strong.

Word study: Friction from *frictus* (L.), to rub.

Force Any push or pull that causes an object to move, or to change its speed or direction of motion.

Friction A force that opposes motion.

Suggestion: Demonstrate sliding friction and rolling friction. Compare the forces needed to maintain motion. If an air track or air table is available, air friction can be demonstrated.

FORCES

Great discoveries in science are often made when someone asks the right question. Scientists always ask questions. Before Newton, the question usually asked about motion was, "Why do objects move?" Experiments seemed to show that a push or pull was needed to cause motion. Any push or pull is called a **force.** People saw that an object with no *force* acting on it did not move. However, Netwon saw the problem differently. He asked the question, "Why do objects *stop* moving?"

Newton thought that moving objects are usually stopped by a force. We call this force **friction.** *Friction* is caused by two surfaces rubbing together. For example, there is a force between your shoes and the floor. If there were no friction, you would have trouble walking. See Fig. 2–9. Have you ever slipped on a polished floor? Smooth surfaces reduce friction.

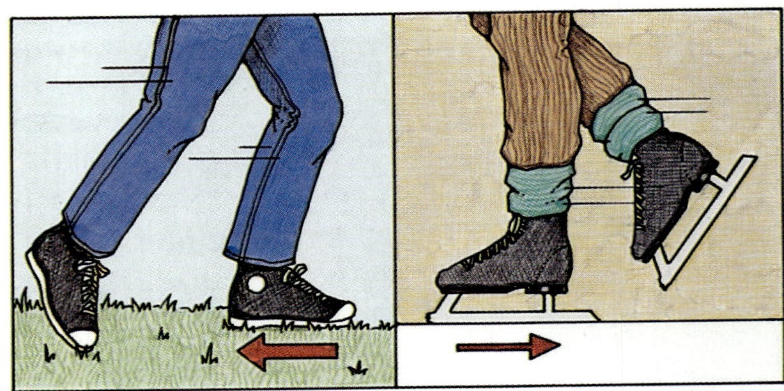

Fig. 2–9 The force of friction between the floor and your shoes helps you to walk. A lack of friction makes it hard to walk on a slippery surface such as ice.

Wheels can also reduce the amount of friction. Have you ever fallen at a roller skating rink? Friction can also be reduced by using a slippery substance like oil. This is why we put oil on the moving parts of machines. We can only reduce friction. We cannot get rid of it altogther. There is always some friction present. How would moving objects behave without friction?

THE FIRST LAW OF MOTION

Newton thought that a moving object with no friction or other force acting on it will continue to move in the same direction at the same speed forever. This statement is his first law of motion: *Every object remains at rest or moves at a constant speed in a straight line unless acted upon by some outside force.*

Newton's first law of motion says that a force is present whenever you see a change in speed or direction. If a car moves at a constant speed, no force is needed. To go faster, you press the accelerator. To slow down, the brakes supply a frictional force against the moving wheels. When a car turns a corner, a force is also needed. Every change in motion requires an outside force. This resistance to any change in motion, described by Newton's first law, is called **inertia.** A moving object, in the absence of friction, continues to move because of its *inertia.* An object that is not moving needs a force to overcome its inertia and start moving. The amount of inertia depends on the mass of the object.

Suggestion: Use Newton's first law of motion to remind students to always wear seat belts.

Inertia The resistance of objects to any change in their motion.

Word study: Inertia (L.), lack of skill.

The first law of motion should remind you always to use a seat belt when riding in a car. Suppose that you are not wearing a seat belt. The car stops suddenly. You keep moving forward. You might hit the windshield or dashboard. A seat belt makes it less likely that you will be hurt. It supplies the force needed to hold you firmly in the seat. See Fig. 2–10.

Fig. 2–10 If you are riding in a car that stops suddenly, you tend to keep moving forward. Seat belts provide the opposite force to stop this motion.

You know that a force is present when you see something move, or change speed or direction. Remember that the first law says that motion in a straight line at a constant speed does not need a force. However, it is not always true that no forces are present if you do not see motion or a change in motion. Two forces might act on an object. Two equal forces that act in exactly opposite directions are *balanced.* Balanced forces do not cause a change in motion. For example, two teams in a tug of war might be well matched. No motion will occur. See Fig. 2–11. Although balanced forces do not change motion, they may have another effect. For example, the balanced forces in a tug of war might break the rope. Because forces can act on an object without causing motion, you should know the direction in which they are acting. Then you can predict how the forces will affect the object.

Fig. 2–11 If the forces are equal and opposite, there will be no motion.

THE SECOND LAW OF MOTION

All forces act in some direction. Also, forces exist in different sizes. Scientists measure the size of a force in *newtons* (N). You would need a force of about 9.8 newtons to lift an object with a mass of 1 kilogram. Newton said that the size of a force acting on an object determines how its motion will change. This is his second law of motion: *The acceleration of an object is determined by the size of the force acting and the direction in which it acts.* The greater the mass of the object, the greater the force needed to accelerate it. Newton's second law of motion can be expressed as force (F) equals mass (m) multiplied by acceleration (a): $F = ma = 1\ \text{kg} \times 1\ \text{m/s}^2 = 1\ \text{N}$

Enrichment: Newton's first law of motion can be thought of as a special case of Newton's second law ($F = ma$). If the force is zero, the acceleration is zero and, therefore, there is no change in motion.

Enrichment: In using Newton's second law of motion, if the mass is in kilograms and the acceleration is in meters per second per second, the force will be in newtons (N).

Fig. 2–12 If a larger force is exerted on the same mass, the acceleration is larger.

In other words, a force of 1 N is needed to accelerate a mass of 1 kg by 1 m/s^2.

Fig. 2–12 shows an example of Newton's second law of motion. Suppose you have to push a stalled car to get it started. One person can supply only a small force. You might not be able to accelerate the car enough to make it start. If ten people push, the force is large. The car will accelerate enough to start. Remember that the direction of the force is also important. If five people pushed the car one way, while five pushed the other way, what would happen?

Enrichment: Most amusement or carnival rides illustrate the first and second laws of motion in various ways. Ask students to apply the laws of motion to explain their sensations during the rides they may have taken.

Fig. 2–13 The people whirling around on this ride tend to move off in a straight line. The inward force supplied by the supports keeps them moving in a circle.

Fig. 2–14 The object on the end of the string exerts an outward force on your hand. An equal and opposite force is supplied by your hand.

Skill: Demonstrate this *problem solving* technique. Divide each side of the equation $F = ma$ by m to get $a = F/m$.

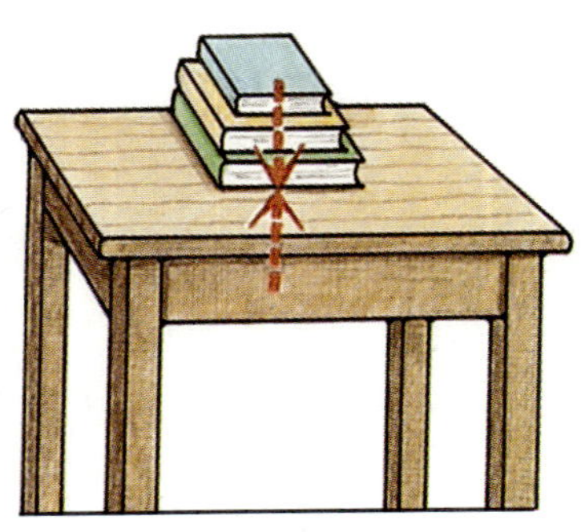

Fig. 2–15 The force of gravity causes the books to exert a downward force on the table. This force is equal to the weight of the books. At the same time, the table exerts an equal upward force on the books.

The mass of the car is also a factor. Ten people supply a force to a large four-door car. It accelerates. The same ten people supply the same force to a small compact car. The acceleration will be greater. You can see this by rearranging the formula: $F/m = a$

If the force remains the same and the mass decreases, the acceleration will increase. What will happen to the acceleration if the mass increases?

A popular ride in amusement parks also illustrates the laws of motion. People stand near the edge of a circular caged platform. See Fig. 2–13. They stand with their backs against a support. The platform starts to turn. The riders begin to feel the support push against their backs. Newton's second law of motion says that a force is needed to make something move in a curved path. On this ride, the force is supplied by the support behind the riders. Without this force, the riders would tend to move in a straight line. This is what the first law of motion says. As the ride turns faster, the riders feel a larger force. This is because the acceleration has increased.

THE THIRD LAW OF MOTION

Whirling an object in a circle on the end of a string is similar to the ride. See Fig. 2–14. You pull inward on the string. This pull supplies the force needed to move the object out of a straight-line path and into a curved path. You also feel another force pulling outward on the string. There are really two exactly opposite forces. One force is exerted by the string on the object to make it follow a curved path. The other force is exerted by the string on your hand. This example shows that no force exists by itself. Forces always exist in pairs.

Newton discovered that forces never exist alone. This is the principle of his third law of motion: *For every force there is an equal and opposite force.* The weight of a book pushes down on a table with a certain force. The table pushes up on the book with an equal but opposite force. See Fig. 2–15. One force acts on the table. The second force acts on the book.

A jet or rocket engine works on the principle of equal and opposite forces. In both cases, hot gases are forced out the rear of the engine. See Fig. 2–16. The engine exerts a force on the gases to push them out. The gases exert an equal and opposite force on the engine. This force moves the jet forward.

Fig. 2–16 According to Newton's third law of motion, the downward force of the escaping gases pushes the space shuttle and its solid rocket boosters upward.

SUMMARY

In the 17th century, Isaac Newton discovered three laws that describe motion. The first law deals with the cause of motion. The second law accounts for changes in motion. The third law describes pairs of forces that act on different objects.

QUESTIONS

Use complete sentences to write your answers.

1. What is a force? What happens to a moving object when a force acts on it?
2. What force is needed to lift a 2-kilogram mass? What force is needed for a 5.5-kilogram mass?
3. What is inertia? What determines the amount of inertia?
4. In your own words, state Newton's three laws of motion. Give an example of each.

1. A force is any push or pull. When a force acts on a moving object, the object will speed up, slow down, or change direction.
2. It takes 9.8 newtons of force to lift 1.0 kg, 19.6 newtons to lift 2.0 kg, and 53.9 N to lift 5.5 kg.
3. Inertia is the name given to the resistance of an object to a change in motion. The amount of inertia depends on the mass of the object.
4. Answers will vary. Make sure students use the correct terms and give a reasonable example of each law.

SKILL-BUILDING ACTIVITY

See teacher's commentary for teaching hints, safety, and answers to questions.

FORCE AND ACCELERATION

PURPOSE: You will make measurements to find how the size of a force affects the acceleration of an object.

MATERIALS:

recording timer
clock with sweep secondhand
recording tape (2.5 m)
spring scale
metric ruler
cart or roller skate

PROCEDURE:

A. Hook the spring scale to the cart.

B. Pull on the cart so that the spring scale reads 0.5 newton. See Fig. 2–17. Copy the table below.

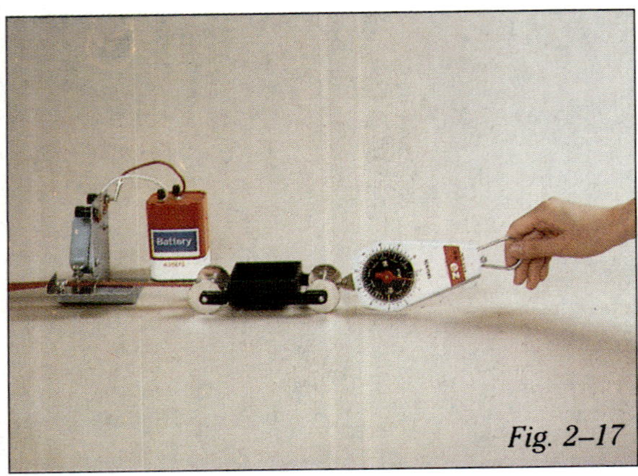

Fig. 2–17

Trial	Interval Number	Time (s)	Speed (mm/s)

C. Fasten a piece of recording tape to the other end of the cart. Put the recording tape through the timer. See Fig. 2–18.

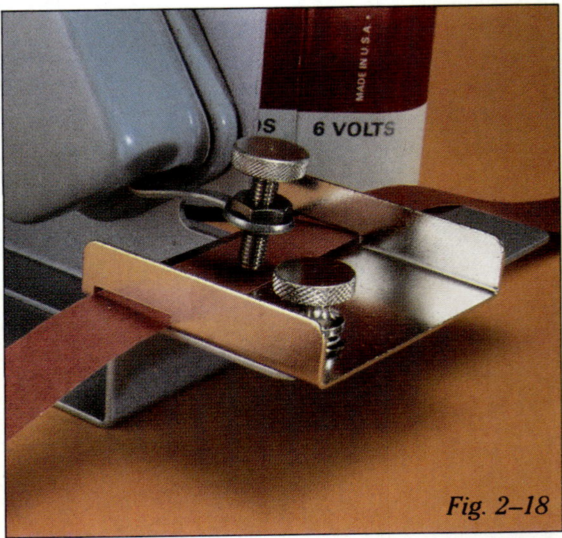

Fig. 2–18

D. Have a partner work the timer while you pull the cart. The spring scale should read 0.5 newton. Label this tape "0.5 N."

E. Repeat step J using new tape. This time the scale should read 1.0 newton. Label this tape "1.0 N."

F. Find the speed of the cart for the tenth interval of the tape labeled "0.5." Record.

G. Find the speed of the cart for the tenth interval of the tape labeled "1.0." Record. The acceleration of the cart is the change in speed during a given time. The cart started at rest. Therefore, the speed in steps F and G is also the acceleration.

CONCLUSIONS:

1. Based on your observations, how does the size of the force applied affect the acceleration of the cart?
2. What would the distance during the tenth interval be if the scale reading was 1.5 newtons?

2-3. Gravity

At the end of this section you will be able to:

- Show how to apply the law of gravitation.
- Describe how to measure the gravitational force acting upon an object.
- Compare mass and weight.

The first colony on the moon might look like Fig. 2–19. A base on the moon could be used to mine minerals. How would your life be different if you lived and worked on the moon? One big difference would be the way gravity affects you.

Fig. 2–19 In the next century, colonists from earth may live and work on the moon. They will have to become accustomed to the moon's weak gravity.

GRAVITY

Word study: Gravity from *gravitas* (L.), heaviness.

Every day you feel many different forces. In a moving car, you feel forces as the car starts, stops, and changes direction. These forces usually do not last very long. However, there is one force that is with you every minute of your life. That is the force called **gravity.** *Gravity* tends to pull all objects toward the center of the earth. You feel the force of gravity as weight.

Gravity The force that tends to pull all objects toward the center of the earth.

THE LAW OF GRAVITATION

Law of gravitation The gravitational force between two objects is directly proportional to the product of their masses and inversely proportional to the square of the distance between them.

Word study: Mass from *massa* (L.), lump.

Mass The amount of matter in an object.

In his study of motion, Newton discovered a rule that describes gravity. It is called the **law of gravitation.** Newton's *law of gravitation* has three parts. First, it says that any two pieces of matter will pull on each other with a certain gravitational force. For example, two objects hanging from strings will feel a gravitational force acting to pull them together. See Fig. 2–20. Second, the amount of matter in the objects determines the size of the force. The force between the objects in Fig. 2–20 would be very small.

The amount of matter in an object is called its **mass.** As the *mass* of objects increases, the size of the gravitational force pulling them together gets larger. See Fig. 2–21. The earth has the greatest mass of any object close to us. So we feel the earth's gravity as a large force. At the same time, the mass of your body pulls on the earth. The earth and the moon also attract each other. The greater mass of the earth causes its effect on the moon to be larger than the moon's effect on the earth. However, the moon's gravitational force is large enough to cause tides on earth.

Third, the law of gravitation describes how the size of the gravitational force between two objects changes as the distance between them changes. Newton found that increasing the distance between two objects greatly reduces the gravitational force. Bringing the same objects closer causes the gravitational force to increase. Doubling the distance reduces the force by four times. Moving the objects to half the distance causes the force to increase by four times. See Fig. 2–22.

Fig. 2–20 A small force tends to pull these two objects together. The force is too small for you to observe directly.

Fig. 2–21 The larger the mass of the two objects, the larger the gravitational forces between them.

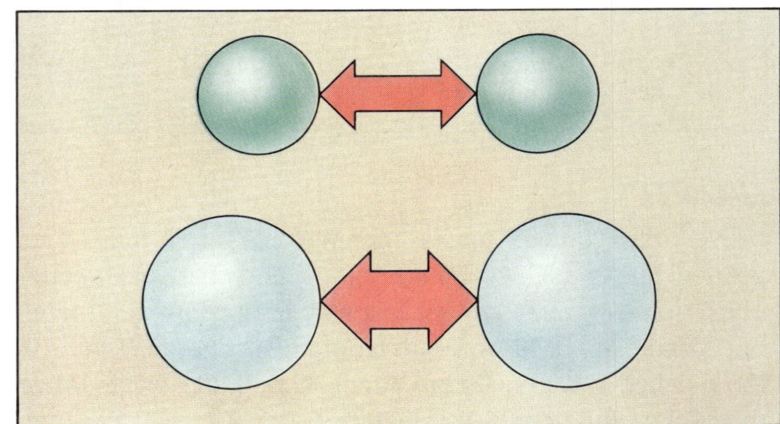

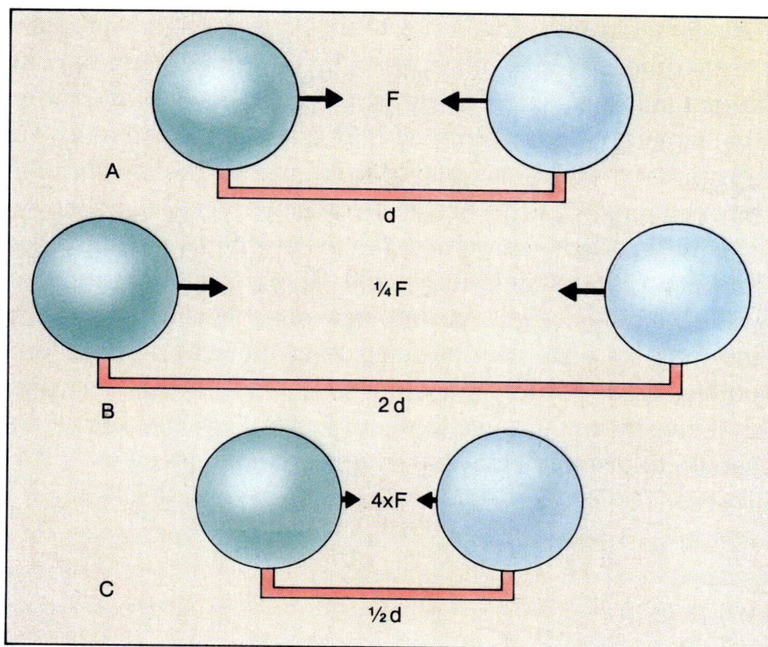

Fig. 2–22 The gravitational force between two objects varies as the square of the distance between the two objects.

All parts of Newton's law of gravitation can be expressed in mathematical form. The gravitational force between two objects changes in proportion to:

$$\frac{\text{mass of one object } (m_1) \times \text{mass of second object } (m_2)}{(\text{distance between objects})^2 \ (d)^2}$$

Like many scientific laws, the law of gravitation predicts how some part of the natural world works. It does not explain what causes gravity. The law of gravitation is a scientific tool. It helps explain the effects of gravitational forces. For example, Newton's law predicts that the gravitational force on the surface of the moon will be about one-sixth of that on the earth. This is because the moon's mass is only about one-sixth the mass of the earth. On the moon, you would weigh only about one-sixth of what you weigh on earth. You could jump six times higher. You could leap six times farther. How do you think this would affect you if you lived on the moon?*

Suggestion: For ordinary-size objects the gravitational force is very small. It is usually measured using the force need to twist a thin fiber. You can demonstrate the size of this force by hanging a ruler at its center from 50 cm of nylon thread. The force needed to twist the thread is more than the force between two 1 kg objects 10 cm apart.

*Student answers will vary. Use this as the basis of a discussion.

MASS AND WEIGHT

When you weigh yourself, you measure the size of the gravitational force acting on your body. The gravitational force on an object is called **weight.** A bathroom scale measures the gravitational force pulling on a person. See Fig. 2–23. Scientists

Weight A measurement of the gravitational force acting on an object.

usually measure force in newtons. Since gravity is a force, it is also measured in newtons. A person with a mass of 50 kilograms weighs 490 newtons. On the surface of the moon, the same person would weigh 81.6 newtons. This does not mean that the person's mass has changed. The *weight* of an object changes as the size of the gravitational force changes. The mass, or amount of matter in the object, does not change. As long as you stay in one place, an object with more mass will have more weight. At any place on earth, you can measure the mass of an object by measuring the gravitational force pulling on it. For this reason, "mass" and "weight" are used as if they mean the same thing. However, scientists are always careful to distinguish between weight and mass.

Enrichment: 1 pound = 4.45 newtons.

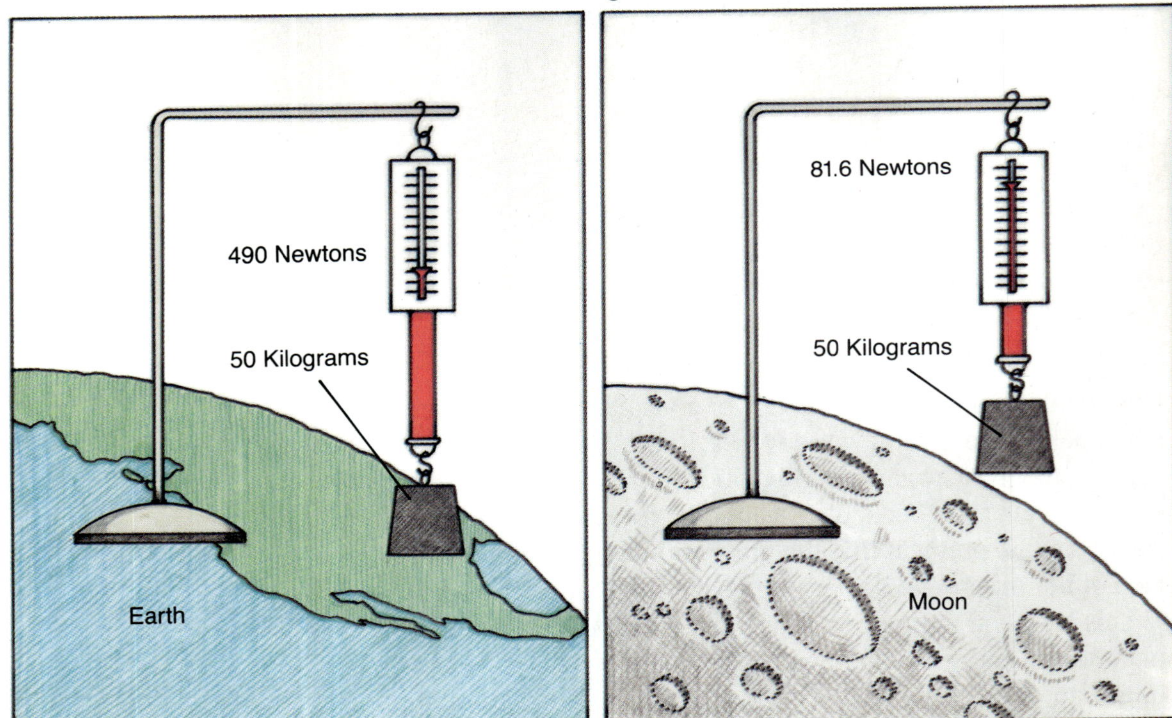

Fig. 2–23 A scale measures the gravitational force pulling on your body. Since the moon's gravity is less than the earth's, your weight would be less on the moon than on earth. Your mass, however, would remain the same.

The weight of an object can change. Its mass cannot change. The mass of an object is important when it is moving. Think about the force needed to accelerate a bicycle and a car to 8 km/h. See Fig. 2–24. A larger force is needed for the massive car than for the bicycle. The mass of an object determines the size of the force needed to produce acceleration. This is part of Newton's second law of motion.

Fig. 2–24 The smaller mass of the bicycle means that a smaller force is needed to produce the same acceleration.

Suppose you drop a heavy and a light rock at the same time. Will the heavy one fall faster? The heavy rock has a greater mass. A larger gravitational force is acting on it. But the greater mass also needs a larger force to produce a given acceleration. The lighter rock has less mass. It can reach the same acceleration with a smaller gravitational force pulling on it. For example, suppose one rock has ten times the mass of the other. It has ten times as much force pulling it down. But it is also ten times harder to accelerate. So both rocks fall togther. A heavy and a light rock will fall with the same acceleration due to gravity in the absence of air resistance.

SUMMARY

Newton described the force called gravity in his law of gravitation. This law says that the gravitational force acting between two objects changes depending upon their masses and the distance between them.

QUESTIONS

Use complete sentences to write your answers.

1. How does the gravitational force between two objects change in relation to the distance between the objects?
2. How can you measure the gravitational attraction between two objects? What unit would you use?
3. How is mass different from weight?

1. The gravitational force changes with the square of the distance between the objects, getting smaller as the distance increases.
2. The gravitational attraction between a person and the earth can be measured by stepping onto a bathroom scale. The force will probably be measured in pounds, but could also be in newtons.
3. Mass measures how much matter there is in an object while weight measures the force of attraction between the object and the earth.

SCIENCE INPUT

As you learned in Chapter 2, motion in a straight line does not need force to continue. The path of a satellite, however, is not a straight line. It revolves around the earth. For it to remain in orbit around the earth, force must be applied to maintain a particular speed. If the speed decreases, the satellite's orbit will decay and the craft will fall to earth. If speed increases, the satellite may possibly pull away from the earth. By controlling the satellite's engines, we can adjust its speed and maintain a proper orbit.

COMPUTER INPUT

NASA uses computers to assist in adjusting the position of satellites in orbit. Since computers can process a great deal of information in short periods of time, changes can be made as quickly as is necessary. NASA computers continually receive information from the satellite's instruments about its speed and position. In response, the computers direct the satellite's motion by accelerating or decelerating, thereby using a certain number of pounds of fuel per mile per second.

WHAT TO DO

Program Satellite is a game which uses the computer to simulate or model the movement of a satellite in orbit. The object of the game is to reach the speed necessary to maintain orbit, 18,250 mph, before running out of fuel.

Type the following program into your computer. Save it on disk or tape and run it. You must decide either to accelerate (A) or decelerate (D). You must also decide how many seconds you want your engine to burn fuel. After your decisions, the computer will tell you what speed you have achieved and how much fuel you have left. (HINT: Burn time can be fractions of seconds as well as whole seconds.)

On a separate piece of paper make a copy of the data chart and record your data.

GLOSSARY

PROGRAM	a list of step-by-step instructions that a computer reads and follows
RUN	the BASIC command that starts the program you have entered
HARDWARE	the computer itself, along with keyboard, screen, storage unit
SOFTWARE	the programs
BASIC, PASCAL, LOGO	the names for several high-level computer languages. A high-level language uses everyday words to represent basic commands. Machine language is a pattern of ones and zeros (a binary number system).

MAINTAINING MOTION: PROGRAM SATELLITE

PROGRAM

```
100  REM SATELLITE
110  F = 100: S = 13250: FB =
     INT(RND(1) * 50) + 50
120  PRINT
130  PRINT "NEED SPEED = 18250 + -1
     MPH": PRINT "SPEED = ";S;
     "MPH": PRINT "FUEL = ";F;" LBS":
     PRINT "FUEL BURN = ";FB;
     "MILES/POUND/SECOND"
140  IF F < 1 THEN PRINT "ORBIT
     DECAY - OUT OF FUEL": END
150  IF S > 18249 AND S < 18251 THEN
     PRINT "YOU ARE IN PERMANENT
     ORBIT": END
160  INPUT "ACCELERATE OR
     DECELERATE (A/D) ";C$
170  IF C$ = "A" THEN AD = 1: GOTO
     200
180  IF C$ = "D" THEN AD = -1: GOTO
     200
190  GOTO 160
200  INPUT "HOW LONG ENGINE BURN?
     (1-60 SEC) ";C$
210  C = VAL(C$): IF C < .000001 OR C >
     60 THEN GOTO 200
220  S = (AD * FB * C) + S: F = F - C
230  GOTO 120
```

Data Chart

	1	2	3	4
Speed				
Remaining Fuel				
Your decisions (A or D)				
Engine Burn Time				

PROGRAM NOTES

This program is based on mathematical formulas you learned in the chapter on motion regarding speed and acceleration. You could play the same game doing the mathematical calculations by hand. What are some of the advantages and disadvantages of playing the computer game?

BITS OF INFORMATION

Thinking of buying a computer? Try a little reading and window shopping first. You want a computer which will fit the family budget and be able to do what you need to have done. You might want it to be compatible with your school computer, as well. For a 50-page illustrated guide to home computers (no price information included), write:

"How to Buy a Home Computer"
Electronics Industries Association
P.O. Box 19100
Washington, D.C. 20036

Be sure to send a stamped self-addressed envelope. (It needs 54¢ postage and must be 6" × 9" or larger.)

INVESTIGATION

See teacher's commentary for teaching tips, safety, and answers to questions.

MEASURING GRAVITATIONAL ACCELERATION

PURPOSE: You will find a value for the acceleration caused by gravity by using the period of a pendulum.

MATERIALS:

string, 1.5 m long
eraser or rubber stopper
watch with second hand
metric ruler

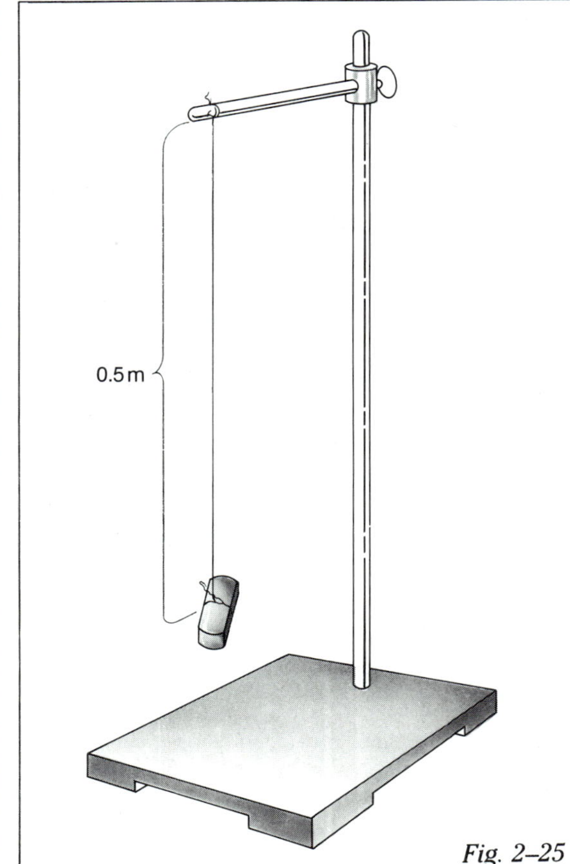

Fig. 2–25

PROCEDURE:

A. Set up a pendulum. See Fig. 2–25.

B. Copy the following table.

Trial	Length (l)	Time (t)	Swings	Period (T)

C. Pull the eraser 10 cm to one side and release it.

D. Count the number of complete swings the eraser makes in 60 seconds. Record.

E. Find the period *(T)* of your pendulum. This is the number of seconds needed to complete one swing:

$$T = \frac{60 \text{ seconds}}{\text{number of swings}}$$

Record.

F. Repeat steps C through E at least three times. Find the average period of your pendulum.

G. Find the value of the gravitational acceleration (g). Use the following formula:

$$g = 4\,\pi^2\, l/T^2$$

In this formula, $\pi = 3.14$, l = length of pendulum, T = period of pendulum.

CONCLUSIONS:

1. What is the acceleration caused by gravity in your classroom?
2. Suppose you did this experiment on top of a high mountain. Would the value of g be different? Explain.

TECHNOLOGY

HUMAN-POWERED VEHICLES (HPV)

Even though we are constantly looking for new sources of energy to power complicated machines, we are still fascinated by the energy of the human machine. Running, riding a bike, skating, hang gliding and bobsledding are all activities that have challenged the power and ability of the human body to move. In each of these activities, simple machines are harnessed to human direction and energy. What engineers and bicycling enthusiasts are aiming for is a vehicle, powered by one or more persons, which will reach speeds previously reached only by machines using nonhuman energy.

How fast have you ridden on your bicycle? The world speed record for all existing human-powered vehicles is 62.92 m/h, set by David Grylls and Leigh Barzewski in 1980. Mr. Grylls, riding alone, went 58.64 m/h in the same year. This vehicle, called "Vector," looks a lot different from your bike, although it is also driven through the use of pedals. As you can see in the photo, "Vector" is designed as a thin shell built close to the ground with the rider pedaling in a reclining position.

Other human-powered vehicles look like shark fins and torpedoes. Some are shaped like bananas and cigars. Some are custom designed and built; others are built around commercially manufactured racing bicycles. At a recent competition, there was a vehicle 42 feet long with a bullet-shaped nose. A crew of five sat in reclining positions, two facing the rear. Four operated hand cranks as well as foot pedals. The pilot of this cigar-on-wheels wore special goggles that were connected to a nine-foot system of fiber optic cables. Still another HPV held a crew of four. It was forty feet long and was designed to be extremely light as well as very strong.

In the competition, however, neither vehicle went over forty m/h. Racing bicyclists routinely achieve this speed. Why didn't these vehicles break the record? Critics cited a number of reasons. Having more than one rider increases power but also increases the number of people who can make errors. Besides that, increasing the number of riders does not increase speed by the same number. If you double the number of riders, speed will only increase by 10 percent. The basic problem lies in the *aerodynamics* of these machines. Aerodynamics is the study of the motion of air and of the forces acting on bodies in motion. The secret of success for human-powered vehicles does not appear to be in the number of operators nor in the force they generate. Success will be achieved by the design that offers the least resistance as it moves through the air and, at the same time, gives the rider the greatest opportunity to use his or her own strength and ability. What are your predictions for the future of the HPV? If they were easily pedaled and reasonably fast, might they replace cars for short-distance travel?

CHAPTER REVIEW

See teacher's commentary for answers.

VOCABULARY

On a separate piece of paper, match the word with the number of the phrase that best explains it.

acceleration	speed	weight	inertia
gravity	velocity	friction	motion
force	mass		

1. Force that tends to pull all objects toward earth's center.
2. Force caused by two surfaces rubbing together.
3. Combination of both speed and direction.
4. Gravitational force acting on an object.
5. Motion in which change occurs in speed, acceleration, or both.
6. Resistance of objects to any change in position or motion.
7. Any push or pull.
8. Amount of matter in an object.
9. Describes an object that is changing its position compared to a reference point.
10. Measure of distance moved in a period of time.

QUESTIONS

Give brief but complete answers to each of the following questions. Unless otherwise indicated, use complete sentences to write your answers.

1. Why is a reference point needed to tell if an object is moving? Give an example.
2. Explain the difference between speed and velocity. Give an example.
3. Give an example of accelerated motion in which (a) only the speed changes; (b) only the direction changes.
4. How are acceleration and terminal speed related for a freely falling object?
5. What is the acceleration of a train starting from rest and speeding up to 100 km/h in 50 seconds?
6. If there were no friction or other force acting on a moving body, what would happen to its motion?
7. Use an example to tell what is meant by inertia.
8. How much force is needed to lift a mass of 2.5 kilograms?
9. A 1.0-newton force causes an object to accelerate 1.0 m/s^2. What acceleration would a 2.0-newton force cause on the same object?
10. How do mass and distance affect the gravitational force between two objects?
11. The earth attracts a person with a force of 400 newtons. With what force does the person attract the earth?

12. Two objects attract each other with a gravitational force of 100 newtons. (a) What would be the force if the distance between them were cut in half? (b) What would be the force if the distance between them were doubled?
13. Two objects attract each other with a gravitational force of 100 newtons. (a) One object is replaced by an object with twice as much mass. What is the new gravitational force between them? (b) Both objects are replaced by objects with twice as much mass. What is the new gravitational force?
14. Give an example to show how mass is different from weight.

APPLYING SCIENCE

1. Find the speed of cars on a nearby street. Mark off a 50-meter distance. Measure the time it takes a car to travel that distance. Calculate the speed of the cars in kilometers per hour.
2. Roll a skate, toy car, or similar object down a slanted board. Find a way to measure its acceleration and terminal speed. Change the slant of the board by raising or lowering the end. Again measure the acceleration and terminal speed. Do this several times. Record and report all your results. Look for and report any pattern in the data you collect.
3. Compare the rates at which heavy and light objects fall through thick syrup. A marble and a ball bearing of the same size are ideal. Use a tall glass jar. Thin the syrup with a small amount of water and compare the rates. Continue to thin the syrup until both objects fall too quickly for you to time them. Record and report all your results. State a hypothesis to answer the question, "How would the rates of fall the two objects compare if there were no syrup or air in the jar?"
4. Set up an experiment to find the acceleration of a lead sinker or similar object as it falls freely through the air. Use your school or public library for references.

BIBLIOGRAPHY

Cherrier, F. *Fascinating Experiments in Physics.* New York: Sterling, 1978.

Covault, C. "Aerobatics at Mach 25." *Science 81,* May 1981.

Dalton, S. *Caught in Motion.* New York: Van Nostrand Reinhold, 1982.

Drake, S. "Galileo and the Rolling Ball." *Science Digest,* October 1978.

Taubes, G. "Einstein's Dream." *Discover,* December 1983.

Von Braun, W. and F. I. Ordway. *History of Rocketry and Space Travel.* New York: Crowell, 1975.

CHAPTER

3

This photo shows industrial robots at work. Robots are machines. Like all machines, robots help make our work easier. Technology is changing how we live and work in many ways.

WORK

CHAPTER GOALS

1. Explain how to find the amount of work done by a machine.
2. Explain the difference between work and power.
3. List eight simple machines and describe how they work.
4. Find the mechanical advantage and efficiency of a machine.
5. Explain what is meant by technology and tell how it affects our lives.

3-1. What Is Work?

At the end of this section you will be able to:

- Explain how a force can do work.
- Measure the amount of work done per unit of time.

Lifting a heavy box is work. Washing the dishes or taking out the trash is also work. You always use energy whenever you do work.

FORCES AND WORK

At least one force is pulling on you right now. It is the force of gravity. The size of the gravitational force is equal to your weight. If you are sitting in a chair, an equal force is pushing on you. This force acts in the opposite direction from the gravitational force. This equal and opposite force is supplied by the chair.

Think about climbing a flight of stairs. Your muscles supply a force to lift your body up each step. See Fig. 3–1. The forces acting on you sitting in a chair do not cause motion. On the other hand, the force used to climb stairs does cause motion.

When a force causes motion, you always observe some kind of change. For example, suppose that you push hard against a wall. You probably will not move the wall or see any change in it. But if you push a chair just as hard, you would expect the chair to move. See Fig. 3–2. The difference between the two forces is that the force moving the chair does **work**. In science, *work* means that a force causes something to move. Work can always be observed and measured. The amount of work *(W)* done is equal to the size of the force *(F)* multiplied

Work The work done by a force is equal to the size of the force multiplied by the distance through which the force acts.

Fig. 3–1 When you climb a flight of stairs, you exert an upward force to overcome the downward force of gravity.

by the distance *(d)* the object moves. Thus work can be described by the following formula:

$$\text{work } (W) = \text{force } (F) \times \text{distance } (d)$$
$$W = F \times d$$

Suppose you push on a chair with a force equal to two newtons. You move the chair one meter across the floor. The amount of work done is:

Skill: Practice *problem solving* by doing sample problems on the board and discussing them.

$$W = F \times d = 2\text{ N} \times 1\text{ m} = 2\text{ newton-meters (N} \cdot \text{m)}$$

The *newton-meter* (Nm) is the unit most commonly used to measure work. It is given the name *joule* (J). This unit is named for the English physicist James Prescott Joule. In the example above, two joules (2 J) of work were done to push the chair.

Suggestion: Illustrate the amount of work in 1 joule: 102 grams lifted 1 meter requires 1 joule of energy.

Fig. 3–2 No matter how hard you push, the wall will not move. No work is being done. But you can move the chair. Work is being done.

WORK AND TIME

What changes when work is done to move an object? When you do work on an object, you can change its **energy**. For example, if you lift a box, you are doing work on it. You are using *energy*. You are also adding energy to the box. The amount of energy added can be found by measuring the amount of work done. Since energy can do work, the units used to measure work and energy are the same. Both are measured in joules.

Energy The ability to do work. It is commonly expressed in joules.

Word study: Energy from *energos* (Gr.), active, at work.

Often, we want to know how fast work is being done. The rate at which work is done is called **power**. To find the *power*, we measure the amount of work done per unit of time:

$$\text{power} = \frac{\text{work}}{\text{time}} = \frac{\text{force} \times \text{distance}}{\text{time}}$$

Power The rate at which work is being done. Power = work ÷ time. It is expressed in joules per second (J/s).

For example, suppose you exert a force of one newton over a distance of one meter for one second. The power would be:

$$\text{power} = \frac{\text{force} \times \text{distance}}{\text{time}} = \frac{1\ \text{N} \times 1\ \text{m}}{1\ \text{s}} = 1\ \text{N m/s} = 1\ \text{J/s}$$

Fig. 3–3 Horses were once used to help pump water out of mines. When engines replaced them, the power of the engine was compared to the number of horses needed to do the same job. This gave rise to the term "horsepower."

Fig. 3–4 An electric meter measures the kilowatt hours of electrical energy used.

The amount of power is therefore one joule per second (1 J/s). One joule per second is equal to one **watt**. The *watt* is the SI unit of power. It is named after James Watt who invented the steam engine. You are probably more familiar with the *kilowatt*. One kilowatt (kw) is equal to 1,000 watts. Fig. 3–3 shows another way to measure power.

The rate at which a light bulb uses energy is usually expressed in watts (W). For example, light bulbs are labeled 40 W, 60 W, 100 W, and so forth. The total amount of energy used by the bulb depends on how long it operates. A 60-W light bulb burning for one hour uses 60 W × 1 h = 60 watt-hours (Wh) of electricity.

The total electrical energy used is measured in kilowatt hours. A meter such as that shown in Fig. 3–4 measures energy used. Periodically, the electric company reads the meter. Subtracting the previous reading from each new one tells how many kilowatt hours of electricity were used. For example, the last meter reading was 6,530 kWh. The meter now reads 6,845 kWh. The energy used is 6,845 kWh − 6,530 kWh = 315 kWh.

Watt The SI unit of power. It is equal to one joule per second (1 W = 1 J/s).

SUMMARY

When a force causes motion, work is done. The amount of work depends on the size of the force and the distance the object moves. Energy is always used when work is done. Power measures how fast work is done.

QUESTIONS

Use complete sentences to write your answers.

1. What two things are needed to do work?
2. How can you find the amount of work done?
3. What are joules and watts? How are they related?
4. Complete the following table:

Force (N)	Distance (m)	Work (J)	Time (s)	Power (W)
3	2	(a)	3	(b)
15	8	(c)	4	(d)
–	–	(e)	3	40
–	–	(f)	5	100

1. To do work a force must act through a distance.
2. The amount of work is the product of the force and the distance.
3. Joules are units of energy and watts are units of power. One watt of power is used when one joule of energy is used each second.
4. (a) 6, (b) 2, (c) 120, (d) 30, (e) 120, (f) 500

INVESTIGATION

See teacher's commentary for teaching hints, safety, and answers to questions.

FORCE AND WORK

PURPOSE: You will measure the amount of force and work needed to move a book.

MATERIALS:

spring scale
book
string, about 1 m
metric ruler

PROCEDURE:

A. Tie the string around the book. See Fig. 3–5.

B. Hook the spring scale to the string so that you can pull the book across a table.

C. Copy the following table.

Object	Force (N)	Distance (mm)	Distance (m)	Work (J)
Book				

D. Find the force needed to pull the book across the table. Record the force.

E. Pull the book across the table at different, but constant, speeds.

1. How does the speed affect the amount of force needed?
2. How much work is done in pulling the book 1.0 meter? 1.6 meters? Record.

F. Use the spring scale to find the force needed to lift the book. Record this measurement in your table.

G. Calculate the amount of work needed to lift the book from the floor to the height at which you normally carry your books. Record.

CONCLUSION:

1. How can you find the amount of work, in joules, needed to lift a book to a height of 1.5 meters?
2. In your own words, explain the relationship between force and work.

Fig. 3–5

3-2. Simple Machines

At the end of this section you will be able to:

- ☐ Explain how a *lever* can change the size of a force.
- ☐ List and describe the kinds of simple machines.
- ☐ Compare the amount of work done by any simple machine to the amount of work put into it.

Fig. 3–6 and Fig. 3–7 These people are both using levers to make their work easier.

Simple machine A device that can be used to change the direction and size of forces.

Enrichment: Have students identify any simple machines they can find in the classroom.

A large force is needed to lift a car. Ordinarily, one person cannot supply such a large force. However, one person can easily lift a car by using a jack. See Fig. 3–6. The jack can increase the force you apply to the handle. This larger force is transferred to the car. Sometimes your muscles cannot supply enough force to do the work you want done. Then you can use some kind of **simple machine**. A *simple machine* is used to change the size or direction of a force. For example, moving a heavy boulder probably requires more force than you can supply alone. You might not be able to move it at all by pushing on it. However, by applying the same force to a pole or bar placed under the boulder, you can move it. If the pole is used as shown in Fig. 3–7, you can produce a large force to move the heavy load. A rigid pole or bar used to move a load is a kind of simple machine called a *lever*. The automobile jack shown in Fig. 3–6 is also a kind of lever.

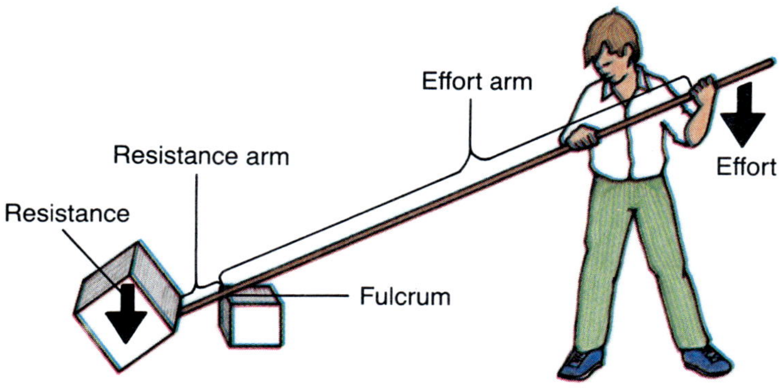

Fig. 3–8 This diagram shows the parts of a lever.

USING LEVERS

It might seem that a simple machine such as a lever can supply more work than is put into it. This is not true. The work done in moving one end of a lever is always equal to the work done on the load at the other end. This means that a lever only transfers work. A lever does not increase the amount of work done. However, by using a lever you can do the same amount of work with less force. Remember, work depends only on the force applied and the distance moved. A lever always turns on a fixed point. This fixed point is called a *fulcrum*. The fulcrum is the place where the lever is supported. For example, look at the lever shown in Fig. 3–8. The length of the lever between the fulcrum and the load is called the *resistance arm*. From the fulcrum to the end of the lever where the force is applied is the *effort arm*. You can see that the effort arm is much longer than the resistance arm. When the end of the effort arm is pushed down, the end of the resistance arm moves up a shorter distance. Thus, the effort force acts over a greater distance than the resistance force.

Enrichment: The mechanical advantage of a lever is found by dividing the effort distance by the resistance distance. The mechanical advantage of the lever increases as the effort distance increases.

In Fig. 3–8, the input work is equal to the output work. Since work equals force times distance:

$$\text{input work} = \text{output work}$$

$$\text{effort force} \times \text{effort distance} = \text{resistance force} \times \text{resistance distance}$$

$$F_e \times d_e = F_r \times d_r$$

Therefore, if the effort force is less than the resistance force, the effort distance must be greater than the resistance distance. For example, suppose you use a lever to lift a load of 8 newtons. You apply a force of 2 newtons and lift the load 0.5 meters. How far would you have to push the lever?

$$F_e \times d_e = F_r \times d_r$$
$$2\text{ N} \times d_e = 8\text{ N} \times 0.5\text{ m}$$
$$d_e = \frac{8\text{ N} \times 0.5\text{ m}}{2\text{ N}}$$
$$d_e = 2\text{ m}$$

The resistance force *(F_r)* is four times larger than the effort force *(F_e)* you applied. However, your effort force moved four times farther than the load was lifted. Thus a lever can change the size of a force but it cannot supply more work than is put in to it.

KINDS OF LEVERS

By using a lever, you can do the same amount of work with less force. The position of the fulcrum determines how the lever works. For example, the lever shown in Fig. 3–7 has the fulcrum between the effort applied and resistance to be moved. This kind of lever is called a *first-class lever*. A *second-class lever* has the resistance located between the effort and the fulcrum. A lever in which the effort is applied between the resistance and the fulcrum is called a *third-class lever*. A first-class lever can change the size of the applied force. It also reverses the direction of the applied force. Second- and third-class levers can change the size but not the direction of the applied force. You probably have seen many examples of all three kinds of levers. See Fig. 3–9.

Enrichment: Display various common tools such as a screwdriver, a can opener, and a staple remover. Ask students to point out the levers in these tools and explain how the lever helps with applied forces.

Fig. 3–9 The three classes of lever. The diagrams show where the fulcrum (F), resistance (R), and effort (E) are located.

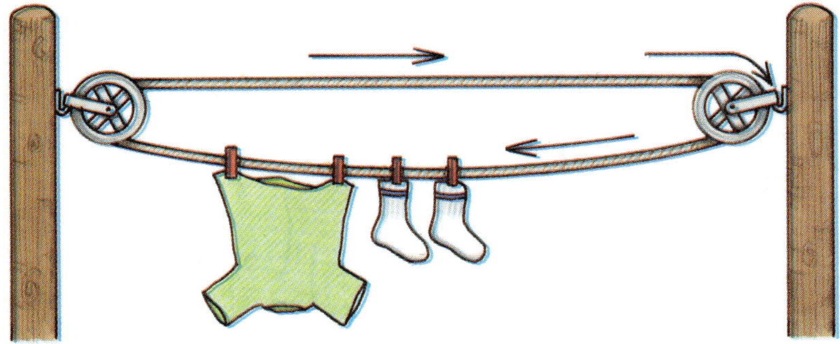

Fig. 3–10 A single fixed pulley changes the direction of a force.

PULLEYS

Not all kinds of levers are made of straight poles or bars. For example, the simple machine called a *pulley* is a lever in the form of a wheel. A single pulley, like those shown in Fig. 3–10, can be thought of as a kind of lever supported at the axle. This arrangement simply changes the direction of the force used. Two pulleys will lift the load only half as far as the length of rope pulled down. Then, ideally, the force applied must be equal to half the weight lifted. Other pulley arrangements are also possible that supply even greater forces. See Fig. 3–11.

Fig. 3–11 Several pulleys are often used in combination on ships. As shown in this photo, two pulleys are used to lift a weight.

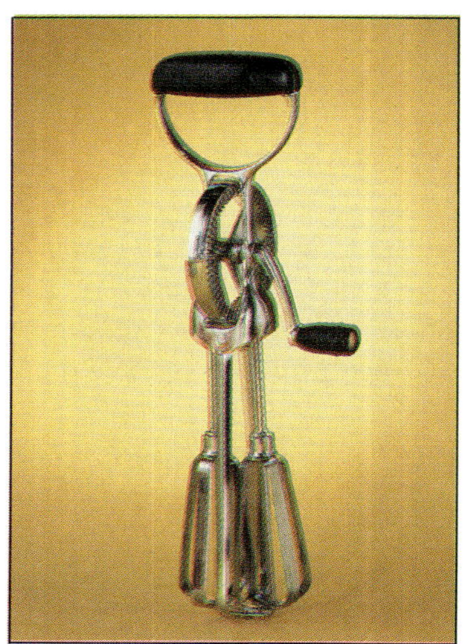

Fig. 3–12 An eggbeater uses gear wheels. When you turn the handle, the gears cause the blades to turn faster than the handle.

GEARS

Another simple machine using a wheel as a lever is the *gear wheel*. When two gears operate together, work is transferred. There is no change in the size of the forces used. If the gear wheels are of different sizes, the larger wheel always turns more slowly than the smaller. An egg beater shows how gear wheels work. It has a large gear wheel with a crank handle. See Fig. 3–12. Two smaller gears whose teeth fit into the large gear are attached to the beaters. The small gears make many turns for each complete turn of the large gear. Thus the beaters can turn very rapidly. However, the turning force of the small gears is less than the turning force of the large gear wheel. Speed, not force, is increased.

Fig. 3–13 A steering wheel is a wheel and axle, which is a type of lever. The center of the steering wheel is the fulcrum.

WHEEL AND AXLE

A *wheel and axle* also is a machine in which a wheel acts as a lever. The steering wheel of a car is an example of a wheel and axle. A large circle, the wheel, is attached to a small circle, the axle. A force turning the wheel also turns the axle. However, the force on the axle is greater than that applied to the wheel. See Fig. 3–13. The wheel of a wheel and axle may also be a crank. The effort force applied to the crank handle moves in a large circle. The axle then moves through a small circle. Therefore, a larger force pulls on the rope to lift the weight. A doorknob is also an example of a wheel and axle. The doorknob is the wheel and the rod is the axle.

HYDRAULIC PRESS

One kind of simple machine uses liquids to transfer forces. It consists of two *pistons* of different sizes. See Fig. 3–14. When the small piston is pushed down, the liquid pushes up on the large piston. The large piston moves up a shorter distance than the small one moves down. The force delivered by the large piston is greater than the force applied to the small. A machine that works this way is called a *hydraulic* (hie-**draw**-lik) *press*. The brakes on most cars use a hydraulic press. It increases the size of the force applied to the brake pedal. This larger force is transferred to the wheels to stop the car's forward motion. Hydraulic machines are used in many industries where large forces are needed.

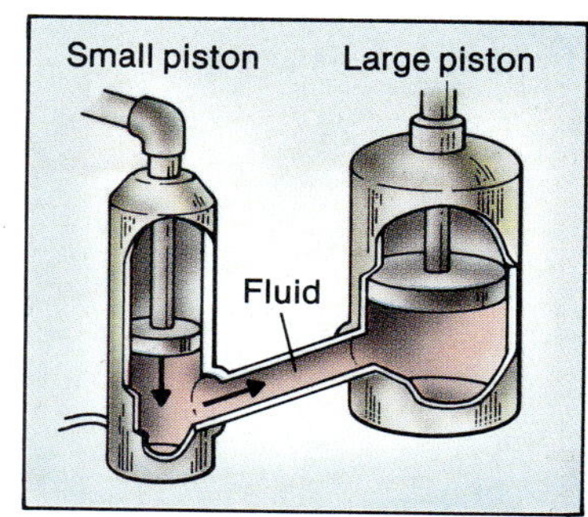

Fig. 3–14 This diagram shows the relationship between the pistons in a hydraulic press.

Word study: Hydraulic from *hydraulos* (Gr.), a water pipe.

Fig. 3–15 The ramp shown here is an inclined plane. It increases the distance but reduces the force needed to raise a load.

INCLINED PLANE

An *inclined plane* is a simple machine with no moving parts. An inclined plane increases the distance over which the applied force acts. It is a sloping surface like the ramp shown in Fig. 3–15. Using an inclined plane, you can move a load using less force than would be needed to lift the same weight. Stairs are a kind of inclined plane. The force needed to move you to the top of the stairs is spread over a large distance.

An inclined plane wrapped around a cylinder makes a *screw*. See Fig. 3–16. Screws are very useful because the length of the inclined plane can be spread over a large distance. The more tightly wound the screw is, the larger the distance.

1. A simple machine can either increase or decrease the force applied to it. A simple machine also transfers work.
2. Eight simple machines are the lever, the inclined plane, the hydraulic press, the pulley, the wheel and axle, the wedge, the screw, and the gear wheel. The screw and the wedge are types of inclined plane. The gear wheel, wheel and axle, and pulley are types of lever.
3. The amount of work done by a machine is equal to the amount of work put into it. Effort force × effort distance = resistance force × resistance distance.
4. The work to be done is 10 N × 1.5 m = 15 J. The distance to be moved is 3 m. Therefore the effort force is 15 J / 3 m = 5.0 N. This assumes 100% efficiency.

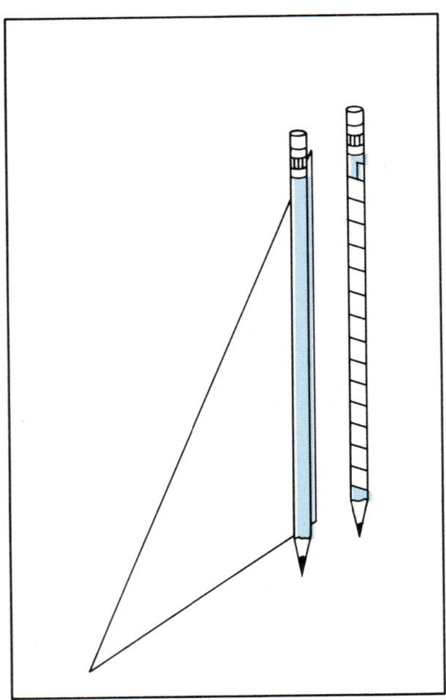

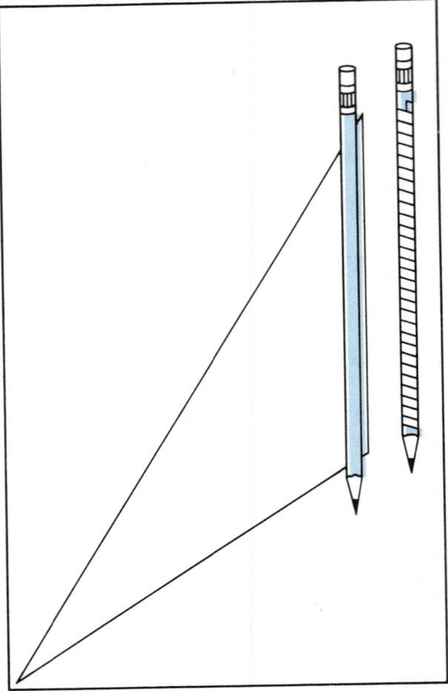

Fig. 3–16 As shown in the diagram, a screw is an inclined plane wrapped around a cylinder. The more tightly wound screw has a smaller pitch *and the incline is longer.*

Two inclined planes put together make a *wedge*. When a wedge is used to split a log, as shown in Fig. 3–17, the two inclined planes move the resistances apart on each side. A knife is a kind of very narrow wedge.

Fig. 3–17 As a downward force is applied, the wedge splits the log apart.

SUMMARY

A simple machine can be used to change the size or direction of a force. Different kinds of simple machines are used to make work easier. A simple machine cannot produce more work than is put into it.

QUESTIONS

Use complete sentences to write your answers.

1. State two things that a simple machine can do.
2. List eight simple machines. Which four are related to each other? Explain.
3. How does the amount of work that is put into a machine compare to the amount of work that is done by the machine? Explain.
4. You want to move a load of 10 newtons onto a truck 1.5 meters high. If your ramp is three meters long, how much effort must you use?

3-3. Machines at Work

At the end of this section you will be able to:

- ☐ Explain how to find the *mechanical advantage* of some simple machines.
- ☐ Compare the work input and output of a machine.
- ☐ Explain the meaning of technology.

How would your life be different if you had a robot to help you? Robots are machines. They can do some things that are usually done only by people. No one has yet invented a robot that can completely replace a person. However, many other kinds of machines can also help you. Each one is made of two or more parts. Each is designed to do certain jobs.

MECHANICAL ADVANTAGE

A lever can be used as a simple machine to multiply forces. For example, a lever can have the fulcrum closer to the load than to the effort. See Fig. 3–18. This lever increases the effort force because the effort arm is longer than the resistance arm. The amount by which the lever increases the effort force can be found by dividing the length of the effort arm by the length of the resistance arm. This number is called the **mechanical advantage** of the lever. *Mechanical advantage* compares the output force of a machine with the input force:

Mechanical advantage The relationship of the output force of a machine to its input force.

$$\text{mechanical advantage} = \frac{\text{output force}}{\text{input force}} =$$

$$\frac{\text{effort distance}}{\text{resistance distance}} = \frac{\text{resistance force}}{\text{effort force}}$$

For example, the length of the effort arm of the lever in Fig. 3–18 is two meters. The length of the resistance arm is 0.5 meter. The mechanical advantage can be found as follows:

$$\text{mechanical advantage} = \frac{\text{effort distance}}{\text{resistance distance}} = \frac{2\text{ m}}{0.5\text{ m}} = 4$$

The lever has a mechanical advantage of 4.0. In other words, the lever multiplies the effort force by four. The mechanical advantage can also be less than one. A machine can increase speed rather than force. For example, turn the handle of an eggbeater. The blades turn faster than the handle.

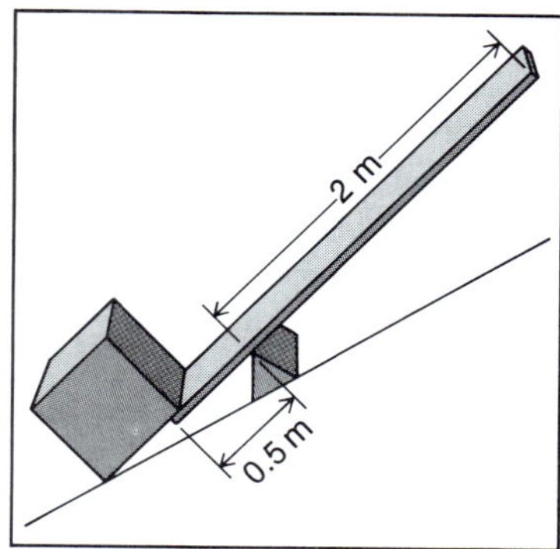

Fig. 3–18 The effort arm of this lever is longer than the resistance arm. The lever has a large mechanical advantage.

FRICTION

Friction is a force caused by two surfaces rubbing together. It opposes and slows the motion between two objects in contact with each other. For example, suppose that you used an inclined plane to help lift a heavy box as shown in Fig. 3–19. The mechanical advantage of an inclined plane is found by dividing its length by its height. If the length of the inclined plane is ten meters and its height is two meters, the mechanical advantage is:

$$\text{mechanical advantage} = \frac{10\text{ m}}{2\text{ m}} = 5$$

So the force needed to push the box up the inclined plane should be only one-fifth of the force needed to lift the box directly. However, there is friction between the box and the surface of the inclined plane. More force is needed to overcome the friction.

The mechanical advantage a machine would have if there were no friction is called its *ideal mechanical advantage*. All machines have some friction. Therefore, the *actual mechanical advantage* of a machine is always less than its ideal mechanical advantage.

Fig. 3–19 The actual mechanical advantage of this inclined plane is less than its ideal mechanical advantage because some force is used to overcome friction.

EFFICIENCY

The mechanical advantage of a machine can often be increased by combining it with other machines. For example, look at the bicycle shown in Fig. 3–20. The pedals are attached to levers. The levers turn the gear wheel, which pulls on the chain. The chain turns a smaller gear wheel and transfers force to the rear wheel. Thus levers and gears are among the

Fig. 3–20 A bicycle is an example of a machine that is made up of several simple machines.

most important parts of a bicycle. What other examples of simple machines can you find on a bicycle?

A bicycle is an example of a machine made up of two or more simple machines. Machines always have moving parts. Therefore, they have to overcome friction. Some of the work put into a machine with moving parts is used to overcome friction. Therefore, a machine always puts out less work than is put in. A comparison of the work input and work output of a machine is called its **efficiency**. The *efficiency* of a machine is usually expressed as a percent. For example, suppose a bicycle has an efficiency of 87 percent. This means that only 87 percent of the work done by the rider can be used to move the bicycle. If you put six joules of energy into a machine, and two joules are used to overcome friction, the efficiency of the machine is:

Efficiency Percentage found by comparing the work output of a machine with work input.

$$\text{efficiency} = \frac{\text{work output}}{\text{work input}} = \frac{6\ \text{J} - 2\ \text{J}}{6\ \text{J}} = \frac{4\ \text{J}}{6\ \text{J}} = 0.67 = 67\%$$

The efficiency of a machine can be increased by reducing friction. Friction can be reduced in many ways. Oils and greases make the surfaces of moving parts slide more easily. Bearings, such as the ball bearings on bicycle wheels, can reduce friction between rotating parts. However, friction can also be useful. For example, there must be friction between bicycle tires and the road surface. Otherwise the bicycle would not be able to move. Have you ever tried to ride a bicycle on a slick, wet road with low friction?

PEOPLE AND MACHINES

Reinforcement: Show pictures of people in different parts of the world using simple machines.

No one knows when the first simple machine was used. About three thousand years ago, the Egyptians used levers to lift water for crops. As the centuries passed, more complicated machines were invented. They were needed to do many of the jobs that support a more civilized life. By the 15th and 16th centuries, machines were used to mill grain, saw wood, and pump water. These machines began the great change known as the Industrial Revolution. During the 19th century, machines replaced human and animal labor in manufacturing, transportation, and building. This was made possible by the application of scientific knowledge to the solution of practical problems. The ways in which science can be used to produce useful products is called **technology**. *Technology* means applying scientific discoveries to make tools and machines that serve some useful purpose. As modern science has developed over the past 300 years, technology has also grown. This growing technology has helped to create the civilization in which we now live.

Technology The application of scientific knowledge to solve practical problems.

Without **engineers** there would be no technology. *Engineers* use scientific knowledge to produce useful products or to solve practical problems. A scientist tries to discover new knowledge whether it is practical or not. An engineer applies all kinds of scientific knowledge to meet the needs of people. See Fig. 3–21(a) and Fig. 3–21(b).

Engineer A person who uses technology to make new products or to solve problems.

Fig. 3–21 (a) This photo shows several examples of technology. Two astronauts on the space shuttle Challenger *left their ship to retrieve and repair the Solar Max satellite. They then returned the satellite to its proper orbit.*

Fig. 3–21 (b) This photo shows an astronaut in the cargo bay of the Challenger. *The satellite and the mechanical arm that was used to retrieve it are also visible.*

SUMMARY

The mechanical advantage of any machine relates its output force to the input force. Some of the work put into a machine is used to overcome friction. Two or more simple machines are often combined to make a more complicated machine. Our technological civilization is based on the use of machines.

QUESTIONS

Use complete sentences to write your answers.

1. What is meant by the mechanical advantage of a simple machine?
2. If you pull down with a force of two newtons on a pulley to raise a load of seven newtons, what is the mechanical advantage of the pulley?
3. Give an example of a machine made up of two or more simple machines.
4. What is meant by the efficiency of a machine?
5. What is technology? How does technology affect your life? Give some examples.

1. The amount by which a machine increases the effort force is called its mechanical advantage.
2. MA = resistance force ÷ effort force = 7 N / 2 N = 3.5.
3. A bicycle is an example of a complex machine. (Other examples are also acceptable.)
4. The efficiency of a machine is a comparison of the work input and work output.
5. Technology includes all the different ways that science is used to produce useful products. Most of the things you see around you are the result of technology. Automobiles, clocks, books, just to name a few, are the results of technology.

¡COMPUTE!

SCIENCE INPUT

We use machines to help us do work. The machine transfers energy from one place to another, multiplies force, multiplies speed, or changes direction of force. The six types of simple machines—the lever, the pulley, the wheel and axle, the inclined plane, the screw, and the wedge—are described and explained in your text. Most other machines are combinations of these six simple machines. The mechanical parts of robots are made of combinations of these simple machines or modifications of them. A great deal of engineering research and design goes into the making of a robot. However, robots need more than well-engineered parts to perform their work.

COMPUTER INPUT

Humans use the computer to help them do work as well, but the computer is a different kind of machine. Some people say it acts as if it were intelligent because the computer has the ability to remember and to recall information in a manner similar to the human brain. In robots, a computer, programmed with the correct data, acts to direct the mechanical parts of the machine which then performs the required task. The Technology Feature in this chapter discusses robots in greater detail.

WHAT TO DO

In this activity you will learn how the computer acts as an artificial intelligence. You will program the computer to recognize the special talent of the people in your class and to greet them!

Make your data chart on a separate sheet of paper or use the classroom chalkboard. In the first column, write an identifying number for each student. In the next column, write the first and last names of everyone in your class. In the third column, next to the appropriate name, list a two word description of the person. (The words should be chosen by each student for himself or herself. No two people may use the same description.) If the student is a female, include the letter "F" at the end of your description. If the student is male, include the letter "M" at the end of your description. Several examples are given below.

GLOSSARY

REM — short for remark; a command in BASIC, written for the user, not the computer. REM statements help the user understand the program, but they are not read by the computer

DATA — a command in BASIC that instructs the computer to store information for use in the program

READ — a command in BASIC that instructs the computer to read a value from a data statement and give that value to a variable in the program. You *must* have a read statement or the data will not be included in the working of the program

RECALL — to bring back stored data for use in a program

INTELLIGENT MACHINES: PROGRAM HELLO

PROGRAM

```
100  REM HELLO
110  DIM F$(39), L$(39), S$(39), I$(39)
120  FOR X = 1 to 25: PRINT: NEXT
130  FOR M = 1 to 39
140  PRINT TAB(15) "HELLO WHO:      "
     :PRINT:
150  PRINT M; "INPUT INFORMATION"
160  PRINT: INPUT "FIRST NAME ——→";
     F$(M)
170  INPUT "LAST NAME ——→"; L$(M)
180  INPUT "SEX (M or F) ——→" S$(M)
190  IF S$(M) < > "M" AND S$(M) < >
     "F" THEN GOTO 180
200  INPUT "FEATURE ——→"; I$(M)
210  IF LEN (I$(M)) > 35 THEN I$(M) =
     LEFT $ (I$(M), 35)
220  FOR X = 1 to M
230  PRINT X; "  "; I$(X)
240  NEXT
250  PRINT: PRINT "WHICH CHOICE?
     (1 - " ;M; ")";: INPUT "——→"
     C$: C = VAL(C$)
260  IF C < 1 OR C > M+1 THEN PRINT:
     GOTO 220
270  IF C = M + 1 THEN GOTO 340
280  A$ = "MISS"
290  IF S$(C) = "M" THEN H$ = "MR."
300  FOR X = 1 TO 17: PRINT NEXT
310  PRINT "HELLO"; H$; "  "; L$(C)
     PRINT: PRINT F$(C); "YOUR
     OUTSTANDING FEATURE IS ":
     PRINT I$(C): PRINT
320  PRINT: PRINT TAB (15) "MR.
     MICROCOMPUTER": PRINT
330  PRINT: INPUT "TYPE 'Y' TO
     CONTINUE"; Y$: IF Y$ = 'Y' GOTO
     350
335  GOTO 220
340  NEXT
350  END
```

Data Chart

N	Name	Descriptions
1	James Elliot	FAST RUNNERM
2	Arlene Furst	MATH WIZARDF
3	Joe Barker	GREAT SHOULDERSM
Etc.		

PROGRAM NOTES

Line 110 tells you how many spaces have been saved in the memory for data. Program Hello has been written so that it can contain information for up to 39 people. (In line 110, F stands for first name, L for last name, S for sex of student, and I for outstanding feature.) If there are more students in the class, change the numbers in lines 110 and 130.

BITS OF INFORMATION

A robot or "artificial intelligence" can only "recognize" data that it has been programmed to recognize.

Very often users are neither programmers nor engineers. Therefore, they are not aware of the amount of human work that must be done before a computerized machine can operate. This lack of awareness sometimes causes people to think of these "intelligent machines" in more human-like terms than they deserve. They cannot, however, know what no one has told them.

SKILL-BUILDING ACTIVITY

See teacher's commentary for teaching hints, safety, and answers to questions.

MACHINES

PURPOSE: You will compare the effect of simple machines on the force needed to move an object.

MATERIALS:

board, 50 cm × 15 cm
spring scale
laboratory cart
books
string
single pulley

PROCEDURE:

A. Copy the table below. Use it to record your measurements.

Object	Condition	Number of Books	Force (N)
cart	alone		
cart	pulley		

B. Use the spring scale to lift the cart. Record the scale reading.

1. What force, in newtons, is needed to lift the cart?

C. Use a pulley and spring scale as shown in Fig. 3–22 to lift the cart. Record the force needed to lift the cart.

2. What force, in newtons, is needed to lift the cart using a pulley?

D. Set up an incline as shown in Fig. 3–23. Without using the pulley, find the force needed to pull the cart up the incline at a slow but constant speed. Record.

E. Repeat step D. This time use a pulley as shown in Fig. 3–23. Record the force needed to pull the cart.

F. You may wish to make one or more of the above measurements again. Always record your observations.

CONCLUSIONS:

1. What effect does a pulley have on the force needed to move an object?
2. What is the effect of an incline on the force needed to move an object?
3. What is the effect of using a pulley and an incline together to move an object?
4. Compare your answers to questions 1 and 2 with your answer to question 3.

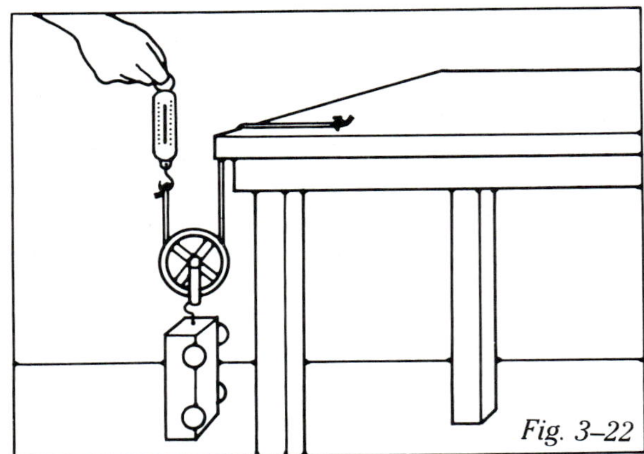

Fig. 3–22

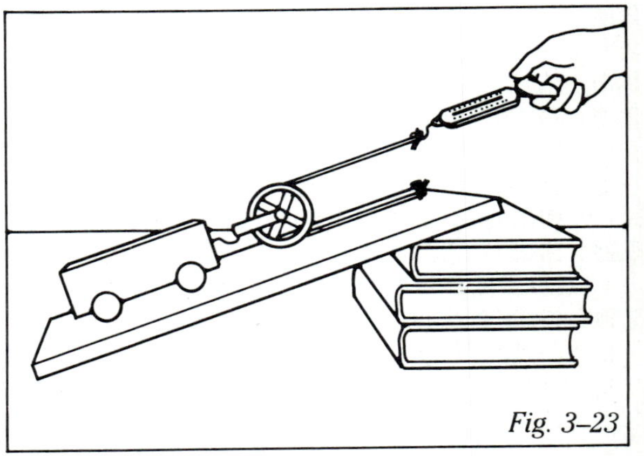

Fig. 3–23

TECHNOLOGY

THE ROBOTS ARE COMING

Thousands of robots are at work today helping to perform tasks that are particularly boring or difficult or dangerous for human beings. Robots perform repetitive tasks more reliably and with greater speed than humans, who often make mistakes if work requires that they repeat the same tasks over and over. Robots can also withstand heat and fumes that may be harmful to humans, thus freeing humans from having to work in dangerous environments. Robots are being built with three fingers to grasp objects the same way a human hand does; with two hands that can work together; and with six legs that can walk. They are used in a variety of industries, by marine geologists exploring the ocean bottom, and by medical researchers who need to put sterile hands into certain environments. A few companies have designed robots that not only do household tasks, but can serve dinner as well! And some robots are designed to be toys.

A popular image of robots is of machines that look and act something like humans. But a robot is more generally defined as any automatic device that performs tasks ordinarily done by human beings or that operates with what appears to be almost human intelligence. Industrial robots are most common. They assemble parts of larger machines, load or unload work pieces or tools, paint, and even inspect finished work. A special type of robot, a robotruck, is used in certain kinds of manufacturing systems to transport work pieces.

The main problem for developers of robots is the capability of the computers that are the brains of robots. A robot does not "think" as people do. It can only do work it is "programmed" to do; it can only recognize objects or information that is stored in its memory banks or circuits. Engineers are working to develop robots that can recognize objects in three dimensions; they want a robot to "see", to interpret what it sees, and to recognize that there is a problem that needs solving. Science fiction movies make us think that robots such as this already exist. But creating this type of robot is very difficult. In order for the robot to know what it sees, the object on the outside must be the same or similar to one described in its memory banks. And, because a robot must sift through millions of bits of information stored in its memory, it takes a robot two to three minutes to see and recognize a simple cube or sphere.

What is needed are computers that work thousands of times faster than those we are using today. Computer scientists and engineers working with robots (called roboticists) believe that with a new generation of computers, robots will be exploring planets, mining the sea floor, performing rescues in nuclear power plants, and perhaps even building other robots. Then, our problem may be the management of robots!

CHAPTER REVIEW

See teacher's commentary for answers.

VOCABULARY

On a separate piece of paper, match the number of the statement with the term that best completes it. Use each term only once.

simple machine	efficiency	engineer	technology
work	energy	power	mechanical advantage
watt			

1. Force multiplied by distance is ______.
2. The work done lifting a book gives the book more ______.
3. ______ is the rate of doing work.
4. The power when one joule of work is done in one second is called one _____.
5. The ______ of a lever is the ratio of the effort distance to the resistance distance.
6. A comparison of work output to work input is called the ______ of a machine.
7. ______ is the different ways that science can be used to solve practical problems in our daily lives.
8. An ______ applies scientific knowledge to produce useful products.
9. A device that can be used to change the direction or size of forces is called a ______.

QUESTIONS

Give brief but complete answers to each of the following questions. Unless otherwise indicated, use complete sentences to write your answers.

1. In addition to a force being applied, what else is necessary in order for work to be done? What is the formula used to find work?
2. No simple machine will give you more work than you put into it. If this is so, why are machines useful?
3. List eight simple machines and give an example of how each is used.
4. Draw a diagram of a lever. Label your diagram to show that work input equals work output.
5. The effort arm of a lever is 3.0 meters long. The resistance arm is 0.30 meter long. What is the effort force required to move a 4,469-newton load?
6. You put 4 joules of work into a machine. If 1.5 joules are used to overcome friction, what is the efficiency of the machine? Another machine uses 1.0 joule to overcome friction. Compare the efficiency of the two.
7. Define technology. How would your life be different without technology?

8. Are you doing work when you sit and read a book? Are you doing work when you walk to school? Explain your answers.
9. Find the amount of work done when a 446-newton person walks up a flight of stairs four meters high.
10. How much more energy will the person in question 9 have after walking up the stairs?
11. A pile of 1,000 bricks is moved by a forklift machine in 30 seconds. The machine does 15,000 newton-meters of work. A person moves the bricks at a rate of one brick each ten seconds. The person does the same amount of work. Compare the power of the forklift with the power of the person.
12. One horsepower equals 746 watts. How many horsepower do you use if you use 373 watts running up stairs?
13. An electric heater marked 1,250 watts is on for six hours. If electric energy costs ten cents per kilowatt hour, what did the energy used by the heater cost?
14. Use drawings to show the three kinds of levers. Label each drawing and give an example of each lever.
15. In a pulley system, the effort applied to pull the rope 2.0 meters raises a load 0.1 meter. What is the mechanical advantage of the system?

APPLYING SCIENCE

1. Describe three situations in which the forces acting are balanced and no work is being done. Describe all the forces acting in each case. Use diagrams.
2. List the electric devices in use in your home during a one-hour period in the evening. Check the power rating of each device. Find the total kilowatt-hours used and the cost. (Ask your parents what the kilowatt-hour cost is.)
3. Visit a local auto garage or service station that has a hydraulic lift. Find out how it works. Report your findings to the class. Include a labeled diagram.

BIBLIOGRAPHY

Adkins, J. *Moving Heavy Things*. Boston: Houghton Mifflin, 1980.

Gross, A.C. "The Aerodynamics of Human-Powered Land Vehicles." *Scientific American*, December 1983.

Kerrod, R. *The Way It Works: Man and His Machines*. New York: Mayflower, 1980.

Soloman, S. "Amazing Machines." *Science Digest*, November–December 1980.

CHAPTER

4

These windmills change the energy of the wind into electrical energy. We are all dependent on energy in our daily lives. Wind is just one possible source of energy that we may use in the future.

ENERGY

CHAPTER GOALS

1. Explain what is meant by energy and state the law of conservation of energy.
2. Compare potential and kinetic energy.
3. List the six forms of energy and explain how energy can change form.
4. Give three examples of renewable and nonrenewable energy sources.

4-1. Energy Causes Motion

At the end of this section you will be able to:

- ☐ Identify the property of matter that enables it to do work.
- ☐ Explain how potential energy is different from kinetic energy.
- ☐ Describe an experiment to show that energy is neither created nor destroyed.

People have often dreamed of making a perpetual motion machine. The word "perpetual" means "continuing forever." Such a machine could run forever. A so-called perpetual motion machine is shown in Fig. 4–1. This machine is a wheel with curved sections. Each section holds a metal ball. The balls on the right roll to the outside. Their weight tends to pull the wheel around. As the wheel turns, the balls roll toward the center. Thus they can roll outward again and keep the wheel turning. Once started, the machine is supposed to keep turning by itself. Can this, or any other, perpetual motion machine work?

WHAT IS ENERGY?

The secret of perpetual motion machines can be found in the scientific laws that describe **energy**. *Energy* is the capacity to do work. The concept of energy is the basis of almost all scientific laws and theories. The common definition of energy says that an object has energy if it can do work. As you know, work is done only when an object moves through a distance

Energy The capacity to do work.

Fig. 4–1 The machine on the left is an example of a perpetual motion machine. The diagram on the right shows how the wheel is supposed to keep turning.

($W = F \times d$). Thus the definition of energy really says that energy causes motion.

Scientists who study energy observe the changes it causes. Almost all the changes you see in the world are the result of energy. Energy can cause an object to move. For example, the breeze you feel is caused by energy from the sun warming the air. Solar energy can change into wind energy. The wind energy can then cause motion by pushing against the sails of a sailboat. See Fig. 4–2.

Fig. 4–2 These billowing sails capture the wind's energy and push the boats forward.

POTENTIAL AND KINETIC ENERGY

Try this experiment: Stand with your feet firmly on the floor. Hold your book in both hands. With your eyes closed, slowly raise and lower the book several times. You feel a force pulling the book down. This force is the weight of the book caused by gravity. Now think of a spring holding the book to the floor. See Fig. 4–3. If you try hard, you will be able to see the spring stretch as you raise the book. Now think about the energy added to the spring as it stretches.

Fig. 4–3 The stretched spring represents the energy stored in the book as it is held above the floor. The energy is released when the book is dropped.

A stretched spring has energy stored in it. We know it is there because the spring can apply a force over a distance as it returns to its normal shape. That is, it can do work. See Fig. 4–4. Energy stored in an object as a result of any change in its position is called **potential energy**. A spring gains *potential energy* when it is stretched. If you lift a book against the force of gravity, you are adding energy in much the same way. The energy you use to raise the book is stored in the book as potential energy. The amount of potential energy stored in the book is equal to the amount of work done to lift it. The work

Word study: Potential from *potens* (L.), powerful.

Potential energy Energy stored in an object as a result of a change in its position.

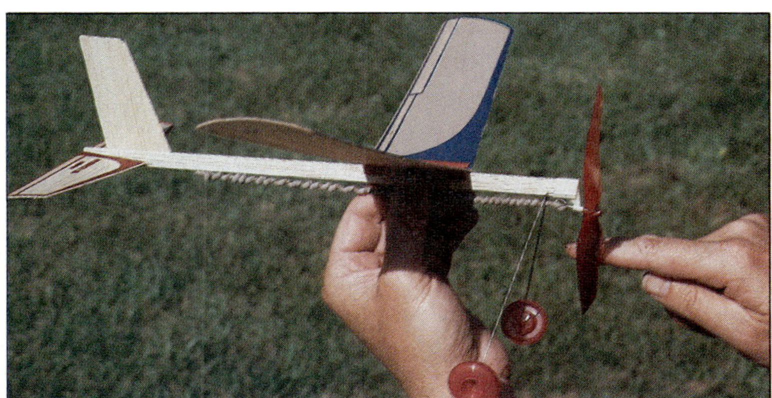

Fig. 4–4 Just as a stretched spring can do work, this wound-up rubber band will turn the plane's propeller when it is released.

Skill: Write several sample problems on the board to find gravitational potential energy and kinetic energy.

done is equal to the weight of the book times the height to which it is lifted. Thus the amount of gravitational potential energy (PE) in an object depends on its weight (mass × gravitational force) and the distance (h) it is lifted: PE $= mgh$.

When relaxed, a stretched spring gives up the potential energy stored in it. A book on a shelf gives up its potential energy if it falls. The potential energy stored in the book changes into energy of motion as it falls. Energy that an object has as a result of its motion is called **kinetic energy**. Any moving object has *kinetic energy*. See Fig. 4–5.

Kinetic energy Energy that moving things have as a result of their motion.

Word study: Kinetic from *kinetikos* (Gr.), putting in motion.

Fig. 4–5 A diver has a certain amount of potential energy that depends on his or her weight and the height of the board. When the diver hits the water, the energy will be changed into kinetic energy.

How can the amount of kinetic energy of a moving object be measured? Think about the kinetic energy of the falling book. Its kinetic energy determines how hard it will hit the floor. A heavy book will hit harder than a light book. Also, the farther the book falls and the faster it is moving, the harder it will hit. Thus the amount of kinetic energy (KE) a moving object has depends on its mass (m) and speed (v). This is shown as follows: KE $= \frac{1}{2} mv^2$.

Notice that the increase in kinetic energy depends on the square of the speed (v^2). For example, doubling the speed of a car from 40 km/h to 80 km/h more than doubles its kinetic energy. The amount of kinetic energy increases by four times. This means that at 80 km/h the distance needed to stop the car by putting on the brakes will also be about four times greater than at 40 km/h. See Fig. 4–6.

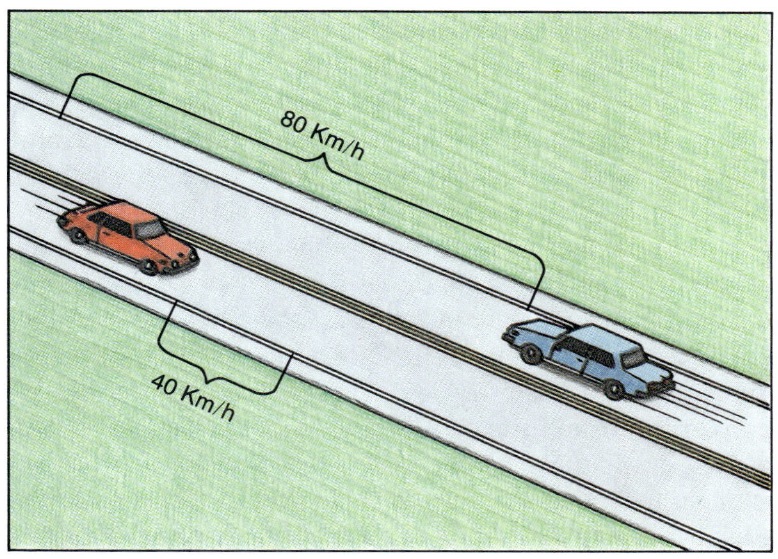

Fig. 4–6 If the speed of the car is doubled, the distance needed to stop the car increases by about four times.

CAN ENERGY DISAPPEAR?

Have you ever ridden a roller coaster? First, the car is pulled to the highest part of the track. At the top of the track, the car has potential energy. See Fig. 4–7. As you roll down the first steep slope, some of the potential energy changes into kinetic energy. At the bottom, all of the potential energy has changed into kinetic energy.

As the car climbs to the top of the next hill, the kinetic energy changes back into potential energy. This process is

Fig. 4–7 On a roller coaster, potential energy is constantly changing into kinetic energy.

Suggestion: A weight oscillating on a spring is a good demonstration of conservation of energy. Exchanges of spring potential energy, gravitational potential energy, and kinetic energy are easily seen with very little energy loss.

repeated over and over. Potential energy changes to kinetic and back again on each hill. After the first hill, the car moves without outside help. Each time it coasts down a hill it gains enough kinetic energy to climb the next one. However, some energy is lost in overcoming friction. For this reason, each hill in the ride is a little less high than the one before it.

When scientists measure energy changes in a system such as a roller coaster, they find that when energy disappears in one form, an equal amount appears in another form. In other words, energy is neither created nor destroyed. It only changes form. This is a basic law of nature. It is called the **law of conservation of energy.** The law says, for example, that all of the gravitational potential energy stored in an object changes to kinetic energy as the object falls. A book on a high shelf has a certain amount of potential energy. The book has this energy as a result of its height above the floor. If the book falls from the shelf, the potential energy changes into kinetic energy. The *law of conservation of energy* says that as the book's potential energy decreases, its kinetic energy increases. When the book hits the floor, all of the potential energy it had on the shelf is lost. It is changed into kinetic energy. Some energy is used to overcome air resistance.

Law of conservation of energy A scientific law that says energy cannot be created or destroyed but may be changed from one form to another.

Word study: Conservation from *com* (L.), together, and *servare* (L.), to keep.

Can you use the law of conservation of energy to decide whether a perpetual motion machine will work? Remember that all machines use some energy to overcome friction.

SUMMARY

Energy can do work as it changes form. Gravitational potential energy changes to kinetic energy as an object falls from a height. Energy is always conserved as it changes form.

QUESTIONS

Use complete sentences to write your answers.

1. In your own words, explain what is meant by energy.
2. How are potential energy and kinetic energy related?
3. Describe the changes in energy that occur during a roller coaster ride.
4. Describe the changes in energy that occur in a swinging pendulum.

1. Answers will vary. Energy is usually defined in terms of what it does rather than what it is.
2. Stored energy is called potential energy; energy of motion is called kinetic energy. Potential energy changes into kinetic energy as an object falls from a height.
3. Answers may vary. As the car moves to the top of the roller coaster track it gains potential energy which changes to kinetic energy as it rolls down the hill. The energy is supplied by an electric or gas motor. The energy changes to heat when the car stops.
4. When a pendulum is at the end of its swing the energy is stored as potential energy. As the bob swings down, some potential energy changes to kinetic energy. In time air friction will cause the pendulum to stop.

SKILL-BUILDING ACTIVITY

See teacher's commentary for teaching hints, safety, and answers to questions.

POTENTIAL AND KINETIC ENERGY

PURPOSE: You will compare the potential and kinetic energy of a laboratory cart on an incline.

MATERIALS:

laboratory cart
board, 50 × 15 cm
stop watch
metric ruler
books
chalk
spring scale

PROCEDURE:

A. Set up an incline as shown in Fig. 4–8.

B. Measure the mass of the cart in kilograms. Also measure the height of the incline in meters.

C. Copy the table below and use it to record your data.

D. Calculate the potential energy the cart has at the top of the incline. The energy will be in joules (newton meters).

E. Place the cart at the bottom of the incline. The back wheels should be just off the incline. Measure a distance of 0.3 m from the front of the cart. Put a chalk mark at this point on the table top.

F. Place the cart at the top of the incline and release it. Measure the time that it takes the cart to move from the bottom of the incline to the chalk mark.

G. Find the speed of the cart at the bottom of the incline ($v = d \div t$).

H. Calculate the kinetic energy as the cart leaves the incline.

1. How much kinetic energy did the cart have at the bottom of the incline?
2. About how much potential energy did the cart lose when it rolled down the incline?
3. Why would you expect the kinetic energy to be slightly less than the potential energy?

CONCLUSION:

1. In your own words, explain how potential energy can change to kinetic energy. Show the equations and the units used.

Mass (kg)	Height (m)	Speed (m/s)	Gravitational Force	Potential Energy	Kinetic Energy
			9.8		

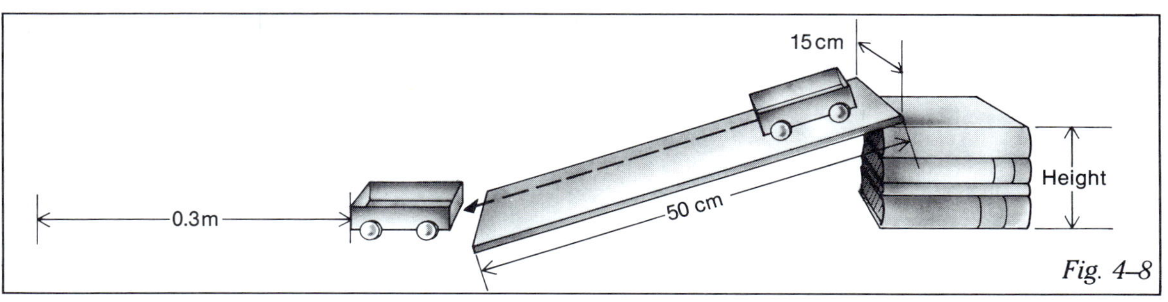

Fig. 4–8

4-2. Forms of Energy

At the end of this section you will be able to:

- Give several examples to show that energy exists in different forms.
- Describe six forms of energy.
- Classify sources of energy as either renewable or non-renewable.

At some time in the future, a huge solar energy collector might be in orbit around the earth. See Fig. 4–9. The satellite will stay above the same point on the earth. Energy from the sun will fall on the satellite. This energy will be changed into radio waves. These waves are similar to the waves used to cook food in microwave ovens. Stations on earth will pick up the radio waves and change them into electric power. We will be able to collect solar energy in space to produce electricity on earth. We will be able to do this because energy can change from one form to another.

Fig. 4–9 This is an artist's idea of what a solar energy collector in orbit around the earth might look like.

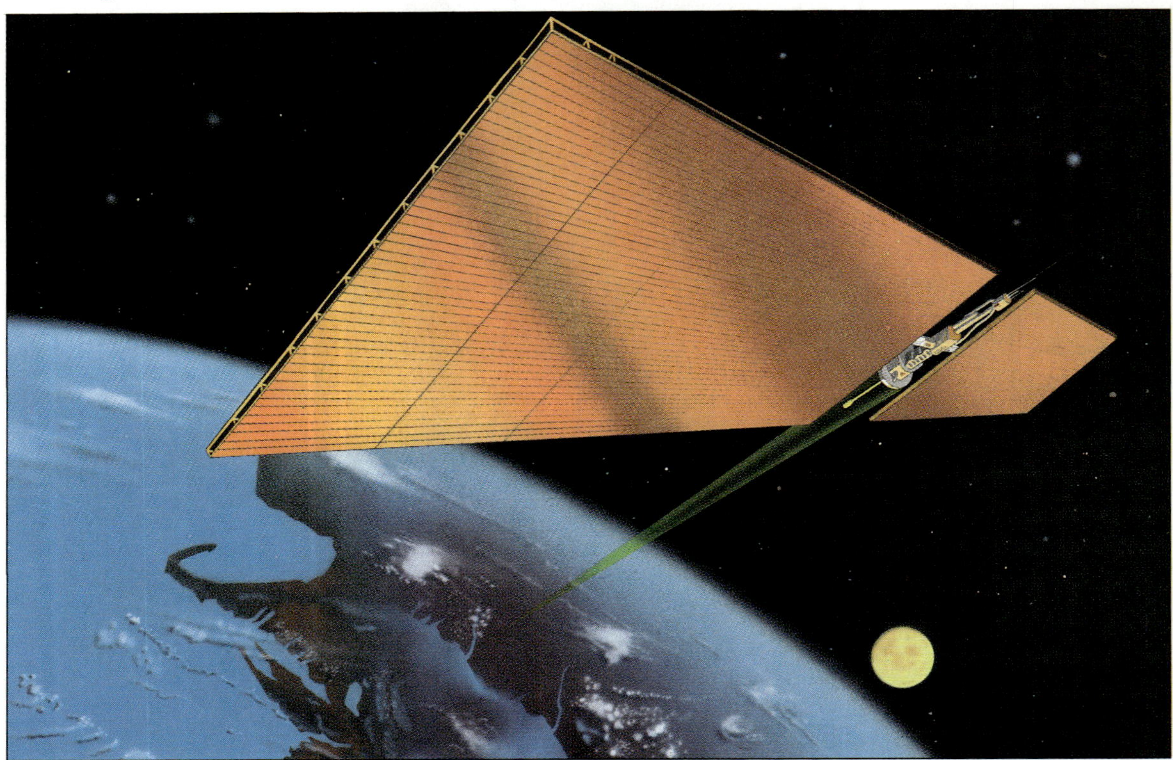

Fig. 4–10 This drawing illustrates some of the ways in which energy can be changed from one form to another. For example, an electric iron changes electric energy into heat energy and a hot-air balloon changes heat energy into mechanical energy. Try to think of other examples in which you have observed energy change form.

TYPES OF ENERGY

Look around you. You can see the many ways by which energy changes form. As rivers flow to the sea, the kinetic energy of falling water can be used to make electricity. Wind energy can turn windmills. Windmills also produce electricity. What forms of energy can describe all these changes? Scientists have found that there are at least six forms of energy. These six forms account for all the changes in energy we see around us. See Fig. 4–10. The six forms of energy are described below. You will study more about them in later chapters.

1. Mechanical energy. This energy is due to the position or motion of an object. It includes all forms of kinetic energy. An example of mechanical energy is the motion of the moving parts of a car engine. The energy of a hammer hitting a nail is also mechanical.

2. Electric energy. Comb your hair. Now quickly hold the comb close to small pieces of paper. Often the pieces of paper will jump towards the comb. They may briefly cling to it. The energy to move the paper came from electricity built up in the comb. Electric energy often builds up when two materials such as your hair and a comb are rubbed together. See Fig. 4–11. Electric energy can be carried through many materials including, for example, copper wires. Magnets attract many metal objects just as a comb can attract paper. Magnetic energy can also produce forces. Experiments show that magnetic energy and electric energy are closely related.

Fig. 4–11 Lightning is an example of electric energy.

3. Chemical energy. When a piece of paper burns, energy is given off. The paper is also changed into another material, the ashes. When one kind of matter is changed into another kind of matter, the source of the energy given off is chemical energy.

4. Nuclear energy. Matter can also be changed in a different way to produce energy. Changes in the cores, or *nuclei*, of atoms release nuclear energy. The nucleus of some kinds of atoms can be split into two or more parts. This is the most common way in which we release nuclear energy. When the nucleus is split, some matter disappears. This matter is changed into energy. Nuclear energy is the most concentrated form of energy.

Fig. 4–12 Laser light is a form of radiant energy. This concentrated energy can be used to cut metal.

5. Radiant energy. A laser can cut through metal. See Fig. 4–12. This laser beam shows the energy that can be carried by light. Energy that passes through space in the form of waves such as light is called radiant energy or *electromagnetic* energy. This type of energy includes radio waves and X-rays as well as visible light. Laser light is also a form of electromagnetic energy.

6. Heat energy. When your hands are cold you can warm them by holding them against something hot. Heat is the form of energy that causes temperature changes in any form of matter. Heat energy always flows from a hot object to a colder object.

Enrichment: Each field of science deals with a great number of specific forms of energy. Each of these forms can be grouped under one of the forms given here. For example, heat of vaporization, heat of fusion, and heat of solution are a few forms of heat energy that chemists deal with.

Fig. 4–13 How many kinds of energy can you find in these pictures? Is the energy changing form?

USES OF ENERGY

How many forms of energy do you use every day? Even a brief answer to this question quickly shows that our lives are built around energy. See Fig. 4–13. For example, you need the chemical energy supplied by food. You would find it hard to live without heat energy to warm your house and to cook your food. Large amounts of energy run machines to make consumer products. A great deal of energy is used for transportation. The average person uses about eight times as much energy as could be produced by muscle power alone. In a developed country such as the United States, each person uses ten times more energy than the average person in most other parts of the world. See Fig. 4–14.

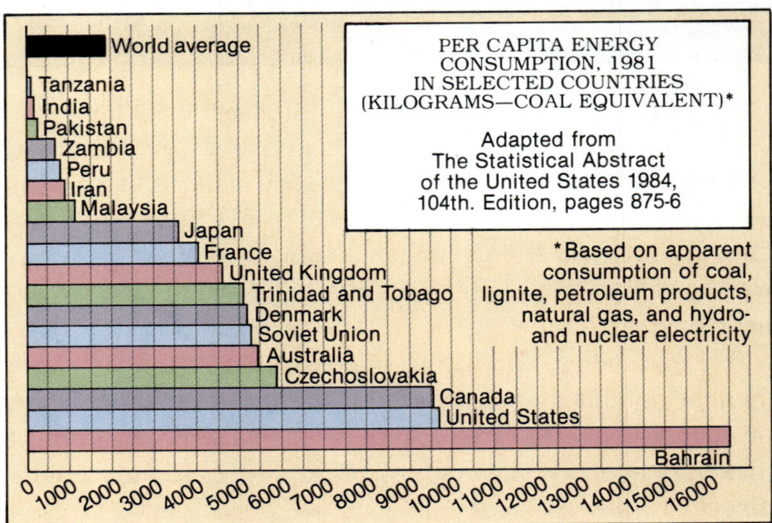

Fig. 4–14 This graph shows the amount of energy used by each person in different countries in the world in one year.

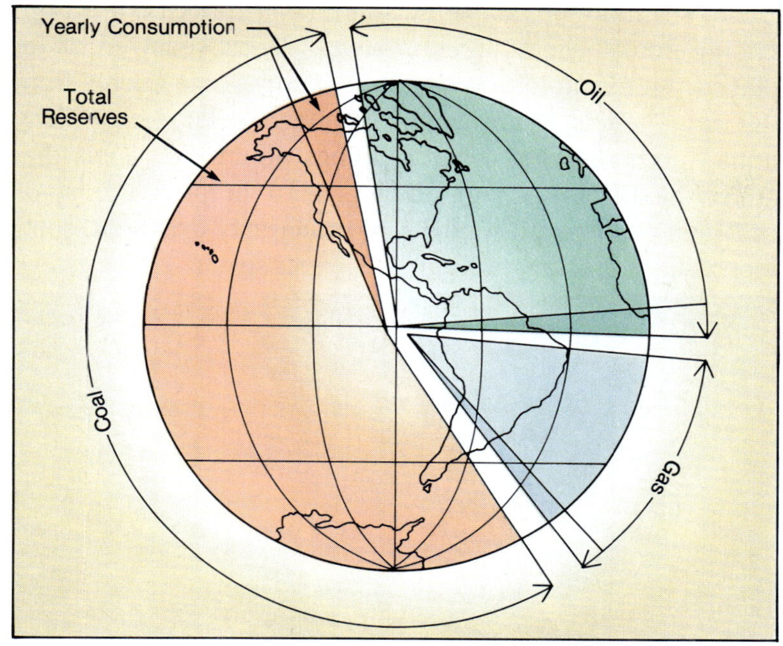

Fig. 4–15 This diagram shows the remaining amounts of coal, oil, and gas reserves in the world.

Most of these energy needs are now met by burning fuels. These fuels include petroleum, coal, and natural gas. The supply of these fuels is limited and will be gone some day. See Fig. 4–15. In the future, people will learn to meet growing energy needs by using other sources. Some of these future sources are water power, nuclear energy, wind, and heat from inside the earth. All together these sources now supply only a small amount of the world's energy needs.

FUTURE SOURCES OF ENERGY

Suggestion: Energy awareness should lead to a discussion of energy conservation.

Supplies of energy come from two sources. First, there are the sources that cannot be renewed or replaced. Petroleum, coal, and natural gas are examples of *nonrenewable* energy sources. These fuels were formed millions of years ago in the earth's crust. They are examples of *fossil fuels*. Fossil fuels are the remains of long-dead plants and animals. Once they are used up, there is no way to make new supplies of these fuels. No one knows exactly how much petroleum and natural gas remain in the earth. But the total reserves now known to exist will probably be used up in about 50 years. Petroleum is becoming more expensive as the world's supply runs out. There seems to be enough coal to last a few hundred years.

The second kind of energy source can never be used up. Energy from these sources is always being renewed or replaced. An example of *renewable* energy is the energy from the sun. There is no limit to the amount of solar energy. Many homes, schools, and other buildings now have panels that collect heat from the sun. See Fig. 4–16. In the future, *solar cells* that can change sunlight into electricity may be in common use. At present, they are very expensive.

Fig. 4–16 Since this home can be partially heated by solar energy, the amount of other fuels, such as gas or oil, that must be used can be reduced.

Fig. 4–17 This ship uses computer-controlled sails in addition to its engines.

Wind can also provide a renewable source of energy. At one time, sailing ships driven only by wind power were common. Modern ships are powered mainly by fossil fuels. However, these expensive fuels can be conserved by building ships with sails to help the engines. See Fig. 4–17.

Heat stored deep within the earth is also a renewable energy source. It may help meet our future energy needs. Deep wells drilled in certain parts of the earth can bring hot water and steam to the surface. Generators can then use that energy to produce electricity. See Fig. 4–18.

Fig. 4–18 The energy released from inside the earth in the form of steam and hot water can be used to make electricity.

Ocean tides may also be used as an energy source. Large dams can be built across the mouths of some bays. Water is carried into the bay by the rising and falling tides. This tidal energy can then turn electric generators.

Nuclear energy can almost be thought of as a renewable source of energy. Nuclear power plants need a supply of uranium fuel, which is used up in the process of producing nuclear energy. Only a limited amount of uranium exists on earth. However, these plants produce a large amount of energy from a small amount of uranium. See Fig. 4–19. Thus it is not likely that the supply of uranium will be used up soon. There is another problem, however. Nuclear power plants produce radioactive wastes. A safe way to dispose of these dangerous wastes is needed.

Fig. 4–19 The small amounts of uranium in these fuel rods produce a great deal of energy. However, many people feel that nuclear energy is too dangerous to use.

At some time in the future, our energy needs must be met by renewable energy sources. However, fossil fuels will supply most of the energy we need for many years. As the fossil fuels become more scarce and expensive, renewable sources will slowly replace them.

SUMMARY

Energy exists in six different forms. Each form can change into other forms. Nonrenewable energy sources are being used up. Most future energy needs will be met by renewable energy sources.

QUESTIONS

Use complete sentences to write your answers.

1. Describe three ways in which energy is changed from one form to another.
2. List six forms of energy. Give an example of each.
3. Name three sources of energy that are nonrenewable.
4. Name four possible sources of energy for the future.

1. Examples of energy changes include solar energy changes to electric energy, wind energy changes to mechanical energy, water in rivers changes potential energy to kinetic energy and then to electric energy.
2. Answers will vary. See pages 92 and 93.
3. Petroleum, coal, and natural gas are nonrenewable energy sources.
4. Nuclear energy, solar energy, wind energy, tides, and heat from within the earth may be sources of energy for the future.

CAREERS IN SCIENCE

PHYSICS TEACHER

Physics teachers working in secondary schools, colleges, and universities conduct classroom lectures, assist students with research projects, supervise laboratory sessions, and advise students on their goals and progress. They may also conduct research projects in their areas of specialization, supervise assistants, and perform administrative duties. Many teaching physicists write textbooks or reference works, report on current research for professional journals, and act as consultants to industries such as electrical or scientific instruments manufacturers or the aerospace industry.

At the secondary school level jobs may be obtainable with a bachelor's degree alone, providing state certification requirements for teachers are met. A Ph.D. is generally required to teach in a college or university.

For further information, contact: American Association of Physics Teachers, Graduate Physics Building, SUNY, Stony Brook, NY 11794.

CONSUMER ENERGY ANALYST

Consumer energy analysts help people find ways to make the most efficient use of limited energy resources. Homeowners come to them to learn how to cut fuel bills in the winter. Architects and designers consult them for advice on the best materials for insulating new buildings. Furniture manufacturers ask for their suggestions on how to conserve wood in the manufacturing process.

Good preparation for this field is a background in construction or engineering, but many employers readily hire teachers or scientists for this job. Training in public speaking and familiarity with computers is also very helpful.

The demand for energy analysts is growing. Most analysts work for public utilities, but industry and government have begun to make increasing use of their services.

For further information, contact: Con Edison, Consumer Education Division, 4 Irving Place, New York, NY 10003.

CHAPTER REVIEW

See teacher's commentary for answers.

VOCABULARY

On a separate piece of paper, match each term with the number of the statement that best explains it. Use each term only once.

chemical	heat	nuclear	fossil fuels
electric	kinetic	potential	mechanical
radiant	conservation of energy	renewable	energy

1. Energy an object has because of its position.
2. Energy an object in motion has.
3. The law that states that energy is never created or destroyed.
4. Energy due to position or motion of an object.
5. Energy that causes bits of paper to stick to a comb after you have used it to comb your hair.
6. The source of energy when one kind of matter changes to another kind.
7. The energy that comes from within atoms.
8. Laser light and X-rays are examples of this form of energy.
9. Energy that always flows from a hot object to a colder object.
10. Petroleum, coal, and natural gas are examples of this form of energy.
11. Sources of energy that are never used up or that replace themselves.
12. The capacity to do work.

QUESTIONS

Give brief but complete answers to each of the following questions. Unless otherwise indicated, use complete sentences to write your answers.

1. Discuss the changes in energy when a batter hits a baseball to center field.
2. Describe in detail all energy changes that occur when you pick up a baseball in center field and throw it to home plate.
3. How might solar energy received by a satellite be sent to earth?
4. Name three forms of radiant energy. How are they used?
5. Give two examples in which one form of energy is changed to another form of energy.
6. What two things determine the amount of gravitational potential energy an object has? Give an example.
7. What is the source of energy when iron changes into rust?
8. What is the source of nuclear energy? How do we use nuclear energy? Is it renewable or nonrenewable?

9. What kind of energy is closely related to magnetic energy?
10. In your own words, state the law of conservation of energy.
11. What form of energy causes changes in temperature?
12. Name at least five forms of energy and describe how you use them.
13. Draw a sketch of a simple roller coaster. Label at least two places on the track where the kinetic energy is high and two places where the gravitational potential energy is high.
14. Using key words from the chapter, write a paragraph summarizing the two sections of this chapter.
15. How could you show someone how one form of energy can be changed into another form? Describe the equipment you would need.

APPLYING SCIENCE

1. Does your family use more electric energy during the day or at night? If possible, read the electric meter in your house when you first get up in the morning and again at sunset. Keep a record of the readings for a week. Suggest ways your family can decrease the use of electric energy. Compare your results with those of other students.
2. Write a report on some historical examples of perpetual motion machines. Describe each proposed machine. Why would the machines eventually stop? Would they work in outer space or on another planet?
3. Show that light energy can be changed to heat energy. Use a light source, two cans, and two thermometers. Remove the labels from both cans. Spray one can black. Use plastic tops for insulation. Explain any temperature changes.

BIBLIOGRAPHY

Congdon, R.J., ed. *Introduction to Appropriate Technology: Toward a Simpler Life-Style*. Emmaus, PA: Rodale, 1977.

Davis, G. *Your Career in Energy-Related Occupations*. New York: Arco, 1980.

Drake, S. "Galileo and the Rolling Ball; Excerpt from Galileo at Work." *Science Digest*, October 1978.

Naar, John. *The New Wind Power*. New York: Penguin, 1982.

Park, Jack. *The Wind Power Book*. Palo Alto, CA: Cheshire Book, 1981.

Satchwell, J. *Energy At Work*. New York: Lothrop, 1981.

CHAPTER

5

This photograph is a thermogram. The different colors represent different temperatures. The reds and yellows are the hottest areas. The blues and greens are the coolest areas.

HEAT

CHAPTER GOALS

1. Explain why heat is considered a form of energy and how heat affects the particles that make up matter.
2. Compare the three methods of heat transfer.
3. Give an example that shows how temperature is different from heat.
4. Compare the Fahrenheit and Celsius temperature scales.

5-1. Heat Energy

At the end of this section you will be able to:

- ☐ Explain why heat is a form of energy.
- ☐ Predict what will happen to particles of matter when heat energy is added.
- ☐ Describe how heat energy can be changed into mechanical energy.

Imagine primitive humans sitting around a fire in their cave. They must have wondered why fire is hot. Where does the heat come from? This question puzzled scientists for hundreds of years. Their search for an answer led them to some important discoveries.

WHAT IS HEAT?

About two hundred years ago heat was described in this way: "Heat is an invisible and weightless fluid. It soaks into an object when the object is heated. Cooling is caused by the heat fluid draining away." The heat fluid was called *caloric*. According to this theory of heat, ice changes into water as more caloric is added. Adding still more caloric causes the water to change into steam. If you burned your hands by sliding too quickly down a rope, the burns were caused by caloric squeezed out of the rope.

The caloric theory did explain some observations about heat. For example, heat seems to move from a hot object to a cold object. Heat leaves a warm house in cold weather. It must be replaced constantly. This observation seems to support the

Enrichment: The caloric theory of heat is surprisingly difficult to disprove since the caloric fluid is defined as invisible and weightless. Challenge students to suggest an experiment (other than Rumford's) that would disprove the caloric theory.

idea that heat "flows" from place to place. However, the caloric theory could not pass the most important test of a scientific theory: The caloric theory did not stand up under experiment. Experiments showed that heat could not be any kind of substance such as caloric fluid.

One such experiment was done in 1798 by Benjamin Thompson. Thompson was an American who became a government official in England. There he was called Count Rumford. At one time, he was in charge of a cannon factory. In those days, cannons were made by drilling machines run by horses. See Fig. 5–1. Rumford noticed that the cannons became very hot during the drilling. He wondered why this happened. To find out, he set up the following experiment: A cannon was drilled in a box full of water. After several hours of drilling, the water began to boil. It continued to boil as long as the drilling went on. The experiment showed that the supply of heat was unlimited. Thus it could not be the result of caloric stored in the metal of the cannon. Rumford decided that heat was a form of energy added to the cannon by the work of the horses. Rumford's experiment, and others that were done later, finally proved that work can be changed into heat in many different ways. If other kinds of energy can change into heat, then heat itself must be a form of energy.

Fig. 5–1 At the time Rumford did his experiment, it was thought that heat was a fluid. This fluid, called caloric, was thought to be present in the metal of the cannon. Rumford's experiment proved that heat is really a form of energy.

HEAT IS MOTION

If heat is energy, how is this energy contained in a hot object? Scientists think of all matter as being made up of small particles called *molecules*. Molecules are too small to be seen. They are in constant motion. When heat energy is added to an object, these small particles vibrate faster. For example, a drop of water contains a huge number of individual water molecules. All of these molecules are vibrating. When the water is heated, the molecules vibrate faster. Thus they bump into each other more often. See Fig. 5–2. You cannot watch one water molecule to see if heating or cooling changes its speed. Only the results of the motion of a large number of water molecules can be seen. You may have noticed that food coloring put into water slowly spreads through the water. Put a drop of ink or food coloring into a glass of water. Do not stir the water. In time, you will see the motion of the molecules of water and the dye. The color will spread evenly throughout the water in the glass.

Fig. 5–2 When the water in this pan is heated, the water molecules begin to vibrate faster. They bump into each other more often and the water begins to boil.

Fig. 5–3 The expansion joint on a bridge, as shown here, allows for the expansion and contraction of the metal as it is heated and cooled.

Let's look at another example. A bar of iron looks as if none of its parts are moving. However, the particles of iron are in constant motion. When the iron is heated, its particles move faster. The piece of solid iron expands because the heated particles of iron are speeded up. This causes them to move farther apart. When the iron cools, the particles slow down. The piece of iron will shrink. See Fig. 5–3. If you have ever seen railroad tracks, you have seen a space where the pieces of track come together. This space between the ends of the

Reinforcement: Some students will know that you can loosen a tight jar lid by running it under hot water. Relate this to the expansion of a metal when heated. Ask for other examples of expansion.

Enrichment: Some students may bring up the unusual case of water, which expands when it freezes. Point out that the general rule that materials expand when heated applies only if there is no change of state.

rails allows them to expand and shrink as they are heated and cooled. Similar spaces can be seen on many bridges and highways. All kinds of matter expand when heated because their particles move faster.

HEAT AND WORK

Because heat is a form of energy, it can do work. Machines can change heat energy into useful mechanical energy. For example, a steam engine uses the heat energy contained in the moving water particles that make up the hot steam. The earliest steam engines used steam to push against a metal plate called a *piston*. The piston moved up and down inside a tube called a *cylinder*. As the engine worked, steam from a boiler pushed the piston to the top of the cylinder. Cool water was then sprayed into the cylinder. The cooled steam in the cylinder changed back into water. The piston returned to the bottom of the cylinder and the process was repeated. This kind of engine used only a small part of the heat energy in the steam. Most of the energy was wasted.

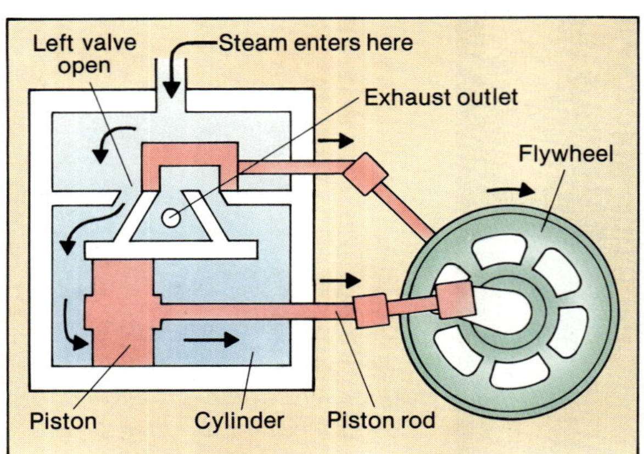

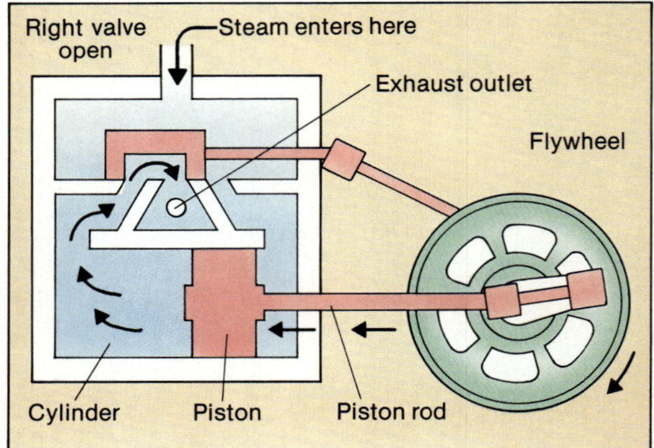

Fig. 5–4 In Watt's sliding-valve steam engine, the piston moved both ways in the cylinder. This improvement increased the efficiency of the machine.

In the late 1700's, James Watt, an instrument maker in Scotland, invented an improved steam engine. Watt's engine used the steam to push the piston both ways in the cylinder. See Fig. 5–4. Watt's steam engine was far more powerful than the early wasteful models. It made possible the use of steam power for locomotives and factories. The Industrial Revolution of the 19th century was powered by the heat energy of steam.

Modern steam engines do not use the back-and-forth motion of a piston in a cylinder. Instead, the steam pushes against the blades of a *turbine*. A turbine turns like a high-speed windmill. See Fig. 5–5. Turbines work smoothly and do not waste much of the energy in the steam.

Automobile engines also use heat energy. A burning fuel produces hot gases inside the cylinders. The hot gases push pistons. Jet engines also use hot gases produced by burning fuels. However, in a jet engine the hot gases run a turbine. The turbine forces hot air at high speed out the back of the engine. The engine then works in the same way as a rocket. The hot gases leaving the rear of the engine push the engine ahead, demonstrating Newton's third law of motion: For every force there is an equal and opposite force.

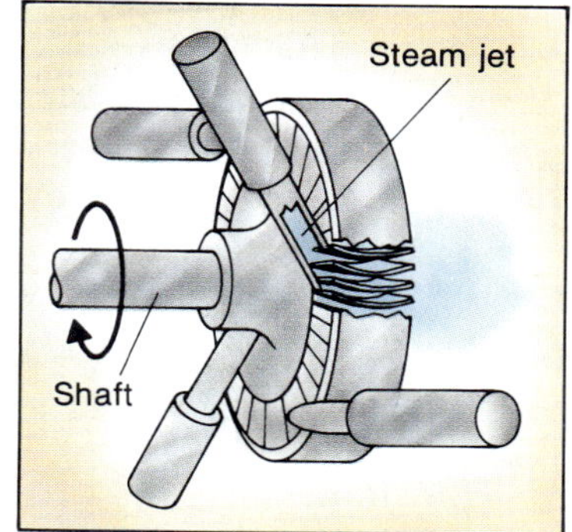

Fig. 5–5 The wheel of a turbine turns when steam pushes against the blades.

All engines that work by burning some kind of fuel are examples of **heat engines**. A *heat engine* is a machine that changes heat energy into mechanical energy. However, there is a problem in using all heat engines. Much of the heat energy is wasted. There is no way to use all of the energy in the moving particles of hot gases. A typical car engine, for example, is only 30 percent efficient. No one can make a heat engine that will change *all* of the heat energy supplied to it into mechanical energy. In other words, no engine is 100 percent efficient.

Heat engine A machine that changes heat energy into mechanical energy.

SUMMARY

Experiments show that heat is a form of energy. When a substance is heated, energy is added to its particles. This causes the particles to move faster. Heat engines are machines that change some of the energy of moving particles into motion.

QUESTIONS

Use complete sentences to write your answers.

1. Why is heat considered a form of energy?
2. Describe what happens to the atoms of a metal pan as the pan is heated and then cooled.
3. Describe how heat energy can be changed into mechanical energy.
4. What did Count Rumford's experiment show about heat?
5. Name three types of heat engines. How does each one use heat energy?

1. Experiments show that work and other forms of energy can be changed into heat. Therefore, heat must also be a form of energy.
2. As heat is added to the pan, the metal atoms move faster. When the pan cools, the atoms move more slowly.
3. Heat energy can be changed into mechanical energy by steam engines and steam turbines, for example.
4. Count Rumford's cannon drilling experiment showed that heat is a form of energy since heat was produced as long as work was being done.
5. The steam engine uses steam to push on the piston of the engine. The steam turbine uses steam to turn the turbine like a windmill. An automobile engine uses the hot gases from burning fuel to push pistons.

SKILL-BUILDING ACTIVITY

See teacher's commentary for teaching hints, safety, and answers to questions.

MOTION OF PARTICLES

PURPOSE: You will observe evidence that particles of water are moving. You will also find the effect of heat on that motion.

MATERIALS:

3 small beakers
dark food coloring
2 medicine droppers
ice cube
hot water

Fig. 5–6

PROCEDURE:

A. Fill a small beaker about two-thirds full of water at or near room temperature.

B. Place one drop of dark food coloring on the surface of the water. See Fig. 5–6. Do not stir. Observe the coloring and water from the top and sides of the beaker for two to three minutes.

1. Describe, in your own words, the changes you observed after you added the food coloring to the water.
2. Write a hypothesis that tells what effect you think hot or cold water would have on the rate at which the coloring mixes with the water.

C. Fill a second beaker about two-thirds full of water. Add an ice cube to the water. Leave it in the water for two to three minutes. Then remove the ice cube.

D. While the water is cooling, fill a third beaker two-thirds full of hot water.

E. Place the two beakers side by side.

3. In which beaker (hot or cold) are the water particles moving faster?

F. Wait a minute for the water currents to stop. Then add one drop of dark food coloring to each beaker at the same time. Observe the reactions in each beaker.

4. In which beaker (hot or cold) did the mixing appear to take place faster?

CONCLUSION:

1. In your own words, explain your observations in terms of the motion of water particles.

5-2. Heat Transfer

At the end of this section you will be able to:

- Give an example to show that heat energy can move from one material to another.
- Compare how heat is transferred by *conduction*, *convection*, and *radiation*.
- Describe four ways that sunlight can be used as a source of energy.

A metal cooking pan put over a fire takes on some of the heat from the fire. People sitting near the fire feel the heat. A bird perched in a tree above the fire also feels some of the heat. How does heat move from one place to another? Does the heat move to the pan in the same way as it moves to the people and the bird?

HOW HEAT MOVES

A metal pan put directly on a fire is heated by **conduction** (kun-**duk**-shun). Transfer of heat by direct contact is called *conduction*. It is the simplest method of heat transfer. See Fig. 5–7. The metal in the pan, like all other substances, is made up of particles. The rapidly moving particles of the burning wood in a fire bump the particles in the metal and make them vibrate faster. Each particle of metal bumps its neighbors in the cooler parts of the pan. This continues until all the particles

Conduction Transfer of heat by direct contact.

Fig. 5–7 This pan is being heated by conduction.

in the metal pan are moving about an equal amount. If you touch the handle of the pan, you will be burned. The heat is also transferred to your skin by conduction.

Suggestion: Different metals conduct heat at different rates. You can demonstrate this with a conductometer. Science supply houses have such conductometers.

The metal in a pan conducts heat very well. Not all materials conduct heat as well as metals. Wood, for example, is a poor *conductor* of heat. That is why the handles of pans and other metal objects are often made of wood. Liquids, gases, and nonmetallic solids are all poor conductors of heat. They are called *insulators*. Insulators are used in houses and other buildings to prevent heat from escaping. An insulated house also stays cooler in summer because heat cannot enter. Clothes shield our bodies against loss of heat. They can do this because air trapped under clothes acts as an insulator. Many layers of clothes with air spaces between each layer provide better insulation than one heavy layer. See Fig. 5–8.

Enrichment: The air trapped by clothing has the same effect as the air pockets in house insulation. Air does not conduct heat energy very well. The R-values of insulation measure their effectiveness.

How does heat from a fire reach a bird in a tree above the fire? The answer depends on the way air acts when it is heated. The air over the fire becomes hot. This hot air expands because its particles start to move faster. Thus each particle collides with its neighbors with greater force. These collisions cause the average distance between the particles to increase. Therefore, the heated air takes up more space. Expansion of the heated air makes it less dense than the surrounding air because there is more empty space between its particles. The

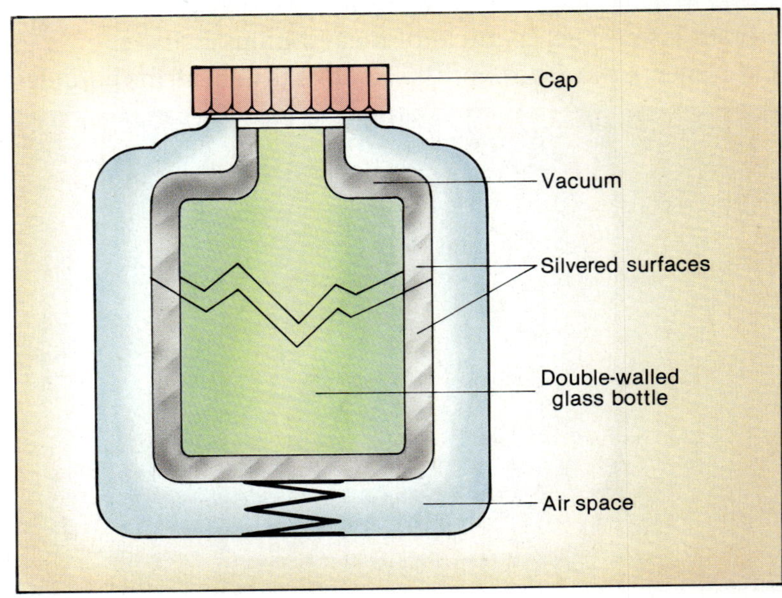

Fig. 5–8 A thermos bottle can keep liquids hot or cold because it is well insulated.

less dense warm air moves up toward the bird. See Fig. 5–9. Transfer of heat by the movement of a heated gas or liquid is called **convection** (kun-**vek**-shun). *Convection* occurs when a gas such as air or a liquid such as water is heated unevenly. The heated part of the gas or liquid becomes less dense and floats upward. Heat transfer by convection can take place only in gases or liquids.

Convection Transfer of heat by movement of a heated gas or liquid.

Enrichment: Gliders use rising air currents to lift them to great heights so that they can have time to enjoy their flights. Birds also use these air currents to save energy.

Fig. 5–9 The top illustration shows an early version of a hot-air balloon. These balloons make use of convection. As the air in the balloon is heated, it becomes less dense and rises. The balloon rises also.

An open fire in a fireplace is usually a poor source of heat for a room. Convection carries most of the heat up the chimney. On the other hand, some room heaters make use of convection. For example, steam or hot water moves through a heater and heats some of the air in the room. This warm air rises and moves to the cooler parts of the room. The cool air sinks and moves toward the heater where it is heated again. See Fig. 5–10.

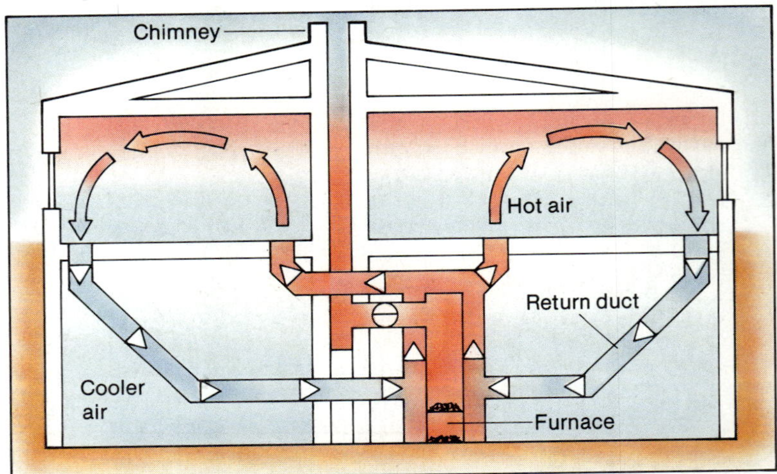

Fig. 5–10 This diagram shows how a hot-air heating system heats a home by means of convection.

Convection transfers heat when the heated part of a gas or liquid moves. A third method of heat transfer is very different. It is called **radiation** (rade-ee-**ay**-shun). *Radiation* transfers heat through empty space. The heat energy is carried by waves similar to radio waves. All waves that move through empty space are called *electromagnetic waves*. You will learn about electromagnetic waves in Chapter 8. The electromagnetic waves that transfer heat energy are called *infrared* waves.

Radiation Transfer of heat through space by infrared waves.

Sources of heat, such as a fire, send out these invisible infrared waves. When the waves reach your skin or other material, they are changed into heat. Infrared waves are responsible for some of the warmth you feel when you are near a hot object. Radiation is a very important method of heat transfer. The earth receives heat energy from the sun by radiation. See Fig. 5–11. You feel warm while sitting in the sun because you are receiving heat by radiation. The sun is an average of 150 million kilometers from the earth. This distance is mostly empty space. Thus it is impossible to receive heat from the sun by conduction or convection.

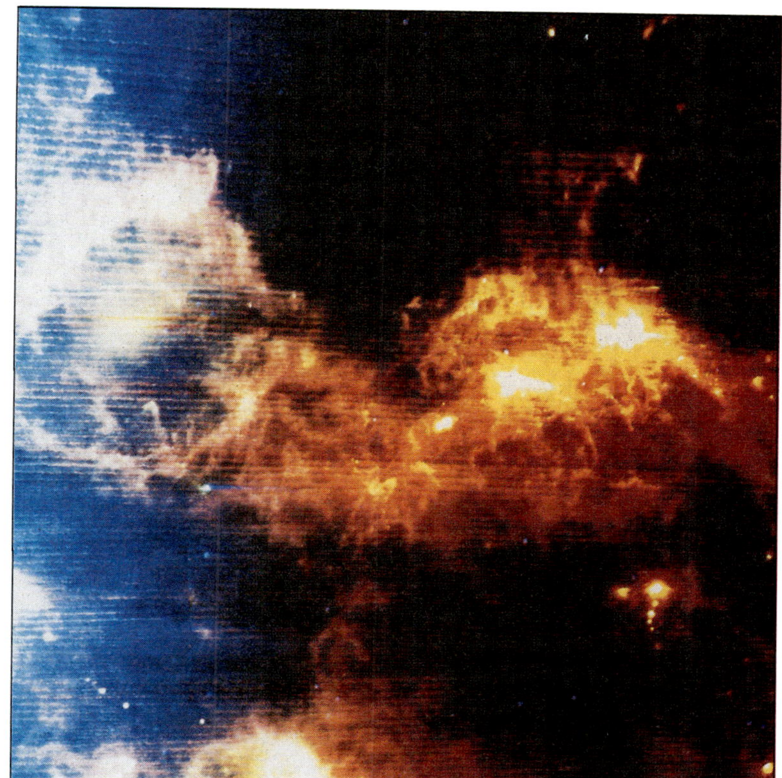

Fig. 5–11 The infrared radiation given off by objects in space can be studied by astronomers. This is an infrared photo of the Orion nebula.

Suggestion: Discuss the different types of heating systems (forced air, convection, radiant) used in schools and homes as well as the different types of fuel (wood, coal, gas, electricity).

KEEPING WARM

As you now know, an open fireplace is not an efficient way to heat a home. Much of the heat is lost by convection as the hot air goes up the chimney. Standing in front of the fire warms only the side of you that receives radiation. The other side will still be cool. A great improvement in home heating was made in the 1740's. Benjamin Franklin invented an iron stove that fitted inside a fireplace. The Franklin stove heated room air by conduction. This allowed heat to spread through the room by convection. In time, the iron stove itself held the fire and was moved out of the fireplace. The stove was then given its own stovepipe chimney. See Fig. 5–12.

Today, many houses are heated by burning a fuel such as oil or natural gas. Oil or gas burners are usually located in the basement or in a special room of the house. Heat is moved through the house by heated water or air. You have already seen how convection can be used to move hot air or water through a heating system. Some systems also use pumps to

Fig. 5–12 A modern wood-burning stove such as the one shown can help to heat a house.

Fig. 5–13 Insulating a home helps to reduce heat loss and to lower fuel bills.

help move the hot water. If heated air is used, convection is usually speeded up by a fan. Steam can also be used. Boiling water in the furnace sends steam into radiators. There the steam changes back into water and gives up the heat it gained when it became steam. The water then returns to the boiler.

No matter what method is used to heat a home, much heat is wasted if the house is poorly insulated. One method of preventing heat loss is to fill the spaces around the walls and ceiling with an insulator. Sealing the openings around doors and windows also helps to prevent the loss of heat by convection. See Fig. 5–13.

You can see if a building is well insulated by using a special camera that records infrared waves. See Fig. 5–14. The colors in the photographs show places where heat is being lost. This type of photograph is called a *thermogram* (from the Greek words *therme* meaning "heat" and *gramma* meaning a "drawing" or "record").

Fig. 5–14 This thermogram shows where heat is being lost because of inefficient insulation.

USING SOLAR ENERGY

Each year the United States receives five hundred times as much energy from the sun as is used. Trapping only a small part of the solar energy available can meet all our energy needs. However, the solar energy must be collected before it can be used. At the present time, four methods are used to collect solar energy. First, some solar-energy collectors reflect sunlight from a large area to a smaller surface. Mirrors follow the sun and reflect the light onto a boiler. The steam that is

Fig. 5–15 The mirrors reflect sunlight onto a boiler on top of the tower. The steam that is produced is used to generate electricity.

Fig. 5–16 The water in the pipes in these solar collectors is heated by the sun. The hot water is then used to heat the house.

Fig. 5–17 This passive solar home collects the sun's energy through strategically placed windows and skylights.

Fig. 5–18 Solar cells convert sunlight directly into electricity. Panels of solar cells are often used to provide energy for spacecraft.

produced can be used to generate electricity or to heat buildings. See Fig. 5–15. A second method of collecting solar energy uses flat plates. See Fig. 5–16. Water or air can be heated in the plates. The heated water or air moves through the building by convection or by using pumps. Many houses have flat-plate collectors on their roofs to help supply hot water instead of heating the water by burning a fuel.

A third method of collecting solar energy has no moving parts. Sunlight enters a house or other building through large windows. The infrared waves in the sunlight then heat the inside of the building. The windows are placed so that the summer sun is blocked. This keeps the house cool in summer. See Fig. 5–17. In the fourth method for collecting solar energy, sunlight generates electricity. Special cells change the solar energy directly into electricity. See Fig. 5–18. Each cell produces only a small amount of electricity. Therefore, many cells are put together in panels. These panels combine the output of all the cells.

All of these methods of collecting solar energy allow it to be used as a *renewable* energy resource. A renewable energy resource is one that is never used up. Fuels that supply energy by being burned must be replaced by finding new sources. In the future, the renewable supply of solar energy can replace many of the fuels now used to produce heat.

SUMMARY

Heat can be transferred in three ways: (1) by conduction, (2) by convection, and (3) by radiation. Most methods of heating the inside of a building transfer heat in more than one way.

QUESTIONS

Use complete sentences to write your answers.

1. How do you know that heat energy can move from one material to another? Give an example.
2. Define conduction and give an example.
3. Define convection and give an example.
4. Define radiation and give an example.
5. Discuss one method by which sunlight can be used as a source of energy.

1. Answers may vary. Touching a hot object is a simple example. Any answer showing conduction should be accepted.
2. Conduction is the name given to heat transfer by direct contact. Setting a pan on a fire is one example of conduction.
3. Convection is the name given to heat transfer by the movement of a gas or liquid. Warming your hands by holding them over a fire is an example of convection.
4. Radiation is the name given to heat transfer by means of infrared waves. Sunlight is one example of radiation.
5. There are four examples given in the text for using solar radiation.

5-3. Temperature and Heat

At the end of this section you will be able to:

- Explain the difference between the Fahrenheit and Celsius temperature scales.
- Compare temperature and heat.
- Describe how to use a calorimeter to measure heat.
- Define specific heat capacity.

Which of the following accidents is more dangerous? (1) You spill a cup of hot tea on your hand. (2) While pouring the tea, the cover of the teapot falls off and all of the hot water in the teapot spills on your hand. You will find the answer to this question in this section.

WHAT DOES TEMPERATURE MEASURE?

Temperature Measurement of the average motion of the particles of matter.

Dip your finger into a glass of warm water. Then touch an ice cube. You would probably say that the **temperature** of the water is higher than the *temperature* of the ice. Warm water has more heat than the same weight of ice. See Fig. 5–19. You

Fig. 5–19 Heat from inside the earth is released through natural vents on the ocean floor. This heat raises the temperature of the water around the vents.

Fig. 5–20 The Celsius scale is commonly used by scientists to measure temperature. It is also widely used in many parts of the world.

now know that heat energy is the result of the movement of particles of matter. The particles of warm water in the glass are moving faster than the particles in the ice cube. When you measure the temperature of an object, you measure the average amount of movement of one atom of the object. The quantity of heat depends on the sum of the motion of all the atoms in the object.

Do you think other people would always agree with your observations of temperature based only on your feeling? In order to have the same meaning for everyone, temperature must be measured with an instrument. A *thermometer* is an instrument used to measure temperature. Materials expand

Word study: Thermometer from *therme* (Gr.), heat.

Enrichment: The Fahrenheit scale was based on the lowest temperature available at the time. With this temperature as zero, body temperature was set at 100°F. Today, 32°F and 212°F are the freezing and boiling points of water.

Enrichment: The temperature of molten metal is measured by comparing its color with the color of an electrically heated wire.

when heated and shrink when cooled. The most commonly used kind of thermometer is based on this principle. A liquid is sealed in a glass tube. Alcohol is often used and so is the liquid metal, mercury. When a thermometer is heated, the liquid expands and rises in the tube. Cooling causes the liquid to shrink and fall.

The thermometer tube must have a scale. Many thermometers use the Fahrenheit scale. On the Fahrenheit temperature scale, water freezes at 32° and boils at 212° at sea level. The temperature scale now used in most scientific work is the Celsius scale. On the Celsius scale, water freezes at 0° and boils at 100° at sea level. See Fig. 5–20.

Not all thermometers use a liquid in a glass tube. One kind of thermometer, called a *thermostat*, uses a strip made of two different metals sandwiched together. The metals expand and shrink by a slightly different amount when the temperature changes. This causes the metal strip to bend. See Fig. 5–21. Another kind of thermometer, called a *thermocouple*, measures temperature by its effect on the flow of an electric current. See Fig. 5–22. These thermometers are often used to measure body temperature since they respond quickly to temperature changes.

Fig. 5–21 A thermostat is used to regulate temperature in a building. The middle diagram shows that the bimetallic strip bends when it is heated. This breaks the circuit and turns off the heat.

Fig. 5–22 The second diagram shows how a thermocouple is used to register temperature in an electronic thermometer.

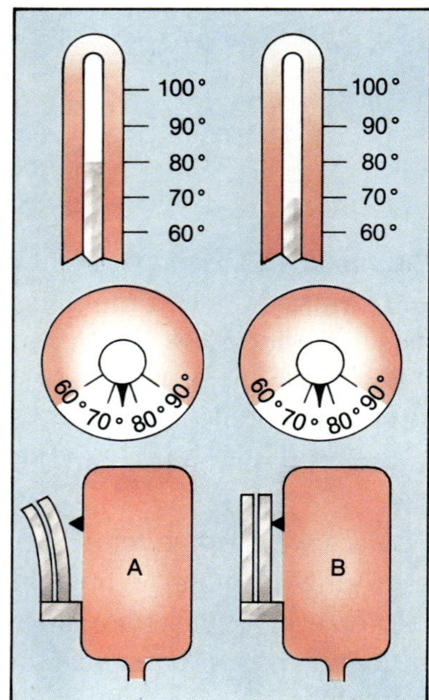

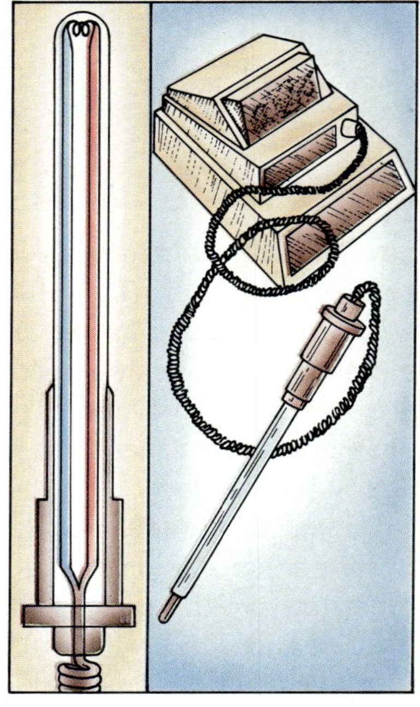

MEASURING HEAT

Now look at the question asked at the beginning of the section. A teapot full of boiling water and a cup of boiling water both have the same temperature, 100°C. The water particles in both the pot and the cup are moving at the same average speed. However, the pot contains more water than the cup. The larger amount of water in the pot holds more heat. This is the reason why a pot of hot water would cause a more serious burn than a cup of water at the same temperature. In order to measure heat, you must include the mass of material heated as well as its temperature change.

Suggestion: The Skill-Building Activity following this section deals with the distinction between temperature and heat. If students do not do the Activity, be sure to discuss the distinction carefully.

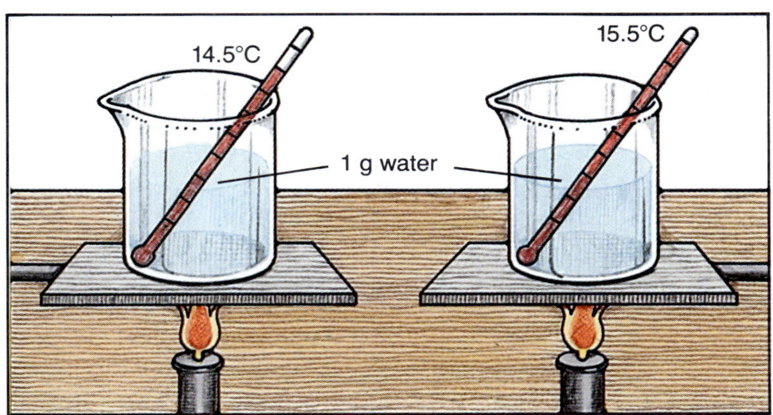

Fig. 5–23 One calorie is the amount of heat needed to raise the temperature of one gram of water from 14.5°C to 15.5°C.

Heat is often measured by a unit called a **calorie** (**kal**-uh-ree). A *calorie* measures both the mass of material and the temperature change. For example, the amount of heat needed to raise the temperature of one gram (g) of water by one degree Celsius (1°C) is one calorie (cal). See Fig. 5–23. Suppose that you put 500 grams of water into an electric coffee maker. The water has a temperature of 20°C. When the coffee maker is started, the water is heated to 100°C. The change in temperature (ΔT) is the difference between 100°C and 20°C, which is 80°C. One calorie of heat is needed to increase the temperature of each gram of water by one degree Celsius. So the amount of heat produced by the coffee maker is:

Calorie The amount of heat needed to raise the temperature of one gram of water by one degree Celsius.

$$\text{mass (grams)} \times \text{temperature change (°C)} = \text{heat (calories)}$$

$$M \times \Delta T = H$$

$$500\text{ g} \times (100°C - 20°C) = H$$

$$500\text{ g} \times 80°C = H$$

$$40{,}000\text{ cal} = H$$

Skill: Discuss several problems using calories and the conversion of calories to joules; 1 calorie = 4.18 joules.

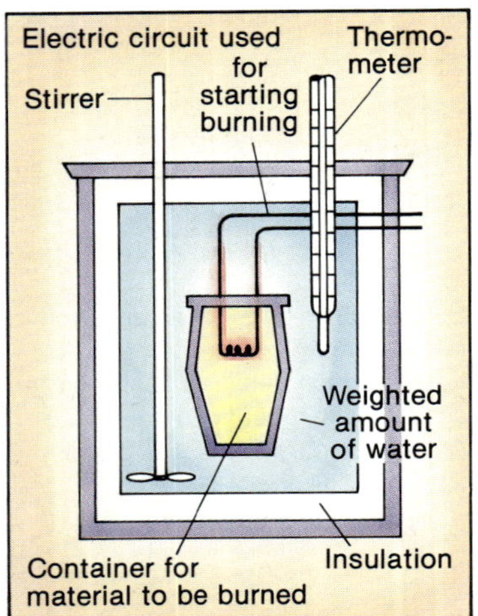

Fig. 5–24 This diagram shows a cross-section of a calorimeter used to measure the amount of heat energy in different foods.

Enrichment: One slice of bread contains approximately 100 kilocalories (Calories) of energy. This is the energy needed for a 50 kg (110 lb) person to climb 800 meters (straight up).

Enrichment: The BTU (British thermal unit) is a unit of heat in the English system. One BTU is the amount of heat needed to raise the temperature of one pound of water one degree Fahrenheit; 1 BTU = 252 calories.

You can see that a thermometer tells only part of the information needed to measure heat. The mass of material being heated must also be known. Heat is usually measured by using a device called a *calorimeter* (cal-uh-**rim**-uh-ter). A calorimeter holds a known mass of water in an insulated container. The amount of heat used to warm the water is measured in the calorimeter. The temperature change is measured with a thermometer. For example, the heat energy in food can be measured with the kind of calorimeter shown in Fig. 5–24. A sample of food is combined with oxygen. The amount of heat released is measured in calories. The number of calories is the energy content of the food.

You are probably familiar with the use of calories to express the energy content of different foods. The "calorie" commonly used to measure food energy is actually a *kilocalorie*. A kilocalorie is a thousand times larger than a calorie. (Remember that "kilo-" means 1,000 times a unit.) Sometimes a kilocalorie is called a "Calorie" with a capital "C" to distinguish it from the ordinary calorie.

The SI unit for heat energy is the joule. One calorie is equal to 4.19 joules. This unit is named after James Prescott Joule. Joule was an 18th-century English scientist who did many experiments showing that heat is a form of energy. Remember that you learned in Chapter 3 that the joule is the unit for both energy and work.

HEAT CAPACTIY

People often wrap food in aluminum foil to keep it moist when it is heated in the oven. When the hot food comes out of the oven, you can touch the foil without burning yourself. Although the food gets very hot, the aluminum does not hold much heat. This shows an important fact about different materials. The capacity of different materials to hold heat is not the same. For example, experiments show that it takes only 0.21 calorie to change the temperature of each gram of aluminum by one degree Celsius. Compare this with the heat capacity of the water in moist food. Each gram of water absorbs one calorie of heat to raise its temperature by one degree Celsius. Therefore, the moist food holds about five times as much heat as the aluminum. The amount of heat needed to raise the temperature of one gram of a material by one degree

Celsius is called its **specific heat capacity**. Aluminum has a *specific heat capacity* of 0.21 cal/g°C. Water has a specific heat capacity of 1.00 cal/g°C. Table 5–1 lists the specific heat capacity of some common materials.

Specific heat capacity The amount of heat needed to raise the temperature of one gram of a substance by one degree Celsius.

SPECIFIC HEAT CAPACITY OF SOME COMMON MATERIALS		
	(cal/g°C)	(J/g°C)
Water	1.00	4.18
Ice	0.50	2.09
Wood	0.42	1.76
Iron	0.11	0.46
Copper	0.09	0.39
Aluminum	0.22	0.92

Table 5–1

SUMMARY

Thermometers measure temperature, which is related to the motion of particles. The amount of heat energy in a material depends on both temperature and the mass of the material. Both the mass of material and the change in temperature determine heat energy measured in calories or joules.

QUESTIONS

Use complete sentences to write your answers.

1. How does the Fahrenheit temperature scale differ from the Celsius temperature scale?
2. Which is larger, a Fahrenheit degree or a Celsius degree?
3. Give an example to show the difference between heat and temperature.
4. How many calories of heat energy does it take to raise the temperature of 150 grams of water from 15°C to 80°C? Show your calculations.
5. What is the answer to question 4 in joules? Show your calculations.
6. Explain what is meant by specific heat capacity.

1. On the Fahrenheit scale water freezes at 32° and boils at 212°. On the Celsius scale water freezes at 0° and boils at 100°.
2. A Celsius degree is larger than a Fahrenheit degree.
3. Answers will vary. A cup of boiling water and a pail of boiling water are at the same temperature, but the pail of water contains much more heat energy.
4. $M \times \Delta T = H$
$150 \text{ g} \times (80°C - 15°C) = 9{,}750 \text{ cal.}$
5. $9{,}750 \text{ cal} \times 4.18 \text{ J/cal} = 40{,}755 \text{ J}$
6. Specific heat capacity is the amount of heat needed to raise the temperature of one gram of a material by one degree Celsius.

¡COMPUTE!

SCIENCE INPUT

When you add heat (calories) to water, the temperature increases. When you remove heat from water the temperature decreases. Under ordinary circumstances it takes one calorie of heat to raise the temperature of one gram of water one degree Celsius. Therefore, we can write the formula,

$$H = (T_2 - T_1)M$$

Where H is the amount of heat in calories, $(T_2 - T_1)$ is the change in temperature, and M is the amount of water in grams.

Using this formula, we can determine the number of calories exchanged when raising or lowering the temperature of a specific amount of water.

COMPUTER INPUT

A computer can also be used to calculate the amount of heat in calories. The equation above needs only a simple program. Such a program would have three parts to it: THE INPUT, which allows the user to put information into the computer; THE CALCULATION, which is the manipulation of this information; and THE OUTPUT which is the result of the calculation and which appears on the screen. A diagrammatic view of a simple computer program is:

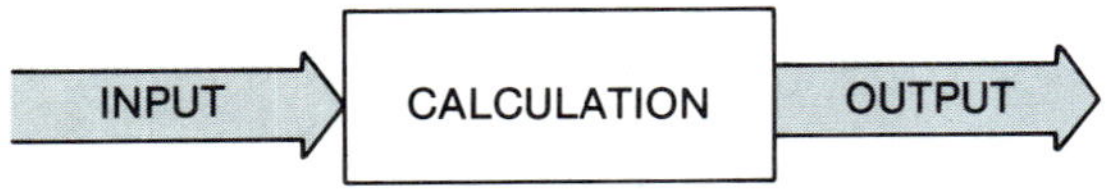

WHAT TO DO

A simple program for changing feet into inches is listed below: Type the program into the computer, save, and then run it.

```
100  REM EXAMPLE
110  INPUT "DISTANCE (FEET ONLY)?"; F
120  I = F *12
130  PRINT "THAT =    "; I; "INCHES"
```

Remarks to user (100)
User input (110)
Computer language instructions
Calculation (120)
Output (130)

When you ran the program, what information were you asked to input?

Let's try two other simple programs. The first one will determine the number of calories needed to change the temperature of water. The second will convert Fahrenheit temperatures to degrees Celsius. Identify the input statements, the calculation statements, and the output statements.

Remember to save your programs on disk or tape before running them.

A SIMPLE CALCULATION: PROGRAM CALORIC ENERGY

GLOSSARY

USER — the person(s) inputing and/or running the program.

STATEMENT — any line of instructions within a program.

MODEM — a device that allows your computer to communicate with other computers over telephone lines (See Bits of Information.)

PROGRAM

```
100  REM CALORIC ENERGY
105  INPUT "HOW MANY GRAMS OF
     WATER?";M
110  INPUT "WHAT IS THE STARTING
     TEMPERATURE?";T1
115  INPUT "WHAT IS THE FINAL
     TEMPERATURE?";T2
120  TC = T2 - T1
125  H = TC * M
130  PRINT "FOR TEMPERATURE
     CHANGE OF ";TC
135  PRINT "THE EXCHANGE IS  ";H;
     " CALORIES"
140  PRINT
150  END
```

```
100  REM CELSIUS CONVERSION
105  INPUT "TEMPERATURE IN
     FAHRENHEIT = " ;T
110  C = 5 * (T - 32)/9
120  PRINT T " DEGREES = ";C;
     " DEGREES CELSIUS "
130  END
```

PROGRAM NOTES

In order to run a program, you do not have to understand the calculations, but in order to write a program you must. In Programs Caloric Energy and Celsius Conversion what scientific and mathematical information did the programmer need to write the program?

BITS OF INFORMATION

Users are always looking for new programs and video games to run on their computers. Young computer users can exchange and buy software through the Young Peoples' Logo Association (YPLA). YPLA lists programs in a number of computer languages. For membership information, write YPLA, 1208 Hillside Drive, Richardson, Texas 75801.

You can also exchange software or other ideas via computer if you have a modem. You could even set up a computer game competition between your school and one that is across town or even in another state. It's possible, if both locations have computers and modems. A modem (short for Modulator/Demodulator) changes the electronic impulses inside your computer into vibrations that a telephone can understand. These telephone vibrations are then changed back again into electronic impulses to the other computer where the message appears on the screen. With a modem you can talk to other computers and even play games with other computer users. Communication can be very fast. It is important that your modem be compatible with the one with which you're communicating, that is, both must operate with the same electronic requirements.

SKILL-BUILDING ACTIVITY

See teacher's commentary for teaching hints, safety, and answers to questions.

TEMPERATURE AND HEAT

PURPOSE: You will compare and contrast temperature and heat.

MATERIALS:

2 250-mL beakers
Bunsen burner
matches
container of water
ringstand and ring
wire gauze square
thermometer
sweep second hand clock
stirring rod
water

PROCEDURE:

A. Label one beaker A. Fill it about one-fourth full of tap water.

B. Label the second beaker B. Fill it about three-fourths full of tap water.

C. Copy the data table shown below.

	Beaker A	Beaker B
Temperature, initial (T_i)		
Temperature, final (T_f)		
Temperature change ($\Delta T = T_f - T_i$)		

D. Measure the temperature of the water in each beaker. Record this as the initial temperature (T_i).

E. Place beaker A on the ringstand. Light and adjust the burner before placing it under the ring. Heat the beaker and water for one minute. CAUTION: Wear goggles.

F. After one minute, remove the beaker from the ringstand. Stir the water three or four times with the stirring rod. Measure the temperature. Record this as the final temperature (T_f).

G. Remove the burner from the ringstand but do not change the flame.

1. If the same amount of heat energy were added to beaker B, what temperature change would you expect to occur?

H. Repeat steps E and F with beaker B.

I. Record the temperature change for each beaker.

2. How did the temperature change in beaker A compare with the temperature change in beaker B?
3. If you followed the same series of steps for both beaker B and beaker A, compare the amount of heat added to each beaker of water.
4. Explain why the change in temperature was different for each beaker.

J. Calculate the amount of heat added to each beaker of water.

5. What additional measurement did you have to make?

CONCLUSION:

1. Using the information obtained from this activity, explain how the terms "temperature" and "heat" differ in meaning.
2. Use your results to explain why the amount of heat added to each beaker depends on both the mass of water and the temperature change.

TECHNOLOGY

CRYOGENICS: THE TECHNOLOGY OF COLD

The lowest air temperature ever recorded on earth was −125 degrees F. This was recorded in Antarctica. But man-made temperatures fall far below even that mark. In fact, −125° F seems warm compared to the temperatures reached every day in many factories where air is liquefied at temperatures of about −310° F. This is the world of cryogenics, the branch of physics involved in producing very low temperatures.

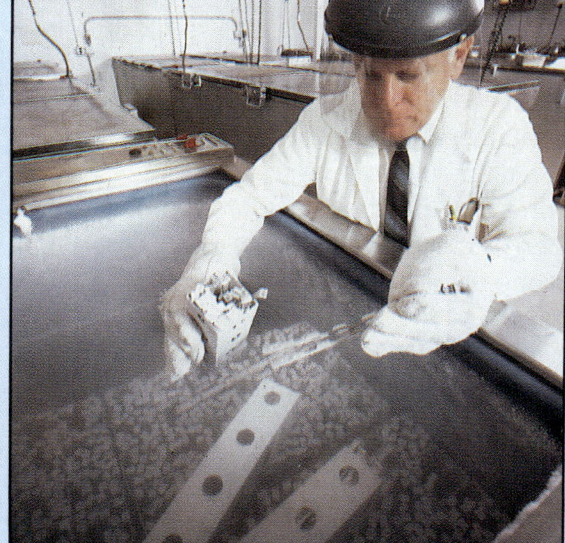

Why study low temperatures? Temperature is an important factor in determining the state and characteristics of a substance. Consider, for example, water. At high temperatures, it becomes a gas and evaporates. At low temperatures it becomes a solid, ice. Each state serves a different purpose. In its liquid form, water satisfies thirst. As a gas (steam), it may clear a congested chest or provide energy to move a ship. As a solid, it can prevent a knock on the head from becoming a bump or it may preserve food. Other substances change states and characteristics as well. Under extreme cold, some even become superconductors of electricity.

Many of the principles learned from the research of low-temperature physics are being applied in other sciences today. A scalpel cooled by liquid nitrogen can cut so sharply and accurately that it can separate one or two cells. Cryosurgery is the name of the branch of medicine that uses low temperatures. The scalpel or "probe" as it is called, can cut away or destroy diseased tissue while leaving healthy tissue one millimeter away unharmed. Cryosurgery has other benefits as well. Blood vessels can be sealed by the probe. A surgeon does not have to clamp or stitch vessels. Operations can be almost bloodless and, therefore, much safer.

Liquid nitrogen is also used to store both animal and human sperm. The scientist shown on this page is lowering vials of bull sperm into liquid nitrogen storage tanks. With this technology a breed can be improved or even saved from extinction. Human sperm banks use the same techniques.

Liquid helium is also used in the giant particle accelerator of the Fermi National Laboratory. Physicists use the accelerator to study the smallest particles of matter in the universe. The accelerator controls these particles by using 1,000 "super conducting magnets," that is, magnets which are amazingly excellent conductors of electricity. The only way the metal in the magnets can become a superconductor is by cooling it to −450° F. This is done with liquid helium.

What does the future hold in store? Research is being conducted on refrigerators and air conditioners without moving parts and on computers with supercooled parts that may operate faster while using less electrical power. The technology of cold is already affecting our lives and many more practical benefits of cryogenics will definitely be in our future.

CHAPTER REVIEW

See teacher's commentary for answers.

VOCABULARY

On a separate piece of paper, match each term with the number of the statement that best explains it. Use each term only once.

calorie	convection	radiation	temperature
conduction	heat engine	specific heat capacity	

1. Changes heat energy to mechanical energy.
2. Transfer of heat by infrared rays.
3. Transfer of heat by direct contact.
4. The number of calories needed to raise the temperature of one gram of a substance one degree Celsius.
5. Transfer of heat by movement of a gas or liquid.
6. A measurement of movement of particles in matter.
7. Heat needed to raise the temperature of one gram of water one degree Celsius.

QUESTIONS

Give brief but complete answers to each of the following questions. Unless otherwise indicated, use complete sentences to write your answers.

1. What was the importance of Count Rumford's cannon-boring experiment?
2. Describe how you could demonstrate that heat energy added to water causes the water particles to move faster.
3. What happens to the atoms of a solid when it is heated?
4. Give an example of a heat engine. Explain how it works.
5. Name and give examples of the three methods of heat transfer.
6. Give an example to show that heat energy can move from one object to another.
7. How can sunlight be used as a source of energy?
8. What does the temperature of an object measure?
9. Normal room temperature is 70°F. What is this temperature in degrees Celsius?
10. How does temperature differ from heat?
11. An automobile runs at a temperature of 190°F. What is this temperature in degrees Celsius?
12. Compare the Fahrenheit and Celsius temperature scales. Draw a diagram.
13. Compare the heat needed to change 100 g of water from 35°F to 40°F with the heat needed to change 100 g of water from 70°C to 75°C.
14. If you were given a thermometer with no scale marks, how would you calibrate it to read in degrees Celsius?

15. How does the amount of heat needed to change 50 g of water from 20°C to 30°C compare with the amount of heat needed to change 10 g of water from 20°C to 70°C? Show your answer in calories and in joules.

APPLYING SCIENCE

1. The Kelvin scale is the official temperature scale in SI units. Write a report on the Kelvin temperature scale. Explain why absolute zero temperature (0°K = −273°C) has never been reached. Discuss the method used to find that −273°C is the absolute minimum temperature.
2. Build an air thermometer and calibrate it. One way to calibrate it is to immerse the thermometer in ice water and then in boiling water. Make several readings and compare them with a laboratory thermometer.
3. Find out how the heat of fusion of water is determined and try the measurements yourself. One method involves melting a piece of ice of known mass in a styrofoam cup of water of known mass. The amount of heat needed to melt the ice comes from cooling the water. Find the number of calories needed to melt one gram of ice. Also express your answer in joules.
4. Read the instruction book for an electric range to find the number of watts one burner uses. From this, calculate the number of calories the burner uses in three minutes. Put a measured amount of water into a pot and put it on the burner for three minutes. Measure the initial and final temperatures of the water to determine how many calories actually were added to the water. Calculate the efficiency of the burner. (Remember, efficiency = work output ÷ work input.)

BIBLIOGRAPHY

Adler, Irving. *Hot and Cold: The Story of Temperature from Absolute Zero to the Heat of the Sun*. New York: John Day, 1975.

Kavaler, Lucy. *Life Battles Cold* (Wonders of Cold Series). New York: Harper, 1973.

Kentzer, Michael. *Cold* (Young Scientists Series). Morristown, NJ: Silver Burdett, 1976.

Kentzer, Michael. *Heat* (Young Scientists Series). Morristown, NJ: Silver Burdett.

Wade, H. *Heat.* Milwaukee: Raintree, 1979.

UNIT 2

WAVES

CHAPTER

6

These antennas are part of a large network. They receive waves from outer space. There are many types of waves. As you will see, all waves are alike in some ways. Waves carry energy.

WAVE MOTION

CHAPTER GOALS

1. Describe two kinds of waves.
2. Name three properties of all waves.
3. Compare the causes of reflection and refraction.
4. Explain and give an example of the Doppler effect.

6-1. Waves

At the end of this section you will be able to:

- Describe two kinds of waves that may be produced when energy travels through a medium.
- Identify four properties that describe a wave.

Think of a surfer riding a wave in to the beach. Energy is needed to move the surfer. Where does this energy come from?

WAVES AND ENERGY

Drop a fishing line and sinker into a lake or pond. Watch what happens. You will see **waves** travel across the surface of the water. The *waves* spread out from the point where the sinker hit the water. See Fig. 6–1. These waves are caused by energy traveling through the water. Where do you think the energy came from? Remember that an object in motion has kinetic energy. The sinker flying through the air has kinetic energy. When the sinker hits the water, some of the kinetic energy is transferred to the water. This energy causes the individual water particles to start moving in circular paths. This movement, in turn, causes neighboring water particles to move. See Fig. 6–2. As the water particles move in small circles, their energy moves through the water. The result is seen as a wave on the surface of the water.

Wave A disturbance caused by the movement of energy through a medium.

When a wave moves through open water, the water itself does not move along with the wave. For example, a cork floating on water will not move along with passing waves. It stays in almost the same place and moves up and down. This shows that the wave is a disturbance moving through the water. The water is the *medium* that carries the wave. Any substance through which energy is transferred by wave motion is called

Suggestion: A ripple tank can be used to demonstrate many features of waves such as frequency, wavelength, and velocity. Put the light below the tank and project onto the ceiling for the whole class to see.

Fig. 6–1 A drop of water strikes the surface of the water. Immediately, circular waves move out from the point of impact.

a medium. A liquid such as water can be a medium for waves. Gases like those in the atmosphere, as well as solids like iron, can also be a medium for waves. Only the energy that causes the wave moves through the medium. For example, the energy in an ocean wave can be used by a skillful surfer to move over the water. The surfer is pushed along by keeping just ahead of the moving wave. The energy in the wave was added to the water by winds blowing across the surface of the sea.

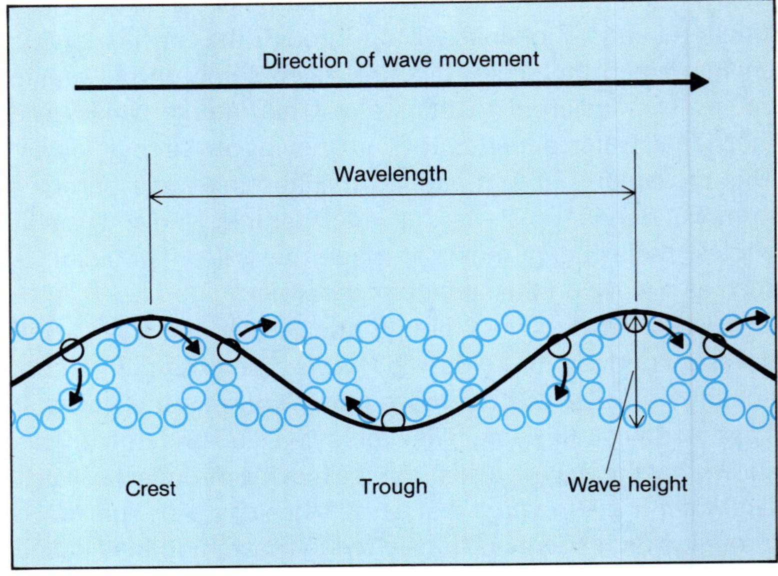

Fig. 6–2 As a wave moves through the water, the individual water particles move in circles.

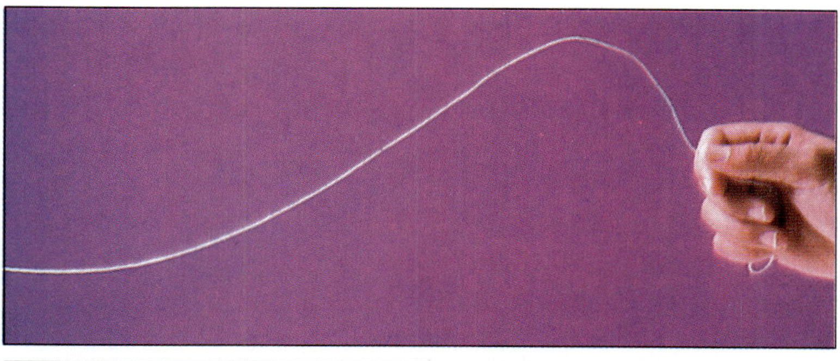

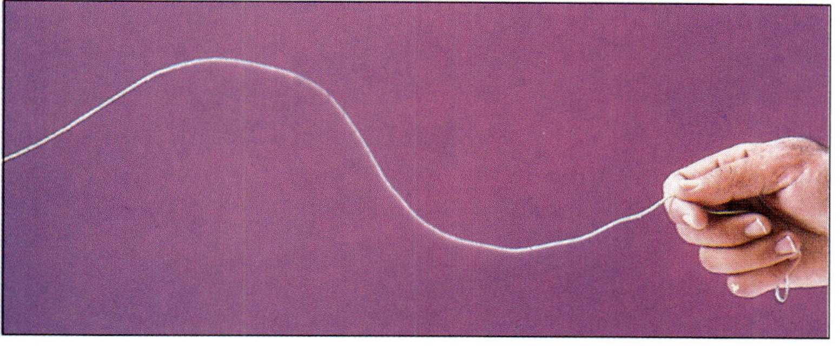

Fig. 6–3 These photos show how a wave moves from right to left as the rope moves up and down.

Waves are always the result of energy moving from one place to another. You can see how this happens if you hold the end of a rope tied to a doorknob. If you move your hand up and down, you add energy to the rope. The energy travels along the rope as a wave. See Fig. 6–3. Notice that the wave moves along the rope as the rope moves up and down. A wave can also move along a spring. See Fig. 6–4. The wave in the rope is the result of up-and-down motion. In the spring, the wave is caused by back-and-forth motion.

Suggestion: In the Investigation following this section, students use a coiled spring to study waves. If students do not do the Investigation, you should at least demonstrate some of the properties.

The kind of wave produced by the up-and-down motion of a rope is called a *transverse wave*. "Transverse" means "across." In a transverse wave, the material moves across, or at right angles to, the direction in which the wave moves. Another kind of wave can be shown with a spring stretched

Reinforcement: A flag moves with transverse waves in a strong wind.

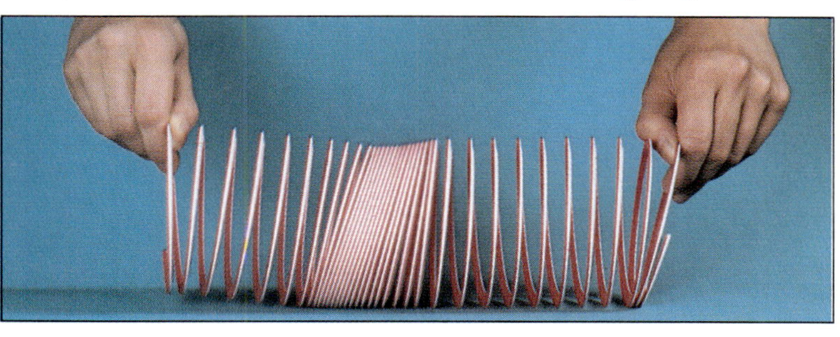

Fig. 6–4 The wave in this spring is shown by the compression of the coils. The wave is moving from left to right.

out on the floor. A pulse can be made to move along the spring by gathering a few coils of spring together. When the coils are released, a pulse made up of back-and-forth motions will travel along the spring. The movement of the pulse along the spring is a wave. The back-and-forth motion of a wave in a spring is called a *longitudinal wave*. "Longitudinal" means "lengthwise." A longitudinal wave travels along a spring as the coils are squeezed together and then spread apart. The part of the wave where the coils are squeezed together is called a *compression*. For this reason, this type of wave can also be called a *compression wave*. The part where the coils are spread apart is called a *rarefaction* (rare-eh-**fak**-shun). Notice that the individual coils of the spring move only a short distance back and forth. Only the energy represented by the wave moves along the spring.

Suggestion: Draw a longitudinal wave on the board and discuss the various parts (crest, trough, wavelength, and amplitude).

PROPERTIES OF A WAVE

Wavelength The distance between two neighboring crests or troughs of a wave.

All kinds of waves have some properties in common. First, a wave always has a certain **wavelength**. For transverse waves, the *wavelength* is the distance between two neighboring *crests* (high parts) or between two neighboring *troughs* (low parts). For longitudinal waves, the wavelength is the distance between two neighboring compressions or between two neighboring rarefactions. Wavelengths of transverse and longitudinal waves are compared in Fig. 6–5. Wavelengths are usually measured in meters for longer waves. Shorter waves can be measured in millimeters. The symbol for wavelength is the Greek letter lambda (λ).

Amplitude The distance a wave rises or falls from a normal rest position.

Fig. 6–5 also shows a second feature of a wave. This is the **amplitude** of the wave. The *amplitude* shows the amount of

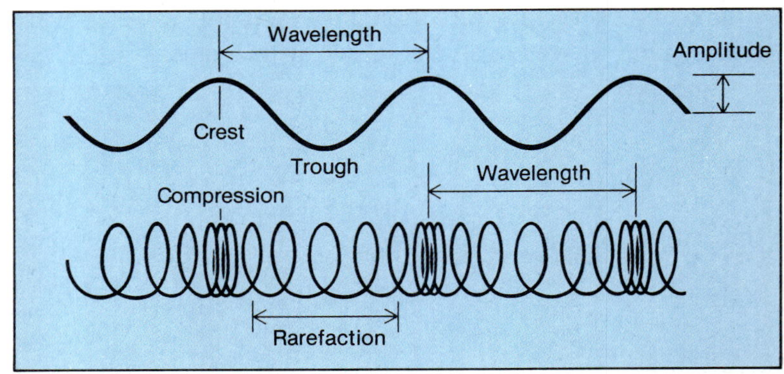

Fig. 6–5 This diagram shows how wavelength is measured in a transverse and a longitudinal wave.

energy carried by the wave. The larger the amplitude, the more energy the wave carries.

A third feature of a wave is a result of its movement. Since waves always move, they have a speed. The speed (v) can be determined by measuring how fast a certain point on the wave moves. For example, the speed of a wave on water can be measured by observing one crest. The distance the crest moves in one second is measured. Wave speed is usually measured in meters per second (m/s).

A fourth way of describing a particular wave involves counting the waves that pass a point in one second. For example, you can count the number of crests or troughs of a water wave passing in one second. This number is called the **frequency** (**free**-quen-see) of the wave. One complete wave passing during one second measures a *frequency* (f) of 1 wave/s. Frequency is measured in **hertz** (Hz). The unit *hertz* is named after the German scientist Heinrich Hertz, who was one of the first to study light waves. One hertz means a frequency of one complete wave passing a point each second (1 Hz = 1 wave/s). The Greek letter nu (ν) is also used to indicate frequency.

Frequency The number of complete waves that pass a point each second.

Hertz A unit used to measure the frequency of waves. A frequency of 1 Hz means that one complete wave passes a point each second (1 wave/s).

Suppose you want to observe waves in a rope. You move the rope up and down twice in one second. Two complete waves are produced in one second. Thus the frequency of the waves in the rope is 2 Hz (2 waves/s). You measure how fast the waves travel along the rope. The speed of the waves is found to be 2 m/s. This means that after one second the first wave is two meters from your hand. The second wave is one meter away. See Fig. 6–6. The distance between two neighboring crests of the waves is one meter. Therefore, each wave has a wavelength of one meter.

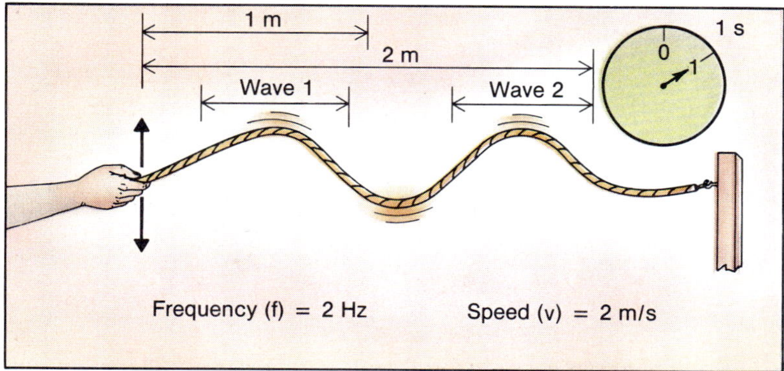

Fig. 6–6 This diagram shows how speed, frequency, and wavelength are related.

Skill: Solve several sample problems on the board for speed, wavelength, and frequency.

The relationship between wavelength, speed, and frequency of waves is expressed in the following equation:

$$\text{wavelength } (\lambda) = \text{speed } (v) \div \text{frequency } (f)$$

$$\lambda = \frac{v}{f} = \frac{2 \text{ m/s}}{2 \text{ waves/s}}$$

$$\lambda = 1 \text{ m}$$

The formula $\lambda = v/f$ also can be written as $v = f \times \lambda$. You can use this equation to find the speed if you know the wavelength and the frequency. The speed (v) of waves is equal to their frequency (f) multiplied by wavelength (λ). For example, suppose that you are fishing from a stationary boat. Several waves pass by the boat. You could find the speed of those waves by counting the number that pass in one second (frequency) and measuring the length of one wave. If the frequency is 2 waves/s (2 Hz) and the wavelength is 0.5 meter, the speed is given by: $v = f \times \lambda$

$$v = 2 \text{ waves/s} \times 0.5 \text{ m/wave} = 1.0 \text{ m/s}$$

SUMMARY

Waves are the result of energy moving from one place to another. There are two types of waves. All waves have wavelength, speed, and frequency.

QUESTIONS

Use complete sentences to write your answers.

1. Name two types of waves that may be produced when energy travels through matter. Give an example of each.
2. Compare the two types of waves you named in question 1.
3. Name three features that describe any kind of wave. Explain how to measure each one.
4. Complete the following table.

Speed (m/s)	Frequency (Hz)	Wavelength (m)
0.4	0.2	(a)
300	4.0	(b)
(c)	0.1	0.2
(d)	2.0	0.035
100	(e)	0.4
0.3	(f)	0.03

1. Two types of waves are transverse and longitudinal. Waves on a rope are transverse while compressional waves in a coiled spring are longitudinal.
2. In transverse waves, the material carrying the wave moves at right angles to the direction the wave is moving. In longitudinal waves, the material carrying the wave moves back and forth in the same direction the wave is moving.
3. The three features are speed, frequency, and wavelength. Speed is a measure of how fast the wave travels. Frequency is the number of waves generated each second. Wavelength is the distance between two neighboring crests or troughs.
4. (a) 2, (b) 75, (c) 0.02, (d) 0.07, (e) 250, (f) 10.

INVESTIGATION

See teacher's commentary for teaching hints, safety, and answer to questions.

WAVES IN A SPRING

PURPOSE: You will determine the conditions that affect the motion of waves in a coiled spring.

MATERIALS:

paper
pencil
coiled spring

PROCEDURE:

A. With one person on each end, stretch the coiled spring to about five or six meters on a smooth floor. Do not release the spring when it is stretched or it will tangle.

B. While one person holds one end very still, the person at the other end can send a wave along the spring by moving the end sharply to one side and back. If this is done quickly, a well-defined transverse wave will be made and will travel along the spring. Practice doing this until you can do it easily. See Fig. 6–7 (a).

C. Send several transverse waves and observe what happens as they travel down and back.

1. Does the wave travel at a nearly constant speed?
2. Does the wave change shape?
3. How does the speed of a large wave compare with that of a small wave?
4. Does stretching the spring more affect the speed of the wave?

D. You can send longitudinal waves along the spring by gathering about 15 to 20 coils in your free hand and suddenly releasing them. Be sure you hold on to the end of the spring after releasing the coils. See Fig. 6–7 (b).

5. Is the speed of the longitudinal waves constant?
6. How does the speed of a small wave (a few coils) compare to the speed of a large wave (many coils)?

CONCLUSION:

1. How can you make transverse and longitudinal waves in a coiled spring?
2. What affects the way a wave travels along a spring?

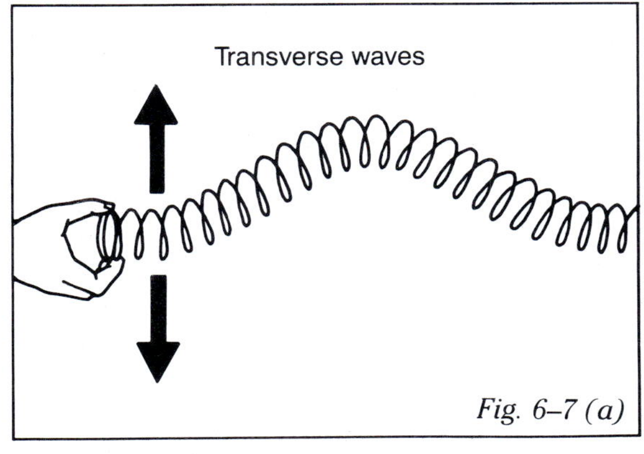

Fig. 6–7 (a)

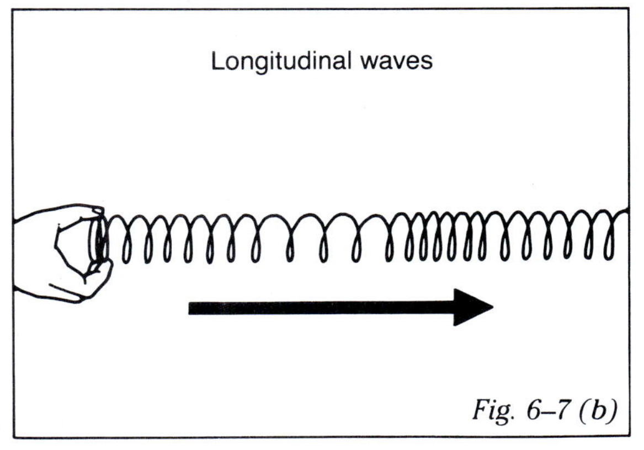

Fig. 6–7 (b)

6-2. *Wave Interactions*

At the end of this section you will be able to:

- Predict what will happen when a wave meets a barrier in its path.
- Explain what happens to a wave when its speed changes.
- Explain and give examples of the *Doppler effect*.

Reinforcement: A billiard ball bounces from the side of a pool table with nearly equal angles of incidence and reflection.

What happens when a moving ball hits a barrier such as a wall? The ball usually bounces off the wall and continues to move. But its direction is different than it was before it hit the barrier. See Fig. 6–8.

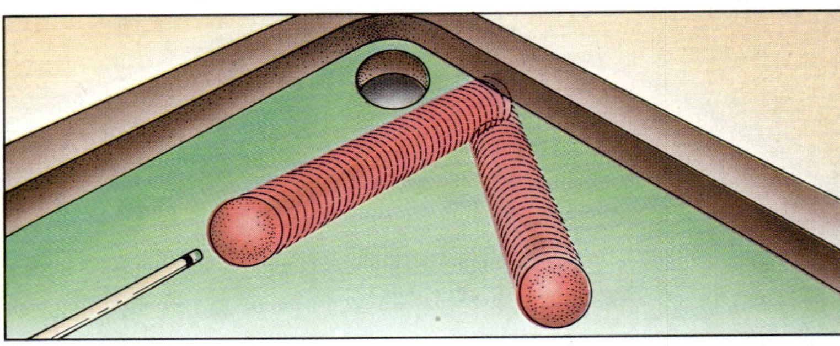

Fig. 6–8 When a moving ball hits a barrier in its path, it bounces off the barrier and keeps moving in a different direction.

CHANGING THE DIRECTION OF WAVES

Reflection The process in which a wave is thrown back after striking a barrier that does not absorb its energy.

Like a ball, waves also can change direction if they meet a barrier in their path. If the barrier does not absorb the energy of the wave, **reflection** (rih-**fleck**-shun) will occur. *Reflection* causes the wave to bounce off the barrier and move away in a different direction. For example, a wave moving down a rope will be reflected back along the rope if the end of the rope is tied down. See Fig. 6–9. In this case, the direction of the wave is reversed. Only a small amount of the energy carried by the wave is absorbed by the post. Thus the energy travels back along the rope as a reflected wave.

Suggestion: Standing waves can be generated on a small diameter (2.0 cm) coiled spring. Anchor one end to a door knob and, while stretching it a little, generate waves from the other end. Start at a low frequency and gradually increase the frequency until standing waves are present. This is also the subject of the Investigation following this section.

Suppose that you continue to send waves along the rope while the waves are being reflected. When waves with the same wavelength and frequency moving in opposite directions meet, they combine. Then the rope will move twice as much in some places. Other parts of the rope will not move at all. See Fig. 6–10. Waves in a rope that is moving in this way are called *standing waves*.

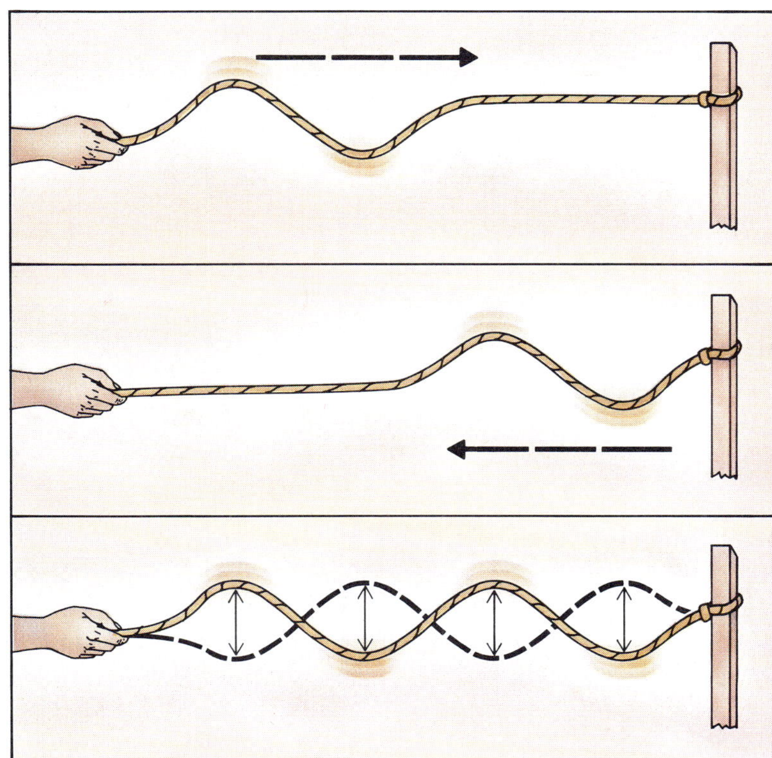

Fig. 6–9 The top two diagrams show how a wave in a rope is reflected from a post.

Fig. 6–10 When reflected waves meet waves moving in the opposite direction, standing waves are formed.

A wave may strike a barrier straight on like a wave in the rope. Then reflection sends the wave back in a directly opposite direction. A wave that strikes a barrier at an angle is reflected back at the same angle. This can be seen with water waves by using a *ripple tank*. In a ripple tank, ripples, or small waves, are made in a shallow layer of water. The tank holding the water has a glass bottom. A light shines downward through the water onto a sheet of white paper. Ripples in the tank cause a shadow of the wave pattern to fall on the white paper. See Fig. 6–11. Waves reflected from a barrier can be studied easily with a ripple tank. For example, waves can be observed as they strike a barrier at an angle. The incoming waves are called the *incident waves*. Reflected waves bounce off the barrier. The angle between the incident waves and a line at a right angle to the barrier is the *angle of incidence*. The angle of the reflected waves is measured in the same way. This angle is the *angle of reflection*. Observation of waves in a ripple tank shows that the angle of incidence is always equal to the angle of reflection. See Fig. 6–12.

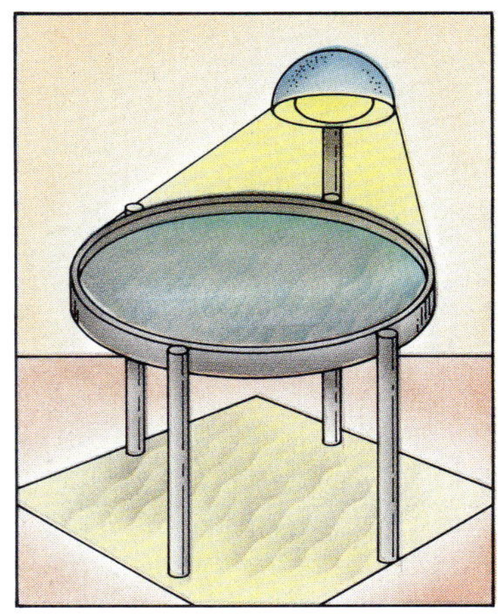

Fig. 6–11 Wave motion can be studied with a ripple tank.

Incident wave
Angle of incidence
Wooden barrier
Angle of reflection
Reflected wave

Fig. 6–12 When moving waves are reflected from a barrier, the angle of incidence and the angle of reflection are always equal.

CHANGING WAVE SPEED

Word study: Refraction from *refractus* (L.), to turn aside.

Refraction The process in which a wave changes direction because its speed changes.

A ripple tank also can be used to observe the effect of changing the speed of waves. This can be done by putting a flat piece of glass in the ripple tank. Waves moving into the shallow water over the sheet of glass slow down. You can see them change direction. See Fig. 6–13. When waves change the direction in which they are moving because of a change in speed, the process is called **refraction** (rih-**frak**-shun). Waves in water show *refraction* when the depth of the water changes. The speed of waves is slower in shallow water. As each wave approaches the shallow water at an angle, one side

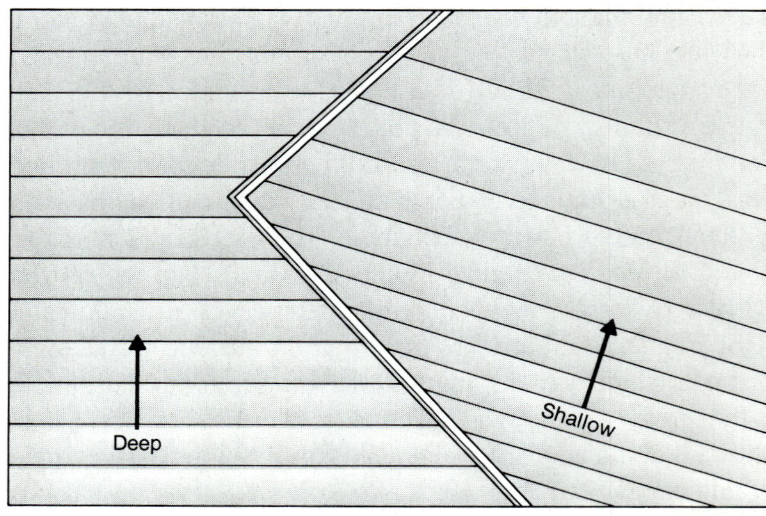

Fig. 6–13 When waves move from deep water into shallow water, they slow down. This change in speed causes them to change direction.

reaches the shallow water first and slows down. As the wave moves, more and more of it slows as it reaches the shallow water. This finally causes the entire wave to swing around and move in a different direction.

On the shore of an ocean or lake, you often can observe refraction of the waves. As you watch the waves approach the shore, you can see that the direction in which they move changes. Waves almost always approach the shore at an angle. But they strike the shore almost straight on. Their direction usually changes as the waves move closer to the shore. See Fig. 6–14. This change of direction takes place as the waves slow down and are refracted as they reach the shallow water near the shore.

Fig. 6–14 As waves move into shallow water near shore, they slow down and are refracted.

CHANGING WAVE FREQUENCY

Sometimes the frequency of waves appears to change. This can happen if you look at waves while you are moving. For example, think of watching water waves from a moving boat. Waves appear to strike the boat more often as the boat heads into the waves. Many waves hit the boat each second. Thus the frequency of the waves appears to be high. However, fewer waves hit the boat when it is moving in the same direction as the waves. The frequency of the waves appears low to the observer in the boat. To someone watching the waves from shore, the frequency never appears to change. An apparent change in the frequency of waves caused by motion is called the **Doppler effect**.

Doppler effect An apparent change in the frequency of waves caused by the motion of either the observer or the source of the waves.

Suggestion: Swing a tuning fork around your head on the end of string while it is vibrating to illustrate the Doppler effect. You could also swing a whistle on the end of a piece of rubber tubing while using the tube to blow the whistle.

The *Doppler effect* also occurs when an observer is stationary and the source of the waves is moving. For example, the sound of an approaching car horn becomes lower as the car goes past you. As a source of sound moves toward you, the sound waves seem to have a high frequency. As the source moves away, the apparent frequency of the sound waves is lower. See Fig. 6–15.

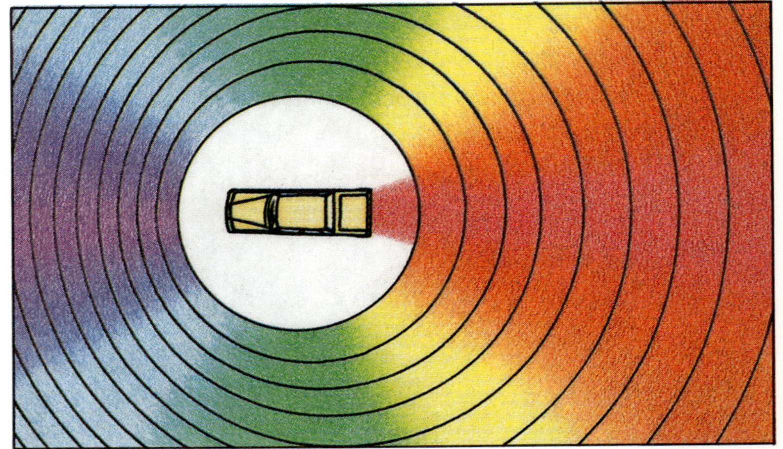

Fig. 6–15 The frequency of waves appears to change when either the source of the waves or the observer is moving.

SUMMARY

The next time you are at the beach, or watching a film of waves hitting a beach, remember what you have learned in this section. A barrier, such as a dock or pier, will change the direction of the waves. Waves also change direction as they slow down near the beach. Finally, if you are in a moving boat, the frequency of the waves appears to change.

QUESTIONS

Use complete sentences to write your answers.

1. What happens when a wave changes speed?
2. What happens when a wave strikes a barrier? How could you demonstrate this?
3. What causes the Doppler effect?
4. Give an example of the Doppler effect.
5. What is the relation between the angle of incidence and the angle of reflection when a wave hits a barrier? Show this in a diagram.

1. When a wave changes its speed, the wavelength gets shorter and the wave is refracted.
2. When a wave strikes a barrier, it is reflected. You could demonstrate reflection by sending a wave down a rope that is tied to a barrier and letting it strike the barrier.
3. The Doppler effect is caused by either the source of waves or the observer moving.
4. Rowing a boat with the waves and against the waves would demonstrate the Doppler effect. A moving car or train going by while blowing its horn is also an example of this effect.
5. Diagrams will vary. The angle of incidence is equal to the angle of reflection.

INVESTIGATION

See teacher's commentary for teaching hints, safety, and answers to questions.

STANDING WAVES

PURPOSE: You will generate standing waves in a coiled spring. You will then measure the speed of the waves that caused the standing waves.

MATERIALS:

coiled spring
meter stick
paper
pencil
clock

PROCEDURE:

A. Work in groups of three or more. Let one person hold one end of the coiled spring on the floor so that it does not move.

B. Have a second person hold the other end of the spring and stretch it out on the floor to a length of 5 to 6 meters.

C. Move one end of the spring from side to side. Move it slowly at first. See Fig. 6–16. Gradually increase the frequency of the motion until you observe a standing wave pattern. Standing waves result when the waves moving forward meet the reflected waves.

D. Continue increasing the frequency until you observe three or four standing waves.

E. When three standing waves are present between the ends of the spring, count complete back and forth motions to find the frequency of the waves.

   1. What is the frequency of the waves?

F. Have the third person measure the wavelength from crest to crest of the three standing waves. The wavelength of the standing waves is half the wavelength of the traveling waves that cause them.

   2. What is the wavelength of the waves that caused the standing waves?

G. Calculate the speed of the traveling waves.

   3. What is the speed of the waves?

CONCLUSIONS:

1. Describe how you can generate standing waves in a coiled spring.
2. How can you use standing waves to find the wavelength and speed of the traveling waves that caused them?

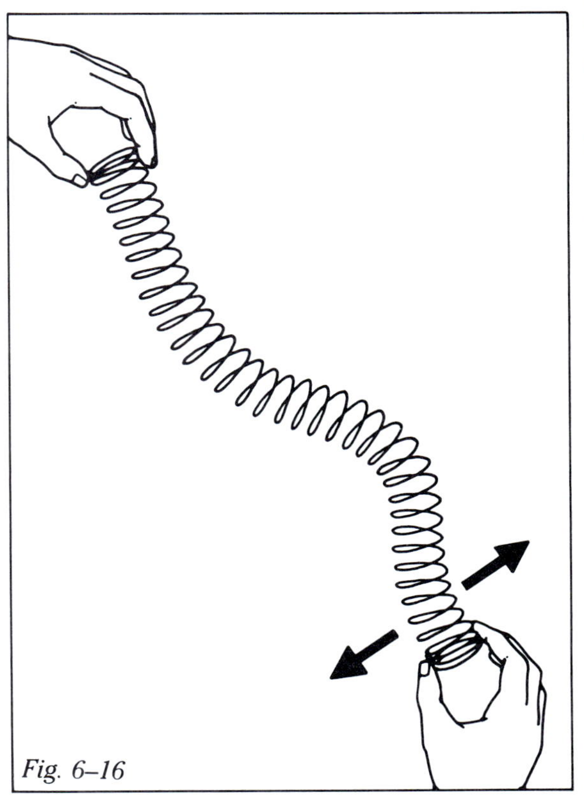

Fig. 6–16

SKILL-BUILDING ACTIVITY

See teacher's commentary for teaching hints, safety, and answers to questions.

REFLECTION OF WATER WAVES

PURPOSE: You will observe how waves reflect from a curved barrier.

MATERIALS:

small beaker
eye dropper
shallow round dish
water

PROCEDURE:

A. Put enough water in the dish to completely cover the bottom no more than 5 mm deep.

B. Fill the eye dropper with water. Hold the eye dropper about 30 cm over the middle of the dish. Allow one drop of water to strike the water in the dish near the center of the dish. See Fig. 6–17.

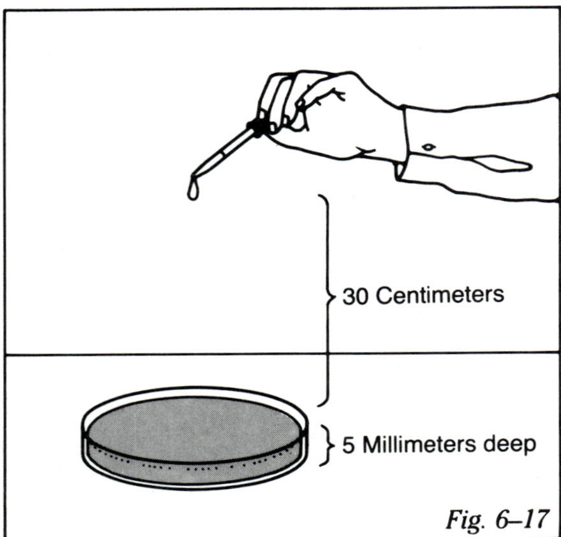

Fig. 6–17

1. What happens when a drop of water strikes the surface of the water?
2. Describe the shape of the wave formed when the drop of water strikes the surface of the water.
3. What happens to the wave when it strikes the side of the dish?
4. What is the shape of the wave after it reflects from the side of the dish?

C. Look back at Fig. 6–12 on page 142 showing the reflection of a water wave from a straight barrier.

5. What is the relation between the angle at which the wave hits a barrier and the angle at which it reflects?
6. Explain the kind of wave formed in step B in relation to your answer to question 3.

D. Repeat step B. Watch closely as the wave reflects off the side of the dish. Do this several times if necessary.

7. Draw a diagram showing what happens to the wave as it reflects. Use arrows to show the direction of the wave.
8. State a hypothesis to explain what would happen if you let a drop of water fall closer to the side of the dish.

E. Observe what happens to the reflected wave as you release a drop of water closer to one side of the dish. Repeat this several times.

9. Do your observations confirm your hypothesis? Explain your observations.

CONCLUSION:

1. In order to explain what you observed in this activity, what is the relationship between the angle at which any wave strikes a barrier and the angle at which it reflects?

CAREERS IN SCIENCE

PHYSICAL OCEANOGRAPHER

Physical oceanographers are physicists or geophysicists who specialize in the ocean. They examine its currents, waves, and tides as well as its physical properties such as density and temperature. They plot the movement of pollutants and determine how the relationship between the sea and the atmosphere affects the weather.

Less than 3,000 persons are employed as oceanographers, although the government estimates that by 1985 there will be a need for about 4,000. Competition for jobs is keen.

The minimum requirement for beginning jobs in oceanography is a bachelor's degree, with a strong background in mathematics, physics, chemistry, geophysics, and meteorology. Most jobs require some graduate training, however.

For further information, contact: International Oceanographic Foundation, 3979 Rickenbacker Causeway, Virginia Key, Miami, FL 33149.

RADAR TECHNICIAN

Radar technicians repair, test, and maintain radar equipment. Testing to diagnose the cause of a malfunction or to ensure that the equipment is still in top form requires a knowledge of the fundamental operation of various radar units and systems and employs complex testing devices such as oscilloscopes and signal generators. The technician is also expected to maintain records of repairs, maintenance service, and tests performed.

Licensing, and most top-level technicians' jobs, requires a high school education with a strong background in mathematics, physics, schematic reading, electricity, and basic electronics. Beyond this, it is usually necessary to spend one to two years training on the job. The military services offer this training as part of a tour of duty.

For further information, contact: Institute of Electrical and Electronic Engineers, 345 East 47th Street, New York, NY 10017.

CHAPTER REVIEW

See teacher's commentary for answers.

VOCABULARY

On a separate piece of paper, match each term with the number of the statement that best explains it. Use each term only once.

wave	frequency	wavelength	amplitude
Doppler effect	reflection	hertz	refraction

1. The distance a wave rises or falls from a normal rest position.
2. The number of complete waves that pass a point each second.
3. The process in which a wave is thrown back after striking a barrier.
4. A disturbance caused by the movement of energy from one place to another.
5. The process in which a wave changes direction because its speed changes.
6. The name of a unit used to measure the frequency of a wave.
7. The effect of an apparent change in the frequency of waves caused by the motion of the source or the observer.
8. The distance between two neighboring crests or troughs of a wave.

QUESTIONS

Give brief but complete answers to each of the following questions. Unless otherwise indicated, use complete sentences to write your answers.

1. What is a wave? Draw a wave and label a crest, a trough, and a wavelength.
2. What is a transverse wave? Give an example of a transverse wave.
3. What properties can be used to describe any wave?
4. Define each of the properties you named in question 3.
5. Define the terms reflection and refraction. What do they have in common?
6. What happens when a wave is refracted?
7. Draw a diagram to compare the angle at which a wave strikes a barrier with the angle at which it is reflected.
8. How does the depth of water affect the speed of waves?
9. Draw a diagram to show how a wave is refracted.
10. How could you generate a longitudinal wave?
11. Find the speed of waves with a frequency of 60 Hz and a wavelength of 5 m.
12. Water waves have a frequency of 15 Hz and a speed of 30 cm/s. What is their wavelength?
13. Give one common example of the Doppler effect. What do you hear in this case?
14. Why do ocean waves approach the shore head on?

15. Describe how a water wave would change when (a) it strikes a barrier in its path, (b) it enters shallow water.

APPLYING SCIENCE

1. You probably have heard about earthquakes in different parts of the world. Perhaps you have experienced an earthquake yourself. Scientists who study earthquakes measure the different kinds of waves produced by the earthquakes. Go to the library and look up information about the three types of earthquake waves. What kinds of waves are they? Where are they reflected, refracted, or absorbed? How does studying these waves help scientists to learn more about earthquakes?
2. Find several ways in which you can demonstrate the Doppler effect. For example, you can swing a whistle on the end of a hollow rubber tube while blowing through the other end of the tube. Or you can swing a tuning fork on the end of a heavy cord. Can you think of any other demonstrations?
3. Police radar units make use of the Doppler effect to measure the speed of cars on the highway. Interview a member of your local police department or highway patrol to find out how the Doppler works. Report your findings to the class.
4. Use a ripple tank and a tuning fork to measure the frequency of water waves. While holding the tuning fork by the stem, tap it against the heel of your shoe so that it begins to vibrate. Dip the vibrating tuning fork into the water in the ripple tank. Count the number of waves that strike the side of the tank in 30 seconds. Divide the number of waves by 30 to find the frequency of the waves in hertz.

BIBLIOGRAPHY

Bascom, Willard. *Waves and Beaches: The Dynamics of the Ocean Surface.* New York: Doubleday, 1980.

Kentzer, Michael. *Waves.* (Young Scientists Series). Morristown, NJ: Silver Burdett.

LeBond, P. H., and L. A. Mysak. *Waves in the Ocean.* New York: Elsevier, 1981.

McCormick, Michael E. *Ocean Wave Energy.* New York: John Wiley, 1981.

Pierce, John R. *Almost All About Waves.* Cambridge, MA: MIT Press, 1974.

Ross, D. *Energy from the Waves.* New York: Pergamon, 1981.

CHAPTER

7

This photograph is a hologram reconstruction of a vibrating guitar. By studying these images, scientists hope to improve the sound of guitars and other musical instruments.

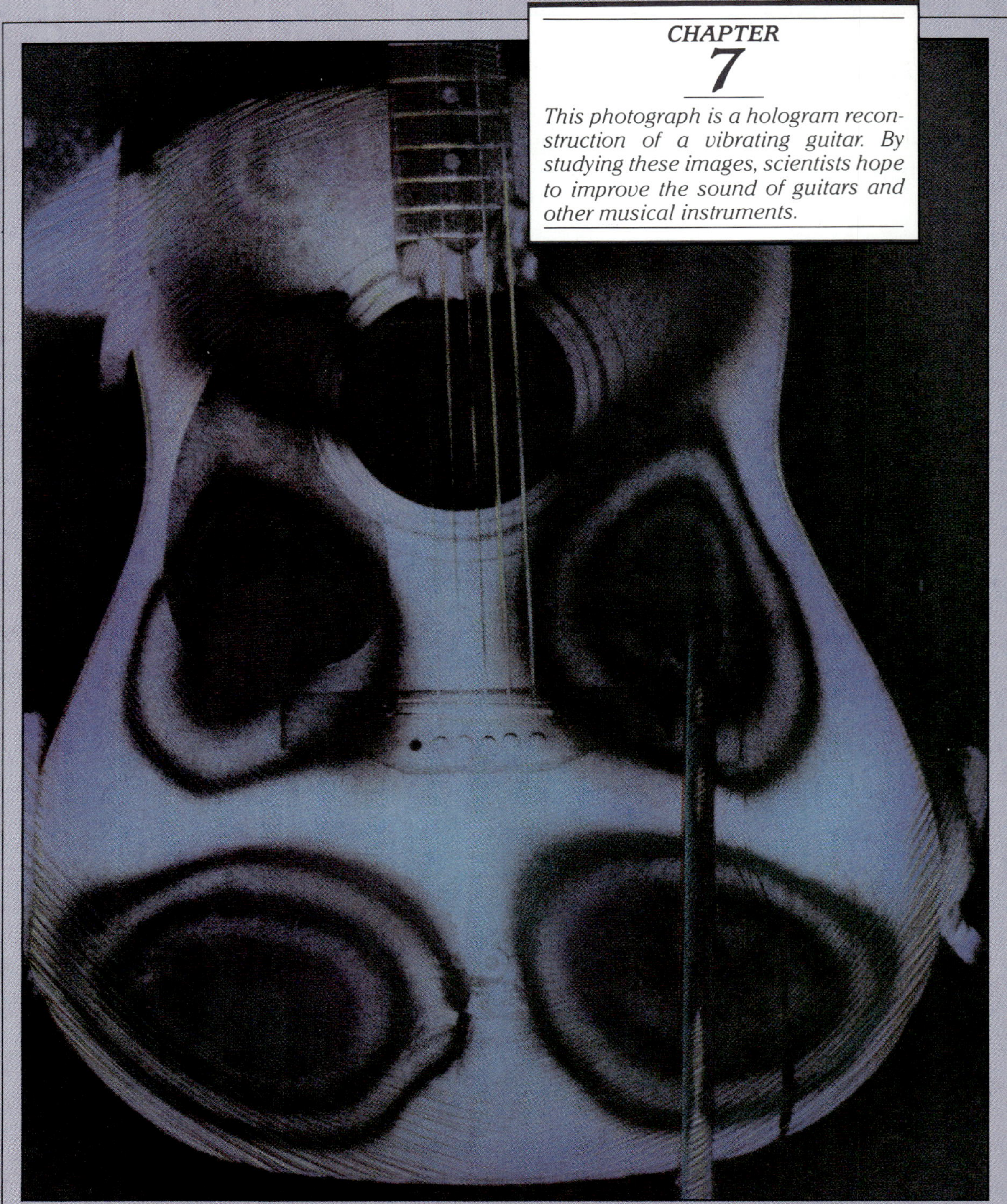

SOUND

CHAPTER GOALS

1. Compare the similarities and differences of sound waves and other types of waves.
2. Explain the difference between a musical and a nonmusical sound.
3. Describe how musical instruments produce sound.

7-1. Sound Waves

At the end of this section you will be able to:

- Identify the properties of a sound wave.
- Relate the properties of sound waves to the way we hear sound.
- Describe some of the ways sound waves are used.

An old riddle asks this question: "If a tree falls in a forest, and no one is there to hear it, will there be a sound?" An answer can be found in this section.

WHAT IS A SOUND WAVE?

Without air there would be no familiar sounds. This is because sound moves through air the way ripples move through water if you drop a pebble into a quiet pool. A sound begins when a vibrating object pushes on air particles. These particles of air then push on other particles. It is like a long line of people standing close together. The person at one end pushes the next, and that one pushes the next, and so on. Can you imagine a disturbance passing to the head of the line without any person moving forward? Something that vibrates steadily, such as a guitar string, sends out a series of disturbances through the air. See Fig. 7–1. The sound is carried through the air by the back-and-forth motions of the particles of air. This motion is similar to the way waves move through a spring. So it is called a longitudinal wave. Since sound moves through air, or some other medium, it can be said to be made up of **sound waves**. As *sound waves* move through the air, the air particles are alternately crowded together and spread

Suggestion: Demonstrate longitudinal waves on a coiled spring. Stretch the spring, gather in a few coils, and release them to generate a longitudinal wave.

Sound wave A longitudinal wave moving through air or some other medium.

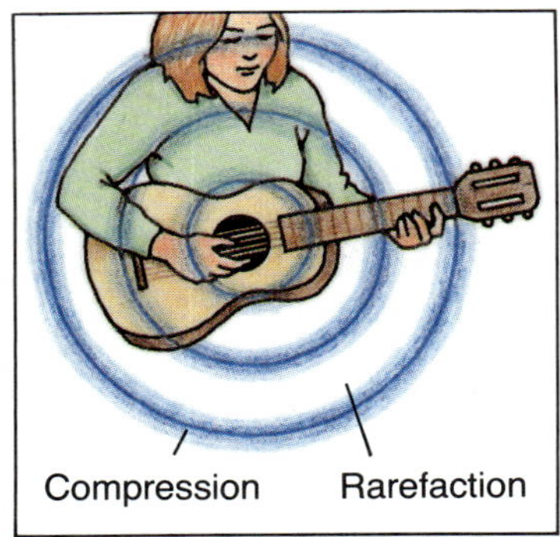

Fig. 7–1 When a guitar string is plucked, it sends out a series of sound waves through the air.

apart. See Fig. 7–2. Compare this to the compression and rarefaction of waves in a spring.

SPEED OF SOUND

Sound waves travel much faster than water waves. In air at 0°C, sound waves have a speed of 331 m/s. As air gets warmer, the speed of sound increases. The speed of sound in air increases by about 0.6 m/s for each 1°C increase in temperature. At 20°C, the change in the speed of sound can be given by: $0.6 \text{ m/s} \cdot {}^\circ\text{C} \times$ temperature increase above 0°C

$$0.6 \text{ m/s} \cdot {}^\circ\text{C} \times 20^\circ\text{C} = 12 \text{ m/s}$$

This means that the speed of sound at 20°C is 343 m/s (331 m/s + 12 m/s).

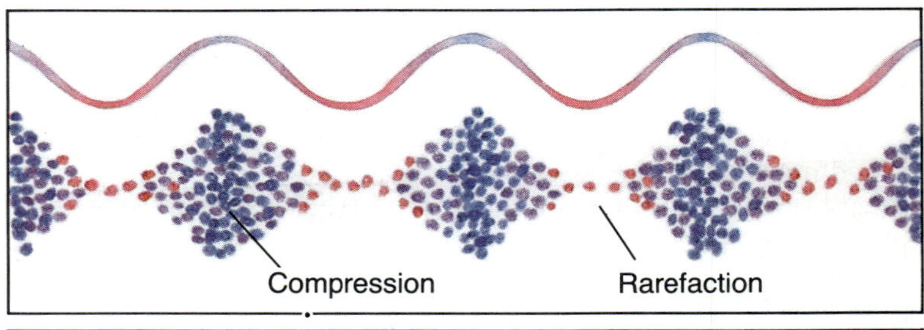

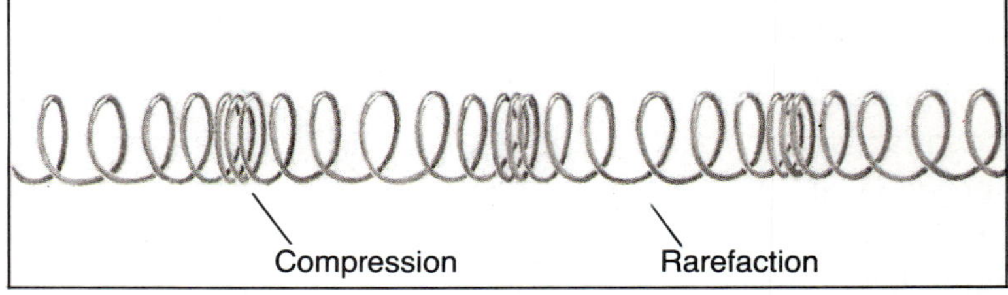

Fig. 7–2 This diagram compares the compression and rarefaction of sound waves with the movement of waves in a spring.

You can use the speed of sound to find the distance to a source of sound. For example, you can determine the distance to a lightning flash. Start counting the number of seconds when you see the lightning. Stop counting when you hear the sound of thunder from the lightning. Then multiply this time by 350 m/s. Suppose you hear thunder three seconds after you see lightning. The lightning was 350 m/s × 3 s = 1,050 m (about 1 km) away.

Reinforcement: A film loop called "Shock Waves" from Ealing Films shows how a sonic boom develops.

A jet airplane flying at the speed of sound makes a powerful sound wave called a *sonic boom*. Any object moving through the air makes a sound wave by pushing the air ahead of it. See Fig. 7–3. A plane moving slower than the speed of sound never catches up with this disturbance. At less than the speed of sound, the air easily moves away from the path of the plane. In order to move faster than the speed of sound, the plane must thrust the air aside. It must break through a "sound barrier." This makes a powerful sound wave. This sonic boom sounds like thunder to someone on the ground.

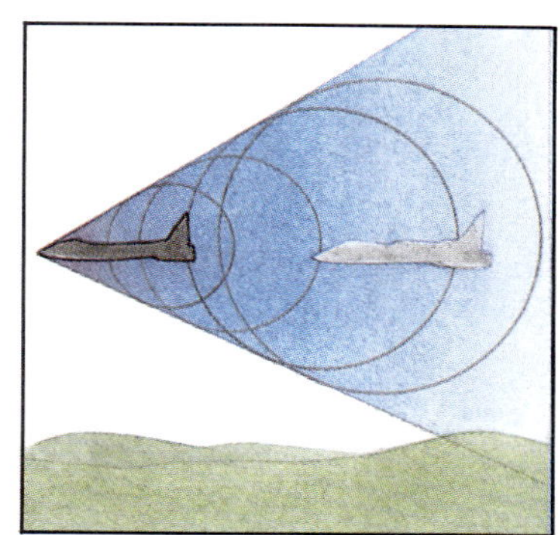

Fig. 7–3 A jet plane moving faster than the speed of sound breaks through a barrier of air and creates a sonic boom.

Sound waves have different speeds in different materials. For example, in water at 20°C, sound moves at a speed of about 1,460 m/s. In steel at the same temperature, the speed of sound is about 5,000 m/s. In general, sound moves faster in solids and liquids than in air. The particles of matter in solids and liquids are closer together than they are in gases such as air. This makes it easier for vibrations making up sound waves to be passed along. See Table 7–1.

THE SPEED OF SOUND IN SEVERAL COMMON SUBSTANCES AT 25°C	
Medium	**Speed (m/s)**
Air	346
Water	1,497
Wood	1,850
Glass	4,540
Aluminum	5,000
Iron (Steel)	5,200

Table 7–1

Many solids and liquids also conduct sound waves much better than air. For example, hit two stones together underwater. Someone swimming underwater can hear the sound many meters away. You can hear a train approaching by listening to the sound waves through the steel rails. You can hear the sound through the rails long before you hear the train noise through the air. This is because air absorbs more of the sound energy than steel does.

HEARING SOUNDS

When a tree falls, it disturbs the air. Thus there is a sound. But if there is no one around to receive the sound waves, is there really a sound? Without sound waves, there can be no

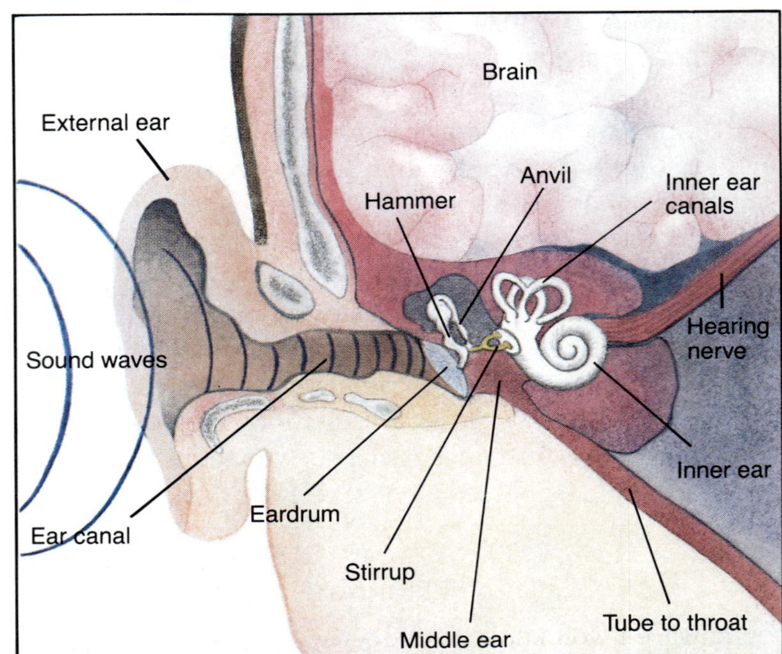

Fig. 7–4 Sound waves cause the eardrum to vibrate. The vibrations are magnified and sent to the inner ear. Here they become pressure waves. The hearing nerve changes the pressure waves to electric signals, which are sent to the brain.

Enrichment: Children have a better capacity for hearing high-frequency sounds than adults. Apparently, the sensitivity of the nerves of the inner ear decreases with age because of constant exposure to loud sounds. Many animals have the ability to hear high-frequency sounds far beyond the range of the best human ears. Dogs can hear up to 50,000 Hz. Porpoises and bats have a frequency range of well over 100,000 Hz.

sounds. But sound is both the sound waves and the effect they have on our sense of hearing. The properties of the sound waves determine how we hear the sound. See Fig. 7–4.

Like all waves, each sound has a particular frequency. Sounds are made by vibrations. For example, a vibrating guitar string produces a sound. Your voice is produced by the vibration of your vocal cords. The frequency of the sound waves depends on the speed of the vibration. For example, a tuning fork vibrates when it is struck. See Fig. 7–5. The fork vibrates 440 times each second. The frequency of the sound waves produced is 440 waves/s or 440 Hz. The average person can hear sounds with frequencies from about 20 to 20,000 Hz. However, the average ear is most sensitive to sounds with frequencies between 2,000 and 4,000 Hz.

Pitch A property that describes the highness or lowness of a sound; it is determined primarily by the frequency of the sound waves.

If the frequency of a sound is high, the sound is said to have a high **pitch**. *Pitch* describes the way the sound is heard. For example, a short guitar string vibrates very rapidly. It produces a high-frequency sound that is said to be high-pitched.

Because of the Doppler effect, the pitch of a moving source of sound seems to change. A locomotive horn, for example, will seem to have a higher pitch when it is coming toward you than when it is moving away. The Doppler effect causes the

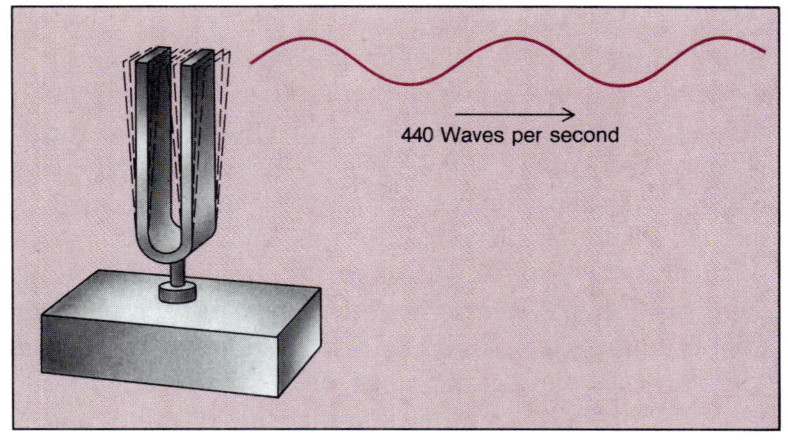

Fig. 7–5 The frequency of the sound produced by this tuning fork is 440 waves per second or 440 Hz.

frequency of the sound waves to increase as the source moves toward you. As it moves away, the frequency decreases and so the pitch is lowered.

Since sound waves always move at the same speed through air at a certain temperature, you can find the wavelength of a sound wave if you know its frequency. For example, find the wavelength of the sound waves with a frequency of 440 Hz produced by a tuning fork at 20°C. The relationship among speed, frequency, and wavelength is:

$$\text{speed } (v) = \text{frequency } (f) \times \text{wavelength } (\lambda)$$

$$\lambda = \frac{v}{f} = \frac{343 \text{ m/s}}{440 \text{ waves/s}} = 0.78 \text{ m/wave}$$

Skill: To practice *problem solving,* work out several sample problems on the board.

As the frequency of a wave increases, its wavelength decreases. Thus a high-pitched sound is made of waves with short wavelengths. A low-pitched sound has longer wavelengths. See Fig. 7–6.

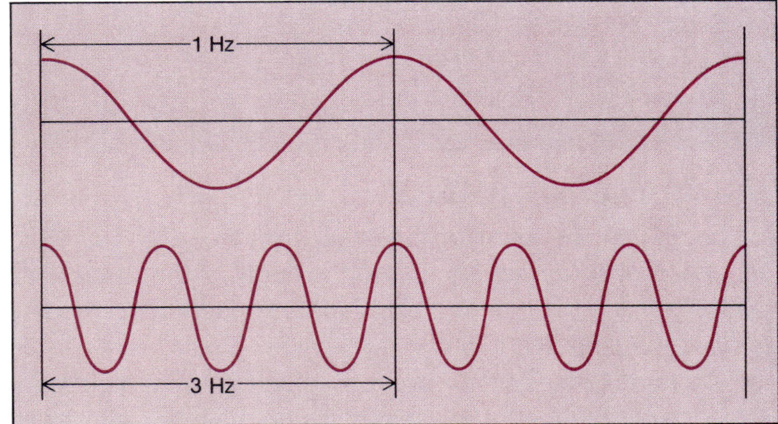

Fig. 7–6 As the wavelength of a sound increases, its frequency decreases.

Fig. 7–7 An echo is produced when sound waves are reflected from a barrier.

Sound waves carry energy. The amount of energy carried by sound waves helps to determine the *loudness* or *intensity* of the sound. You have probably heard sounds like a sonic boom that were loud enough to shake walls. Most sound waves, however, carry only a small amount of energy. Sound energy is carried by the vibration of the particles of the medium through which the sound travels. This back-and-forth motion is usually not very great. Therefore, the energy involved is not large. Also, sound waves spread out. As you move farther away from a source of sound, less energy from the waves reaches your ear. The sound grows fainter as the distance increases. Sometimes sound waves hit a barrier that does not absorb their energy. Then the waves are reflected and you hear an *echo*. See Fig. 7–7.

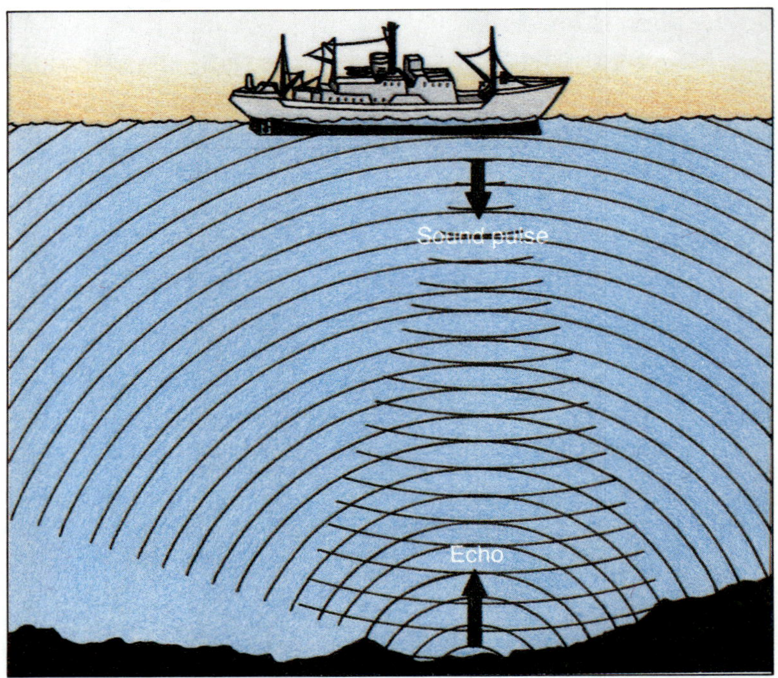

Fig. 7–8 To find the depth and shape of the ocean bottom, sound waves from the front of the ship are directed to the sea floor. The reflected sound waves are picked up by a receiver at the rear of the ship.

USING SOUND WAVES

Echoes can be used to measure distance. Ships use the echoes from sound waves to find the depth of the water. This device is called *sonar.* See Fig. 7–8. A sonar "pinger" in the front of the ship sends out sound waves. These waves strike the sea floor. Some of the waves are reflected back to the ship. A receiver in the rear of the ship picks up the reflected waves.

The time needed for the reflected waves to return as an echo is measured. For example, suppose the sound waves were sent and received as an echo in one second. The speed of sound in water is 1,460 m/s at 20°C. Thus the total distance the sound traveled in a complete trip from the ship to the bottom and back to the ship would be about 1,460 meters. Then the depth of the water would be half of that distance, or 730 meters.

Sonar can be used to map the sea floor and to find objects underwater as well as to measure depth. Porpoises and whales use a method similar to sonar to locate objects in the water.

Word study: Ultrasonic from *ultra* (L.), beyond, and *sonus* (L.), sound.

Sound waves with frequencies above 20,000 Hz have many special uses. These very high-frequency sounds are called **ultrasonic**. The human ear cannot hear *ultrasonic* sound waves. See Table 7–2.

Ultrasonic Sound waves with frequencies above 20,000 Hz.

FREQUENCIES RECEIVED AND PRODUCED BY PEOPLE AND SOME OTHER ANIMALS		
Animal	Frequency Heard (hertz)	Frequency Produced (hertz)
Human	20–20,000	85–1,100
Dog	15–50,000	452–1,800
Cat	60–65,000	760–1,500
Bat	1,100–120,000	10,000–120,000
Porpoise	150–150,000	7,000–120,000
Frog	50–10,000	50–8,000
Robin	250–21,000	2,000–13,000

Table 7–2

Ultrasonic waves are used in industry for cleaning. The objects to be cleaned are put into a liquid. Ultrasonic waves are sent through the liquid. This causes the particles of the liquid to vibrate. The rapid vibration of the particles in the liquid can easily scrub the object. Ultrasonic waves can also be sent through solid objects to find cracks or other hidden flaws. The waves are reflected from the cracks. Ultrasonic waves are also used in medicine. They can be reflected from internal parts of the body to give an image like that produced

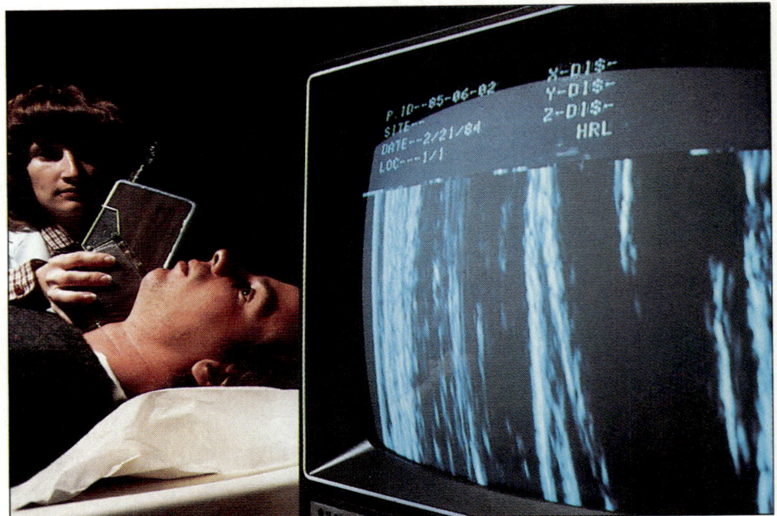

Fig. 7–9 Doctors use ultrasound waves to form images of the inside of a human body.

by the use of X-rays. See Fig. 7–9. These ultrasound pictures are helpful in examining unborn babies and in the diagnosis of kidney stones.

SUMMARY

Sound waves consist of back-and-forth motions of the particles of the medium through which the sound moves. The way we hear sound depends on the properties of the sound waves. Reflection of sound waves through water and other materials makes them useful in navigation, industry, and medicine.

QUESTIONS

Use complete sentences to write your answers.

1. What is a sound wave?
2. What is the pitch of a sound?
3. Describe how a sound is made.
4. Sound travels at 350 m/s in air. If you hear the echo of a sound in 6.0 s, how far away is the reflecting surface?
5. How can ultrasonic sound waves be used?
6. Sound travels at 1,460 m/s in water. Suppose sonar equipment aboard a ship sends out a signal and receives it back from the ocean bottom 0.5 s later. How deep is the ocean at that point?

1. A sound wave is a longitudinal wave moving through air or some other medium.
2. The pitch is the highness or lowness of a sound. It is determined by the number of vibrations per second that a person hears.
3. Sound is generated by a vibrating object.
4. $d = v \times t = 350\ \text{m/s} \times 6.0\ \text{s} = 2{,}100\ \text{m}$. The distance to the surface is then $\frac{1}{2} \times 2{,}100\ \text{m} = 1{,}050\ \text{m}$.
5. Ultrasonic sound waves can be used to clean objects by causing them to vibrate. They can also be used to detect cracks and flaws in objects.
6. In 0.5 s the sound travels 730 m (1,460 m/s × 0.5 s). Therefore the ocean bottom is 365 m deep (730 m × ½).

SKILL-BUILDING ACTIVITY

See teacher's commentary for teaching hints, safety, and answers to questions.

SOUND

PURPOSE: You will observe some of the properties of sound.

MATERIALS:

tuning fork	shoe box
wad of aluminum foil	balloon
string	meter stick
beaker of water	metal rod
rubber band	straight pin

PROCEDURE:

A. Gently tap the tuning fork on the rubber heel or sole of your shoe. Observe the results.

1. What do you observe? Record your observations in your notebook.

B. Tap a tuning fork and let it touch a small ball of aluminum foil hanging from a string.

2. What happens to the ball?

C. Tap the tuning fork again and carefully let the prongs touch the surface of the water in the beaker.

3. What happens to the water? Why?

D. Stretch a rubber band across the narrow end of an open shoe box. Pull the rubber band slightly to the side and release it. See Fig. 7–10.

4. What do you observe about the rubber band?

E. Now stretch the rubber band across the wide end of the shoe box. Pluck the rubber band as in step D.

5. What is the effect of stretching the rubber band more?

F. Blow up a balloon. Stretch the neck of the balloon and allow air to escape.

6. What do you observe at the neck of the balloon?
7. State a hypothesis explaining each of your observations in step A through step F.

G. Use a meter stick and a metal rod of the same length. Place the stick on a table so that one end extends over the edge.

H. Have a partner tap one end of the meter stick with a straight pin. Place your ear at the other end of the stick.

8. Can you hear the tapping?

I. Replace the stick with the metal rod and repeat step H.

9. Can you hear the tapping better through the metal rod or the meter stick?
10. Which medium transmits sound better, wood or metal?

CONCLUSION:

1. In your own words, describe how sound is produced and tell how the medium affects the sound traveling through it.

Fig. 7–10

7-2. Music and Noise

At the end of this section you will be able to:

- Compare a musical and a nonmusical sound.
- Explain how two or more sound waves affect each other.
- Describe how an instrument produces a musical sound.

Fig. 7–11 shows two musical instruments. Below each is an electronic trace of the sound waves produced by the instrument. In what way are the sounds produced by the instruments alike?

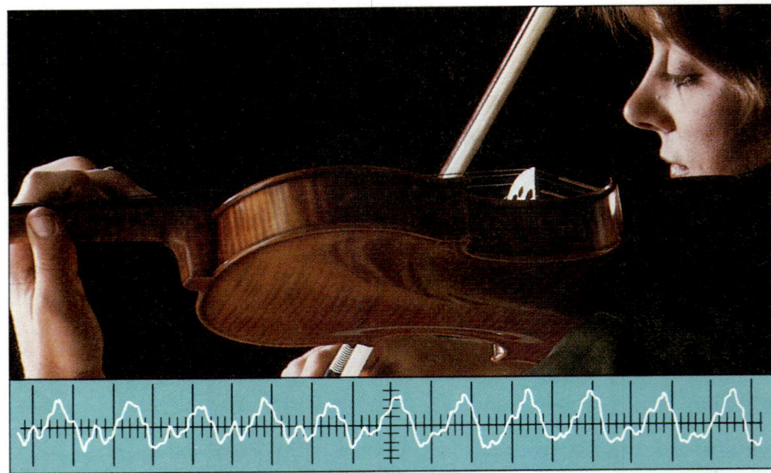

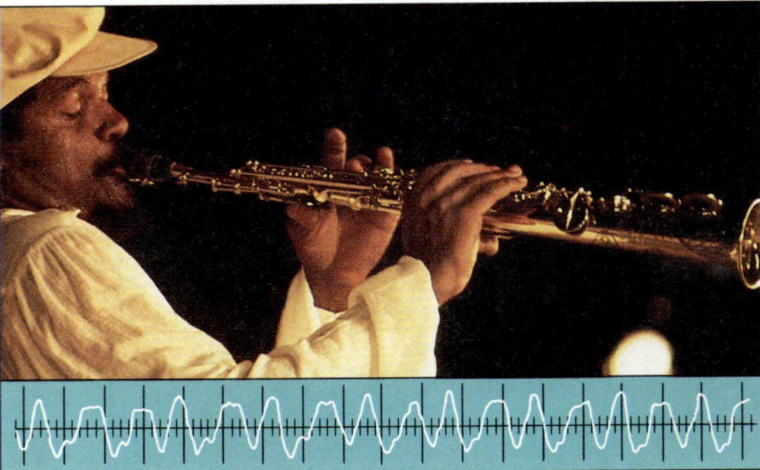

Fig. 7–11 The oscilloscope traces beneath the violin and the clarinet show the characteristic sound waves produced by each instrument.

MUSICAL SOUNDS

What is the basic difference between a musical sound and a nonmusical sound? All sounds are made by a series of waves. Do the waves that make up music have some special property that makes them different from other sound waves? One way to study sound waves is with an electronic device called an *oscilloscope*. An oscilloscope looks somewhat like a small television set. The screen of the oscilloscope shows a picture of sound waves. See Fig. 7–12. The sound wave is shown as if it is a transverse wave so that its properties can be seen more easily.

Fig. 7–12 This photo shows what an image on an oscilloscope screen looks like.

If you compare the waves making up different musical sounds, you will see that they are alike in one way: Every musical sound is made up of a regular wave pattern. For example, a tuning fork makes a musical tone when struck. Its sound is made by waves of only one frequency. A fork tuned to middle C vibrates at 256 Hz. Each wave produced by the fork repeats the same frequency. As the fork slowly stops vibrating, the sound dies away. But the sound waves keep the same pattern while they become less energetic. Most music is not made up of waves with the same frequency. What happens to these sound waves when they meet?

Enrichment: Demonstrate the use of an oscilloscope to analyze the sounds of a tuning fork and a voice.

INTERFERENCE

When two or more waves arrive at the same place at the same time, they will affect each other by a process called **interference** (int-er-**fir**-unts). Two waves that are identical, or in phase, will combine to make a single wave. The new wave has higher crests and lower troughs. This is called constructive interference. See Fig. 7–13. Two sound waves with the same wavelength will make a louder sound with nearly the same pitch. Suppose two waves whose crests and troughs are out of phase come together. If their wavelengths are the same, these waves will tend to cancel each other. This is called destructive interference. See Fig. 7–14. Waves that have different wavelengths can also combine to produce a new wave. See Fig. 7–15. The new wave has a wavelength that is different from either of the original waves.

Interference The effect two or more waves have on each other if they overlap.

Enrichment: Two point sources producing circular waves in a ripple tank will produce an interference pattern. Interference can also be demonstrated outdoors using two speakers placed about two meters apart. Play a constant 600 Hz signal from an oscillator through the speakers. Students can move around and hear regions of loud sound and regions of little sound.

Interference affects the way we hear musical sounds. Most music is a mixture of waves whose frequencies are related in

Fig. 7–13 The diagram on the left shows an example of constructive interference.
Fig. 7–14 The middle diagram shows an example of destructive interference.
Fig. 7–15 The diagram on the right shows how two waves can combine to form a more complicated wave.

some simple way. Interference between the waves then produces a repeating pattern in the overall sound. For example, suppose that you strike two piano keys at the same time. One key produces a note with a basic frequency of 262 hertz. The second key produces a note with a frequency of 524 hertz. The frequency of the second note is twice that of the first. The relationship between their frequencies can be expressed by the simple ratio 1:2. Thus the combined sound wave has a repeating pattern. It therefore sounds musical.

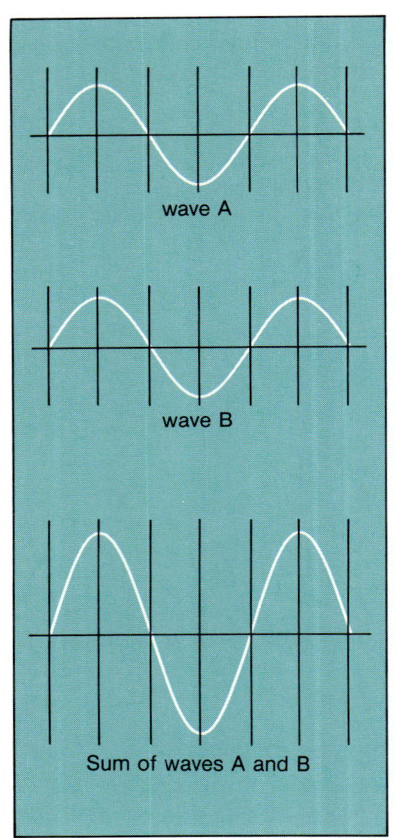

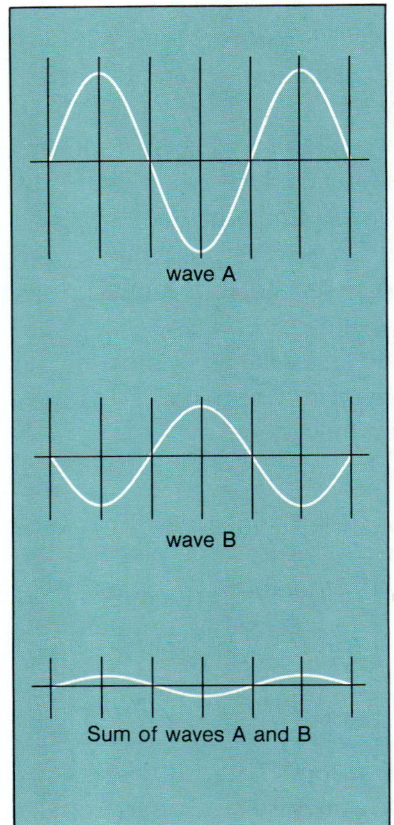

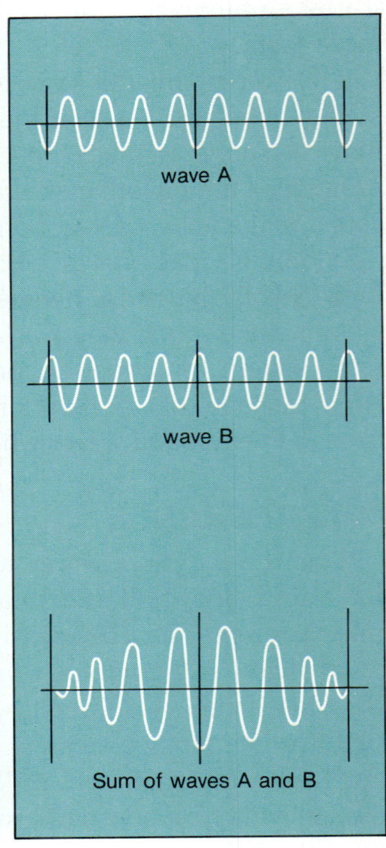

ACOUSTICS

Interference also affects the way we hear music in a concert hall. Many auditoriums have "dead spots" where it is hard to hear the music. These spots are the result of destructive interference in which the sound waves cancel each other. Engineers called acoustical engineers try to design concert halls with no dead spots. The science of sound is *acoustics*. Acoustics is also concerned with the way sound waves are reflected from the walls of a hall. A *reverberation* is a combination of many reflected waves, or echoes. A long reverberation time gives musical sounds a chance to blend properly. In a good concert hall, the reverberation time should be about one second. See Fig. 7–16.

Fig. 7–16 In this room, scientists can study the way sounds are produced and reflected.

MUSICAL INSTRUMENTS

Enrichment: Analyze the sound from several musical instruments by playing a single pitch into a microphone connected to an oscilloscope.

All musical instruments can be classified into one of three groups. Each group of instruments produces musical sounds in a different way. One group is the *stringed* instruments such as a guitar or violin. They use vibrating strings. Pianos also have strings which vibrate by being struck with hammers. A second group is the *wind* instruments, including the trumpet

Fig. 7–17 The fundamental tone combines with overtones to produce the sounds of stringed instruments.

and clarinet. These instruments cause a column of air to vibrate. A third group of instruments produces vibrations when struck. These are the *percussion* instruments like drums and chimes. The word "percussion" means "beating" or "striking."

1. Stringed Instruments. A stretched rubber band vibrates when you pluck it. In the same way, a piece of stretched wire in a violin will vibrate when plucked or scraped with a bow. The wire, called a string, can vibrate along its whole length. It then produces a musical tone called its *fundamental*. However, if the string is plucked near one end, it can also vibrate in parts. For example, a string plucked one-fourth of the way from one end will vibrate in two parts. It vibrates in two parts at the same time that it is vibrating as a whole. See Fig. 7–17. As the string vibrates in two parts, it produces a second, higher pitched, sound called the first *overtone*. The overtone blends with the fundamental to produce a musical sound. The string can be plucked at different spots to produce many different overtones. See Fig. 7–18.

Resonance The ability of objects to respond to sounds of certain frequencies.

One vibrating object can make something else vibrate without touching it. You probably have noticed that loud sounds cause loose windows and small objects to rattle. This ability of objects to respond to sounds with certain frequencies is called **resonance**. The frequency of a sound must be just right to cause *resonance* in an object. A loose window, for example, will only vibrate in response to sounds with a certain frequency. The window then vibrates with the same frequency. The sound it produces adds to the original sound to make it louder.

Many musical instruments use resonance. For example, the body of a violin vibrates in sympathy with the sounds produced by the strings. See Fig. 7–19. These vibrations add to the mixture of sound waves that are characteristic of the violin. A piano has a sounding board that adds to its sound by resonance. A note played on a violin sounds different from the same note played on a piano. We say that the *quality* of the sound is different. The quality of an instrument depends on its fundamental tone and overtones.

Fig. 7–18 By shortening or lengthening the strings, a player can produce many different sounds from a guitar.

2. Wind Instruments. Blow across the top of an empty bottle. You will make a sound. This sound is a result of resonance in the column of air inside the bottle. If you put some water into the bottle, a different sound results. This is because the air column is now shorter. The length of the column of air in the bottle determines the frequency of its resonance.

Wind instruments also produce sound by resonance in a column of air. For example, a trumpet player makes a buzzing noise with his or her lips on the mouthpiece. These vibrations cause sympathetic vibrations in the air trapped inside the instrument. The player changes the pitch by changing the vibrations of the lips. However, the air column in the instrument can only respond to a limited number of frequencies. The player produces many different notes by changing the length of the air column with valves. See Fig. 7–20. Other wind instruments, such as the clarinet, use vibrations produced by a reed or thin piece of material held against the mouthpiece. The vibrations of the reed cause resonance in the air column inside the clarinet. A system of holes and valves along the instrument changes the length of this air column. There are many different kinds of wind instruments. But they all produce their music by causing resonance in a column of trapped air.

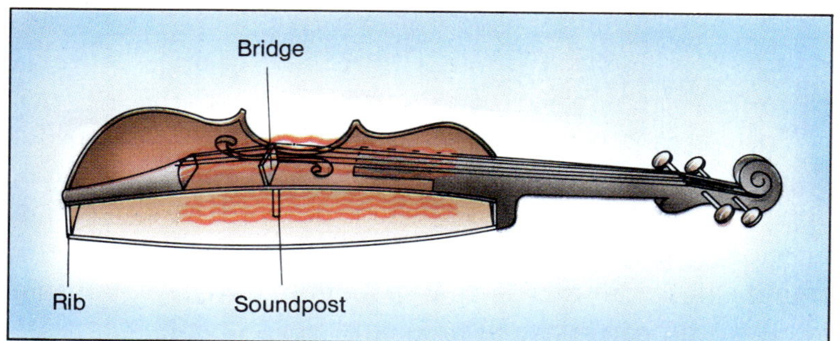

Fig. 7–19 The body of a violin vibrates in resonance with the vibration of the strings to produce the sound associated with a violin.

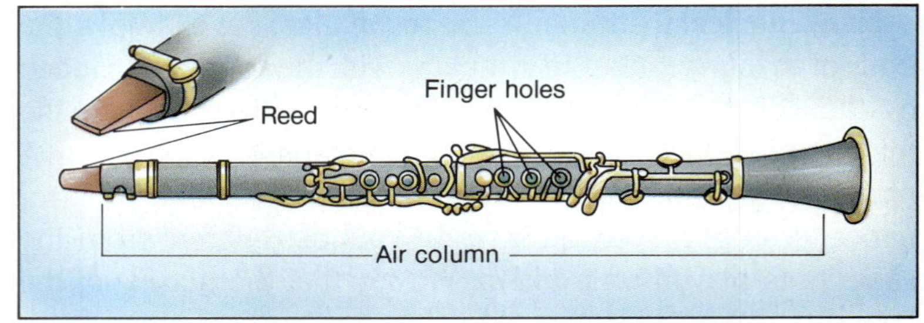

Fig. 7–20 In a clarinet, closing and opening the holes changes the length of the air column and thus the pitch of the sound that is produced.

3. Percussion Instruments. A drum is the oldest kind of musical instrument. Drums are made by stretching a piece of thin material across a wooden or metal frame. This is called the *head* of the drum. The head vibrates when it is struck. See Fig. 7–21. The sound waves produced are unlike other musical sounds. A drum produces a burst of waves with no particular frequency. Usually, the waves have a low pitch. The sound quickly dies out unless the head is struck again. Other percussion instruments, such as chimes, make sounds when a solid material such as brass is struck.

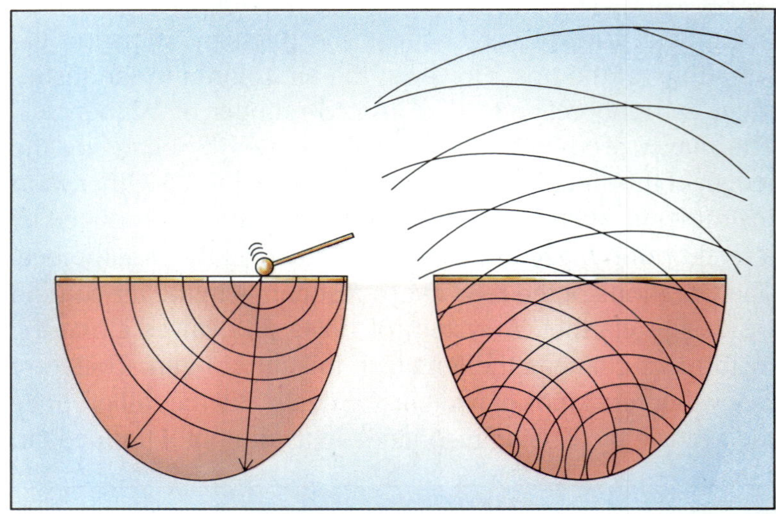

Fig. 7–21 Striking the head of a drum produces sound waves, which are reflected from points inside the drum. These reflected waves combine and the sound bounces out of the top of the drum.

NOISE REDUCTION

Music and noise are both made up of sound waves. But noise is a random mixture of frequencies with no pattern. Sounds without a repeating pattern do not have a pleasant effect. However, noise can be more than just an unpleasant sound. Noise can be a form of pollution. Constant exposure to noise can cause health problems. For example, exposure to loud noise can cause a permanent loss of hearing. Loudness of sounds is measured in units called *decibels* (dB). Each increase of 10 dB doubles the loudness of the sound you hear. Exposure to sound levels above 90 dB can cause hearing

Enrichment: If a decibel meter is available, have students monitor sound levels at various places around your school. Street noises and plane traffic might also provide interesting results.

THE DECIBEL LEVELS OF SOME COMMON SOUNDS		
Transportation and Industry Noise Levels	Loudness (decibels)	Community Noise Levels
Jet plane at takeoff	135	Air-raid siren
	130	Thunder
New York subway	120	
Chain saw	115	Rock concert
Loud motorcycle	110	
Snowmobile	125	Loud conversation
Loud outboard motor	100	Power mower
Air hammer	95	Police siren
Farm tractor	90	Loud singing
	85	
Heavy traffic	80	Noisy restaurant
Average factory	75	Vacuum cleaner
Average car accelerating	70	Noisy office
	65	Normal conversation
Busy freeway	60	Average office
	55	Background music
Light traffic	50	Average home
	45	Quiet street
	30	Quiet auditorium
	20	Faint whisper
	10	Rustling leaves
	0	

Table 7–3

damage. Usually the ability to hear high-frequency sounds is lost. Constant exposure to loud noise also can cause high blood pressure. Sounds of 160 dB can cause permanent loss of hearing. Table 7–3 shows the typical decibel rating of some sounds.

It is hard to shut out noise from a building. However, there are ways to control noise pollution. One way is to close off openings to the outside. Some buildings are made without windows to help control noise. Acoustical engineers also try to reduce noise levels in buildings by using special materials. These materials absorb some of the sound energy. Another method of reducing noise is to stop it at its source. For example, automobiles have mufflers to reduce the noise produced by their engines. Engineers try to make jet engines that produce the least amount of noise. But there are so many different sources of noise, particularly in cities, that control is not easy. It is also important to remember that any loud sound, even loud music, can cause hearing problems.

SUMMARY

Musical sounds are made up of waves with a characteristic pattern. The way we hear sound is affected by interference and resonance. Each kind of musical instrument produces sound in one of three ways. Exposure to loud noise or music can cause hearing loss and other health problems.

QUESTIONS

Use complete sentences to write your answers.

1. Compare the sound of a person whistling with the sound of a person scratching fingernails on a chalkboard.
2. Describe an example of the interference of sound waves.
3. Explain how interference affects the way you hear music in a concert hall.
4. What is the difference between a reverberation and an echo?
5. Describe how each of the following musical instruments produces a sound: (a) violin, (b) trumpet, (c) drum.
6. How does resonance affect the ways a violin produces sound?

1. Whistling is a musical sound caused by regular vibrations of air; scratching is a nonmusical sound caused by irregular vibrations of the vibrating object.
2. Two sound waves of the same frequency can interfere with each other to produce a louder sound or softer sound. When crests combine with crests the sound is louder. If crests combine with troughs the sound is softer.
3. Destructive interference in a concert hall can cause "dead spots" where it is hard to hear the music.
4. A reverberation is a combination of many echoes.
5. (a) A violin uses vibrating strings to produce sound. (b) A trumpet uses a vibrating column of air to produce sound. (c) A drum uses a vibrating membrane to produce sound.
6. Resonance in the body of a violin causes it to vibrate in sympathy with the vibrating strings. These vibrations add to the mixture of sound waves characteristic of the violin.

CAREERS IN SCIENCE

ACOUSTICAL ENGINEER

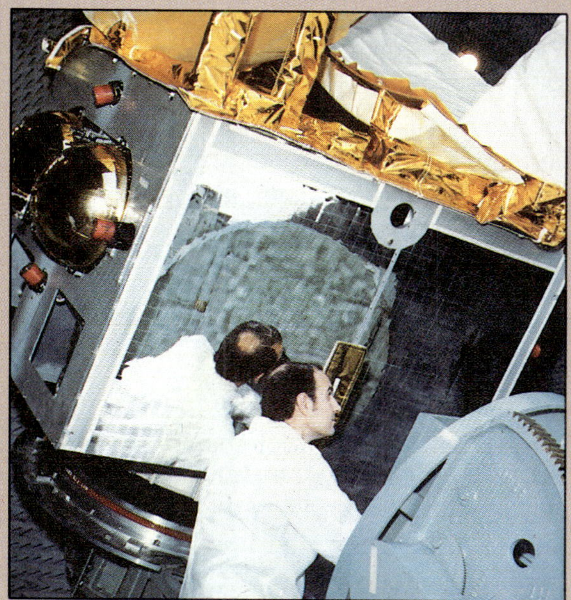

Engineering uses the principles and theories of science to solve practical technical problems. Acoustical engineers concentrate on sound. Perhaps their best-known work is the design of theaters and concert halls so that the sounds made on stage project most effectively to the audience. But acoustical engineers also find ways to reduce noise, design detection systems for ships and submarines, create ultrasonic diagnostic equipment to help doctors look inside the human body, engineer instruments used to check manufactured products for hidden defects, and produce acoustical microscopes.

Most acoustical engineers have degrees in electrical or mechanical engineering with a specialization in acoustics. Career opportunities in this field are expanding, as more electronic devices contain synthesized voice components.

For further information, contact: National Society of Professional Engineers, 2029 K Street NW, Washington, DC 20006.

ULTRASOUND TECHNICIAN

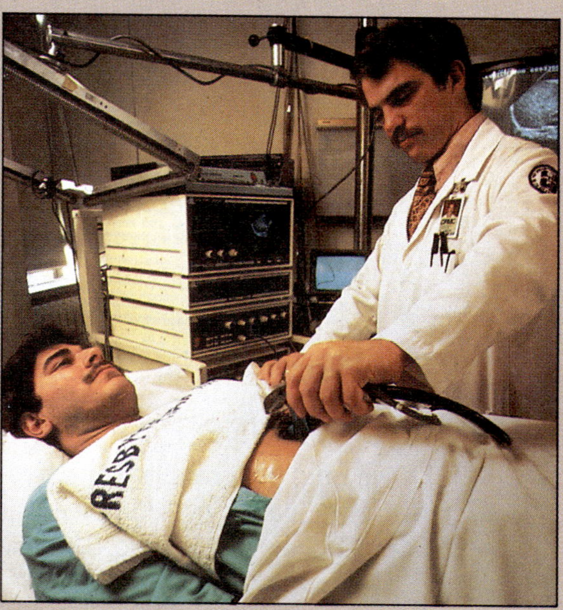

Ultrasound is a medical diagnostic technique that uses sound waves to create images of what is going on inside the human body. Ultrasound technicians, or sonographers, work primarily in obstetrics, providing information about the growth and development of unborn babies. In addition, they employ their skills to scan internal organs. Ultrasound helps to detect cysts and tumors in the brain. It can measure the functioning of the valves and chambers in the heart. In the eye, it is used to check for detached retinas.

Sonographers must complete a one-year training program and are usually required to have completed high school and two years of college before entering training. College preparation should emphasize mathematics and the life sciences.

For further information, contact: American Society of Ultrasound Technical Specialists, Box 1676, University of Kansas, Medical Center, Kansas City, KS 64103.

CHAPTER REVIEW

See teacher's commentary for answers.

VOCABULARY

On a separate piece of paper, match each term with the number of the statement that best explains it. Use each term only once.

interference resonance ultrasonic sound wave
pitch

1. A longitudinal wave moving through air or some other medium.
2. A property that describes the highness or lowness of a sound; it is determined mainly by the frequency of the sound waves.
3. Sound waves with frequencies above 20,000 hertz.
4. The effect two or more waves have on each other if they overlap.
5. The ability of objects to respond to sounds of certain frequencies.

QUESTIONS

Give brief but complete answers to each of the following questions. Unless otherwise indicated, use complete sentences to write your answers.

1. Choose a wave motion other than sound and describe how it is similar to sound waves and also how it differs from sound waves.
2. Describe the motion of the air particles as a sound wave passes.
3. How does the speed of sound in steel and other materials compare with the speed of sound in air?
4. Give an example of a musical sound and a nonmusical sound. Explain why one is musical and the other is not.
5. Describe how the loudness of sound can affect people. Have you ever been affected by sound in this way? Describe your experience.
6. What is an echo?
7. What is the speed of sound in air at 0°C? At 30°C?
8. You see an explosion and 15 seconds later hear the noise. How far away is the explosion? Show how you got your answer.
9. Find the wavelength of a sound wave with a frequency of 400 Hz (a) if the temperature is 20°C, (b) if the temperature is 30°C.
10. Name three types of musical instruments. Describe how each type produces its sound.
11. How does the speed of sound change when the temperature changes?
12. How are ultrasonic sound waves used to clean objects? How else can ultrasonic waves be used?

13. Describe a longitudinal wave and explain how it differs from a transverse wave. Give one example of each.

APPLYING SCIENCE

1. Visit a local audio store and collect brochures on phonographs and tape recorders. Using simple diagrams, explain how each one operates. How is a phonograph record different from a tape?
2. Hold a tuning fork over a piece of large diameter (4 to 5 cm) tubing. When you strike the tuning fork, you may hear a magnified sound. The length of the tubing must be "just right." The length is related to the wavelength of the sound. Report on and demonstrate what you observe.
3. Look up the work of Robert A. Moog and the Moog Electronic Music Synthesizer. Find a recording that uses the Moog Synthesizer and play part of it for your class. Write a report on the synthesizer.
4. How is a recording of an orchestra concert made? How does a studio recording differ from a live recording?
5. Do sound waves travel through a vacuum? Place a battery-operated buzzer or doorbell in a bell jar connected to a vacuum pump. Can you hear the buzzer after the air is pumped out of the bell jar? Demonstrate this result to the class.
6. Find the speed of sound in air. Have two people stand at least 45 meters apart. One person should make a sound by hitting two pieces of wood together. (Other sources of sound are also possible.) The other person should use a stopwatch to measure how long it takes to hear the sound. Divide the distance by this time to find the speed.

BIBLIOGRAPHY

Deutsch, D. "Musical Illusions." *Scientific American*, October 1975.

Dunkle, T. "The Sound of Silence." *Science 82*, April 1982.

Knight, D.C. *Silent Sound*. New York: Morrow, 1980.

Rossing, T.D. *Science of Sound: Musical, Electronic, Environmental*. Reading, MA: Addison-Wesley, 1981.

Tannenbaum, B., et. al. *Understanding Sound*. New York: McGraw-Hill, 1973.

Wade, H. *Sound*. Milwaukee: Raintree Publications Ltd., 1977.

Wilson, R. *The Voice of Music*. New York: Atheneum, 1977.

CHAPTER

8

These glass tubes are carrying light waves. Many tubes or fibers can be combined into fiber optic cables to provide telephone communication to cities and towns at the speed of light.

LIGHT

CHAPTER GOALS

1. Name and describe the six waves that make up the electromagnetic spectrum.
2. Describe the motion of light waves and explain how to calculate the index of refraction of a substance.
3. Explain the differences in the way a lens and a mirror produce an image.
4. Compare and contrast two types of lenses.

8-1. The Electromagnetic Spectrum

At the end of this section you will be able to:

- Use examples to show that light behaves like waves.
- Explain what is meant by *electromagnetic waves* and the *electromagnetic spectrum.*
- Name and give the characteristics of six parts of the electromagnetic spectrum.

Have you ever seen a rainbow? The colors in a rainbow are only a small part of a much larger group of waves. All of these waves carry energy. Some of them can be used to cook food in microwave ovens. Others carry AM, FM, and television signals. We cannot see these waves. We only can see the narrow strip of colors that make up visible light.

WAVE-PARTICLE THEORY OF LIGHT

To begin your study of light waves, try this experiment. Make a small pinhole in an index card. Look through the pinhole at a light some distance away. If the hole is very small, you will see the light spread out. That is, the light will appear to be larger than the pinhole through which it is coming. This strange effect can be explained if light is thought of as a series of waves.

This behavior of light is called *diffraction.* Light is diffracted when it passes through a small opening. An example of diffraction is shown in Fig. 8–1. Water waves and sound waves also undergo diffraction. Therefore, scientists believe that light is a result of energy moving as waves.

Other experiments, however, give different results. For example, experiments show that light always transfers energy in the form of small particles. These particles all carry the same amount of energy. These small particles of light energy are called *photons*.

Some experiments show that light is made up of waves. Other experiments show that light is a stream of small particles. This result is often called the *wave-particle theory of light*. However, most of the behavior of light can be explained by thinking only of light waves.

Fig. 8–1 The light from the sun is diffracted when it passes through the small spaces between the branches of these trees.

SPEED OF LIGHT

Light has many of the properties of waves, such as diffraction, reflection, and refraction. See Fig. 8–2. However, light waves have some important differences from other waves. For example, unlike sound, light can move through empty space. Light waves also move much faster than sound waves. Moving with the speed of light, you could make about 7.5 trips around the world in one second. Such great speeds are very hard to measure. It took scientists many centuries to find a way to measure the speed of light.

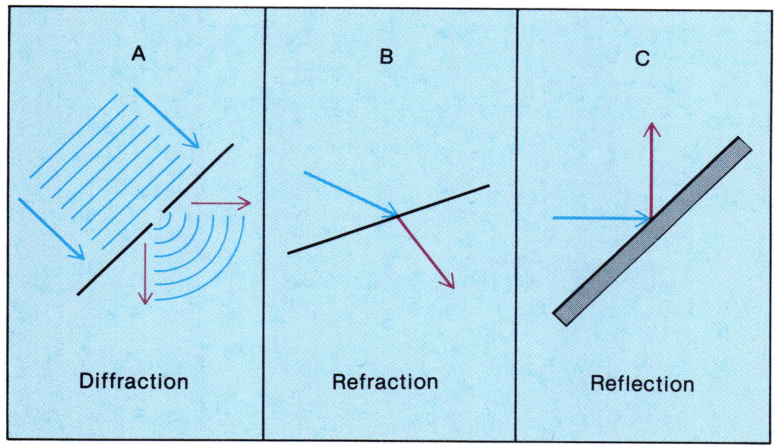

Fig. 8–2 Light is diffracted when it passes through a small opening (a), refracted when its speed changes as it moves from one medium to another (b), and reflected when it hits a barrier (c).

The Italian scientist Galileo tried to measure the speed of light in the 16th century. He tried to measure the time it took light to travel about two kilometers. However, light covers this distance almost instantly. Galileo had no way to measure such a short time. A Danish astronomer named Friedrich Roemer was more successful. In 1675, he was able to measure the time it took light to travel a great distance. He measured the time it took for light from one of Jupiter's moons to travel across the diameter of the earth's orbit. This is how he did it. Roemer observed the times when some of the moons were eclipsed by passing into Jupiter's shadow. The brightest moon of Jupiter is eclipsed every seven days. Roemer found that the eclipse occurred earliest when the earth was nearest Jupiter. When the earth was farthest away, the eclipse was seen a little later. This was because the light had to travel an additional distance equal to the earth's orbit. See Fig. 8–3. Dividing the diameter of the earth's orbit by the greatest difference between

Fig. 8–3 When Jupiter is farther away from the earth, as shown in the right diagram, it takes longer for the light from its moon to reach the earth. Roemer was able to use this time difference to find a value for the speed of light.

the times of the eclipses gave Roemer a value for the speed of light. His result was not accurate because the exact diameter of the earth's orbit was not known in his day. Modern scientists now have very accurate ways to measure light's great speed. This speed has been found to be 3.0×10^8 m/s in a vacuum. (The number 3.0×10^8 means that the decimal point is moved eight places to the right: $3.0 \times 10^8 = 300,000,000$.)

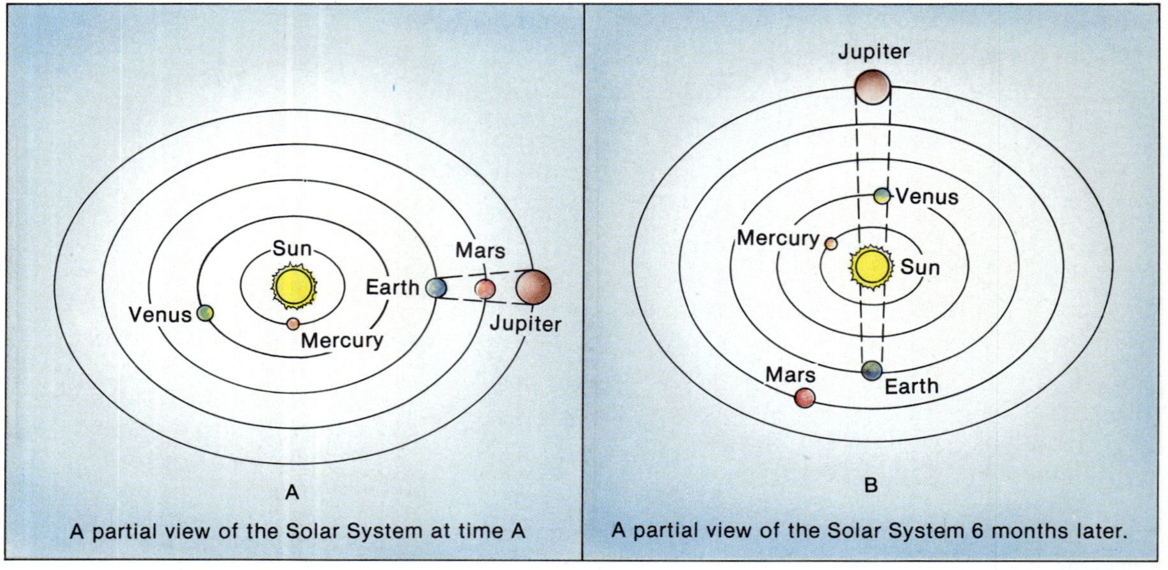

ELECTROMAGNETIC WAVES

Electromagnetic waves A form of energy that moves through empty space at a speed of 3.0×10^8 m/s.

Waves that can move through empty space at the speed of light are called **electromagnetic** (ih-**lek**-troe-mag-*net*-ik) **waves.** Visible light waves are not the only form of *electromagnetic waves.* Radio waves also move through empty space at 3.0×10^8 m/s. Thus radio waves are also electromagnetic waves. There are many other electromagnetic waves. For example, microwaves used to cook food are electromagnetic waves.

Different electromagnetic waves are usually identified by their frequencies. (Remember, frequency is the number of complete waves passing a point in one second.) All of these waves have frequencies between 10^4 and 10^{21} hertz (Hz). Visible light has a frequency of about 10^{14} Hz. The frequency of microwaves is about 10^9 Hz. We can see only those electromagnetic waves with a frequency around 10^{14} Hz.

PARTS OF THE ELECTROMAGNETIC SPECTRUM

All electromagnetic waves known to exist are part of the **electromagnetic spectrum.** A chart of the *electromagnetic spectrum* is shown in Fig. 8–4. The major parts of the electromagnetic spectrum are:

Electromagnetic spectrum All of the electromagnetic waves.

1. Radio waves. These waves include the parts of the electromagnetic spectrum with low frequencies. Ordinary AM radio broadcasts use frequencies between 535 kilohertz (kHz) and 1,605 kHz. (A kilohertz is 1,000 waves per second.) A layer of the atmosphere, called the *ionosphere*, reflects AM waves back to the earth's surface. Thus AM radio broadcasts can be received far away from the station. FM radio waves have much higher frequencies. These waves have frequencies between 88.1 megahertz (MHz) and 107.9 MHz. (One megahertz is 1,000,000 waves per second.) FM radio waves are not reflected from the atmosphere. This means that FM waves cannot be received as far away as AM waves. Like FM, TV broadcasts also use high-frequency radio waves. For this reason, TV signals cannot travel far. But satellites can relay radio and TV signals half-way around the world. See Fig. 8–5. Each radio or TV station is assigned a certain frequency. Your receiver must be tuned to each frequency. When you change radio stations or TV channels, you are making this adjustment.

Fig. 8–4 This chart shows all the major parts of the electromagnetic spectrum.

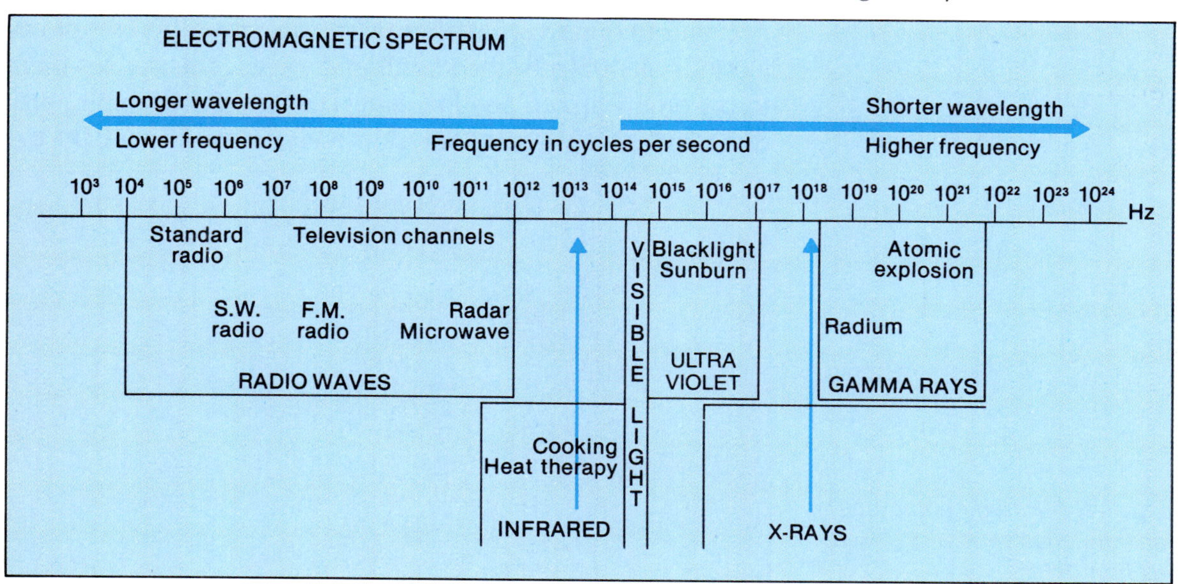

Fig. 8–5 Radio and TV signals can be sent over long distances by reflection from the ionosphere. They can also be relayed by communications satellites.

Radar waves have higher frequencies than FM or TV. Waves at these frequencies are reflected by many materials. For example, most metals reflect radar waves. Reflected radar waves are like reflected sound waves that are heard as an echo. A radar "echo" can be used to "see" objects through darkness or fog, or at a great distance. For this reason, radar is used on ships and planes.

Microwaves, unlike radar, pass through or are easily absorbed by many materials. For example, microwaves pass through glass but are absorbed by water. When a material absorbs microwaves, it is heated. Thus moist food can be heated in a microwave oven in a glass dish. The food gets hot, but the glass dish does not.

Word study: Infrared from *infra* (L.), below, and the color red.

2. Infrared waves. Infrared waves are given off by hot objects. Cooler objects absorb infrared waves. This causes them to become warmer. See Fig. 8–6. The sun, for example, produces infrared waves. Your skin feels warm in sunlight be-

Fig. 8–6 Infrared heat lamps like the ones shown are used as hair dryers.

cause it absorbs infrared waves. A dark surface absorbs infrared waves better than a light-colored surface. This is the reason that light-colored clothing feels cooler in hot summer sunlight.

3. Visible light waves. A very narrow band of frequencies higher than infrared can be seen with the eye. We see different frequencies within this narrow band as different colors. The lowest frequencies of visible light are seen as red. The highest frequencies appear as blue or violet. Electromagnetic waves with frequencies above or below the visible part of the spectrum cannot be seen by the human eye. The colors we see in a rainbow are part of the visible spectrum. You will learn more about how we see color in Chapter 9.

Word study: Ultraviolet from *ultra* (L.), beyond, and the color violet.

4. Ultraviolet waves. The waves in this part of the electromagnetic spectrum are at frequencies just above visible light. Ultraviolet waves in sunlight cause *sunburn*. Too much ultraviolet light can be dangerous. It may cause serious skin damage, including skin cancer. But ultraviolet light can also kill germs. It is often used for this purpose in hospitals.

Enrichment: Get some exposed and discarded X-ray film from a doctor or hospital. Display the film on an overhead projector to show the different absorption by bones and tissues of various organs.

5. X-rays. These high-frequency electromagnetic waves are very useful in medicine. X-rays easily pass through skin and other tissues, but not through bone. They can produce a photograph on film or a picture on a screen. This means that X-rays can be used to see inside your body. You probably have had X-ray photographs made of parts of your body by a doctor or dentist. See Fig. 8–7. However, too much exposure to X-rays can kill living cells. Machines that produce X-rays must be used only by trained persons.

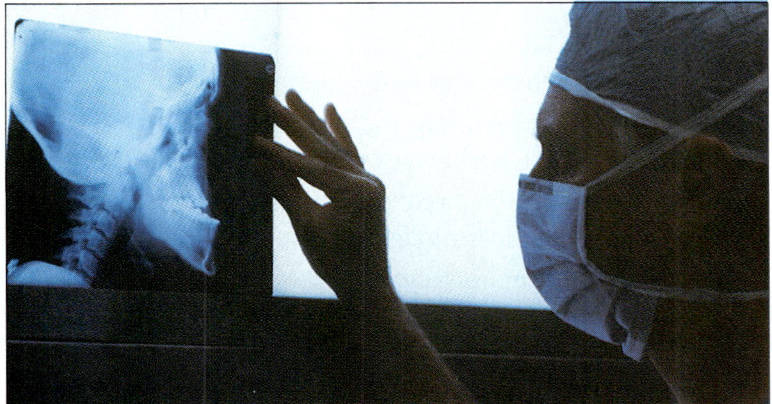

Fig. 8–7 This surgeon is studying an X-ray photograph of a human skull.

6. Gamma rays. Gamma rays are similar to X-rays. However, they are much more dangerous. They can pass through matter more easily. Gamma rays are useful in fighting cancer. Cancer cells are more easily killed by gamma rays than are normal cells. Beams of gamma rays can be aimed at the location of the cancer. See Fig. 8–8. The rays can pass deep into the body to reach and kill the cancer cells.

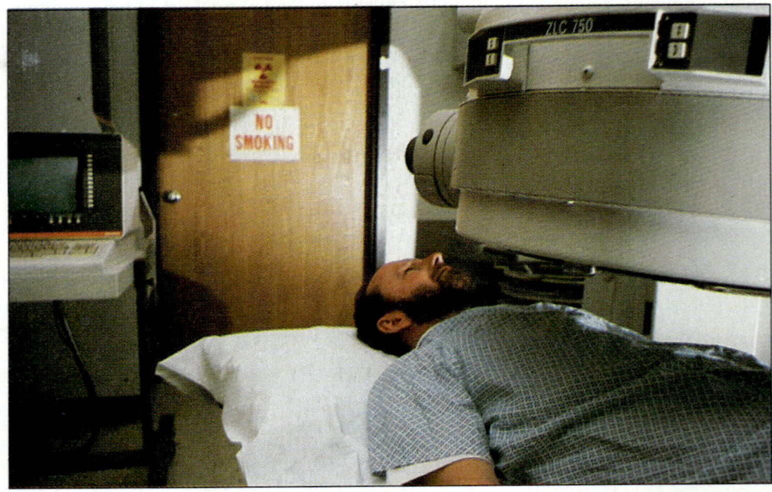

Fig. 8–8 This device uses gamma rays to kill cancer cells. The gamma rays can be focused only on the cancer cells and will not harm normal cells.

SUMMARY

Light has properties that cause it to act as if it were made up of waves. Other properties of light are best explained if it is thought of as a stream of photons. Light moves through empty space and travels at very high speeds. The electromagnetic spectrum is made up of light waves of different frequencies.

QUESTIONS

Use complete sentences to write your answers.

1. Describe one experiment that you could do to show that light behaves the way waves do.
2. Name six electromagnetic waves in the order of their frequencies in the electromagnetic spectrum.
3. Choose three electromagnetic waves. Write a brief paragraph describing how these waves are important in your daily life.
4. Why does a microwave oven heat the food but not the dish?

1. Look at a light source through a pinhole in an index card. The light will appear spread out around the hole because of diffraction.
2. The electromagnetic spectrum contains radio waves, infrared waves, visible light, ultraviolet waves, X-rays, and gamma rays.
3. Answers will vary.
4. Microwave ovens heat the water in food but pass through materials like glass dishes.

INVESTIGATION

See teacher's commentary for teaching hints, safety, and answers to questions.

INFRARED WAVES

PURPOSE: You will measure the heating effect of infrared waves from the sun on a light and a dark surface.

MATERIALS:

white cloth or paper
black cloth or paper
2 thermometers

PROCEDURE:

A. Place a piece of white cloth or paper in direct sunlight. Next to the white cloth, place a piece of black cloth or paper.

B. Place a thermometer under each piece of cloth. See Fig. 8–9.

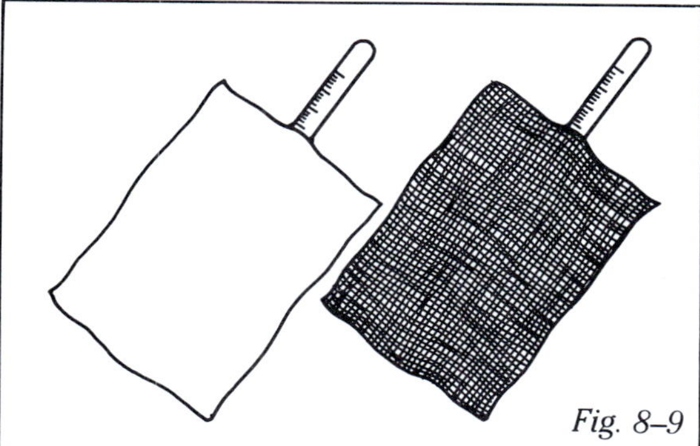

Fig. 8–9

C. Leave both pieces of cloth in the sunlight for four minutes. Read the thermometers.

D. Copy the table below. Record your observations in your notebook.

Covering	Thermometer Reading at Start	Thermometer Reading After 4 Min
White Cloth		
Black Cloth		

1. Which piece of cloth is warmer?

CONCLUSION:

1. Based on what you know about infrared waves, explain why one piece of cloth is warmer than the other.

EXTENSION: You will compare how different colors absorb heat from the sun.

MATERIALS:

3 squares of different colored cellophane
rubber bands
ice cubes
glass plates
clock

PROCEDURE:

A. Wrap an ice cube in each of the cellophane squares. Use a rubber band to secure the wrapping. See Fig. 8–10.

B. Place each ice cube on a glass plate in direct sunlight.

C. Measure how long it takes for each ice cube to melt. Record.

D. Repeat steps A through C two more times.

CONCLUSIONS:

1. Which color absorbed heat fastest?
2. Which color clothing would keep you coolest on a hot, sunny day?

Fig. 8–10

8-2. Movement of Light

At the end of this section you will be able to:

- List several observations showing that light moves in straight lines.
- Name and compare three kinds of mirrors.
- Calculate the *index of refraction* of a substance, given the speed of light in the substance.

Everything we see is visible because light bounces off a surface back to our eyes. High above the earth's atmosphere, the sky is black, not blue. There is nothing in space to reflect light waves. See Fig. 8–11.

Fig. 8–11 There is no atmosphere in outer space to scatter light and produce the blue skies we see on earth. As shown in this photo, the sky above the earth's atmosphere is black.

LIGHT RAYS

Suggestion: A pinhole camera (sometimes called a *camera obscura*) can be used to demonstrate that light travels in straight lines.

Try this experiment. Cut a small hole in the center of four or five index cards. Place them in front of a light. If all the holes are lined up, you can look through the holes and see the light. If you move one card to the side, however, you will not be able to see the light. This simple experiment shows that light waves move in straight lines. The holes must be lined up in a straight path in order for you to see the light.

Light seems to move in a straight path through the air. See Fig. 8–12. The motion of light can be shown by straight lines called **rays.** The *rays* show the path that light follows through a substance such as air.

Rays Straight lines showing the path followed by light.

Fig. 8–12 *The beams of sunlight and shadows in this photo show that light travels in straight lines.*

REFLECTION IN MIRRORS

When light rays strike the surface of a mirror, they are reflected. If the mirror is flat and smooth, it is called a *plane mirror*. Light rays falling on a plane mirror are reflected at the same angle at which they strike the mirror. The incoming rays are the *incident rays*. The angle made by the incident rays and reflected rays are measured from a line at right angles (90 degrees) to the mirror. See Fig. 8–13. The angle of incidence is always equal to the angle of reflection.

When light rays strike a plane mirror, the pattern of the rays is not changed. Each ray is reflected at the same angle at which it strikes. Thus, when you look in a flat mirror, you see an image of everything in front of the mirror. The image is formed by the reflected rays reaching your eyes. The image seems to be the same height as the object. It also seems to be as far behind the mirror as the object is in front of the mirror. See Fig. 8–14. The image seen in a plane mirror is called a *virtual* image. "Virtual" means "not real." A virtual image can be seen only in the mirror. It cannot be projected onto a screen. Look at the path of the rays in Fig. 8–14 as they are reflected. You can see that the image is reversed from right to left when compared with the object. For example, stand in front of a mirror. Reach out with your right hand as if to shake hands with your image in the mirror. Which hand does the image reach out?*

* The image reaches out its left hand.

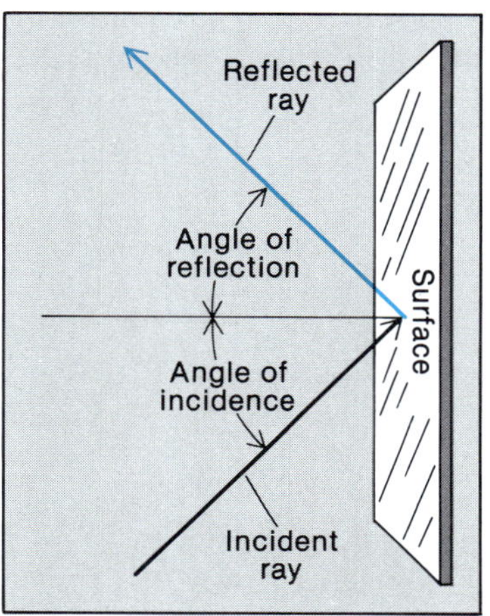

Fig. 8–13 *When light is reflected from a surface, the angle of incidence is equal to the angle of reflection.*

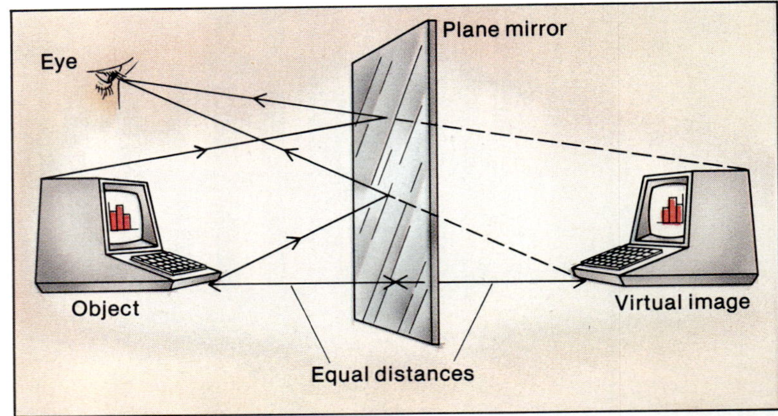

Fig. 8–14 A plane, or flat, mirror forms a virtual image. The image is reversed and appears to be as far behind the mirror as the object is in front of the mirror.

Suppose that the surface of a mirror is not flat but curved. The images in a curved mirror are different from those in a plane mirror. There are two kinds of curved mirrors. One kind of mirror curves inward. This is a **concave mirror**. The other kind of mirror curves outward. It is called a **convex mirror**. The inside of a tennis ball has a *concave* shape. The outside of the ball has a *convex* shape.

Concave mirror A mirror whose surface curves inward.

Convex mirror A mirror whose surface curves outward.

Light rays striking a curved mirror are reflected in the same way as in a plane mirror. However, the curved surface causes the reflected rays to form different kinds of images. For example, a concave mirror causes the reflected rays to come together. See Fig. 8–15. The point in front of the mirror where the reflected rays meet is called the **focus.** The image you see in a concave mirror depends on how far you are from the

Focus A point at which light rays come together.

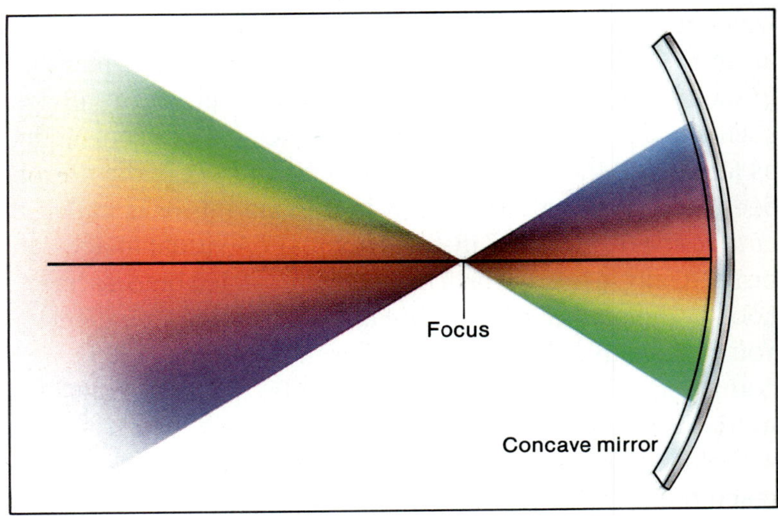

Fig. 8–15 A concave mirror brings light rays to a focus at a point in front of the mirror.

mirror. You will see a magnified virtual image if your eye is between the *focus* and the mirror. For example, hold a concave mirror close to your face. (Shaving mirrors and makeup mirrors are concave.) You will see a virtual image that is larger than your face. Now hold the concave mirror farther away. If your eye is outside the focus, you will see an upside-down image. This image seems to be in front of the mirror. It is called a *real* image. A real image can be projected on a sheet of paper held in front of the mirror. You can see this type of image by looking at the inside of a large, shiny spoon.

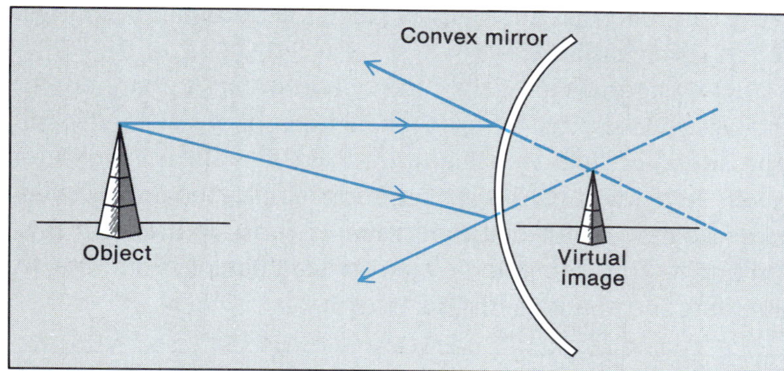

Fig. 8–16 A convex mirror forms a virtual image behind the mirror. The image appears smaller than the object.

Fig. 8–17 A rear-view mirror gives the driver a wide view of objects behind the vehicle.

A convex mirror causes reflected rays to spread out. See Fig. 8–16. The image in a convex mirror is always a virtual image. It is smaller than the object. Everything seen in a convex mirror looks farther away than it really is. However, you can see a wide area in the mirror. You have probably seen convex mirrors used in stores. They are also used as rear-view mirrors on cars and buses. See Fig. 8–17.

Fig. 8–18 As the reflected light rays move from water into air, they are bent, or refracted, into a new path.

REFRACTION

When light rays move from one material into another, their speed changes. For example, when light moves from air into water, it slows down. Light waves travel about 25 percent slower in water than in air. Light moving from water to air speeds up. This change of speed causes light entering or leaving the water to be *refracted*. This means that the light rays are bent into a new path. See Fig. 8–18. Refraction of light makes objects underwater appear to be closer to the surface than they really are. See Fig. 8–19. Refraction also makes water seem less deep than it really is since the bottom looks closer to the surface than it is.

Some materials slow light more than water. A diamond, for example, slows light to less than 50 percent of its speed in air. The speed of light in a diamond is 1.24×10^8 m/sec. As a result, light rays entering a diamond are refracted through very large angles. A cut diamond refracts most of the light rays striking it. Thus most of the rays are sent back to your eyes. A cut diamond sparkles for this reason.

Fig. 8–19 Because light is refracted when it moves from water into air, underwater objects appear closer to the surface than they really are.

The amount by which a material can bend light is given by its *index of refraction*. The index of refraction for any material is found by dividing the speed of light in air by the speed in that material. For example, the index of refraction for a diamond is given by:

$$\text{index of refraction} = \frac{\text{speed of light in air}}{\text{speed of light in diamond}}$$

$$= \frac{3.00 \times 10^8 \text{m/s}}{1.24 \times 10^8 \text{m/s}} = 2.42$$

The index of refraction of some common materials is given in Table 8–1. A large index of refraction means the greatest change in the path of light rays. In other words, the light rays are bent the most.

INDEX OF REFRACTION OF SOME COMMON SUBSTANCES	
Substance	**Index of Refraction**
Air	1.00
Water	1.33
Ice	1.31
Glass (ordinary)	1.52
Glass (heat resistant)	1.61
Diamond	2.42

Table 8–1

FIBER OPTICS

You may have noticed an unusual example of refraction of light rays while swimming. If you swim underwater and look up, the surface of the water acts like a mirror. This happens because many light rays moving from water to air are bent back into the water. This effect is called *internal reflection*. One of the light rays in Fig. 8–18 shows total internal reflection. These light rays are reflected back into the water. They make the water surface look like a mirror when seen from below.

Suggestion: If you hold a glass of water so that you are looking at the underside of the water surface, you can see the phenomenon of total internal reflection.

A kind of "light pipe" can be made by using this method of reflecting light rays. A thin fiber of clear glass or plastic is used. A ray of light can be kept inside the fiber as shown in Fig. 8–20. The light ray zigzags by reflecting first off one side and then the other. The use of fibers to carry light in this way

Enrichment: Some decorative displays use fiber optics. A student may be able to bring one from home and explain to the class how it works.

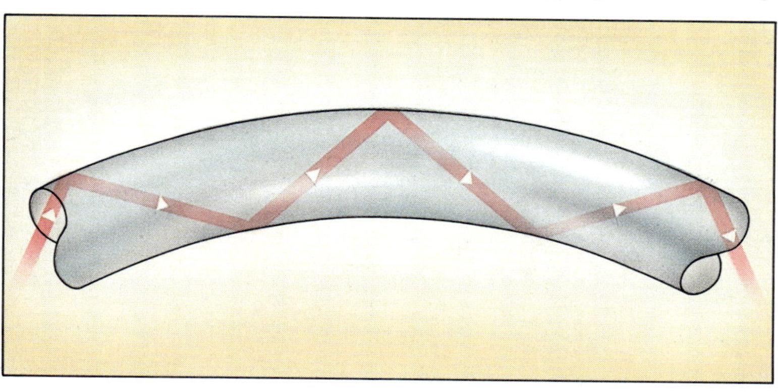

Fig. 8–20 A ray of light is totally internally reflected inside a thin glass or plastic fiber.

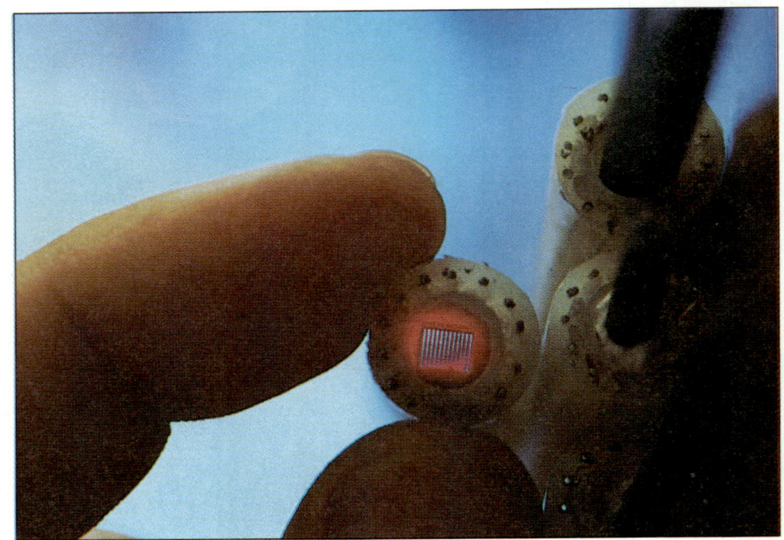

Fig. 8–21 Fiber optic cables like the ones shown here are used in telephone communication systems.

is called *fiber optics*. See Fig. 8–21. Light can be used to carry messages along fiber optic cables. For example, did you know that all of the telephones in downtown Miami use fiber optic cables? Other devices using fiber optics can be used to look inside the human body.

Refraction of light explains the appearance of *mirages* (muh-**rah**-zhez). Mirages are optical illusions. These illusions cause distant objects to seem to be upside down or floating in the air. Mirages occur when light is refracted while passing through air layers of different temperatures. On a warm day, the air close to the ground is warmer than the air at higher levels. Light is refracted by the warm air. This refraction makes distant objects appear to be upside down. See Fig. 8–22. When this happens, you may see a mirage like the one shown in Fig. 8–23. Such mirages are often seen in the desert.

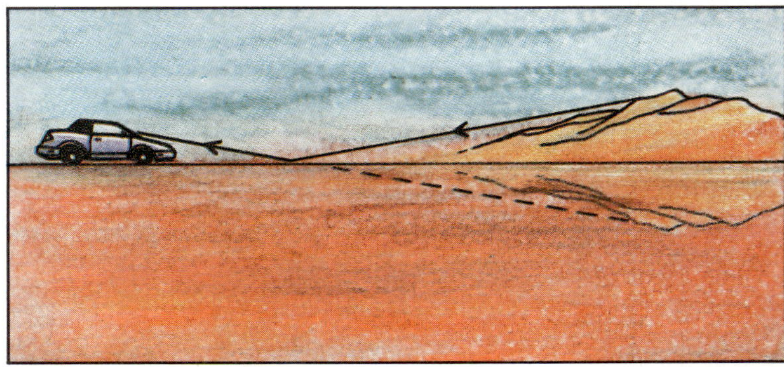

Fig. 8–22 This diagram shows how a mirage is formed when the air close to the ground is warmer than the layer of air above it.

Fig. 8–23 Mirages are often seen in the desert because the air near the ground is hotter than the air above it.

SUMMARY

Light travels in straight lines. A ray is a straight line showing the path followed by light. Reflected light rays from plane or curved mirrors form virtual or real images. Refraction of light occurs when it changes speed in passing from one material to another.

QUESTIONS

Use complete sentences to write your answers.

1. Give three examples to show that light travels in straight lines.
2. Describe three kinds of mirrors and how they differ.
3. The speed of light in a liquid is 2×10^8 m/sec. What is the index of refraction of the liquid? Look at Table 8–1 and name the material.
4. Explain why the water in a clear pool appears to be less deep than it really is.
5. Calculate the speed of light in water and in diamonds.
6. Describe a situation in which an image is behind a mirror. How is the image related to the object? Draw a diagram to show your answer.
7. How does a virtual image differ from a real image? Give an example of each.

1. All of the following show that light travels in straight lines: sighting along the edge of a board to check whether it is straight; looking through holes in several cards; light shining through trees; the sharp shadows cast by a light bulb. Many others may be given.
2. A plane mirror is flat, a convex mirror curves outward, and a concave mirror curves inward.
3. Index of refraction $= \dfrac{3 \times 10^8 \text{ m/s}}{2 \times 10^8 \text{ m/s}} = 1.5$
The substance might be ordinary glass.
4. The path of light reflected from the bottom of the pool is refracted when it moves from the water into the air. This makes the bottom appear closer to the surface.
5. Speed in water $= \dfrac{3 \times 10^8 \text{ m/s}}{1.33} = 2.26 \times 10^8$ m/s
speed of light in diamond $= \dfrac{3 \times 10^8 \text{ m/s}}{2.42} = 1.24 \times 10^8$ m/s
6. If you stand in front of a plane mirror, your image appears to be behind the mirror. The image is reversed left for right. See Fig. 8–14.
7. A real image can be projected on a screen while a virtual image cannot be projected.

SKILL-BUILDING ACTIVITY

See teacher's commentary for teaching hints, safety, and answers to questions.

CONCAVE MIRRORS

PURPOSE: You will measure the focal length of a concave mirror and observe how images in it differ from an image in a plane mirror.

MATERIALS:

light bulb	large white index card or paper
socket	meter stick
110 V outlet	plane mirror
concave mirror	

PROCEDURE:

A. Look at yourself in a plane mirror.
   1. Is your image right side up or upside down?

B. Move closer to the mirror.
   2. What happens to the image as you move closer?
   3. Is your image smaller, larger, or the same height as you?

C. Look at yourself in a concave mirror. Move closer and then farther away from the mirror.
   4. How does your image appear when you are close to the mirror?
   5. Describe any change in the image as you move away from the mirror.

D. Move to the opposite side of the room from the windows. Hold the concave mirror so that the concave surface is facing the windows. Have a partner hold a white index card in front of the mirror. Move the card until you see a clear image of trees or buildings outside the room. Measure the distance from the mirror to the card. This is the focal length of the mirror.
   6. What is the focal length of your mirror?

E. Place a light bulb next to the index card. Turn on the light. Move the concave mirror away from the light until you see a sharp image of the light bulb on the card. Measure the distance from the mirror to the card. See Fig. 8–24.

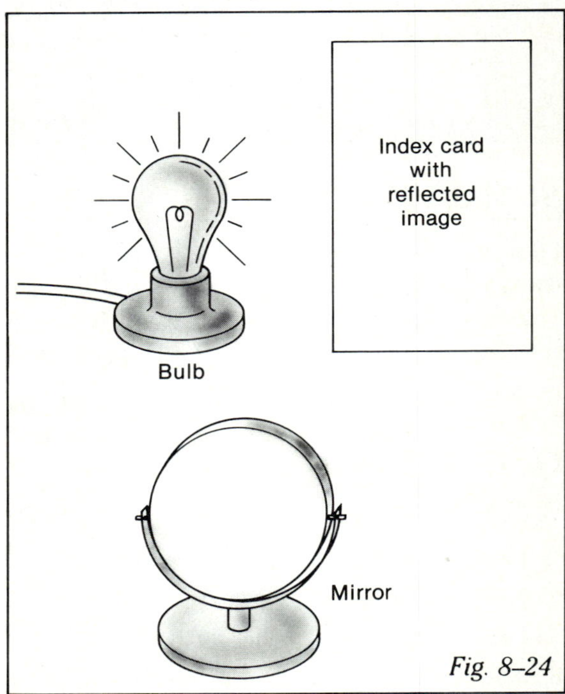

Fig. 8–24

   7. How does this distance compare with the focal length of the mirror?
   8. Is the image right side up?

CONCLUSIONS:

1. How do images in a concave mirror differ from those in a plane mirror?
2. Explain how to find the focal length of a concave mirror. Draw a diagram to show your answer.

8-3. Lenses

At the end of this section you will be able to:

- Explain how a lens produces an image.
- Name and describe the properties of two different kinds of lenses.
- List some of the ways lenses are used.

Fig. 8–25 shows how an image is formed in your eyes. In this section you will learn why everything you see is upside down.

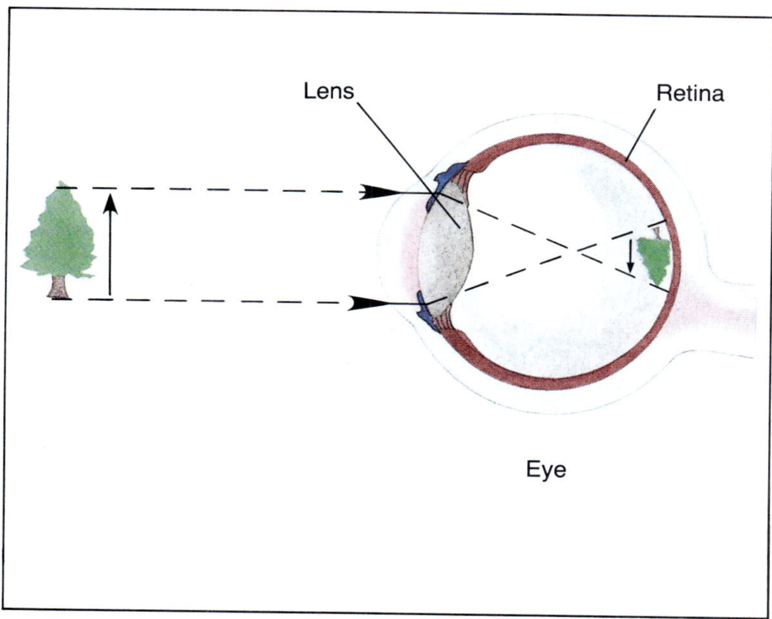

Fig. 8–25 The image formed on the retina by the lens in your eye is upside down. The brain, however, interprets everything as right side up.

LENSES

A camera is like your eye. In a camera, light falls on film. The film records the picture. In your eye, light falls on special kinds of nerve cells in the *retina*. An image is formed on the retina. Your eye then sends the image to the brain. Both a camera and an eye have a **lens** that forms an image. See Fig. 8–26. A *lens* is a piece of transparent material. Although some lenses are flat, a lens usually has curved surfaces. A lens refracts light rays that pass through it. The lens in a camera is made of glass or plastic. In your eye, the lens is made of living tissue.

Lens A piece of transparent material, often with at least one curved surface, that refracts light passing through it.

Fig. 8–26 This diagram shows how a camera lens forms an image on film in the same way that an eye lens forms an image on the retina.

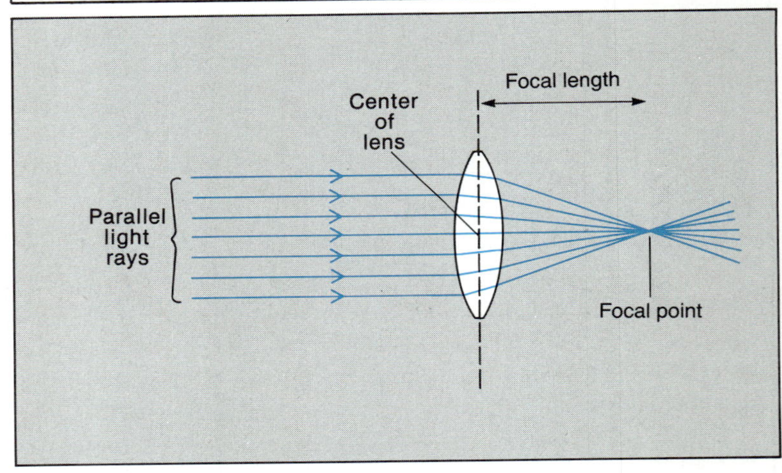

Fig. 8–27 A convex lens refracts light rays to a point called the focal point.

CONVEX LENSES

To see how lenses work, look at a simple magnifying glass. A magnifying glass usually has at least one curved surface. Most magnifying glasses have two curved surfaces. The surfaces curve outward just like the surface of a convex mirror. This makes the edges of the lens thinner than the center. See Fig. 8–27. This shape is called a **convex lens.** A *convex lens* refracts parallel light rays so that they come together. The rays meet at a point called the **focal point.** The distance from the center of the lens to the *focal point* is called the **focal length.** A convex lens that is very thick in the middle has a short *focal length*. Thinner lenses have longer focal lengths. Try holding a convex lens close to the printing on this page. Then move the lens closer to your eye. You will see a large image of the

Convex lens A lens with at least one curved surface that curves outward.

Focal point The point at which parallel light rays meet after being refracted by a convex lens.

Focal length The distance from the center of the lens to the focal point.

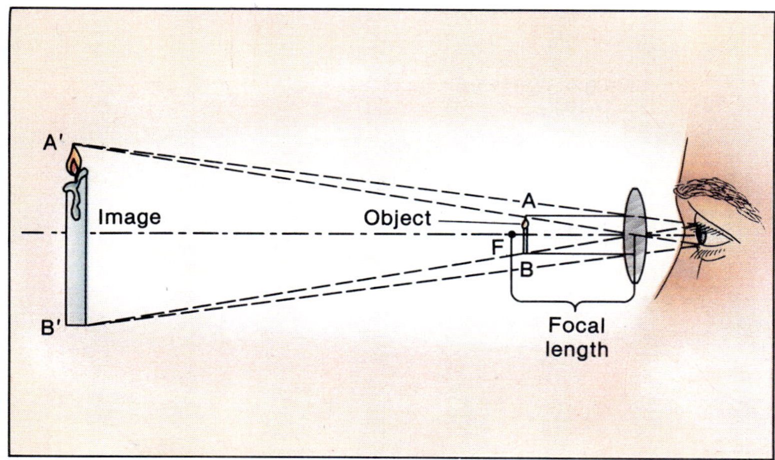

Fig. 8–28 When an object is within the focal length of a convex lens, the lens will form a magnified image of the object. The image is right side up.

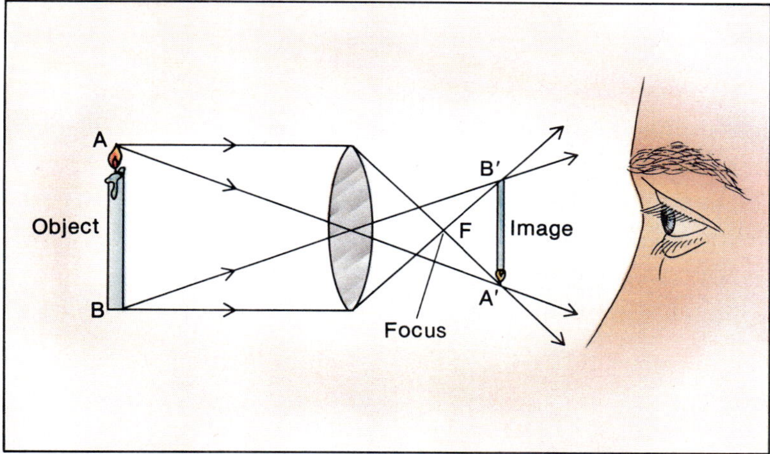

Fig. 8–29 When an object is beyond the focal length of a convex lens, the lens will form a real image that is upside down.

printing. A convex lens can be used as a magnifier. Fig. 8–28 shows the paths of the rays through a magnifying lens. By following the rays, you can see how a convex lens magnifies an image. In order to magnify the image, the lens must be held so the object is within the focal length. Then you see a virtual image that is larger than the object and is right side up.

When you hold a convex lens in front of your eye and look at a distant object, you see a different kind of image. Close to your eye, you can see only a blur through the lens. Moving the lens away from your eye produces an upside-down image. See Fig. 8–29. This is a real image. Unlike a virtual image, a real image can be projected on a sheet of paper held behind the lens. A convex lens will produce a real image only when the object is beyond the focal length.

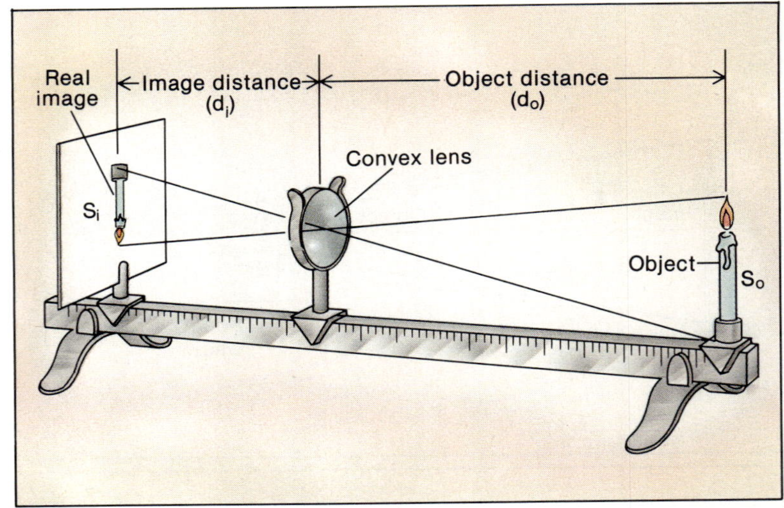

Fig. 8–30 This diagram shows how the size and distance of a real image formed by a convex lens are related to the size and the distance of the object.

Fig. 8–30 shows how a convex lens can be set up to produce a real image. The size of the image depends on the distance between the lens and the object. The distance between the lens and the object is d_o. The size of the object is s_o. The size of the image is s_i. The relationship of these values is shown as follows:

$$\frac{\text{distance of object}}{\text{distance of image}} = \frac{\text{size of object}}{\text{size of image}}$$

$$\frac{d_o}{d_i} = \frac{s_o}{s_i}$$

This relationship can be used to find any one of the values if you know the other three. For example, suppose an object 4 cm tall is placed 20 cm from a convex lens. The image is formed 15 cm from the lens. What is the size of the real image? Substituting known values gives:

$$\frac{d_o}{d_i} = \frac{s_o}{s_i}$$

$$\frac{20 \text{ cm}}{15 \text{ cm}} = \frac{4 \text{ cm}}{s_i}$$

$$s_i = \frac{4 \text{ cm} \times 15 \text{ cm}}{20 \text{ cm}} = \frac{60 \text{ cm}^2}{20 \text{ cm}} = 3 \text{ cm}$$

The convex lens of a camera produces a real image that is recorded on film. The lens has a certain focal length. Thus, it must be able to move toward and away from the film in order to form images of both close and distant objects. Most cameras have lenses that can be moved. The lens is moved closer to

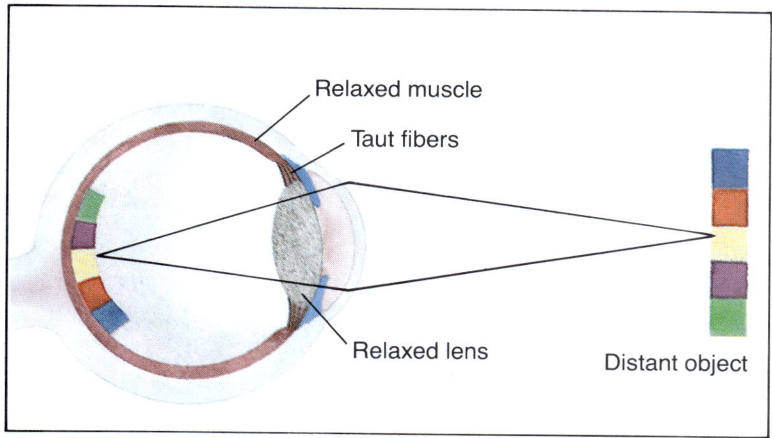

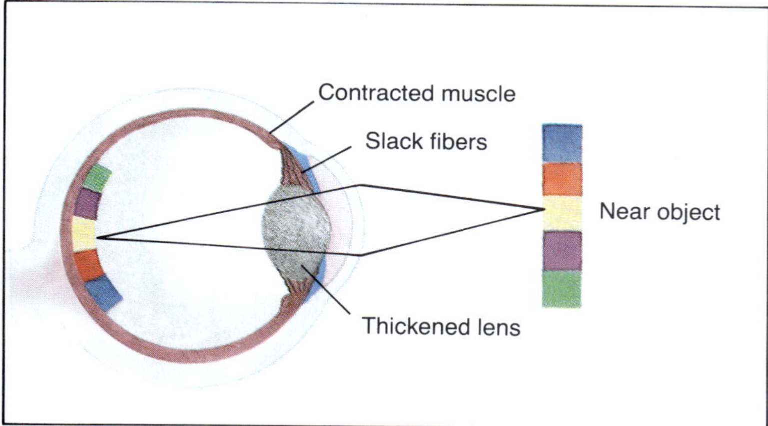

Fig. 8–31 This diagram shows how the lens of the eye changes shape to bring near or distant objects into focus.

the film to produce an image of a distant scene. When photographing a close object, the lens is moved away from the film. Thus sharp images of both near and distant scenes can be produced.

How do your eyes produce clear images of both near and distant objects? The convex lens of your eye is not hard and rigid. It is soft and can easily change its shape. It can be pulled into a thin shape with a long focal length to produce images of distant objects. Or it can shrink into a thick shape with a short focal length to look at close objects. Small muscles change the shape of the lens. Light rays from both near and far objects are refracted to form an image on the back of the eye. See Fig. 8–31. The images produced by the convex lenses in your eyes are always upside down. Your brain corrects the upside-down image seen by the eyes. Therefore, you see the world right side up.

CONCAVE LENSES

Concave lens A lens in which the curved surface curves inward and the edges are thicker than the middle.

Not all lenses have a convex shape. One common type of lens is thicker at the edges than in the middle. The surfaces of the lens curve inward just as a concave mirror curves inward. This type of lens is called a **concave lens.** Light rays are spread apart by a *concave lens*. An image seen through a concave lens is a virtual image. You can see the image only when you look through the lens. It cannot be projected on a screen. The image is always smaller than the object and is right side up.

USING LENSES

Enrichment: Eyeglasses, cameras, binoculars, field glasses, and telescopes can be inspected if they are available.

1. Eyeglasses. Some people's eyes cannot form clear images of everything they see. A person may be able to see distant objects more clearly than near objects. Such people are said to be *farsighted*. The lenses of the eyes do not refract the light rays enough. Eyeglasses with convex lenses can correct this problem. See Fig. 8–32 (a). A *nearsighted* person can see near objects more clearly than distant objects. The light rays are refracted too much. Nearsighted people wear eyeglasses with special concave lenses. See Fig. 8–32 (b).

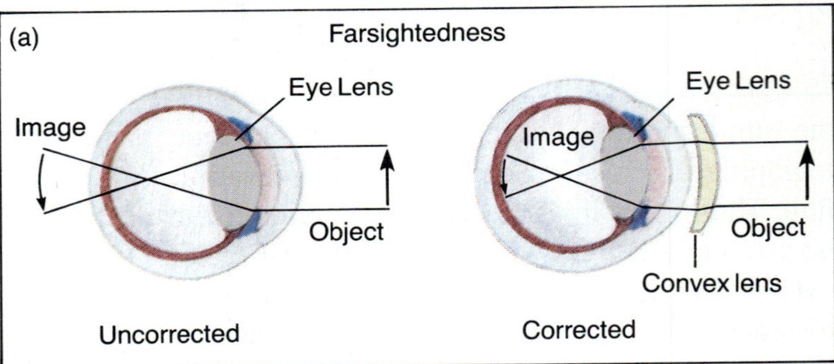

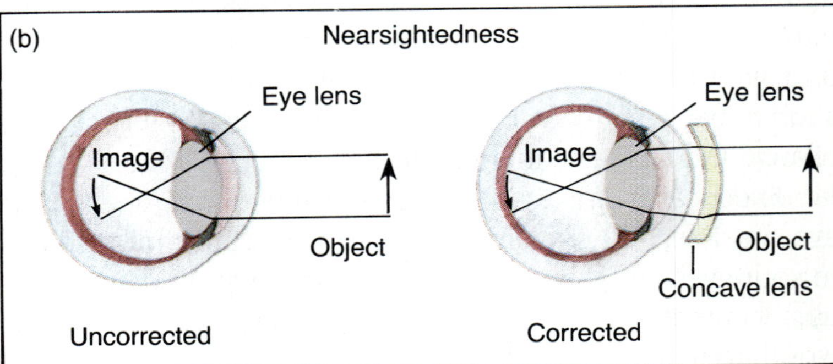

Fig. 8–32 In a farsighted person, the image of nearby objects is formed behind the retina (a). In a nearsighted person, the image of distant objects is formed in front of the retina (b).

Fig. 8–33 When a lens with a short focal length is used, a camera forms a small image of a wide area (a). When a lens with a long focal length is used, it forms a large image of a small area (b).

2. Cameras. Just as in the eye, the most important part of a camera is the lens. Most camera lenses are made up of several separate lenses. A single convex lens cannot focus light rays as well as a combination of lenses. The focal length of a camera lens determines the size of the image on the film. A lens with a short focal length produces a small image. Because the image is small, such a lens includes a wide area in the picture. See Fig. 8–33 (a). On the other hand, a camera lens with a long focal length produces a large image. This kind of lens is useful for taking pictures of distant scenes. However, because of the larger image, only a small part of the scene can be included. See Fig. 8–33 (b). The lenses on many cameras can be changed according to the focal length needed. Some cameras have lenses with adjustable focal lengths called zoom lenses.

3. Telescopes. A telescope uses at least two lenses. The simplest kind of telescope has a convex lens with a long focal length, called the *objective*, at one end of a tube. This lens produces a real image near the other end of the tube. A second, smaller convex lens, called the *eyepiece*, magnifies the real image produced by the objective. See Fig. 8–34. Thus a distant object is seen as much larger than when seen with the eye alone. However, the image seen through a simple telescope is upside down. This is no problem when viewing stars or other objects in the sky. Can you explain why this is true? Some telescopes have lenses that allow the image to be seen right side up. Astronomers need telescopes with a large objective lens to receive the faint light from distant stars. But it is difficult to make these large lenses. Thus astronomers often use a *reflecting* telescope. A concave mirror is used in place of an objective lens. Large mirrors are easier to make than large lenses. In a reflecting telescope, the mirror produces a real image. The real image is magnified by an eyepiece lens. See Fig. 8–35.

Fig. 8–34 The left diagram shows how an image is formed by a refracting telescope.

Fig. 8–35 The right diagram shows how an image is formed by a reflecting telescope.

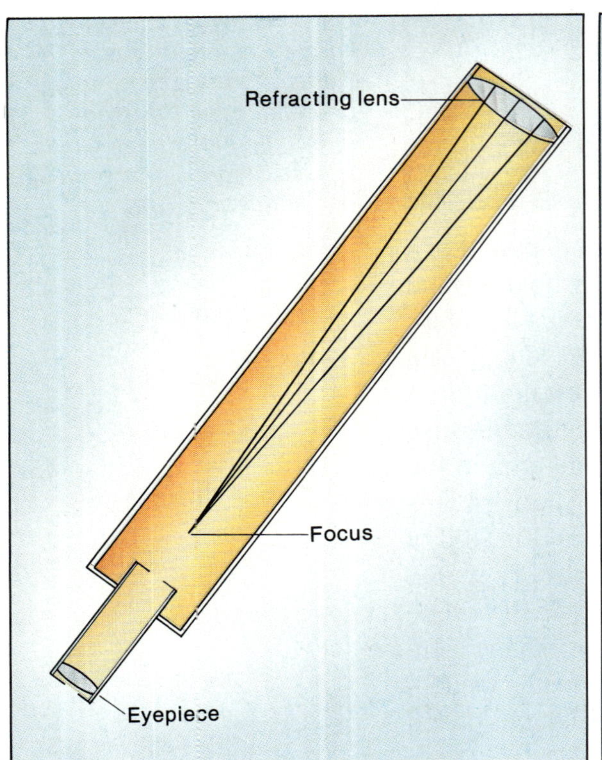

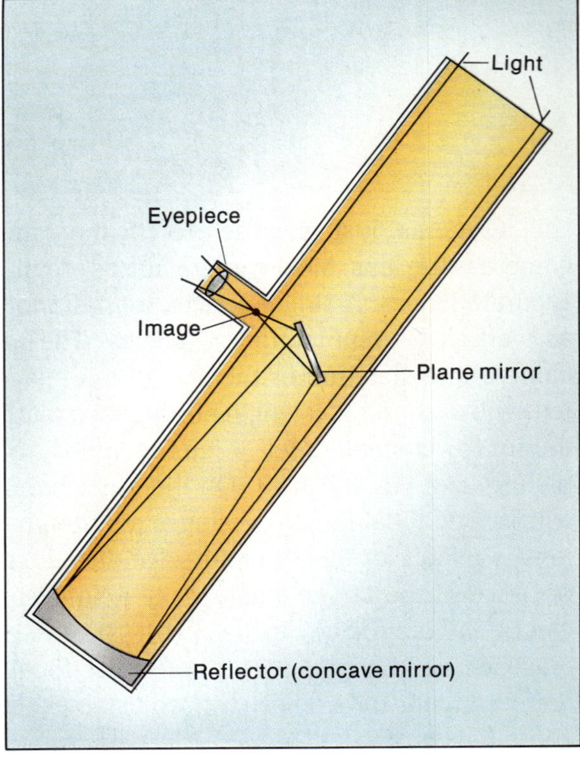

4. Microscopes. Microscopes use lenses to view objects that are very small. Like a telescope, a microscope also uses at least two convex lenses. One lens with a very short focal length is placed at the end of a tube. This is the objective lens of the microscope. When a small object is placed very close to the focal point of the objective lens, a large real image is formed near the top of the tube. See Fig. 8–36. Because of the short focal length of the objective lens, the object distance is small. Remember the relationship between object size, object distance, image distance, and image size:

$$d_o/d_i = s_o/s_i$$

A small object distance will always produce an image size greater than the object size. A microscope has an eyepiece lens that further magnifies the real image produced by the objective. Most microscopes have a concave mirror below the objective to reflect the light onto the object viewed.

Fig. 8–36 This diagram shows how an image is formed by a microscope.

SUMMARY

Lenses refract light passing through them. Depending on the shape of the lens, light rays may be brought together or spread apart. The lens of the eye is an example of the kind of lens that produces a real image. Lenses are used in eyeglasses, cameras, telescopes, and microscopes.

QUESTIONS

Use complete sentences to write your answers.

1. How does a lens affect light rays in order to form an image?
2. Name two kinds of lenses and describe how they differ.
3. Name four instruments that use lenses. Explain what the lenses do in each.
4. Copy the following table. Use the equation $d_o/d_i = s_o/s_i$ to complete the table.

d_o (cm)	d_i (cm)	s_o (cm)	s_i (cm)
75.0	25.0	6.0	(a)
(b)	10.0	5.0	2.5
100.0	(c)	10.0	2.0
30.0	12.0	(d)	1.6

1. A lens refracts light rays in order to form an image.
2. A convex lens bends light rays toward each other while a concave lens bends light rays away from each other.
3. Lenses are used in eyeglasses, cameras, telescopes, and microscopes. Students may name many other examples. They should describe how the lenses refract light to form an image in each case.
4. (a) 2.0 cm (b) 20 cm (c) 20 cm (d) 4.0 cm

INVESTIGATION

See teacher's commentary for teaching hints, safety, and answers to questions.

LENSES

PURPOSE: You will observe what a lens does.

MATERIALS:

piece of window glass	white cardboard
small magnifying lens	paper
	ruler

PROCEDURE:

A. Lay a piece of flat window glass on top of a page in your book. Look through the glass and move it slowly away from the page.

1. What happens as you move the glass away from the printing on the page?

B. Lay a small magnifying lens on top of the same page. Look through the lens and move it slowly away from the page.

2. What happens as you move the lens away from the page?

Fig. 8–37

C. Stand near the center of the room. Hold a piece of white cardboard as shown in Fig. 8–37.

D. Hold the lens between the cardboard and the window, about 1 cm from the cardboard. Slowly move the lens away from the cardboard.

E. When an image of the window frame is clear, study it carefully.

3. Is the image larger or smaller than the window frame itself?
4. Is the image right side up or upside down?

F. Move the lens farther from the cardboard.

5. What happens to the image?

G. Now stand on the side of the room opposite the windows.

H. Hold the lens so that you can see the windows clearly on the cardboard. Measure the distance from the lens to the cardboard. This is nearly the focal length of the lens.

6. What is the focal length of the lens you are using?

I. Cover one-half of the lens with a piece of paper or cardboard. Then try to form an image of the windows.

7. Describe the image formed.

CONCLUSIONS:

1. Explain how you can use the lens to form an image.
2. Is the image a real image or a virtual image? Explain.
3. How can you find the focal length of a lens?

TECHNOLOGY

NEW PATHS FOR COMMUNICATIONS

It's possible that copper cable and overland radio transmitters, with their antennas, may already be out of date! A cable, made up of many hair-sized optical fibers, can carry up to 240,000 conversations at the same time. In fact, even a single fiber can carry more communications than one copper cable can. Light, not electricity, transmits these messages. And tiny fibers of glass, not copper, are being used as cables. This new material and technology provides significant advantages over our existing systems.

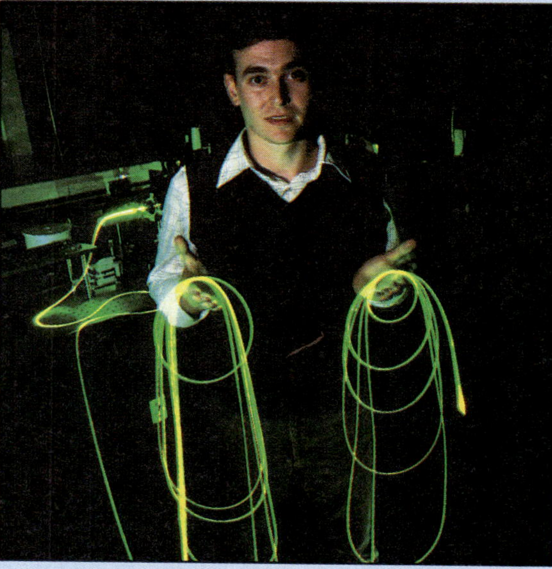

Optical fibers, though extremely tiny, act as a pipeline for laser light which transmits the information. This process is much faster than sending sound waves. But speed alone is not enough of an advantage. Using the traditional copper cable, sending more messages means laying more cable. Our cities' streets already have a gigantic underground maze of cable, which is difficult and costly to repair. Optical fibers provide a solution because one tiny optical fiber replaces many bulky copper cables. Small lasers have been developed with special switching devices which enable the pulses of light to send different messages within the same extremely thin glass fiber. A single fiber can, therefore, carry the information for many individual telephone conversations.

Satellite communication is also important in the future elimination of cables. The newest communication satellites can carry more than 33,000 telephone conversations plus two television channels at the same time between the U. S. and Europe. Future satellites, now being developed, will increase this capacity. The U. S. alone will place more than 200 communication satellites in orbit in the next ten years. Some communications experts believe that satellites will completely eliminate the need for overland cables in many parts of the world.

One of the more fascinating ways optical fibers are being used is in lightwave telecommunications. Businesses and medical professionals, especially, have made use of this system in a process called "teleconferencing." Several individuals in different states, or even different countries, arrange to speak together. Voice communication may be joined with a video screen so that they can see each other as well. This is particularly valuable in medicine where specialized and delicate surgery can be performed by a surgeon in one country and viewed by surgeons in another part of the world who can then ask questions or make suggestions right on the spot!

Perhaps the next step will be cars with satellite navigation systems which pinpoint locations and guide the driver to his or her destination or a teleconferencing system that you will be able to use at home! Do you think these innovations would change the way you carry on your daily activities? Would you like to be able to see the people with whom you speak on the phone?

¡COMPUTE!

SCIENCE INPUT

Light travels at the astonishing speed of 300,000 km/s. It takes only 1¼ s for light to reach the earth from the moon, and about 8 min and 20 s to reach earth from the sun. The early calculations of the speed of light made by Roemer took a great deal of time and research effort. Tools of observation were nowhere near as precise as they are today. Even early versions of calculators were mechanical and slow. It is much easier today to find out how long it would take light to travel from an object in the atmosphere or outer space to earth and this information could be helpful in calculating the possibility of light wave communications between space stations and earth. On a more ordinary basis you could calculate the time it would take for the lights from an airplane to reach the surface of earth.

COMPUTER INPUT

The computer can make extremely fast calculations. This capacity for mathematical calculation can be combined with other computer capabilities to provide the additional information necessary to solve research problems. For example, the computer can be used as a time-lapse machine. This means that it is capable of registering a period of time and in this sense, it acts as a clock.

To be combined, these two capacities of the computer, doing quick calculations, and registering a time period, require instructions from the software as well as the instructions built into the hardware. There is a looping mechanism built into the circuitry of your computer. There is also a processor which changes program language into machine language. The machine language contains several instructions describing the path the information should take around the loop. The computer hardware runs each part of the loop in approximately the same time. Once you know what that period of time is, you can, in your program, multiply it by any number in order to produce the desired time.

WHAT TO DO

On a separate piece of paper, make a data chart similar to the one shown. List five objects of varying distances from earth in the first column. Write the approximate distance (in kilometers) from earth to the object in the second column. Three examples are given. Enter Program Computerclock.

For the first part of the program you will need a watch with a second hand. The computer will run through the looping mechanism in your machine and will ask you to time the machine.

In the second part of the program you will use the computer to calculate how long it takes for light to reach earth from the objects you listed in your chart. Then, if you choose, the computer will use the looping mechanism to "count out" that time.

Data Chart

Object	Distance (KM) from Earth	Time for Light to Travel
1. Sun	150,000,000	
2. Pluto	5,800,000,000	
3. Bolt of Lightning	3	

SPEED OF LIGHT: PROGRAM COMPUTERCLOCK

GLOSSARY

GOTO	a command in BASIC that instructs the computer to return to a previous statement or to go to another part of the program
LOOP	a subroutine in a program which gives directions to repeat steps instead of going straight on
PERIPHERALS	computer accessories. A peripheral might be a printer, a joystick, the TV screen, or the keyboard. Everything except the actual electronic circuits are peripherals.

PROGRAM

```
100  REM COMPUTERCLOCK: PART I
105  FOR X = 1 TO 24: PRINT: NEXT
110  PRINT "GUESS HOW MUCH TIME
     BETWEEN 'START TIMING' AND
     'STOP'?"
115  PRINT
120  FOR T = 1 TO 5000: NEXT
130  PRINT "START TIMING ——→ ";
140  FOR T = 1 TO 15000: NEXT
150  PRINT "STOP"
160  INPUT "HOW MANY SECONDS DID
     THAT TAKE?";LT$: LT = VAL(LT$)
170  IF LT <1 OR LT> 60 THEN GOTO
     130
180  TV = INT(15000/LT)
190  INPUT "GUESS AGAIN (Y/N)? ";C$;
     IF C$ = "Y" THEN GOTO 130
200  REM SPEED OF LIGHT: PART II
210  PRINT: INPUT "DISTANCE TO LIGHT
     SOURCE (KM)? ";D$: D = VAL(D$)
215  REM T = TIME D = DISTANCE
220  T = D/300000; TT = T * TV
225  IF T < .001 THEN PRINT "TIME LESS
     THAN 1 HUNDREDTH SECOND ":
     GOTO 210
230  IF T > 600 THEN PRINT "TIME
     GREATER THAN 10 MINUTES"
240  INPUT "DO YOU WANT TO
     DETERMINE TIME (Y/N)? ";C$: IF C$
     = "N" THEN GOTO 290
250  IF C$ < > "Y" THEN GOTO 240
260  PRINT "GO ——→ ";
270  FOR N = 1 TO TT: NEXT
280  PRINT "STOP"
290  PRINT "TIME = ";INT (T/60);" MIN
     AND "T - INT(T/60) * 60;"   SEC"
300  END
```

PROGRAM NOTES

The "loop" defined in the glossary is different from the looping mechanism in the circuitry. If you read Program Computerclock carefully, you will see several statements directing the computer to go someplace other than the next step if certain conditions are true. These "loops" are written into the software by the programmer.

BITS OF INFORMATION

Through a combination of precision mirrors, computerized telescope-to-earth communications, and other marvels of advanced engineering, the Hubble space telescope, to be launched on the Space Shuttle, will enable us to see stars 14 billion light years away. The light images, which will be transmitted to earth via computer, may even tell us how our galaxy was formed.

CHAPTER REVIEW

See teacher's commentary for answers.

VOCABULARY

On a separate piece of paper, match each term with the number of the statement that best explains it. Use each term only once.

convex mirror	electromagnetic spectrum	lens	convex lens
focal point	electromagnetic waves	focus	concave lens
focal length	concave mirror	rays	

1. The series of waves with many properties similar to those of light.
2. The distance from the center of a lens to the focal point.
3. Straight lines showing the path followed by light.
4. A lens that is thicker in the center than at the edges.
5. A piece of transparent material that refracts light passing through it.
6. A lens that is thinner in the center than at the edges.
7. The point where parallel light rays meet after being refracted.
8. A form of energy that moves through empty space at a speed of 3.0×10^8 m/s.
9. A curved mirror whose surface curves outward.
10. A point at which light rays come together.
11. A curved mirror whose surface curves inward.

QUESTIONS

Give brief but complete answers to the following questions. Unless otherwise indicated, use complete sentences to write your answers.

1. Name six electromagnetic waves and state how each is useful to us.
2. What does light passing through a pinhole in an index card show about the behavior of light?
3. Why can AM radio waves be received directly over longer distances than FM radio waves?
4. Describe your image in a plane mirror.
5. How do lenses and mirrors differ in the way in which they produce images?
6. What kind of lens is used in eyeglasses (a) for a farsighted person? (b) for a nearsighted person? Explain.
7. Use an example to show how fast light travels. How fast is this in kilometers per hour?
8. Use the formula given in Chapter 6 to find the wavelength, in meters, of visible light and radio waves.

9. From the fact that light travels 25 percent slower in water than in air, show how to find the index of refraction of water.
10. The index of refraction of some artificial diamonds is 2.00. (a) How does this compare with the index of refraction of real diamonds? (b) What is the speed of light in the artificial diamonds?
11. A picture is taken of a tree 50 m away from the camera. The image is formed in the camera 5.0 cm from the lens. The image of the tree is 2.5 cm tall. Find the height of the tree.
12. Compare and contrast convex and concave lenses. Give an example of one way in which each is used.

APPLYING SCIENCE

1. Investigate and report on the advantages and disadvantages of using a microwave oven for cooking. Include some safety precautions for using a microwave oven. A dealer will probably be able to give you an advertising pamphlet and some information.
2. "Black light" makes some materials glow in the dark. What is "black light"? What is it used for? How is it related to visible light?
3. Double convex, double concave, and plano-convex are some types of lenses. What other types can you find? What do the names mean? What are the various lenses used for?
4. Find out what is meant by polarized light and demonstrate polarization to the class. Stick three or four pieces of transparent tape at various angles on top of each other. Place the tape between two polarizing lenses such as those used in sunglasses. The resulting display of colors is caused by a property called *photoelasticity.* Polarized light can be used in many ways to test materials.

BIBLIOGRAPHY

Boraiko, A. A. "Miracles of Fiber Optics." *National Geographic,* October 1979.

Boraiko, A. A. "The Laser: A Splendid Light." *National Geographic,* March 1984.

Branley, F. M. *The Electromagnetic Spectrum.* New York: Crowell, 1979.

Caulfield, H. J. "The Wonder of Holography." *National Geographic,* March 1984.

Goodwin, D. V. "The Sorcerer of Strobe Alley." *Science '82,* June 1982.

Schneider, H. *Laser Light.* New York: McGraw-Hill, 1978.

CHAPTER

9

This photo shows a close up of some of the colorful pigments used to make paints. We can see color because of the way light is reflected and absorbed by different materials.

COLOR

CHAPTER GOALS

1. Describe the spectrum of visible light.
2. Show how a spectrum can be formed with a prism.
3. Compare ordinary light with laser light.
4. Describe the difference between the primary colors of light and the primary colors of paint.

9-1. Light and Color

At the end of this section you will be able to:

- Show how white light can be separated into a visible spectrum by using a prism.
- Explain what causes a rainbow.
- Compare the light produced by lasers with light from other sources.

Have you ever heard the expression "All cats are gray in the dark"? What does it mean? To find out, try this experiment. Put on a bright-colored shirt or sweater. Now go into a dark closet and shut the door. With the light off, can you still see the color of your shirt? What happens to color in the dark? Where does color come from?

THE VISIBLE SPECTRUM

All color comes from light. A simple experiment can show that all colors we see are found in white light. This experiment was first performed by the great scientist Sir Isaac Newton. When a ray of light passes from air into glass, its speed changes. This change in speed causes the ray to be bent, or *refracted*. The amount of bending depends on the frequency of the ray. Light rays with high frequencies are bent the most. A specially shaped glass called a **prism** will spread out the rays according to how much they are refracted. A common *prism*, seen from one end, has the shape of a triangle. When a ray of white light passes through the prism, the light spreads out as a band of colors. This band of colors is called the **visible spectrum**. See Fig. 9–1.

Prism A specially shaped piece of glass that can divide white light into its separate colors.

Visible spectrum The band of colors produced when white light is divided into its separate colors.

Fig. 9–1 This photograph shows how a prism separates white light into the colors of the visible spectrum.

Reinforcement: Show how a prism is used to produce a spectrum of light. Hold the prism in the beam of a slide projector so that the spectrum falls on a screen.

A prism can separate white light into a *visible spectrum* because each color of light has a different frequency. The higher the frequency, the more the ray will be bent by passing through the prism. Red light has the lowest frequency. It is bent the least by passing through the prism. Thus the red light is seen at one end of the visible spectrum. Violet light has the highest frequency and is bent the most, or refracted through the largest angle. It is seen at the opposite end of the spectrum. Yellow, green, and blue light appear in the middle of the visible spectrum. A diamond acts like a prism. Different parts of a cut diamond refract white light striking the gem from almost any direction. See Fig. 9–2.

Fig. 9–2 The facets of a diamond act like tiny prisms that refract light into many colors.

RAINBOWS

Sunlight contains a nearly equal mixture of all the visible frequencies of light. Sometimes you can see the colors in sunlight spread out in a rainbow. A rainbow is made when drops of rain act like natural prisms. A raindrop is not shaped like a prism. However, its round shape spreads out the white sunlight striking the drop into a tiny spectrum. See Fig. 9–3. As you look up from the ground at a rainbow, you see only one color from each little spectrum. Looking at the highest raindrops, you see only the color bent the least amount, which is red. As a result, the top of the rainbow is seen as a band of red. Below the red band you see bands of orange, yellow, green, blue, and violet. See Fig. 9–4. All of these colored bands have a curved shape.

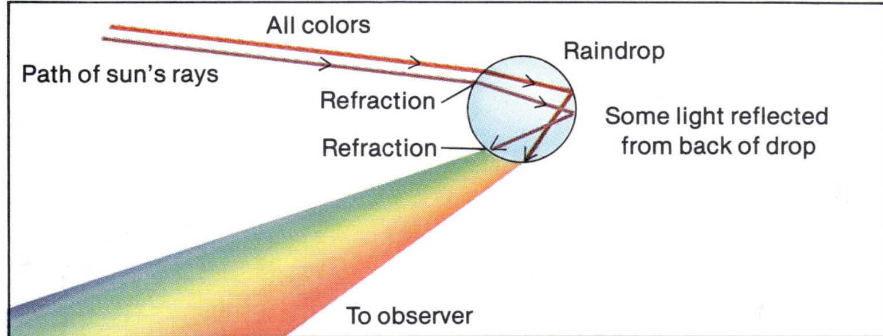

Fig. 9–3 A ray of sunlight is refracted as it enters and leaves a raindrop. As in a prism, this causes the white light to spread out into a spectrum of colors.

Fig. 9–4 When sunlight is refracted by raindrops, an observer on the ground sees a rainbow.

WHY IS THE SKY BLUE?

Separation of sunlight into colors also gives the sky its color. At noon, the sun is high in the sky. The white light from the sun passes directly through the atmosphere. However, particles of air and bits of dust reflect and scatter some of the sun's rays. The light with the highest frequency, in the blue part of the visible spectrum, is scattered most. You see these scattered blue rays when you look at the sky. The sky is deepest blue when the air is clean and dry. When there is a great deal of dust or water vapor in the air, more frequencies of light are scattered. The sky then looks whiter.

Fig. 9–5 The colors of this sunset are a result of the way light is scattered in the earth's atmosphere.

At sunrise and sunset, the sun is lower in the sky. At those times, the white light from the sun passes through more of the atmosphere. The atmosphere scatters the blue, green, and violet frequencies more than it scatters red, yellow, and orange. Therefore, red, yellow, and orange pass through the air most easily. When the sun is near the horizon it appears red or orange. See Fig. 9–5.

SOURCES OF LIGHT

Word study: Luminous from *lumen* (L.) a light.

Some objects such as the sun, the stars, and light bulbs produce visible light. They are called *luminous bodies*. The word "luminous" means "giving off light." Most objects are not luminous. You can see them only because they reflect some of the light falling on them. The paper on which this page is printed is visible only because light rays are reflected from its surface back to your eyes. A change in conditions can cause an object that is not luminous to give off light. For example, paper can produce light when it burns.

A material that gives off light when it is heated is said to be **incandescent**. A light bulb has a fine wire, or filament, that becomes *incandescent* when it is heated by an electric current passing through it. See Fig. 9–6. Many kinds of lamps produce light by making some material incandescent. The color of light from an incandescent source usually depends upon the temperature of the heated material. For example, a piece of iron can be heated until it gives off a dull red glow. Further heating can cause the iron to produce yellow and, finally, white light. At this point, it is "white hot."

Incandescent Giving off visible light as a result of being heated.

Some light sources do not depend upon heat. An example is the light produced by neon signs. The light comes from a gas that is sealed inside a glass tube. See Fig. 9–7. When an electric current is passed through the gas, the gas gives off colored light. However, the gas remains cool. The color of the light depends upon the kind of gas. Neon gas gives a bright red color. Other gases, such as helium, produce different colors.

Many streets and highways are lighted by mercury vapor lamps. They produce a violet-green light that does not produce much glare. Sodium vapor lamps that give a bright yellow-orange light are now replacing mercury vapor lamps. Sodium lamps use less electricity than mercury lamps.

Fluorescent lamps also use mercury vapor. However, most of the visible light from a fluorescent lamp does not come directly from the mercury vapor. Instead, the mercury vapor is used mainly as a source of ultraviolet rays. The invisible ultraviolet rays strike a coating on the inside of the lamp, causing it to glow.

Fig. 9–6 The photo on the right shows an example of an incandescent bulb. The filament produces light when it is heated.

Fig. 9–7 The photo on the left shows neon lights. Different gases in the tubes produce different colors when an electric current passes through them.

The outdoor lighting in large cities can cause an unusual form of light pollution. The telescopes used by astronomers may be made nearly useless by light pollution if they are located near cities. The glare from the city lights blocks out some of the light from the stars. However, the problem can be helped by using outdoor lights that do not produce the frequencies of light that interfere with the light from the stars.

Laser A device that produces an intense beam of light of nearly a single frequency.

Word study: Laser from the first letters of *l*ight *a*mplification by *s*timulated *e*mission of *r*adiation.

LASERS

A **laser** produces a light unlike that from other common light sources just described. Almost all the light you see, from the sun, a fire, or a light bulb, is made up of a mixture of different frequencies and wavelengths. A *laser* produces a very intense beam of light made up almost completely of a single frequency. This type of light is called *coherent*. The waves in coherent light are all "in step." See Fig. 9–8. Thus, a beam of laser light has a very bright, pure color. See Fig. 9–9. If light waves produced sound, ordinary light would be noise made up of a jumble of frequencies. Laser light, on the other hand, would sound like a musical tone of just one frequency.

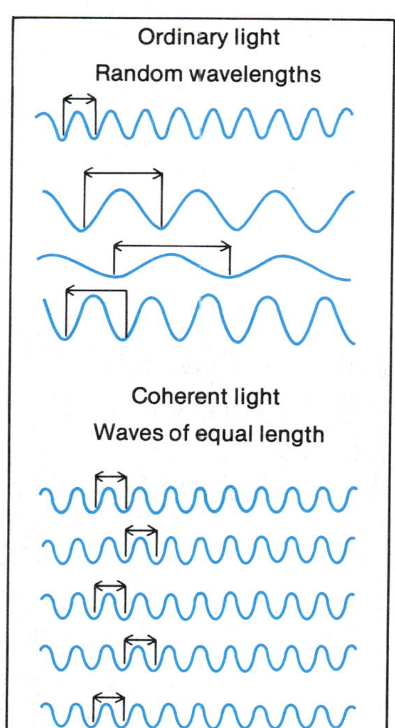

Fig. 9–8 Laser light is coherent, that is, it is made up mostly of one frequency. The light waves are all "in step."

Fig. 9–9 The color of a laser beam is bright and pure. Laser light does not contain a mixture of colors.

Laser light can be produced in different ways. A common kind of laser is a tube filled with gas. One end of the tube holds a mirror. At the other end is a mirror that reflects only part of the light. Some of the light can pass through this mirror. An electric current passed through the gas produces light. This is similar to the way light is produced in a neon sign. The light is reflected from the mirrors. It bounces back and forth inside the tube and causes the gas to produce more light. Finally, the light gains so much energy that it passes through the partly transparent mirror. Then a powerful beam of coherent light waves emerges from the laser. See Fig. 9–10.

Enrichment: If a laser is available, place a lens in the beam to spread the light and let students try to read by laser light. They will have difficulty because the laser light reflects from the fibers in the paper and sets up an interference pattern.
CAUTION: Do not look into the laser beam.

High-voltage power supply
Mirror (100% reflective)
Gas mixture
Mirror (95% reflective)

Fig. 9–10 This diagram shows the operation of a gas laser. The gas in the tube is a mixture of carbon dioxide, helium, and neon.

The waves in a laser beam are all moving parallel to each other and are "in step." As a result, laser light has the following important properties: First, a laser beam can travel great distances without spreading out. A laser beam may spread less than one centimeter after traveling one kilometer. You have probably seen how a beam from an ordinary flashlight spreads out after traveling only a few meters. A laser beam sent to the surface of the moon (a distance of 392,000 km) will spread out to make a spot only several kilometers across. Second, the energy in a laser beam can be concentrated in a small area. If you hold your hand in a patch of sunlight, a certain amount of energy from the sun falls on your hand. A laser beam can deliver as much as ten billion times more energy to the same area. If this amount of energy falls on the surface of a sheet of steel, it can cut through the steel almost instantly. See Fig. 9–11.

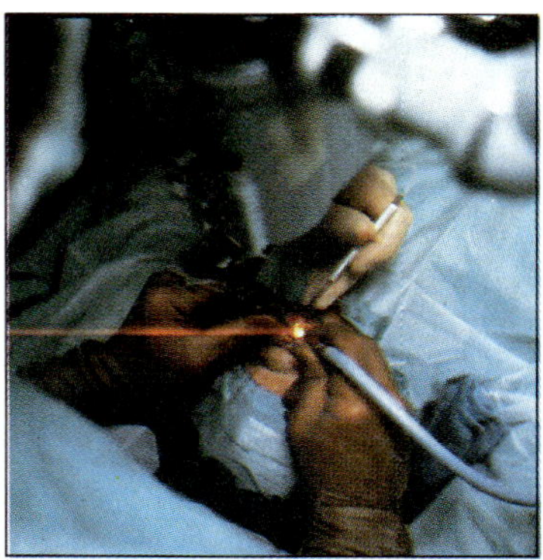

Fig. 9–11 Although some laser beams are very powerful, lasers can also be used for delicate surgery. They cause little bleeding and can be used with great precision.

The unusual properties of laser light make it very useful. For example, you have probably seen lasers used to record prices at checkout counters in stores. A laser beam scans the bars and stripes of a code marked on the package. The laser light is reflected from the bar code. A computer picks up the reflections and prints out the name and price of the product. Only laser light can produce the very narrow beam needed to scan the bar code as the package is quickly passed over the scanner. A tiny beam of laser light is also used to read the information stored on a videodisc. See Fig. 9–12. A videodisc does not have grooves like a phonograph record. Instead, it is covered with billions of tiny pits. The pits hold the information that makes the TV picture and sound. Each pit is so small that it would take one hundred to equal the diameter of a hair. To play the videodisc, a laser beam scans the pits. The laser beam picks up information from the pits on the videodisc like a needle tracking the grooves of a phonograph record.

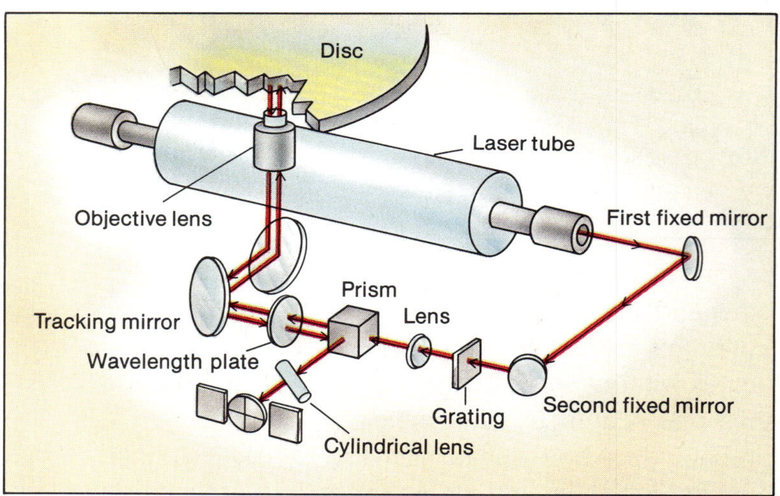

Fig. 9–12 A series of prisms, lenses, and mirrors focus a laser beam on the videodisc.

Word study: Hologram from *holos* (Gr.), whole, and *graphia* (L.), writing.

One of the most unusual uses of laser light is in the making of *holograms*. A hologram is a picture that can be seen from all directions. See Fig. 9–13 (a). That is, looking at a hologram is like looking through an open window. By looking through different parts of the window, you can see the same scene from different angles. In a hologram, you can see all sides of an object by changing your angle of view. See Fig. 9–13 (b). In the future, it may be possible to make holographic TV and movies that will let you feel as if you are actually in the picture.

Enrichment: Display a hologram. They are available from science supply houses. White light holograms also have been produced. See the cover of *National Geographic*, March, 1984.

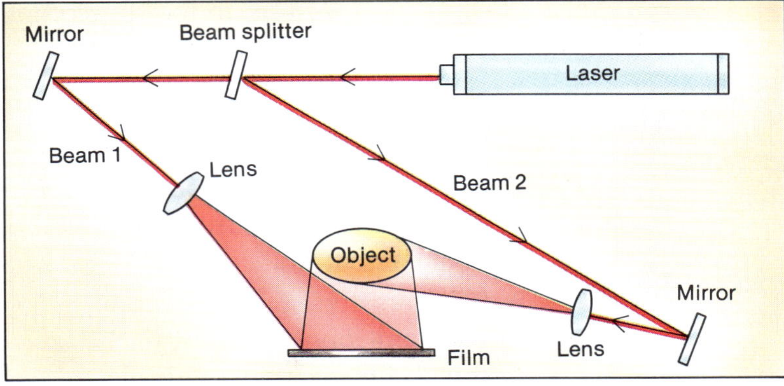

Fig. 9–13 (a) A hologram is a three-dimensional image that is made by using laser light. (b) This diagram shows how a hologram is made. A beam splitter splits the laser beam in two. Both of the beams are aimed by a mirror and spread out by a lens. One beam shines on the object. The second beam shines directly on the photographic plate.

SUMMARY

By using a prism, you can show that white light is made up of different frequencies. Each frequency is a color in the visible spectrum. Sometimes you can see many of the different colors in sunlight in a rainbow. There are various types of light sources. Unlike light from these common sources, laser light is coherent.

QUESTIONS

Use complete sentences to write your answers.

1. Using a diagram, explain what causes a rainbow.
2. Name the main colors in the visible spectrum in order of decreasing frequency.
3. Describe how you could use a prism to produce a spectrum of visible light.
4. How does laser light differ from ordinary light?
5. Describe three uses of lasers.

1. A ray of light is refracted as it enters and when it leaves a raindrop. This causes the ray to be broken into different colors. Student diagrams should look like Fig. 9–3.
2. Red, orange, yellow, green, blue, and violet.
3. Hold a prism so that a ray of white light passes through it. The white light will be broken into a spectrum as it passes through the prism. See Fig. 9–1.
4. Laser light has one frequency; ordinary light has many frequencies. Ordinary light has a tendency to spread out; laser light does not.
5. Lasers can be used for delicate surgery, for use in light shows, for playing video discs, and for producing holograms.

INVESTIGATION

See teacher's commentary for teaching hints, safety, and answers to questions.

THE VISIBLE SPECTRUM

PURPOSE: You will describe and compare the spectrum as viewed through a prism and through a diffraction grating.

MATERIALS:

glass prism
diffraction grating
light source

PROCEDURE:

A. Using the setup shown in Fig. 9–14 (a), look through the prism toward the light bulb. The light enters one surface of the prism and follows the path shown in the diagram. See Fig. 9–14 (b).

B. Turn the prism through various angles until the spectrum is spread out as much as possible.

1. Name the colors you see in the order they appear. Record your observations in your notebook.

C. Look through the plastic diffraction grating at the light bulb. Turn the diffraction grating so that the colors are to the left and right of the bulb.

2. Do you see more than one spectrum to the right of the bulb? (Are the colors repeated?)

3. How do the colors to the left of the bulb compare with those to the right?

D. Look at the spectrum to the right of the bulb.

4. Name the colors from left to right.

CONCLUSIONS:

1. In your own words, describe how you can produce a spectrum of the colors contained in white light.

2. Compare the spectrum produced by the diffraction grating with the spectrum produced by the prism.

EXTENSION:

E. Repeat steps A through D using different light sources. Describe each spectrum you observe.

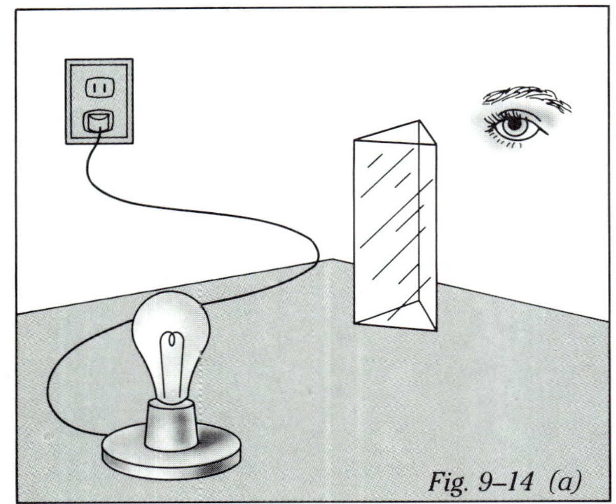

Fig. 9–14 (a)

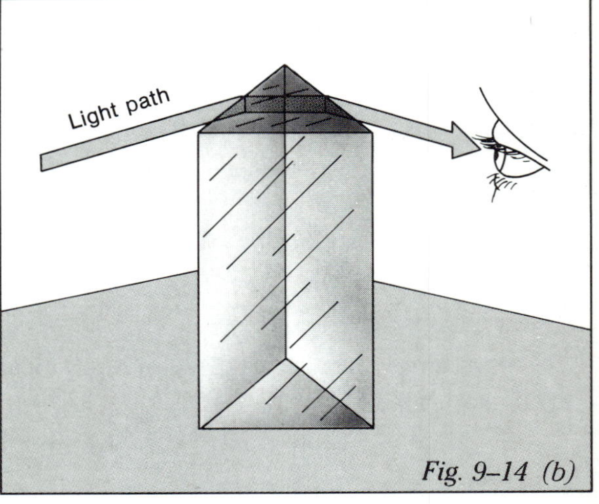

Fig. 9–14 (b)

9-2. Seeing Color

At the end of this section you will be able to:

- Compare the results of mixing colored light with the results of mixing colored paints.
- Describe how *interference colors* are produced.
- Explain how color images are made.

Fig. 9–15 shows an American flag. However, this flag is unusual. Try this experiment. Stare at a star in the lower right of the flag for at least one minute. Then quickly look at a sheet of blank white paper. What do you see?

Fig. 9–15 This flag is printed in colors that are complementary to the normal red, white, and blue of the American flag.

COLORED LIGHT

When most people try the experiment described above, they see the flag with its normal colors on the blank white paper. This experiment tells you an important fact about the way we see color. All colors that we see are a result of frequencies of light waves and how our eyes respond to those light waves. For example, suppose that three beams of colored light are projected on a screen. One beam is red, the second is green, and the third is blue. You can see other colors where the beams overlap. See Fig. 9–16. Mixing any two colors produces a new color. Red light plus green light makes yellow light. Blue light plus red light makes purple light. Green light plus blue light makes blue-green (cyan) light. All three colors of light combine to make white light. Scientists call red, green,

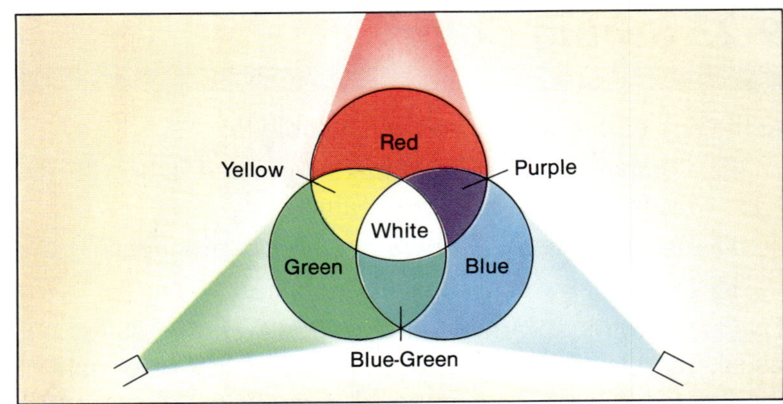

Fig. 9–16 This diagram shows the colors that are produced when the primary colors of light are combined.

Primary colors (of light) Red, green, and blue light. These colors of light can be added together to produce any other color.

and blue the **primary colors** of light. The *primary colors* can be mixed to produce light of any color. All other shades of color can be produced by making each primary color weaker or stronger as they are mixed. You can make pink, for example, when you mix all three beams of primary colors, provided the red light is slightly stronger. Red light plus weak green light gives a brown color. Any other color of light can be made by mixing red, green, and blue in different ways.

Look at Fig. 9–16. You can see that if you add yellow light to blue, the result is white. In other words, yellow light contains all the primary colors except blue. Any two colored lights, such as yellow and blue, that can be combined to produce white are called **complementary colors**. Green and purple are also *complementary colors*. Can you identify one more pair of complementary colors? *

Complementary colors A pair of colors of light that combine to produce white.

* Red and blue-green (cyan) are also complementary colors.

Reinforcement: Color disks, some of which are adjustable, are available from science supply houses. When the disks are spun in white light the three primary colors combine to produce white or at least near white. Primary color filters can be used in a slide projector to give similar results.

Look at the flag at the beginning of this section. It is printed in complementary colors. If you stare at one of a pair of complementary colors, then look away, you will see the other color of the pair. This effect is caused by the way our eyes see color. Special cells in the eye called rods and cones receive each of the primary colors. In the same way colored lights are mixed together, signals from the eye are combined in the brain. Thus we can see all possible colors. Staring at a certain color causes the eye to become fatigued for that color. Then if you suddenly look at white, you will not see that color. The missing color taken from the white produces its complementary color. This is the reason that you see the normal colors of the flag if you look at a piece of white paper after staring at the complementary colors.

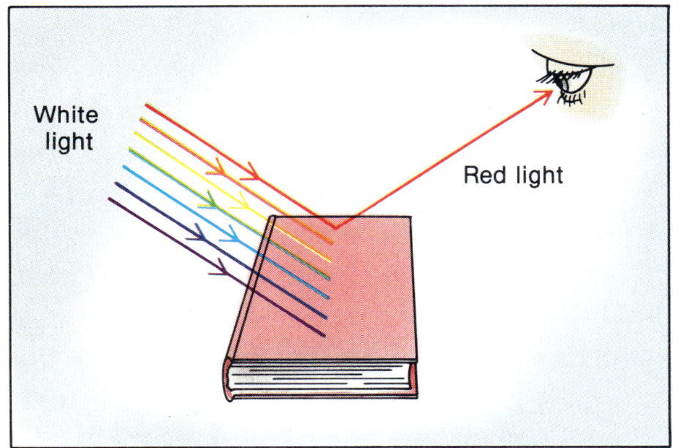

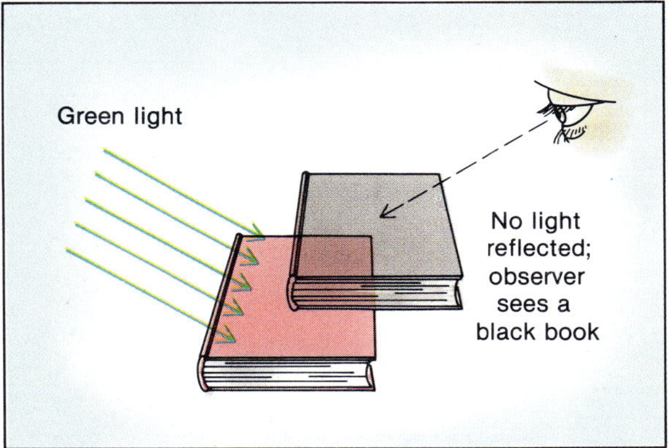

Fig. 9–17 As shown in the left diagram, when white light shines on a red object, the object appears red because only red light is reflected.

Fig. 9–18 If green light shines on a red object, as shown in the right diagram, there is no red light for the object to reflect. Thus the object appears black.

Most light that reaches your eyes has been reflected from the surface of an object. The color of the object depends on the color of the reflected light. For example, if white light falls upon a red object, all frequencies except red are absorbed. Red light is reflected. See Fig. 9–17. You say that the object is red. Most objects reflect more than one frequency. The color you see is the combination of those reflected colors. Only those colors present in the light falling on an object can be reflected. White light contains all colors. Thus if white light shines on a red object, the object appears red. The object also appears red if only red light shines on a red object. But if only green light shines on a red object, the object appears black. See Fig. 9–18. For example, suppose you wear a red coat in a room in which there is only green light. There is no red light for the coat to reflect. Therefore, it appears black.

COLORED PAINT

Paints have a certain color because they absorb certain frequencies of light and reflect others. Thus mixing colored paints does not give the same result as mixing colored lights. For example, mixing blue and yellow paint produces green. Blue paint absorbs red and yellow light but reflects green. At the same time, yellow paint absorbs blue and red and also reflects green. Thus a mixture of blue and yellow paint will reflect only green light. This mixture appears green to the eye. All colors of paints can be produced by mixing blue, yellow, and red. See Fig. 9–19. Thus blue, yellow, and red are the primary colors of paint. Mixing all three primary paint colors produces black. Can you explain why?

* When blue, yellow, and red are mixed, all the colors are absorbed. None is reflected and so the mixture appears black.

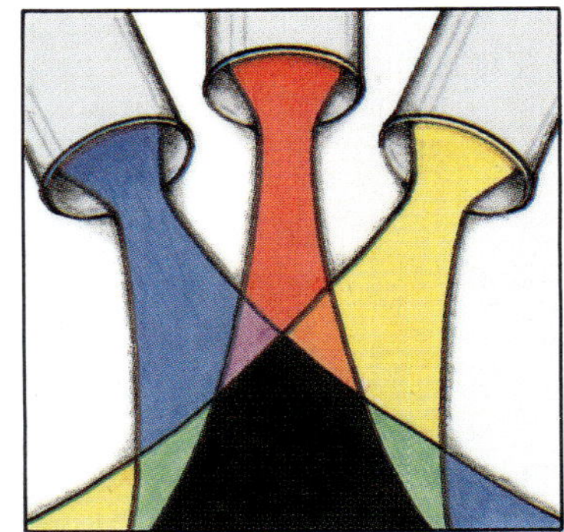

Fig. 9–19 When the primary colors of paint are combined, the result is black.

Reinforcement: Soap solutions sold in toy stores make bubbles that show the effects discussed here. Have students look for the colors. Ask them to explain why the top of the bubble eventually does not reflect any light.

INTERFERENCE

The color of reflected light is not always caused by the absorption of certain frequencies. Sometimes reflected light rays interfere with each other to produce colors. The colors of soap bubbles are an example of this way of producing color. See Fig. 9–20. A soap bubble has a thin, transparent skin. White light is reflected from both the inner and outer surfaces of the skin. Incoming light waves reflected from the inner surface travel slightly farther than the waves reflected from the outer surface. The crests and troughs of the two reflected waves line up to produce a stronger wave with the same frequency. See Fig. 9–21. This is an example of *interference*

Fig. 9–20 The colors reflected by these soap bubbles are a result of the interference of light waves.

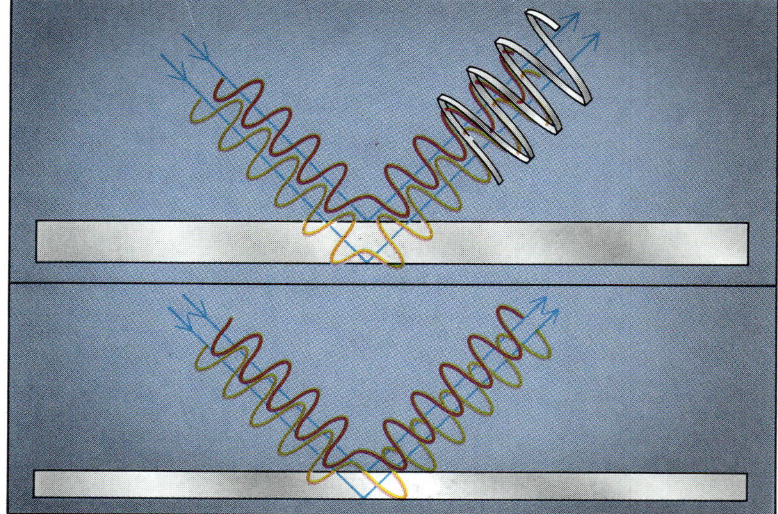

Fig. 9–21 This diagram shows how a thin film, such as a soap bubble, produces interference of light waves.

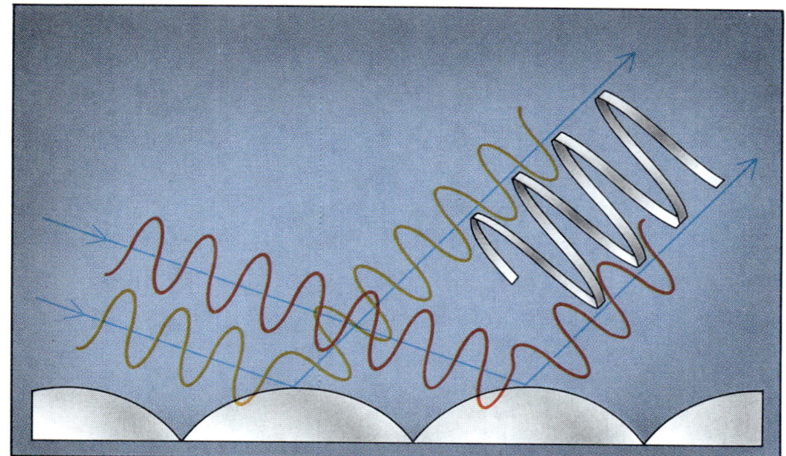

Fig. 9–22 This diagram shows how a surface made up of ridges, such as a diffraction grating, also produces interference of light waves.

Fig. 9–23 The ridges on the surface of this videodisc act like a diffraction grating to produce interference colors.

between the waves. The wave produced by interference between the reflected waves is seen as a color. It is called an **interference color**. The thickness of the soap bubble film is not always the same. Thus, you see several *interference colors* as different frequencies are produced by the reflected waves. Thin films of oil on water also show interference colors.

Interference color Color produced when reflected light waves combine to strengthen or cancel each other.

Light rays reflected from surfaces with many closely spaced ridges also show interference. When the waves hit the ridges at certain angles, they may line up as shown in Fig. 9–22. The strongly reflected wave has the frequency of a certain color. Waves striking the ridges at different angles can produce several colors. You can often see interference colors when white light is reflected from the ridges on the surface of a phonograph record or videodisc. See Fig. 9–23.

Reinforcement: Have a phonograph record or videodisc available so that students can see light reflected from the ridges on the surface.

COLOR IMAGES

Color images can be made by mixing colored light. A color TV picture is an example of a color image made with light. If you look at a color TV tube with a magnifier when the set is turned off, you will find that the face of the tube is covered with tiny lines. These lines are arranged in groups of three. When the set is on, one line in each group gives off red light, blue light, or green light. See Fig. 9–24. These are the primary colors that can be combined to produce any color of light. When the set is on, the lines glow red, blue, and green. In this way, three separate pictures are made in each of the primary colors. The lines are so close together that you do not see each colored line. Your eyes blend the lines together so that you see one picture in all of its different colors.

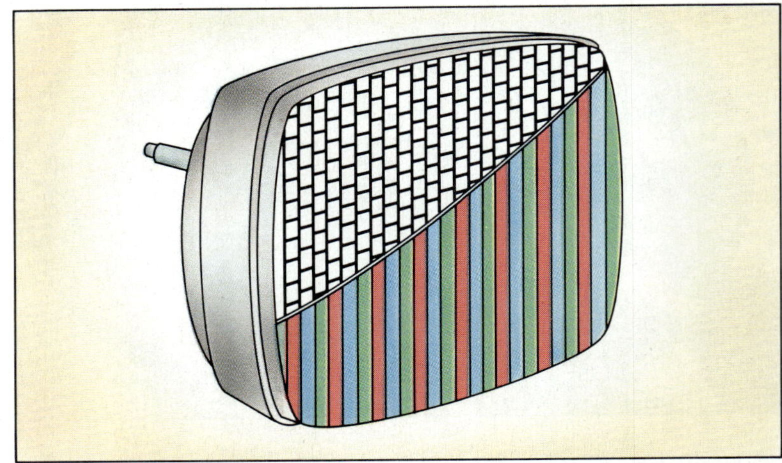

Fig. 9–24 In a color TV, electron guns focus an electron beam on vertical red, green, and blue lines.

Printed color pictures like the ones in this book are made by using colored inks. The inks absorb and reflect light the way colored paints do. The picture to be printed is first separated into the primary colors of blue, yellow, and red. The paper is first printed with the yellow picture. Then the blue and red pictures are added. The colors now are close to those in the original picture. However, the combined inks do not absorb colors perfectly. Black must be added to help darken the colors. The steps in printing a color picture are shown in Fig. 9–25. Various combinations of color pigments are used to produce different colors of paints and inks. Chemists use a method called *chromotography* to separate materials into their basic colors.

Fig. 9–25 A color picture is printed by first separating the picture into blue, yellow, and red images. When black is added, the four colors combine to reproduce all the colors of the original picture.

COLORBLINDNESS

Not all people see colors in the same way. About 8 percent of men and less than 1 percent of women have trouble seeing certain colors. This condition is called *colorblindness*. Colorblind people usually see all colors normally except those that are shades of red and green.

People with normal color vision can sense the three basic colors of red, green, and blue. Colorblind people have reduced ability to see red or green, or both. A red-blind person will confuse red and green and has trouble seeing a red object if it is on a black background. Any color that is a mixture of red, such as orange or purple, is seen by the red-blind person as

Fig. 9–26 *This is a standard test for colorblindness. Can you see the numbers in this photo?*

if there were no red present. Thus orange looks yellow and purple is seen as blue. A green-blind person sees a green object as gray. In a mixture of colors, the green will not be seen. For example, a blue-green object will appear to be pale blue. See Fig. 9–26.

SUMMARY

The primary colors of light can be mixed to produce all other colors. Colors we see are the result of light that is reflected from a surface. The color is a result of absorption of certain frequencies. Since the colors of paints are a result of the way light is reflected, their primary colors differ from those of colored light. Color images may be made by combining colored lights or colored inks.

QUESTIONS

Use complete sentences to write your answers.

1. Using examples, explain how the mixing of light colors differs from the mixing of paint colors.
2. What are complementary colors?
3. Describe a situation in which interference of light waves produces color.
4. How are the colored pictures in this book printed? Why are these pictures called "four-color" pictures?

1. When light colors are mixed the colors are added. When paint colors are mixed most of the colors are absorbed. For example, green is a primary light color. Mixing blue and yellow paint gives green since that is the only color that both blue and yellow paint reflect.
2. Complementary colors are two colors that combine to produce white.
3. A soap bubble (or oil film on water) reflects light from both the inner and outer surfaces of the film to produce a spectrum.
4. The pictures are printed using the three primary paint colors plus black. Because of this, they are called "four-color" photographs.

SKILL-BUILDING ACTIVITY

See teacher's commentary for teaching hints, safety, and answers to questions.

COLOR PIGMENTS

PURPOSE: You will predict which pigment colors are present in black ink.

MATERIALS:

black felt-tip pen
strip of filter paper
beaker, 400 mL
water
cardboard cover for beaker
transparent tape

PROCEDURE:

A. Place a dot of black ink from the felt-tip pen about 2 cm from one end of the paper strip.

B. Tape the other end of the strip to the beaker cover so that the inked end will hang down into the beaker when the lid is on.

C. Put about 3 cm of water in the bottom of the beaker.

D. Place the lid on the beaker so that about 1 cm of the paper strip is under water. See Fig. 9–27 (a).

1. Based on what you know about the primary colors of paint, what colors do you predict are in black ink?

E. Observe carefully as the water soaks up into the paper strip.

2. Describe what happens during the next 10 minutes.
3. What color pigments are in the black ink? Was your prediction correct?

CONCLUSION:

1. Describe a method for separating the pigments in an ink so you can see which colors are present.

EXTENSION:

F. Repeat steps A through E using different colored inks. Record your results and compare them with the results obtained using black ink. See Fig. 9–27 (b).

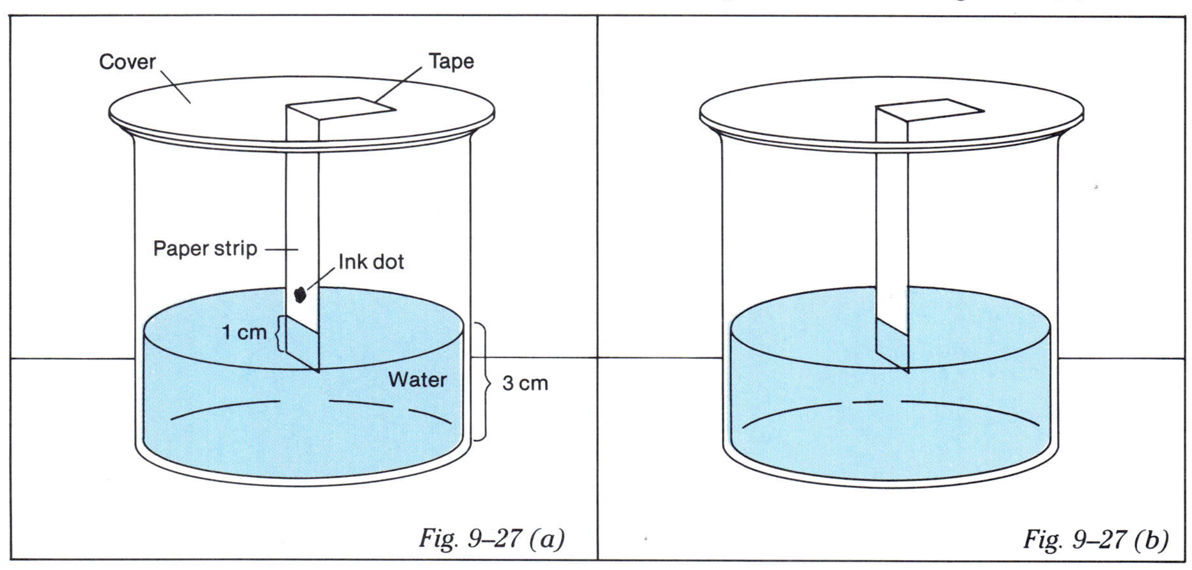

Fig. 9–27 (a)

Fig. 9–27 (b)

INVESTIGATION

See teacher's commentary for teaching hints, safety, and answers to questions.

SEEING COLOR

PURPOSE: You will observe how objects of various colors look in red, green, and blue light.

MATERIALS:

various objects
light source (slide projector)
red, green, and blue filters

PROCEDURE:

A. Copy the table below.

Object	Color	Color of Filter		
		Red	Green	Blue

B. In the first column, list each object that you will observe. Write the color of the object in the second column.

C. Your teacher will set up a slide projector so that a beam of white light can shine on each object. Place one object at a time in the white light. See Fig. 9–28 (a).

1. What effect does the white light have on the color of each object?

D. Now place the red filter in the path of the light. See Fig. 9–28 (b).

2. What is the color of the light shining on the object?
3. What color does the object appear in this light? Record in your table.

E. Repeat step D using the green filter and then the blue filter. Record your observations in your table.

CONCLUSION:

1. In your own words, explain why an object appears to be different colors when seen in red, green, or blue light.

Fig. 9–28 (a)

Fig. 9–28 (b)

TECHNOLOGY

COMPUTER GRAPHICS

The art and science of creating images with a computer lies in the ability to translate form, texture, and color into a series of instructions that a computer can understand. These instructions are called algorithms or mathematical models. These models and others like them are explained in the Technology Feature called "Digitization" in Chapter 12. Here we will explain the nature of what you see in a computer-generated picture.

Look at the computer graphic shown in the photo. Notice the squarish and jagged edges of the image. Most graphics programs currently in use contain pictures with squared or jagged edges. They do not produce smooth, rounded images because of the method by which the video screen produces its image. The screen is made up of picture elements called "pixels." These are rows and columns of squares similar to the boxes in a crossword puzzle. Just as the directions for the crossword tell what letter goes into each box, so the instructions for the computer tell what color goes into each pixel. The picture, or computer graphic, is made by filling in all the boxes on the screen. The number of pixels on a screen determines how round or square the graphic will be. The greater the number of pixels on the screen, the more realistic the picture is. This same principle applies to different kinds of print. Look at a picture in this book, then look at a picture on the front page of a newspaper. The book picture is clearer, the objects are more defined. To find out why, look at each again with a magnifying glass. There are more dots and fewer spaces in the book. The newspaper picture is printed with 60 dots of ink per square inch. But the textbook picture is printed with 120 dots of ink per square inch.

To add color to an image, the computer mixes what is called a palette from the three primary colors with red, blue, and green sources of light. Black is, of course, the absence of all three. The palette is stored as information in the memory of the computer.

Computer graphics are being used for a number of purposes, video games being only one of them. Advertising is currently the heaviest user of computer graphics and may continue to be for some time. They are also used to produce charts, graphs, and illustrated tables and simulations in business, medicine, the military, and education. They are used by the military for what are called "simulations." (A simulation is a model or game that resembles the actual thing very closely.) Science fiction and fantasy films are also making heavy use of this technology as well. With computer graphics they can create worlds that would be very expensive (or impossible) to actually manufacture or engineer.

What will the future bring? Suppose a computer could produce a perfect picture of you standing either next to the President of the United States or at the scene of a crime. Then could we still say seeing is believing?

CHAPTER REVIEW

See teacher's commentary for answers.

VOCABULARY

On a separate piece of paper, match each term with the number of the statement that best explains it. Use each term only once.

complementary colors interference colors laser visible spectrum
incandescent primary colors prism

1. A pair of colors of light that combine to produce white.
2. Produced when white light is divided into its separate colors.
3. Able to divide white light into its separate colors.
4. Gives off visible light when heated.
5. Colors that are produced when reflected light waves combine to strengthen or cancel each other.
6. A device that produces a beam of light that is made up almost completely of a single frequency.
7. Red, blue, and green.

QUESTIONS

Give brief but complete answers to each of the following questions. Unless otherwise indicated, use complete sentences to write your answers.

1. Describe how a prism produces a spectrum from white light. Draw a diagram and label the colors produced.
2. Why does the sky appear blue at midday and red at sunset?
3. What is meant by, "If light waves were like sound, ordinary light would be noise while laser light would be a pure tone"?
4. List three light sources and describe how they produce light.
5. What would the American flag look like if seen (a) in green light? (b) in red light?
6. Describe an experiment to determine the complement of red light.
7. Name the primary light colors and state how they differ from the primary paint colors.
8. Explain how a color TV picture is produced.
9. How do we know that light from the sun is composed of many colors?
10. Explain why the outer band of a rainbow is red.
11. How does the spectrum produced by a soap film (or oil film on water) differ in the way it is produced from the spectrum produced by white light going through a prism?

12. In your own words, describe how a laser produces coherent light. What is coherent light?
13. What color would a red sweater appear to be if you saw it in green light? What color would a green sweater appear in green light?
14. Draw a diagram to show how a prism separates white light into a spectrum of colors. Label the colors of the spectrum. Which color has the highest frequency? Which color has the lowest frequency?

APPLYING SCIENCE

1. Studies have been made of the effect of colors on humans. Some colors create a "cool" atmosphere while others create a "warm" atmosphere. Colors may make you feel happy, sad, excited, calm, and so forth. Write a report on which colors create these moods and suggest ways to improve the color schemes around you.
2. Demonstrate the difference between photos taken in sunlight and photos taken in infrared light. Do you need special film for infrared light? Explain. Show how photos differ when various kinds of light filters are used. Explain what the filters do to the light.
3. Get a copy of the Ishihara Colorblindness Test and check yourself and other members of your class to find out if they see the same colors as you see. Report on the theory of how people see color.
4. Calculate the wavelengths of all six parts of the electromagnetic spectrum. Use the formula velocity = frequency × wavelength. From your results, explain why X-rays and cosmic rays penetrate matter more easily than visible light.

BIBLIOGRAPHY

Bova, B. *Amazing Laser*. Philadelphia: Westminster Press, 1972.

Branley, F. M. *Color: From Rainbows to Lasers*. New York: Thomas Y. Crowell, 1978.

Maurer, A. *Lasers: Light Waves of the Future*. New York: Arco, 1982.

Nassau, K. "The Causes of Color." *Scientific American*, October 1982.

Scientific American. *Light and Its Uses: Making and Using Lasers, Holograms, Interferometers, and Instruments of Dispersion*. San Francisco: Freeman, 1980.

Simon, H. *The Magic of Color*. New York: Lothrop, Lee, and Shepard, 1981.

UNIT

3

CURRENTS AND CIRCUITS

CHAPTER
10

This photo shows how important electricity is in our lives. Electricity lights our homes and office buildings. We use electricity in many different ways each day in homes, schools, and offices.

ELECTRICITY

CHAPTER GOALS

1. Explain what causes an object to have an electric charge.
2. Describe how electrically charged objects affect each other.
3. Explain how an electric current flows in a conductor.
4. Compare direct current and alternating current.
5. Explain the difference between a series circuit and a parallel circuit.

10-1. Static Electricity

At the end of this section you will be able to:

- ☐ Use examples to show how a person or an object can have an electric charge.
- ☐ Predict the behavior of objects that have electric charges.
- ☐ Explain what causes a change in the electric force between charged objects.

Have you ever walked across a carpet and then felt a shock when you touched a metal doorknob? Have you ever heard a small crackling sound when you combed your hair? Perhaps you have noticed that while combing or brushing your hair, the hair seems to cling to the comb or brush. These experiences are the result of electric charges.

KINDS OF ELECTRIC CHARGE

Try this experiment. Rub a comb briskly with a piece of cloth. Then quickly bring the comb near some small bits of paper. The pieces of paper will usually be attracted to the comb. The comb can attract the paper because it picked up an electric charge when you rubbed it with the cloth. Rubbing two different materials together often causes the materials to become electrically charged. See Fig. 10–1. When you walk across a carpet, the friction of your shoes on the carpet may cause your body to pick up an electric charge. When electric charges build up, they produce *static electricity*. The word "static" means "stationary." Static electricity is caused by electric charges that are stationary, or fixed in one place.

Reinforcement: Vinyl rubbed with wool takes on a strong negative charge. Acetate rubbed with cotton becomes strongly positive. Demonstrate both attraction and repulsion to illustrate the text material. Point out that only repulsion can establish that both objects are charged.

Fig. 10–1 Static electricity causes these bits of paper to cling to the comb.

Objects with an electric charge affect each other in one of two ways. (1) Two charged objects may pull toward each other. (2) Two charged objects may push away from each other. For example, a hard rubber rod rubbed with fur is touched to a light-weight ball hanging on a string. See Fig. 10–2. After touching the rod, the ball is pushed away. When charged objects push away from each other, they are said to *repel* each other. The suspended ball is repelled when the rubber rod is near it. If a glass rod is rubbed with a silk cloth, the ball is attracted to the glass rod. This is shown in Fig. 10–3.

Observations like these have led scientists to the conclusion that there are two kinds of electric charges. Experiments show that two objects with the same kind of electric charge will repel each other. Since the ball touched the rubber rod, it picked up the same charge as the rubber rod. The ball and the rod then repelled each other. Objects with different charges attract each other. The ball was attracted to the glass rod because a glass rod takes on a different charge than a rubber rod. The behavior of objects with electric charges can be described by a simple rule: *Like charges repel each other; unlike charges attract.* See Fig. 10–4. Can you apply this rule to explain what is happening in the photo? All of the hairs on the girl's head seem to be repelling each other. Later in this section you will find out why.

Fig. 10–2 When the rubber rod is rubbed with a piece of fur, it picks up a negative electric charge and repels the ball.

Fig. 10–3 When the glass rod is rubbed with a piece of silk, it picks up a positive charge and attracts the ball.

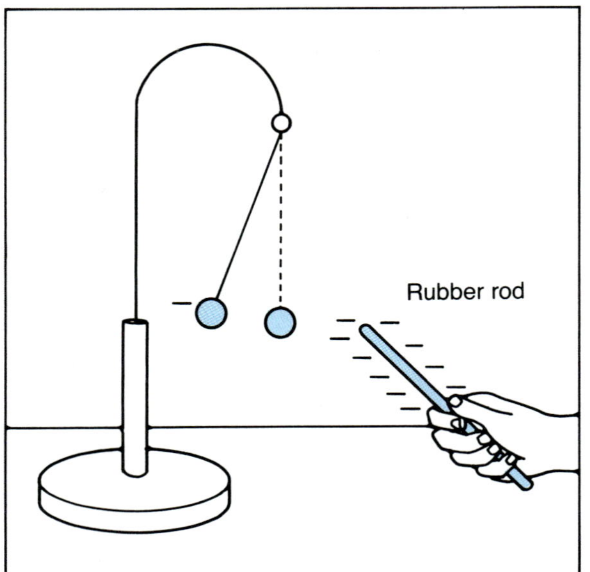

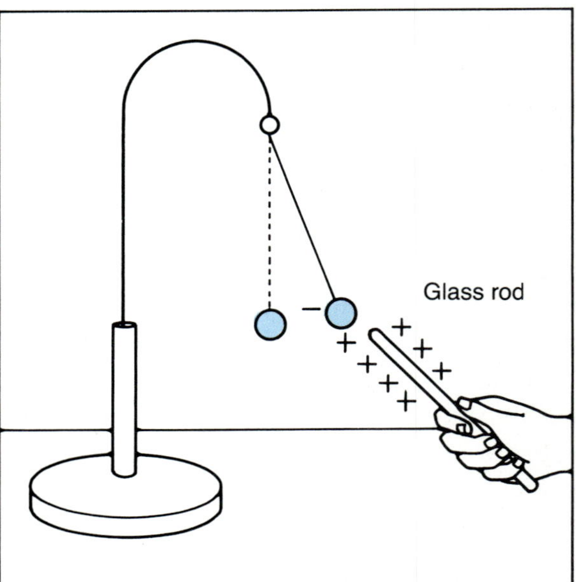

Fig. 10–4 The hairs on the person's head all picked up the same kind of electric charge from the machine shown. The hairs are repelling each other.

One of the scientists who studied electricity was Benjamin Franklin. In addition to being a statesman and author, Franklin was an outstanding scientist. Much of his scientific work was done with electricity. One of his most famous electrical experiments showed that lightning is a form of electricity. In 1752, Franklin flew a kite on a thin wire into a thunderstorm. (CAUTION: Do *not* attempt to repeat this experiment.) The lower end of the wire was attached to a string that held a metal key. Franklin knew that holding the wire directly could be dangerous because the lightning charge could travel down the wire to the key. However, a spark did jump from the key to his hand. See Fig. 10–5. This proved that the clouds contained an electric charge. The spark from Franklin's key was similar to the shock you sometimes feel when you walk on a carpet and then touch a metal object. However, the charges causing lightning are very large. Franklin's experiment could easily have killed him in spite of his safety measures.

Like other scientists of his time, Franklin thought that electricity was an invisible fluid. The electric fluid was supposed to flow from one object to another. He thought that the two kinds of electric charges were the result of the amount of this electric fluid in an object. Franklin was wrong about the cause of electric charges. However we still use his method of naming the two kinds of electric charges.

Fig. 10–5 Franklin's experiment showed that lightning is a form of electricity. Why was this a dangerous experiment?

Positive charge The electric charge given to a glass rod when it is rubbed with a silk cloth.

Negative charge The electric charge given to a hard rubber rod when it is rubbed with fur.

Neutral The term describing an object that has equal amounts of positive and negative electric charge.

Franklin suggested that the two kinds of electric charge be called **positive** (+) and **negative** (−). The charge on the rubber rod rubbed with fur is a *negative* charge. The charge on a glass rod rubbed with silk is *positive*. Following Franklin's system for naming electric charges, we say that all objects that behave like the glass rod are positively charged. All objects that behave like the rubber rod are said to be negatively charged. When an object has neither a positive nor a negative electric charge, the object is **neutral.** An object that is electrically *neutral* has an equal number of positive and negative charges that cancel each other. See Fig. 10–6. Most objects are neutral. However, the electric charges within materials such as steel are also important. The attraction between opposite charges gives steel its strength.

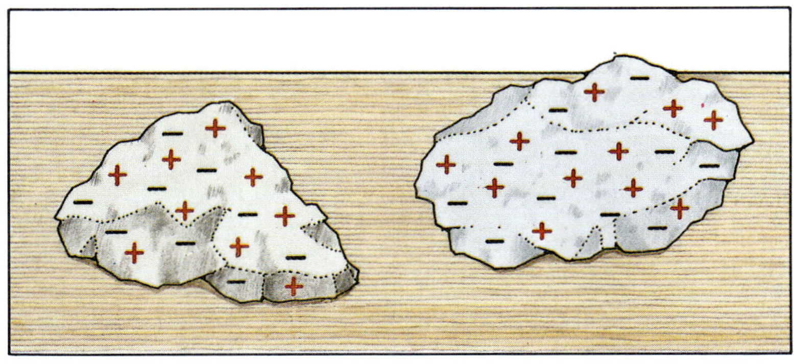

Fig. 10–6 Most objects have about the same amount of positive and negative charge and are therefore neutral.

ELECTRIC FORCE

You have learned that a force is any push or pull. Thus when two electrically charged objects attract or repel each other, a force is acting upon them. This force is called the **electric force.** *Electric forces* cause charged objects to attract or repel each other based on the kind of charge they have.

Electric force The force that causes two like-charged objects to repel each other or two unlike-charged objects to attract each other.

Electric force works at a distance. That is, two electrically charged objects can be affected by an electric force even when they are some distance apart.

Two things affect the size of electric forces. First, the more an object is rubbed to give it an electric charge, the stronger the electric force produced. For example, rub a plastic ruler once with a cloth. Then hold the charged ruler about one centimeter away from another charged object such as a hanging ball. The ruler will attract or repel the ball only slightly. Now rub the same ruler ten times. The amount of charge increases. The ruler will now attract or repel the ball with much greater force. *The strength of the electric force between two objects increases as the amount of electric charge on one or both objects increases.*

It is difficult to build up very large electric charges by rubbing a ruler with a cloth. However, there are machines that can build up very large electric charges. An example of a machine that produces static electricity is a Van de Graaff generator. The way the machine works is shown in Fig. 10–7. If you touched an operating Van de Graaff generator, you would pick up a very large static electric charge. This would cause all of the hairs on your head to have the same charge. The hairs would then repel each other to produce the effect seen in Fig. 10–4. Scientists use Van de Graaff generators and similar machines to help study the structure of atoms.

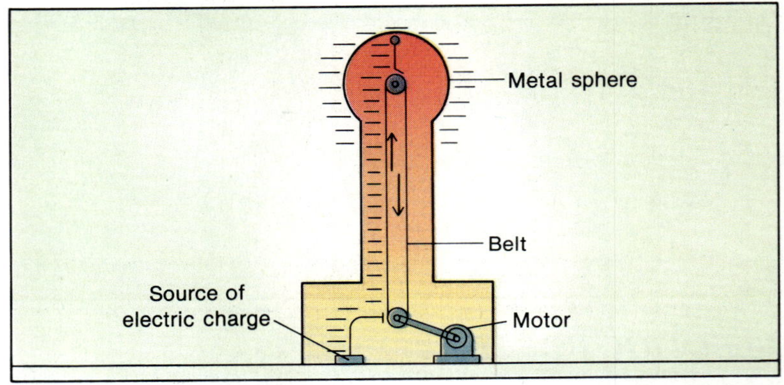

Fig. 10–7 This diagram shows how a Van de Graaff generator like the one shown in Fig. 10–4 produces electric charges.

Distance also affects the size of an electric force. Charged objects have a greater effect on each other as they come closer together. If the two charged objects are 100 cm apart, reducing the distance between them to 50 cm causes the electric force to become four times greater. In other words, cutting the distance in half causes the force to become four times greater. In the same way, moving the objects 200 cm apart reduces the force to one-quarter of what it was. The relationship between electric force and the distance between charged objects is shown in Fig. 10–8 (a) and Fig. 10–8 (b).

Skills: Problem solving skills can be reinforced with Coulomb's law problems. Vary the amount of charge on each object and the separation of the objects.

This relationship is known as *Coulomb's law* after the French scientist Charles Coulomb. Coulomb's law can be stated:

$$F = k\frac{q_1 q_2}{d^2}$$

In other words, the force between two charged objects is directly proportional to the amount of charge on each object (q_1 and q_2). The force is inversely proportional to the square of the distance between the two objects (d^2).

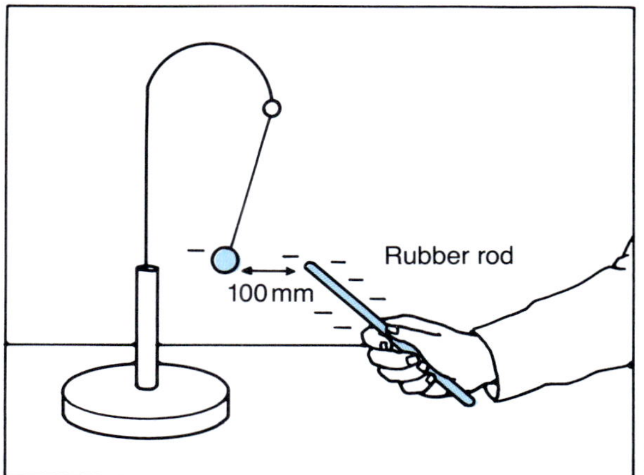

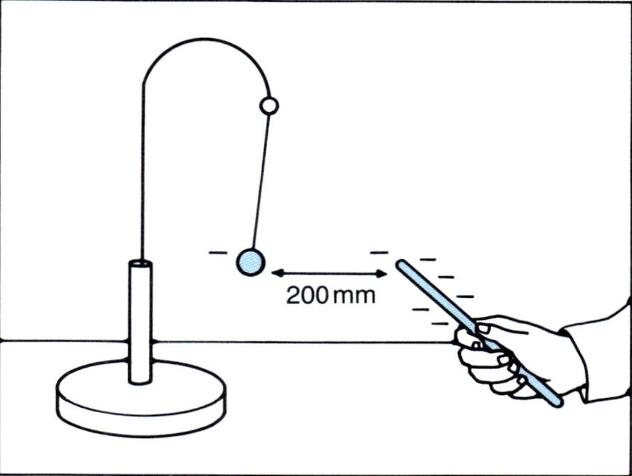

Fig. 10–8 The closer the rod is to the ball, the stronger the electric force between them (a). As the distance between the rod and the ball increases, the electric force between them becomes weaker (b).

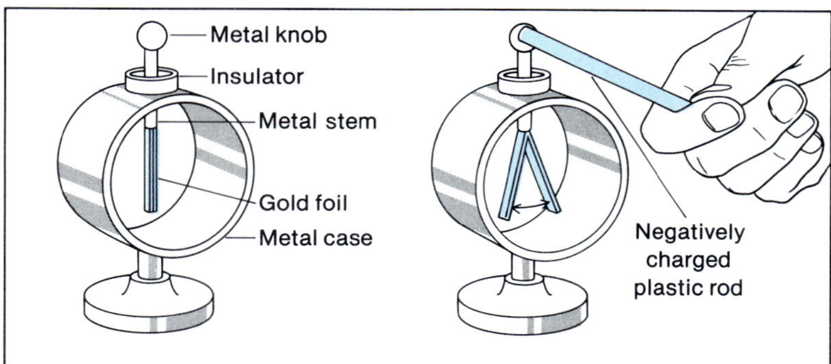

Fig. 10–9 This diagram shows how an electroscope can be charged by contact with a negatively charged rod.

An instrument called an *electroscope* shows the presence of static electric charges. An electroscope contains two thin metal strips. These strips are often made of gold because gold can be made very thin. When the electroscope has no charge and is neutral, the two metal strips hang down. However, when a charged object touches the top of the metal rod supporting the strips, the strips pick up part of the charge. The electric force between the two charged metal leaves pushes them apart. See Fig. 10–9. The electrons move from the plastic rod to the knob and down the stem to the gold strips.

Since electric forces work at a distance, there is a space around every charged object in which the electric force can be measured. Such a region of space is called an **electric field.** The *electric field* surrounds the charged object in all directions. As you have already seen, the size of the electric force becomes smaller as the distance becomes larger. Finally, at some specific distance, the electric field grows too weak to be noticeable.

Electric field The region of space around an electrically charged object in which an electric force is noticeable.

USING STATIC ELECTRICITY

The behavior of electrically charged objects is useful in many ways. For example, most copying machines use static electricity. (1) A flat plate made of a conducting material is given a positive charge. (2) A light projects an image of the material to be copied onto the plate. The parts of the plate on which the light falls lose their electric charge. The dark areas remain charged. (3) A powder carrying negative charges is sprinkled over the plate. This power sticks to the positively charged parts of the plate. (4) A piece of paper is then laid on the plate and given a positive charge. (5) The negative powder sticks to the paper, creating a copy of the original printing. Heating the paper melts the powder and permanently attaches it to the paper. These steps are shown in Fig. 10–10. Copying by this method is called *xerography*. Xerography means "dry writing." It comes from the Greek words *xeros* meaning "dry" and *graphein* meaning "to write."

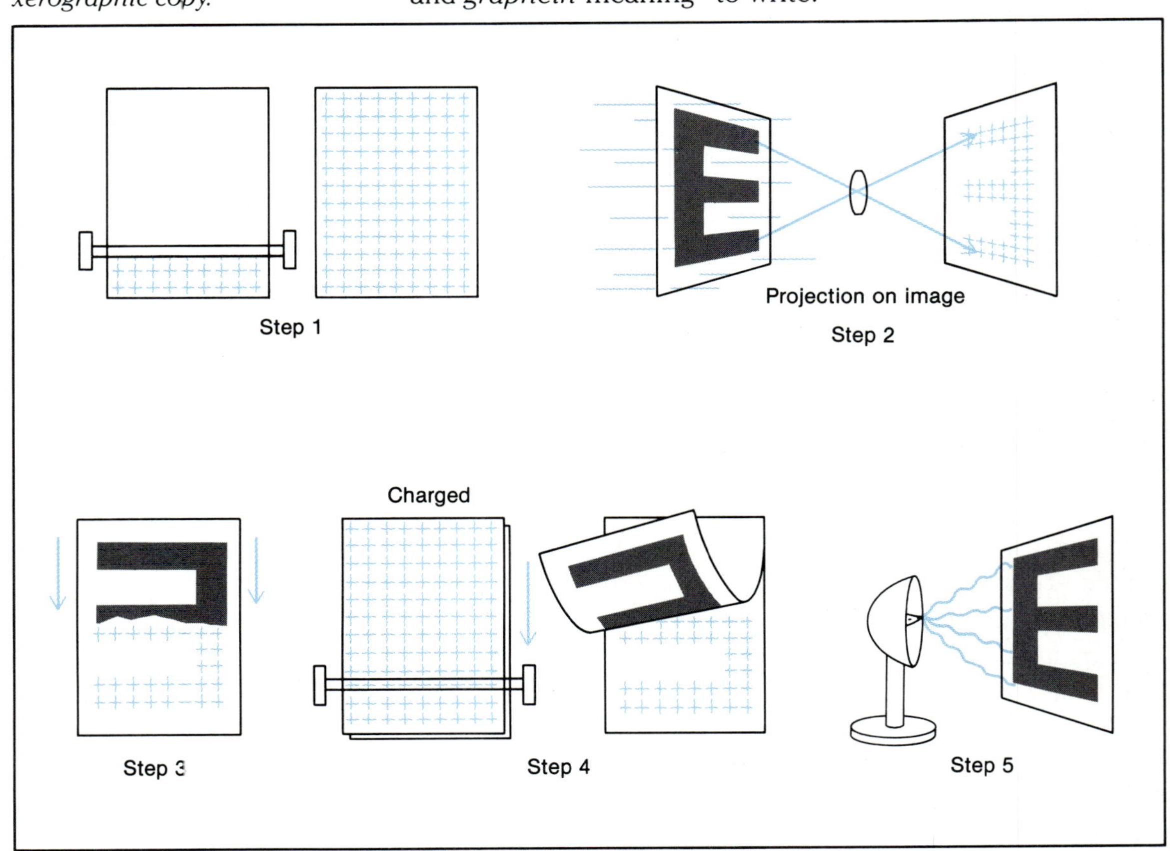

Fig. 10–10 This diagram shows the steps in making a xerographic copy.

Electric charges can also be used to filter unwanted solid materials from the air. Smoke particles, for example, carry electric charges. The smoke particles can be removed from the air by passing the air over a filter containing electrically charged wires or plates. See Fig. 10–11. The charged particles are attracted to either the positively charged or negatively charged parts of the filter. Removal of solid particles from smoke greatly reduces the pollution caused by the smoke. However, only particles are removed. Harmful gases passing out of the smokestack are not removed by this process. Some of these gases can cause acid rain.

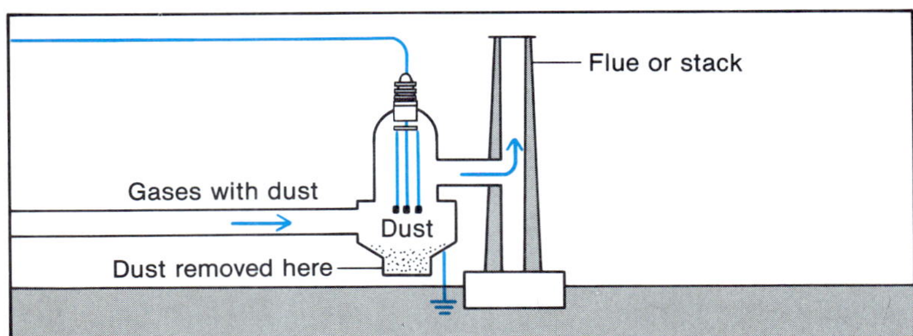

Fig. 10–11 An electrostatic precipitator uses static electricity to remove dust particles from smokestack gases.

SUMMARY

There are two kinds of electric charges. Objects with the same charge repel each other while objects with different charges attract each other. The size of the force causing attraction or repulsion changes in size when the charge on the objects or the distance between them changes. Any object with an electric charge is surrounded by an electric field.

QUESTIONS

Use complete sentences to write your answers.

1. Explain how an object can pick up an electric charge. Give two examples.
2. How do two electrically charged objects act if (a) both objects have a positive charge? (b) one object is positive and the other is negative?
3. When is an object electrically neutral?
4. What two things affect the force between charged objects? Describe the effect of each.
5. Describe two practical uses of static electricity.

1. Rubbing an object is one way to give it an electric charge. Combing your hair and walking across a rug are two examples.
2. (a) The objects will repel each other. (b) The objects will attract each other.
3. When an object has the same amount of positive charge as it has negative charge, it is neutral.
4. The amount of charge on the objects and the distance between the objects affect the force between charged objects. Increasing the charge will increase the force. Increasing the distance will decrease the force.
5. Static electricity is used in most copying machines and also in air filters to remove smoke particles.

INVESTIGATION

See teacher's commentary for teaching hints, safety, and answers to questions.

ELECTRIC CHARGES

PURPOSE: You will observe the effect of forces caused by electric charges and compare these forces.

MATERIALS:

2 plastic rulers
nylon thread
waxed paper or wool
paper
chalk eraser
piece of aluminum foil
transparent tape

PROCEDURE:

A. Tie one end of a nylon thread around the center of one plastic ruler.

B. Hold the ruler at the center and rub both ends with a piece of waxed paper or wool. Rub fairly hard.

C. Hang the ruler by the thread so that the ruler is balanced. See Fig. 10–12. You can hang the ruler from a ringstand or from the edge of a table.

D. Hold the second plastic ruler by one end. Rub the other end with waxed paper.

E. Bring the end of the second ruler near one end of the hanging ruler.

   1. Is there a force acting on the rulers?
   2. Does the force attract or repel the rulers? (Note: If the rulers are attracted, repeat steps B through E.)

F. Bring the second ruler near the other end of the hanging ruler.

   3. Is the reaction at this end different from that at the other end?

G. Bring your hand near one end of the hanging ruler.

   4. Do your hand and the ruler attract each other?

H. Rub the second ruler with other materials such as paper, a chalk eraser, your shirt, or anything else handy. Now bring the second ruler close to the first ruler.

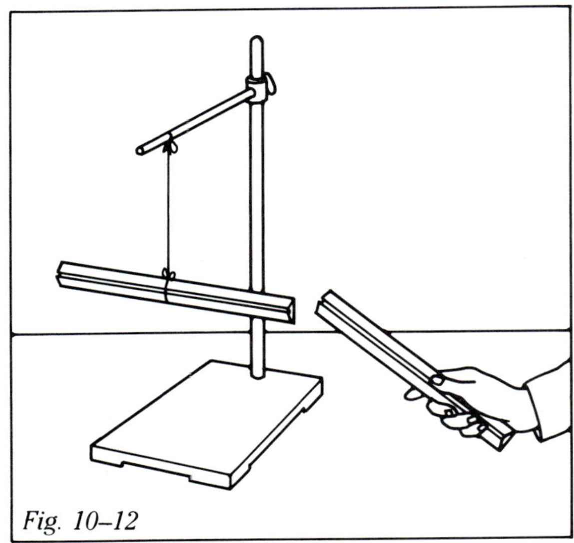

Fig. 10–12

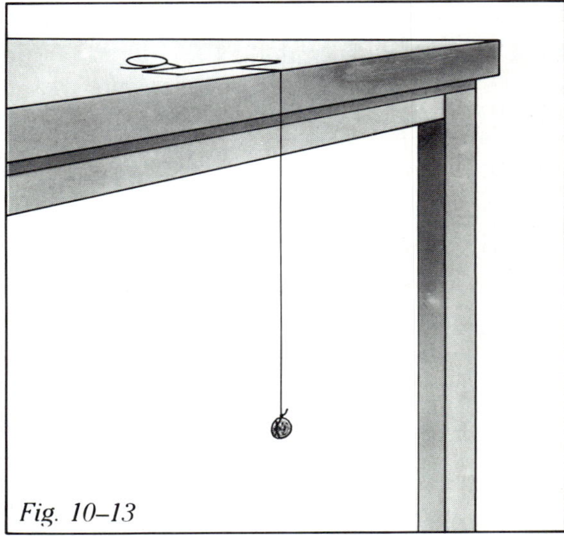

Fig. 10–13

5. Do the rulers attract or repel each other?

I. If there is no reaction, charge the first ruler with waxed paper again and repeat step H.

J. Crush a piece of aluminum foil into a ball about 0.5 cm in diameter. Tie a piece of thread around the ball. Tape the end of the thread to the edge of your desk. See Fig. 10–13.

K. Rub a ruler briskly with waxed paper. Bring the ruler near the aluminum ball.

6. When you first bring the ruler near the ball, is the ball attracted or repelled by the ruler?

L. Move the ruler back and forth so that the ball touches the ruler at several places. Continue rubbing the ruler and touching it to the ball until they repel each other forcibly.

M. After the ball and the ruler repel each other, hold the ruler 5 cm from the ball. Slowly move it closer. See Fig. 10–14 (a).

7. Describe the effect on the ball as the ruler gets closer.

8. What does this effect tell you about the force acting on the ball?

N. While the charged ball and the ruler are repelling each other, touch the charged ball with an uncharged aluminum ball hanging from a thread. See Fig. 10–14 (b).

9. Does changing the charge on the ball change the force?

CONCLUSIONS:

1. Explain how you can produce an electric charge on a plastic object.
2. Explain how the amount of charge and the distance between two charged objects affects the force between them.

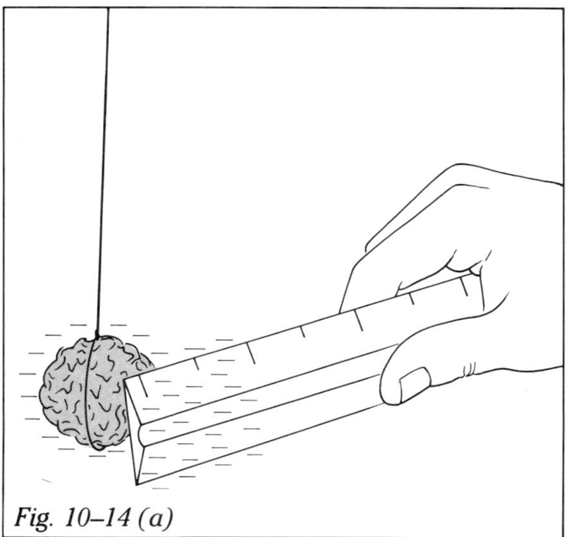

Fig. 10–14 (a)

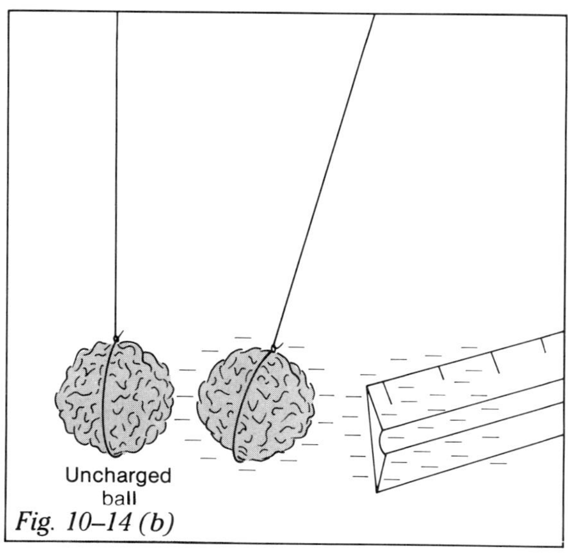

Fig. 10–14 (b)

10-2. Electric Current

At the end of this section you will be able to:

- Explain what is meant by a *scientific model.*
- Describe what causes an *electric current.*
- Compare a conductor and an insulator and give three examples of each.

A bolt of lightning has tremendous power. A single flash of lightning can heat the air to a temperature higher than the surface of the sun. See Fig. 10–15. Holes have been melted in church bells struck by lightning. Chains have been melted into iron bars. Potatoes in a field struck by lightning have been cooked in the ground. For all its great power, lightning is basically the same as the feeble spark that jumps from your hand to a doorknob when you walk across a carpet.

Fig. 10–15 Every year, many people are killed or seriously injured by being struck by lightning.

Fig. 10–16 Electric charges can build up on your body when you walk across a rug. When you touch a doorknob, the charges can jump from your hand to the metal knob.

MOVING ELECTRIC CHARGES

Scuffing your feet across a carpet may give your body an electric charge. You are not aware of the charge unless you touch a metal object. Then you suddenly feel a small electric shock. See Fig. 10–16. The shock you feel is the result of the electric charge moving from your body to the metal object. You cannot see the electric charge as it moves. Sometimes it may make a small spark, but the charge itself is not visible. When scientists want to study something that cannot be seen, they often use a **scientific model.** A *scientific model* is a sort of mental picture of something that cannot be seen directly.

Scientific model A kind of mental picture used by scientists to describe something that cannot be seen.

One scientific model is used to explain how objects become electrically charged. It also explains how charges can move from one place to another. It is called the **electron** (ih-**lek**-tron) model. An *electron* is a negatively charged particle of matter that is so small it is invisible. The fact that many objects can pick up an electric charge when they are rubbed with another material can be explained by the electron model. Rubbing two materials together causes electrons to be torn away from one material and added to the other. For example, clothes taken from a dryer often cling together because they are electrically charged. This results from the different kinds of cloth rubbing together as the clothes are tumbled in the dryer. The rubbing causes electrons to move from one garment to another. The clothes that have picked up added electrons take on a negative charge. See Fig. 10–17.

Electron A particle of matter with a negative charge that is so small it is invisible.

Fig. 10–17 Has this ever happened to you? Static electricity makes the clothes cling together after they are removed from the dryer.

Objects do not usually have an electric charge even if electrons are present. Those objects are neutral because they also contain particles with positive charges. Such particles are found in all matter. These particles are called **protons (proe-tons)**. A *proton* is a very small particle of matter with a positive electric charge. Matter, then, is usually neutral because it contains an equal number of protons and electrons. Normally, you do not have an electric charge. You are neutral because the negative electrons in your body are cancelled by the positive protons. When you walk across a carpet, you pick up extra electrons. Then your body has a negative charge.

Proton A very small particle of matter with a positive electric charge.

ELECTRIC CURRENT

In some ways, electrons behave like water. Water can flow from one place to another. Usually, gravity causes water to flow downhill. Electrons can also move or "flow" from one place to another. It is not gravity, however, that causes electrons to move. Electrons move from a place where there are a greater number of them to a place where there are fewer. This movement of electrons causes an **electric current** to flow. An *electric current* is the result of electrons moving from one place to another. For example, you may pick up extra electrons from a carpet or similar material. When you touch something that has no extra electrons, such as doorknob, some electrons may flow from you to the doorknob. A small electric current flows between you and the doorknob. While you cannot feel an electric charge, you feel an electric current as a shock.

Electric current The result of electrons moving from one place to another.

LIGHTNING

Lightning is a common example of the movement of a large number of electrons. Some clouds are like the Van de Graaff machines that build up large amounts of electric charge. Scientists still do not fully understand how clouds are able to build up electric charges. One theory says that the top of a cloud holds negatively charged raindrops and positively charged ice particles. The raindrops fall through the cloud causing its lower parts to become negative. Thus, the lower part of the cloud builds up a huge supply of negative electrons. These electrons may suddenly move from one part of the cloud to another. Or they may jump from the cloud to the ground. This large number of electrons moving through the air cause the air to become very hot. The heated air gives off brilliant light. We see this as a flash of lightning. At the same time, the heated air rushes outward to make sound waves that we hear as thunder.

Buildings can be protected from lightning by lightning rods. Lightning rods are pointed metal rods. They are placed on the highest part of a building. These rods are connected to the earth by a heavy wire. A lightning rod can protect a building in two ways: (1) If electrons move from the cloud to strike the building, they strike the lightning rod first. The building itself is not struck by the lightning. The wire then carries the electric charge from the lightning rod to the earth. (2) Some parts of a cloud are positively charged. Electrons can flow from the earth to the cloud through the lightning rod. See Fig. 10–18. This neutralizes the charge on the cloud.

Fig. 10–18 This diagram shows two ways in which a lightning rod can protect a home from lightning: (a) by transferring the charge to the earth (right) or (b) by neutralizing the charge on the cloud and preventing lightning (left).

In a house not protected by lightning rods, a TV antenna may be struck by lightning. This can cause a fire and seriously damage the electric wires in the house. A person standing close to any part of a house struck by lightning can be injured or killed. For the same reason, you should stay away from trees and tall structures when outdoors in a thunderstorm. If you are standing in an open field, you may be struck directly. A large building with a steel frame is safe from lightning. The metal in the building acts like a lightning rod. The inside of an automobile is also safe. The metal body keeps the charges outside of the car.

INSULATORS AND CONDUCTORS

Insulator A material that does not allow electrons to flow through it easily.

Conductor A material that can carry an electric current because electrons can move through it easily.

Lightning would not happen if electrons could move easily through the air. Air is an example of an **insulator** (**in**-suh-late-ur). Any substance that does not allow electrons to flow easily through it is called an *insulator*. If air were not an insulator, electrons could not build up in clouds. Instead, they would leak away through the air. Most substances that are not metals are insulators. Examples of such substances are plastics, glass, and rubber. Some materials, like the metal in a doorknob, allow electrons to flow freely. These materials are called **conductors** (kun-**duk**-turz). Any *conductor* carries electric current because electrons can easily move through it. For example, see Fig. 10–19. When a conductor joins the two wires, the circuit is completed and the bulb will light. The bulb will not light if the material is an insulator. Metals such as copper, aluminum, and silver are the best conductors. See Fig. 10–20. Just as the flow of heat from a house can be

Fig. 10–19 This diagram shows how to test for insulators and conductors. A conductor will complete the circuit and the bulb will light.

controlled by using insulation, the flow of electrons from a conductor can be stopped by using an insulator. For example, a metal wire can be covered with an insulator such as rubber to prevent the electrons from escaping when an electric current flows through the wire.

Fig. 10–20 Which of the objects in this photo are conductors? Which are insulators?

SUMMARY

Scientists use the electron model to help explain how electric charges move. All matter contains both electrons and protons. Objects can become electrically charged when electrons are added or removed. The movement of electrons produces an electric current. Some materials allow electrons to pass through them freely while other materials do not.

QUESTIONS

Use complete sentences to write your answers.

1. What is a scientific model?
2. How does the electron model explain how objects can become electrically charged?
3. In what way do electrons behave like water?
4. Describe what is meant by an electric current.
5. How does an insulator differ from a conductor? Give three examples of each.

1. A scientific model is a mental picture of something that cannot be seen directly.
2. The electron model says that negatively charged particles can move from one place to another. An object can pick up these particles and become electrically charged.
3. Water can flow from one place to another. In a similar fashion, electrons can flow from one place to another producing an electric current.
4. An electric current is the movement of electrons from one place to another.
5. An insulator does not allow charges to move easily through it. A conductor allows charges to move easily through it. Plastics, glass, and rubber are insulators. Copper, aluminum, and silver are conductors.

SKILL-BUILDING ACTIVITY

See teacher's commentary for teaching hints, safety, and answers to questions.

INSULATORS AND CONDUCTORS

PURPOSE: You will classify various materials as insulators or conductors.

MATERIALS:

battery (6 V)
light bulb
3 insulated wires with clips
wood
plastic
staple
pencil
paper clip
glass
chalk
eraser

PROCEDURE:

A. Set up a battery, a light bulb, and wires as shown in Fig. 10–21.

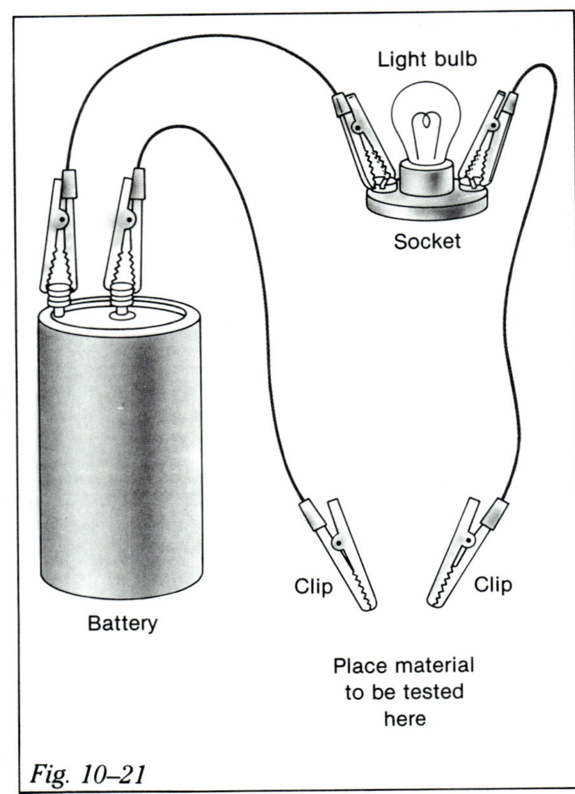

Fig. 10–21

B. Copy the data table below.

Material	Insulator	Conductor
Wood		
Plastic		
Staple		
Glass		
Chalk		
Eraser		
Pencil		
Paper clip		

C. Place the object to be tested between the clips on the wires as shown in the diagram in Fig. 10–21.

1. What will happen if the object tested is a conductor? Explain.
2. What will happen if the object tested is an insulator? Explain.

D. Test each object listed, as well as any other materials you have handy. Record all your results in the data table.

CONCLUSIONS:

1. Of the materials you tested, list three conductors and three insulators.
2. In your own words, describe how you can classify materials as insulators or conductors.
3. Explain why the wires you used in this activity are surrounded by an insulator, such as rubber.
4. Why are electrical wires made of a metal such as copper?

10-3. Electric Circuits

At the end of this section you will be able to:

- ☐ Describe the flow of an electric current.
- ☐ Explain the difference between *direct current* and *alternating current*.
- ☐ Compare a *series circuit* with a *parallel circuit*.

It can be very dangerous to touch a wire that is carrying an electric current. A large number of electrons can travel from the conductor through your body. The result can be fatal. However, birds and squirrels often sit safely on wires carrying a large electric current. See Fig. 10–22. Why are these animals safe from the electric current? You will find out in this section.

Fig. 10–22 These birds are not harmed by the large electric current flowing through the wires. Why not?

THE PATH OF AN ELECTRIC CURRENT

What do switching on a light and turning on a faucet have in common? Opening the faucet lets water flow from the pipe. Turning on an electric light switch permits electrons to flow through the wires. See Fig. 10–23. Water will not flow in the pipe, however, unless a force is present to move it. That force could be supplied by gravity causing the water to flow downhill. A pump could also supply the energy needed to move the water. Electrons flowing through a conductor also need a force to cause them to move.

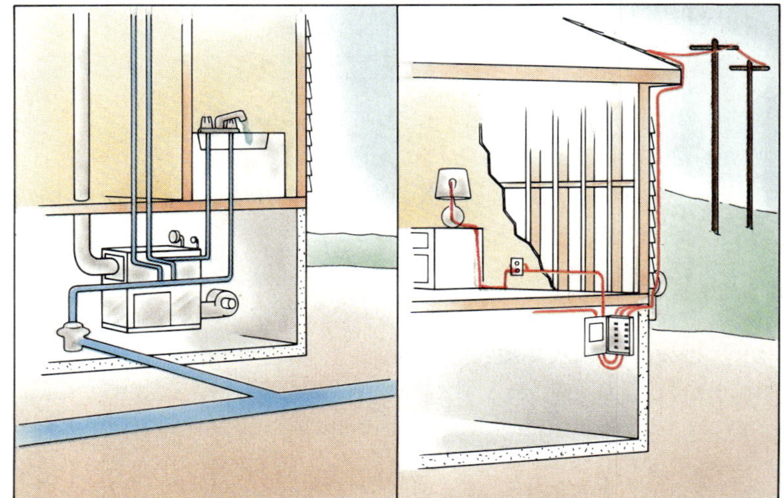

Fig. 10–23 When you turn on a faucet, water flows in the pipes. Similarly, when you turn on a light switch, electric current flows in the wires.

About the year 1800, an Italian scientist named Alessandro Volta discovered a way to make electrons flow through a conductor. Volta found that a combination of two different metals and salt water could make electrons move through a conductor. A chemical reaction between the metals and the salt solution caused the electrons to move. This arrangement of two materials together with a solution causing a flow of electrons is called an *electrochemical cell*. An automobile battery is made up of several electrochemical cells. See Fig. 10–24. Electrical energy in the battery is changed into chemical energy and stored in the cells. Later, the cells in the battery can change the stored chemical energy back into electricity.

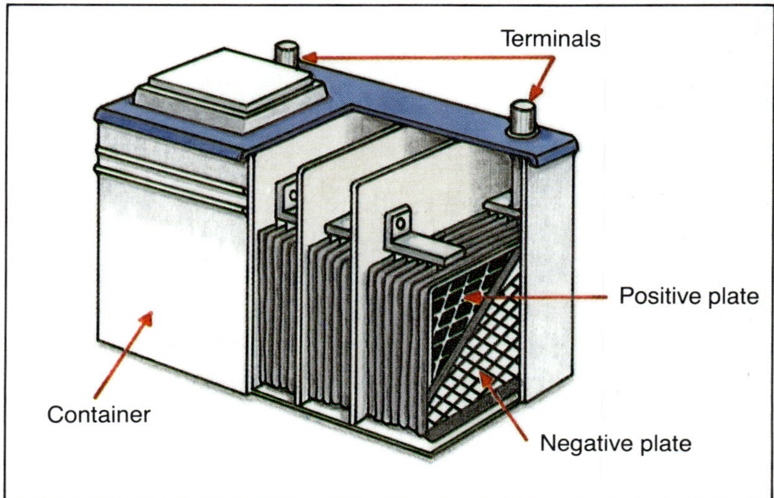

Fig. 10–24 As shown in this diagram, an automobile battery is made up of several electrochemical cells.

An ordinary flashlight battery is also a kind of electrochemical cell. It is often called a *dry cell* because it does not contain a liquid. A moist chemical mixture is used instead of the liquid.

Chemical changes taking place inside the dry cell cause part of the cell to build up a supply of extra electrons. This part of the cell is called the *negative terminal* (−). Another part of the cell lacks a normal supply of electrons. This part of the cell is called the *positive terminal* (+). Wires can be attached easily to the negative and positive terminals of a cell or battery.

ELECTRIC CIRCUITS

If you connect a wire or other conductor between the negative and positive terminals of a cell, the extra electrons at the negative terminal will have a path to get to the positive terminal where electrons are lacking. Electrons will immediately start to flow between the two terminals. You have made an **electric circuit**. An *electric circuit* is a complete path allowing electrons to flow and produce an electric current.

Electric circuit A complete path through which an electric current flows.

When you plug a lamp into an electric outlet and turn on the switch, you are completing an electric circuit. See Fig. 10–25. The two parts of the plug and a pair of wires provide a complete circuit. An electric current can then flow through the lamp that is plugged into the outlet.

Reinforcement: Draw several electric circuits on the board and trace the paths of the current to show complete circuits.

Fig. 10–25 When you turn on an electric switch, you are completing an electric circuit and allowing current to flow.

An electric circuit may also be completed by allowing the electrons to flow into the earth. This is what happens when a lightning rod is struck by lightning. If you touch a conductor carrying an electric current, the electricity may flow through your body to the ground. This might happen if you touched a wire carrying an electric current and also touched a metal pipe at the same time. The electrons could then flow through you to the pipe and then into the ground. You could be seriously injured or killed. It is never safe to allow a wire or other conductor carrying an electric current to touch any part of your body. If this is so, why are the birds shown in Fig. 10–22 not harmed by the large electric currents in the wires? The answer is that they are not part of an electric circuit. They are touching only one wire. The birds could not safely touch two different wires at the same time. If the current could travel through the birds to the earth, the birds would be killed.

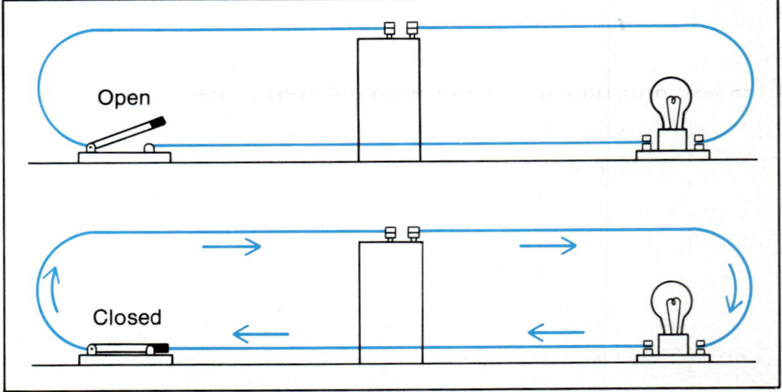

Fig. 10–26 When the switch is open, an electric current cannot flow through the circuit. Closing the switch completes the circuit.

DIRECT AND ALTERNATING CURRENT

Electric circuits in a house are controlled by switches. The circuit is broken when the switch is turned off. When the switch is on, the circuit is complete. See Fig. 10–26. Electrons flowing in a complete circuit are like water flowing in a pipe. However, there is one difference. If you could follow one electron along a wire carrying a current, you would find that the electron itself moves very slowly. It travels only a fraction of a centimeter per second. Yet when you switch on a light, the electric current takes effect and the light goes on almost instantly. You do not have to wait for the electrons to move along the wires. This is because the electrons repel each other.

Electrons repel each other because they all carry a negative charge. An electron in a wire repels other electrons in the wire. Electrons all along the wire pass along this movement from one to the next. This effect travels rapidly along the wire. This is what is meant when electrons are said to "flow" along a conductor.

Electrons do not always flow in the same direction in all electric circuits. When a circuit is made with a dry cell, the electrons always move from the negative terminal to the positive terminal. This is called **direct current** (DC). In a circuit carrying *direct current*, the electrons always flow in one direction. However, the most commonly used current is not direct current. Electric current supplied by power stations changes direction many times each second. This is called **alternating** (**awl**-tur-nay-ting) **current** (AC). *Alternating current* continuously alternates, or changes, its direction of flow. The electric current supplied by power stations in the United States is 60 hertz (Hz) AC. This means that it is alternating current that changes its direction 60 times each second. Some other countries use alternating current with a different frequency.

Direct current An electric current that flows in one direction in an electric circuit.

Alternating current An electric current that changes its direction of flow constantly.

Conductor

Switch

Fuse

Ground

Battery of cells in parallel

Battery of cells in series

Resistor

Symbols Used in Diagrams of Electric Circuits

Fig. 10–27 These are some of the symbols used in electric circuit diagrams.

KINDS OF CIRCUITS

An electric circuit is made up of several parts. There must be a source of electrons to be moved through the circuit. Conductors, usually wires, are needed to connect all the parts. These parts include switches and the appliance to be operated, a light for example. See Fig. 10–27. These items can be

Series circuit An electric circuit in which all the parts are connected one after another.

connected one after another. This arrangement is called a **series circuit.** In a *series circuit*, all parts of an electric circuit are connected one after another. See Fig. 10–28. There is only one path the electrons can follow. A series circuit can cause some problems. Suppose, for example, that light bulbs are arranged in a series circuit. If one bulb fails, the circuit is broken and all the bulbs go out. See Fig. 10–29. No part of a series circuit can be switched off without turning off the whole thing. If the lights in a house were connected in series, they would all have to be on or off at the same time.

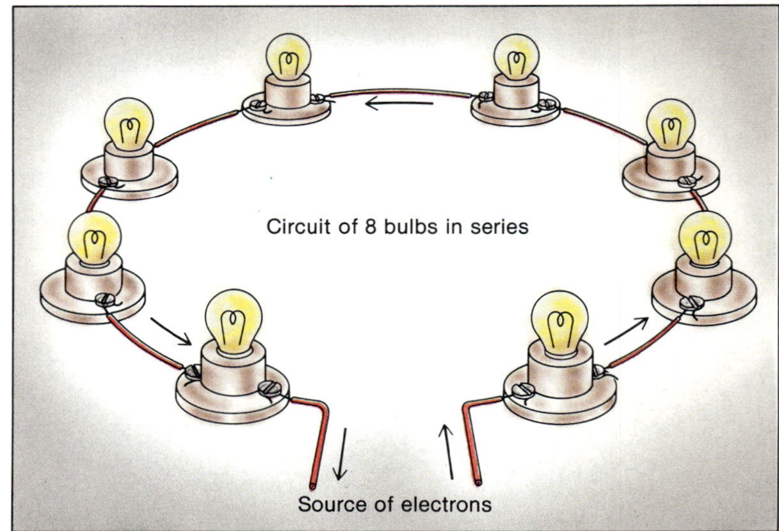

Fig. 10–28 This diagram shows a series circuit. If one bulb goes out, all of the other bulbs will also go out.

Fig. 10–29 Are these bulbs part of a series circuit? How do you know?

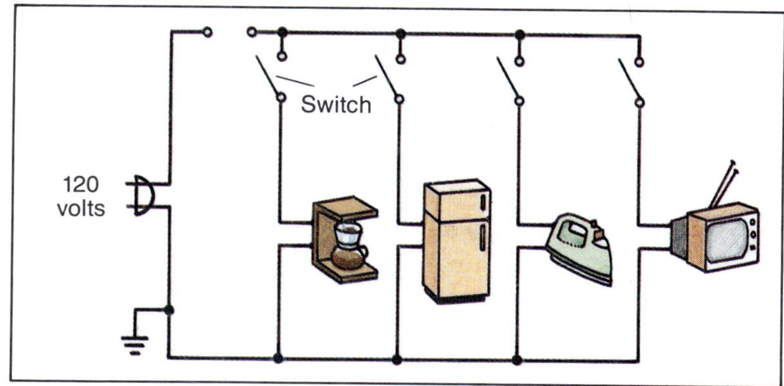

Fig. 10–30 These appliances are arranged in a parallel circuit. You can turn one of them off without affecting the others.

Another way to connect the parts of a circuit is shown in Fig. 10–30. This arrangement is called a **parallel circuit.** In a *parallel circuit*, the different parts are on separate branches. Each branch of a parallel circuit can be switched off without affecting the other branches. The different circuits in a house are arranged in parallel. In this way, many appliances can be used at the same time. They do not all have to be on at the same time.

Parallel circuit An electric circuit in which all the parts are on separate branches.

Reinforcement: Draw several series and parallel circuits on the board. Trace the paths of the current in each circuit.

SUMMARY

A complete electric circuit using a dry cell can be made by connecting the negative and positive terminals of the cell with a conductor. Current from a dry cell is called direct current since it travels in only one direction. Current used in home appliances is called alternating current since it changes direction rapidly. The parts of a circuit can be connected either in series or in parallel.

QUESTIONS

Use complete sentences to write your answers.

1. Describe what happens to the electrons when you complete a circuit by turning on a wall switch, causing an overhead light to go on.
2. How can the earth be made part of an electric circuit? How can this be dangerous?
3. Contrast the flow of electrons in an AC circuit with the flow of electrons in a DC circuit.
4. Explain how a series circuit and a parallel circuit differ.

1. When the switch is thrown, electrons can move in the complete circuit. The movement of electrons heats the filament of the light bulb, causing the filament to glow.
2. The earth can act as a conductor to complete a circuit. If this happens when you are holding a wire carrying a current, you could receive a serious electric shock.
3. In an AC circuit the electrons move first in one direction and then in the other direction. In a DC circuit the electrons always move in the same direction.
4. In a series circuit all of the current travels through all parts of the circuit. In a parallel circuit separate branches can be switched on and off without affecting the other branches.

INVESTIGATION

See teacher's commentary for teaching hints, safety, and answers to questions.

SERIES AND PARALLEL CIRCUITS

PURPOSE: You will determine how the number of batteries and light bulbs affect the amount of current that flows in a series and a parallel circuit.

MATERIALS:

2 batteries (1.5 V)	3 sockets
battery holders	4 insulated wires
3 light bulbs	

PROCEDURE:

A. Set up a circuit with one battery and a light bulb. Notice how bright the light bulb is. The brighter the bulb, the greater the current.

   1. How do you know that a current is flowing in the circuit?

B. Connect two batteries in series with the bulb. See Fig. 10–31.

   2. When the circuit is complete, is the bulb brighter than in step A?
   3. When two batteries are connected in series with a light bulb is the amount of current greater or less than with one battery?

C. Add a second bulb to the circuit in series with the first bulb.

Fig. 10–31

   4. With two batteries and two bulbs in series, how does the brightness compare with one battery and one bulb?
   5. When two batteries and two bulbs are in series, how does the amount of current compare with one battery and one bulb?

D. Based on your observations in steps A through C, predict how bright the bulbs will be when three bulbs are connected in series to two batteries in series.

   6. What is your prediction?

E. Set up the circuit and make the final connection to check your prediction.

   7. Was your prediction correct?

F. To see the effect of connecting two bulbs in parallel, set up an electric circuit as in step A. Observe the brightness of the bulb.

G. Put a second bulb in the circuit, in parallel with the first. If the current is the same across both bulbs as it is across one bulb, the two bulbs will be just as bright as the single bulb.

   8. How does the current through each bulb compare to the standard current with one battery and one bulb?

CONCLUSIONS:

1. Explain how the number of batteries and the number of bulbs in a series circuit affects the amount of current that flows in the circuit.
2. How is the current affected when two bulbs are put in parallel compared to one battery and one bulb?

CAREERS IN SCIENCE

ELECTRICAL TECHNICIAN

Electrical technicians install, maintain, and repair electrical systems and equipment such as telephones, motors, wiring, and alarm systems. They locate electrical malfunctions and repair them by replacing burned-out elements or rewiring motors. They also test and inspect equipment such as generators or circuits for safety and efficiency and adjust them to conform with building codes and safety regulations.

More than half of all electrical technicians are employed as construction crafts persons or maintenance mechanics. Their pay, usually on an hourly basis, is the highest in this field, but the work is seasonal and slacks off when construction work slows down.

Apprenticeship training is the traditional method of learning this skilled trade. Electrical technicians are generally well paid, and the field is expected to expand.

For further information, contact: International Brotherhood of Electrical Workers, 1125 15 Street NW, Washington, DC 20002.

COMPUTER SYSTEMS ENGINEER

Computers must be designed with specific jobs in mind. That is the work of the computer systems engineer. The engineer works with the designer to develop hardware such as circuits, boards, and keyboards. Engineers study what is to be required of the computer and meet with clients and project managers to determine the limitations of existing equipment. They analyze this information to plan a new type of computer, or a change to existing equipment. About 80 percent of an engineer's time is spent in developing new hardware (machinery) and the rest is used to write specifications or work with other engineers and draftsmen.

A bachelor's degree in computer science or engineering is required for the job. Most people enter the field as assistant engineers and become full engineers after a minimum of two year's work experience.

For further information, contact: Association of Computer Users, P.O. Box 9003, Boulder, CO 80301.

CHAPTER REVIEW

See teacher's commentary for answers.

VOCABULARY

On a separate piece of paper, match each term with the number of the statement that best explains it. Use each term only once.

alternating current	electron	positive charge	negative charge
electric circuit	insulator	proton	electric force
electric current	neutral	scientific model	conductor
electric field	parallel circuit	series circuit	direct current

1. The charge on a glass rod rubbed with silk.
2. Equal amounts of positive and negative charge.
3. Present in the space around a charged object.
4. Used by scientists to study something that they cannot see.
5. A negatively charged particle that is too small to be seen.
6. A positively charged particle of matter.
7. The movement of electrons.
8. Charges cannot move easily through it.
9. The path along which electrons move.
10. The current reverses at regular time intervals.
11. All charges travel through all parts.
12. Has branches that are independent of each other.
13. An electric current that flows in one direction in an electric circuit.
14. A material that can carry an electric current because electrons can move through it easily.
15. The electric charge given to a hard rubber rod when it is rubbed with a silk cloth.
16. The force that causes two like-charged objects to repel each other or two unlike-charged objects to attract each other.

QUESTIONS

Give brief but complete answers to each of the following questions. Unless otherwise indicated, use complete sentences to write your answers.

1. What was Benjamin Franklin's contribution to the study of electricity?
2. Describe how you could demonstrate electrical attraction between two objects.
3. Explain one use of a scientific model.
4. Describe one way you could convert the energy of motion into electric energy and pick up an electric charge.

5. How are electrons related to electric current?
6. Explain why matter can be either positive, negative, or neutral.
7. Classify the following list of materials as insulators or conductors: plastic ruler, copper wire, rubber rod, aluminum pan, glass window, iron skillet, silver ring, cover on electric wire, plastic spoon.
8. How does a lightning rod work if clouds are (a) negatively charged or (b) positively charged?
9. Why is it dangerous to touch a water pipe while also touching a wire carrying an electric current?
10. How does alternating current differ from direct current?
11. What is the benefit of using a parallel circuit?
12. Explain how a Van de Graaff generator works.
13. Why do most power companies in the United States supply 60 Hz AC electricity?

APPLYING SCIENCE

1. Draw a wiring diagram and set up a display to show how an electric light can be controlled from two different switches. Use batteries and flashlight bulbs.
2. Build an electroscope and use it to test several kinds of material. Determine the kind of electric charge that is produced when each material is rubbed with various other materials. For example, vinyl rubbed with wool cloth produces one kind of charge while acetate rubbed with cotton cloth produces the opposite charge. Demonstrate your results to the class.
3. In a dark room, rub a fluorescent light bulb with a piece of fur or wool cloth. Describe what happens. State a hypothesis to explain your observations.
4. Write a research report on the development and use of xerography.

BIBLIOGRAPHY

Asimov, Isaac. *How Did We Find Out about Electricity?* New York: Walker, 1973.

Chapman, Phil. *Electricity.* (Young Scientists Series). Tulsa: EDC, 1976.

Epstein, S. *The First Book of Electricity.* New York: Franklin Watts, 1977.

Leon, George. *The Electricity Story: 2500 Years of Discoveries and Experiments.* New York: Arco, 1983.

Math, I. *Wires and Watts, Understanding and Using Electricity.* New York: Scribners, 1981.

Mileaf, H. *Electricity One.* Rochelle Park, NJ: Hayden, 1976.

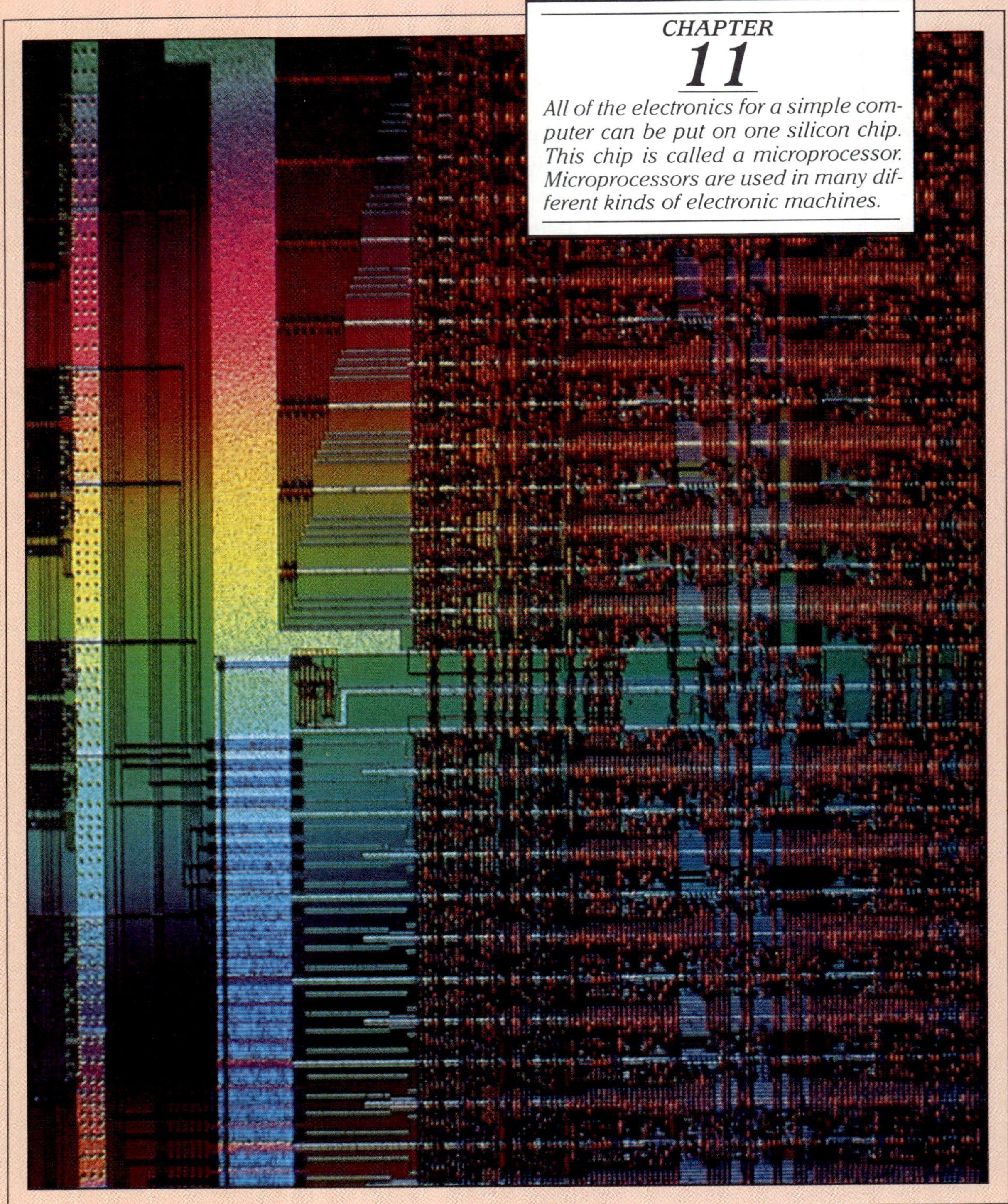

CHAPTER

11

All of the electronics for a simple computer can be put on one silicon chip. This chip is called a microprocessor. Microprocessors are used in many different kinds of electronic machines.

USING ELECTRICITY

CHAPTER GOALS

1. Explain how volts, amperes, and ohms are related.
2. Describe how electricity is made available for safe use in the home.
3. Describe how at least two electronic devices work.
4. Give some examples of the importance of computers.

11-1. Measuring Electricity

At the end of this section you will be able to:

- ☐ Define the terms *volt*, *ampere*, and *ohm*.
- ☐ Describe how *volts*, *amperes*, and *ohms* are related.

The water behind a dam has potential energy. It gained this energy by being lifted above sea level. A dry cell also has potential energy stored in it. This energy cannot be used until the dry cell is connected to an electric circuit. Then the flow of electrons in the circuit releases some of the energy of the cell. How could you find out how much potential energy is stored in a dry cell? You would need some way to measure this energy. The potential energy of water trapped behind a dam is determined by the height of the dam. In the same way, the potential energy (E) of electrons in a dry cell is measured in **volts** (V). A *volt* measures the potential of electrons to do work. We can use volts to measure the amount of work done if electrons are moved between two points in an electric circuit. This is often called the *potential difference*. If we compare the flow of electrons to water running down a hill, then voltage is a measure of how high the hill is. An ordinary flashlight battery gives 1.5 volts of energy. This would compare to water held behind a low dam. The 1.5-V battery is also similar to water flowing down a low hill. A larger battery gives 6 volts of energy. This would be like water behind a high dam. The 6-V battery is also similar to water flowing down a higher hill. In other words, the 6-V battery has the potential to do four times as much work as the 1.5-V cell. A 6-V battery *pushes* the electrons harder than a 1.5-V battery.

Enrichment: While charge is not stored in an electric circuit, a *capacitor* stores positive charge on one metal plate and an equal amount of negative charge on another, nearby, metal plate. The energy stored in this way can be used later to do work.

Volt A measure of the electrical potential for doing work in an electric circuit. One volt is equal to one ampere flowing with a resistance of one ohm.

The voltage of an electric circuit can be measured by an instrument called a *voltmeter.* A voltmeter can be attached to an electric circuit. Then the voltage of the circuit can be read on the dial of the voltmeter. A voltmeter can also be used in an automobile. This voltmeter tells the driver if there is enough voltage in the car's electrical system to run the starter, lights, and other parts of the car.

Ampere A measure of the amount of current moving past a point in an electric circuit in one second. One ampere is equal to one volt per ohm of resistance.

For most electric circuits, we want to know not only the voltage, or how hard the electrons are pushed, but also how many electrons are flowing. This is called the current (I). To measure the amount of current, we use **amperes** (**am**-pirz). An *ampere* (A) measures the amount of charge moving past a point in a circuit in one second. An ampere is often called "amp" for short. Measurement of both voltage and amperage describes the behavior of an electric current. For example, a circuit may have high voltage with low amperage. This would be like a very narrow but swiftly flowing stream. On the other hand, a circuit with high amperage but low voltage would be like a wide but slow-moving river.

The amount of current in a circuit can be measured by attaching a meter called an *ammeter* to the circuit. An ammeter in a car tells whether the battery is being charged (electrons flowing in) or drained (electrons flowing out).

Enrichment: Have students calculate the number of electrons moving past a point in a wire when 1.5 amperes is flowing in the wire as follows:
1 ampere = 1 coulomb/s
1 coulomb = 6.25×10^{18} electrons

A voltmeter and an ammeter each has a coil of wire in a magnetic field. When a current flows through the coil, the coil moves a pointer on a scale. The scale shows the number of volts or amperes. In an ammeter, all the current flows through the coil. In a voltmeter, a small current that is proportional to the voltage flows through the coil.

Suppose that water is flowing through a wide pipe. Suddenly, the pipe becomes much narrower. What will happen to the amount of water that can flow through the pipe? The flow of water will slow down because the pipe becomes narrower. When water flows through pipes, the size or shape of the pipe can change the ease with which the water moves. This is also true of electrons. When electrons move through any material, they meet **resistance** (rih-**zis**-tunts). *Resistance* (R) is the term used for all conditions that limit the flow of electrons in an electric circuit. For example, a light bulb adds resistance to an electric circuit.

Resistance Any condition that limits the flow of electrons in an electric circuit, for example, a light bulb in a circuit.

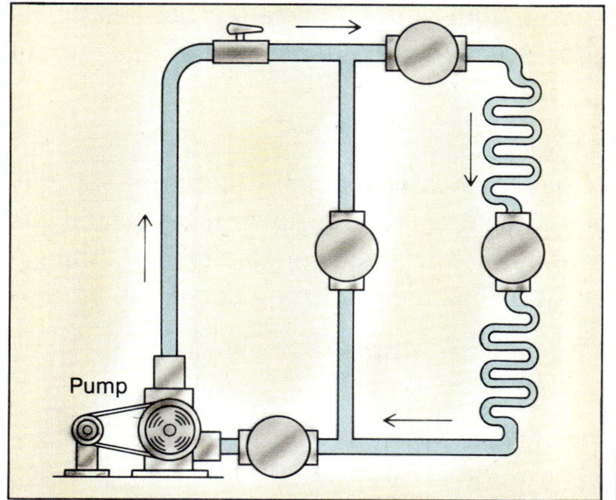

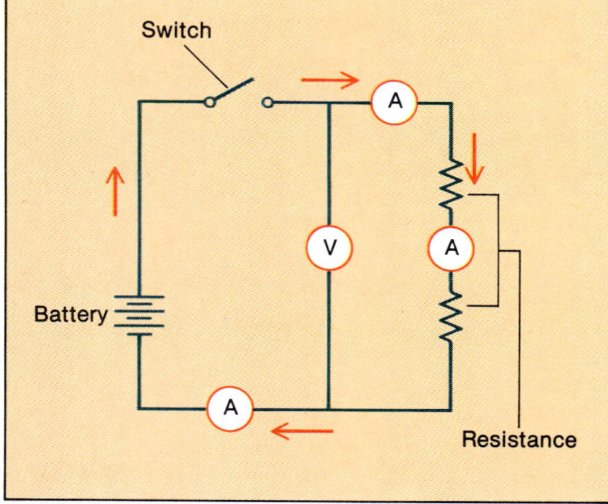

Fig. 11–1 The flow of water in a system of pipes (a) can be compared to the flow of electricity through a circuit (b).

The amount of current that flows in a particular electric circuit is also affected by the voltage. Again, think of water flowing through a pipe. See Fig. 11–1 (a). The amount of water that will pass through the pipe is affected by the force pushing the water. Suppose that the water flows through a narrow pipe. Less water could then pass through the pipe. The narrow pipe has the same effect on the flow of water as resistance in an electric circuit has on the flow of electrons. If electrons flow through a part of the circuit where the resistance is high, then the amount of current flowing through the entire circuit is reduced. See Fig. 11–1 (b). Resistance is measured in **ohms** (Ω). A resistance of one *ohm* means a potential of one volt per one ampere of current. The symbol for ohm is the Greek letter omega Ω.

Ohm A measure of the amount of resistance in an electric circuit. One ohm is equal to a potential difference of one volt per ampere of current flow.

OHM'S LAW

The voltage, current, and resistance in an electric circuit are related to each other by a rule known as *Ohm's law*. This relationship was discovered by a German schoolteacher, Georg Ohm, in the early 1800's. Ohm experimented with electric circuits made of wires having different amounts of resistance. He discovered a general rule that describes the relationship among voltage, current, and resistance in a circuit. This rule, now known as Ohm's law, can be written as:

$$I = \frac{E}{R} \qquad \text{amperes} = \frac{\text{volts}}{\text{ohms}}$$

Enrichment: Care must be taken in using Ohm's law. Most materials do not have an unchanging resistance. The resistance may increase with a change in current. Also, some electrical parts, such as semiconductors, may have a different resistance when the current flows in different directions.

For example, an automobile with a 12-V battery has headlights whose resistance is 4 Ω. When the lights are on, the current needed is:

$$I = \frac{E}{R} = \frac{12\ V}{4\ \Omega} = 3\ A$$

Most automobile batteries can supply 3 A of current for only a few hours. Thus, a battery can run down if the headlights are left on for several hours while the engine is not running.

By rearranging the terms, the preceding equation can also be written:

$$\text{volts} = \text{amperes} \times \text{ohms}$$

$$E = IR$$

or

$$\text{ohms} = \frac{\text{volts}}{\text{amperes}}$$

$$R = \frac{E}{I}$$

SUMMARY

A dry cell is like water behind a dam. Both have potential energy. For the dry cell, potential energy, or potential difference, is measured in volts. When the energy of a dry cell sends current through a circuit, the amount of current is measured in amperes. Whatever resistance the current meets is measured in ohms.

QUESTIONS

Use complete sentences to write your answers.

1. Explain what is measured by volts, amperes, and ohms. How are these units related?
2. If the resistance of a material increases, what will happen to the amount of current flowing through it? Explain.
3. The starter on an automobile has a resistance of 0.06 ohms. The battery is 12 volts. How much current will flow when starting the car?
4. Find the resistance of a toaster if it uses 5.5 amperes of current when plugged into a 110-volt circuit.
5. Calculate the number of volts it will take to make a motor run properly if the motor needs 7.0 amperes of current and has a resistance of 15 ohms.

1. Volts measure the potential of electrons to do work. Amperes measure the amount of current flowing in an electric circuit. Ohms measure the resistance in an electric circuit. Volts, amperes, and ohms are related to each other by Ohm's law: I = E/R.
2. When the resistance of a material increases, the amount of current flowing through it decreases. Since according to Ohm's law I = E/R, if E remains the same and R increases, I decreases.
3. Current = volts/ohms
Current = 12 V/0.06 Ω = 200 amperes
4. Resistance = volts/amperes
Resistance = 110 V/5.5 A = 20 ohms
5. Volts = amperes × ohms
Volts = 7.0 A × 15 Ω = 105 V

SKILL-BUILDING ACTIVITY

See teacher's commentary for teaching hints, safety, and answers to questions.

VOLTS, AMPERES, AND OHMS

PURPOSE: You will find how voltage, resistance, and current are related in a circuit.

MATERIALS:

ammeter (0-1 amp)
voltmeter (0-3 V)
6 wires with clips
2 resistors (equal)
2 batteries (1.5 V)

PROCEDURE:

A. Copy the table below and use it to record your data.

Number of Batteries	Number of Resistances	Volts	Amperes

B. Set up an electric circuit like the one shown in Fig. 11–2. After you make the final connection, read the voltmeter and ammeter. Do not leave the battery connected after you read the meters. Record.

C. Set up a series circuit like the one shown in Fig. 11–3. Read the voltmeter and ammeter and record the readings in your data table.

D. Move the voltmeter so that it reads the voltage across the second resistance. Record the reading.

E. Set up a circuit like the one shown in Fig. 11–4. Read both meters and record.

F. Set up a series circuit like the one shown in Fig. 11–5. Read both meters and record. Move the voltmeter and record.

G. Study the data table and then answer the following question.

1. When two resistances of equal value are in series in a circuit, how does the voltage across one resistance compare with the voltage across the other?

CONCLUSIONS:

1. How is the current in a circuit related to the voltage?
2. How is the current in a series circuit related to the amount of resistance?
3. Using Ohm's law, find the value in ohms of each resistance used.

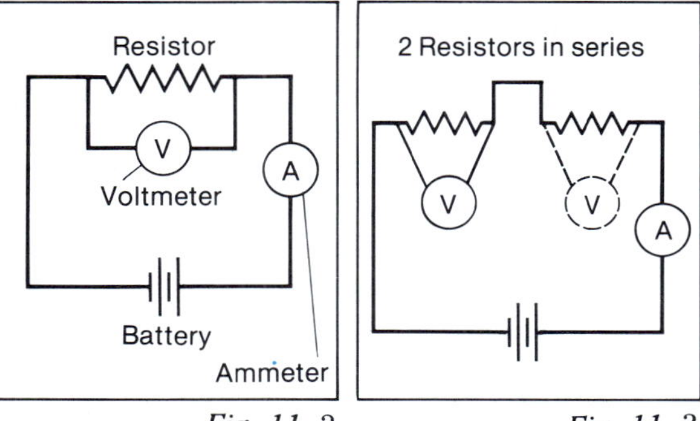

Fig. 11–2 *Fig. 11–3*

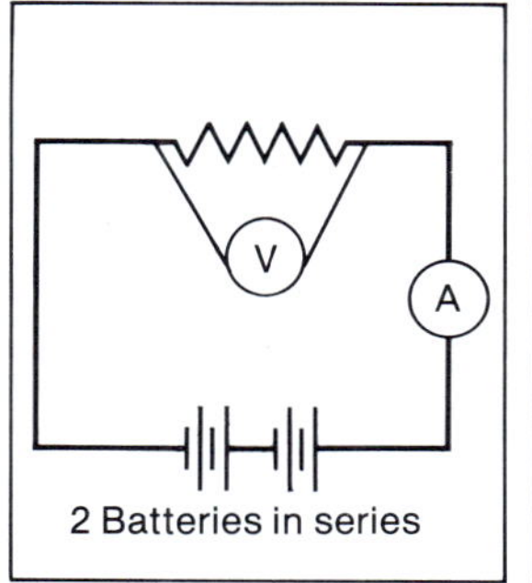

Fig. 11–4

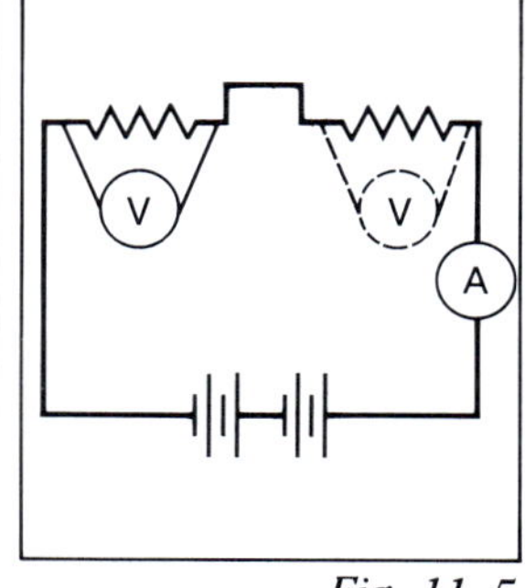

Fig 11–5

11-2. Electric Power

At the end of this section you will be able to:

- ☐ Describe what a *transformer* does.
- ☐ Describe how electric circuits carry electric power throughout a home.
- ☐ Discuss the role of fuses and circuit breakers in making electric circuits safe.

Enrichment: A field trip to a local generating plant would be of interest to students. Such tours are usually part of the company's public relations program.

Have you ever experienced a power blackout? Think about the last time the electric power went off at your house. How were you affected?

Fig. 11–6 During the blackout of July 1977, the famous skyline of New York City took on an unfamiliar darkness.

PROVIDING ELECTRICITY

Suggestion: Discuss the many areas of daily life that depend on electricity.

The photograph in Fig. 11–6 was taken during a power blackout in New York City in July 1977. The electricity suddenly went off for as long as 24 hours in many parts of the area. Is your life changed when the electricity goes off? We usually do not realize how much we depend upon this form of energy until it goes off. When the power fails, lights go out, the television is dead, food spoils in the refrigerator, and even most clocks stop. A city becomes helpless. Traffic signals stop working, elevators stop, airports close, and computers lose their memories as the flow of electricity stops.

Fig. 11–7 We use electricity in so many ways that we sometimes take it for granted.

Electric energy is used in so many different ways for several reasons. The most important reason is that electricity can be changed into almost any other form of energy. Electric motors change electricity into energy of motion. Lamps change electricity into light energy. The temperature inside buildings is controlled by air conditioners and heaters run by electricity. Your voice can be carried great distances by telephone. See Fig. 11–7.

Another reason electric energy is widely used is because it can be sent over long distances through wires. Because of this property, factories can be located far from a source of power. The same wires also allow different buildings to be connected to a source of energy. Think about how your life would change if those wires did not bring electricity to your home.

To provide a building with electricity, at least two wires must be connected to the power lines. The voltage sent out through the main power lines is very high. The electric company sends out high-voltage alternating current because it is the cheapest way to send large amounts of electric energy over long distances. This high voltage must be reduced to a safe lower voltage by use of a **transformer**. A *transformer* is used to change the voltage of alternating current. You may have seen the transformers on power poles. See Fig. 11–8. These transformers change the high voltage into 110-V current used in homes. Some household appliances, such as electric stoves and clothes dryers, use 220 V. To provide this doubled voltage, as well as more current, three wires are often connected to large appliances.

Transformer A part of an electric circuit that changes the voltage of an alternating current in the circuit.

Word study: Transformer from *transformare* (L.), to change the form of.

Fig. 11–8 A transformer lowers the voltage in the power lines for use in our homes.

The electricity supplied to homes is alternating current. Alternating current changes its direction of flow many times each second. If it is called 60 hertz AC, the current changes its direction 60 times each second.

Wires bringing electricity into a home are connected to parallel circuits in the home. See Fig. 11–9. To use the electric energy, an appliance is connected to one of the circuits. For example, a toaster is plugged into a wall socket. The plug and the cord on the toaster make the toaster a part of the circuit. An electric current flows through special wires in the toaster that have high resistance. When the current meets resistance, some of the energy is lost. The lost energy is changed into heat. The wires become red hot and the heat toasts the bread.

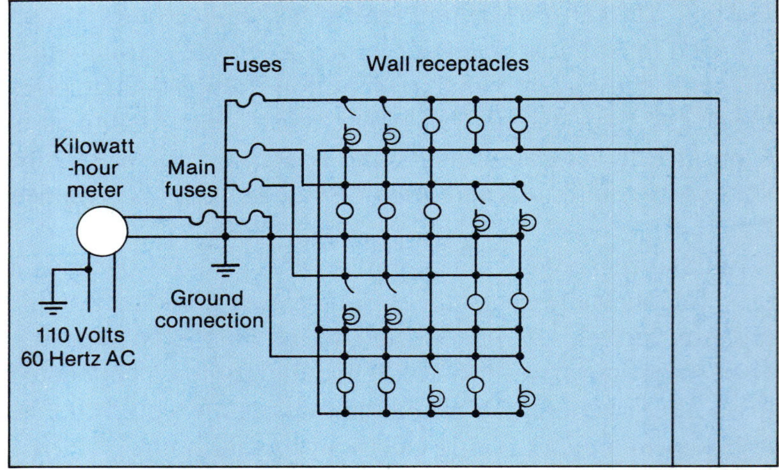

Fig. 11–9 Each appliance in your home is only one part of the entire electrical system. This toaster is connected to a parallel wiring system.

ELECTRICAL SAFETY

Many common appliances, such as electric stoves and irons, change electric energy into heat energy. When the current flowing through an appliance meets high resistance, the electric energy is changed into heat. A common electric light bulb also works this way. The bulb contains a thin metal wire. Because of its high resistance, this thin wire becomes hot enough to give off a bright light. Too much current flowing in a house circuit is dangerous. For example, if you connect a toaster, a steam iron, and an electric coffeemaker to the same circuit, more than 20 A of current would be needed. The wires of the circuit could become overheated and start a fire. See Fig. 11–10. To prevent this overheating, each circuit in a house can be provided with a **fuse**. A *fuse* in a circuit prevents too much current from flowing. See Fig. 11–11. A fuse contains a part that melts and breaks the circuit if too much current is flowing. More commonly, a special switch called a **circuit breaker** is used instead of a fuse. See Fig. 11–12. The *circuit breaker* shuts off when too much current flows. All home circuits must have some kind of overload protection to prevent the threat of serious fire.

Reinforcement: Students can have their parents help them determine the maximum current that each fuse or circuit breaker in the house can carry. From that they can determine the maximum current for the house. Newer houses are usually built for higher current; 300 amperes is typical.

Fuse A part of an electric circuit that prevents too much current from flowing.

Circuit breaker A switch that turns off if too much current flows in a circuit.

A *short circuit* can also cause a circuit to overheat and start a fire. A short circuit can happen if two wires accidentally touch each other. Worn insulation can allow two wires to touch. Instead of flowing to the appliance, the current then flows back to the outlet, causing it to overheat.

Enrichment: Have one or two students set up a simple circuit of two D cells in series, a 2-cell flashlight bulb, and a 0.5 ampere fuse. Have the class watch as they short out the bulb by connecting a wire from one terminal of the bulb to the other. The bulb will go out. When the wire is removed the bulb will not light because the fuse will have melted. Fuses are available from local electronic supply houses.

Fig. 11–10 When too many wires are plugged into an outlet, there is danger of an electrical fire.

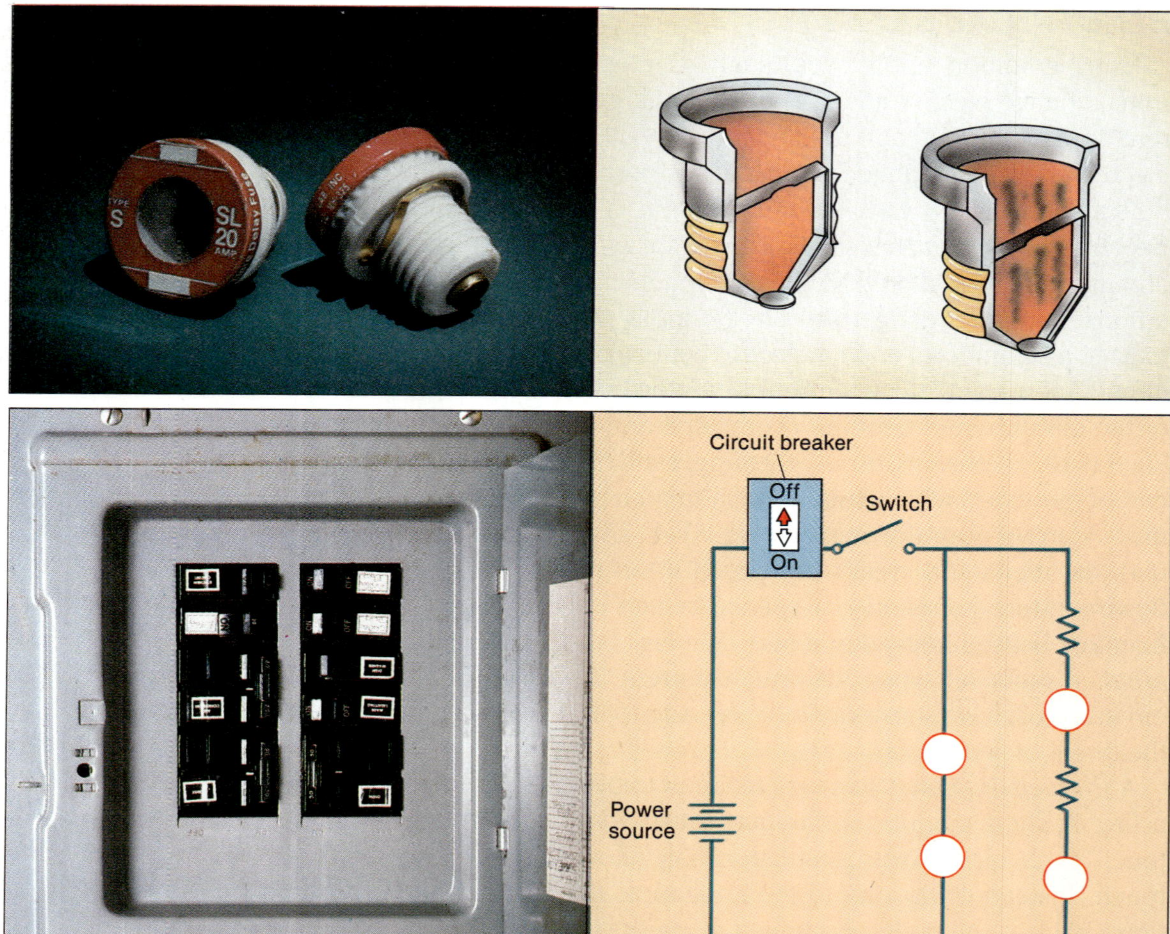

Fig. 11–11 When a circuit is overloaded, the center part of a fuse melts, breaking the circuit. When this happens, the fuse must be replaced.

Fig. 11–12 When too much current flows through a circuit, the circuit breaker automatically flips to the off position. This opens the switch and stops the flow of current. Then the circuit breaker can be reset. The circuit breaker does not have to be replaced.

It is possible to receive dangerous electrical shocks from house current. The danger increases as the amount of current that flows through your body increases. To prevent contact with dangerously large currents, you should always follow these safety rules:

1. Never touch any part of an electric circuit such as a switch when you are wet or standing in water. Moisture lowers the resistance of your skin to the flow of current.

2. Do not use electric appliances while you are also touching a metal object, such as a water pipe, that is connected to the earth. This may allow an electric current to flow through you to the earth.

3. Never come close to the wires on power poles by climbing the poles or nearby trees and buildings. These wires often carry very high voltages. Never touch wires that have fallen from power poles or buildings.

4. Never put anything but the appropriate plug into an electrical outlet. Don't put objects into appliances that are plugged into an electrical outlet.

5. Never allow electric cords to become worn.

6. Never overload an electric outlet.

Fig. 11–13 The energy guide on an electrical appliance tells you how much energy the appliance uses and how efficient it is.

CONSUMING ELECTRICITY

The appliances we use in our homes consume different amounts of electricity. See Table 11–1. You can easily find out how much electric energy an appliance uses. For example, light bulbs are marked as 60, 75, or 100 watts. Remember that a *watt* (W) is the unit of electric power. It measures the rate at which electric energy is changed to other forms. Watts are useful in measuring how much electric energy is consumed. The amount of power used by a light bulb, for example, depends on two things: (1) how fast the bulb used the electricity by changing it into light energy and (2) how long the bulb was turned on. For example, a 100-W light bulb burning for one hour uses 100 *watt hours* of electricity. A watt hour is a small amount of electric energy. It is more common to use a **kilowatt hour** (kWh) which is a thousand times larger. A *kilowatt hour* is the amount of energy supplied in one hour by one kilowatt of power. A home has a meter attached to its lead-in wires. The meter measures the amount of electricity consumed in kilowatt hours.

Reinforcement: Thoroughly discuss the basic safety rules for working with electricity. A safety quiz that everyone must pass would be a good requirement for this section.

Kilowatt hour The amount of energy supplied in one hour by one kilowatt of power. It is used to measure how much electric energy is consumed.

ELECTRICITY CONSUMED IN HOMES	
Activity	Percentage of Electricity Consumption
Space and water heating	28%
Refrigeration	24%
Lighting	11%
Air conditioning	11%
Television	9%
Cooking	7%
Washing and drying clothes	4%
Miscellaneous	6%

Table 11–1

Appliance	Typical Wattage
Color television	300 W
Hair dryer	1,000 W (1 kW)
Refrigerator	400 W
Toaster	750 W
Range/oven	3,000 W (3 kW)
Vacuum cleaner	500 W

Table 11–2

Enrichment: Have students calculate the hourly cost of operating various electrical appliances.

Most electric appliances have labels attached, telling how many watts of electricity they use. See Fig. 11–13. Table 11–2 shows the typical wattage of some common appliances. At $0.12 per kilowatt hour, how much would it cost to run each appliance for two hours? In order to find the cost of operating an appliance, first multiply its wattage times the number of hours it is used. This gives you the number of watt hours. Then divide this result by 1,000 to find the number of kilowatt hours. Multiply the number of kilowatt hours by the amount the electric company charges per kilowatt hour. For example, if electricity costs $0.12 per kilowatt hour, a 300-W television set operating for five hours would cost:

$$300 \text{ W} \times 5 \text{ h} = 1{,}500 \text{ Wh}$$

$$\frac{1{,}500 \text{ W h}}{1{,}000 \text{ W/kW}} = 1.5 \text{ kWh}$$

$$1.5 \text{ kWh} \times \$0.12/\text{kWh} = \$0.18$$

SUMMARY

Electricity is one of the most commonly used forms of energy. It is useful mainly because it can be changed into other forms of energy so easily. Electricity can also be sent over long distances. It is supplied in a home by several low-voltage circuits connected to the power lines. Each circuit must be protected from overloads.

QUESTIONS

Use complete sentences to write your answers.

1. A transformer is needed in the electric power system to your house. Explain why this is so.
2. Discuss the reason why parallel circuits are used in the wiring of your home.
3. Electric circuits in your home have safety devices to protect them. What are these devices called? What do they do? Where are these devices in your home?
4. Where is the electric meter in your home located? What does it measure?
5. In your own words, state at least five safety rules you should follow in using electricity in your home.

1. The electricity is delivered at a dangerously high voltage on the power poles. A transformer is needed to lower the voltage to that used in your home. (110 volts is most common.)
2. Parallel circuits are used in homes so that an overload on one circuit won't cause a blackout. They also give a constant voltage that wouldn't be available if series wiring were used.
3. The safety devices are called circuit breakers (or fuses). They keep the wiring from overloading and becoming hot. Students should know where fuses or circuit breakers are located.
4. Locations will vary. The electric meter measures the number of kilowatt hours of electric energy delivered to the home.
5. (1) Do not touch electrical appliances while in water. (2) Do not touch electrical appliances while also touching a metal pipe. (3) Do not touch wires on power poles. (4) Do not put metal objects into electrical outlets. (5) Do not use appliances with worn electric cords. (6) Never overload an electrical outlet by plugging several appliances into it.

INVESTIGATION

See teacher's commentary for teaching hints, safety, and answers to questions.

PARALLEL CIRCUITS

PURPOSE: You will determine why parallel wiring is used in homes.

MATERIALS:

2 flashlight bulbs and sockets	4 wires
	2 batteries and holders

PROCEDURE:

A. Set up a circuit as shown in Fig. 11–14. Notice how bright the light is.

B. Set up a series electric circuit as shown in Fig. 11–15.

1. What do you notice about the brightness of the bulbs?

C. While both lights are on, unscrew one of the bulbs.

2. What effect does unscrewing a bulb have in a series circuit?

D. Set up a circuit with three light bulbs in series.

3. How does the brightness of the bulbs compare with the previous circuits?

E. Set up a parallel electric circuit as shown in Fig. 11–16.

F. While the lights are on, unscrew one of the bulbs.

4. What effect does unscrewing a bulb have in a parallel circuit?

CONCLUSION:

1. What is the advantage of using parallel circuits in wiring a home?

Fig. 11–14

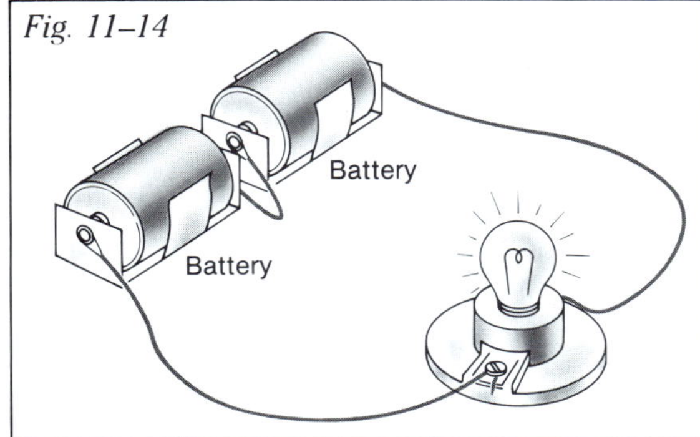

Fig. 11–15

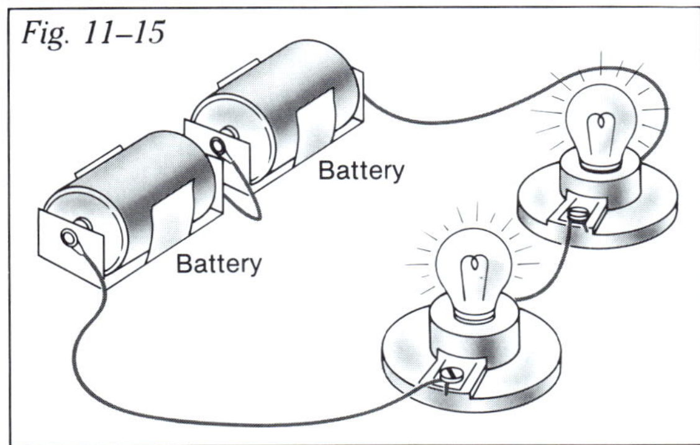

Fig. 11–16

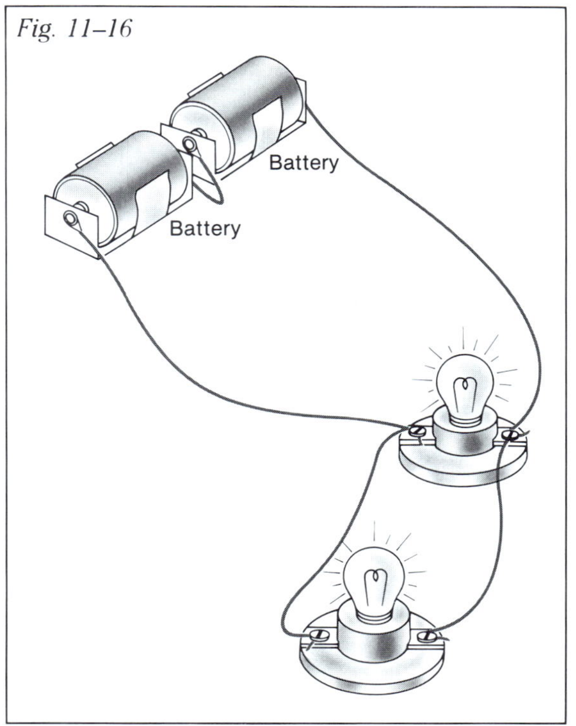

11-3. Electronic Devices

At the end of this section you will be able to:

- Discuss how three electronic devices are used for communication.
- Describe how a television picture is produced.
- Explain what a computer does and how it can be used.

If you ever play video games, you always have many partners. See Fig. 11–17. They are invisible but dependable and hard workers. These unseen helpers are electrons. A video game is an example of an electronic device. In this section you will see that a video game is only one example of the work done by electronic devices.

THE TELEGRAPH

You have seen how electrons moving through conductors make an electric current that can deliver energy. Electric currents can also be used to send information. The first use of electricity for communication was the *telegraph*. The first practical American telegraph was invented by Samuel F. B. Morse in 1840. Morse used a simple arrangement. Signals were sent along a wire by making or breaking an electric circuit. Each time the current went on or off, it operated an electromagnet at the place where the message was received. See Fig. 11–18 (a). In time a code, called the Morse code, was developed. Morse code used dots (currents lasting a short time) and dashes (currents lasting longer). Letters and numbers were signaled by using combinations of dots and dashes. See Fig. 11–18 (b). Skillful telegraph operators heard the clicks made by the movements of the magnet as dots and dashes. They memorized the code, which allowed them to recognize letters and write out the message. A message was sent by using a switch or key to produce the on-off currents that made up the dots and dashes.

The first telegraph line was built between Baltimore and Washington, D.C., a distance of 60 kilometers. The first public use of this line was on May 24, 1844. Modern telegraph systems incorporate computers, communications satellites, and laser communication systems.

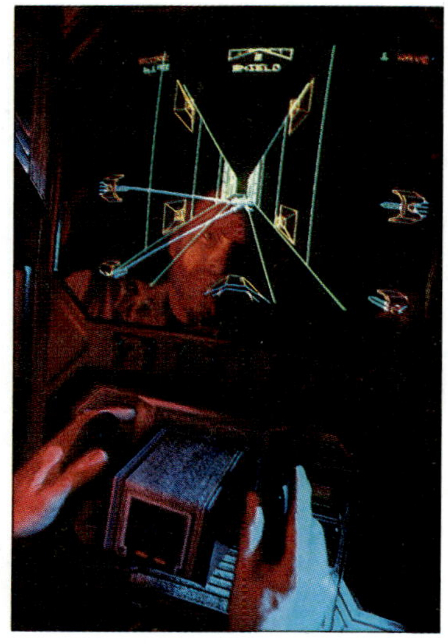

Fig. 11–17 A video game is one example of an electronic device.

MORSE CODE

AMERICAN MORSE CODE[1]						INTERNATIONAL CODE[2]							
A	•—	N	—•	1	•——•	A	•—	N	—•	Á	•——•—	8	———••
B	—•••	O	• •	2	••—••	B	—•••	O	———	Ä	•—•—	9	————•
C	•• •	P	•••••	3	•••—•	C	—•—•	P	•——•	É	••—••	0	—————
D	—••	Q	••—•	4	••••—	D	—••	Q	——•—	Ñ	——•——	,	——••——
E	•	R	• ••	5	———	E	•	R	•—•	Ö	———•	.	•—•—•—
F	•—•	S	•••	6	••••••	F	••—•	S	•••	Ü	••——	?	••——••
G	——•	T	—	7	——••	G	——•	T	—	1	•————	;	—•—•—•
H	••••	U	••—	8	—••••	H	••••	U	••—	2	••———	:	———•••
I	••	V	•••—	9	—••—	I	••	V	•••—	3	•••——	'	•————•
J	—•—•	W	•——	0	—	J	•———	W	•——	4	••••—	–	—••••—
K	—•—	X	•—••	,	•—•—	K	—•—	X	—••—	5	•••••	/	—••—•
L	—	Y	•• ••	.	••——••	L	•—••	Y	—•——	6	—••••	paren	—•——•—
M	——	Z	••• •	&	• •••	M	——	Z	——••	7	——•••	U-line	••——•—

[1]Formerly used on landlines in the U.S. and Canada; now largely out of use.

[2]Often called the continental code; a modification of this code, with dots only, is used on ocean cables.

Fig. 11–18 The telegraph was a great innovation in electronic communication. Messages were sent by using a series of dots and dashes called Morse code.

THE EDISON EFFECT

In 1883, while trying to improve his recently invented electric light, Thomas A. Edison discovered a new behavior of electrons. He removed the air from a glass bulb to produce a vacuum. Inside the bulb, along with the heated wire that produced light, he placed a metal plate. To his surprise, Edison observed an electric current flowing between the hot wire and the plate. See Fig. 11–19. Scientists now know that this current is made up of electrons that leave the hot wire like steam given off from boiling water. The electrons move through the vacuum and strike the plate to produce the electric current observed by Edison.

Although Edison did not apply his discovery, other scientists used it to make the first electronic devices called *vacuum tubes*. In a vacuum tube, electrons from a heated filament move through a vacuum to a plate. One kind of vacuum tube allows electrons to move in one direction only. See Fig. 11–20. Because this tube allows electrons to move in only one direction, it is used to change the back-and-forth flow of alternating current into direct current moving in a single direction. A second kind of vacuum tube adds a third part, called a *grid*, between the hot filament and the plate. See Fig. 11–21. A small electric charge on the grid controls the amount of

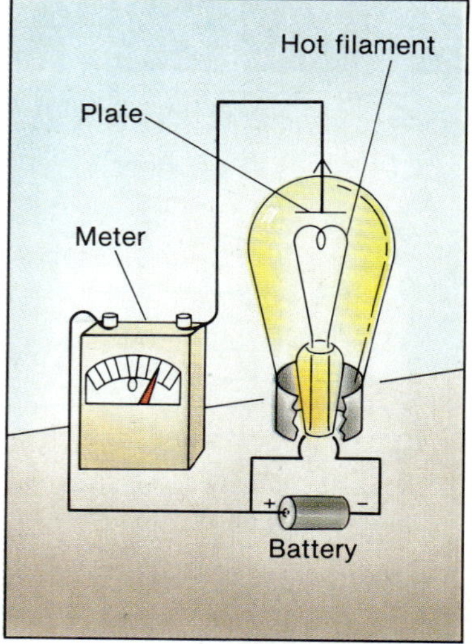

Fig. 11–19 The diagram on the left shows the Edison effect in a vacuum tube.

Fig. 11–20 The diagram on the right shows a filament and a plate in a diode vacuum tube.

Fig. 11–21 A triode vacuum tube contains a grid in addition to a filament and a plate.

current that flows through the tube. This means that the tube can be used to make a very small electric current control a large one. In other words, the tube acts as an *amplifier*. For example, a sound from a musical instrument can be changed into a small electric current. That weak current is fed into an amplifier tube. The current coming from the plate of the tube is much stronger than the weak current from the original sound. But the stronger current has the same pattern as the original sound. Thus the amplified current can be changed back into a sound that is louder than the original.

Enrichment: Have a student who is familiar with electronic devices (radios, games, TVs, computers) explain how they work and demonstrate them.

In the 1940's, the *transistor* was invented. Like vacuum tubes, transistors can be used to amplify currents and to change AC to DC. However, transistors use *semiconductors* to control electric currents. A semiconductor is a material, such as silicon, with a resistance to the flow of current that is easily controlled. Transistors have two great advantages over vacuum tubes. First, transistors do not use hot filaments. Thus transistors do not require much energy to operate and they produce very little heat. A second advantage of transistors is their size. They can be made very small. A very large number of transistors and the electric circuits they control can be put on a tiny chip. See Fig. 11–22. **Electronic devices** such as radios, television sets, calculators, watches, and computers are made with electric circuits using these chips. An *electronic device* always uses electric circuits in which part of the current flows through a semiconductor, a vacuum, or a gas.

Electronic device A device that uses electric circuits in which part of the current flows through a semiconductor, a vacuum, or a gas.

Fig. 11–22 These tiny chips can store and process a great deal of information. They take up a fraction of the space needed for vacuum tubes.

COMMUNICATION BY ELECTRONICS

1. Telephone. Before the telegraph, almost all communication over large distances was by letter. The telegraph was much faster. However, it was still a slow way to send information. Think about how slowly you would talk to someone if it was necessary to say each letter of every word.

The word *telephone* comes from the Greek words *tele,* meaning far, and *phone,* meaning sound. Alexander Graham Bell and Elisha Gray, both working in the United States from 1872 to 1875, developed similar telephone instruments. However, Bell was granted a patent in 1876. Commercial use of Bell's telephone began in 1877. The carbon-resistance transmitter that is used in all telephones today was patented by Thomas Edison. The first commercial telephone switchboard was put into service in Connecticut in January 1878.

The telegraph sent pulses of electric current through wires to make a simple click. The telephone also uses electric currents sent through wires. However, the telephone uses a changing current that can reproduce the sound of your voice. The telephone into which you talk is part of an electric circuit that reaches to the telephone of the person who hears you at the other end. Your call must pass through at least one telephone exchange. Each exchange has the switches necessary to make the connections that complete the circuit to the place you are calling. When you speak into the mouthpiece of the telephone, the sound waves cause a small container filled with carbon grains to vibrate. As the carbon grains are pressed together by the vibrations, their electric resistance drops. When the grains spread apart, their resistance increases. Thus the vibrations of the sound waves change the strength of an electric current flowing through the carbon grains. The changing current is passed along wires to the other telephone. There the current flows into the receiver. A small electromagnet in the receiver causes a metal disc to vibrate. These vibrations make sound waves that are like those made by your voice in the mouthpiece. See Fig. 11–23.

Telephone lines are also used for other purposes. For example, telegraph and television signals and data can also be transmitted over telephone lines. In addition, information can be sent in a form that can be fed directly into processing

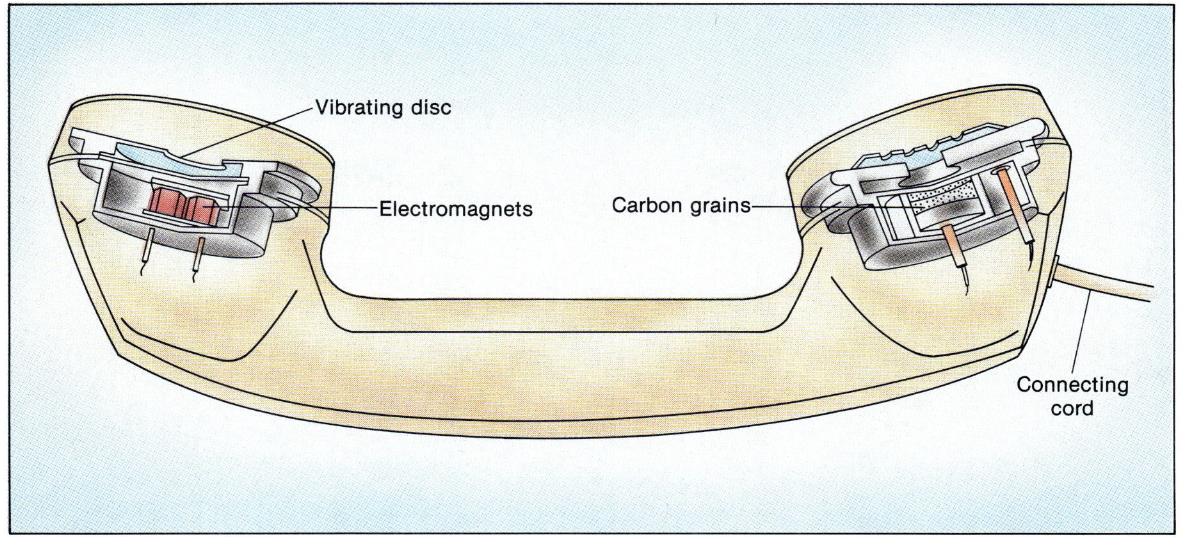

Fig. 11–23 The parts of a telephone handset allow speech patterns to be converted to electric signals which are then changed back into sound waves.

devices. In other words, computers can "talk" to each other over telephone lines.

2. Radio. Communication without wires can be done by using electromagnetic waves. As you know, electromagnetic waves are a form of energy that can travel through space. Electric currents moving through a conductor such as a wire produce these waves. When an electric current builds up in a wire, a magnetic field forms around the wire. Remember that moving electric currents always produce a magnetic field. At the same time, a moving magnetic field makes electricity. This means that an electric current moving along a wire is surrounded by both a magnetic and an electric field. If the electric current moves rapidly back and forth, a series of electromagnetic waves are created and move out through space.

Radio waves are electromagnetic waves made by sending a very rapidly changing electric current through a broadcasting antenna. See Fig. 11–24. This high-frequency current causes radio waves that are the same frequency as the current. As you have seen, changing the strength of an electric current in telephone wires can create sound. In the same way, changing the strength of the current produces radio waves that can carry different kinds of signals. The radio waves are picked up by a receiving antenna. An electric current produced the electromagnetic radio waves. In the receiving antenna, the process is reversed. A very weak electric current is created in the

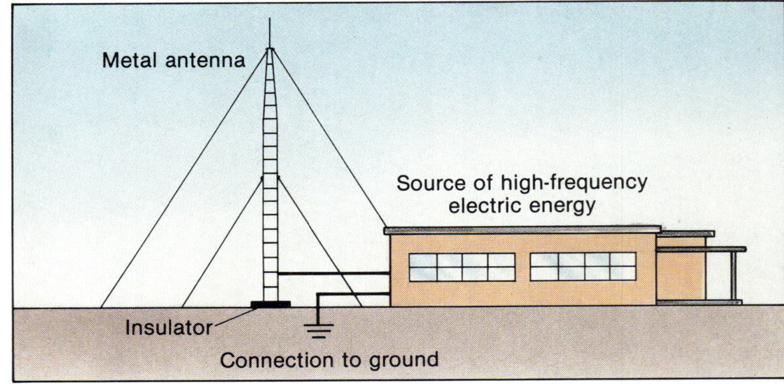

Fig. 11–24 Radio waves are broadcast from a metal antenna at a radio station.

receiving antenna. This weak current is amplified by an electronic receiver. The amplified current then produces the sounds or other signals that were carried by the waves.

The first demonstration that sound could be transmitted by radio took place in 1915. In that year, speech signals were transmitted across the Atlantic from Arlington, Virginia to Paris. The first commercial broadcasts were made in November 1920. Radio is now used for a variety of scientific, industrial, and personal uses. For example, citizen's band (CB) radio can be used for personal communication over distances of 16 to 24 km. Radio frequencies are also used to open garage doors by remote control. One of the most important scientific uses of radio is in radio astronomy. Radio signals from the sun and other stars are picked up by antennas. Previously unknown objects such as quasars and pulsars were discovered in this way.

3. Television. Television pictures and sound are among the most common signals sent out by electromagnetic waves. A television picture starts with a television camera. The camera changes an image into an electric current. The current is made stronger and then sent to the television station's broadcast antenna. When the electromagnetic waves sent from the station are received, they are changed back into an electric current. The television set contains a picture tube. In the back of the picture tube is an *electron gun*. The electron gun shoots a narrow beam of electrons toward the front of the tube. The electron beam is about the size of a pencil lead. The inside of the picture tube is coated with a substance that gives off light when it is struck by the electron beam. The beam moves back

and forth across the face of the tube. It is controlled by magnetic coils in the back of the tube. See Fig. 11–25. Remember that the negative charge on electrons causes them to be affected by a magnet. The strength of the electron beam is controlled by a signal sent from the station. To make the bright parts of the picture the beam is made stronger. A strong beam of electrons makes the material on the face of the tube glow brighter. Dark areas are made by making the beam weaker. The electron beam sweeps from top to bottom of the picture tube. It acts like a brush painting a picture 30 times each second. These pictures are made so quickly that your eyes see them as a moving picture.

Early television sets all depended on some form of mechanical system. The first all-electronic television was demonstrated in 1932. Regular broadcasts began in the United States in 1941. Color sets were first introduced in the 1960's.

A color TV picture tube has three electron guns. One beam of electrons is produced for each of the primary colors (red, green, blue). There are three different substances on the face of the tube arranged as rows of tiny dots or in vertical lines. Each substance glows with one of the primary colors. Each electron beam strikes only the dots or lines that produce one of the primary colors. All colors can be produced by the three electron beams sweeping across the tube at the same time.

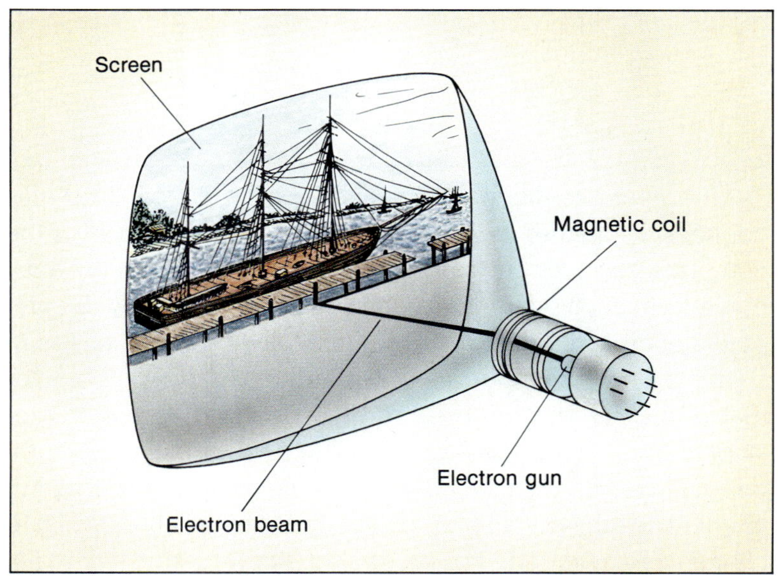

Fig. 11–25 The picture on a television screen is produced by a beam of electrons from an electron gun.

COMPUTERS

Enrichment: Demonstrate computer capabilities in word processing and repeated calculations.

Sometimes computers are called "electronic brains." This description says two things about computers. First, all computers are electronic devices that use many different kinds of electric circuits. Even a small computer such as a calculator contains thousands of circuits. Second, computers use electricity flowing through circuits as a way of recording and processing information. Your brain also is able to record and process information. For example, as you look at the words printed on this page, your brain receives signals from your eyes. The brain processes this information and you know what the words mean. However, a human brain is far better at processing information than any computer.

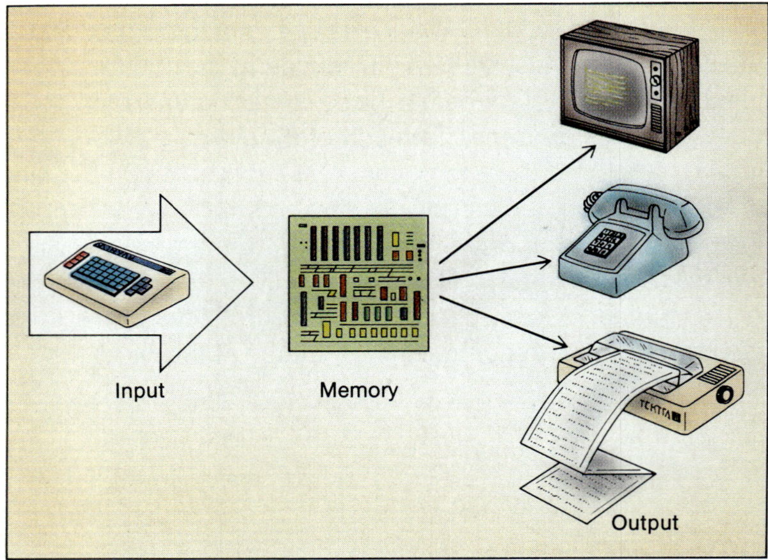

Fig. 11–26 All computers have some form of input, a memory bank, and some form of output.

A computer contains several kinds of electronic devices connected together by wires. See Fig. 11–26. One part of the computer receives the information or *input*. The input may come from a keyboard like a typewriter keyboard. Small computers such as calculators usually receive input by means of separate keys. The input goes into another part of the computer that processes the information. This is done by a series of steps that make up the *program*. The program tells the computer what to do with the information. For example, a program might direct the machine to divide an input number by 100 to change it to a percent. Programs are usually made up of many steps. Computers also have a *memory bank* that stores information. The memory bank stores the information until it can be processed and then records the results. The results are put into a useful form by the *output* section of the computer. This can be a screen like a television tube or a printer that prints out a record on paper.

Fig. 11–27 Computers are becoming an increasingly important part of our daily lives. Many people today own personal computers.

USES OF COMPUTERS

Computers have become a common part of modern living because they can receive and process large amounts of information very quickly. For example, many stores use computers at the checkout counters. They can add up prices quickly and at the same time keep a record of each item sold. Computers are also used to monitor and control other machines. Many automobiles contain small computers. These computers constantly receive information about the amount of gasoline and air used by the engine. The computer can adjust the flow of fuel and air to make the engine work most efficiently. Computers will never be able to replace people, but they will change the way almost everyone works. See Fig. 11–27.

SUMMARY

Electronic devices use electric circuits that are controlled by vacuum tubes or transistors. Electric currents carry information along wires as in the telephone. Information can also be sent through space by using radio waves. Computers are electronic devices that receive and process information.

QUESTIONS

Use complete sentences to write your answers.

1. Describe how a telegraph uses an electric current to send information over a distance.
2. Explain how a beam of electrons produces a picture on a TV screen.
3. Give two reasons why transistors rather than vacuum tubes are used in electronic devices.
4. Describe two uses that can be made of a computer.
5. Name the four parts of a computer and explain the purpose of each part.

1. The telegraph sends pulses of electric current to a receiver. The current activates an electromagnet which makes movements that can be heard as clicks. The message is received as a series of dots and dashes, or short and long clicks.
2. A beam of electrons sweeps across the face of the TV tube from top to bottom. The face of the tube is coated with a material that glows where the electrons hit. The beam is strong for bright areas and weak for dark areas. The light and dark areas make up the picture.
3. Transistors operate at a lower temperature than vacuum tubes and therefore use less energy. Transistor devices are also smaller.
4. Answers will vary. Accept any two uses of computers.
5. The input section receives information. The program section processes the information as it is instructed. The memory bank holds information while it is being processed. The output section puts the results on a screen or prints it out on paper.

INVESTIGATION

See teacher's commentary for teaching hints, safety, and answers to questions.

THE COST OF ENERGY USE

PURPOSE: You will calculate the cost of operating electrical appliances, and estimate the cost of using electricity for one month.

MATERIALS:

pencil paper

PROCEDURE:

A. In your notebook, copy the data table shown below.

B. List all the electrical appliances you can find in your home or classroom. Record the power needed to operate each one. (NOTE: The power needed is printed on a plate connected to each item or on the item itself. See Fig. 11–28.) Unplug any item that you need to move.

C. Convert the watts to kilowatts for each appliance and record.

D. Estimate the number of hours per day each appliance is used and record. Calculate the number of kilowatt hours of energy each appliance uses.

E. Find the total energy in kilowatt hours used each day.

F. Find the average amount of your home electric bill and the number of kilowatt hours used. Calculate the cost per kilowatt hour.

G. From your estimate of daily use and the cost per kilowatt hour in step F, calculate the estimated daily cost.

H. Convert the estimated cost per day into estimated cost per month.

CONCLUSIONS:

1. Compare the amount of your home electric bill for an average month, in step F with the estimate in step H.
2. How can you account for any differences between the two numbers?

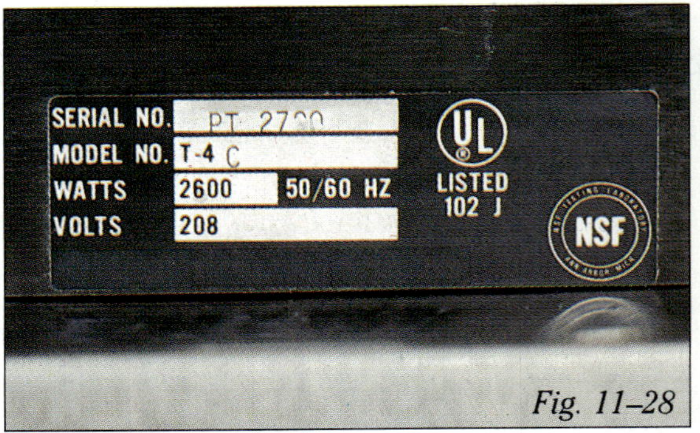

Fig. 11–28

Appliance	Watts (W)	Kilowatts (kW)	Hours Used (h)	Kilowatt hours (kWh)
Television				
Lamp				
Toaster				
Clock				
Etc.			Total:	

TECHNOLOGY

CIRCUITS, CHIPS & WAFERS: ELECTRONIC FAST FOOD

Next to oxygen, silicon is the most abundant element found on earth. This substance, manufactured into a flat, square shape small enough to fit through the eye of a needle, has changed the way we live. Digital-calculator watches, cameras that focus automatically and talk, pocket calculators, and microcomputers all exist today because of silicon chips and the tiny circuits that these chips contain.

The development of silicon chips and their applications is the product of years of research and the desire to find faster means of communication and information storage. Early computers were huge machines occupying an entire room. Silicon chips, which have circuits etched (engraved) on them, store as much information on a tiny piece of silicon as was stored in these huge early computers. The more densely you pack the circuits (the closer the circuitry on the chip), the greater is the capacity of the machine and the faster it will work.

The chip itself is only one part of the hardware; it is the place where the messages are collected and stored. A great deal of research has also gone into controlling and directing the electrical impulses that are the message. Scientists had to learn to direct the movement of electrons, to convert sound waves, radio waves, and even light into a flow of electrons, and then to amplify the strength of these signals. We have gone from minicircuits to even smaller microcircuits. Smaller is faster, the shorter the distance an electrical impulse has to travel and the smaller the control elements are, the faster the circuit can operate. This greater speed means that a circuit can process more information in less time. Only after scientists had developed more accurate means of controlling the flow of electrons could they develop a chip a sixth of an inch long and an eighth of an inch wide that was actually a computer!

How are chips made? Minicircuits were once individually wired together by technicians working through microscopes. Microcircuits are now printed by photographic methods. The chips are coated with a thin photosensitive film. Then a negative, which has been reduced from a large drawing, is placed over the surface and exposed to light. The next step is to etch (or eat away) the portion that has been exposed to light in a chemical bath. By repeating this process a number of different times, thousands of different pathways and controls can be put on a chip about the size of your smallest toenail. The next step may be to etch circuits on one large wafer instead of on a series of silicon chips. Lasers would be used to achieve this precision circuitry. Computer scientists and the computer industry are engaged in an effort to achieve this goal. Microcomputers are helping scientists to concentrate on solving problems rather than spending hours on calculations.

¡COMPUTE!

SCIENCE INPUT

In this chapter you learned Ohm's law, which states the relationship among the three aspects of electricity: volts, ohms, and amperes. The formula for this relationship is:

$$\text{amperes} = \frac{\text{volts}}{\text{ohms}}$$

If you know any two of the three quantities you can determine the unknown third quantity. All you have to do is change the formula depending on the unknown.

If the unknown is volts, then the formula is:

$$\text{amperes} \times \text{ohms} = \text{volts}$$

If the unknown is ohms, the formula is:

$$\text{ohms} = \frac{\text{volts}}{\text{amperes}}$$

COMPUTER INPUT

A program is written according to a system of logic. For the computer, being logical does not mean being reasonable; it means following a specific set of instructions. These instructions must take two things into consideration: the purpose of your program and the electronic capabilities of the machine. A flowchart acts as a diagram of the steps the computer must take to run the program. A programmer designs a flowchart before writing the program. It helps to organize his or her thoughts by providing an overview of the program. For a short program a flowchart may not seem necessary. But when writing long programs, of a hundred lines or more, even professional programmers can lose sight of their overall goals. A flowchart is also useful in taking the "bugs," or errors, out of the program. Matching the flowchart to the steps in the program can show where the logic may have been incorrect.

WHAT TO DO

Program Quick Check will give you two of the three quantities in Ohm's law and will ask for the unknown third. After you have entered your answer, the computer will give you the correct answer. After giving you five problems, it will tell you how many correct answers you had. (Your answers must be rounded off to the nearest tenth or they will be counted as "wrong answers.") Study the flow chart to help understand the program.

GLOSSARY

start or stop

shows path program will take

a single step

input or output

a decision point. A question must be answered or a decision made before the next step can be taken.

ELECTRICITY CONVERSION: PROGRAM QUICK CHECK

PROGRAM

```
100  REM QUICK CHECK
110  K = 0: C = 0
120  REM SELECT QUESTIONS
130  N = INT(RND(1) * 3 + 1)
140  K = K + 1: PRINT: PRINT K
     " QUESTION"
150  IF N = 1 THEN 0 = INT(RND(1) *
     100 + 1): X = 110/0: GOTO 210
160  IF N = 2 THEN 0 = INT (RND(1) *
     100 +1): A = INT(RND(1) * 10 + 1):
     X = A * 0: GOTO 200
170  A = INT(RND(1) * 10 + 1): X = 110/
     A
180  REM ASK QUESTION
190  PRINT "VOLTS = 110": PRINT
     "AMPERES = ";A: INPUT "HOW
     MANY OHMS? ";R$: R = VAL(R$):
     GOTO 230
200  PRINT "OHMS = ";0: PRINT
     "AMPERES = ";A: INPUT "HOW
     MANY VOLTS? ";R$: R = VAL (R$):
     GOTO 230
210  PRINT "VOLTS = 110 ": PRINT
     "OHMS = ";0 : INPUT "HOW MANY
     AMPERES? ";R$: R = VAL(R$)
220  REM CORRECT ANSWER
230  IF INT (X * 10 + .5) / 10 = R THEN C
     = C + 1
240  PRINT "ANSWER = "; INT(X * 10 +
     .5) / 10
250  IF K < > 5 THEN GOTO 130
260  REM PRINT RESULTS
270  PRINT: PRINT: PRINT "     RESULTS:
     ";C " CORRECT ANSWERS"
280  END
```

PROGRAM NOTES

Program Quick Check labels the counters "K" and "C". They could have been labeled with any other letters. They are simply the programmer's identification for what is being counted. "K" stands for the questions, and "C" stands for the number of correct answers.

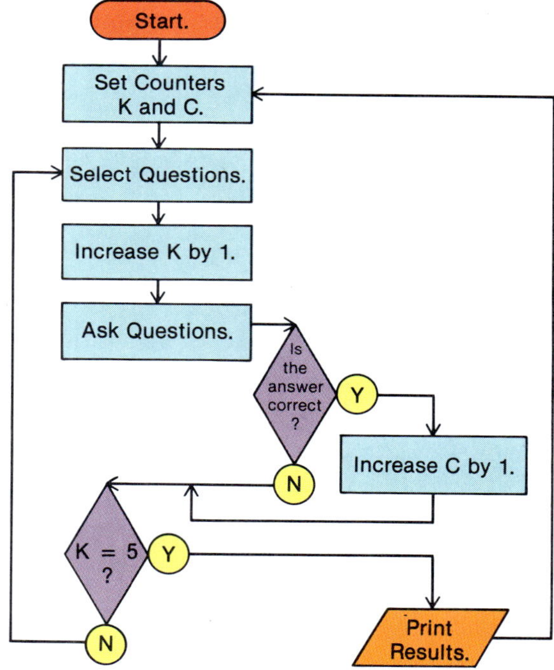

BITS OF INFORMATION

Not all computers use the same words for command functions. Check your computer manual to make sure you are using the correct terms for your machine!

CHAPTER REVIEW

See teacher's commentary for answers.

VOCABULARY

On a separate piece of paper, match each term with the number of the statement that best explains it. Use each term only once.

ampere	kilowatt hour	transformer	resistance
circuit breaker	ohm	volt	fuse
electronic device			

1. A measure of the electric potential for doing work in an electric circuit.
2. A measure of the amount of current moving past a point in an electric circuit in one second.
3. Any condition that limits the flow of electrons in an electric circuit.
4. A measure of the amount of resistance in an electric circuit.
5. A part of an electric circuit that changes the voltage of an alternating current in the circuit.
6. A part of an electric circuit that prevents too much current from flowing in the circuit.
7. A switch that turns off if too much current flows in a circuit.
8. A unit that is used to measure how much electric energy is consumed.
9. A device that uses electric circuits in which part of the current flows through a semiconductor, a vacuum, or a gas.

QUESTIONS

Give brief but complete answers to each of the following questions. Unless otherwise indicated, use complete sentences to write your answers.

1. Why do automobiles have voltmeters (or indicator lights)?
2. All electric circuits have some resistance. What is the effect of the resistance?
3. Complete the following table:

E (volts)	I (amperes)	R (ohms)
12		0.05
6	4.0	
	5.5	20.0

4. List the reasons that electricity is used in so many different ways.
5. Which is easier to repair, a string of Christmas tree lights in which the lights

are in series, or a string of lights in which the lights are in parallel? Why? How is this related to the wiring in a house or building?

6. In what way is the electrical wiring in your home protected from an overload?
7. State several reasons why computers are an important part of our lives.
8. Draw a simple circuit that contains a battery, a switch, a resistance, a voltmeter, and an ammeter.
9. Suppose electricity costs $0.12 per kilowatt hour. If your family used 546 kilowatt hours of electricity in one month, what would be the amount of your electric bill?
10. Explain how the information to produce the television sound and pictures is sent from the TV station to your home.
11. Describe how a telephone transmits your voice.
12. At $0.12 per kilowatt hour, how many hours of television can you watch for $1.00 if your TV uses 240 watts of energy?

APPLYING SCIENCE

1. Using diagrams, explain the workings of a common household appliance such as a steam iron, toaster, or electric coffeemaker.
2. Set up a display using batteries, flashlight bulbs, and switches to show how the wiring in a house works. Explain why parallel wiring is used.
3. Set up a simple electric circuit using a voltmeter, ammeter, batteries, and a piece of nichrome and iron wire. Calculate and compare the resistances of both the nichrome and the iron wire.
4. The units amperes, ohms, and volts are named for three famous scientists: André Marie Ampere, Georg Ohm, and Alessandro Volta. Look up information about these scientists in the library. Write a short biography of each.

BIBLIOGRAPHY

Englebardt, S. L. *Miracle Chip: The Microelectronic Revolution.* New York: Lothrop, 1979.

Heller, R. S. and C. D. Martin. *Bits 'n Bytes about Computing: A Computer Literacy Primer.* Rockville, MD: Computer Science, 1982.

Math, I. *Wires and Watts: Understanding and Using Electricity.* New York: Scribners, 1981.

Renmore, C.D. *Silicon Chips.* New York: Beaufort, 1980.

CHAPTER

12

This photo of an aurora was taken by the Dynamics Explorer satellite. The aurora is caused by charged particles from the sun (the solar wind) that are trapped by the earth's magnetic field.

MAGNETISM

CHAPTER GOALS

1. Describe the behavior of magnets.
2. Compare the earth with a magnet.
3. Explain and give an example of the relationship between electricity and magnetism.
4. Compare an electric motor with an electric generator.

12-1. Magnets

At the end of this section you will be able to:

- ☐ Explain how magnets are similar to objects with electric charges.
- ☐ Use examples to explain what magnetic poles are.
- ☐ Describe a magnetic field.

A lodestone, which means "leading stone," was a small natural magnet used on sailing ships as part of a compass. In the days of sailing ships, before modern methods of navigation, sailors depended upon magnetism to tell direction. Today, magnets are still as important to us as they were to the sailors four hundred years ago.

Suggestion: Have a piece of magnetite (natural magnet) available and demonstrate its properties.

MAGNETIC FORCES

A common kind of magnet is made of a straight bar of iron. With two of these bar magnets you can quickly discover one important way that magnets behave. When you hold them close together, you can feel a force acting between the two magnets. The magnetic force can both attract and repel. In this way, magnetic force and electric force are alike. The part of a magnet where the magnetic forces seem to be strongest is called a **magnetic pole.** Every magnet has at least two *poles*. In a bar-shaped magnet, the poles are at the ends. This is why two magnets will push or pull on each other strongly when their ends are brought together. Magnets with other shapes may have poles anywhere. See Fig. 12–1. Some magnets have several sets of poles.

Magnetic pole The part of a magnet where the magnetic forces are strongest.

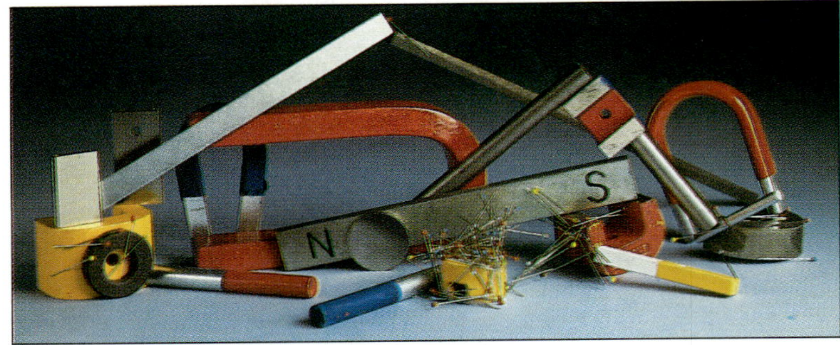

Fig. 12–1 Magnets can have many different shapes and sizes.

Magnetic force is similar to electric force in other ways. First, both kinds of force work at a distance. Two magnets do not need to touch each other in order to attract or repel. Second, both magnetic force and electric force become weaker as the distance between two magnets or two electrically charged objects increases. As two magnets are brought closer together, the push or pull between them becomes much greater. Third, a magnet will attract an unmagnetized object just as an electrically charged object attracts a neutral object.

Suggestion: Tie a string around the center of a bar magnet so that it lines up with the magnetic field in the room. The direction may vary from the earth's magnetic field because of metal in the building. You should still be able to identify the north-seeking pole of the magnet.

MAGNETIC POLES

A simple experiment shows another important fact about magnets. See Fig. 12–2. In this experiment, a bar-shaped magnet is allowed to swing freely. In this case, the magnet will always point in a north-south direction. One pole points north. The other pole then points south. Because magnets always act in this way, the pole of the magnet pointing north is called its *north pole.* The opposite pole is called the *south pole* of the magnet.

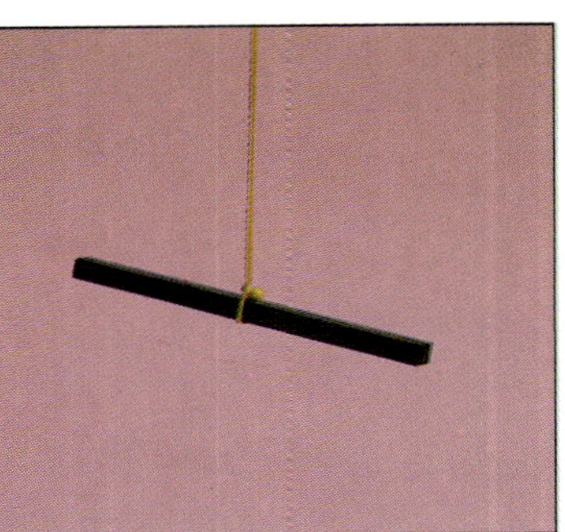

Fig. 12–2 Because a magnet always aligns itself in a north-south direction, its two poles are called its north pole and south pole.

There is an important difference between electricity and magnetism. As you learned in Chapter 10, an object can have an electric charge. It can be either positive or negative. The same is not true of magnets. A magnet cannot have only a south pole or a north pole. As you will see, a magnet always has one north pole and one south pole. A particle with one pole is called a magnetic *monopole.* Many scientists are searching for magnetic monopoles. One theory says that they may have been made at the time of the Big Bang. If so, scientists hope to detect them with special instruments. Although research is still going on, no magnetic monopoles have definitely been found.

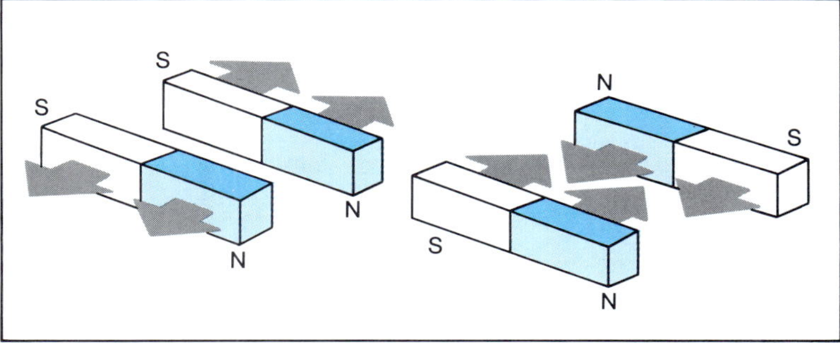

Fig. 12–3 Two north poles or two south poles repel each other. A north pole and a south pole attract each other.

Experiments with magnets prove that like poles repel and unlike poles attract. If the north pole of one magnet is brought near the north pole of a second magnet, there will be a repulsive force between them. If the north pole is brought near the south pole of the second magnet, there is an attractive force between them. See Fig. 12–3.

Suggestion: Place a magnet on an overhead projector. Place a sheet of plastic over it. Sprinkle iron filings on the plastic to show the magnetic field.

The observation that magnets can affect each other without touching shows that they are surrounded by a **magnetic field.** A *magnetic field* is a region of space around a magnet in which magnetic forces are noticeable. Electrically charged objects, as you remember, are surrounded by electric fields. You can see the shape of a magnetic field if you sprinkle small pieces of iron around a magnet. See Fig. 12–4.

Magnetic field The region of space around a magnet in which the magnetic forces are noticeable.

Try this experiment. Place two bar magnets on a sheet of white paper. Bring the north pole of one magnet near the south pole of the other magnet. Now sprinkle iron filings around both magnets. What does the shape of the magnetic field tell you about the magnetic poles of the magnets?* Repeat the experiment with the two north poles together.

* The magnetic field as outlined by the iron filings shows that the north and south poles attract each other. The two north poles repel each other.

Fig. 12–4 This horseshoe magnet has a circular magnetic field. Like all magnets, the field is strongest at the magnetic poles.

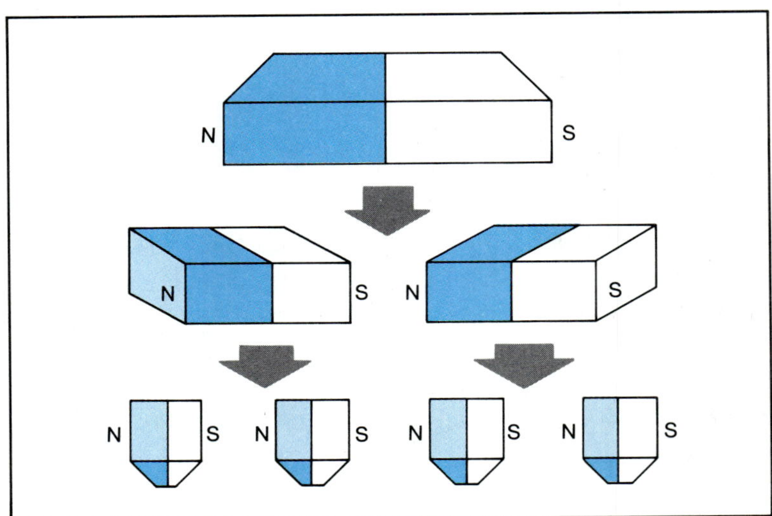

Fig. 12–5 Each piece of the bar magnet still has a north and a south pole.

MAKING A MAGNET

What would happen if you cut a bar magnet in half? You might think that the north pole would be in one piece and the south pole would be in the other piece. The actual result is shown in Fig. 12–5. Each piece becomes a complete magnet with both north and south poles. If the pieces are cut into even smaller ones, the smallest piece will still be a complete magnet with a north and south pole. Each magnet seems to be made of many small magnets.

Fig. 12–6 In an unmagnetized bar of iron, the particles are arranged randomly (a). In a magnet, the particles are aligned into magnetic domains (b).

In a bar of iron that is not a magnet, each small particle of iron acts like a tiny magnet. However, these small magnetic particles are not arranged in a pattern. See Fig. 12–6 (a). They are like a crowd of people sitting in a park and facing in all directions. When the iron bar is magnetized, each of the magnetic particles lines up into regions called *magnetic domains.* See Fig. 12–6 (b). They are more like people sitting in a theater in rows. Within the magnetic domains, the poles all point in the same direction. This makes the whole iron bar into a single large magnet. You can easily turn a steel needle into a magnet. Rub one end of a magnet along the needle, always in the same direction. This rubbing disturbs the particles in the steel. The particles then arrange themselves into magnetic domains. This causes the needle to be magnetized. In Section 12–3, you will learn another way in which a piece of iron can be made into a magnet.

MAGNETIC MATERIALS

The lodestone mentioned at the beginning of this section is a natural magnet. It is a form of iron ore called magnetite. The Greeks knew about natural magnets as early as 800 B.C. Lodestone was mined in the Greek province of Magnesia in Thessaly. This may have led to the name magnet.

Some metals, such as soft iron, can be easily changed into magnets. The small magnets within the soft iron can be lined up without much difficulty. However, soft iron magnets also lose their magnetism easily. For example, hammering on such a magnet can cause the small magnets to lose their orderly arrangement. Magnets that lose their magnetism easily are called *temporary magnets*. Some harder metals, such as steel, are harder to magnetize but tend to keep their magnetism better. A magnet made of material that tends to keep its magnetism is called a *permanent magnet*. Most permanent magnets are made of a mixture of iron, aluminum, nickel, and cobalt that is called alnico. Small permanent magnets are useful for such purposes as making latches to keep cupboard doors closed.

In 1600, William Gilbert published *De Magnete*. It contained everything that was then known about magnets. You will learn about one of Gilbert's discoveries in the next section.

SUMMARY

A magnet always has a north pole and a south pole. The poles can attract or repel each other. Each magnetic pole is surrounded by a magnetic field. The force between magnetic poles decreases as the separation between them increases.

QUESTIONS

Use complete sentences to write your answers.

1. Describe three ways in which magnets are similar to objects with electric charges.
2. Given a metal bar and a piece of string, how could you tell if the bar is a magnet?
3. How could you show that a magnet has two poles?
4. Describe how you can use iron filings to show the shape of a magnetic field.

1. Magnets attract and repel. Magnets can be weak or strong. Magnets exert forces that vary with distance.
2. Hang the magnet by a string in the earth's magnetic field and see if the magnet lines up north and south.
3. A magnet can be shown to have two poles by testing it with another magnet. The south poles and the north poles will repel each other.
4. Place the magnet on a sheet of white paper and sprinkle iron filings around it. The filings will show the shape of the magnetic field.

INVESTIGATION

See teacher's commentary for teaching hints, safety, and answers to questions.

OBSERVING THE MAGNETIC FORCE

PURPOSE: You will use two magnets to observe magnetic force.

MATERIALS:

2 bar magnets
plastic wrap
various objects (pencil, eraser, paper, glass, plastic, paper clip, aluminum foil, staple, chalk, iron nail)

PROCEDURE:

A. Mark one end of each magnet with the letter A. Mark the opposite ends B.

B. Place both magnets on a flat surface. See Fig. 12–7 (a).

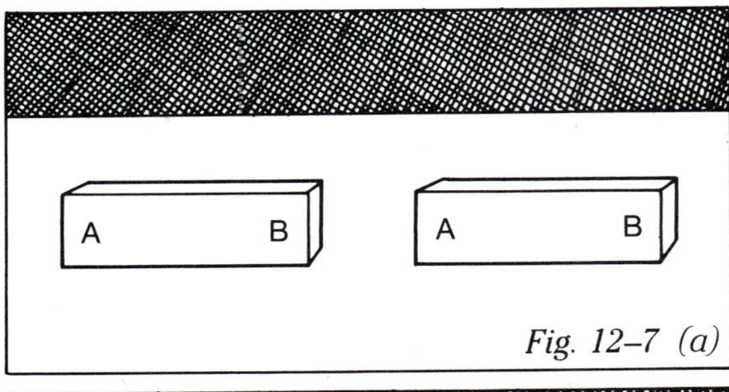

Fig. 12–7 (a)

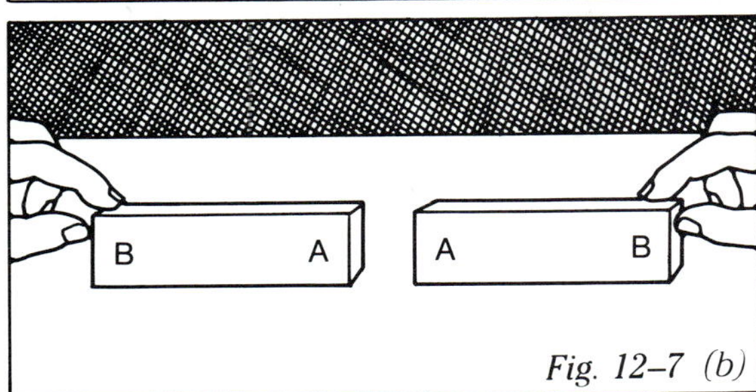

Fig. 12–7 (b)

C. Bring end A of one magnet near end A of the second magnet. See Fig. 12–7 (b).

1. Do the magnets attract each other or repel each other?

D. Now bring end A of the first magnet near end B of the second magnet.

2. Do the magnets attract or repel each other?
3. Do both ends of the magnet behave the same or are they different?

E. Cover one of the magnets with a piece of plastic wrap and repeat steps C and D.

4. Does the plastic have any effect on the attraction or repulsion of the magnets?

F. Copy the table below in your notebook.

Object	Attracted	Repelled	No Effect
Pencil lead			X
Eraser holder on pencil			X
Eraser			X
Paper			X
Glass			X
Plastic			X
Paper clip	X		
Aluminum foil			X
Staple	X		
Chalk			X
Nail	X		

G. Bring a magnet near each of the materials listed in the table. Record the results in the table.

CONCLUSION:

1. What kind of materials were attracted by the magnet?

12-2. Earth As a Magnet

At the end of this section you will be able to:

- ☐ Explain how to make a compass.
- ☐ Use a compass to demonstrate that the earth acts like a magnet.
- ☐ Explain why a compass does not point directly north and south.

When you use an ordinary compass, you are making use of two magnets. One of these magnets is small. That is the needle of the compass. The other magnet is very large. That magnet is the earth. See Fig. 12–8.

Fig. 12–8 A compass can help you find your way because it always points north.

MAGNETS AND COMPASSES

Any magnet that can turn freely will swing around so that its poles point toward the north and south. For example, magnetize a steel needle by rubbing it with one end of a magnet. Then place the needle on a cork floating in a bowl of water. The bowl should be made of glass or another nonmetal. A metal bowl weakens the effect of the earth's magnetic field on the needle. See Fig. 12–9. The needle will turn to point in a north-south direction. This is the kind of compass used by sailors hundreds of years ago. A lodestone was used to magnetize the compass pointer from time to time. The lodestone used in early compasses is a mineral that is a natural magnet.

Fig. 12–9 The magnet on the floating cork is pointing in the same direction as the compass needle.

According to the laws of magnetic attraction and repulsion, a compass always points in one direction because the earth acts like a magnet. Imagine a giant magnet inside the earth. See Fig. 12–10. A compass points north and south because its magnetic poles are attracted to the opposite poles of the magnet in the earth. Of course, there is not really a giant magnet buried in the earth. Scientists do not yet know why the earth acts like a magnet. They think it may be a result of slow movements of very hot metals deep inside the earth. Whatever the cause of the earth's magnetism, its effect is the same as that of a huge magnet buried within the earth.

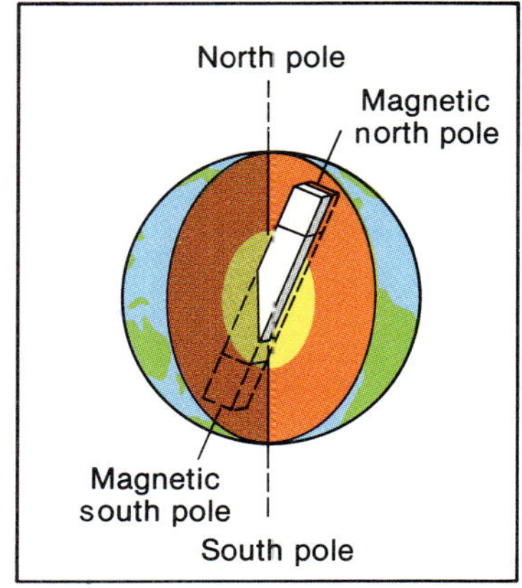

Fig. 12–10 A magnetic compass always points north because the earth acts like a giant magnet.

Today, it seems reasonable to use the earth's magnetism to explain the behavior of compasses. However, compasses were used for centuries before this idea was suggested. In 1600, William Gilbert, who was the physician of Queen Elizabeth I of England, first proposed that the earth is a magnet. He predicted that the earth would be found to have magnetic poles. When those poles were discovered, the laws of magnetic attraction and repulsion were not completely understood. Thus the magnetic pole of the earth to which the north pole of a compass needle points was incorrectly named the "north" magnetic pole. However, this magnetic pole of the earth is actually a south pole since it attracts the opposite pole of a compass needle. See Fig. 12–11. Likewise, the earth's "south" magnetic pole is also incorrectly named. It would be too confusing to try to correct this error now. Thus the earth's magnetic poles are named according to their locations near the imaginary axis marking the true north and south geographic poles.

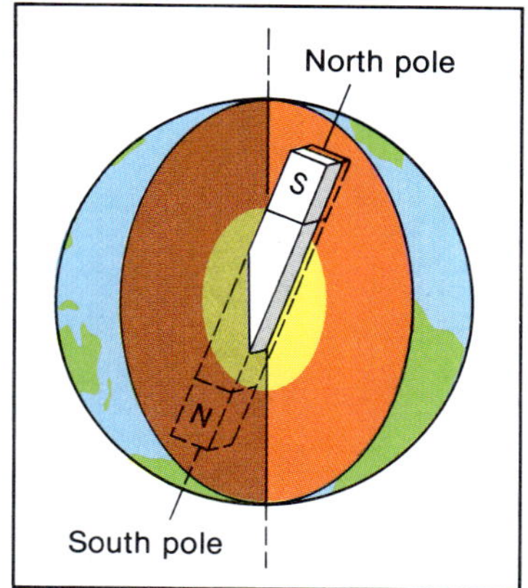

Fig. 12–11 The north pole of the earth is really a south magnetic pole.

LOCATING THE EARTH'S MAGNETIC POLES

Look again at Fig. 12–10. You can see that the imaginary magnet in the earth is not exactly lined up with the true north and south geographic poles. In other words, earth's magnetic poles are not in the same place as the true geographic poles. The magnetic pole in the north, for example, is in northeastern Canada about 1,600 km from the geographic north pole. This creates a problem in navigation. Since compasses point toward the earth's magnetic poles, a compass needle does not necessarily show true geographic north and south. This error in a compass is called **magnetic variation.** See Fig. 12–12. The difference caused by *magnetic variation* is not always the same. Close to the equator, the error is small. There, the distance to the poles is great. Therefore, the magnetic pole and the geographic pole seem closer together. The closer you get to either pole, the greater the amount of error. Magnetic variation must be taken into account if you use a compass to find accurate directions.

Magnetic variation The error in a compass caused by the difference in location of the earth's magnetic and geographic poles.

Enrichment: The earth's field is not horizontal at all places. Use a dipping needle to show the vertical component of the earth's magnetic field.

Word study: Variation from *variatus* (L.), to change.

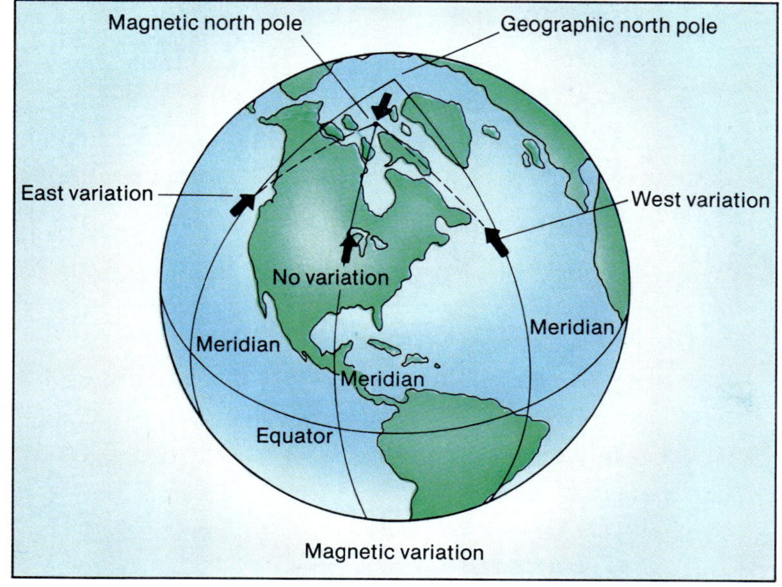

Fig. 12–12 Magnetic variation is greatest near the poles and least at or near the equator.

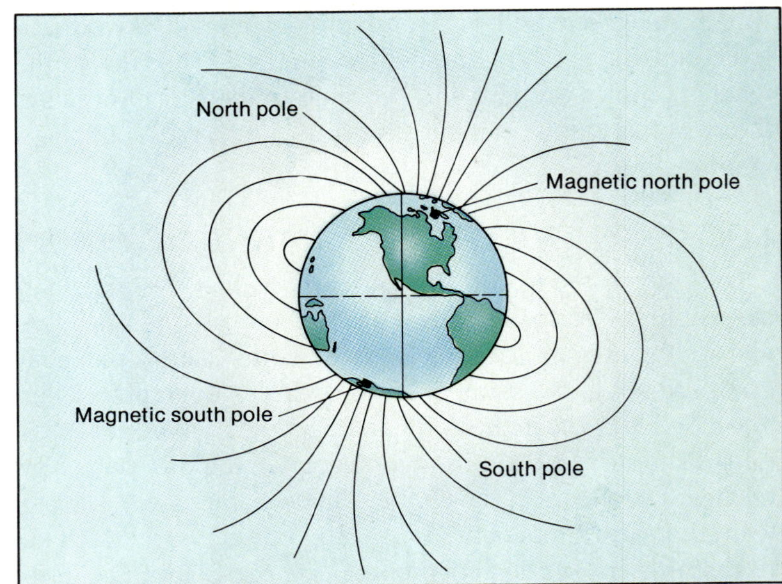

Fig. 12–13 Like other magnets, the earth has a magnetic field that is strongest at the poles. Many stars and other planets also have magnetic fields.

Enrichment: Steel objects that remain in the same position in the earth's magnetic field for a long time may become magnetized. For example, the steel frames of students' chairs may be magnetized. Iron rails and fences often are magnetized. Students could use a compass to test various iron or steel objects for magnetism. Remember that the only true test for magnetism is repulsion.

Like all magnets, the earth is surrounded by a magnetic field. You can see a field around a small magnet if you sprinkle small pieces of iron on a piece of paper over the magnet. If there were some way to do this for the earth, you would have a picture of its magnetic field. See Fig. 12–13. The earth's magnetic field causes the beautiful and mysterious northern lights, as you will learn in the next section.

SUMMARY

To make a compass all you need is a magnet that can swing freely. This kind of compass works because the earth acts like a magnet. Since the magnetic poles and the geographic poles of the earth are not in exactly the same places, a compass does not point to true geographic north and south.

QUESTIONS

Use complete sentences to write your answers.

1. Describe how you could make a compass using a steel needle.
2. How could you use a compass to show that the earth acts like a magnet?
3. Explain why a compass needle does not point directly north and south.

1. You can make a needle into a compass by stroking the needle in one direction with one pole of a magnet and then hanging it from a thread. Stroking the needle causes the magnetic domains to line up, making the needle a magnet.
2. A compass contains a magnet that points north and south. This shows that the earth acts like a magnet and has a magnetic field.
3. A compass needle does not point directly north and south because the earth's magnetic poles are not located exactly at the geographic poles.

INVESTIGATION

See teacher's commentary for teaching hints, safety, and answers to questions.

MAKING A COMPASS

PURPOSE: You will magnetize a needle and find out how to use it as a compass.

MATERIALS:

bar magnet
steel needle
nylon thread, 50 cm
transparent tape
paper clip

PROCEDURE:

A. Place a needle on the top of your desk.

B. Hold down the eye end of the needle with your finger.

C. Starting near the eye end of the needle, stroke the needle with the south pole of a magnet. Do not move the magnet back and forth. Stroke in one direction only. Repeat this 15 times. See Fig. 12–14 (a).

D. Tie a thread around the center of the needle. Hang the needle by the thread so that it swings freely.

1. In what direction does the needle point? (Note: If the needle does not point in any particular direction, stroke it with the magnet several more times.)
2. What kind of a magnetic pole is the point of the needle?

E. Twist the thread in one direction about 20 times while the needle is hanging from it. See Fig. 12–14 (b).

3. Does the needle point in the same direction as before?

F. Bring a paper clip near the hanging needle.

4. Does the paper clip affect the direction of the needle?
5. How do you think rubbing the needle with the north pole of a magnet (see step C) would affect the magnetism of the needle?

CONCLUSION:

1. In your own words, describe how to make a compass and explain the limitations of that compass.

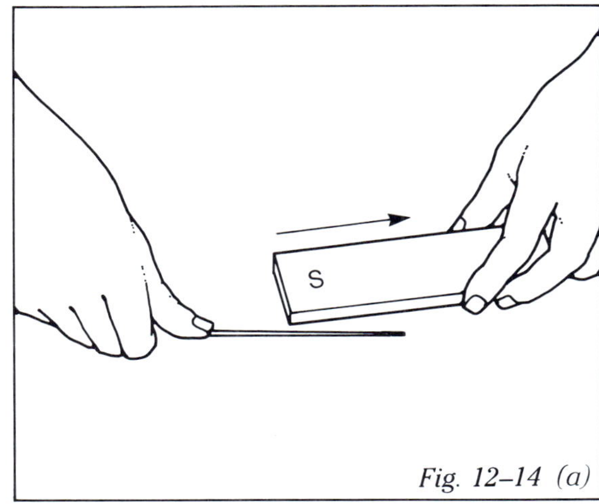

Fig. 12–14 (a)

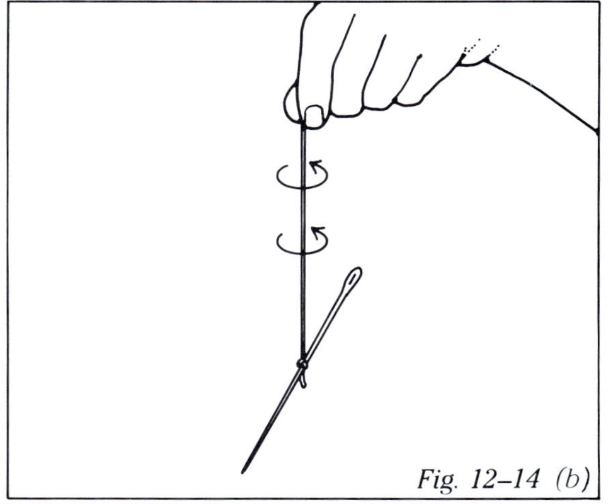

Fig. 12–14 (b)

12-3. Electromagnetism

At the end of this section you will be able to:

- ☐ Explain how magnetism and electricity are related.
- ☐ Describe how an electric motor works.
- ☐ Discuss the relationship between an electric motor and an electric generator.
- ☐ Describe how a transformer affects an electric current.

At certain times of the year, the night sky near the north or south pole is filled with colored streaks or curtains of light. See Fig. 12–15. These colored lights dance over the sky, growing dim or bright as they change shape. After a while, the lights fade away, leaving only a faint glow. What is the explanation of these "northern lights" and "southern lights"?

Fig. 12–15 An aurora can be a spectacular sight, whether it is seen from the ground (as in this photo) or from outer space (as on page 292).

ELECTRICITY AND MAGNETISM

Aurora The northern or southern lights.

Word study: Aurcra, in Roman mythology, the goddess of dawn.

The colorful displays of the northern and southern lights are called **auroras** (uh-**rore**-uhz). *Auroras* are most often seen in the far north or far south of the earth. Auroras occur as a result of the shape of the earth's magnetic field. The magnetic field curves around the earth, meeting near the poles. See Fig. 12–16. Experiments have shown that the auroras are caused by electrified particles from the sun. These particles are part of the *solar wind* blown out from the sun.

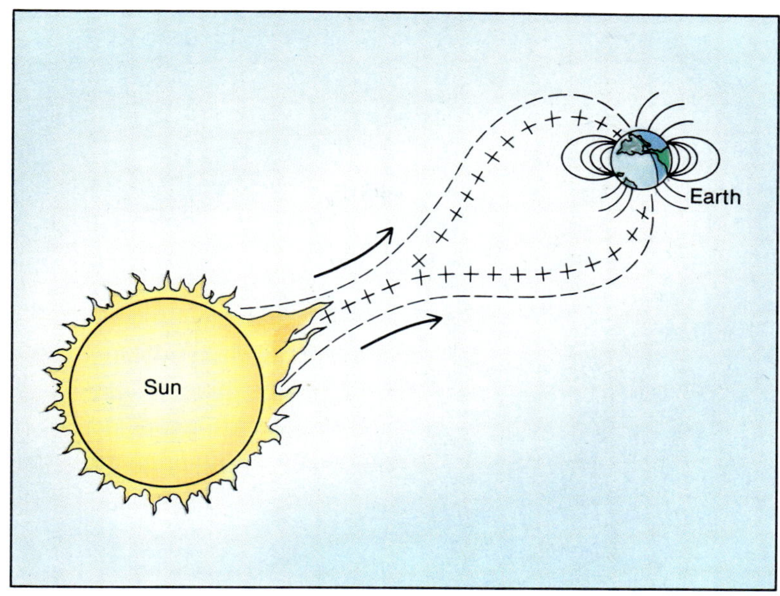

Fig. 12–16 An aurora is created when electrically charged particles in the solar wind interact with the earth's magnetic field.

When these electrically charged particles reach the earth they are guided toward the poles by the earth's magnetic field. As the charged particles fall into the earth's atmosphere, they give off visible light.

Any moving object with an electric charge is affected by a magnetic field. There is a connection between magnetism and electricity. The first scientist to discover this connection was Hans Christian Oersted. In 1820, Oersted found that an electric current passing through a wire caused a nearby compass needle to move.

When an electric current moves through a wire, that wire becomes surrounded by a magnetic field. The field spreads out over a long wire and can be concentrated by turning the wire into a coil. If a piece of iron is put inside a coil of wire, a very strong **electromagnet** can be made. An *electromagnet* is a temporary magnet made by wrapping a coil of wire around a piece of iron. When an electric current flows through the wire, the iron becomes a magnet. See Fig. 12–17 (a). An electromagnet is different from a permanent magnet in two important ways. First, an electromagnet can be made stronger or weaker by changing the amount of current flowing through the wire coil. Second, an electromagnet can be turned off and on. See Fig. 12–17 (b). It is a strong magnet only when the current is on. At very low temperatures, a *superconducting*

Electromagnet A temporary magnet made when an electric current flows through a coil of wire wrapped around a piece of iron.

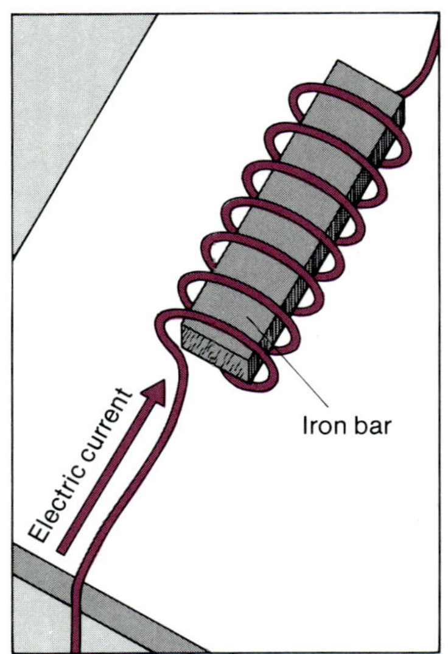

Fig. 12–17 (a) When current flows in the wire, the iron bar becomes magnetized. (b) A strong electromagnet is made when a strong electric current is flowing.

magnet can be made. At very low temperatures, for example in liquid helium at −269°C, some metals have almost no electric resistance. This low resistance means that large currents can flow through these cold conductors. The current continues to flow without any loss of energy. The coil carrying the current acts like a permanent magnet. Superconducting magnets operating at very low temperatures are important tools in scientific research. They are used in particle accelerators to guide beams of charged particles. High magnetic fields may also be used to confine a plasma of charged ions at a temperature of 100,000,000°C.

ELECTRIC MOTORS

Electromagnets are different from permanent magnets in one other way. The poles of an electromagnet can be reversed. If you connect an electromagnet to a dry cell, you can use a compass to tell which are its north and south poles. See Fig. 12–18. If you then switch the connections to the dry cell, the current reverses direction. The compass will then show that the poles of the electromagnet have also reversed. This ability to reverse the poles in an electromagnet explains the operation of electric motors.

Electric motor A device that uses a current in a magnetic field to produce motion.

An **electric motor** is made up of two magnets. One magnet is fixed in one spot on the frame of the motor. See Fig. 12–19. The other magnet is made by sending a current through a loop of wire on a rotating shaft. This causes the wire loop to form a north and south pole. The loop will then turn to line up its poles near the opposite poles of the outer magnet. If the current continued to flow in the same direction through the loop, nothing else would happen. But an automatic switch causes the current in the loop to reverse. Now the poles of the loop are unlike the poles of the outside magnet. The wire loop will be repelled and thus cause the shaft to turn. The switch reverses the current in the loop to keep the shaft turning. The motor will keep turning as long as the electric current flows, first one way and then the other, through the loop of wire.

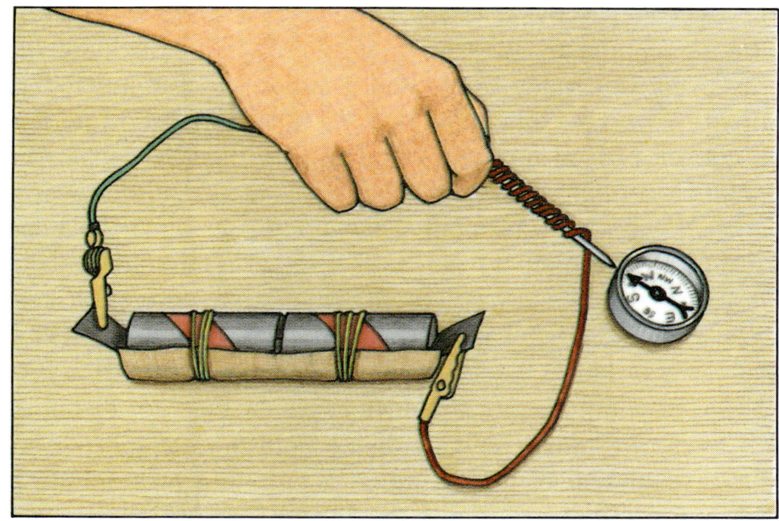

Fig. 12–18 You can use a compass to find the north and south poles of an electromagnet. Changing the direction of the current causes the poles to reverse.

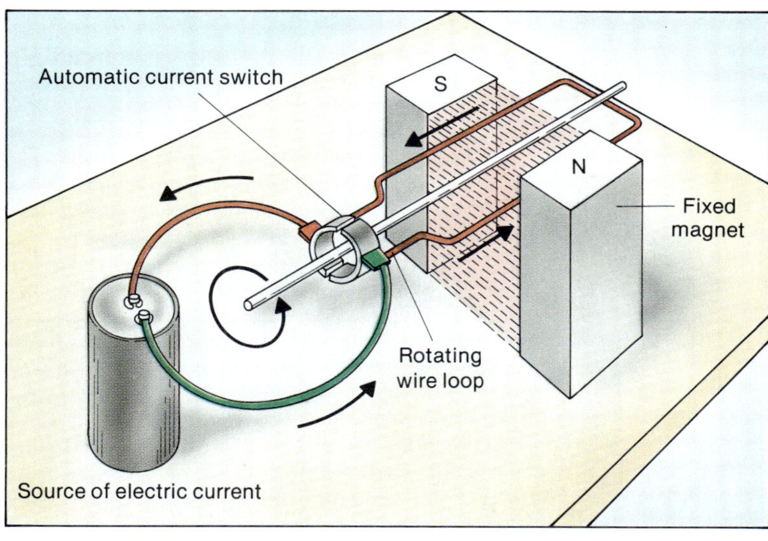

Fig. 12–19 As the direction of the current in the wire loop changes, the loop rotates to align with the poles of the fixed magnet.

Fig. 12–20 This food processor contains a small electric motor.

Electric motors have many wire coils attached to the rotating shaft. The current flowing through each coil of wire keeps the shaft turning smoothly. The outer magnet is usually also an electromagnet. The current always flows in the same direction through it. Many different kinds of electric motors are used. But no matter how they are made, all electric motors use magnetic forces caused by electric currents. Electric motors are used in many household appliances. See Fig. 12–20.

GENERATING ELECTRICITY

Electricity can produce magnetism. Can magnetism also produce electricity? This question was first answered at about the same time by two different scientists. In England, the discovery was made by Michael Faraday, a bookbinder's apprentice who became a famous scientist. Faraday found that a current passed through a coil of wire creates a magnetic field. In turn, the magnetic field causes a current to flow in a second wire coil. In America, a mathematics teacher named Joseph Henry made the same discovery. He found that a current was produced in a coil of wire when a magnet was brought near it. Both Faraday and Henry had discovered that magnetism can produce electricity when a magnetic field and an electric conductor move relative to each other. For example, when a wire moves in a magnetic field, an electric current flows in the wire. This generation of current is an example of what is called **electromagnetic induction** (ih-**lek**-troe-mag-**net**-ik in-**duk**-shun). An electric current produced by *electromagnetic induction* is always the result of motion in a magnetic field. When a wire moves past a magnet, a current will flow

Electromagnetic induction Production of an electric current by motion of a conductor in a magnetic field.

Word study: Induction from *inductio* (L.), a bringing into.

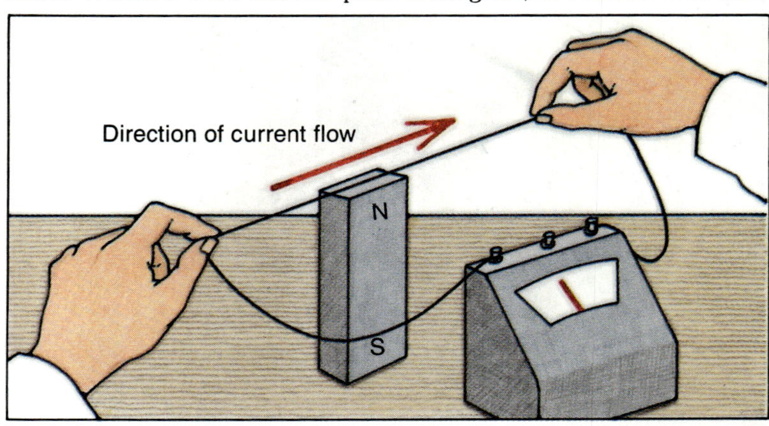

Fig. 12–21 Electromagnetic induction. When a wire is moved in a magnetic field, an electric current is induced in the wire.

in the wire. If the wire is held still and the magnet moves past, a current also flows in the wire. The only requirement for producing a current in this way is to cause motion within the magnetic field. Experiments with a wire moving past a magnet show that the current flows in one direction. See Fig. 12–21. If the wire moves in the opposite direction, the direction of current flow reverses.

Electromagnetic induction can be used to produce electricity in an electric **generator**. A loop of wire is put into a magnetic field. See Fig. 12–22. As the wire loop is turned, an electric current is produced. Spinning the loop produces a current that is fed into wires.

Generator A device that uses the motion of a wire in a magnetic field to produce an electric current.

Remember that the direction of current flow changes with the direction of movement of a wire in a magnetic field. When one side of a wire loop moves down in a magnetic field, the current produced will flow in one direction. When the same side moves up during the other half of its turn, the current flows in the opposite direction. As a result, the current flows first in one direction and then the other. This change of direction produces *alternating current.*

The big *generators* in power plants have many loops of wire spinning inside large electromagnets. The speed of the generators is carefully controlled. The direction of current flow reverses 60 times each second. This change of direction produces the form of electricity we commonly use. This form of electricity is alternating current with a frequency of 60 Hz (cycles per second). Automobiles are equipped with small generators called *alternators* to supply the energy needed to run the car's electrical system.

Enrichment: The alternator in an automobile actually generates alternating current (AC). A rectifier changes this to direct current (DC) that can be used by the battery and other equipment.

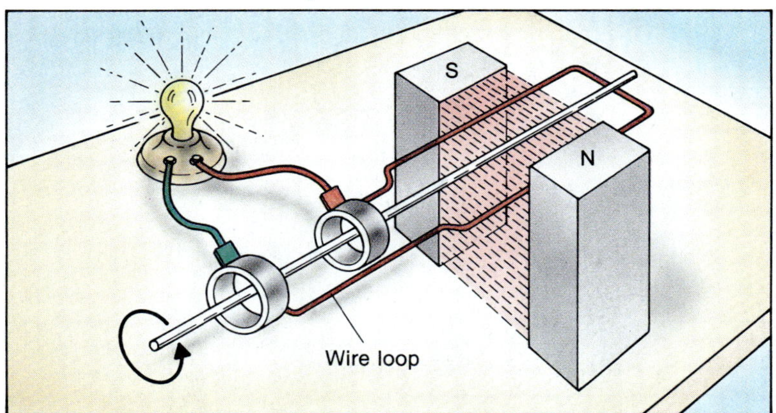

Fig. 12–22 Spinning the wire loop in the magnetic field induces an electric current in the wire.

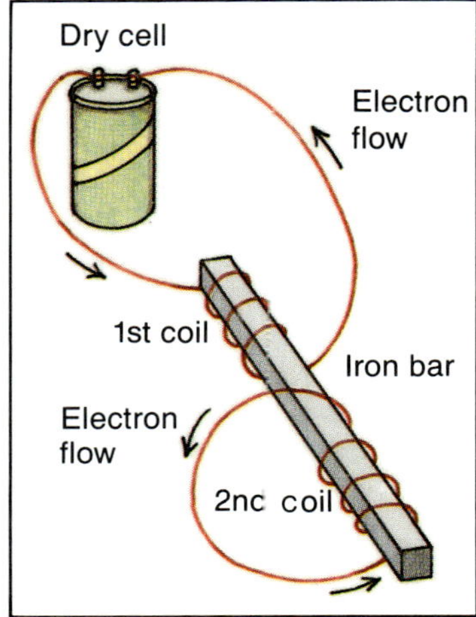

Fig. 12–23 When an electric current flows in one coil of wire, the iron bar is magnetized. A current is then induced in the second coil of wire.

Transformer A device in which a current in one coil induces a current in another coil.

Enrichment: The ignition coil in an automobile is a transformer that sends out a 15,000- to 30,000-volt pulse each time the 12-volt primary is pulsed by the ignition system.

TRANSFORMERS

You have seen how an electric current can be generated by moving a wire past a magnet. A current may also be produced by electromagnetic induction when a magnet moves past a stationary wire. A third method of electromagnetic induction needs no visible motion.

Suppose two coils of wire are wound around opposite ends of an iron bar. See Fig. 12–23. One of the coils is attached to a source of electric current. When the current begins to flow through the wire coil, the iron bar is magnetized. The second coil of wire then acts as if a magnet were suddenly pushed into it. The effect on the second coil of wire is the same as if a magnet had moved past it. Electromagnetic induction causes an electric current to flow in the second coil. Each time a current changes in the first coil, a current is produced in the second wire coil.

This principle is the basis of an electrical **transformer**. A *transformer* consists of two coils of wire wrapped around the same iron core. Transformers are useful because they can change the voltage of alternating current. If the number of turns in the two coils of wire is the same, the voltage produced in the second coil will be the same as that flowing in the first coil. If the second coil has *twice* as many turns, its voltage will be *twice* that in the first coil. See Fig. 12–24. Although the voltage is doubled, the current is cut in half. If there are fewer turns in the second coil, the output voltage will be less than the input voltage. Transformers can only be used to change

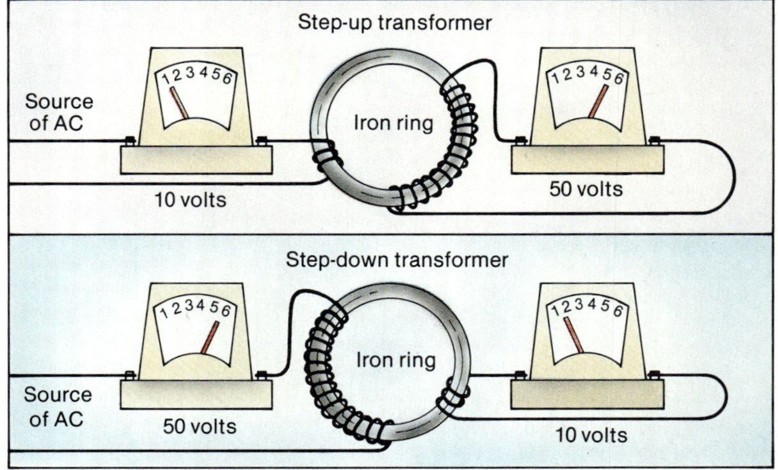

Fig. 12–24 (a) A step-up transformer increases the voltage. (b) A step-down transformer decreases the voltage.

the voltage of alternating current. Only alternating current has the start-and-stop action needed to produce the changing magnetic field required for electromagnetic induction.

In Chapter 11 you learned that transformers produce the many different voltages needed to operate all kinds of electrical machinery and appliances. The very high voltages needed to send electric currents long distances in power lines are produced by transformers. Other transformers then reduce the voltage again for ordinary use.

Enrichment: The transformer (ignition coil) in an automobile operates on DC current. A switch cuts off the current from the battery at the instant a spark plug is to fire. The collapsing magnetic field in the coil connected to the battery then induces a high voltage in the secondary coil of the transformer.

Electromagnetic induction might seem to break the law of conservation of energy. One part of this law says that energy cannot be created. When a wire moves through a magnetic field, the electric energy in the wire seems to come out of nowhere. However, remember that the wire must be moving. If the motion stops, the electric current stops. The electric energy really comes from the energy of motion. An electric generator needs a source of energy to cause motion. This source of energy may be heat energy from burning fuel. Energy released by falling water can also turn generators. Nuclear energy is becoming more important as a way to produce electricity.

SUMMARY

Electromagnets show that electricity can produce magnetism. An electric motor works on this principle. Similarly, magnetism can be used to produce electricity. An electric generator works on this principle. A motor and a generator are similar in construction. Transformers change the voltage of alternating current.

QUESTIONS

Use complete sentences to write your answers.

1. Give another name for the northern lights and explain how they are produced.
2. How is magnetism related to electricity?
3. Using Fig. 12–19, describe how an electric motor works.
4. Using Fig. 12–22, describe how a generator works.
5. Draw a diagram to explain what a transformer is and what it does.

1. The northern lights are also known as the auroras. They are the result of electrical particles from the sun being concentrated by the earth's magnetic field as they enter our atmosphere.
2. By wrapping a coil of wire around a piece of iron and running an electric current through the wire, the iron can be magnetized.
3. The electric current is fed into a wire loop in a magnetic field. A force causes the wire loop to turn. An automatic current switch reverses the current flow after every half turn of the loop. This causes the loop to turn completely in the magnetic field.
4. The wire loop in a generator turns through a magnetic field, producing an electric current. As the wire moves back through the magnetic field, the current reverses.
5. A transformer contains two coils of wire wound around an iron core. It can be used to change the voltage of an alternating electric current. If the number of turns in the input coil is twice the number in the output coil, the voltage will be cut in half. Diagrams should be similar to Fig. 12–23 or 12–24.

¡COMPUTE!

SCIENCE INPUT

As you have learned in this chapter, the earth is like a great magnet. If you traveled around the earth with a compass, it would always point to the closest source of the earth's magnetism, either the North Pole or the South Pole. Therefore, by using a series of these compass readings, it is possible to pinpoint the true location of the magnetic pole.

COMPUTER INPUT

The computer may be used for simulation or modeling. In this case, a program has been written, using a game format, to produce a model of a magnetic source. This was done by using the computer's capacity to generate a random number to represent the position of the source on a map.

A random number is one that has the same probability of being chosen as any other number. For example, lottery numbers are always chosen randomly to ensure that every ticket has an equal chance of being chosen. Each time you play the game the computer generates 2 random numbers; one represents the vertical axis of a map and the other represents the horizontal axis. The magnetic source is located where the vertical and horizontal axes meet. In this way, a new magnetic source is produced for each game.

WHAT TO DO

In this adventure game you will try to locate the magnetic source on a map. You will have 10 tries to locate the source. On each try you will tell the computer where you think the magnetic source is located by indicating 2 map positions, one vertical and one horizontal. If you haven't pinpointed the source with your guess, the computer will tell you in what direction your compass is pointing. Use this information to direct your next guess.

Using a separate piece of graph paper for each run (or different colored pencils on the same piece of paper), record you position and the direction of the pole. See the data chart example. (The vertical or (x) axis represents longitude, a north to south marking, and the horizontal or (y) axis represents latitude, an east to west marking.)

This game can be played by individuals or by teams within a class.

GLOSSARY

RND a command in BASIC which instructs the computer to generate a random number

DIM short for dimension. This instruction tells the computer how many spaces in the computer's memory need to be reserved for the program's information. For example, if you wanted to set aside space for a map with 20 vertical and 20 horizontal lines, you could type DIM L (20,20). See line 110 of Program Compass.

PROGRAM

```
100  REM COMPASS
110  DIM L (20,20)
120  FOR Z = 1 TO 41
130  X = INT (RND(1) * 20)
135  Y = INT (RND(1) * 20)
140  L(X,Y) = 1
```

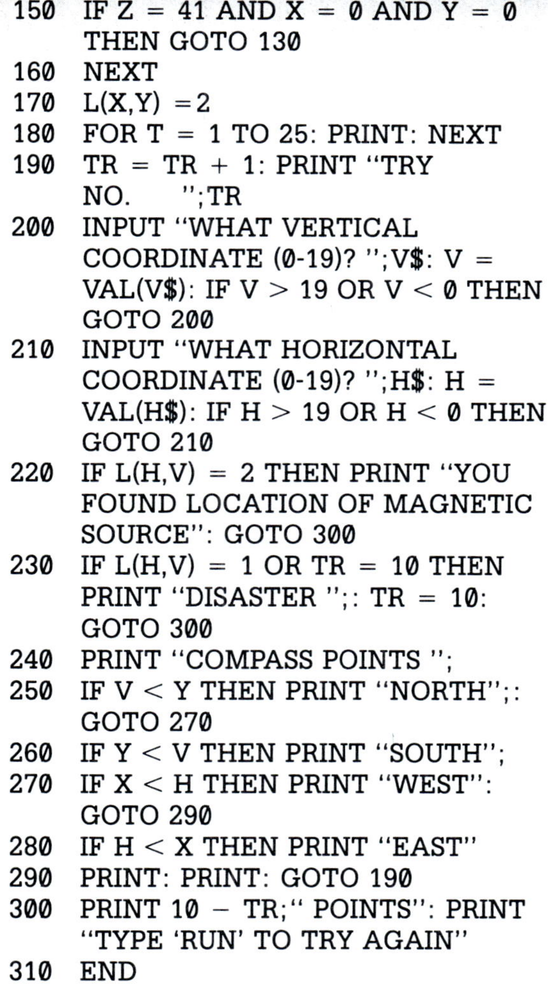

```
150  IF Z = 41 AND X = 0 AND Y = 0
     THEN GOTO 130
160  NEXT
170  L(X,Y) =2
180  FOR T = 1 TO 25: PRINT: NEXT
190  TR = TR + 1: PRINT “TRY
     NO.     ”;TR
200  INPUT “WHAT VERTICAL
     COORDINATE (0-19)? ”;V$: V =
     VAL(V$): IF V > 19 OR V < 0 THEN
     GOTO 200
210  INPUT “WHAT HORIZONTAL
     COORDINATE (0-19)? ”;H$: H =
     VAL(H$): IF H > 19 OR H < 0 THEN
     GOTO 210
220  IF L(H,V) = 2 THEN PRINT “YOU
     FOUND LOCATION OF MAGNETIC
     SOURCE”: GOTO 300
230  IF L(H,V) = 1 OR TR = 10 THEN
     PRINT “DISASTER ”;: TR = 10:
     GOTO 300
240  PRINT “COMPASS POINTS ”;
250  IF V < Y THEN PRINT “NORTH”;:
     GOTO 270
260  IF Y < V THEN PRINT “SOUTH”;
270  IF X < H THEN PRINT “WEST”:
     GOTO 290
280  IF H < X THEN PRINT “EAST”
290  PRINT: PRINT: GOTO 190
300  PRINT 10 – TR;“ POINTS”: PRINT
     “TYPE ‘RUN’ TO TRY AGAIN”
310  END
```

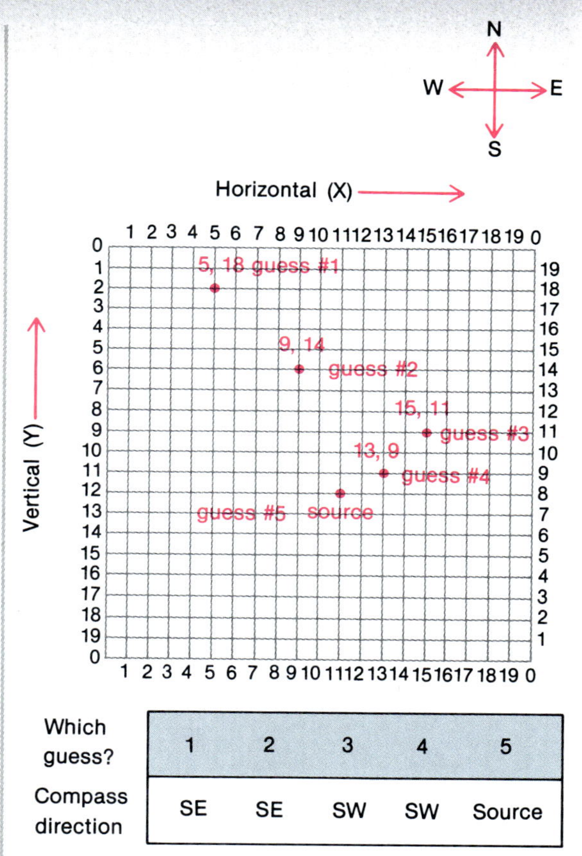

Which guess?	1	2	3	4	5
Compass direction	SE	SE	SW	SW	Source

PROGRAM NOTES

This program is written for a “map” with 20 vertical lines and 20 horizontal lines; that is its array of numbers. Where is that indicated in the program? How could that be changed?

BITS OF INFORMATION

Can you imagine a computer, small enough to sit on your lap, which would let you write letters or make notes and do programming? Such computers are available, some weighing as little as 9 pounds. This innovation makes computing a very portable possibility and users are no longer confined to a particular space to do their work.

SKILL-BUILDING ACTIVITY

See teacher's commentary for teaching hints, safety, and answers to questions.

MAGNETISM AND ELECTRICITY

PURPOSE: You will study the cause and effect between electricity and magnetism.

MATERIALS:

nail
wire, 1.5 m
2 batteries
2 wire connectors
light bulb and socket
paper clip
compass
pencil
bar magnet

PROCEDURE:

A. Wrap 30 turns of wire around a nail. Set up an electric circuit as shown in Fig. 12–25. Do not make the final connection yet.

B. Bring the nail head near a paper clip.

1. Does the nail attract the paper clip?

C. Connect the final wire.

2. What evidence do you see that a current is flowing?

D. While the current is flowing, bring the head of the nail near a paper clip.

3. Does the nail attract the paper clip?

E. Bring the head of the nail near the south and then the north pole of a compass.

4. Does the head of the nail attract or repel the south pole of the compass?
5. Does the head of the nail attract or repel the north pole of the compass?

F. Test the north and south pole of the compass with the point of the nail.

6. How do the poles of the compass react to the point of the nail?

G. Wrap one end of the wire around a compass so that 5 loops go over the top and under the compass needle. Wrap the wire into another coil around a pencil. Make about 15 coils. Then remove the pencil.

H. Join the loose end of the wire to the end of the wire near the compass. The two coils should be at least 15 cm apart.

I. Arrange the compass so that the compass needle is pointing in the same direction as the wires in the coil around it.

J. Insert the magnet in the coil of wire you made around the pencil. Quickly pull the magnet from the coil.

7. What do you observe when you pull the magnet out of the coil? Is an electric current flowing?

CONCLUSIONS:

1. Explain how you can use a battery, wire, and a nail to make a magnet.
2. Describe how you can use a magnet and a piece of wire to cause a current to flow in the wire.

Fig. 12–25

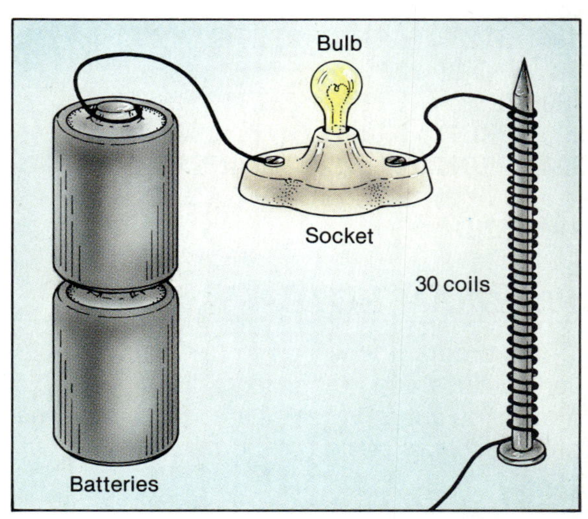

TECHNOLOGY

"DIGITIZATION"

Many of the technologies described in the Special Features sections, such as computer graphics, lightwave communication, and robots, rely on "digital" techniques. **Digitization** is the name of the process that changes sound, pictures, or print into numbers and then back again into sound, pictures, or print.

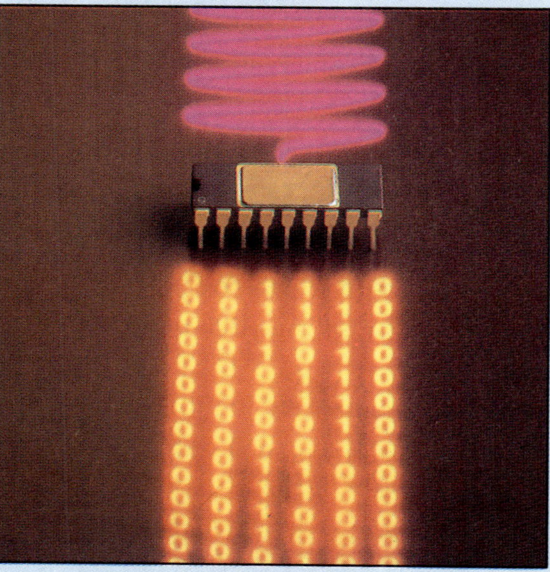

Imagine singing into a microphone. The microphone changes the sound waves into a flow of electrical signals. The pattern of electrical signals is *similar* to the sound waves. They both flow with a certain speed, frequency, and amplitude. No part of the sound wave is actually separate from another part. No part of the flow of electrical signals is separate from another part. This information or data is said to be continuous. Sound waves and the electrical signals both represent continuous data. Things that are similar to one another are said to be *analogous*. Therefore, machines based on changing sound waves to electrical impulses use "analog systems." Analog systems of information processing are often very open to noise, static, and interference because the characteristics of these distortions are usually very similar to the original signal. If the information could be broken up into pieces that could be converted to machine language and manipulated by mathematical equations, these problems could be solved. How can we change the flow of electricity or continuous sound waves to separate pieces of information? We take samples of that information at different times and give each sample or "bit" a number. This is done with a device called an analog-to-digital converter (A/D). (The photo shows the device and depicts the process we are explaining.) The A/D converter details how the amplitude of the sound wave should be translated into a pattern of pieces of information called "bits." When this sample of information has been taken, we have a digital system.

The numbers, or digits, the computer uses are **binary** numbers. A binary system has only 2 separate numbers: 0 and 1. Combinations of these 2 digits are used to identify pieces of information. How is this done? Wherever electricity flows, as it did through the microphone, it creates a magnetic field. The computer "reads" this magnetic field. In other words, the computer recognizes the presence (1) or absence (0) of a magnetic field. All information is coded either 1 or 0 or combinations of these two numbers. These binary numbers, or digits, become the impulses used by the particular technology. Digital clocks "read" the digits representing the times and change this information to an "electric read out." Digital impulses appear on the CD or compact disc as little "pits" on a reflective plastic disc which are read by a small laser and changed back into sound. Television has also begun going digital. In fact, modern electronic technology and digital systems go hand in hand.

CHAPTER REVIEW

See teacher's commentary for answers.

VOCABULARY

On a separate piece of paper, match each term with the number of the statement that best explains it. Use each term only once.

aurora
electromagnet
generator
electromagnetic induction
magnetic variation
magnetic field
magnetic poles
motor
transformer

1. The parts of a magnet where magnetic forces are strongest.
2. Formation of an electric current by motion of a conductor in a magnetic field.
3. A device in which a current in one coil induces a current in another coil.
4. The error in a compass caused by a difference in location of the earth's magnetic and geographic poles.
5. Uses a current in a magnetic field to produce motion.
6. A region of space around a magnet in which magnetic forces are noticeable.
7. The northern and southern lights.
8. A temporary magnet made when an electric current flows through a coil of wire wrapped around a piece of iron.
9. A device that uses the motion of a wire in a magnetic field to produce electricity.

QUESTIONS

Give brief but complete answers to each of the following questions. Unless otherwise indicated, use complete sentences to write your answers.

1. In what ways do magnets behave like objects with electric charges?
2. How could you demonstrate that magnetic poles always seem to come in north-south pairs?
3. Explain why a compass does not point true north. What is the error called?
4. Describe three ways in which an electromagnet differs from a permanent magnet.
5. What happens when a wire is moved in an electric field? What is this called?
6. What is the difference between an electric motor and an electric generator?
7. Explain the difference between a magnetized piece of iron and an unmagnetized piece.
8. What is meant by the north and south poles of a magnet? Where are they located?
9. Describe how you would make a simple compass.

10. What is the relationship between magnetism and electricity? How could you demonstrate this relationship?
11. Explain what causes an aurora.
12. Discuss how reversing the poles of an electromagnet helps explain how an electric motor works.
13. Describe the parts of a transformer and explain how it works. Give an example of how the number of turns of wire affects the transformer's output.

APPLYING SCIENCE

1. Construct a simple electric motor and demonstrate it to the class. Use simple materials such as nails, wire, and tape. How do AC and DC motors differ from each other?
2. Build a sensitive magnetic compass and use it to monitor the magnetic field around your home or school. The needle will need to be longer than the usual compass needle. Keep a record of any changes in the magnetic field. Report your observations to the class. Write a hypothesis to explain your observations.
3. Any steel structure that is in a magnetic field for a long period of time may become magnetized. Use a compass to test the steel chairs in your classroom for magnetism. Remember that the only sure test for magnetism is repulsion.
4. Draw a diagram or build a model to show how an electric meter, such as an ammeter or a voltmeter, works. Demonstrate your model to the class.
5. Michael Faraday and Joseph Henry each discovered electromagnetic induction at about the same time, although Faraday is usually credited with the discovery. Write a short report on the work of Faraday and Henry.

BIBLIOGRAPHY

Adler, David. *Amazing Magnets.* Mahwah, NJ: Troll, 1983.

Fleming, June. *Staying Found: The Complete Map and Compass Handbook.* New York: Random, 1982.

Geary, Don. *Step in the Right Direction: A Basic Map and Compass Book.* Harrisburg, PA: Stackpole, 1980.

Kentzer, Michael. *Power* (Young Scientist Series). Morristown, NJ: Silver Burdett, 1979.

Math, Irwin. *Wires and Watts.* New York: Scribner, 1981.

UNIT

4

MATTER

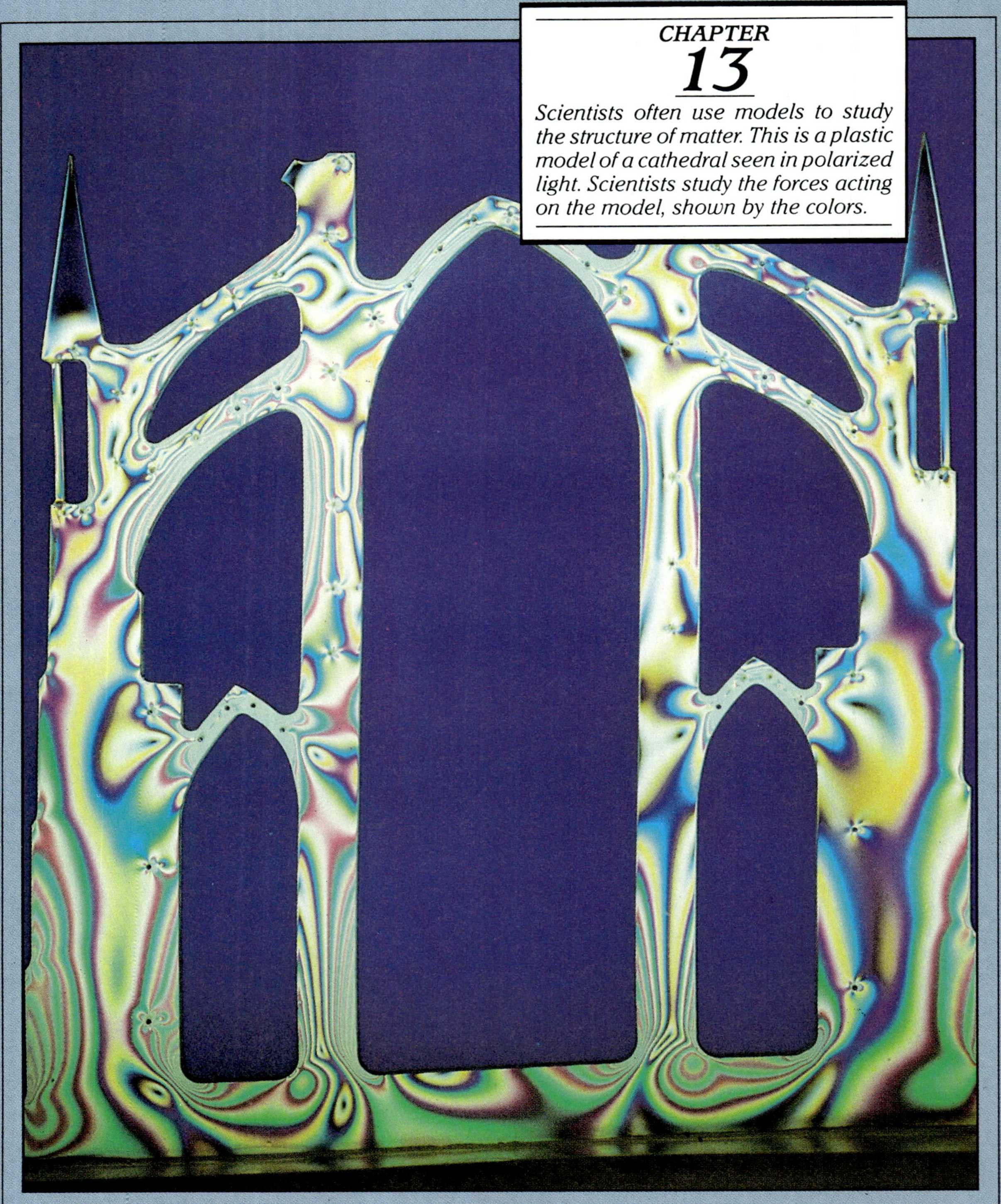

CHAPTER
13

Scientists often use models to study the structure of matter. This is a plastic model of a cathedral seen in polarized light. Scientists study the forces acting on the model, shown by the colors.

THE STRUCTURE OF MATTER

CHAPTER GOALS

1. Define the term *molecule.*
2. Distinguish between physical and chemical properties and compare physical and chemical changes in matter.
3. State the kinetic theory of matter and use it to describe solids, liquids, and gases.
4. Explain the melting of solids and the boiling of liquids in terms of the motion of molecules.

13-1. Matter

At the end of this section you will be able to:

- Describe what happens when matter is divided into smaller and smaller parts.
- Explain what is meant by a *molecule.*
- Compare how molecules move in solids, liquids, and gases.

Imagine that you are a skydiver. With your parachute strapped on securely, you jump from an airplane. For a short time you fall freely. Then at a certain height, the parachute opens and you float gently down to the ground.

What might you see on such a jump? At first you would see the whole landscape beneath you. You would see fields, highways, even whole towns. Coming down closer, you would see a smaller area in greater detail. You would be able to see trees, cars on the highway, and individual houses. Finally, on landing you would see grass, soil, and twigs on the ground around you. See Fig. 13–1.

In this chapter, you will be a "skydiver" studying matter. You will begin with a view of a whole "landscape" of matter. Then you will look closely at the behavior of small particles that make up the different forms of matter.

As you will learn in this chapter, all kinds of matter are made up of particles that are in constant motion. The amount of motion of the particles determines the structure of matter. Different kinds of matter have different properties.

Fig. 13–1 This photo of Baltimore was taken from a satellite far overhead. Closer to the ground, you would be able to see trees and houses. Matter is also made of smaller parts.

Suggestion: The idea of molecules as small invisible particles can be demonstrated by evaporating a material with a strong but pleasant odor at the front of the classroom. Point out that the odor can be detected some distance away because small particles are able to travel through the air to the students' noses.

Molecule The smallest particle of a substance, such as water, that is still identified as that substance.

Enrichment: Most chemists use the term molecule exclusively for covalently bonded substances. In this approach, molecules do not include ionic substances (salts), metallic elements, or the noble gases.

MOLECULES OF MATTER

Matter is defined as anything that takes up space and has mass. Everything you see around you is made of matter. Just as the details on the earth's surface become clearer to a falling skydiver, a closer look at matter shows that it is made up of smaller parts.

Try dividing a glass of water as many times as you can. First pour out half the water. You still have half a glass of water. Then divide that in half, and so on. What would happen if you could keep dividing the remaining amount of water in half? Imagine that you could keep pouring out more and more water. You would finally have one tiny particle that would still be water. That small particle of water is called a water **molecule** (**mohl**-i-kyool). The word "molecule" comes from the Latin *molecula* meaning "little mass." A water *molecule* is the smallest particle of water that is still water. Generally speaking, all water molecules are alike. A water molecule in a rain drop is the same as a water molecule in the ocean. However, if you could divide a single water molecule, you would no longer have water. You would then have two different kinds of matter. This means that a water molecule is made up of two separate parts that combine to produce the substance we call water.

Actually it would be impossible for you to separate out just one water molecule. Water molecules are small. It would take about 60 million water molecules side by side to reach across a penny! If you could make a drop of water as big as a football field, you would be able to see billions and billions of water molecules.

What would happen if you could divide a liquid such as alcohol in the same way as you imagined you did water? Eventually you would come to the smallest particle that is still alcohol. This particle would be a molecule of alcohol.

PHYSICAL AND CHEMICAL PROPERTIES OF MATTER

You can tell the difference between different kinds of matter by their different properties. For example, suppose you have two test tubes. Each tube is partly filled with a liquid. One test tube contains water. The other test tube contains vinegar. You could easily tell which test tube contains vinegar because vinegar has a different odor than water. By carefully sniffing each test tube, you could identify the vinegar. Also, red vinegar has a color that could help you distinguish between the two liquids. Properties of matter such as odor and color are **physical properties.** Other examples of *physical properties* are taste, hardness, density, melting point, and boiling point. You can observe any physical property of matter by using only your senses. See Fig. 13–2.

Physical property A characteristic of matter that can be observed by using any of your senses.

Fig. 13–2 How many different physical properties can you identify in this photo?

Chemical property A description of how one kind of matter behaves in the presence of another kind of matter.

Enrichment: Physical properties can be observed without changing a substance. Chemical properties can only be observed when the substance is changed by a chemical reaction.

Suggestion: Comparing the behavior of acid-base indicators with water and vinegar may also be used to demonstrate the difference in chemical properties.

Chemical properties, on the other hand, can be observed only when one kind of matter is mixed with another. For example, when you add vinegar to baking soda, a gas is released. If you slowly add vinegar to the soda until no more gas is produced, you will find that you can no longer observe the odor and other physical properties of the vinegar. A *chemical property* describes how one substance reacts with other substances. The behavior of vinegar with baking soda is an example of a chemical property of the vinegar. Water does not share this chemical property with vinegar. If you mix water with baking soda, no gas will be produced. Thus you could also use their chemical properties to distinguish between water and vinegar.

Vinegar, like water, is made up of separate molecules. Vinegar molecules, however, are different from water molecules. A huge number of different substances exists in the world. Each has its own kind of molecules. Therefore, there are many different kinds of molecules. These different molecules give different substances their individual physical and chemical properties.

STATES OF MATTER

Matter is either a *solid*, a *liquid*, or a *gas*. Each of these states of matter is made up of molecules. To understand how the individual molecules behave in solids, liquids, and gases, a comparison is helpful. Think of all the people sitting in rows in a theater as individual molecules. During the performance, everyone is seated in an orderly arrangement. This arrangement is like molecules in a solid. Molecules in a solid stay in a fixed pattern just like people sitting in a theater. When the performance is over, people leave their seats and start to move out of the theater. The moving people then resemble the motion of molecules in a liquid. Finally, the crowd leaves the theater and everyone moves off in a different direction. This movement is similar to the way molecules of a gas spread out to fill space. Whether matter is a solid, a liquid, or a gas depends on the motion of its molecules. See Fig. 13–3. The top diagram shows the motion of molecules in a solid. The middle diagram shows how molecules in a liquid move. The bottom diagram shows widely spaced gas molecules.

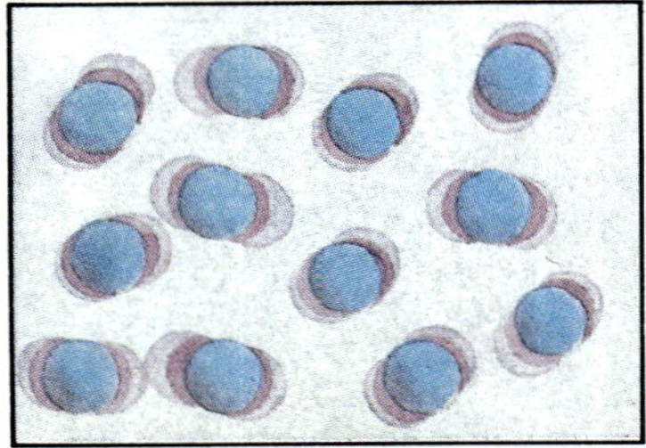

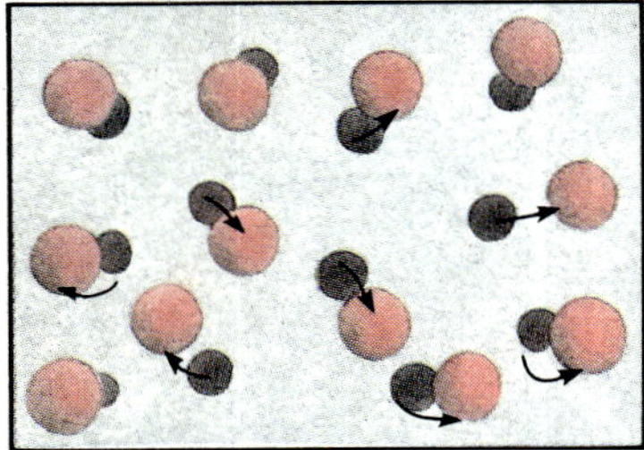

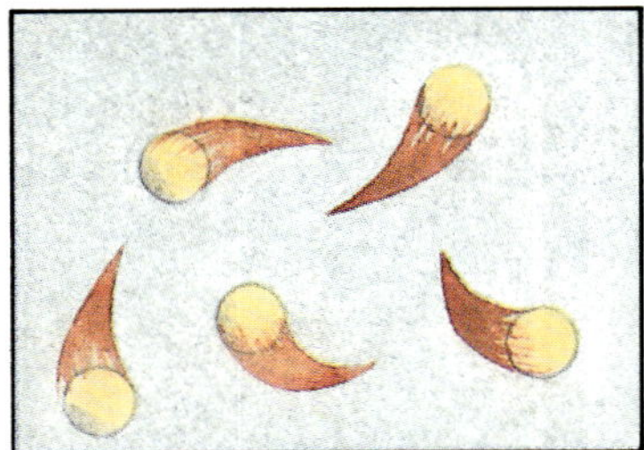

Fig. 13–3 The motion of molecules is different in a solid, a liquid, and a gas.

You know from experience that water is not always a liquid. You can freeze liquid water to make solid ice. You can also boil water and change it into a gas. See Fig. 13–4. Are the water molecules changed into different kinds of molecules when they are frozen or boiled? Try this experiment at home. Fill an empty ice cube tray with water. Put the tray in the freezer. After the water freezes, remove the tray and let the ice melt. Does the melted ice look the same as the water before it froze? Does it taste the same as the water before it froze? Do you think that the water molecules were changed by freezing and melting? This experiment shows that melted ice has the same physical properties as the water before it was frozen. Water molecules in liquid water, ice, and steam are all alike. The changes of water from a liquid to a solid to a gas are examples of a **physical change.** After a *physical change,* each of the molecules in a substance is the same as it was before the change.

Suggestion: Prepare a display of several pairs of substances such as aluminum and copper, sulfur and carbon, water and vinegar, sugar and salt, and paraffin and soap. Ask students to select physical and chemical properties that could be used to distinguish between the substances in each pair. Have each student describe the properties on a slip of paper. Mix all the slips together, then have each student pick one and use the description to identify the substance.

Physical change A change in matter in which the individual molecules are not changed.

Fig. 13–4 Water can exist as a liquid, a solid (ice), and a gas (steam or water vapor).

Skill: Students are asked to *compare and contrast* chemical and physical changes.

Boiling, melting, and freezing are examples of physical change. Any change in matter from one state to another is a physical change. Only the motion of the molecules changes.

Not all changes in matter are physical changes. Suppose an iron nail lies on the ground until it becomes rusty. Where did the rust come from? Does the rust have the same properties as iron? If you compare rust with iron, you will find that they have many different properties. For example, the color, hardness, and melting points of rust and iron are different. If rust and iron were made up of the same molecules, they would have the same properties. Therefore, rust must be made up of different molecules than iron. The rusting of iron is an example of a **chemical change.** When one kind of molecule changes into another kind of molecule, a *chemical change* causes a new substance with new properties to be formed. For example, when vinegar is mixed with baking soda, the molecules of both the vinegar and the soda are chemically changed. One of the new substances produced by these chemical changes is the gas that is given off.

Chemical change A change in matter in which one kind of molecule is changed into another kind.

SUMMARY

All matter is made up of small particles called molecules. The molecules that make up a substance determine its physical and chemical properties. A physical change in matter takes place when the molecules are arranged differently but are not changed in any other way. A chemical change causes the molecules to become different kinds of molecules.

QUESTIONS

Use complete sentences to write your answers.

1. What is a molecule of water? Can you see a water molecule? Explain.
2. What properties of water are different from the properties of vinegar? Are these physical or chemical properties? What does this tell you about water and vinegar molecules?
3. Use an example to compare how molecules move in solids, liquids, and gases.
4. How does a physical change differ from a chemical change? Give two examples of a physical change.

1. A molecule of water is the smallest particle of water that is still water. Water molecules are too small to be seen.
2. The smell (and perhaps color) of vinegar is different from water. These are physical properties. Vinegar bubbles when added to baking soda and water does not. This is a chemical property. These properties tell us that water and vinegar are made from different molecules.
3. Molecules in solids, liquids, and gases can be compared to students seated in a classroom, students in a classroom just before class starts, and students out of class moving freely. This comparison holds for the orderliness of the motion as well as the amount of motion.
4. In a physical change, the molecules are not changed. In a chemical change, the molecules change into different molecules. Examples of a physical change are ice melting or water freezing, a glass breaking, etc.

SKILL-BUILDING ACTIVITY

See teacher's commentary for teaching hints, safety, and answers to questions.

PHYSICAL AND CHEMICAL CHANGE

PURPOSE: You will observe and classify physical and chemical changes.

MATERIALS:

4 heat-resistant test tubes
sugar
test tube holder
Bunsen burner
matches
container of water
paraffin
microscope slide
baking soda
water
vinegar

PROCEDURE:

A. Place about 1 gram of sugar in a test tube. Hold the tube with the test-tube holder. Heat the sugar by holding the tube over a Bunsen burner flame. See Fig. 13–5. CAUTION: Wear goggles.

1. What happened to the sugar?
2. Does the substance formed look like sugar?

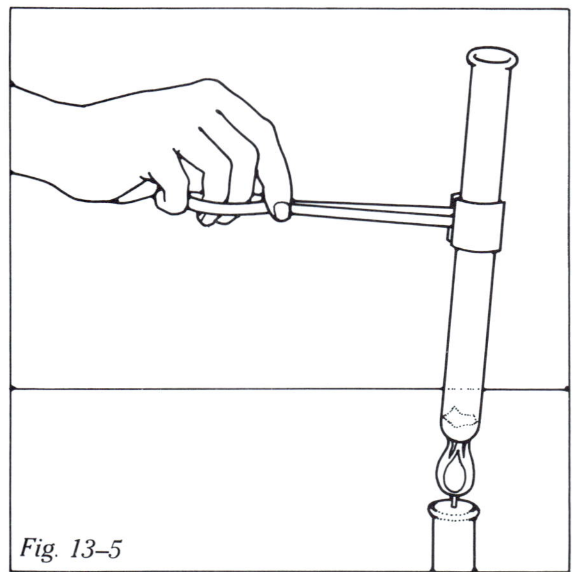

Fig. 13–5

B. Continue heating the test tube.

3. What happened to the substance in the test tube?
4. Does the substance formed look like sugar?
5. Does heating sugar cause a physical or a chemical change?

C. Place about 1 gram of paraffin (wax) in a test tube. Using the test tube holder, hold the tube over the flame of a Bunsen burner to melt the wax.

6. Does the melted wax look like the solid wax?

D. Pour the melted wax onto a microscope slide. Let the wax cool and harden.

7. Does the hardened wax feel like the original solid wax?
8. Are melting and hardening wax physical or chemical changes?

E. Place about 1 gram of baking soda in each of two test tubes. Add several drops of water to one tube and several drops of vinegar to the other. Record your observations in your notebook.

9. In which tube did a physical change take place? In which tube did a chemical change take place? What evidence supports your answer?
10. Can you use this test to distinguish between water and vinegar? Why?

CONCLUSION:

1. In you own words, use your observations to describe the difference between a physical change and a chemical change.

13-2. Gases

At the end of this section you will be able to:

- Use the *kinetic theory* to explain how gases behave.
- Explain why nothing can be colder than *absolute zero*.
- Predict how the volume of a gas will change when the pressure or temperature changes.

Do you know why you should put less air in a bicycle tire in hot weather? See Fig. 13–6. Sometimes, when the tire becomes hot, the air pressure can build up enough to cause the tire to burst. Why do gases such as air change so much when the temperature changes? You will find out in this section.

Word study: Kinetic from *kinetos* (Gr.), moving.

Kinetic theory of matter The scientific principle that says that all matter is made of particles whose motion determines whether the matter is solid, liquid, or gas.

THE KINETIC THEORY

The scientific belief that all matter is made of moving molecules is called the **kinetic theory of matter.** The *kinetic theory* is one of the most important theories of modern science. By using the kinetic theory, scientists have been able to explain and predict the properties of matter. Each of the three states of matter is called a *phase*. See Fig. 13–7. Matter in the solid phase is usually made up of molecules that are in orderly arrangements. The molecules in a solid usually vibrate back and forth but hold their positions close beside their neighbors. Thus, under ordinary conditions, a solid like a pencil does not change its shape or the volume it occupies. In the liquid phase, the molecules are able to move around each other but still remain close together. Thus, liquids may change their shape but still take up a certain volume. Liquid water, for example, can be poured from a tall, narrow glass to a short, wide glass but will occupy the same volume in both glasses. In the gas phase, molecules of matter move very fast and spread apart from each other. Gases have neither a definite shape nor a definite volume.

Fig. 13–6 Air expands when it is heated. You should always allow for this expansion when you put air in a bicycle tire.

PROPERTIES OF A GAS

The kinetic theory applies to all the phases of matter. However, it is particularly useful to explain and predict the behavior of gases. The kinetic theory explains the following observations about gases.

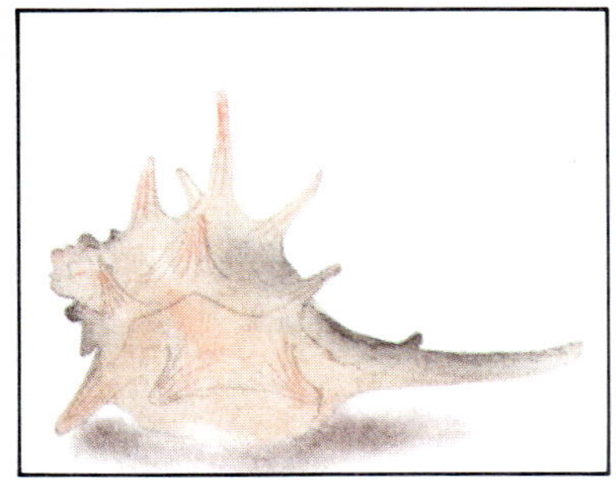

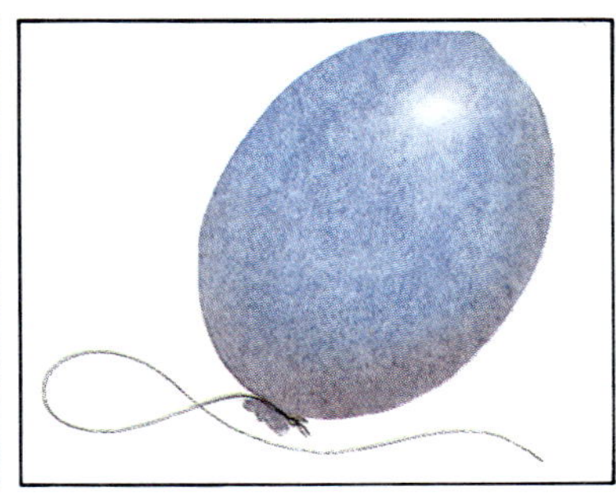

Fig. 13–7 The three phases of matter. A solid has a specific shape and volume. A liquid takes on the shape of its container but has a specific volume. A gas expands to fill the space available.

1. Molecules in a gas are moving very fast with large average distances between them. A gas is mostly empty space. Gas particles move like a swarm of angry bees trapped in a room. Each particle collides with others many times each second. The particles are not affected by these collisions. Gases have no natural shape but will expand to fill any space available.

Skill: *Compare and contrast* the motion of particles in a solid, a liquid, and a gas.

2. Moving gas molecules cause pressure. The rapidly moving molecules of a gas collide with each other. They also strike the walls of their container. This constant bumping by the molecules causes a push or force on the walls of the container. For example, the rubber walls of a balloon filled with air are pushed out by the constant collisions of the air molecules trapped in the balloon. The total area of the walls of the container can be divided into units such as square centimeters. Then each square centimeter receives a certain force from the colliding gas molecules. The amount of force on each unit of area is called the gas **pressure.** For example, the air inside a balloon might produce a *pressure* of 15 newtons on each square centimeter, or 15 N/cm^2.

Pressure The amount of force applied to a unit of area.

Reinforcement: Put a partially inflated balloon inside a bell jar connected to a vacuum pump. Start the pump and observe the behavior of the balloon. Relate this behavior to gas pressure.

3. Gases have no definite volume. Gas molecules can be crowded together. When a gas is squeezed into a smaller space, the pressure of the gas rises. This rise in pressure is a result of the rapidly moving gas particles hitting the walls of the container more often. In the same way, a gas will have lower pressure if it is allowed to expand. See Fig. 13–8.

Enrichment: The unit of pressure in the SI system is the pascal (Pa; 1 pascal = 1 N/m^2 = 0.000145 lb/in^2).

4. The temperature of a gas measures how fast its molecules move. If a gas is heated, the added heat energy causes the gas particles to move faster. A thermometer would show that the temperature of the gas increases. The greater speed of the molecules causes them to move farther apart. The volume of the gas tends to increase. See Fig. 13–9. Faster

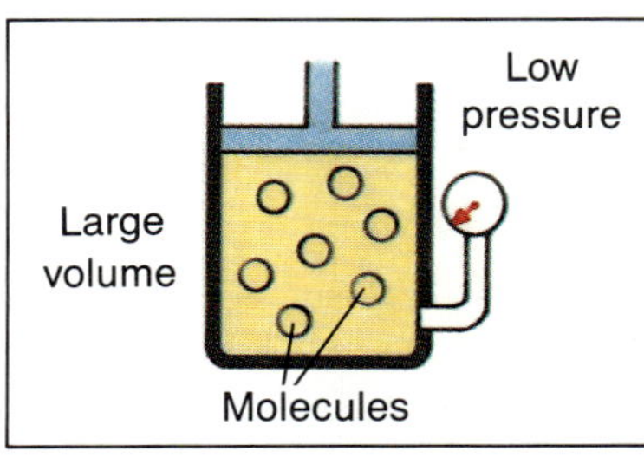

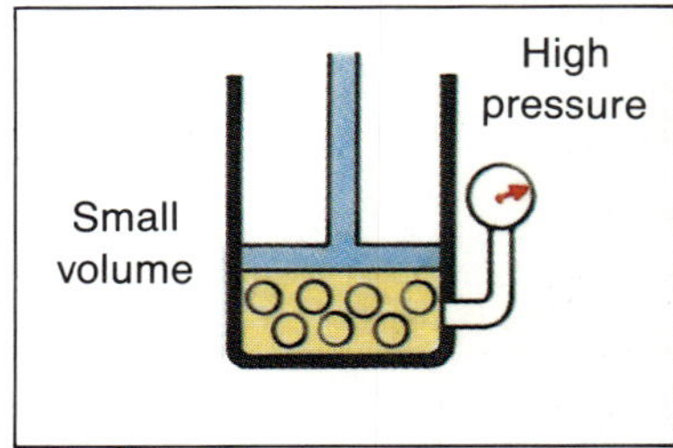

Fig. 13–8 As the volume of a gas changes, its pressure changes.

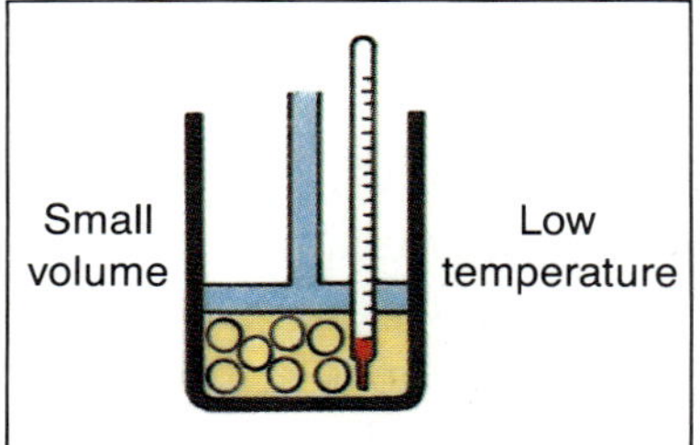

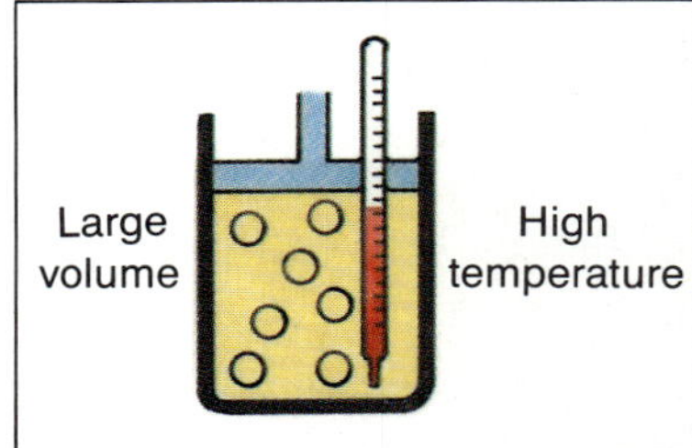

Fig. 13–9 As the temperature of a gas changes, its pressure changes.

moving particles hit the container holding the gas more often. The more frequent collisions cause higher pressure. If the volume is not changed when the termperature of a gas increases, its pressure also increases. For example, the air trapped inside a bicycle tire will increase its pressure on the tire if the temperature goes up. Thus, when the temperature is low, you could pump air into the tire until the pressure on the tire is 60 N/cm^2. Later, when the temperature goes up, the pressure on the tire could increase to 90 N/cm^2. This increased pressure could cause the tire to burst.

Enrichment: Atmospheric pressure = 101 kilopascals (kPa) = 14.7 lbs/in^2.

One kind of gas pressure that is always present is *atmospheric pressure.* The gases that make up the atmosphere have weight. The amount of air filling a classroom, for example, weighs several thousand newtons. The weight of the air in the atmosphere causes a pressure at the earth's surface of about 10 N/cm^2.

Enrichment:

1 N/m^2 = 0.000145 lb/in^2
1 N/m^2 = 1 pascal
1 pascal = 1 Pa
1 Pa = 0.000145 lb/in^2
1 kilopascal = 1 kPa
1 kPa = 0.145 lb/in^2
207 kPa = 30 lb/in^2
atmospheric pressure = 14.7 lb/in^2 = 101 kPa

ABSOLUTE ZERO

A gas such as air will expand when its temperature is raised. In the same way, cooling a gas will cause it to shrink as its particles move more slowly. Using this principle, Galileo, one of the greatest scientists of the sixteenth century, invented an *air thermometer.* The air thermometer is simply a quantity of air trapped by water in a tube. You can use an air thermometer to study the behavior of the trapped air when it is cooled or warmed.

Can you predict what will happen if a gas becomes very cold? As a gas is cooled, its particles move more and more slowly. At what temperature would the particles stop moving? Experiments have shown that this temperature is −273°C. The temperature at which all motion of molecules stops (−273°C) is called **absolute zero.** Since temperature actually measures the amount of molecular motion in a substance, there can be no lower temperature than *absolute zero* because molecules are not moving at this temperature. In other words, there is no kinetic energy at absolute zero. Therefore, absolute zero is the lowest possible temperature. A temperature scale based on absolute zero is often used in scientific observations. This scale is called the **Kelvin (K) temperature scale.** Zero on the *Kelvin scale* is equal to absolute zero.

Absolute zero The temperature (−273°C) at which particles of matter stop moving.

Kelvin temperature scale A scale of temperature on which zero is equal to absolute zero.

GAS LAWS

The following experiment tests the way a gas behaves when the pressure changes. The pieces of equipment used are (1) a plastic syringe called an *air piston,* and (2) some ordinary bricks. The air piston is clamped in an upright position with its outlet closed off. One brick is balanced on top of the piston. See Fig. 13–10. The weight of the brick presses down on the plunger of the piston. This creates pressure on the air trapped inside. When more bricks are stacked on top of the piston, the pressure on the trapped air increases. However, the total pressure also includes the weight of air that is pressing down on the bricks. See Fig. 13–11. The effect of this air pressure is equal to about 1.7 bricks.

Enrichment: There are three types of molecular motion: translational, vibrational, and rotational. Translational motion is the only one related to temperature or kinetic energy. At absolute zero, only the translational motion stops; the vibrational and rotational motion do not stop.

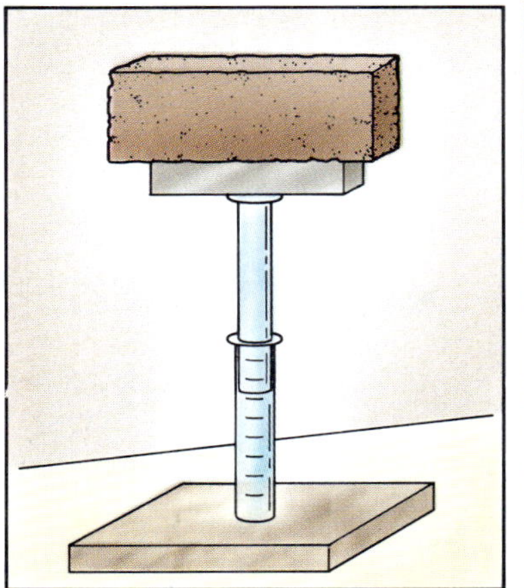

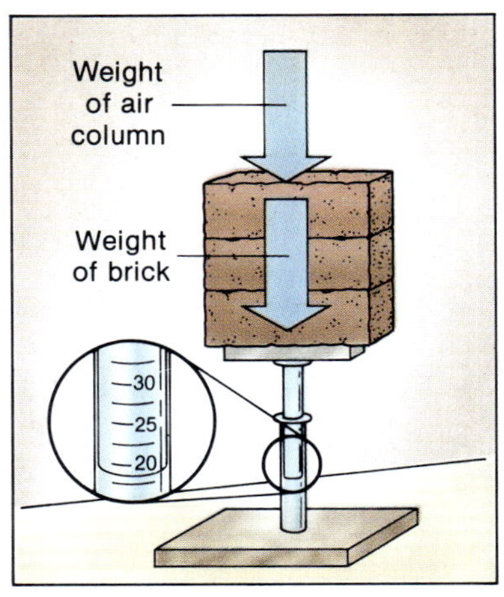

Fig. 13–10 An air piston measures gas pressure. The brick pushes down on the piston.

Fig. 13–11 The weight of the air on top of the bricks also pushes down on the piston.

Pressure Caused by Bricks	Pressure Caused by Air (Bricks)	Total Pressure (Bricks)	Average Volume (mL)
1	1.7	2.7	28.5
2	1.7	3.7	22.5
3	1.7	4.7	17.5
4	1.7	5.7	14.0
5	1.7	6.7	12.0
6	1.7	7.7	10.0
7	1.7	8.7	9.0
8	1.7	9.7	8.0

Table 13–1

During the experiment, bricks are added and the change in the volume of air trapped in the piston is observed. Five bricks are added one by one. After each brick is added, the volume occupied by the trapped air is measured. The experiment is repeated several times and the measured volumes are averaged. Table 13–1 shows the results. You can see that the volume of the air decreases as the pressure increases. The results of the experiment can be seen more clearly in a graph. The graph shows how the volume changes when the pressure changes. See Fig. 13–12. If the experiment is repeated with other gases such as oxygen, hydrogen, or carbon dioxide instead of air in the piston, the results are the same. The experiment shows how any gas responds to changes in pressure. A change in pressure causes a change in volume.

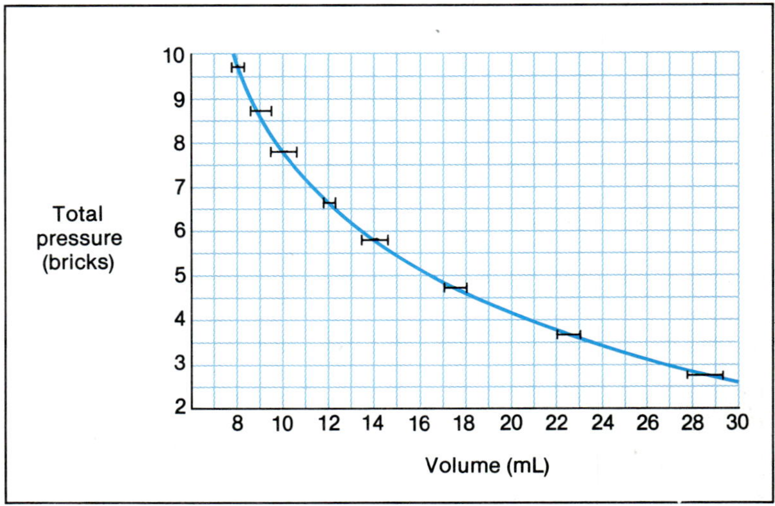

Fig. 13–12 The graph shows that as the pressure of the gas increases, the volume of the gas decreases.

The scientist who first measured how gas volume changes with pressure was Robert Boyle. Boyle lived at the same time as Newton. In 1661, Boyle showed that doubling the pressure on a gas reduced its volume by half. If you look at the graph in Fig. 13–12, you can see that doubling the total pressure always reduces the volume by one-half. This rule is now called *Boyle's law.* Boyle's law can be stated as follows: *The volume occupied by a certain amount of a gas (V_1) multiplied by its pressure (P_1) is equal to its new volume (V_2) times its new pressure* (P_2), or

Suggestion: Work out several problems to show the use of Boyle's law. For example $P = 100$ N/cm^2 and $V = 500$ cm^3. What will be the new volume if the pressure becomes 300 N/cm^2?

$$V_1 \times P_1 = V_2 \times P_2$$

For example, air trapped in an air piston has a volume of 26 mL (V_1) when under a total pressure equal to three bricks (P_1). If the total pressure is increased to 5 bricks (P_2), its new volume (V_2) is given by

$$V_1 \times P_1 = V_2 \times P_2$$

$$26 \text{ mL} \times 3 \text{ bricks} = V_2 \times 5 \text{ bricks}$$

$$\frac{26 \text{ mL} \times 3 \text{ bricks}}{5 \text{ bricks}} = V_2$$

$$\frac{78 \text{ mL-bricks}}{5 \text{ bricks}} = V_2$$

$$15.6 \text{ mL} = V_2$$

The graph in Fig. 13–12 shows slightly different results since it records average values from several different experiments. Boyle's law can only be used if the temperature does not change as the pressure changes. It also does not give accurate results for very high pressures. At high pressures, the molecules in a gas are crowded so close together that they no longer behave like the ideal gas described by Boyle's law.

Another law relates the volume of a gas to changes in temperature. In the late 1700's, a French scientist named Jacques Charles observed that the volume of air increased steadily as the temperature went up. *Charles' law* says that *the volume of a gas increases regularly as the temperature increases if the pressure remains the same.* For example, raising the temperature of a gas by 1°C will cause its volume

Enrichment: T is in kelvins.

Suggestion: Work out several problems to show the use of Charles' law.

to increase by 1/273. Raising the temperature by 2°C increases the original volume by 2/273. When the temperature has risen by 273°C, the volume will have doubled if the measurements are all made at the same pressure. Charles' law can also be written

$$\frac{V_1}{T_1} = \frac{V_2}{T_2}$$

Since he realized that heated air rises because it expands and becomes less dense, Charles used his observations to build the first hot-air balloon.

The behavior of gases can be described by general laws because gas molecules are, on the average, very far apart. Each molecule is independent of its neighbors. Only conditions that affect the way the molecules move, such as temperature and pressure, will change the volume occupied by gases. In liquids and solids, on the other hand, the molecules are close together. Thus the volume taken up by liquids and solids is a result of the size of the individual molecules and the way they affect each other. There are no general laws that describe the way different kinds of liquids and solids will respond to changes in temperature and pressure.

SUMMARY

The kinetic theory of matter describes how molecules move in solids, liquids, and gases. At the lowest possible temperature, there is no motion of particles in matter. The behavior of gases can be described by Boyle's law and Charles' law.

QUESTIONS

Use complete sentences to write your answers.

1. Describe a gas in terms of the kinetic theory of matter.
2. Explain why you would not be able to cool anything below absolute zero.
3. Normal room temperature is 20°C. What is this temperature on the Kelvin scale?
4. If 500 mL of air is under a pressure of 5 N/cm^2 and the pressure is changed to 7.5 N/cm^2, what will the new volume of air be if there is no change in temperature?
5. By how much would the volume of an air sample change if the temperature is raised from 20°C to 25°C?

1. The particles of a gas are in rapid motion with large distances between them. The particles are not affected by collisions. Pressure is the result of collisions between the particles and the sides of the container.
2. Absolute zero is the complete absence of heat at which all (translational) particle motion stops. Therefore it is impossible to cool anything below absolute zero.
3. 292 K.
4. $V_1 \times P_1 = V_2 \times P_2$
$500 \text{ mL} \times 5 \text{ N/cm}^2 = V_2 \times 7.5 \text{ N/cm}^2$
$\frac{500 \text{ mL} \times 5 \text{ N/cm}^2}{7.5 \text{ N/cm}^2} = V_2$
$333 \text{ mL} = V_2$
5. 5/273.

INVESTIGATION

See teacher's commentary for teaching hints, safety, and answers to questions.

MAKING AN AIR THERMOMETER

PURPOSE: You will determine the principles upon which an air thermometer works.

MATERIALS:

small beaker	glass tube
water	ice cube

PROCEDURE:

A. Fill a small beaker about half full with water.

B. Place one end of the glass tube in the water, resting it on the bottom of the beaker.

1. What do you observe?

C. Place your finger over the top end of the tube. See Fig. 13–13. Closing the top traps some water at the bottom of the tube and some air at the top. The top of the tube should be air tight.

D. Keeping your finger over the top of the tube, raise the tube straight up out of the water. Keep it over the beaker.

2. Does the water drip out of the bottom of the tube?
3. Why do you suppose the water tends to drip slowly out of the tube?

E. Watch a drop of water form at the bottom of the tube. Just before the drop falls, touch an ice cube to the side of the tube near the top where you are holding it. See Fig. 13–14.

4. What happens?

F. Remove the ice cube. Heat the air in the tube by cupping your other hand around the tube.

5. Does a drop of water start to form at the bottom of the tube again?
6. What result does warming have on the trapped air?

CONCLUSION:

1. On the basis of your observations, explain what happens to the trapped air when it is first cooled and then warmed.

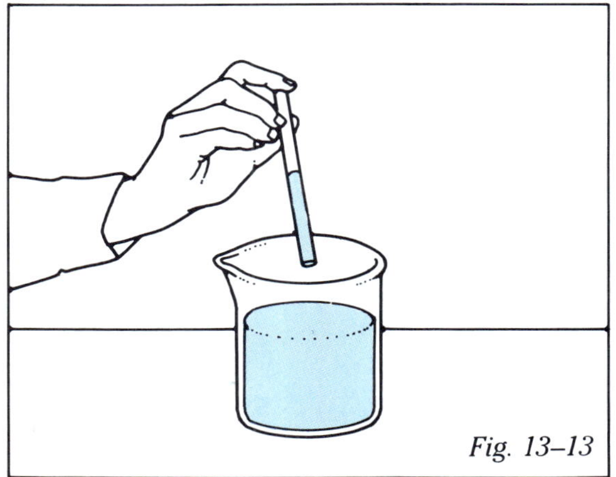

Fig. 13–13

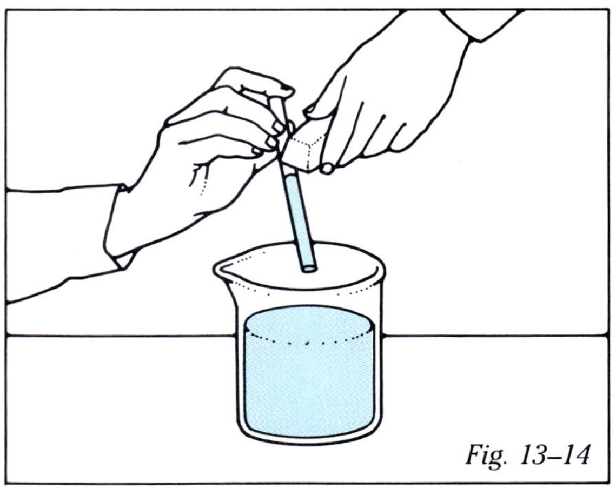

Fig. 13–14

13-3. Solids and Liquids

At the end of this section you will be able to:

- Describe how the particles in most solid materials are arranged.
- Explain what happens when a solid melts.
- Explain what happens when a liquid boils.

Fig. 13–15 shows a diamond in the volcanic rock in which diamonds are often found. Also shown is a diamond that has been cut and polished into a gem. Diamond is the hardest of all solids. If no other solid is harder than diamond, how it is possible to cut and polish this gem?

Fig. 13–15 A rough diamond (top) can be cut and polished into a faceted gem (bottom).

SOLIDS

By watching a diamond cutter at work, you could learn something about the structure of solids. You might be surprised to learn that the diamond "cutter" actually *breaks* a large diamond into smaller pieces. Diamonds are too hard to cut. A large diamond to be "cut" is carefully examined. The diamond is then marked with lines. See Fig. 13–16. The diamond cutter gently taps on a line. If everything has been done properly, the diamond splits evenly. A mistake may cause a valuable large diamond to shatter into many pieces too small and too irregular to be used for jewelry. How does a diamond cutter know exactly where to tap the diamond? The trained eye of a diamond cutter can see in a diamond a characteristic that is found in most solids: They have natural lines along which they will split. This property of a solid is one result of the way its molecules are arranged.

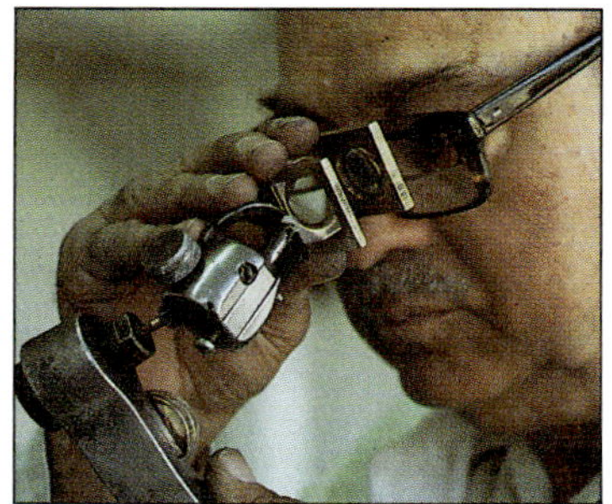

Fig. 13–16 A diamond cutter can break a diamond along fracture lines because diamond has a crystal structure.

Suggestion: Bring several large crystals to class. Students may enjoy growing crystals. Instructions for growing crystals can be found in many books about crystals.

A piece of solid matter cannot change its shape by itself. A diamond, for example, holds its shape unless it is split by a blow. The molecules of a solid are not free to move about. They stay in position. The arrangement of the molecules forming a solid is usually very orderly. For example, when molecules of water freeze to form solid ice, they form a **crystal** of ice. See Fig. 13–17. A *crystal* is a piece of solid matter with a regular shape. A large piece of ice is made up of many small

Crystal A solid whose orderly arrangement of particles gives it a regular shape.

Word study: Crystal from *krystallos* (Gr.), ice.

Fig. 13–17 A snowflake is an example of an ice crystal.

Reinforcement: Crystals can be grown on charcoal briquettes by placing the charcoal in a pan containing a solution made with 50 g of salt, 60 mL of water, 60 mL of laundry bluing, and 15 mL of household ammonia. The solution should not cover the briquettes. Observe the crystals for a period of several days.

ice crystals fitted together like the pieces of a jigsaw puzzle. Almost all solids are made of crystals.

When a diamond is split, it is separated along the surfaces that join its crystals. In many solids the individual crystals are large enough to be seen. However, the crystals of most solids are usually too small to be seen with the eye alone. The shape of an individual crystal is determined by the way its particles are arranged. See Fig. 13–18. For example, in common table salt each crystal is in the form of a cube. See Fig. 13–19. If you could see the molecules in a crystal, each molecule would be found in a regular, orderly position.

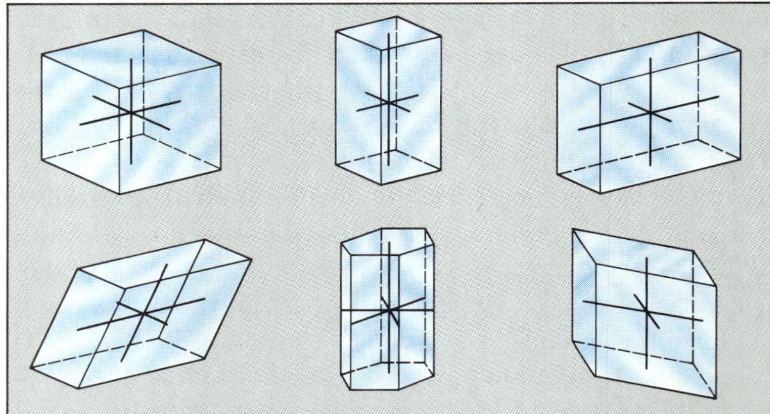

Fig. 13–18 There are six basic crystal shapes.

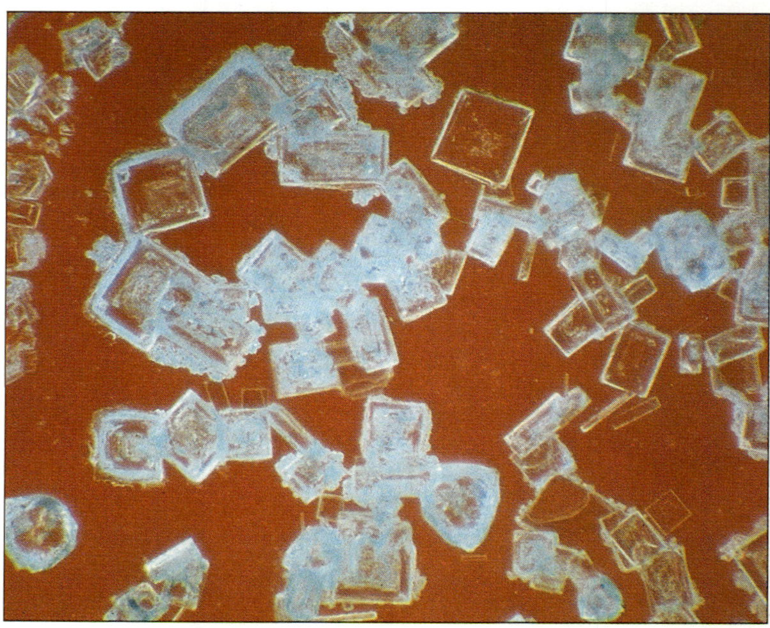

Fig. 13–19 Salt crystals have a cubic shape.

In some solids, the molecules do not have an orderly arrangement. These solids are like liquids in that their molecules are not arranged in crystal patterns. For this reason, they are sometimes called *supercooled liquids.* Glass and some plastics are examples of this kind of noncrystalline solid.

MELTING POINTS OF SOME COMMON SUBSTANCES	
Substance	Melting Point (°C)
iron	1,535
salt	801
lead	328
sugar	186
water	0
mercury	−39

Table 13–2

CHANGE TO A LIQUID

The molecules in a solid are always vibrating. If heat is added to a solid, the molecules vibrate faster and faster as the temperature goes up. At some definite temperature, the motion of the molecules becomes so great that the molecules can no longer hold their orderly arrangement. When this happens, the solid melts and becomes a liquid. See Fig. 13–20. The temperature at which a solid changes into a liquid is called its **melting point.** Each crystalline solid has a particular *melting point.* The melting points of some common substances are given in Table 13–2. Solids such as glass or plastic that are not made of crystals do not have an exact melting point. They soften gradually. A few materials, such as dry ice and moth balls, do not ordinarily melt. They change directly into a gas. The process in which a solid changes into a gas without first becoming a liquid is called *sublimation* (sub-luh-**may**-shun). The Latin word *sublimis* means "to elevate."

Melting point The temperature at which a solid becomes a liquid.

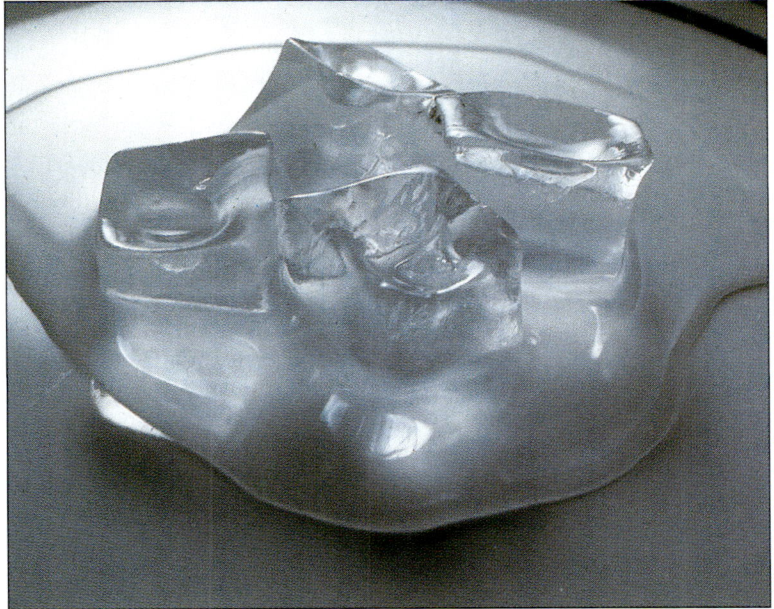

Fig. 13–20 When heat is added to a crystalline solid such as ice, the ice can no longer hold its shape. It melts and becomes a liquid.

Word study: Fusion from *fusio* (L.), a pouring out.

When a solid is heated to its melting point, some extra heat energy is needed to break the bonds that hold its molecules close together. This extra heat energy does not make the molecules vibrate faster and so does not increase the temperature. The heat needed to cause the orderly arrangement of particles in one gram of a solid to change into a liquid is called its **heat of fusion.** For example, 80 calories of heat is needed to change one gram of solid ice at 0°C into one gram of liquid water at 0°C. Thus the *heat of fusion* of water is 80 cal/g (334 J/g). Ice can keep things cool because it absorbs 80 calories of heat when each gram of ice melts. Ice has a higher heat of fusion than most other substances.

Heat of fusion The amount of heat required to change one gram of a solid to a liquid at the same temperature.

CHANGE TO A GAS

As you have seen, the molecules of a liquid move more rapidly than the molecules of a solid. In most liquids at ordinary temperatures, some molecules have enough energy to escape and become a gas. For example, if you leave a pan of water uncovered, the water molecules are constantly leaving the water in the pan and entering the air as water vapor. See Fig. 13–21. If more heat is added to a liquid, the speed of evaporation increases. As you continue to add heat, all the particles of the liquid finally gain enough energy to become a gas. The temperature at which a liquid changes to a gas is called the **boiling point** of the liquid. The exact *boiling point* depends upon two factors: (1) the amount of heat energy needed to make the particles of the liquid separate to become a gas; (2) the pressure of the air. For example, water boils at 100°C at sea level where the air pressure is normal. On a mountaintop, where the air pressure is lower, water boils at a temperature below 100°C. On the other hand, water boils at a temperature above 100°C if the pressure is raised. A pressure cooker uses this principle. At normal pressure, the temperature of boiling water is never above 100°C. Adding more heat to the boiling water cannot make it hotter. The water will only change into water vapor more rapidly. In a pressure cooker, the steam is held in the cooker and the pressure rises. The water must reach a higher temperature in order to boil. This higher temperature cooks the food more quickly. Pressure cookers usually have safety valves to prevent the pressure from reaching a dangerous level.

Boiling point The temperature (at ordinary air pressure) at which the molecules of a liquid have enough energy to become a gas.

Fig. 13–21 When the water in a teapot reaches its boiling point, the liquid water changes to steam.

Extra heat energy is needed to cause the molecules in a solid to form a liquid. In the same way, heat is needed to separate the molecules in a liquid to form a gas. The amount of heat needed to change one gram of a liquid into a gas at the same temperature is called **heat of vaporization.** The *heat of vaporization* of water is 540 cal/g (2,260 J/g). Perspiration evaporating from your skin absorbs its heat of vaporization from your body. This heat loss makes you feel cool.

Heat of vaporization The amount of heat that is required to change one gram of a liquid to a gas at the same temperature.

When a solid changes to a liquid, the temperature does not change. The added heat energy overcomes the forces holding the molecules together. The kinetic energy, and thus the temperature, does not change. Adding more heat energy only makes the solid melt faster. Once the melting point is reached, the temperature stays constant until all the solid becomes a liquid. Similarly, once the boiling point is reached, the temperature stays the same until all the liquid becomes a gas. The temperature does not change during a change of state.

Enrichment: The heat of vaporization of ethyl alcohol is 25 cal/g. Ask students to compare this value with the heat of vaporization of water and explain why alcohol evaporates much more rapidly than water at the same temperature.

SUMMARY

The molecules in most solid materials, such as diamonds, are held together in an orderly pattern. This crystal pattern causes most solids to have a particular melting point. Increasing the temperature of a solid will cause it to melt. Increasing the temperature of a liquid will cause it to boil and become a gas. Some solids change directly into a gas without first becoming a liquid.

QUESTIONS

Use complete sentences to write your answers.

1. What are some of the properties you would look for if you had to decide whether a solid was a crystal or not?
2. Describe what happens to the particles of a solid as it is heated until it melts.
3. An ice cube has a mass of about 40 g. How many joules are needed to melt two ice cubes? How many calories?
4. What two factors determine the exact boiling point of a liquid?
5. How many joules are needed to change 5 g of water into steam? How many calories?

1. You would look for flat surfaces, regular shape, and the ability to break into regularly shaped pieces.
2. As heat is added, the particles vibrate more. At the melting point, the motion of the particles is so great that they cannot hold an orderly arrangement. The solid then becomes a liquid.
3. 80 cal/g × 40 g × 2 = 6,400 calories. 4.18 J/cal × 6,400 cal = 26,752 joules.
4. The two factors are (1) the amount of heat energy needed to cause the particles to separate into a gas, and (2) the air pressure.
5. 540 cal/g × 5 g = 2,700 calories. 4.18 J/cal × 2,700 = 11,286 joules.

¡COMPUTE!

SCIENCE INPUT

Some weather factors are valuable predictors of weather and some are not. Two commonly considered weather variables are temperature, measured with a thermometer, and air pressure, measured with a barometer. Before the use of weather satellites which give forecasters more up-to-the-minute information, the thermometer and barometer, along with past experience, were the chief tools of weather prediction. In this exercise you will use those "old-fashioned" tools to gather data. The modern computer will be used to analyze the data.

COMPUTER INPUT

The speed of a computer's calculations can be valuable for many purposes. When data are collected, there is a great deal of information provided. If it is not organized according to some system none of it will make sense. Imagine, for example, someone asking you to collect data about the students in your class. First, you would have to know what kind of questions you intended to answer with the data.Your point of view and your particular interests would determine how you might classify or sort your data. You could sort by sex and find out if there were more males than females. You could sort by age and find out how close in age members of the class were. You could find out how many are taller than 5′4″ and play a sport. Or you might want to sort by a variety of factors and find out, for instance, how many of those taller than 5′4″ who play a sport are girls. Each sort is a point of view that can show different patterns about the same data.

A computer can manipulate data easily. It can let the facts tell a story from many points of view. In this exercise, you will sort weather data to see if any patterns emerge that can help predict weather in the future.

WHAT TO DO

First, you must collect the data for the computer to sort. At approximately the same time each day, record the temperature (degrees Celsius), the air pressure (millibars), and the present state of the weather (fair, rain, possible rain) for 14 days. Make a chart of this data. An example is given.

Enter Program Weather Sort into your computer. Enter your data in statements 401 to 415. Use the form given in the example shown in statement 401. When you run the program it will ask you how you would like to sort the data, by temperature or air pressure. Try both sorts. After you've analyzed the data decide which instrument was most useful for predicting the weather: the thermometer or the barometer.

GLOSSARY

BIT short for binary digit. A bit is a piece of computer-coded information. The coding process is done by the computer hardware, not the program. The hardware is designed to translate the data input into binary numbers which can be stored electronically in the computer's memory. On most machines 8 bits = 1 byte. (See Chapter 12 for a discussion of digital systems and binary numbers.) The glossary in Chapter 18 defines "byte."

REARRANGING DATA: PROGRAM WEATHER SORT

PROGRAM

```
100  REM WEATHER SORT
110  DIM T$(15), AP$(15), SW$(15)
120  FOR X = 1 TO 15
130  READ T$(X),AP$(X), SW$(X)
135  IF T$(X) = “0” THEN H = X - 1:
     GOTO 150
140  NEXT
150  PRINT: PRINT “1) SORT
     TEMPERATURE & STATE OF
     WEATHER”
160  PRINT “2) SORT AIR PRESSURE &
     STATE OF WEATHER”
170  PRINT: INPUT “ WHICH CHOICE (1
     OR 2)? ”;C$
180  C = VAL(C$)
190  IF C < 1 OR C > 2 THEN GOTO 150
200  K = 0
210  FOR X = 1 TO H - 1
220  IF C = 2 THEN GOTO 240
230  IF VAL(T$(X)) < = VAL(T$(X+1))
     THEN GOTO 290
235  GOTO 250
240  IF VAL(AP$(X)) < = VAL(AP$(X+1))
     THEN GOTO 290
250  T$ = T$(X):T$(X) = T$(X+1):
     T$(X+1) = T$
260  AP$ = AP$(X): AP$(X) = AP$(X+1):
     AP$(X+1) = AP$
270  SW$ = SW$ (X): SW$(X) = SW$(X
     + 1): SW$(X + 1) = SW$
280  K + K + 1
290  NEXT
300  IF K > 0 THEN GOTO 200
310  PRINT “DAY”; TAB(8) “TEMP.”;
     TAB(15) “PRES.”; TAB(25)“STATE OF
     WEATHER”
320  FOR X = 1 TO H
330  PRINT X;
332  IF C = 1 THEN PRINT TAB(8)T$(X);
335  IF C = 2 THEN PRINT
     TAB(15)AP$(X);
337  PRINT TAB(25)SW$(X)
370  NEXT
380  GOTO 150
400  REM PLACE DATA STATEMENTS
     HERE
401  DATA 45, 1010, RAIN
402  DATA 5, 1023, FAIR
500  END
```

Data Chart

Day	Temperature (degrees C)	Air Pressure (millibars)	State of Weather
1	45°	1010	rain
2	55°	1023	fair
3			

PROGRAM NOTES

This program is written for use with 15 items in each data group. Which statements give you that information? How would you change the program to use more or fewer items?

BITS OF INFORMATION

Weather satellites have been sending information to earth via computer since 1968. Right now there are 4 weather satellites in operation. These satellites are responsible for more accurate weather prediction, for early frost warnings for fruit growers, and for saving over 100 lives in search and rescue missions at sea.

INVESTIGATION

See teacher's commentary for teaching hints, safety, and answers to questions.

OBSERVING CRYSTALS

PURPOSE: You will observe the crystalline structure of a substance.

MATERIALS:

table salt	rock salt
plastic sandwich bag	pencil
small magnifying glass	

PROCEDURE:

A. Shake a few crystals of table salt into a plastic sandwich bag.

B. Look at the salt crystals with a small magnifying glass.

1. Are most of the crystals cube-shaped?
2. Describe any crystals you see that are not cube-shaped.
3. Do all the crystals have flat surfaces?

C. A cube is formed when six square surfaces meet, forming 90° angles. See Fig. 13–22. If you place two cubes together, you have a rectangular solid. The surfaces of the rectangular solid still meet to form 90° angles.

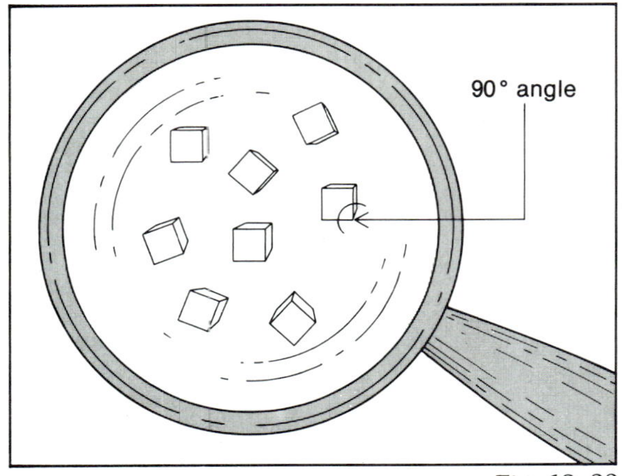

Fig. 13–22

D. Look at the table salt again.

4. Did you find any rectangular crystals?

E. Another feature of crystals is their ability to break apart, forming pieces with flat surfaces. The broken pieces form the same angles as the original crystal. This can be seen in rock salt. Rock salt is made of the same substance as table salt.

F. Pour the table salt from the sandwich bag back into the container provided.

G. Place a few crystals of rock salt in the plastic bag and look at it with the magnifying glass.

5. Do you see any cube-shaped crystals?
6. Do the crystals have flat surfaces?
7. Do the surfaces meet at 90° angles?

H. Now move several rock salt crystals that are *not* cubes to one side of the plastic bag away from the others.

I. Roll your pencil over these crystals to break them up.

J. Look at these pieces of crystals.

8. Do you see any pieces that are shaped like a cube?
9. Do the pieces have flat surfaces?
10. Do the surfaces meet at 90° angles?
11. Look at the crystals that are not shaped like cubes. Compare them with Fig. 13–18. Are any of the crystals shaped like the ones in this diagram?

CONCLUSION:

1. In one or two complete sentences, describe your observations of table salt and rock salt crystals.

CAREERS IN SCIENCE

ELEMENTARY PARTICLE PHYSICIST

Elementary particle physicists concentrate their studies on the particles inside the nuclei of atoms, such as electrons, protons, and neutrons. They examine and study methods of detecting the properties of these particles. They also look at the particles' collisions at high and low speeds as well as their decay and scattering. For their research, physicists employ such tools as particle accelerators, electron microscopes, lasers, electronic computers, and spectrometers. About 40 percent of physicists work in private industry in communications, aerospace, transportation, electronics, and medicine and health. Most of the others are engaged in teaching and research. For a career in this field high school students should take college preparatory programs emphasizing physics and chemistry. A Ph.D. is almost always necessary for top positions in the field.

For further information, contact: American Institute of Physics, 335 East 45th Street, New York, NY 10017.

METEOROLOGIST

When we think of a meteorologist we may picture a television announcer making weather predictions. But weather forecasting is only one branch of this broad science. Meteorologists apply the laws of physics, chemistry, biology, and mathematics to the study of the atmosphere in the hopes of understanding, predicting, and possibly controlling the weather. New tools, such as satellites and electronic computers, are making this atmospheric science more effective and new demands are being placed on it.

Most beginning jobs require a bachelor's degree with a background in physics and mathematics. Advancement usually depends on further training. A good way to get started in this field is through the armed services. They offer special meteorological training programs, often resulting in a degree during a tour of duty, which can provide a base for later job opportunities.

For further information, contact: American Meteorological Society, 45 Beacon Street, Boston, MA 02108.

CHAPTER REVIEW

See teacher's commentary for answers.

VOCABULARY

On a separate piece of paper, match each term with the number of the statement that best explains it. Use each term only once.

absolute zero	crystal	Kelvin temperature scale	molecule
boiling point	heat of fusion		physical change
chemical change	heat of vaporization	kinetic theory of matter	physical property
chemical property	melting point		pressure

1. Smallest particle of a substance that is still that substance.
2. A change in matter in which the individual molecules are not changed.
3. Some examples are color, taste, hardness, and density.
4. One kind of molecule is changed into another kind.
5. Observed when one kind of matter reacts with another.
6. The motion of particles determines whether the matter is solid, liquid, or gas.
7. All particles of matter stop moving.
8. Zero on this scale is equal to absolute zero.
9. The orderly arrangement of particles gives it a regular shape.
10. A solid becomes a liquid.
11. The amount of heat needed to change one gram of a solid into a liquid at the same temperature.
12. The particles of a liquid have enough energy to become a gas at ordinary air pressure.
13. The amount of heat needed to change one gram of a liquid into a gas at the same temperature.
14. The amount of force applied to a unit of area.

QUESTIONS

Give brief but complete answers to each of the following questions. Unless otherwise indicated, use complete sentences to write your answers.

1. Describe two physical changes in matter. Why are they called physical changes?
2. What are the three phases of matter? How are the molecules of a substance different in the three phases?
3. Use the kinetic theory of matter to explain three ways in which gases behave.
4. At what temperature is all kinetic energy absent? Give your answer in two temperature scales.
5. What is a crystal? Give four examples of crystalline solids.
6. Explain the changes in water molecules as water freezes and boils.

7. Is the melting of chocolate a chemical or a physical change? Is the freezing of water a chemical or a physical change? Give some evidence to support your answers.
8. Under constant pressure, what will be the new volume of 300 mL of air if its temperature is changed from 0°C to 91°C?
9. Calculate the number of joules needed to melt five ice cubes each with a mass of 40 grams. How many calories is this?
10. Calculate the number of joules needed to change 150 grams of water from a liquid to a gas. How many calories is this?
11. Give two examples of solids that are not crystalline.
12. What is sublimation? Give an example.
13. Describe what happens to water molecules as water becomes a gas.
14. Use an example to describe how the solid, liquid, and gas phases of matter are different from one another.

APPLYING SCIENCE

1. Allow the air to escape from a spare tire. Cup your hand over the valve as the air comes out. What do you feel happening? How does releasing a gas under pressure help to produce liquified gases? Draw a diagram of the apparatus that is used to liquify gases and explain it to the class. What are liquid gases used for? Why?
2. Design an experiment to determine the densities of some common solids. Use samples of gold, silver, iron, aluminum, wood, and glass. How does the density compare to the heft (how heavy the solid feels for its size) of each solid? Compare your results with values found in a reference book such as *The Handbook of Chemistry and Physics.* What other physical properties of matter are listed in the handbook?
3. Find the heat of fusion of water. Design an experiment to measure this quantity. You will need a balance, a Styrofoam cup, a thermometer, and water. Compare your results with accepted values.

BIBLIOGRAPHY

Holden, Alan, and Phyllis S. Morrison. *Crystals and Crystal Growing.* Cambridge, MA: MIT Press, 1982.

Scheeter, B. "Bubbles that Bend the Mind." *Science 84,* March 1984.

Watson, Philip. *Liquid Magic.* New York: Lothrop, 1983.

CHAPTER

14

A building is made of many kinds of material. The way materials are used depends on their properties. These properties are determined by the way atoms and molecules combine.

THE PROPERTIES OF MATTER

CHAPTER GOALS

1. Compare and contrast mixtures and compounds.
2. Explain how a solution is different from other kinds of mixtures and name three kinds of solutions.
3. Predict the results when a compound is separated into simpler parts.
4. Define a chemical element.

14-1. Mixtures, Compounds, and Solutions

At the end of this section you will be able to:

- ☐ Define and give some examples of a *mixture.*
- ☐ Describe how *solutions* are produced.
- ☐ Explain the difference between a *solute* and a *solvent.*
- ☐ Compare *mixtures* with *compounds* and give some examples of each.

The next time you pour out your morning cereal, look at the package. Somewhere on the box you will find a label that tells what went into making the cereal. You will find that your cereal, like most foods, is made of different substances.

MIXTURES

If you read the labels on packages of food, you will find that they contain different substances such as sugar and salt. Sugar and salt are made up of different molecules. Therefore, the food also contains more than one kind of molecule. Any kind of matter that contains more than one kind of molecule is called a **mixture.** Most foods are *mixtures.* See Fig. 14–1. There are many different kinds of mixture but they all have three things in common. First, a mixture is always made up of at least two substances. Second, the molecules of each substance are not changed when they are mixed together. This means that you can still identify each substance in the mixture. Third, the substances can be put together in any proportion.

Mixture Any matter that contains more than one kind of molecule and that can be separated by a physical change.

Fig. 14–1 Many different foods are mixtures. All mixtures contain more than one kind of molecule.

Reinforcement: Prepare a mixture of sand, salt, and iron filings. Ask students to suggest methods that might be used to separate each substance from the others. Use a magnet to separate the iron filings; mix the remaining sand and salt with water and filter; evaporate the filtrate to recover the salt.

The materials in a mixture can be separated by a physical change. A physical change does not change the materials as they are separated. For example, in a mixture of salt and pepper, the grains of salt and pepper can be seen and separated. You can separate the dark pepper grains from the light salt grains simply by picking them out one by one. Pepper and salt each have their own properties. These properties do not change when pepper and salt are mixed and then separated.

Word study: Solution, solute, and solvent from *solutus* (L.), to loosen.

SOLUTIONS

Suppose that you dissolve a spoonful of sugar in a glass of water. Would you be able to separate the sugar and water easily? When you dissolve sugar in water, the solid sugar crystals disappear in the water. You cannot see the sugar. However, you know that the sugar is mixed with the water because the mixture tastes sweet. The sugar molecules have left the solid sugar crystals and mixed with the water molecules. See Fig. 14–2. A mixture formed when one kind of molecule, such as sugar, fills the spaces between another kind of molecule, such as water, is called a **solution** (suh-**loo**-shun). *Solutions* are mixtures of separate molecules. Something that dissolves to make a solution is called a **solute.** In a solution of sugar and water, the sugar is the *solute.* The water is called the **solvent.** A *solvent* is a substance in a solution that does the dissolving.

Solution A mixture formed when one kind of molecule fills the spaces between another kind of molecule.

Solute The part of a solution that is dissolved.

Solvent The part of a solution that does the dissolving.

Using a liquid solvent such as water makes a *liquid solution.* Usually, a solid solute is dissolved in the liquid solvent. For example, read the label on a bottle of soda. You will see that it is partly a liquid solution of sugar in water. However, you

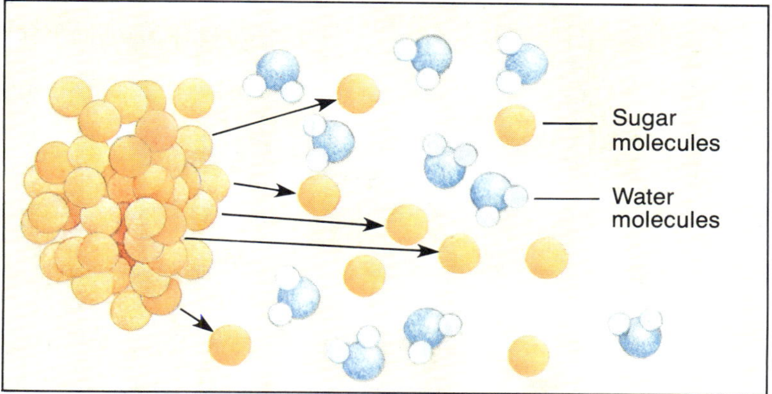

Fig. 14–2 When sugar dissolves in water, the sugar molecules are mixed with the water molecules. Sugar is the solute and water is the solvent.

also know that soda gives off bubbles of carbon dioxide gas. Therefore, gases can also dissolve in liquids to make a solution. See Fig. 14–3. It is also possible to make a liquid solution by dissolving one liquid in another. Alcohol, for example, can dissolve in water. In a liquid solution, the solvent is usually water. Water can dissolve more solutes than any other liquid. For this reason, it is sometimes called the *universal solvent.* However, you also know that some things will not dissolve in water. For example, cooking oil and water will not make a solution. When a substance dissolves in water, the dissolved molecules are mixed very closely with the water molecules. The two kinds of molecules attract each other. This is why they can be mixed together so closely. Oil will not mix with water because the molecules of oil do not attract the water molecules strongly enough.

Enrichment: A solution of water and alcohol occupies a smaller volume than the two liquids occupy separately. Carefully measure 50 mL of ethanol and 50 mL of water into separate beakers. Mix in a 100 mL graduated cylinder. The volume of the resulting solution is about 98 mL. Ask students to explain. (The mixed molecules fit between each other and thus take up a smaller volume.)

RATE OF DISSOLVING

If you want to dissolve a solid in a liquid, there are three ways you could speed up the process. First, you can raise the temperature. The heat will cause the molecules of the solute and solvent to move faster. As a result, the two kinds of molecules mix with each other at a faster rate. Stirring will also increase the speed of dissolving. The stirring motion helps to mix a new supply of solvent molecules with the solute molecules. A third way to speed up the dissolving of a solid is to crush the solid into small pieces. This exposes more of the surface of the solid solute to the liquid solvent. Since the molecules of solute can escape into the solvent only from the surface of the solid, this speeds up the rate of dissolving.

Fig. 14–3 A gas can be dissolved in a liquid. Bubbles of carbon dioxide gas can be seen escaping from the soda in this glass.

Enrichment: Cold tap water that is allowed to warm up to room temperature in a glass will usually produce small bubbles on the walls of the glass as the dissolved air escapes.

GASEOUS AND SOLID SOLUTIONS

Because their molecules are far apart, one gas will easily mix with another to make a *gaseous solution.* Air is an example of a gaseous solution. There is more nitrogen gas than any other gas in air. Thus nitrogen is said to be the solvent. The material that is most abundant in a solution is usually called the solvent. The second most abundant gas in air is oxygen. Air also contains small amounts of many other gases.

Many solids are really *solid solutions.* For example, steel is a solid solution in which carbon is dissolved in iron. The carbon dissolves in the iron when the iron is melted. When the iron cools and changes back to a solid, the carbon remains dissolved in the solid steel. Liquids and gases can also be dissolved in solids in the same way.

MAKING SOLUTIONS

Dilute Describes a solution made by dissolving a small amount of solute in a large amount of solvent.

Concentrated Describes a solution that is made by dissolving a large amount of solute in a solvent.

In order to describe a solution, you must know the solvent and solute used. For example, a salt solution describes a mixture made by dissolving salt in water. You must also know the relative amounts of the materials in the solution. For example, if a small amount of solute is dissolved in a large amount of solvent, the solution is said to be **dilute.** A spoonful of salt in a liter of water makes a *dilute* salt solution. On the other hand, a large amount of solute makes a **concentrated** solution. A cup of salt in a glass of water makes a *concentrated* solution. You may have observed that there is a limit to how concentrated a solution can be at a certain temperature. For

Word study: Dilute from *diluere* (L.), to wash away. Concentrated from *com + centrum* (L.), to bring toward the center. Saturated from *saturatus* (L.), satisfied.

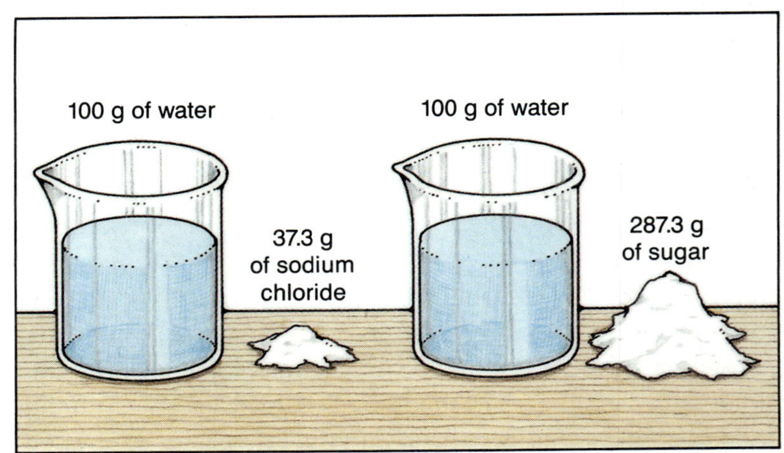

Fig. 14–4 Sugar is more soluble in water than salt. A greater amount of sugar will dissolve in the same amount of water.

example, if you continue to dissolve sugar in iced tea, the solution will become so concentrated that no more sugar will dissolve. When this happens, the solution is **saturated.** A *saturated* solution has all the dissolved solute that it can hold. However, if you raise the temperature, the solution can hold more solute. For example, the amount of sugar needed to make a saturated solution of iced tea is less than the amount needed when the tea is hot. A saturated solution at a certain temperature always contains a definite amount of the solute. The amount of sugar or salt that will make saturated solutions in 100 g of water at 60° C is shown in Fig. 14–4. As you can see, a larger amount of sugar than salt is needed to make a saturated solution at the same temperature. Sugar is said to have greater **solubility** in water than salt. *Solubility* describes the amount of a solute that can be dissolved in a given solvent under given conditions. The solubility of most solids in water increases as the temperature of the water increases. However, the opposite is true for the solubility of gases in water. More gas will dissolve in cold water than in hot water. In other words, gases are more *soluble* in cold water than in hot water.

Saturated Describes a solution that has all the solute that it can hold without changing the conditions.

Enrichment: Careful cooling of a saturated solution produces a supersaturated solution. Disturbing the supersaturated solution or seeding it with a crystal of the solute will cause the excess solute to crystallize out. A state of solution equilibrium will be reestablished.

Solubility Describes the amount of solute that can be dissolved in a given solvent under given conditions.

COMPOUNDS

Like most mixtures, solutions can be broken down by a physical change. The salt and water in a salt solution can be separated by heating the mixture. The water will boil away. The salt will then be left in the form of solid crystals. See Fig. 14–5. The solid salt is the same substance it was before it dissolved. The steam from the boiling solution can be captured, cooled, and changed back into liquid water. That water will also be the same as before it was mixed with the salt.

Pure water, on the other hand, cannot be broken down by a physical change. It can only be broken down by a chemical change. A substance like water that can only be broken down by a chemical change is called a **compound.**

Compounds cannot be broken down into simpler parts by a physical change. For example, aspirin is a compound. If you crushed an aspirin tablet, you would have only smaller particles of aspirin. See Fig. 14–6. A physical change like crushing cannot separate the aspirin into different substances.

Enrichment: Concentration of solid in liquid solutions is often expressed as a percent by weight, liquid in liquid solutions as percent by volume. Specific gravity (sp. gr.), the ratio of the density of a solution compared to the density of water, may also be used.

Enrichment: A supersaturated solution is made by slowly cooling a saturated solution. Excess solute may suddenly precipitate from a supersaturated solution.

Enrichment: Set up a distillation apparatus. Distill a water solution of a food-color dye.

Compound A substance that can only be broken down into simpler parts by a chemical change. A compound contains one kind of molecule.

Fig. 14–5 If a salt solution is boiled, the water will evaporate, leaving behind the solid salt. Like all mixtures, a salt-water solution can be broken down by a physical change.

Fig. 14–6 Aspirin is a compound. Like all compounds, it can only be broken down by a chemical change.

The properties of a compound are usually different from the properties of the elements that make up the compound. For example, sodium is a solid that reacts violently with water. Chlorine is a poisonous gas. When they combine chemically, they form crystals of harmless table salt.

SUMMARY

A mixture contains more than one kind of molecule. A solution is a mixture in which a solute is dissolved in a solvent. In all mixtures, even solutions, the different molecules can be separated by a physical change. Compounds cannot be broken down by a physical change.

QUESTIONS

Use complete sentences to write your answers.

1. Is a combination of sand and sugar a mixture, a compound, or a solution? Explain.
2. Is salt dissolved in water a mixture, a compound, or a solution? Explain.
3. What makes something a mixture? Name at least two mixtures. What makes something a compound? Name at least two compounds.
4. Distinguish between a solvent and a solute. Give an example of each.

1. The combination is a mixture. The two can be separated by a physical means such as dissolving the sugar in water, leaving the sand.
2. The combination is a solution. The salt and water can be separated by a physical means such as evaporating the water, leaving the salt.
3. A mixture is made of two or more different substances. A mixture has a nonuniform composition. Examples are salt and sugar, sugar and sand, etc. A compound is made of only one pure substance. A compound is uniform in composition. Examples are salt, sugar, etc.
4. A solvent is the substance in which a solute is dissolved. In a sugar-water solution, the water is the solvent and the sugar is the solute.

SKILL-BUILDING ACTIVITY

See teacher's commentary for teaching hints, safety, and answers to questions.

MIXTURES AND COMPOUNDS

PURPOSE: You will observe the difference between a mixture and a compound, and you will separate the two materials in the mixture.

MATERIALS:

sand	Bunsen burner
salt	matches
2 beakers	container of water
distilled water	for burned
2 test tubes	matches
test-tube holder	

PROCEDURE:

A. Combine 20 g of sand with 20 g of salt.

1. Is this combination of salt and sand a mixture or a compound?

B. Pour the sand and salt combination into a beaker. Add 200 mL of distilled water. Stir for 2 to 3 min.

C. Pour the liquid into another beaker.

2. In your own words, describe the salt-water solution.
3. Describe what happened to form this solution.

D. Put 1 mL of distilled water in a test tube. Using a test-tube holder, hold the tube above the flame of the Bunsen burner and heat it slowly for several minutes. CAUTION: Wear goggles. See Fig. 14–7.

4. Describe what happens.

E. Put 1 mL of the solution you made in step C into a second test tube. Using the test-tube holder, hold the tube 10 to 15 cm above the Bunsen burner flame. Heat it very slowly for several minutes.

5. In your own words, describe what you observe in the tube.

F. Wait several minutes for the test tube to cool. Add water to the material in the tube.

6. Does the material in the tube go into solution?

CONCLUSION:

1. In your own words, describe how you could separate a mixture of two materials, one of which can be dissolved in water.

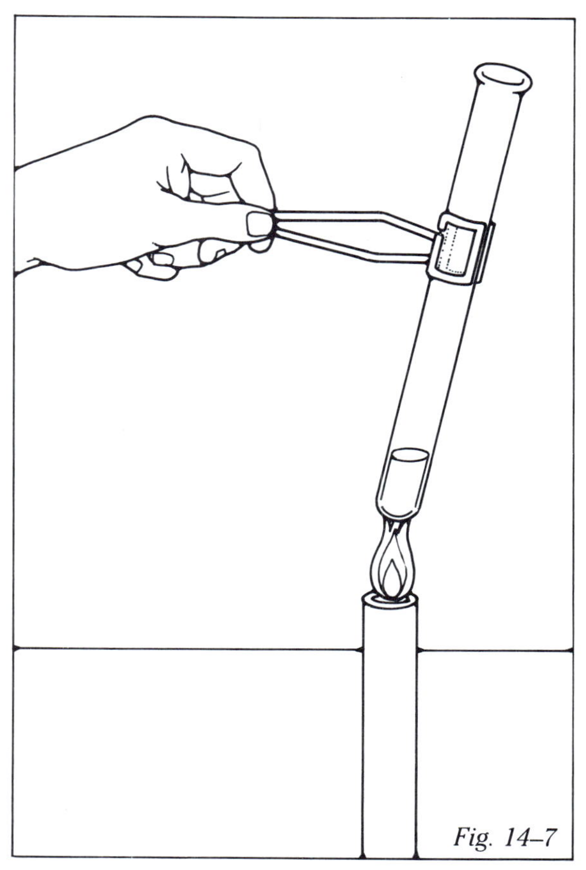

Fig. 14–7

14-2. Elements and Atoms

At the end of this section you will be able to:

- ☐ Describe how a chemical change is produced.
- ☐ Give examples of compounds being broken down into *elements*.
- ☐ Explain how elements and *atoms* are related.

Look at any of the colored pictures in this book with a strong magnifying glass. You will see that each picture is made up of many small colored dots as shown in Fig. 14–8. Suppose that you could look at a compound, such as water, in the same way. You would see that the water is also made up of very small identical molecules. Is each water molecule also made up of even smaller parts?

Fig. 14–8 A colored picture is made up of small dots of color. Matter is also made up of smaller particles.

SEPARATING COMPOUNDS

If you dissolve salt in water, you can later recover the salt. The water can be boiled away. The solid salt that is left is the same as before it was dissolved. A salt solution is a mixture. Therefore, the salt and water can be separated by boiling. Can the molecules of a compound such as water be separated into different materials? If water can be broken down, it would show that water molecules are made up of smaller parts. The following experiment should answer this question.

Equipment such as that shown in Fig. 14–9 is used. The equipment consists of a battery connected to two wires. The current flows through a beaker of water. A small amount of sulfuric acid is added to the water. This is necessary because pure water does not easily conduct an electric current. When the current flows through the water, bubbles of gas form around the wires where the current enters and leaves the water. These gases then bubble up and fill two test tubes. Tests show that one gas is hydrogen. Hydrogen gas burns with an almost invisible flame. The gas in the other test tube is oxygen. Oxygen gas does not burn. But a glowing wooden splint will burst into flame when it is put into the test tube of oxygen.

This experiment shows that water can be broken down into two different substances. The hydrogen and oxygen produced are completely different from the water. The breakdown is an example of a *chemical change*. When a chemical change occurs, one kind of molecule is changed into another kind. In this example, water molecules were broken down into hydrogen and oxygen molecules.

Experiments with compounds other than water show that other compounds can also be changed into different materials. Sugar can be broken down into carbon, hydrogen, and oxygen. You may have seen this happen when sugar burns. The sugar turns into solid black carbon. The hydrogen and oxygen escape in the form of water vapor.

Like water, hydrogen peroxide can be broken down into two different materials. A solution of hydrogen peroxide in water is often used to clean wounds and help prevent infection. Like water, hydrogen peroxide is a compound that is made up of

Reinforcement: Demonstrate the electrolysis of water. Test the resulting hydrogen and oxygen gases for flammability. Show that a larger volume of hydrogen than oxygen is obtained.

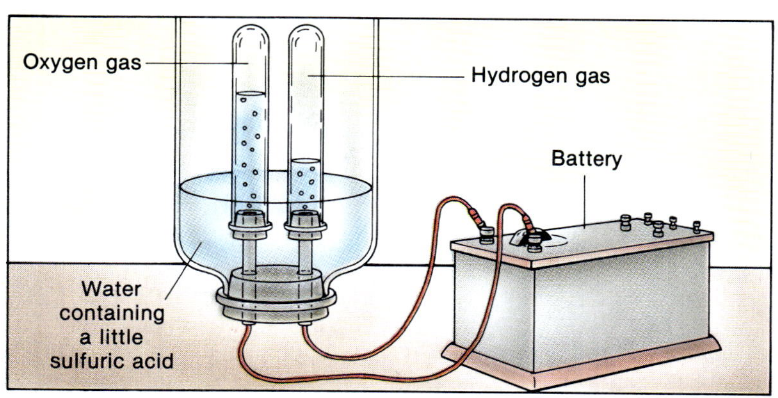

Fig. 14–9 When an electric current passes through the solution in the beaker, it breaks water down into the two gases hydrogen and oxygen. The hydrogen and oxygen are collected in the test tubes.

hydrogen and oxygen. However, hydrogen peroxide contains more oxygen than the same amount of water. Comparing water and hydrogen peroxide shows that different compounds may be made up of the same substances but combined in different proportions.

When a compound is broken down, it always yields the same substances in the same amounts. For example, water is always made up of 11 percent hydrogen and 89 percent oxygen by weight. This means that 20 raindrops with a mass of 2.0 g could be broken down to give 0.22 g of hydrogen and 1.8 g of oxygen. This is shown as follows:

$$\text{hydrogen} = 11\% = 11/100 = 0.11$$
$$\text{mass of hydrogen} = 0.11 \times 2\text{ g} = 0.22\text{ g}$$

$$\text{oxygen} = 89\% = 89/100 = 0.89$$
$$\text{mass of oxygen} = 0.89 \times 2\text{g} = 1.8\text{ g}$$

Fig. 14–10 The lump of coal in the top photo looks very different from the diamond in the bottom photo. But both coal and diamond are made of carbon atoms.

The hydrogen and oxygen in water cannot be changed into simpler forms of matter. Hydrogen and oxygen are the simplest forms of matter in water. Hydrogen and oxygen are examples

COMMON ELEMENTS FOUND IN THE EARTH'S CRUST AND IN THE HUMAN BODY			
Most Common Elements in the Earth's Crust		Most Common Elements in the Human Body	
Oxygen	46.60%	Oxygen	65.0%
Silicon	27.72%	Carbon	18.0%
Aluminum	8.13%	Hydrogen	10.0%
Iron	5.00%	Nitrogen	3.0%
Calcium	3.63%	Calcium	2.0%
Sodium	2.83%	Phosphorus	1.0%
Potassium	2.59%	Potassium	0.3%
Magnesium	2.09%	Sulfur	0.2%
Titanium	0.44%	Sodium	0.15%
Hydrogen	0.14%	Chlorine	0.15%
All others	0.83%	Iron	0.04%
		Magnesium	0.02%
		All others	0.15%

Table 14–1

of **elements.** An *element* is the simplest form of matter. An element cannot be chemically changed into anything else. Up to the present, more than 100 elements have been found. All matter is made up of these elements in different combinations. The most common elements in nature are listed in Table 14–1.

Element The simplest form of matter.

Reinforcement: Samples of common elements such as aluminum, sulfur, copper, silver, and carbon can be displayed. Compare these substances with other common materials that are mixtures or compounds.

Water is made up of water molecules. A water molecule is the smallest particle of water that can still be called water. What happens if an element such as oxygen is broken down in the same way? A small particle that is still oxygen remains. The smallest particle of an element is called an **atom.** The element oxygen, for example, is made up of only oxygen *atoms*. Hydrogen contains only hydrogen atoms. Carbon contains only carbon atoms. See Fig. 14–10.

Word study: Atom from *atomos* (Gr.), indivisible.

Atom The smallest particle of an element that can be identified as that element.

As early as 400 B.C., some ancient Greeks suggested that all matter was made up of atoms. But the modern atomic theory is based on the work of an English schoolteacher named John Dalton. In 1808, Dalton first proposed that atoms join together to make up compounds. The atomic theory that developed from Dalton's ideas is one of the most important scientific theories. You will learn more about atoms and the atomic theory in the next chapter.

Enrichment: Read aloud some of Aristotle's writing on atomic theory.

SUMMARY

Compounds, such as water, are made up of molecules. These molecules can be broken down by a chemical change into elements such as hydrogen and oxygen. Elements, on the other hand, cannot be changed into a simpler kind of matter. Each element is made up of atoms. Atoms are the smallest parts of elements.

QUESTIONS

Use complete sentences to write your answers.

1. Describe what is meant by a chemical change. How does a chemical change differ from a physical change?
2. How can water be broken down into its elements?
3. How can you test for the presence of oxygen gas?
4. Explain how the terms "element" and "atom" are related.
5. One liter of water has a mass of 1,000 g. What is the mass of hydrogen in 1 L of water? What is the mass of oxygen?

1. A chemical change results in a new arrangement of atoms, forming new compounds. A physical change results in a new arrangement of molecules, but no new compounds are formed.
2. An electric current passed through water will change the water into the hydrogen and oxygen of which it is made.
3. A glowing splint placed into an oxygen-rich atmosphere will start to burn.
4. Atoms are the smallest indivisible parts of an element that are still identifiable as that element.
5. 110 g (11%) of hydrogen and 890 g (89%) of oxygen are present in 1 L of water.

INVESTIGATION

See teacher's commentary for teaching hints, safety, and answers to questions.

MAKING OXYGEN FROM HYDROGEN PEROXIDE

PURPOSE: You will break down hydrogen peroxide into water and oxygen. You will then test for the presence of oxygen.

MATERIALS:

test tube	wooden toothpick
hydrogen peroxide	container of water
balance	one-hole rubber stopper
manganese dioxide	
matches	

PROCEDURE:

A. Fill the test tube about 1/3 full of hydrogen peroxide.

B. Look closely at this liquid and answer the following:

1. What does hydrogen peroxide look like? Does it have an odor?

C. When manganese dioxide is added to hydrogen peroxide, the hydrogen peroxide will break down into water and oxygen. Add about 3 to 4 grams of manganese dioxide to the hydrogen peroxide. Swirl the test tube to mix the two liquids.

2. As bubbles form and break, what do you observe?

D. With a match, light one end of a wooden toothpick. CAUTION: Wear goggles. Blow out the flame so that the toothpick glows red. Use the glowing end of the toothpick to break one of the larger bubbles of gas. A glowing piece of wood will break into flames and burn rapidly in oxygen. This is the test for oxygen often used in the laboratory.

3. When the bubble breaks, what happens to the toothpick?

E. Repeat step D several times.

F. Place the one-hole stopper tightly in the test tube. You will use this setup again in 5 minutes.

4. Do you think oxygen itself will burn? Record your prediction.

G. After 5 minutes, try to light the gas escaping from the hole in the stopper using a match. Swirl the liquid in the tube to help make more oxygen. See Fig. 14–11.

5. Does the oxygen burn?

H. Bend a wooden toothpick on one end. Light the bent end of the toothpick. Blow out the flame and use the glowing end to test for oxygen. See step D.

6. Is oxygen coming out of the hole in the stopper?

CONCLUSION:

1. In your own words describe how you can make oxygen gas and then test to find out if oxygen is present.

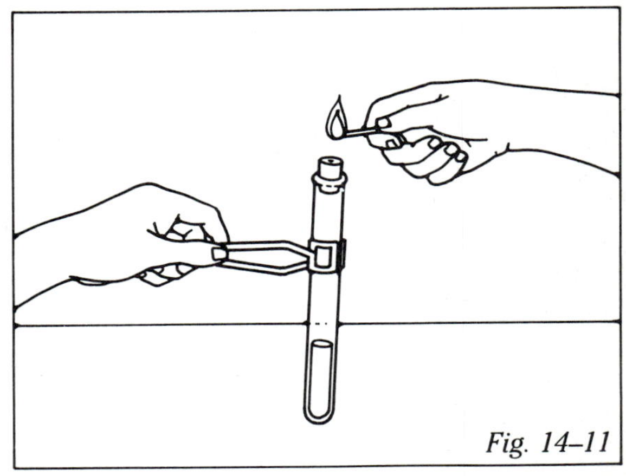

Fig. 14–11

CAREERS IN SCIENCE

ARCHITECT

Architects are responsible for all the work it takes to turn an idea into a physical structure. Although the creative art of an architect's work is done alone, much of an architect's time is spent working with other people, such as engineers, urban planners, and building contractors. Architects have to discuss the project with clients, estimate the cost, design the plans for the building, choose the building materials, supervise the construction onsite, and make certain that the complete work meets specified standards, including state building codes, zoning laws, and fire regulations.

All U.S. architects must be licensed. To qualify, a person must have at least a Bachelor of Architecture degree and three years of approved, on-the-job experience in an architectural office. Most states accept additional experience as a substitute for formal education.

For further information, contact: American Institute of Architects, 1725 New York Avenue NW, Washington, DC 20006.

PHARMACEUTICAL CHEMIST

Pharmaceutical chemists test and prepare products for commercial distribution. They refine, purify, and blend compounds to develop new drugs and medications. These chemists research the actions of drugs, sera, and other medications on the tissues of living organisms to determine their effect on bodily functions. To do this they must also be knowledgeable about the immunological system.

Most pharmaceutical chemists are employed in industry, although U.S. government research organizations such as the Public Health Service also employ pharmaceutical chemists.

Most chemists working in pharmaceutical research have advanced degrees, usually a Ph.D. But it is possible to get entry-level jobs in this field with less formal education and to study on the job in both public agencies and private companies.

For further information, contact: American Chemical Society, 1155 16th Street NW, Washington, DC 20026.

CHAPTER REVIEW

See teacher's commentary for answers.

VOCABULARY

On a separate piece of paper, match each term with the number of the statement that best explains it. Use each term only once.

atom	dilute	mixture	solute	solvent
concentrated	element	saturated	solution	solubility
compound				

1. A mixture formed when one kind of molecule fills the spaces between another kind of molecule.
2. Any matter that contains more than one kind of molecule.
3. A solution containing a large amount of solute.
4. The smallest part of an element that can be identified as that element.
5. A substance that can only be broken down into smaller parts by a chemical change.
6. The substance that is dissolved in a liquid to form a solution.
7. The liquid in which a solute is dissolved.
8. The simplest form of matter.
9. A solution that contains all the solute it can hold at a certain temperature.
10. A solution containing a small quantity of solute.
11. Describes the amount of solute that can be dissolved in a given solvent under a given set of conditions.

QUESTIONS

Give brief but complete answers to each of the following questions. Unless otherwise indicated, use complete sentences to write your answers.

1. Is sand a mixture? How can you tell? Give three examples of mixtures.
2. What are the characteristics of a compound? Give three examples of each.
3. Distinguish between a solute and a solvent and give two examples of each.
4. List three ways to speed up the rate at which a substance dissolves.
5. What is the difference between a concentrated solution and a saturated solution? What is the difference between a concentrated solution and a dilute solution?
6. How does a compound differ from a mixture?
7. Describe how water can be separated into other materials. What are those materials?
8. Explain the relationship between elements and atoms.

9. List the three elements that are found in the greatest amount in the human body.
10. How many common elements in the earth's crust are also common in the human body? Name them.
11. How much oxygen is there in 150 g of water? How much hydrogen is there in 150 g of water?
12. Explain why a crushed aspirin tablet dissolves faster in water than a whole aspirin tablet.
13. What happens to the sugar molecules and the water molecules when you dissolve sugar in water?
14. How could you demonstrate that sugar is more soluble in water than salt?
15. Give one example of each of the following solutions: (a) liquid, (b) gaseous, (c) solid.

APPLYING SCIENCE

1. Adding a solid to water changes the freezing point and the boiling point of the water. Measure the freezing point and boiling point of water before and after adding salt. Report to the class on your findings.
2. Make a display table of several physical properties of some common elements. Some properties to include are specific heat capacity, boiling point, melting point, and density. See the *Handbook of Chemistry and Physics,* published by the CRC Press.
3. Everything around you is either a mixture, a compound, or an element. Make a list of at least 10 items around your home that are mixtures, 10 that are compounds, and 10 that are elements. Also list what is in each mixture, the names of the compounds, and the elements in the compounds listed.

BIBLIOGRAPHY

Arnov, B. *Water: Experiments to Understand It.* New York: Lothrop, 1980.

Gunston, Bill. *Water.* Morristown, NJ: Silver-Burdett, 1982.

Segre, Emilio. *From X-Rays to Quarks.* San Francisco: Freeman, 1980.

Swanson, Glen. *Oil and Water.* New York: Prentice-Hall, 1981.

Trefil, James. "Matter vs. Antimatter." *Science 81,* September 1981.

Trefil, James. *From Atoms to Quarks.* New York: Scribners, 1980.

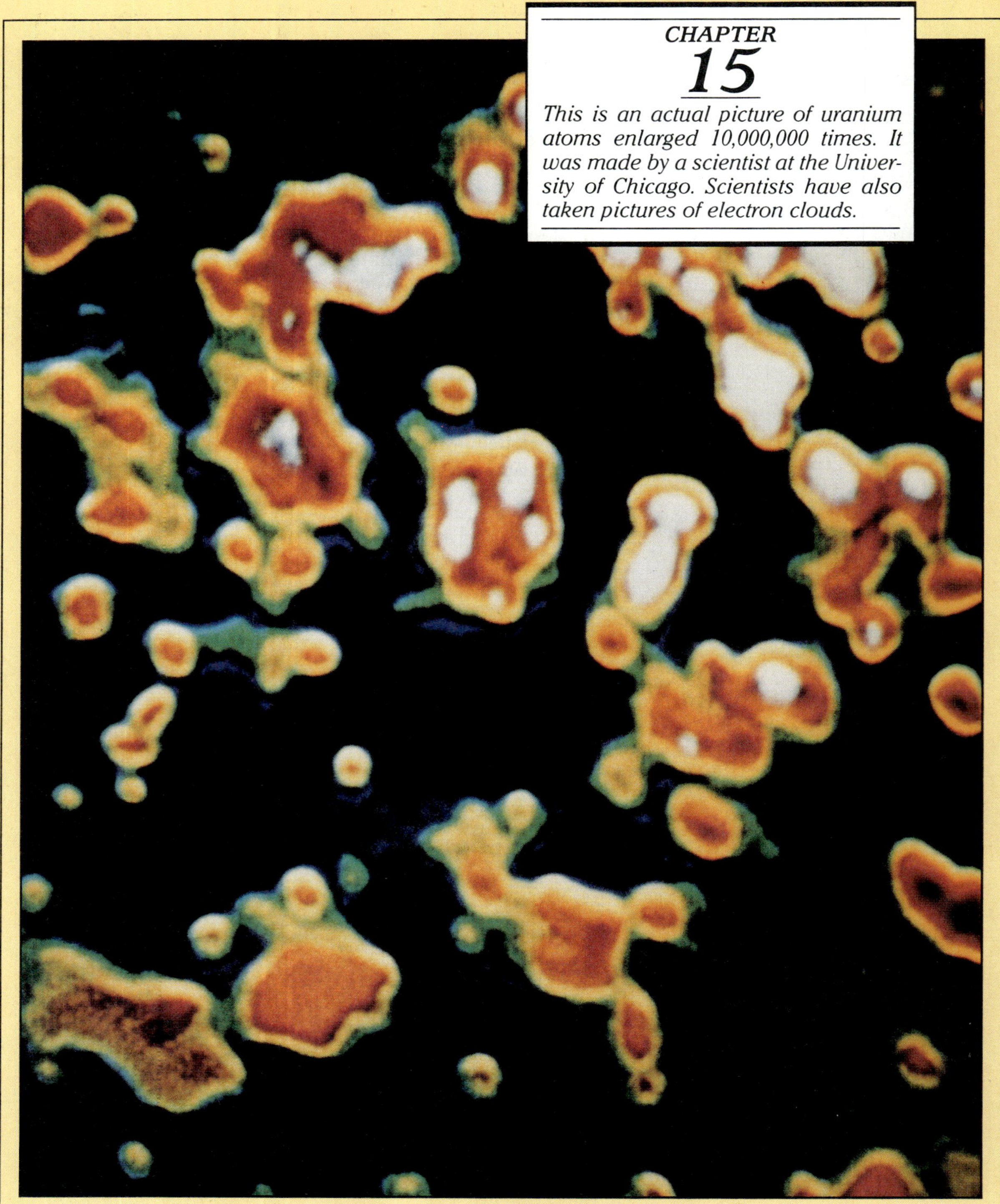

CHAPTER
15

This is an actual picture of uranium atoms enlarged 10,000,000 times. It was made by a scientist at the University of Chicago. Scientists have also taken pictures of electron clouds.

ATOMS

CHAPTER GOALS

1. Name and compare three types of atomic particles.
2. Describe the structure of the atom in terms of electrons, protons, and neutrons.
3. Explain the role of protons and neutrons in determining the mass of an atom.
4. Use the atomic number and mass number to find the number of electrons, protons, and neutrons in an atom.

15-1. Atomic Particles

At the end of of this section you will be able to:

- ☐ Describe three early atomic theories.
- ☐ Compare the properties of three atomic particles.
- ☐ Explain why scientists now use models of atoms.

How big is the smallest thing you can think of? It is probably many times bigger than an atom. For example, think about a soap bubble. A soap bubble is very thin and breaks easily. The thickness of a soap bubble is less than the thickness of a single human hair. However, the surface of a soap bubble is several thousand times thicker than the diameter of an atom.

EARLY THEORIES ABOUT ATOMS

Two thousand years ago, the ancient Greeks believed that all matter was made up of only four materials. These materials were earth, air, fire, and water. Wood, for example, was said to be made of fire and earth. When wood burned, the fire escaped and the earth remained in the form of ashes. One Greek thinker, Democritus, disagreed with this theory. Democritus said that matter was made up of small objects that he called "atoms," from the Greek word *atomos* meaning "cannot be divided." To Democritus, atoms were like hard, solid balls. But people did not believe the teachings of Democritus. The idea that matter was made up of earth, air, fire, and water was taught for nearly 2,000 years. See Fig. 15–1.

Fig. 15–1 The four basic elements of the ancient Greeks: fire, water, air, and earth. The Greeks thought that all matter was made of combinations of these elements.

Enrichment: Dalton experimented in many fields. He was the first to publish a scientific description of color-blindness.

In 1808, John Dalton showed that matter is made up of atoms. His experiments proved that elements such as hydrogen are made up of atoms. He also showed that the atoms of an element such as hydrogen are all alike, but differ in mass from the atoms of other elements. However, Dalton's experiments did not show what atoms are made of. He thought that hydrogen atoms were the smallest bits of matter since they are the lightest atoms.

Reinforcement: Until Thomson proved the existence of electrons, atoms were thought of as the smallest particles of matter. Thomson's discovery showed that atoms were not indivisible.

The first clue that electrically charged particles are hidden within atoms came in 1897. In that year, J. J. Thomson, in England, discovered the negatively charged particles that came to be called *electrons*. The mass of an electron was later found to be 1/1,836 that of a hydrogen atom. It became clear to scientists that there are particles smaller than atoms. Thomson thought that an atom might be a ball of positive electricity with the negative electrons scattered throughout. See Fig. 15–2. The diagram shows a Thomson atom.

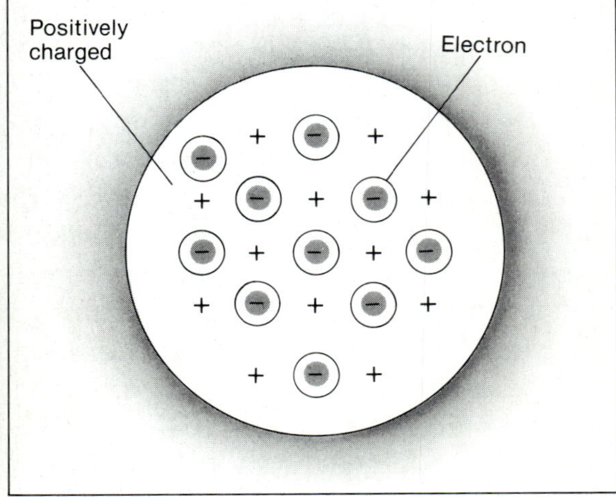

Fig. 15–2 J. J. Thomson (1856–1940) discovered that all atoms contain electrons. He thought that the electrons were scattered randomly throughout the atom.

ATOMIC PARTICLES

Since Thomson's experiments, scientists have found many kinds of particles that are smaller than atoms. However, only three kinds of particles form the basic structure of atoms. See Fig. 15–3. These basic **atomic particles** are listed below:

1. Electrons are extremely light particles. Each electron has a negative electric charge.

2. Protons are positively charged particles. The positive electric charge on each proton is the same size as the negative charge on an electron. Therefore, the charges on an electron and proton cancel each other. Protons are 1,836 times more massive than electrons.

3. Neutrons (**noo**-tronz) are particles that are electrically neutral. A neutron has nearly the same mass as a proton.

An electron in a hydrogen atom is the same as an electron in an oxygen atom. All of the different kinds of atoms that exist are made up of *atomic particles.* Atoms of different elements contain different numbers of electrons, protons, and neutrons.

proton
nucleus
neutron
electron

Fig. 15–3 An atom consists of electrons, protons, and neutrons.

Atomic particles The basic building blocks of atoms.

Enrichment: Electrons, protons, and neutrons are called elementary particles since they make up ordinary atoms. Many other kinds of particles such as photons, neutrinos, positrons, various antiparticles, muons, pions, and quarks have been detected. At the present time there is no completely adequate theory to relate all of the elementary and other particles to each other.

SIZE OF ATOMIC PARTICLES

The three atomic particles differ in electric charge and in mass. All three particles have very small masses. For example, about 6.0×10^{23} protons have a mass of about one gram. A neutron has nearly the same mass as a proton. But an electron has a much smaller mass. These values are so small that scientists use a special unit for the mass of atomic particles. This unit is the **atomic mass unit** (u). Protons and neutrons each have a mass of one *atomic mass unit.* Electrons are much lighter. An electron has a mass of 1/1,836 u. Table 15–1 lists the mass and the electric charge of each of the three atomic particles. Since atoms are made up of atomic particles, the masses of atoms are also given in atomic mass units. The mass of an atom depends only on the number of protons and neutrons it contains.

Atomic mass unit A unit used to express the masses of atomic particles and atoms; $1 \text{ u} = 1.660 \times 10^{-27}$ kg.

Atomic Particle	Mass (u)	Charge
Electron	1/1,836 or 0	1−
Proton	1	1+
Neutron	1,837/1,836 or 1	0

Table 15–1

Reinforcement: Remind students that scientific models are mental models generally used to describe something too small (like an atom) or too big (like the universe) to be seen.

SCIENTIFIC MODELS

A typical atom has a diameter of about 2×10^{-10} m. More than a million atoms side by side would fit across the width of this page. An atom is much too small to be seen clearly. Therefore scientists cannot study atoms directly. Instead, they use scientific models of atoms. Models of atoms are the result of many experiments. Scientists observe the way atoms behave under different conditions. See Fig. 15–4. The earliest scientific models of atoms pictured them as tiny solid balls. But the discovery of electrons and other atomic particles showed that this model could not be correct. In the next section, you will see how a famous experiment led to the development of the modern scientific model of the atom.

Fig. 15–4 Scientists also use models to study stars that are too far away to be observed directly. The diagram shows four theoretical models of the star Epsilon Aurigae.

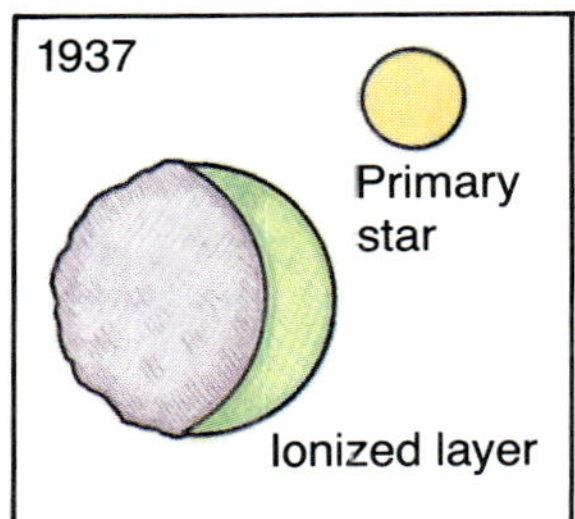

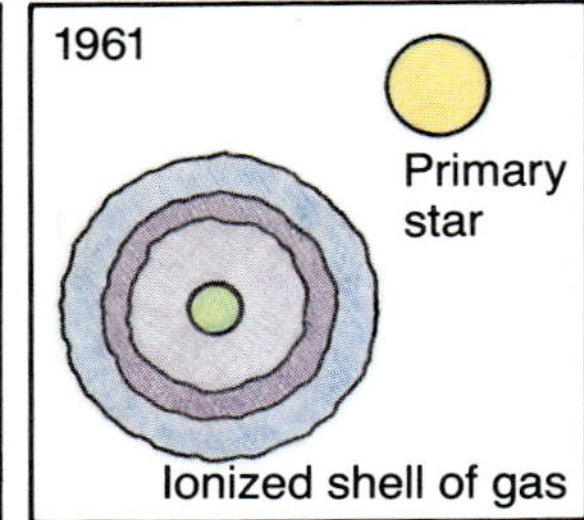

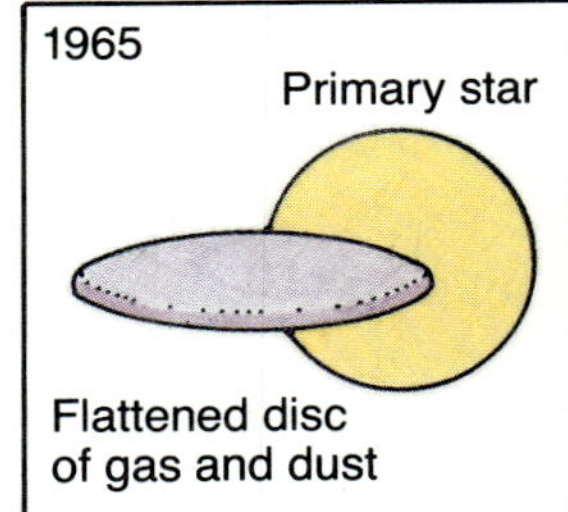

SUMMARY

Atoms are made up of three kinds of particles. These particles are called electrons, protons, and neutrons. Each particle has a specific electric charge and mass. Because atoms are too small to study directly, scientists use models to describe them.

QUESTIONS

Use complete sentences to write your answers.

1. Describe how each of the following people added to our present model of the atom: (a) Democritus, (b) John Dalton, (c) J. J. Thomson.
2. Name three kinds of atomic particles, give their mass in atomic mass units, and the kind of electric charge on each.
3. What is an atomic mass unit? Why is it used?
4. What caused scientists to realize that there were particles smaller than atoms?
5. Why do scientists use models to study atoms?

1. Democritus said that matter is made of indivisible particles (atoms). John Dalton showed that all matter is made of atoms or atoms combined into molecules. J. J. Thomson discovered that atoms contain electrically charged particles.
2. The electron has a mass of 1/1836 u and a negative charge. The proton has a mass of 1 u and a positive charge. The neutron has a mass of 1 u and no electric charge.
3. An atomic mass unit is a unit of mass used for atomic particles. It is equal to the mass of a proton or neutron. Scientists use these units because the mass of the particles is so small.
4. The discovery that the electron has a mass that is 1/1836 of the mass of a hydrogen atom caused scientists to think that the atom must be made up of smaller parts.
5. Scientists use models to study atoms because they cannot see atoms directly and they need to visualize what the atom is like.

INVESTIGATION

See teacher's commentary for teaching hints, safety, and answers to questions.

A SCIENTIFIC MODEL

PURPOSE: You will demonstrate what scientists mean by a scientific model.

MATERIALS:

sealed box containing one object
pencil
paper

PROCEDURE:

A. One object is hidden in the box you have been given. You must find out as much as you can about this object without opening the box. After you have made your observations, you will use a model to describe the object. See Fig. 15–5.

B. Copy the table below in your notebook.

C. Spend about 15 minutes trying as many tests as you can. Ask yourself, "Is the object round? Is it heavy? Is it hard? Is it made of iron?" Then shake the box, turn it upside down, on end, etc., to try to answer your questions. Do not open or otherwise damage the box. Record all your observations.

1. What are some other questions you can test? How would you test them?

D. When you have completed your observations, make a sketch of what you think the object in the box looks like.

E. Trade boxes with other students in the class. Repeat steps A through D.

CONCLUSION:

1. In your own words, describe how you can make a model of something you cannot observe directly.

Fig. 15–5

MYSTERY BOXES					
Box Number	Turning	Shaking	Tilting	Other Observations	Description

15-2. Atomic Structure

At the end of this section you will be able to:

- Describe the atomic *nucleus.*
- Show how to find the number of protons and electrons in an atom from its atomic number.
- Describe the motion of electrons in an atom.
- Use a scientific model to explain how electrons are arranged in atoms.

Suppose that a car could be squeezed until all the electrons, protons, and neutrons in its atoms were pushed against each other. See Fig. 15–6. The entire car would then be about the size of the head of a pin. In this section you will see how the modern scientific model of the atom explains this result.

Fig. 15–6 Do you think it would be possible to squeeze a car until it could fit on the head of a pin?

THE NUCLEAR ATOMIC MODEL

If you were given the parts of a watch, could you put them all together to make a watch that works? A similar problem faced scientists studying the atom in the early part of this century. By 1900, scientists knew that atoms were made up of negatively charged electrons and positively charged protons. However, no one knew how these particles were arranged in an atom. Then, in 1911, a British scientist from New Zealand named Ernest Rutherford reported the results of a brilliant experiment. See Fig. 15–7. The results of this experiment led to the first modern scientific model of the atom.

Fig. 15–7 Ernest Rutherford (1871–1937) worked at the Cavendish Laboratory in England where he made many important discoveries about atoms.

In this experiment, a beam of fast-moving, positively charged particles was used. These particles were aimed at a very thin sheet of gold. Gold metal was used as a target because it can be made into sheets that are only a few atoms in thickness. The purpose of the experiment was to see how the paths of the particles would be changed when they hit the gold atoms. The results of the experiment were very surprising. They showed that most of the particles went straight through the gold as if nothing were there. But a few of the particles bounced off the gold atoms as if they were solid. See Fig. 15–8. Rutherford said, "It was almost as unbelievable as if you fired a 15-inch shell at a piece of tissue paper and it came back and hit you."

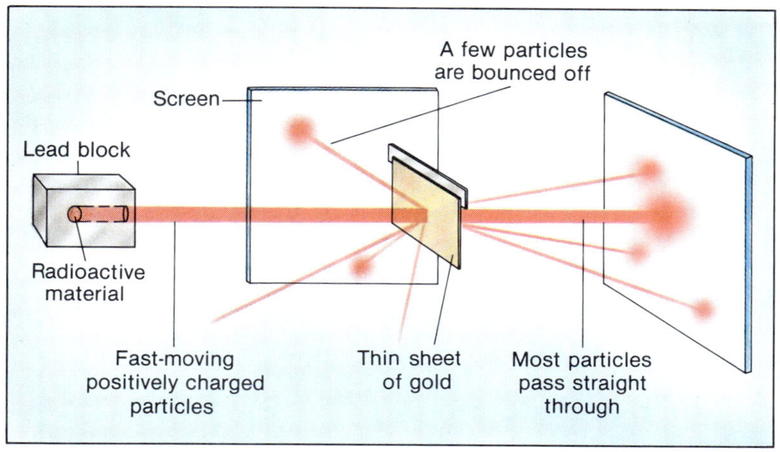

Fig. 15–8 The drawing shows the setup of Rutherford's famous experiment in which the nucleus was discovered.

Reinforcement: Point out that the positively charged (alpha) particles used by Rutherford could only be bounced back by the gold nuclei if those nuclei were also positively charged.

This experiment can be compared to what happens if you throw pebbles at a wire fence. Most of the pebbles go right through the fence because it is mostly empty space. However, a few pebbles may hit wires and bounce back.

Rutherford's experiment led to a new model for the atom. In this model, most of the mass of an atom is found in a very small core at its center. This central core of the atom is called the **nucleus** (plural: nuclei). The rest of an atom is mostly empty space. This is the model of the atom that is used by modern scientists.

Nucleus The small central core of an atom where most of the mass of the atom is located. This core is made up of protons and neutrons.

THE NUCLEUS

All the protons and neutrons in an atom are found in the *nucleus.* The nucleus has a positive charge because it contains the positive protons. The electrons are found in a cloud around the nucleus. See Fig. 15–9. There is an attractive force between the positive nucleus and the negative electron cloud, as you learned in the chapter on electric force.

Word study: Nucleus from *nux* (L.), nut or kernel.

Enrichment: The diameter of a nucleus is not greater than about 8×10^{-15} m.

An atomic nucleus is very small. Picture an atom the size of a football field. The nucleus of that atom would be the size of a flea! Most of the space in an atom is taken up by the electrons around the nucleus. Since electrons are small and light, an atom, like a wire fence, is mostly empty space. Atomic particles shot at an atom, like pebbles thrown at a wire fence, will usually go right through the atom. Since a car is made of atoms, a car is mostly empty space! Therefore, if all the atoms in a car could be squeezed hard enough, they might fit on the head of a pin. See Fig. 15–10.

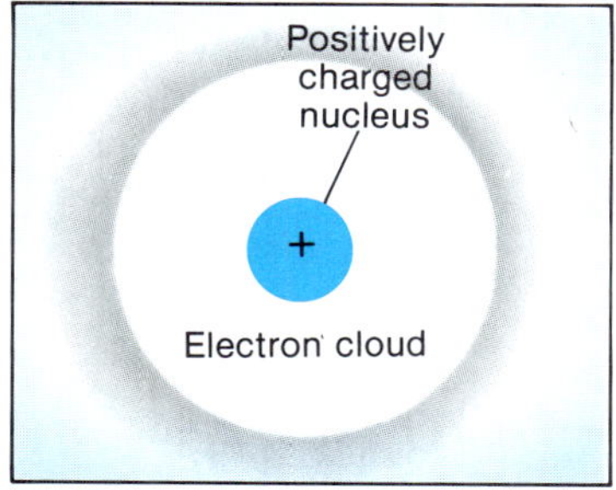

Fig. 15–9 Negative electrons are found in a fuzzy-looking cloud around the positive nucleus.

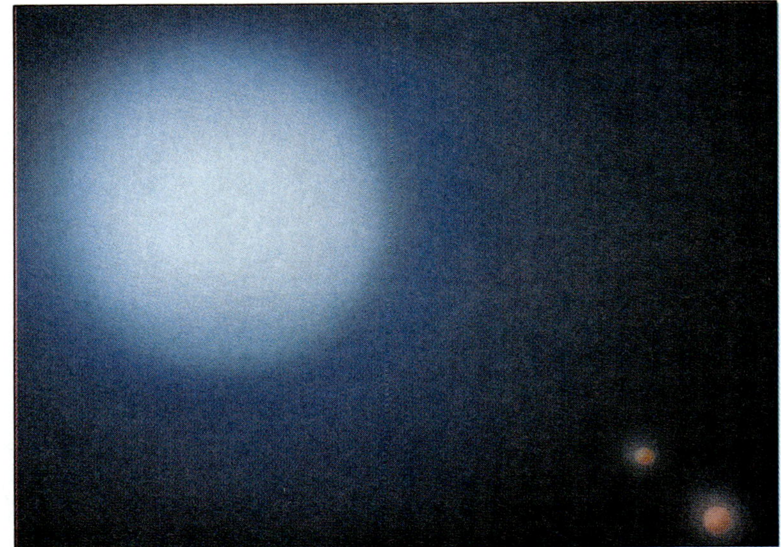

Fig. 15–10 One ton of the material in this superdense white dwarf star would fit in a matchbox. The electrons and protons in the star's atoms have been squeezed together.

Reinforcement: Students should understand that the atomic number of an element must be obtained from a reference source.

Atomic number The number of protons in the nucleus of an atom.

INSIDE A NUCLEUS

All atoms are made up of electrons, protons, and neutrons. Atoms of different elements have different numbers of these particles. For example, hydrogen atoms have one proton in the nucleus. Oxygen atoms have eight protons. See Fig. 15–11. Each element can be described by the number of protons in its nucleus. This number is called the **atomic number** of the element. Hydrogen has an *atomic number* of 1 because all hydrogen atoms have one proton in the nucleus. Since oxygen has eight protons, oxygen has an atomic number of 8. Table 15–2 lists the atomic numbers of the first 20 elements.

Element	Atomic Number	Element	Atomic Number
hydrogen	1	sodium	11
helium	2	magnesium	12
lithium	3	aluminum	13
beryllium	4	silicon	14
boron	5	phosphorus	15
carbon	6	sulfur	16
nitrogen	7	chlorine	17
oxygen	8	argon	18
fluorine	9	potassium	19
neon	10	calcium	20

Table 15–2

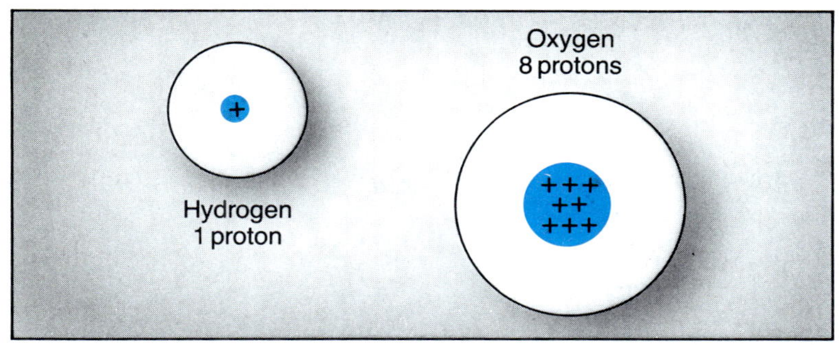

Fig. 15–11 Each element has a different number of protons and neutrons in its nucleus.

Atoms normally do not have an electric charge. The positive charges on the protons in the nucleus exactly cancel the negative charges on the electrons moving around the nucleus. The number of electrons around the nucleus is the same as the number of protons in the nucleus. For example, all hydrogen atoms have an atomic number of 1. Every hydrogen atom has a nucleus that contains one proton. Hydrogen is neutral. This means that each hydrogen atom also has one electron moving around its nucleus. Oxygen atoms have an atomic number of 8. This means that every oxygen atom has 8 protons and 8 electrons. The atomic number of an element tells you the number of electrons as well as the number of protons in each atom of that element.

ELECTRONS IN MOTION

In some ways, the modern atomic model is like the solar system. The sun is at the center of the solar system. An atom has a nucleus at its center. The force of gravity between the sun and the planets causes each planet to follow a certain orbit around the sun. Electric force between the negative electrons and the positive nucleus causes the electrons to move around the nucleus. See Fig. 15–12. But an atom is different from a solar system in one important way. In a solar system, planets can follow many different orbits around the central sun. In a million solar systems, there could be a million different arrangements of the planets. This is not true for electrons moving around a nucleus. For example, each atom of gold (atomic number 79) has 79 electrons around its nucleus. All atoms of gold are alike. All gold atoms would not be alike if the arrangement of the 79 electrons in some gold atoms were different from that in other gold atoms.

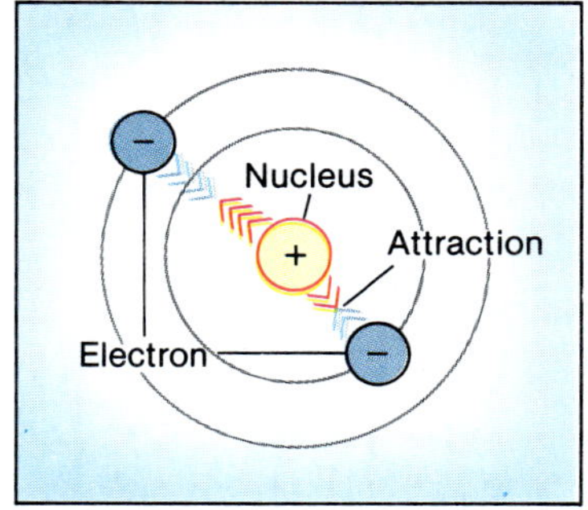

Fig. 15–12 Electrical attraction between the positive nucleus and the negative electrons keep the electrons in orbit around the nucleus.

Fig. 15–13 Niels Bohr (1885–1962) developed an early model of the atom.

In 1913, Niels Bohr, a Danish scientist who worked in Rutherford's laboratory, stated a theory to explain how electrons move around atomic nuclei. See Fig. 15–13. According to Bohr's theory, electrons moving around a nucleus can follow only certain orbits. For example, the electrons in two gold atoms follow orbits that are the same in both atoms. Each electron moves in an orbit that is a certain distance from the nucleus.

This old, simple model is commonly used to show the number of electrons, protons, and neutrons in atoms. Niels Bohr first drew this model with circles to represent the paths of the electrons. This is usually called the Bohr model of the atom. Scientists now use a modern version of this model based on mathematics. This modern model explains much of the chemical behavior of atoms. Figure 15–14 compares the steps in the development of the modern scientific model of the atom.

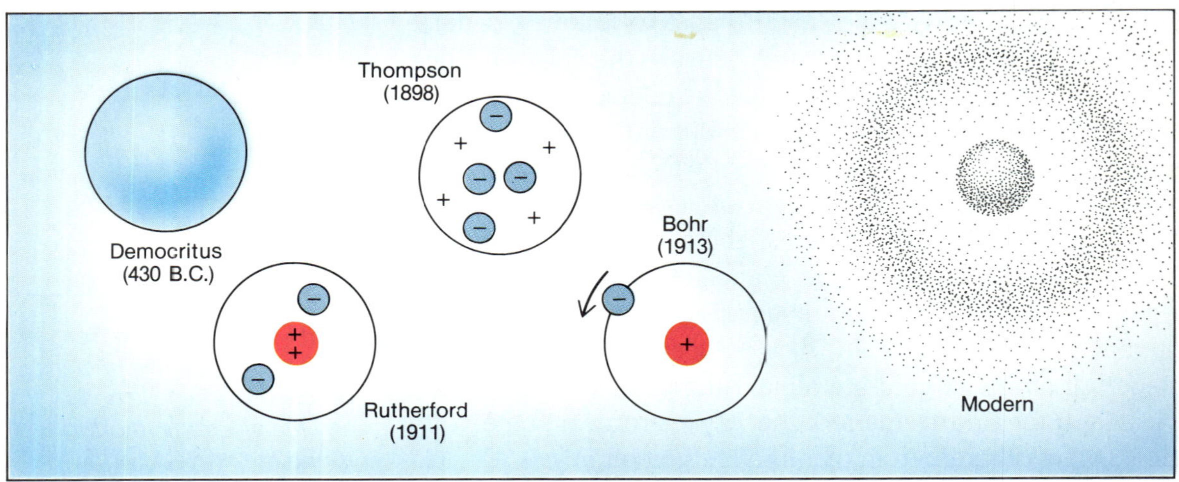

Fig. 15–14 Theoretical models of the atom have changed greatly since the time of Democritus.

ELECTRON ARRANGEMENT IN ATOMS

The first photographs of atoms show fuzzy shapes. See page 364. The fuzziness is a cloud of electrons whirling around the nucleus at high speed. Each electron makes billions of trips around the nucleus in one second. These electrons buzz around the nucleus somewhat like a swarm of bees. But unlike bees, each electron must be part of an **energy level.** An *energy level* describes the space in which electrons can be found as they move around a nucleus at a certain average distance. Within a level, electrons may move in all directions. See Fig. 15–15.

Energy level A region around an atomic nucleus in which electrons move.

Each energy level can only hold a certain number of electrons. The one electron in a hydrogen atom moves around the nucleus in the first level. The two electrons in helium also move in the first level. Two electrons are the limit for this level. The next energy level can only hold eight electrons. Fig. 15–16 shows the electron arrangement of the first 10 elements. This diagram shows the electrons in circles where

Reinforcement: Diagrams of atoms that use circles to represent the position of electrons should not give the impression that an atom is actually a miniature solar system. The circles are a convenient way to show the average position of electrons relative to the nucleus.

Fig. 15–15 Each energy level can hold only a certain number of electrons.

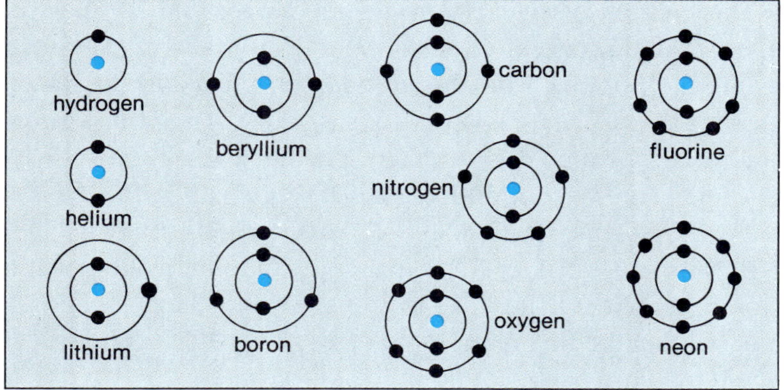

Fig. 15–16 Bohr models showing the electron arrangement of the first ten elements.

each circle represents an energy level. Keep in mind that the levels are *not* flat as shown in the drawings. Table 15–3 shows all the energy levels of the first 20 elements. The smallest number of electrons a level can hold is two in the first level. Eighteen to 32 electrons are found in some of the higher levels. Energy levels can overlap.

Atomic Number	Element	Number of Electrons
1	hydrogen	1
2	helium	2
3	lithium	2 1
4	beryllium	2 2
5	boron	2 3
6	carbon	2 4
7	nitrogen	2 5
8	oxygen	2 6
9	fluorine	2 7
10	neon	2 8
11	sodium	2 8 1
12	magnesium	2 8 2
13	aluminum	2 8 3
14	silicon	2 8 4
15	phosphorus	2 8 5
16	sulfur	2 8 6
17	chlorine	2 8 7
18	argon	2 8 8
19	potassium	2 8 8 1
20	calcium	2 8 8 2

Table 15–3

Enrichment: You may want to introduce electron orbitals at this point and describe the electron arrangements of atoms with atomic numbers larger than 20.

The number of electrons in the electron cloud is different in each kind of atom. To describe any atom you must know its atomic number. The atomic number tells you how many protons are in the nucleus. It also tells you how many electrons are moving around the nucleus. The electrons fill the levels in order. The first level closest to the nucleus is filled first. Then the second level is filled. This goes on until all the electrons are used up. For example, a sodium atom with atomic number 11 has 11 electrons. Two of these electrons are found in the first level. Eight more are in the second level. The remaining one is found in the third level.

SYMBOLS OF ELEMENTS

Up until now, the name of each chemical element has been written out (hydrogen, helium, and so forth). For many years, chemists had to do the same thing. But the Swedish chemist Berzelius (1779–1848) knew that **symbols** are used in algebra

Symbol One or two letters used to represent an atom of a particular element.

SYMBOLS OF SOME COMMON ELEMENTS		
	Name	Symbol
These elements have one-letter symbols.	hydrogen	H
	boron	B
	carbon	C
	nitrogen	N
	oxygen	O
	fluorine	F
	phosphorus	P
	sulfur	S
	iodine	I
These elements have two-letter symbols.	helium	He
	lithium	Li
	beryllium	Be
	aluminum	Al
	silicon	Si
	calcium	Ca
	cobalt	Co
	nickel	Ni
	germanium	Ge
	bromine	Br
	barium	Ba
	magnesium	Mg
	chlorine	Cl
	zinc	Zn
These elements have symbols taken from their Latin names (in parentheses).	sodium (natrium)	Na
	potassium (kalium)	K
	copper (cuprum)	Cu
	gold (aurum)	Au
	silver (argentum)	Ag
	mercury (hydrargyrum)	Hg
	iron (ferrum)	Fe
	lead (plumbum)	Pb
	tin (stannum)	Sn

Table 15–4

and physics. A *symbol* is a form of shorthand. Berzelius suggested that scientists also use symbols for the chemical elements. These symbols consist of one or two letters of the element's name. For example, the symbol for hydrogen is H. The symbol for helium is He. When there are two letters in a symbol, the first letter is capitalized. The second letter is not.

The symbol for mercury is Hg. Does this surprise you? These letters are not part of the word "mercury." The reason is simple. Different languages have different words for mercury. Scientists decided to use the Latin name of the element. "Mercury" in Latin is *hydrargyrum.* Table 15–4 is a list of some common elements and their symbols. The names of newly discovered elements and their symbols are decided by an international committee of scientists.

Try to remember the symbols for these elements. Being able to use the symbols of the elements will make your work in science easier.

SUMMARY

The atomic nucleus is made up of protons and neutrons. The atomic number of an element gives the number of protons and electrons in an atom of that element. Electrons move in energy levels around the nucleus. Each level can hold only a certain number of electrons. Each kind of atom has its own electron arrangement and its own symbol.

QUESTIONS

Use complete sentences to write your answers.

1. Describe where electrons, protons, and neutrons are found in atoms.
2. What does the atomic number of an atom tell you about the number of particles in that atom?
3. Since atoms contain charged particles, how can an atom be neutral?
4. Describe Niels Bohr's model of the atom.
5. Magnesium normally has 12 electrons arranged in three levels. How many electrons are in each level?
6. Write the symbols for five elements and the number of electrons in each of their levels.

1. Electrons are found around the nucleus. Protons and neutrons are found in the nucleus.
2. The atomic number is the same as the total number of protons and electrons.
3. Atoms are usually neutral because they contain the same number of positive protons and negative electrons.
4. According to Bohr, electrons are found in orbits at definite distances from the central nucleus.
5. There are two electrons in the inner level, eight electrons in the next level, and two electrons in the outer level.
6. Answers will vary but should include the symbol of each element and the number of electrons in each level.

SKILL-BUILDING ACTIVITY

See teacher's commentary for teaching hints, safety, and answers to questions.

INFERRING THE STRUCTURE OF AN OBJECT

PURPOSE: You will use some simple tests to infer the structure of a hidden object in the same way that scientists use scientific models to describe atoms.

MATERIALS:

clay ball	paper
paper clip	pencil

PROCEDURE:

A. Use the paper clip as shown in Fig. 15–17 to find out if the clay ball has a hard object hidden in it. Push the probe into or through the clay only 10 times. Probe with care!

1. Is the clay ball the same all the way through or does it contain some kind of hard object?

B. If there is an object hidden in the clay, use the probe to find out as much as you can about the shape of the object.

2. What is the shape of the object?
3. How large is it?
4. Is the object in the middle of the clay ball? If not, where is it located?

C. After 10 probes, draw a sketch of your clay "atom" showing its structure. Show the position and shape of any object in the clay. Label this sketch "Model." Do not go on until you have done this step.

D. Now cut open the clay ball and see how accurate your model was.

5. Were you able to correctly infer the size and shape of the object?

Fig. 15–17

6. Make a sketch of the actual structure of the clay "atom." Label this sketch "Actual."

CONCLUSION:

1. In your own words, describe how you can infer something about an object you cannot observe directly.

EXTENSION: You will draw models of atomic energy levels for ten elements.

A. Using Fig. 15–16 as a guide, draw a model of the energy levels in an atom of sodium. Indicate the correct number of electrons in each level.

B. In the same way, draw models of the energy levels of the remaining elements listed in Table 15–3.

Reinforcement: Students may confuse the mass number (also called atomic weight) of an atom, which is obtained from a reference, with the number of neutrons, which is calculated from the atomic number and mass number.

15-3. Atomic Mass

At the end of this section you will be able to:

- Explain how to find the mass of an atom.
- Find the number of neutrons in an atom, using the *mass number* and the atomic number.
- Explain what is meant by an *isotope.*

All atoms of hydrogen have the same number of protons and electrons. However, they differ in mass as do the three cats shown in Fig. 15–18. How can they differ in mass? In this section you will find out.

Fig. 15–18 All three cats are identical except for their mass. Atoms of hydrogen can also have three different masses.

THE NUMBER OF PARTICLES IN A NUCLEUS

All atoms are made up of electrons, protons, and neutrons. The electrons are found in levels outside the nucleus. The protons and neutrons are found inside the nucleus. Except for the nucleus, an atom is mostly empty space. Most of the mass of an atom is thus made up of the protons and neutrons in the nucleus. The mass of all the electrons in an atom is so small that it can be ignored.

The mass of an oxygen atom depends on the number of protons and neutrons in its nucleus. Protons and neutrons each have a mass of one atomic mass unit (1 u). Look at the diagram of an oxygen atom in Fig. 15–19. Oxygen has eight protons and eight neutrons in its nucleus. Thus the mass of an oxygen atom is 16 u. The mass of an atom, in atomic mass units, is equal to the number of protons and neutrons.

8p
8n

Fig. 15–19 This Bohr model of an oxygen atom shows that oxygen has eight protons and eight neutrons in its nucleus. Oxygen has an atomic mass of 16 u.

If you know the number of protons and neutrons in a nucleus, you know the **mass number** of the atom. You can also use the *mass number* to find the number of neutrons in the nucleus. For example, you know that the atomic number of oxygen is 8. The atomic number tells you the number of protons. The mass of oxygen is 16 u. The mass number is the sum of the protons and neutrons. Thus you can find the number of neutrons in an oxygen nucleus as follows:

$$\begin{aligned} \text{mass number} - \text{atomic number} &= \text{neutrons} \\ (\text{protons} + \text{neutrons}) - (\text{protons}) &= \text{neutrons} \\ 16 - 8 &= 8 \end{aligned}$$

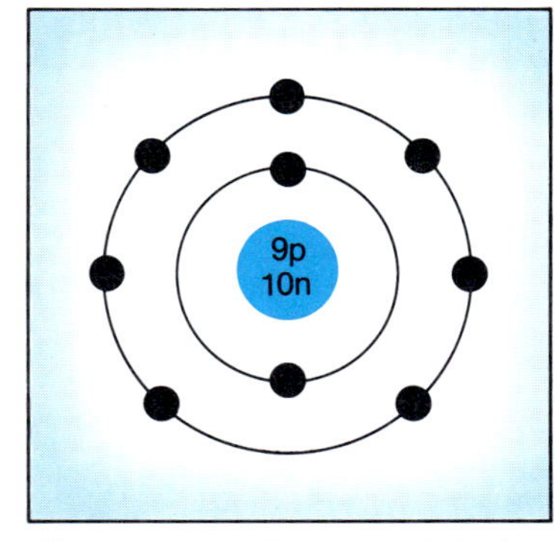

Fig. 15–20 A Bohr model of a fluorine atom. The atomic mass of fluorine is 19 u.

Mass number The sum of the protons and neutrons in the nucleus of a particular kind of atom.

Figure 15–20 shows an atom of fluorine. The atomic number of fluorine is 9. Its mass number is 19. Therefore, fluorine has 10 neutrons.

ISOTOPES

Scientists have found that not all atoms of an element have the same number of neutrons. A hydrogen atom, for example, may have any one of three arrangements in its nucleus. Most hydrogen atoms have only one proton in the nucleus and no neutrons. This is shown in Fig. 15–21 (a). Some hydrogen atoms have one proton and one neutron. This is shown in Fig. 15–21 (b). A very few hydrogen atoms have one proton and two neutrons in the nucleus. This is shown in Fig. 15–21 (c).

The element known as hydrogen is made up of atoms with all three types of nuclei. Each type produces an atom which

Fig. 15–21 The three isotopes of hydrogen. Hydrogen-1 has an atomic mass of 1 u. Hydrogen-2 has an atomic mass of 2 u. Hydrogen-3 has an atomic mass of 3 u.

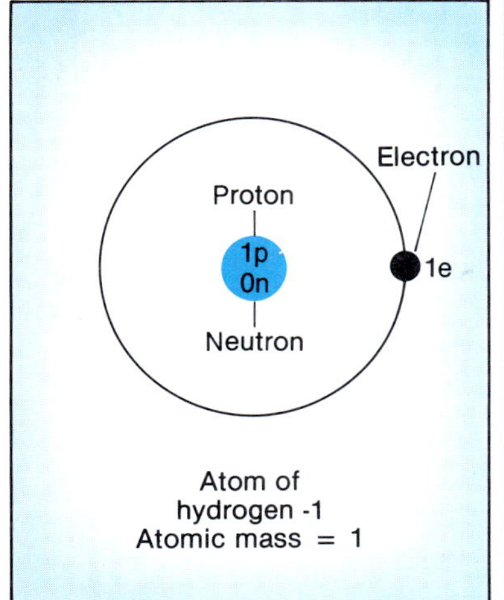

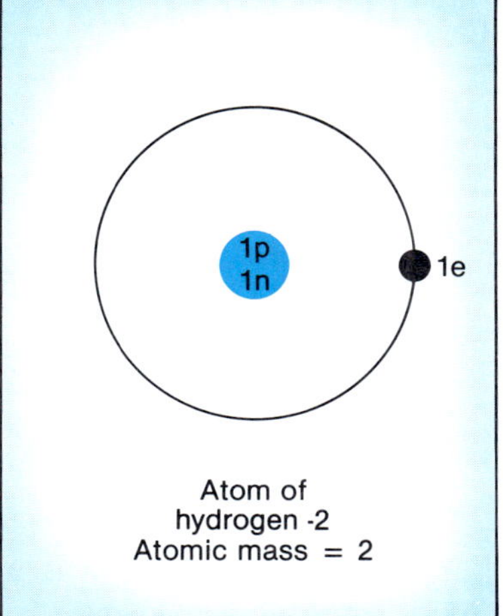

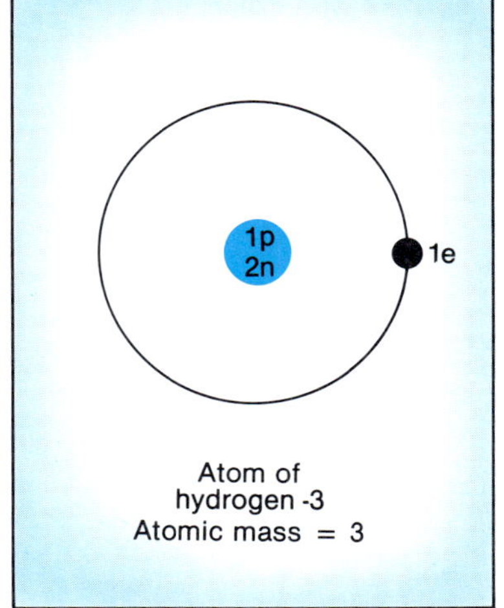

Isotopes Atoms whose nuclei contain the same number of protons but a different number of neutrons.

Atomic mass The average of all the masses of the isotopes of a particular element.

Enrichment: Challenge students to think of a way to measure equal numbers of different kinds of atoms. This is done by measuring amounts of the two elements whose weights are in the same relation as their mass numbers. For example, 1 g of hydrogen contains nearly the same number of atoms as 16 g of oxygen.

is an **isotope** of hydrogen. Hydrogen has three *isotopes:* hydrogen-1, hydrogen-2 *(deuterium),* and hydrogen 3 *(tritium).*

Because they have different numbers of neutrons, isotopes have different masses. Almost all elements have isotopes. For example, lithium exists as lithium-6 and lithium-7. The **atomic mass** of an element is the average of the masses of all the isotopes of that element as they are found in nature. For example, the *atomic mass* of lithium is found to be 6.94 u. This is the average mass of a mixture of the isotope of lithium with a mass of 6 u and the isotope of lithium with a mass of 7 u: $(6 + 7) \div 2 = 13 \div 2 = 6.94$.

The atomic mass of the mixture of lithium-6 and lithium-7 found in nature is 6.94. This is because 93 percent of all lithium atoms have a mass of 7. Only 7 percent have a mass of 6. The atomic mass of the mixture of hydrogen atoms found in nature is 1.008. Often, the atomic mass of an element is rounded off to the nearest whole number. This is equal to the mass number of the element. The number 6.94 can be rounded off to 7. Thus the mass number of lithium atoms is 7. The mass number of an atom is always equal to the sum of its protons and neutrons. For lithium, the mass number 7 = 3 protons + 4 neutrons.

SUMMARY

Most of the mass of an atom is found in the protons and neutrons in the nucleus. The atomic mass is the sum of protons and neutrons. Different atoms of the same element may have different numbers of neutrons in the nucleus. They are called isotopes of the element.

QUESTIONS

Use complete sentences to write your answers.

1. Which atomic particles account for most of the mass of an atom?
2. The atomic number of oxygen is 8 and its mass number is 16. How many neutrons are in the atom? Show how you got your answer.
3. Explain what is meant by an isotope of an atom.
4. Describe two atoms by giving their names and the number of each kind of atomic particle in each atom. Draw a diagram of each atom, labeling each part.

1. Most of the mass of an atom is determined by the total number of protons and neutrons.
2. There are eight neutrons in an oxygen atom. The number of neutrons is equal to the mass number (16) minus the atomic number (8).
3. An isotope of a particular element has the same number of protons but a different number of neutrons.
4. Answers will vary. Check diagrams and labels carefully.

TECHNOLOGY

HIGH ENERGY PHYSICS

Just as Einstein's physics and the theory of relativity changed the ideas we once had about the universe that were based on Isaac Newton's theory of gravity, so particle physics and the technologies developed to carry out its research have begun to change some of the views we have now. Particle physics suggests that the universe is made up of tiny particles of matter moving every which way instead of in consistent patterns. Particle physics also states that these particles can change from being matter to being energy and that, at any given time, we may not know which they are.

Where did these particles originally come from? To explain the origin of these bits of matter and how they work, scientists have been looking for a **G**rand **U**nifying **T**heory or Theories (called **GUT**s). Technologies that help to pinpoint the movement of particles help them to tell which of these GUTs is correct. Theories about how these seemingly different types of matter work often come before the necessary technology is available to prove the theory. To confirm theories, elementary particle physics had to wait for the development of accelerators, huge machines able to speed the collision of matter. With accelerators, scientists are able to see evidence of these collisions, even when they can't see the particles themselves. W and Z particles were discovered in 1983 by physicists of the European Organization for Nuclear Research through the use of one of these machines. That added two more to the list of the smallest bits of matter, which already included alpha, beta, and gamma particles as well as quarks.

The Tevatron is another such machine. Tevatron is the particle accelerator at the Fermi National Accelerator Laboratory outside Chicago. This device is *four miles* in circumference. Superconducting magnets, cooled to −450° F, guide protons and accelerate them to almost the speed of light. These particles are made to collide with other particles, producing the most violent collisions on earth. Because energy and matter are interchangeable, the energy of these collisions can be changed into new forms of matter.

To probe even more deeply into the secrets of nature and to attempt to confirm theories, scientists have proposed that the U.S. government finance a particle accelerator 20 to 40 times more powerful than Tevatron. This "Superconducting Super Collider" would be *120 miles* in circumference and would be the biggest machine ever built, taking ten years and almost two billion dollars to build.

Will this machine be the last word in the technology of physics? Will it prove or disprove all the theories being developed? Probably not. More work will have to be done on the tiny elements of particle physics with the current accelerators and even more amazing technologies will have to be developed to supply answers.

CHAPTER REVIEW

See teacher's commentary for answers.

VOCABULARY

On a separate piece of paper, match each term with the number of the statement that best explains it. Use each term only once.

atomic particles	atomic number	atomic mass	symbol
atomic mass unit	energy level	isotope	mass number
nucleus			

1. A region around an atomic nucleus in which electrons move.
2. The building blocks of atoms.
3. The central core of an atom containing protons and neutrons.
4. The number of protons in the nucleus of an atom.
5. One or two letters used to represent an atom of a particular element.
6. Atoms whose nuclei contain the same number of protons but a different number of neutrons.
7. Unit used to express the mass of atomic particles and atoms.
8. The sum of the protons and neutrons in an atom.
9. The average of the masses of all the isotopes of an element.

QUESTIONS

Give brief but complete answers to each of the following questions. Unless otherwise indicated, use complete sentences to write your answers.

1. Name three atomic particles and state their properties.
2. How do scientists use scientific models?
3. How can a wire fence be used as a model of an atom? How is this related to Ernest Rutherford's experiment with atoms?
4. For each of the following elements, state the atomic number, the number of protons in the nucleus, and the number of electrons around it: (a) hydrogen, (b) helium, (c) carbon, (d) neon, (e) aluminum.
5. How does Bohr's model of an atom differ from a solar system model of an atom?
6. What is the maximum number of electrons in the first, second, and third levels of an atom?
7. Aluminum has an atomic number of 13. How many protons are there in an aluminum atom? How many electrons? Show how you arrived at your answers.
8. Explain what determines the mass of an atom. How is it usually expressed?

9. Can the atoms of an element have different atomic masses? Give an example.
10. Copy and complete the following table:

Element	Atomic Number	Mass Number	Number of Protons	Number of Neutrons	Number of Electrons
Lithium	3	7			
Boron			5	6	
Carbon	6			6	
Neon		20		10	

11. Compare and contrast atomic mass and mass number.

APPLYING SCIENCE

1. Look at Table 15–4 on page 386 of your text. This table lists some common elements and their symbols. How many different elements do you come in contact with each day? Bring to class as many labels (or a list of products) as you can find in your home that list one or more elements as part of their contents. List these elements and their symbols. Find out the purpose of each.
2. Carbon-14 and hydrogen-2 (deuterium) are important isotopes. Write a report on at least five important isotopes, including their uses.
3. There are many subatomic particles in an atom. While it is a useful model, the atom is not simply made up of protons, neutrons, and electrons. Report on current research on subatomic particles. Draw a chart or diagram showing all the subatomic particles known.
4. Using Styrofoam spheres, build models that represent the following historical models of atoms: J. J. Thomson's, Ernest Rutherford's, and Niels Bohr's.

BIBLIOGRAPHY

Asimov, Isaac. *Asimov on Chemistry.* New York: Doubleday, 1974.

Asimov, Isaac. *How Did We Find Out About Atoms?* New York: Walker, 1976.

Trefil, James S. *From Atoms to Quarks.* New York: Scribners, 1982.

Trefil, James S. "They Just Don't Make Protons Like They Used To." *Science 80.* November 1980.

UNIT 5

PATTERNS IN MATTER

CHAPTER

16

Silicon is a metalloid. Integrated circuits are etched on thin slices of silicon to make a chip. Chips are used in computers and other electronic devices such as calculators.

FAMILIES OF ATOMS

CHAPTER GOALS

1. Explain what happens when energy is added to an atom.
2. Use the periodic table of elements to describe a chemical family.
3. Compare the properties of metals and nonmetals.

16-1. Atoms and Energy

At the end of this section you will be able to:

- ☐ Describe what happens to the electrons in an atom when the atom absorbs and then releases energy.
- ☐ Distinguish between an atom and an *ion.*
- ☐ Explain what a noble gas is.

When fireworks explode, they produce beautiful colored lights in the sky. Suppose you could trace each ray of colored light back to its source. You would find that the light comes from atoms that are releasing energy. In this section, you will find out how an atom can release energy.

ATOMS ABSORB AND RELEASE ENERGY

Many cities glow at night from the light of electric signs. One common type of sign is made of thin glass tubes filled with gas. When an electric current passes through the gas, the gas gives off colored light. The atoms of gas produce this light. How do atoms change electric energy into light energy? You can answer this question with the help of a model of an atom. See Fig. 16–1.

Ordinarily, electrons move about the nucleus of an atom without gaining or losing energy. However, what happens if energy in some form is gained from outside the atom? For example, an electric current passing through a gas adds energy to the gas atoms. The added energy causes an electron in each atom to move farther away from the nucleus. This happens because the added energy overcomes the attractive force between the positive nucleus and the negative electron. This allows one or more electrons to jump into an energy level

Fig. 16–1 When an electric current passes through the gas in these tubes, electrons in the gas atoms become excited. The electrons then release the added energy as light.

farther from the nucleus. Usually the outer electrons of an atom make these jumps. Adding energy to an electron, causing it to move away from the nucleus, makes that electron **excited.** The atom is then *unstable.* An *excited* electron will then fall back into its original level or another level closer to the nucleus. The electron falls back because the positive charge on the nucleus always pulls electrons toward it. When an excited electron moves back toward the nucleus, it releases the extra energy it gained. See Fig. 16–2. This energy is generally given off in the form of light. In exploding fireworks, for example, light is produced by chemical changes in the atoms. As a result, energy is absorbed and then released.

Excited electron An electron that has absorbed energy and moved farther away from the atomic nucleus.

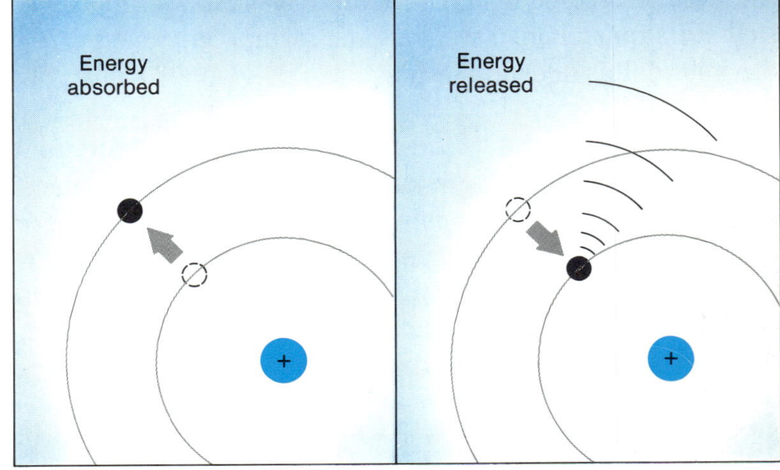

Fig. 16–2 An excited electron absorbs energy and jumps to a higher energy level. When it drops back to a lower level, it releases the added energy.

TYPES OF SPECTRA

If electricity passes through a gas inside a glass tube, as in electric signs, visible light is given off. See Fig. 16–3. The light is made up of certain frequencies or colors. By passing this light through a *spectroscope,* each separate color or frequency appears as a single bright line. For example, hydrogen produces red-orange, blue-green, blue-violet, and violet lines. This arrangement of light frequencies is always produced by glowing hydrogen gas. The atoms of each chemical element produce a distinctive arrangement of lines. This arrangement is called the *spectrum* of the element. Each kind of atom always produces the same spectrum when it gives off light. By observing the spectrum of a star, astronomers can tell what elements are present in the star. The spectrum also shows other conditions in the star.

Enrichment: Have spectrum tubes with several gases set up for students to look at directly and through diffraction gratings.

Word study: The plural of spectrum is spectra.

There are several different kinds of spectra. See Fig. 16–4. A *continuous spectrum* contains all the colors of the rainbow. A rainbow is the most common example of this spectrum. A glowing solid, liquid, or gas under high pressure produces a continuous spectrum. A *bright-line spectrum* results when energy is added to a gas under low pressure. Electrons in the gas atoms are excited and move to higher energy levels. Then, as the electrons fall back to their normal levels, they release light energy. Each kind of atom gives off a particular color of light. When light passes through a cool gas, the gas absorbs the colors that are normally given off when the gas atoms release energy. In this way, a *dark-line* spectrum is formed.

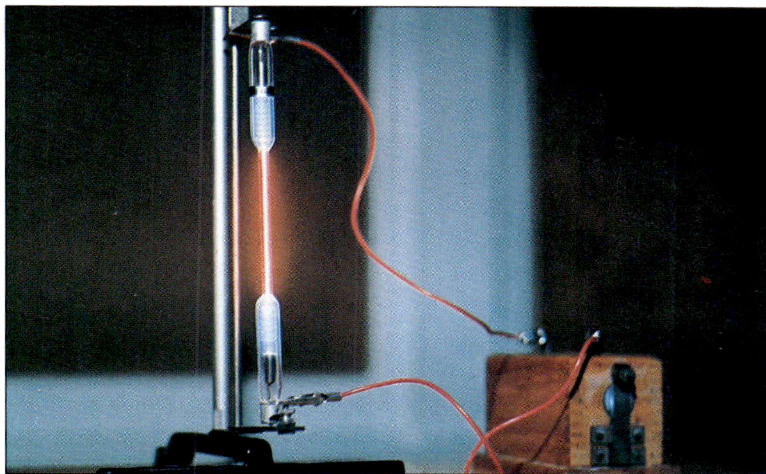

Fig. 16–3 Each kind of gas gives off light of a particular color when an electric current passes through it.

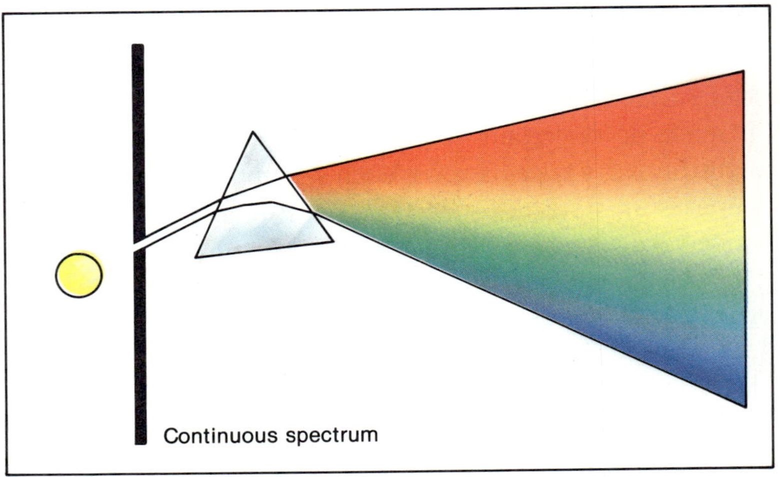

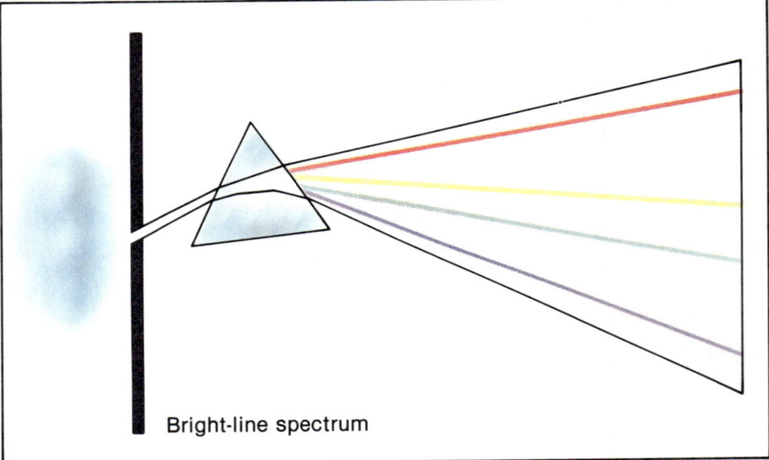

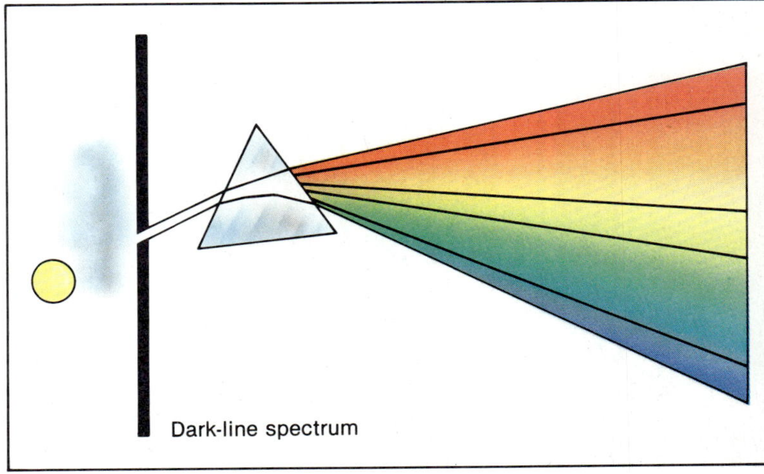

Fig. 16–4 A continuous spectrum (top), a bright-line spectrum (middle), and a dark-line spectrum (bottom).

ATOMS LOSE AND GAIN ELECTRONS

When an atom absorbs a large amount of energy some of its electrons move far away from the nucleus. The energy may be enough to overcome completely the attraction of the positive nucleus for the negative electrons. Then one or more electrons may escape from the atom. When that happens, the number of electrons no longer equals the number of protons in the atom. Normally, the number of electrons moving about the nucleus is the same as the number of protons in the nucleus. The positive and negative charges cancel each other and the atom is electrically neutral.

When an atom loses electrons, it is left with more protons than electrons. An atom with extra protons is a positively charged **ion.** An *ion* is an atom or molecule that has an electric charge. It is also possible for an atom to gain electrons. An atom that gains electrons will have more electrons than protons. The extra electrons give the atom a negative charge. The atom is then a negative ion.

Ion An atom or molecule with an electric charge.

Ions are made in a machine that produces a beam of moving electrons. See Fig. 16–5. The beam of electrons hits a group of target atoms. The electrons in the beam collide with electrons in the outer levels of the target atoms. These collisions knock electrons away from the atom. This loss of electrons changes the neutral atoms into positively charged ions. Ions are also found in nature. For example, the high temperatures that exist in the interiors of stars provide enough energy to ionize the atoms.

Fig. 16–5 This machine fires beams of charged particles at target atoms.

NOBLE GASES

Scientists can measure how hard an electron has to strike an atom in order to change it into an ion. Then they can determine how much energy is needed to remove an electron from the outer level of an atom. These amounts of energy, ranging from hydrogen (atomic number 1) to calcium (atomic number 20), form a pattern. This pattern is shown in the graph in Fig. 16–6. The graph shows that the atoms of the elements helium, neon, and argon need the highest amounts of energy to remove electrons.

Skill: Students should be able to *classify* atoms that are noble gases by studying this graph.

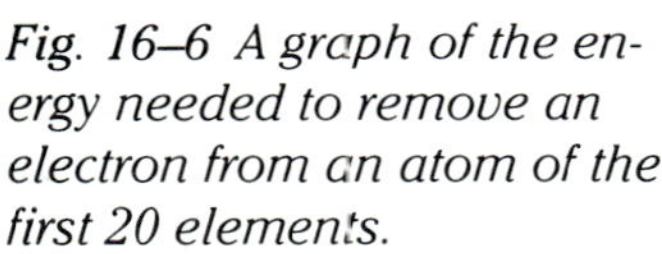

Fig. 16–6 A graph of the energy needed to remove an electron from an atom of the first 20 elements.

Helium, neon, and argon atoms have a tighter hold on their electrons than other atoms. Helium (atomic number 2) has a total of two electrons. Neon has 10 electrons and argon has 18 electrons. Is there something special about the number of electrons in an atom? Remember how many electrons fill each energy level around the nucleus of an atom? The first level is full with two electrons. The second and third levels each fill with eight electrons. Thus helium has all of its electrons in one completely filled level. Neon, with 10 electrons, has filled the first and second levels (2 + 8). Argon, with 18 electrons, has its first, second, and third levels filled (2 + 8 + 8). See Fig. 16–7.

Stable electron arrangement An arrangement in which all of an atom's energy levels are filled.

Noble gases The six elements whose atoms have filled energy levels.

Atoms that have completely filled energy levels do not easily lose electrons. The electron arrangement is **stable.** An atom with a *stable* electron arrangement does not tend to gain or lose electrons since all its energy levels are completely filled. The elements with stable atoms are all gases called the **noble gases.** Experiments have shown that there are a total of six *noble gases* among all the elements. In addition to helium,

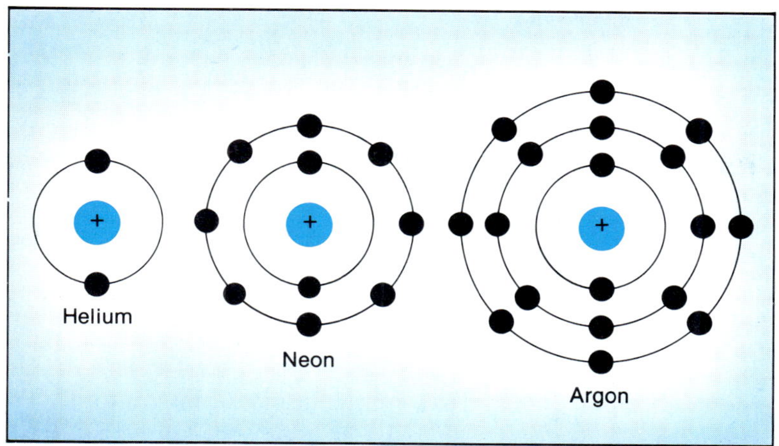

Fig. 16–7 Bohr models showing the electron arrangement in atoms of helium, neon, and argon.

neon, and argon, the other noble gases are krypton, xenon, and radon. Krypton has 36 electrons, xenon has 54 electrons, and radon has 86 electrons. These numbers of electrons completely fill the energy levels of krypton, xenon, and radon.

SUMMARY

When energy is added to an atom, the electrons move to new energy levels. The excited electrons then fall back toward the nucleus and release the extra energy. Electrons can absorb enough energy to escape the atom completely and change the atom into an electrically charged ion. The atoms of noble gases have stable electron arrangements.

QUESTIONS

Use complete sentences to write your answers.

1. What happens to the electrons in a mercury atom when the atom absorbs electric energy?
2. Describe what happens in a mercury atom when it gives up the energy it has absorbed.
3. Compare and contrast what happens to an atom when it becomes a positive ion and when it becomes a negative ion.
4. How are astronomers able to learn about the composition of stars that are far away from the earth?
5. Explain what is meant by a noble gas. Name three noble gases.

1. When a mercury atom absorbs electric energy, one or more electrons move farther from the nucleus.
2. When a mercury atom gives up energy it has absorbed, one or more electrons move back to their original positions, closer to the nucleus.
3. When an atom loses one or more electrons, the atom becomes a positive ion. When an atom gains one or more electrons, the atom becomes a negative ion.
4. By observing the spectrum of light from a distant star, astronomers can tell what elements are present in the star.
5. Elements with stable electron arrangements do not tend to gain or lose electrons and are called noble gases. The nobel gases are helium, neon, argon, krypton, xenon, and radon.

SKILL-BUILDING ACTIVITY

See teacher's commentary for teaching hints, safety, and answers to questions.

CLASSIFYING ELEMENTS

PURPOSE: You will find patterns in the structure of the elements.

MATERIALS:

element cards pencil paper

PROCEDURE:

A. Obtain the set of nine element cards. Each of the nine cards represents a different element. On the front of the card is the name of the element. Below the element's name is the number of electrons in each energy level. See Fig. 16–8 (a). On the back of each card is a description of the element. See Fig. 16–8 (b).

B. Begin with card 1. Read the description of argon on the back of the card.

C. Look at Fig. 16–9. Find the characteristics that describe argon. Follow the arrows. The last box in Fig. 16–9 contains the name of the family of elements to which argon belongs.

D. Write the name of this family in your notebook. List argon under this heading.

E. Follow steps B through D for cards 2 through 9.

1. How many families did you find?
2. What are the names of these families?
3. Which elements are found in each of the families?

F. Now look at the front of each card. Beside the name of each element, write the number of electrons in its outer energy level.

CONCLUSIONS:

1. Describe any pattern you find in the number of outer electrons.
2. Which family has stable elements?

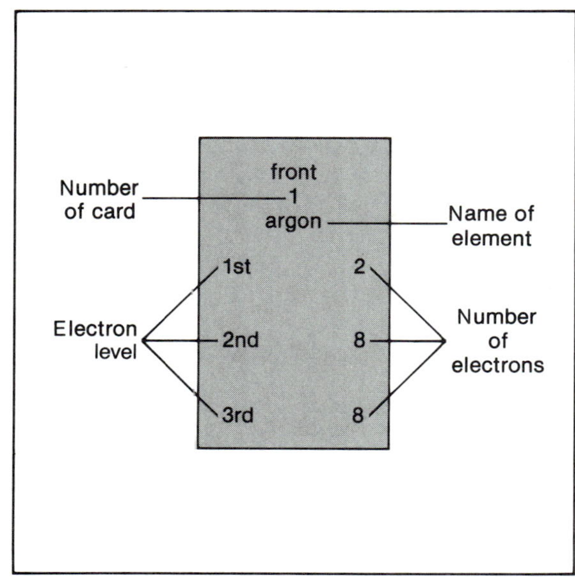

Fig. 16–8 (a)

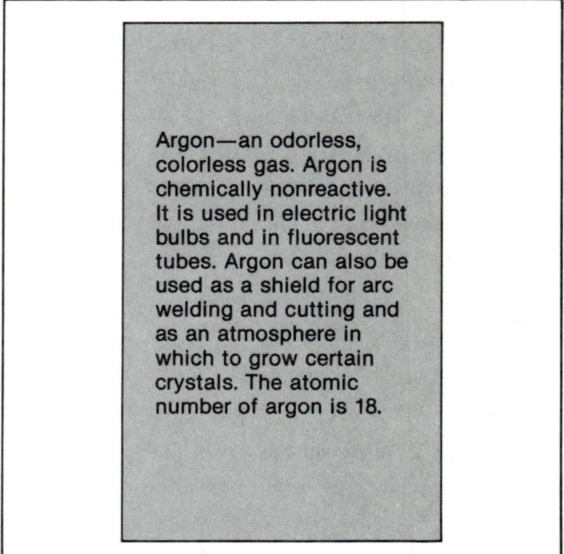

Fig. 16-8 (b)

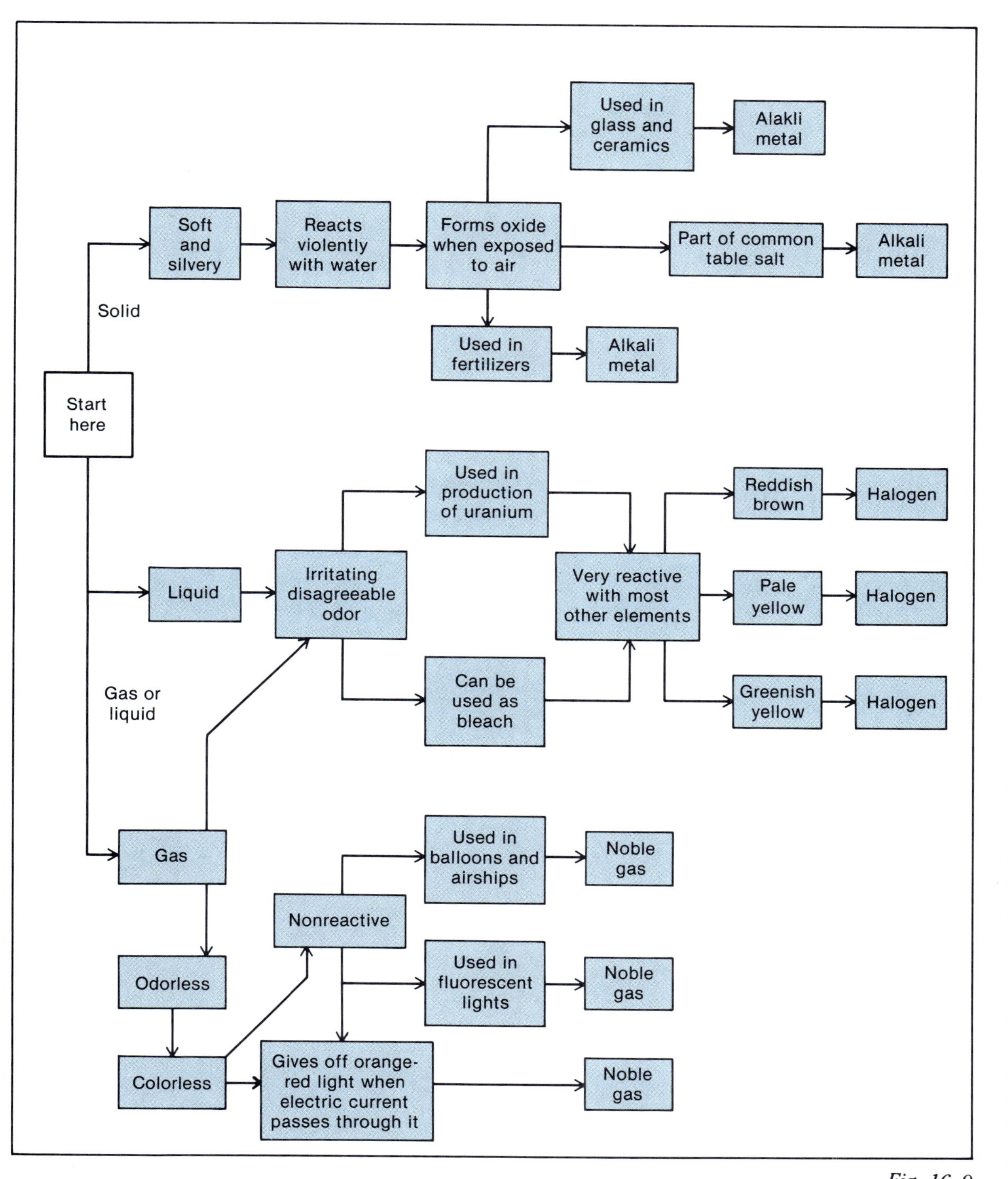

Start here
Solid
Soft and silvery
Reacts violently with water
Forms oxide when exposed to air
Used in glass and ceramics
Alakli metal
Part of common table salt
Alkali metal
Used in fertilizers
Alkali metal
Liquid
Gas or liquid
Irritating disagreeable odor
Used in production of uranium
Can be used as bleach
Very reactive with most other elements
Reddish brown
Halogen
Pale yellow
Halogen
Greenish yellow
Halogen
Gas
Odorless
Colorless
Nonreactive
Used in balloons and airships
Noble gas
Used in fluorescent lights
Noble gas
Gives off orange-red light when electric current passes through it
Noble gas

Fig. 16–9

16-2. Atoms and Chemical Activity

At the end of this section you will be able to:

- ☐ Relate the *chemical activity* of an atom to the number of electrons in its outer energy level.
- ☐ Explain why certain elements can be grouped together into a *chemical family*.
- ☐ Using the *periodic chart*, predict the characteristics of a missing member of two chemical families.

The gas used in a laboratory burner can be dangerous. It is poisonous to breathe and it can cause an explosion if it mixes with the air in a room. The airship shown in Fig. 16–10 is filled with helium gas. Helium is not poisonous and cannot cause explosions because it does not burn. It is safe to use in large amounts in airships. In this section you will learn why helium is not a dangerous gas.

Fig. 16–10 Helium, which is lighter than air and does not burn, is used in all modern airships such as this blimp.

CHEMICAL ACTIVITY

At one time, hydrogen gas was commonly used to fill airships. Hydrogen gas is lighter than air. In order to stay in the air, an airship must be filled with a gas that is lighter than air. The airship then floats in the air in the same way that a piece of wood floats in water. But hydrogen is a dangerous gas. Like the gas used in laboratory burners, hydrogen can burn when mixed with oxygen. Some airships using hydrogen were destroyed when the hydrogen exploded. See Fig. 16–11. Helium is a much safer gas to use in airships. Like hydrogen, helium is also much lighter than air. However, helium does not burn because it does not combine with oxygen. In fact, helium will not take part in any chemical changes. Helium atoms exist separately. They are never part of a molecule. Why is it that helium does not take part in chemical changes?

Fig. 16–11 The dirigible Hindenberg *was the largest airship ever built. It was filled with hydrogen gas. In 1937, it exploded and crashed, probably because a spark ignited the hydrogen.*

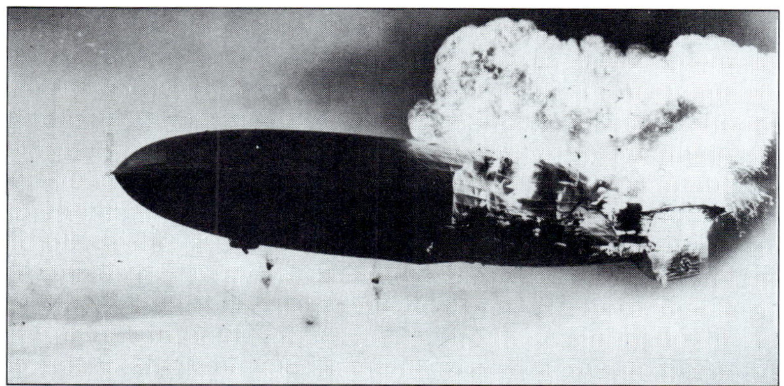

Fig. 16–12 Both hydrogen and helium have only one energy level. Why then is hydrogen more chemically active than helium?

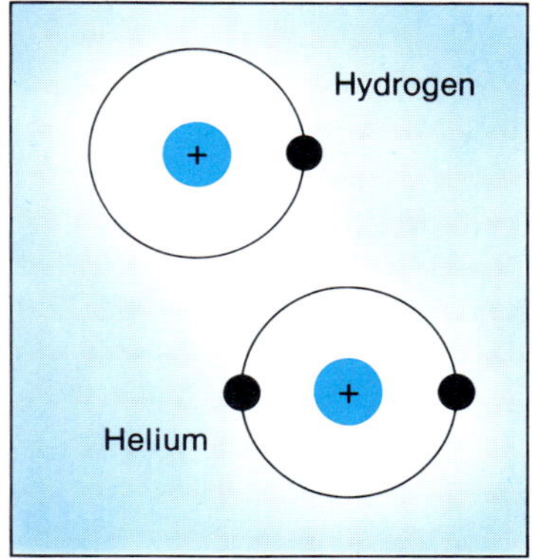

Hydrogen and helium are the only two elements that have only a single energy level. See Fig. 16–12. This level can hold only two electrons. Helium already has two electrons. Therefore, helium has a completely filled level. It does not join with other atoms to form molecules. Hydrogen has only one electron. It needs one more electron to fill the energy level. Therefore, unlike helium, hydrogen reacts with many other atoms to form molecules. The way an atom reacts with atoms of other elements is called its **chemical activity.** Hydrogen, which reacts readily with other elements, is *chemically active.* Helium, which does not react with other elements, is not chemically active. This is the reason helium is called a "noble" gas. It is **inert.** It does not associate with common elements. In nature, all of the noble gases are *inert.*

Chemical activity Describes the way in which an atom reacts with other atoms.

Inert A description of an atom that does not react in nature with other atoms.

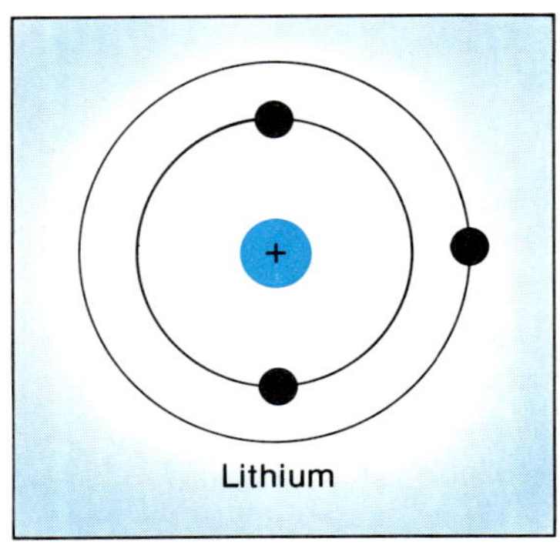

Fig. 16–13 Lithium has three electrons: two in its first energy level and one in its second. Lithium tends to lose the one outer electron.

CHEMICALLY ACTIVE ATOMS

Is it possible that hydrogen and helium behave so differently because of the different number of electrons in their outer energy levels? If this is true, then atoms with the same number of outer electrons should be alike. In the previous section, you learned that atoms with a stable number of electrons do not easily lose or gain electrons. On the other hand, if an atom has one, two, or three electrons *less* than a stable number, it will tend to *add* electrons until a stable number is reached. If an atom has one, two, or three electrons *more* than a stable number, it will tend to *lose* electrons until a stable number is reached. For example, think about a lithium atom. The atomic number of lithium is 3. Therefore, a lithium atom has three electrons. There are two electrons in the first energy level and one electron in the second level. See Fig. 16–13. Thus lithium has one *more* electron than the stable number of two. Lithium will tend to *lose* that one electron to reach the stable number of two. Table 16–1 lists five other elements that can also be expected to lose one electron. This group of elements is called the **alkali** (**al**-kuh-lie) **metals.**

Alkali metals A group of elements whose atoms all have one electron more than the stable number.

THE ALKALI METALS		
Atoms that lose 1 electron easily	Atomic number	Stable electron number after losing 1 electron
lithium	3	2
sodium	11	10
potassium	19	18
rubidium	37	36
cesium	55	54
francium	87	86

Table 16–1

The property of some elements to lose electrons can be used to make an electrochemical cell called a *voltaic cell.* This cell is named after Alessandro Volta, an Italian physicist. In 1798, Volta showed that an electric current could be made by using two different metals. See Fig. 16–14. You can make a simple voltaic cell with strips of zinc and copper, and an ordinary lemon. Make two small cuts in the lemon about 1 cm apart. Push a strip of zinc and a strip of copper into the lemon.

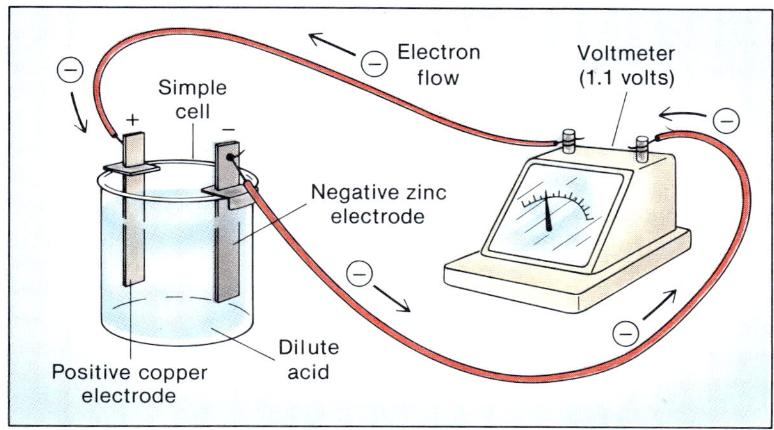

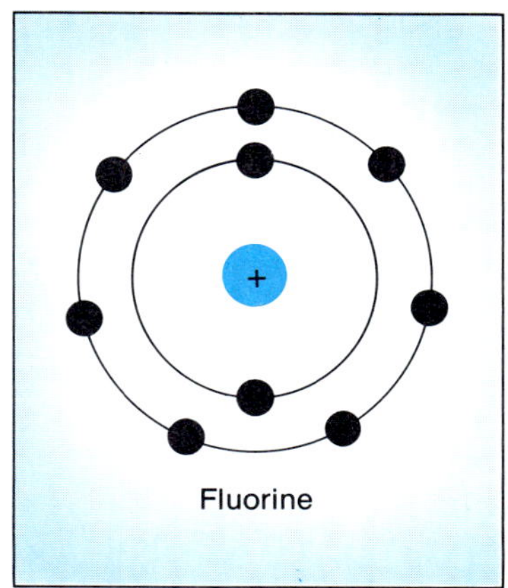

Fig. 16–14 In this electrochemical cell, zinc transfers electrons to copper, causing an electric current to flow.

Fig. 16–15 Fluorine has nine electrons: two in its first energy level and seven in its second. Fluorine tends to add one electron to its outer level.

Connect the zinc and copper strips with a wire. The zinc atoms will lose electrons, which will travel through the wire. Thus an electric current flows through the wire. A dry cell is also a kind of voltaic cell.

Now think about a fluorine atom. The atomic number of fluorine is 9. Therefore, fluorine has a total of nine electrons. As shown in Fig. 16–15, fluorine has two electrons in its first level and seven electrons in its outer level. Fluorine thus has one electron *less* than a stable number of eight in its outer level. Fluorine must *add* one electron to have a stable electron arrangement. Table 16–2 lists four other elements that will gain one electron to become stable. These elements are called the **halogens** (**hal**-uh-juns). Elements like the *alkali metals* and the *halogens* that lose or gain electrons readily are chemically active. In other words they take part readily in chemical changes.

THE HALOGENS		
Atoms that gain 1 electron easily	Atomic number	Stable electron number after gaining 1 electron
fluorine	9	10
chlorine	17	18
bromine	35	36
iodine	53	54
astatine	85	86

Table 16–2

Word study: Halogens from *halo* (Gr.), salt, and *genes* (Gr.), producing.

Halogens A group of elements whose atoms all have one electron less than the stable number.

SOME USES OF NOBLE GASES

The noble gases have filled energy levels and do not gain or lose electrons easily. Thus the noble gases do not readily take part in chemical changes. Although the noble gases are not found in great quantities in nature, their lack of chemical activity makes them very useful. The most abundant noble gas is argon. Argon makes up about one percent of the air. Part of the gas in an ordinary light bulb is argon. The argon in the bulb helps to slow the rate at which the hot wire evaporates. This prevents the inside of the bulb from turning black, so the light bulb stays bright as it is used. Another noble gas, neon, is used in advertising signs. It gives off a bright red light when a high-voltage electric current is passed through it. Different colors are made by mixing neon with other gases. For example, a mixture of neon and helium gives off a yellow color. As you have already seen, helium is used to fill airships and balloons. It is also used in certain kinds of welding. As the weld is made, the helium gas surrounds the hot metal and prevents other gases in the air from reacting with the metal. Deep-sea divers often breathe a mixture of helium and oxygen instead of air. The reason is that when the divers breathe air under high pressure, the nitrogen in the air dissolves in the blood. It can be harmful if the divers return to the surface too quickly. See Fig. 16–16.

Fig. 16–16 If divers return to the surface from a deep dive too quickly, they may suffer from the "bends" as a result of nitrogen gas bubbles forming in the bloodstream. A decompression chamber lowers the pressure gradually to avoid this problem.

CHEMICAL FAMILIES

You probably know members of the same family who look somewhat alike and share the same name. Sometimes these family members even behave alike. Atoms also belong to families. The characteristics of the atoms of an element determine the family to which the element belongs.

Scientists have now identified more than 100 different elements. Additional elements may be discovered in the future. Do you think scientists can easily keep track of such a large number of elements? How would you organize a list of all the different elements? One way to organize a large number of different things is to put them in alphabetical order. For example, your teacher probably keeps an alphabetical list of all the students in your class.

Enrichment: There is some disagreement over the naming of several of the artificial elements, for example, elements 104 and 105. An international meeting of scientists is held every few years to try to resolve such controversies.

In the last section, you learned that some groups of atoms have the same outer electron arrangements. The atoms in one group all have one outer electron. They are called the alkali metals. The members of the alkali metals have similar chemical properties. In another group, the atoms lack one electron in their outer levels. They make up the halogens. The halogens also have similar chemical properties. The noble gases belong to a family whose outer energy levels are completely filled. In nature, all the noble gases are chemically inert. The general name for a group of elements with similar chemical properties is **chemical family.** The alkali metals, halogens, and noble gases are each examples of a *chemical family.*

Chemical family A group of elements that are very similar in their chemical behavior.

THE PERIODIC CHART

As scientists discovered more elements, they began to search for ways to organize these elements. One way to do this was by chemical families.

Skill: Students will find the *classifying* of elements in the periodic chart a valuable tool when they are able to read, understand, and interpret the chart.

During the early 1800's, scientists discovered that each element belongs to a chemical family. They listed the elements in order of their increasing atomic masses. When they did this, the scientists discovered that certain physical and chemical properties were repeated at regular intervals. In other words, elements with similar properties occurred *periodically* in the list the way the days of the week (Sunday, Monday, Tuesday, and so on), occur periodically throughout a calendar month.

Word study: *Periodic* means to repeat at regular intervals.

Fig. 16–17 Dmitri Mendeleev (1834–1907) devised a periodic chart of the elements.

In 1869, a Russian chemist, Dmitri Mendeleev (duh-**meet**-tree men-dl-**ay**-uf), tried to arrange the elements in another way. See Fig. 16–17. He also arranged the elements in the order of their increasing atomic masses. Instead of listing them one after the other, however, he laid them out in rows. The chart in Fig. 16–18 shows what he did.

Mendeleev listed the known elements in a table, or chart. In Mendeleev's chart, the elements were listed in the order of increasing atomic mass. In this order, certain chemical properties were repeated. For example, the elements lithium (Li), sodium (Na), and potassium (K) are next to each other in Fig. 16–18. These three elements belong to the chemical family of alkali metals. Just above these elements are fluorine (F), chlorine (Cl), and bromine (Br). These three elements belong to the chemical family of halogens.

Mendeleev discovered that when he arranged all the elements in a table like this, elements in the same chemical family were found next to each other. Elements in each family are found at particular periods or places when you put them in order. Mendeleev's chart is called the **periodic chart** of the elements.

Periodic chart An arrangement of all the elements, showing chemical families.

			Ti = 50	Zr = 90	? = 180
			V = 51	Nb = 94	Ta = 182
			Cr = 52	Mo = 96	W = 186
			Mn = 55	Rh = 104,4	Pt = 197,4
			Fe = 56	Rn = 104,4	Ir = 198
			Ni = Co = 59	Pd = 106,6	Os = 199
H = 1			Cu = 63,4	Ag = 108	Hg = 200
	Be = 9,4	Mg = 24	Zn = 65,2	Cd = 112	Au = 197?
	B = 11	Al = 27,4	? = 68	Ur = 116	Bi = 210?
	C = 12	Si = 28	? = 70	Sn = 118	Tl = 204
	N = 14	P = 31	As = 75	Sb = 122	Pb = 207
	O = 16	S = 32	Se = 79,4	Te = 128?	
	F = 19	Cl = 35,5	Br = 80	J = 127	
Li = 7	Na = 23	K = 39	Rb = 85,4	Cs = 133	
		Ca = 40	Sr = 87,6	Ba = 137	
		? = 45	Ce = 92		
		?Er = 56	La = 94		
		?Yt = 60	Di = 95		
		?In = 75,6	Th = 118?		

Fig. 16–18 Mendeleev's original periodic chart. He used it to predict the properties of elements that had not yet been discovered.

Modern *periodic charts* are slightly different from the original one made by Mendeleev. In a modern periodic chart, the elements are arranged in order of their increasing atomic numbers and outer energy levels. This causes only small changes from Mendeleev's original arrangement according to atomic mass. Each element in a modern periodic chart is found in a separate box. See Fig. 16–19. The symbol for the element is given in the middle of the box. Above the symbol is the atomic number of the element. Below is the atomic mass. Some periodic charts also show the electron arrangement for an atom of each element. Other information about the properties of the element may be included within the box.

In the periodic chart shown in Fig. 16–19, some of the atomic masses are printed in brackets. This indicates the isotope with the longest known half-life.

USING THE PERIODIC CHART

A street map is helpful if you have to find your way around an unfamiliar city. In the same way, a periodic chart is useful in learning about the chemical elements. Each vertical column of the chart lists elements with similar properties. For example, the noble gases are found in a single column at the right side. Next to the noble gases is the column containing the halogens. The alkali metals are found in a single column at the far left of the chart. All the columns between the right and left sides of the chart list elements with some similarities. The two long rows at the bottom contain elements that would all fit in the third column of the chart. They are placed here to avoid making a very long, single column. Hydrogen is usually put alone at the top of the chart since it resembles both the alkali metals and the halogens. Each horizontal row of the chart is called a *period.* Elements in a period have their chemical activity in the same outer energy level. Within each row or period, the properties of the elements generally repeat periodically. Each row begins with an alkali metal and ends with a noble gas. The elements in the rows between the alkali metals and the noble gases change from metals to nonmetals from left to right across the row. This pattern is repeated periodically within each row. The fourth row contains elements that are unlike any in the above rows. This is the reason for the gap in the top rows of the chart.

Periodic Table of the Elements

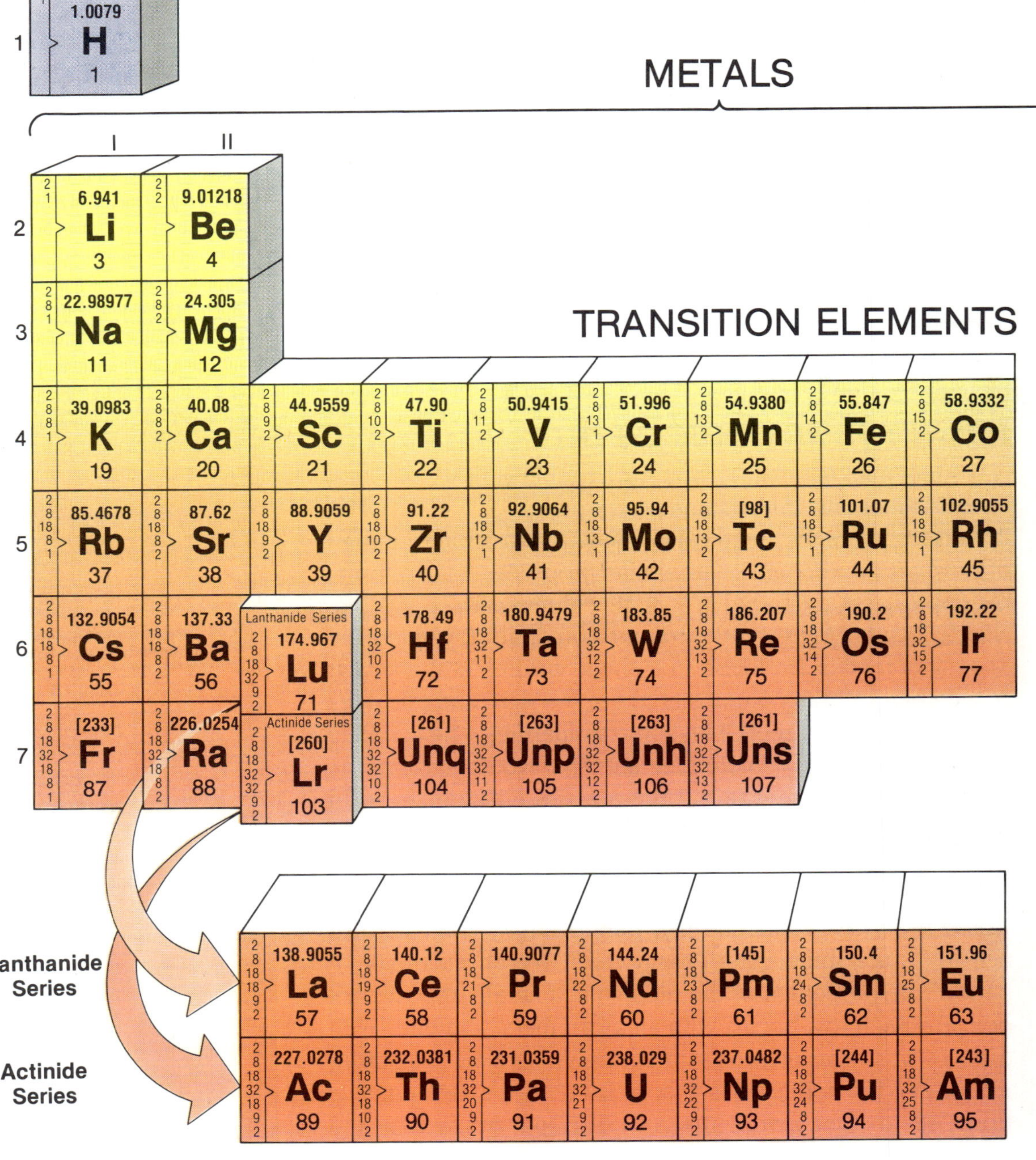

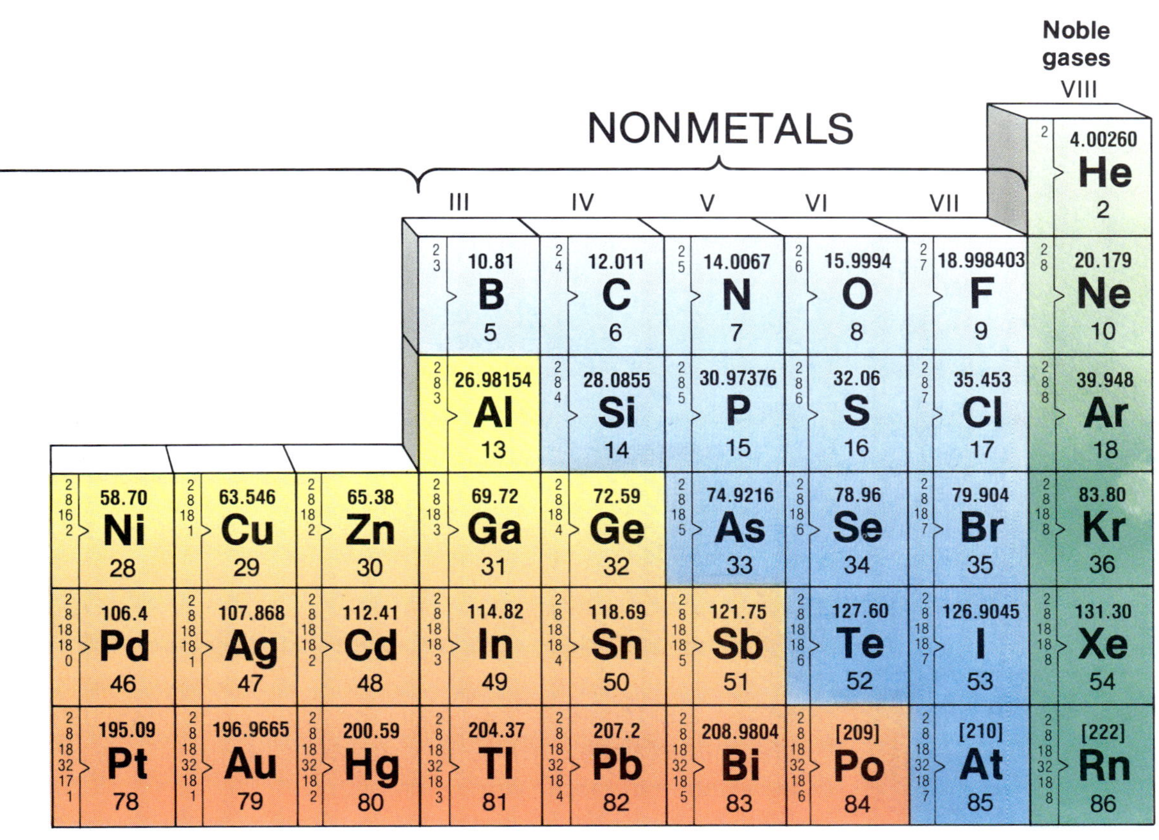

NONMETALS

			III	IV	V	VI	VII	Noble gases VIII
								4.00260 **He** 2 (2)
			10.81 **B** 5 (2,3)	12.011 **C** 6 (2,4)	14.0067 **N** 7 (2,5)	15.9994 **O** 8 (2,6)	18.998403 **F** 9 (2,7)	20.179 **Ne** 10 (2,8)
			26.98154 **Al** 13 (2,8,3)	28.0855 **Si** 14 (2,8,4)	30.97376 **P** 15 (2,8,5)	32.06 **S** 16 (2,8,6)	35.453 **Cl** 17 (2,8,7)	39.948 **Ar** 18 (2,8,8)
58.70 **Ni** 28 (2,8,16,2)	63.546 **Cu** 29 (2,8,18,1)	65.38 **Zn** 30 (2,8,18,2)	69.72 **Ga** 31 (2,8,18,3)	72.59 **Ge** 32 (2,8,18,4)	74.9216 **As** 33 (2,8,18,5)	78.96 **Se** 34 (2,8,18,6)	79.904 **Br** 35 (2,8,18,7)	83.80 **Kr** 36 (2,8,18,8)
106.4 **Pd** 46 (2,8,18,18,0)	107.868 **Ag** 47 (2,8,18,18,1)	112.41 **Cd** 48 (2,8,18,18,2)	114.82 **In** 49 (2,8,18,18,3)	118.69 **Sn** 50 (2,8,18,18,4)	121.75 **Sb** 51 (2,8,18,18,5)	127.60 **Te** 52 (2,8,18,18,6)	126.9045 **I** 53 (2,8,18,18,7)	131.30 **Xe** 54 (2,8,18,18,8)
195.09 **Pt** 78 (2,8,18,32,17,1)	196.9665 **Au** 79 (2,8,18,32,18,1)	200.59 **Hg** 80 (2,8,18,32,18,2)	204.37 **Tl** 81 (2,8,18,32,18,3)	207.2 **Pb** 82 (2,8,18,32,18,4)	208.9804 **Bi** 83 (2,8,18,32,18,5)	[209] **Po** 84 (2,8,18,32,18,6)	[210] **At** 85 (2,8,18,32,18,7)	[222] **Rn** 86 (2,8,18,32,18,8)

RARE EARTH ELEMENTS

157.25 **Gd** 64 (2,8,18,25,9,2)	158.9254 **Tb** 65 (2,8,18,27,8,2)	162.50 **Dy** 66 (2,8,18,28,8,2)	164.9304 **Ho** 67 (2,8,18,29,8,2)	167.26 **Er** 68 (2,8,18,30,8,2)	168.9342 **Tm** 69 (2,8,18,31,8,2)	173.04 **Yb** 70 (2,8,18,32,8,2)
[247] **Cm** 96 (2,8,18,32,25,9,2)	[247] **Bk** 97 (2,8,18,32,26,9,2)	[251] **Cf** 98 (2,8,18,32,28,8,2)	[254] **Es** 99 (2,8,18,32,29,8,2)	[257] **Fm** 100 (2,8,18,32,30,8,2)	[258] **Md** 101 (2,8,18,32,31,8,2)	[259] **No** 102 (2,8,18,32,32,8,2)

A value given in brackets denotes the mass number of the isotope of longest known half-life.

Fig. 16–19

Enrichment: Mendeleev's original periodic chart contained 66 elements. He left blank positions on the chart for those elements that should appear there but had not yet been discovered. Mendeleev was able to predict the properties of germanium, gallium, and scandium accurately.

Mendeleev discovered a valuable tool for scientific research. Each element has its own position on a periodic chart. Thus, if you know the chemical properties of two or three elements, you can predict the properties of a neighboring element. You can even predict the chemical behavior of elements not yet discovered. Mendeleev himself predicted the general properties of several elements that had not yet been discovered. In many cases, when the elements were discovered, they were found to behave almost exactly as Mendeleev had predicted. Next to silicon in Mendeleev's chart is a question mark. No element existed to fill this place. Mendeleev predicted that an element he called "ekasilicon" would be discovered. He said it would have properties similar to silicon. Later, germanium was discovered. Its properties were close to those predicted for ekasilicon by Mendeleev.

SUMMARY

Unstable atoms tend to gain or lose electrons by reacting chemically with other elements. Atoms with the same number of electrons in their outer energy levels have similar characteristics and belong to the same chemical family. In the periodic chart of the elements, the members of a chemical family are found in the same vertical column.

QUESTIONS

Use complete sentences to write your answers.

1. Use the table below to answer the questions that follow.

Atom	A	B	C	D	E	F
Number of outer electrons	7	1	1	7	3	8

   (a) Which atoms are chemically active? (b) Which atoms are not chemically active? (c) Which atom belongs to the same chemical family as atom A? Explain.

2. Explain the three items in each box of the periodic table in Fig. 16–19.
3. State two characteristics of an element that belongs to the same chemical family as (a) lithium or (b) chlorine.

1. (a) A, B, C, D, E. (b) F. (c) D. Both atoms A and D have seven outer electrons.
2. The first number is the atomic number of the element and tells the number of protons in the nucleus of the atom. The letters are the chemical symbol of the element. The third item is the atomic mass of the element and is equal to the sum of the protons and neutrons in the atom.
3. (a) An element in the same family as lithium would lose one electron easily and would react with the same elements as lithium. (b) An element in the same family as chlorine would gain one electron and would react with the same elements as chlorine.

INVESTIGATION

See teacher's commentary for teaching hints, safety, and answers to questions.

VOLTAIC CELL

PURPOSE: You will make a voltaic cell using the metals copper and zinc.

MATERIALS:

zinc plate (approx. 2 cm square)
mixture of ammonium chloride and manganese dioxide paste
copper penny
sandpaper or steel wool
plastic spatula
2 electrical wire leads
flashlight bulb

PROCEDURE:

A. Clean the zinc plate and the penny with sandpaper, if necessary. The mixture of ammonium chloride and manganese dioxide is in the form of a black paste.

B. Use the spatula to coat the piece of zinc with a thin layer of the ammonium chloride-manganese dioxide mixture.

C. Put the penny on top of the paste. See Fig. 16–20. Make sure the penny is only in contact with the paste. The penny and the zinc should not touch each other. The paste prevents electrons from flowing directly from the zinc to the copper.

D. Attach one piece of wire to the zinc and one to the copper penny. You will connect these wires to the light bulb.

1. Why do you think the light bulb is included in the circuit?

E. Fasten one wire to each terminal of the flashlight bulb.

2. What happens to the light bulb when the wires are attached?
3. What does this demonstrate?

F. Draw a diagram of your circuit. Label each part. Draw arrows to indicate the direction of flow of the electrons. Indicate what happens to the light bulb when electrons flow through it.

G. Set up the same circuit using two pieces of copper instead of the copper-zinc combination.

4. Does the bulb light?

CONCLUSIONS:

1. How many metals are necessary in a voltaic cell? Why?
2. Write a paragraph describing how to set up a voltaic cell using zinc and copper.

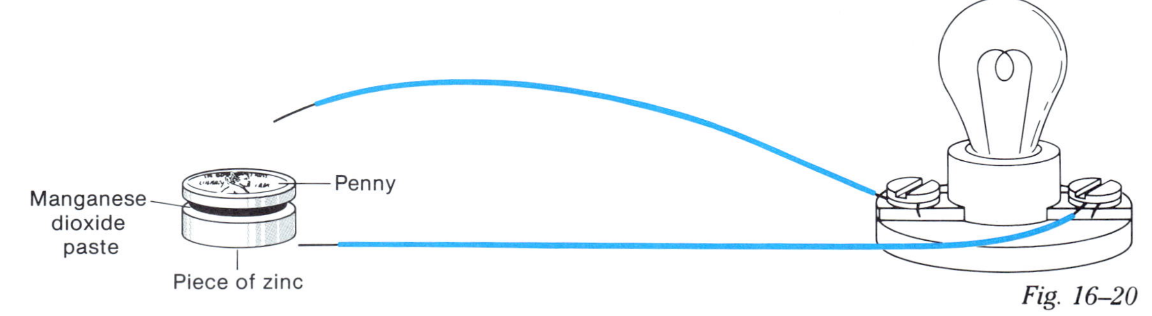

Fig. 16–20

16-3. Metals and Nonmetals

At the end of this section you will be able to:

- List some important properties of all metals.
- Explain what is meant by an *alloy*.
- Describe the difference between a nonmetal and a *metalloid*.

Look at the samples of chemical elements on the shelves of your chemistry storeroom. You will probably find that most of the elements are metals. In this section you will find that most of the elements in nature are also metals.

METALS ON THE PERIODIC CHART

Skill: In this lesson, elements are *classified* as metals, nonmetals, or metalloids.

Look at the periodic chart on pages 414 and 415. You will see a zigzag line near the right side of the chart. This line separates all the elements that are metals from those that are nonmetals. All the elements on the upper right side of this line are nonmetals. Only one element that is not ordinarily considered a metal is found on the left side of the chart. That element is hydrogen. All others on the left of the dividing line are metals. As you can see, about four-fifths of all the elements are metals.

Fig. 16–21 Because steel is malleable, *it can be heated and rolled into thin sheets or other shapes.*

All metals are alike in some important ways. First, they tend to be good conductors of both electricity and heat. Second, they often can be made into different shapes by applying pressure. See Fig. 16–21. Aluminum, for example, can be rolled into very thin foil without breaking. Third, most metals also appear shiny. This shine is called a metallic *luster.* Some metals, such as aluminum and silver, have a white, silvery luster. Other metals, such as gold and copper, have a yellowish luster. However, metals often have a coating that hides their luster. For example, iron is often covered with rust and silver can become tarnished.

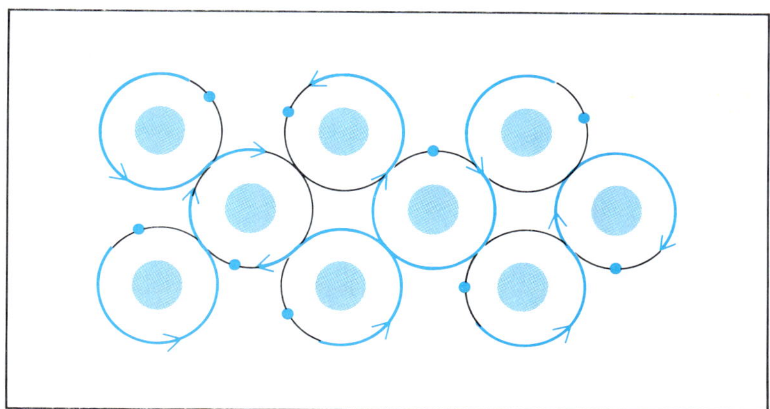

Fig. 16–22 As in all metals, the electrons in gold atoms are free to move among neighboring atoms.

METALLIC ATOMS

Similarity of properties suggests a similarity of structure in the atoms of metals. Close examination of metal atoms shows that the similarity is in the outer level. All metal atoms tend to lose electrons easily. Each atom of gold, for example, has only one outer electron. In a piece of solid gold, each atom does not hold its single outer electron very tightly. As a result, these electrons move freely between the neighboring atoms. See Fig. 16–22. Gold atoms are held together by the freely moving electrons. This is called a *metallic bond.* Atoms held together by a metallic bond are like marbles stuck together with honey. The individual atoms can move around each other, but they are still held together. Because of metallic bonds, metals usually do not break when they are bent. Metal atoms can slide past each other without separating. See Fig. 16–23. This is why most metals can be hammered or made into various shapes without shattering.

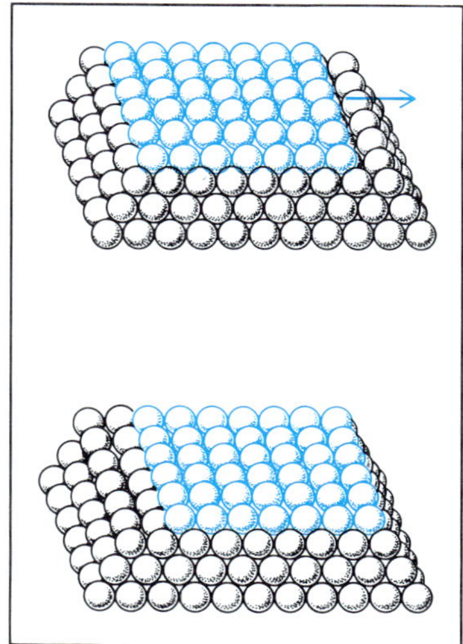

Fig. 16–23 Layers of metal atoms can slide over each other. This is why metals are malleable.

Fig. 16–24 The free electrons in a metal can conduct an electric current. This is why metals are good conductors of electricity.

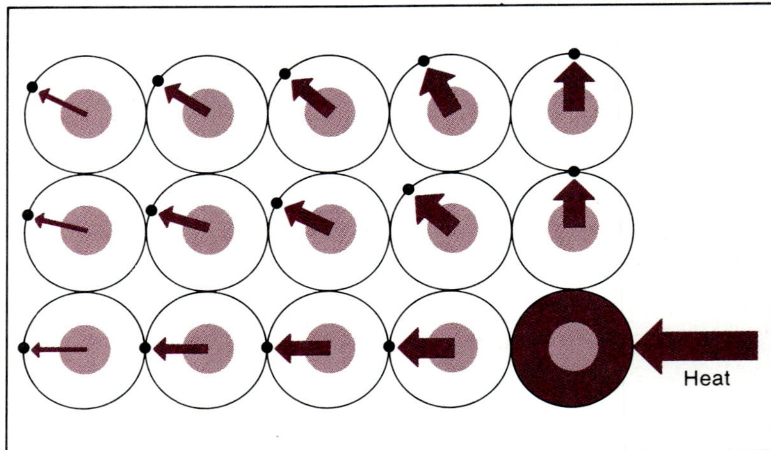

Fig. 16–25 Free electrons transfer heat quickly through metal. This is why metals are good conductors of heat.

The loosely held electrons in metal atoms also explains their ability to conduct heat and electricity. Free electrons drift between the metal atoms. This cloud of moving electrons conducts an electric current through the metal as shown in Fig. 16–24. The same free electrons also conduct heat. As heat is applied to one part of a metal, the free electrons move more rapidly. These electrons move the heat energy quickly through the metal. See Fig. 16–25.

Metals look shiny because their outer electrons absorb light energy. This added energy causes the electrons to vibrate back and forth. Like any moving electric charge, the vibrating electrons give off electromagnetic energy in the form of light. Because of this the metal surface seems to reflect light and looks shiny. See Fig. 16–26.

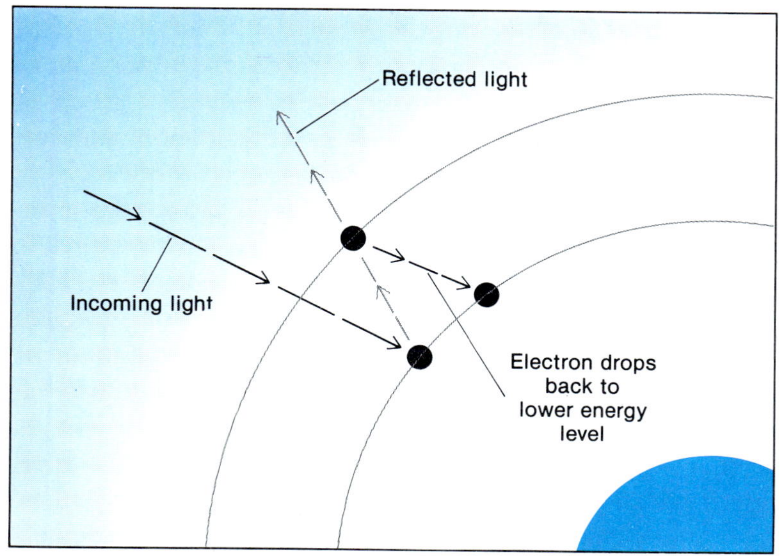

Fig. 16–26 Metals have a shiny luster because their electrons absorb and release energy in the form of light.

CORROSION

Word study: Corrosion from *corrodere* (L.), to gnaw to pieces.

Because metal atoms lose electrons easily, metals take part in many kinds of chemical changes. For example, when iron is exposed to oxygen, rust usually forms. Rusting is one of the most common examples of **corrosion** (kuh-**roe**-zhun). *Corrosion* is the eating away of the surface of a metal by chemical action. Water usually causes corrosion to take place more quickly than it would under dry conditions. A coating such as paint can protect a metal from corrosion. Some metals, such as aluminum and zinc, have a thin protective layer on their surfaces. This protective layer is formed when the metals combine with oxygen.

Corrosion The eating away of the surface of a metal by chemical action.

ALLOYS

Different metals can usually be combined to make **alloys.** An *alloy* is a mixture of two or more metals. For example, bronze is an alloy of copper and tin. Alloys are usually made by melting the metals together. The metals then stay mixed together when they are cooled. The mixture of metals depends upon the properties needed in the particular alloy. For example, chromium can be added to iron to prevent rust. Bronze is harder, and lasts longer, than either of the metals copper or tin. Table 16–3 lists a few common alloys and the metals from which they are made.

Alloy A mixture of two or more metals.

THE COMPOSITION OF SOME COMMON ALLOYS	
Alloys	**Metals**
alnico magnets	aluminum, nickel, cobalt, iron, copper
brass	copper, zinc
bronze	copper, tin
gold (14 carat)	gold, copper, silver
solder	lead, tin

Table 16–3

NONMETALS

Unlike metals, nonmetals do not have many properties in common. The fact that chemists refer to them as a group as *nonmetals* points to one thing they have in common: They are not metals!

Except for some forms of carbon and silicon, nonmetals are poor conductors of heat and electricity. Most nonmetals are brittle and cannot easily be formed into sheets or other shapes. Some nonmetals, such as carbon and sulfur, are solids at ordinary temperatures. Oxygen, nitrogen, and chlorine, on the other hand, are nonmetals that are gases. Bromine is the only nonmetal that is a liquid at room temperature.

Metals usually look alike. Nonmetals, however, can be colorless like oxygen and nitrogen gas, or yellow like solid sulfur. You can see that in studying the nonmetals it is difficult to find many common properties.

Nitrogen and phosphorus are two nonmetallic elements that are very important to living things. Plants require compounds of both of these elements in order to grow. Chemical compounds containing nitrogen and phosphorus are two of the three most important ingredients in fertilizers used in farming. If farmers did not use these chemical fertilizers, much less food could be grown on the world's croplands. Nitrogen and phosphorus are also essential to humans. The proteins that are essential in our diet are compounds containing nitrogen. Phosphorus compounds are needed for normal bone growth as well as for other body processes.

Fig. 16–27 Iron (Fe) is a metal, silicon (Si) is a metalloid, and sulfur (S) is a nonmetal. The photos show crystals of iron oxide (Fe_2O_3), silicon dioxide (SiO_2), and sulfur in calcite ($CaCO_3$).

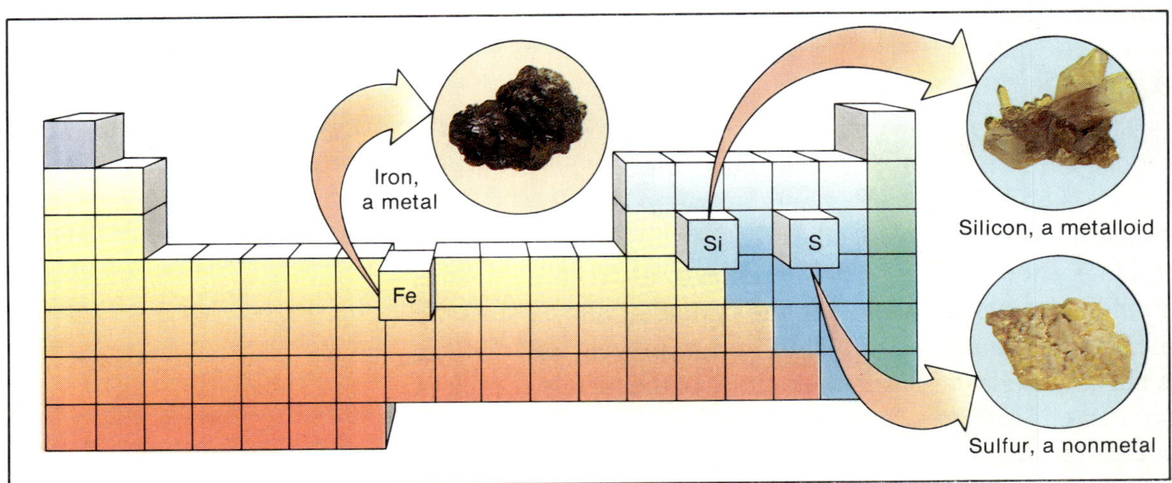

METALLOIDS

The substances called **metalloids** (**met**-l-oidz) have some of the characteristics of metals. For example, silicon is a *metalloid* that makes up about 26 percent by weight of the compounds in the earth's crust. Pure silicon crystals are electrical insulators. However, when small amounts of certain other elements such as arsenic are added to pure silicon, it becomes a *semiconductor.* A semiconductor is a substance that is normally an electrical insulator but can behave like a metal and conduct a current under some conditions. Specially prepared silicon crystals act as semiconductors in many common electronic devices, such as radios and television sets. Another metalloid, germanium, can also be used as a semiconductor. Other metalloids such as boron, arsenic, antimony, tellurium, and polonium also have some properties of both metals and nonmetals. Fig. 16–27 shows the positions of the metals, the nonmetals, and the metalloids in the periodic chart.

Metalloid An element with some properties of both metals and nonmetals.

Word study: Metalloid from *metal eidos* (Gr.), metal form.

SUMMARY

Most of the elements in the periodic chart are metals. The properties of metals are caused by a few outer electrons that are able to move freely among neighboring atoms. Elements such as silicon, oxygen, and sulfur are nonmetals. Almost the only thing nonmetals have in common is that they are not metals. Metalloids have some properties of both metals and nonmetals.

QUESTIONS

Use complete sentences to write your answers.

1. List three important properties of all metals.
2. What is a metallic bond? How does the metallic bond affect the properties of metals?
3. Name three nonmetals and explain how they differ from metals.
4. Why is carbon called a metalloid?
5. Classify each of the following elements as a metal or a nonmetal and give one practical use for it: oxygen, carbon, nitrogen, copper, lead, sulfur, silver.

1. Any three of the following properties: conducts electricity, can be bent, has luster, ductility, few valence electrons, forms bonds by losing electrons.
2. A metallic bond is one in which electrons are free to move between all neighboring atoms. This gives metals their conductivity and allows them to be bent.
3. Oxygen, sulfur, and phosphorus are examples of nonmetals. Nonmetals do not look like or behave like metals. They have no properties in common.
4. Carbon has some properties of metals (it conducts electricity) but not other properties (it cannot be bent).
5. Oxygen: nonmetal, air (20%); carbon: nonmetal, batteries; nitrogen: nonmetal, air (80%); copper: metal, electric wires; lead: metal, solder; sulfur: nonmetal, matches; silver: metal, jewelry.

INVESTIGATION

See teacher's commentary for teaching hints, safety, and answers to questions.

PROPERTIES OF METALS AND NONMETALS

PURPOSE: You will test several different elements to determine whether they are metals or nonmetals.

MATERIALS:

carbon	hammer
lead	anvil
copper	light bulb
sulfur	battery
aluminum	wires with clips

PROCEDURE:

A. Copy the table below in your notebook.

B. Test each of the elements listed in the table to determine if it has the properties of a metal. Remember, *all* of the properties listed in the table must be present if the element is a metal. Use a hammer and anvil to test if the element can be bent into a different shape by pressure. CAUTION: Wear safety goggles.

C. To test for electrical conduction, set up an electric circuit like the one shown in Fig. 16–28. A metal will conduct an electric current. The bulb will light.

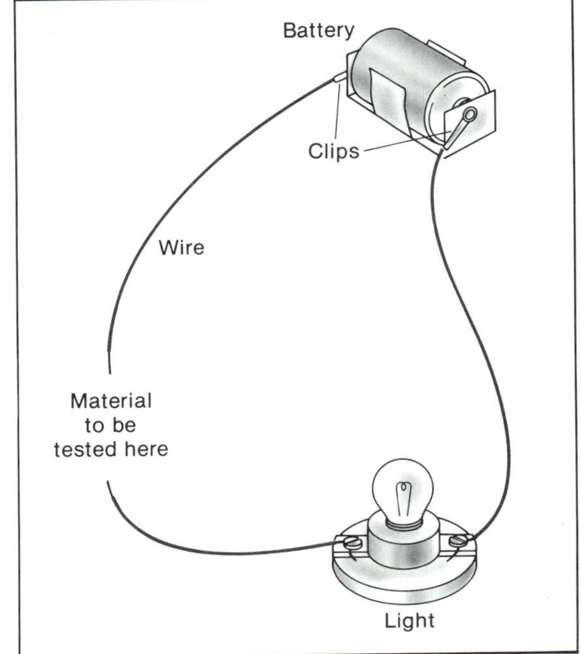

Fig. 16–28

D. Observe if the element is shiny to determine whether it has a metallic luster.

CONCLUSIONS:

1. Which of the elements in the table are metals?
2. Which of the elements are nonmetals?

	Shaped by hammering		Electric conductor		Luster	
Element	Yes	No	Yes	No	Yes	No
Carbon		X	X			X
Lead	X		X		X	
Copper	X		X		X	
Sulfur		X		X		X
Aluminum	X		X		X	

TECHNOLOGY

A NEW VIEW OF THE UNIVERSE

In November 1983, at a NASA press conference, a small group of British, Dutch, and American astronomers described to the world a view of the universe no one had ever seen before. This view was made possible by a small satellite that contained a telescope that could "see" the universe in the infrared portion of the electromagnetic spectrum.

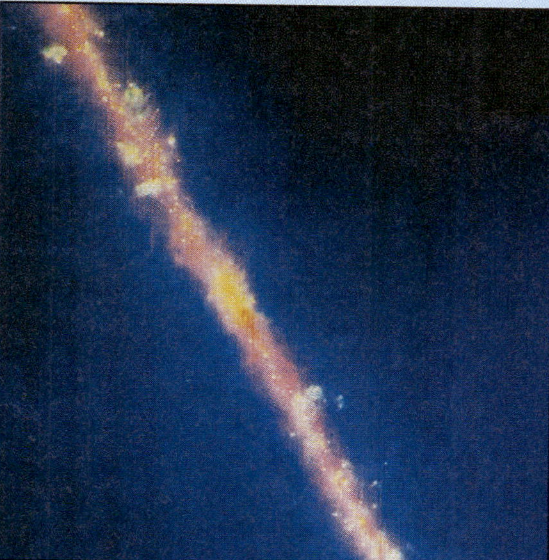

Infrared is that portion of the spectrum we call heat. Every object in the universe emits some infrared radiation (heat), even those with temperatures that may be very close to absolute zero (−273°C). Until the launching of **IRAS**, the Infrared Astronomy Satellite, astronomers were limited to studying the universe in other wavelengths. This is because the human eye is insensitive to infrared, and also because the water vapor in the atmosphere blocks out most of these wavelengths.

IRAS has been described as a "giant thermos bottle of liquid helium" that surrounds a telescope 45 cm in diameter. IRAS was designed to gather data about the universe using infrared or heat sensors. But the satellite itself produced heat in doing its work. Space engineers had to find a way to keep the satellites cool so that the only heat recorded was outside its shell. The liquid helium cooled the telescope so that it did not receive or record its own heat.

Infrared radiation was focused on 62 solid-state chips. These chips were sensitive to four wavelengths of infrared equivalent to between 0°C and −253°C. When stars, planets, and asteroids are being formed, they give off heat in that range of temperatures. When IRAS sensed a heat source, the chips in the satellite produced electrical signals that were received by a radio telescope in Chilton, England. This data was then transmitted to the Jet Propulsion Laboratory in California. The JPL computers sorted, interpreted, and translated this data into visual images. One of these images appears in the photo, which shows a view of the very center of Earth's galaxy.

The list of IRAS discoveries is impressive: five new comets, an asteroid that may be the remains of a comet, streams of dust clouds, stars in the process of forming, 50 stars that appear to have rings of material around them that may become planets, and galaxies that give off so much infrared that they may be forming new stars at remarkable rates.

IRAS passed over Chilton twice each day and transmitted 350 million bits of information for almost eleven months. After that length of time, the liquid helium warmed to a gaseous state and vaporized. IRAS could no longer remain cool enough to work, but so much data was transmitted that it will take years before it can be translated and absorbed! As one NASA scientist said, "A lot of astronomy books will have to be rewritten when all the results are in."

CHAPTER REVIEW

See teacher's commentary for answers to questions.

VOCABULARY

On a separate piece of paper, match each term with the number of the statement that best explains it. Use each term only once.

alkali metals	ion	chemical activity	inert
chemical family	alloy	stable electron	periodic chart
corrosion	metalloid	noble gases	excited electron
halogens			

1. Atoms with one electron less than a stable number.
2. An atom or a molecule with an electric charge.
3. Atoms with one electron more than a stable number.
4. Eating away of the surface of metal by chemical action.
5. Any group of elements that are similar in their chemical behavior.
6. A mixture of two or more metals.
7. Describes an atom that does not usually react with other atoms.
8. Has properties of metals and nonmetals.
9. Arrangement of all elements by atomic number and chemical families.
10. An electron that has absorbed energy and moved farther away from the atomic nucleus.
11. An arrangement in which all of an atom's energy levels are filled.
12. The way in which an atom reacts with other kinds of atoms.
13. The six elements whose atoms have filled energy levels.

QUESTIONS

Give brief but complete answers to each of the following questions. Unless otherwise indicated, use complete sentences to write your answers.

1. How does an electron become excited? What happens to an excited electron?
2. How does an excited electron in an atom give up its extra energy?
3. What is a dark-line spectrum? How is it made?
4. Distinguish between a positive ion and a negative ion.
5. Hydrogen and helium are both lighter than air. Which gas do you think is used in toy balloons? Why?
6. What determines the chemical activity of an element?
7. List the names and chemical symbols of the elements whose atomic numbers are 3, 11, 19, 37, 55, and 87. How are they related?
8. How are the alkali metals and halogens similar and how are they different?

9. State three properties that all metals have but nonmetals do not.
10. How does a metalloid differ from a metal and a nonmetal?
11. What kind of elements are used in making semiconductors? What are semiconductors used for?
12. How do neon signs produce light?
13. Where in the periodic chart are the alkali metals, the halogens, and the noble gases found?
14. What is a metallic bond? Why is it important in determining some of the characteristics of metals?

APPLYING SCIENCE

1. Ozone, O_3, is an isotope of oxygen. It is made up of three oxygen atoms. Find out about the importance of ozone in the atmosphere and report to the class.
2. Use a diffraction grating to study the light given off by mercury vapor street lights, sodium vapor street lights, and neon advertising signs. How many colors are present in the spectrum of each kind of light? Why are various kinds of street lights used?
3. Diamonds (carbon) and sand (silicon dioxide) are both composed of molecules. But unlike most molecular substances, diamonds and sand require extremely high temperatures in order to melt them. How many outer electrons do carbon and silicon have? What kind of bonding exists in these two substances? Why are such high temperatures needed to melt these substances?

BIBLIOGRAPHY

Asimov, Isaac. *Building Blocks of the Universe.* New York: Harper, 1974.

Boraiko, Allen. "The Chip: Electronic Mini-Marvel." *National Geographic,* October 1982.

Coombs, Charles. *Gold and Other Precious Metals.* New York: Morrow, 1981.

Planet Earth Series, *Noble Metals.* Morristown, NJ: Silver Burdett, 1983.

Ley, Willy. *The Discovery of the Elements.* New York: Delacorte.

Lightman, Alan. "The Loss of the Proton." *Science 82,* September 1982.

Trefil, J. S. *From Atoms to Quarks.* New York: Scribners, 1982.

Webb, Michael. *The Magic of Neon: The Rebirth of Light.* Layton, UT: Peregrine Smith, 1983.

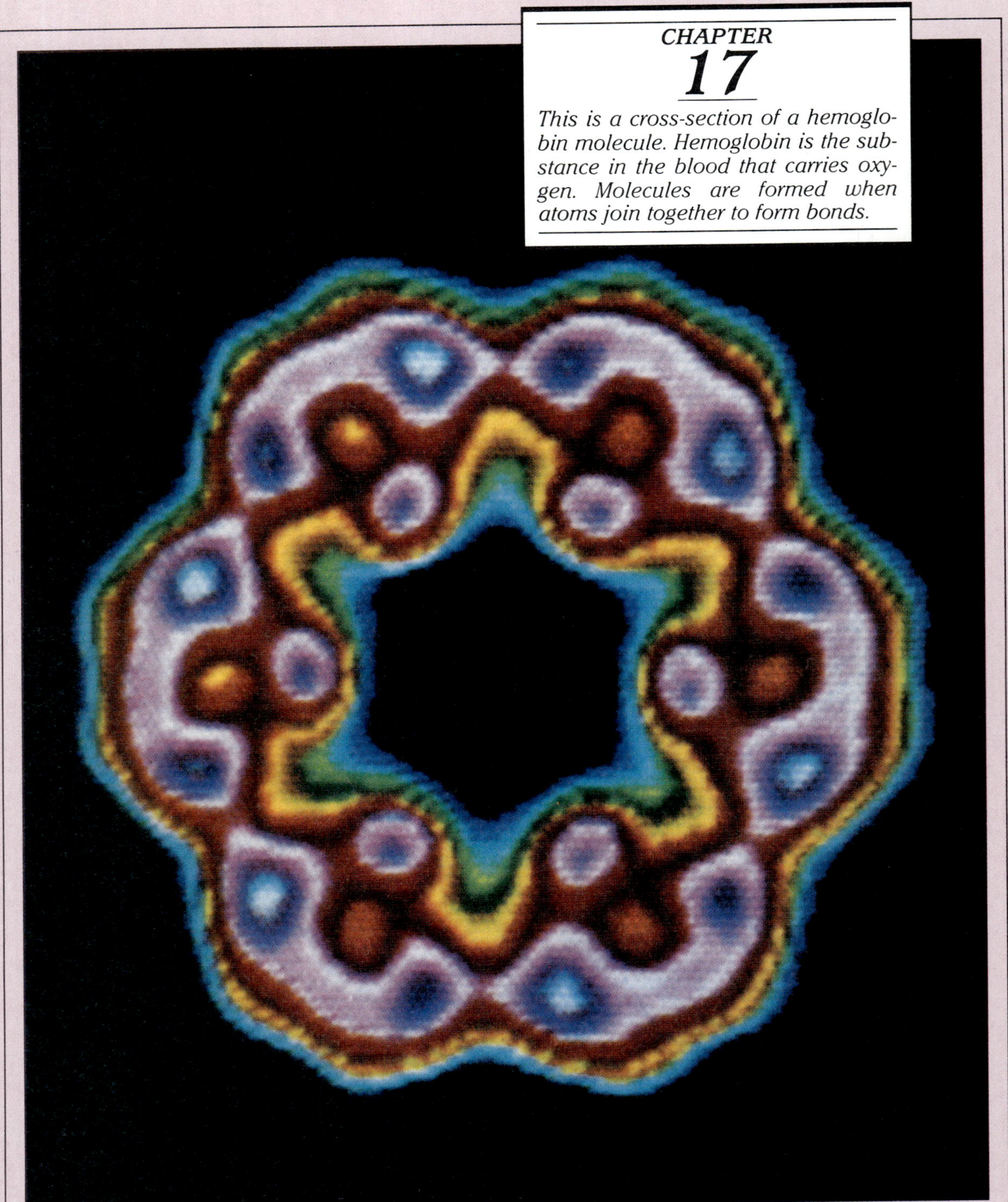

CHAPTER 17

This is a cross-section of a hemoglobin molecule. Hemoglobin is the substance in the blood that carries oxygen. Molecules are formed when atoms join together to form bonds.

ATOMIC BONDS

CHAPTER GOALS

1. Explain how two or more atoms can form chemical bonds.
2. Compare and contrast two kinds of chemical bonds.
3. Use chemical formulas to describe compounds.

17-1. Bonding of Atoms

At the end of this section you will be able to:

- ☐ Explain what is meant by a *chemical bond.*
- ☐ Use *electron dot models* to explain how molecules are formed.
- ☐ Explain the importance of an atom's *outer* electrons in forming a chemical bond.

Have you ever put a jigsaw puzzle together? The separate pieces seem to have no pattern. But you know that the different pieces will fit together if you can match them properly. In this section you will see that atoms are like the pieces of a puzzle. Atoms can join together only in certain ways.

WHAT HOLDS ATOMS TOGETHER?

Diamond is the hardest substance known. A diamond can cut through glass or metal as easily as a knife slices bread. A diamond crystal is made only of carbon atoms. Carbon is also found in other forms besides diamond. The hardness of a diamond is a result of the strength with which the individual carbon atoms cling to each other. Compare carbon, in the form of a diamond, with helium. As you know, helium is a very light gas. In order to change helium into a liquid, its temperature must drop to 4.2 K. This temperature is only a few degrees above absolute zero. This means that helium atoms can cling together only when they are almost motionless. Why do carbon atoms hold so tightly to their neighbors while helium atoms do not? To find an answer to this question, you will take a closer look at hydrogen atoms because they are the simplest of all atoms. You will see how hydrogen atoms combine to form a molecule of hydrogen.

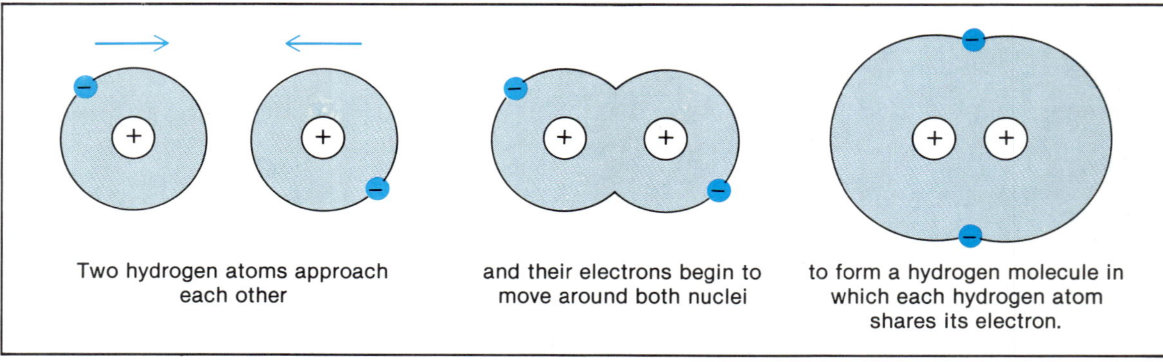

Fig. 17–1 Two hydrogen atoms share their electrons to form a hydrogen molecule.

The following statement describes the general behavior of atoms when they combine. All atoms can be described in one of two general ways: They are either atoms that tend to gain or share electrons to become stable, or atoms that tend to lose or share electrons to become stable. A hydrogen atom has only one electron. Two electrons are needed to fill hydrogen's only energy level. Therefore, a hydrogen atom will tend to gain or share one electron to become stable.

Suppose that two hydrogen atoms come close to each other. Each atom needs one electron to become stable. But each hydrogen atom tends to gain one electron. Neither atom tends to lose its electron. However each hydrogen atom can become stable by sharing its one electron with the other atom. When atoms share electrons, the shared electrons move about the two nuclei. Then the two hydrogen atoms are joined to form a hydrogen molecule. The steps by which they join are shown in Fig. 17–1. No more than two hydrogen atoms can combine because each energy level can hold only two electrons. In a hydrogen molecule, the energy level of each atom is completely filled by the shared electrons.

Chemical bond A force that holds two atoms together.

When each of the two hydrogen atoms shares its electron with the other, the two atoms are joined by a **chemical bond.** Atoms are held together by a *chemical bond* when one or more of their electrons are attracted to, and move around, the nuclei of both atoms. Fig. 17–2 shows how the electrons in a hydrogen molecule are attracted to both nuclei to form a chemical bond.

Compare the behavior of two hydrogen atoms with two helium atoms. Each helium atom has its outer energy level filled with two electrons. Thus a helium atom does not need to share electrons to become stable. In other words, helium atoms will not join in a chemical bond. In nature, helium atoms do not combine with other atoms to form molecules. All members of the noble gas family of elements, like helium, are also stable. For this reason, the noble gases do not tend to join other atoms to form compounds in nature. Scientists have been able to combine some of the noble gases with a few other elements in the laboratory. Noble gas atoms do not combine with each other. They exist as free atoms.

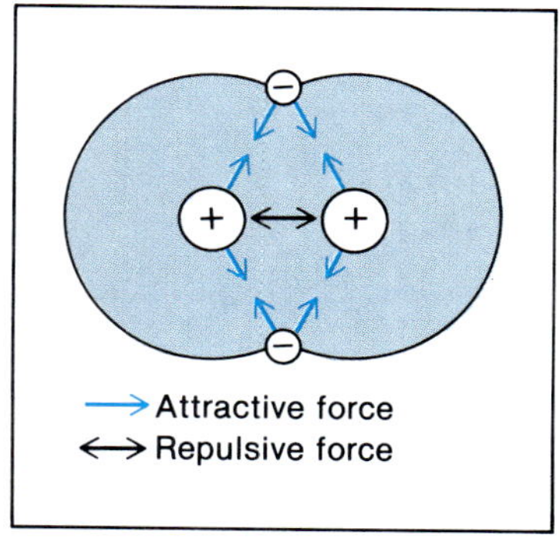

Fig. 17–2 Two hydrogen atoms are held together in a hydrogen molecule because the shared electrons are attracted to the nuclei of both atoms.

MOLECULAR MODELS

In the 1920's, an American scientist named Gilbert Lewis suggested a way of picturing atoms to help explain how they form chemical bonds. In Lewis' system, the symbol for the atom represents the nucleus and the inner electrons. Dots around the symbol represent the outer electrons. This model is called the **electron dot model** of the atom. For example, the *electron dot model* of hydrogen is H·. Fig. 17–3 shows the electron arrangement of a number of atoms along with their electron dot models. This diagram is arranged in the same way as the periodic chart (see pages 414 and 415). It shows that atoms belonging to the same chemical families have the same outer electron arrangement.

Electron dot model A way of picturing the outer electrons of an atom by placing dots representing the outer electrons around the symbol of the atom.

A molecule is always made up of a certain number of atoms. The atoms in a molecule can be shown by their electron dot models. For example, a hydrogen molecule is always made up of two hydrogen atoms. Each hydrogen atom has one outer electron, H·. In a hydrogen molecule, two electrons are shared by two hydrogen atoms. Thus the electron dot model for a hydrogen molecule is H:H.

Two chlorine atoms can also form a chemical bond. As you can see in Fig. 17–3, each chlorine atom lacks one electron to complete its outer level. Thus two chlorine atoms will each share one electron with the other to form a chlorine molecule. The electron dot model of two chlorine atoms joining to form a chlorine molecule can be shown as follows:

$\overset{\cdot\cdot}{\underset{\cdot\cdot}{:Cl}}\cdot$	+	$\overset{\cdot\cdot}{\underset{\cdot\cdot}{:Cl}}\cdot$	=	$\overset{\cdot\cdot}{\underset{\cdot\cdot}{:Cl}}\overset{\cdot\cdot}{\underset{\cdot\cdot}{:Cl}}:$
chlorine atom		chlorine atom		chlorine molecule

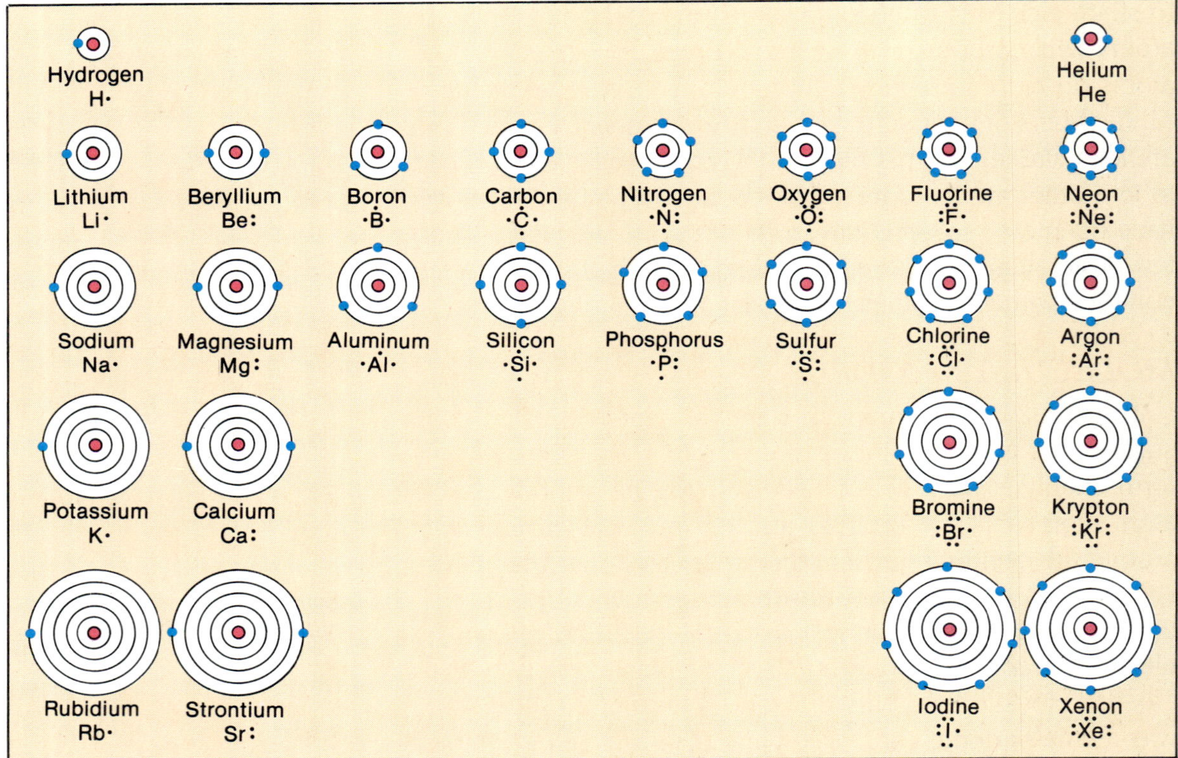

Fig. 17–3 Bohr models showing electron arrangements are compared to electron dot models for the same atoms.

SUMMARY

Two hydrogen atoms can form a hydrogen molecule by sharing electrons. Molecules are made up of atoms held together by chemical bonds. Electron dot models show the outer electrons that are shared to form chemical bonds.

QUESTIONS

Use complete sentences to write your answers.

1. How do atoms share electrons?
2. Using a simple diagram, explain what is meant by a chemical bond.
3. Draw electron dot models of hydrogen, carbon, oxygen, sodium, and chlorine.
4. Using electron dot models, show how two chlorine atoms form a chlorine molecule.
5. Why is the number of outer electrons in an atom important in forming a chemical bond?

1. When an electron is shared by two atoms, the electron moves around the two separate nuclei.
2. See Fig. 17–1.
3. H ·, · C ·, : O :, Na ·, : Cl ·
4. : Cl · + : Cl · = : C : Cl :
5. The number of electrons in the outer level of an atom determines how many electrons are still needed to fill the level and thus which atoms, and how many atoms, it will bond with to gain the electrons it needs.

17-2. Kinds of Chemical Bonds

At the end of this section you will be able to:

- ☐ Explain what is meant by a *covalent bond* between atoms.
- ☐ Compare *covalent* and *ionic* bonds.
- ☐ Explain the importance of *valence* electrons.

If you toss a coin, will it come up heads or tails? The chances are even. There is no sure way to predict which it will be. However, you can predict how atoms will behave when they form chemical bonds. In this section you will learn the properties that determine how atoms will combine. See Fig. 17–4.

SHARING ELECTRONS

Hydrogen and chlorine almost always exist as molecules. Each atom of these elements is missing only one electron to complete its outer level. As a result, two hydrogen atoms or two chlorine atoms each share one electron with the other to form a molecule made up of two atoms. The bond between two hydrogen atoms or two chlorine atoms is called a **covalent** (koe-**vay**-lunt) **bond.** When atoms share electrons to fill their outer levels, they form *covalent bonds.*

Covalent bond A chemical bond formed when atoms share two or more electrons.

As you learned in Section 17–1, hydrogen molecules are formed as follows: H· + H· = H:H. Single atoms of hydrogen (H·) are unstable under most conditions. Hydrogen molecules (H:H) are more stable than separate hydrogen atoms. This is also true of chlorine, oxygen, nitrogen, and fluorine. These gases are found in nature as covalently bonded molecules.

Atoms may share more than one pair of electrons to form a covalent bond. For example, a sulfur atom has six outer electrons. Each sulfur atom needs two electrons to complete its outer level. Thus two sulfur atoms can share two pairs of electrons to form a sulfur molecule. This is shown as follows:

$$\cdot\ddot{\underset{\cdot}{S}}: \;+\; \cdot\ddot{\underset{\cdot}{S}}: \;=\; \ddot{\underset{\cdot\cdot}{S}}::\ddot{\underset{\cdot\cdot}{S}}$$

sulfur atom	sulfur atom	sulfur molecule

Fig. 17–4 You cannot predict with certainty whether a tossed coin will come up heads or tails. However, you can accurately predict how atoms will form chemical bonds.

Different atoms can also form covalent bonds between themselves. For example two hydrogen atoms and an oxygen atom are joined by covalent bonds to make a water molecule. The formation of a water molecule is shown as follows:

$$\mathrm{H}\cdot + \mathrm{H}\cdot + :\ddot{\underset{\cdot}{\mathrm{O}}}\cdot = \begin{array}{l}\mathrm{H}:\ddot{\underset{\cdot\cdot}{\mathrm{O}}}: \\ \quad\;\;\mathrm{H}\end{array}$$

The same kinds of atoms can also form more than one kind of molecule. For example, hydrogen and oxygen can also combine to form hydrogen peroxide. This is shown as follows:

$$\mathrm{H}\cdot + \mathrm{H}\cdot + :\ddot{\underset{\cdot}{\mathrm{O}}}\cdot + :\ddot{\underset{\cdot}{\mathrm{O}}}\cdot = \begin{array}{l}\mathrm{H}:\ddot{\underset{\cdot\cdot}{\mathrm{O}}}: \\ \quad\;:\underset{\cdot\cdot}{\mathrm{O}}:\mathrm{H}\end{array}$$

LOSING AND GAINING ELECTRONS

Look at a model of a sodium atom. Sodium has 11 electrons. Thus, each sodium atom has one outer electron, Na·. Rather than sharing its outer electron, sodium tends to lose one electron to become stable. Suppose that a sodium atom and a chlorine atom come together. The chlorine atom needs to gain one electron to become stable. The sodium atom needs to lose one electron. Therefore, the sodium atom will lose one outer electron to the chlorine atom. See Fig. 17–5. When a sodium atom transfers an electron to a chlorine atom, the sodium atom becomes a positive ion, Na^{+}. The chlorine atom

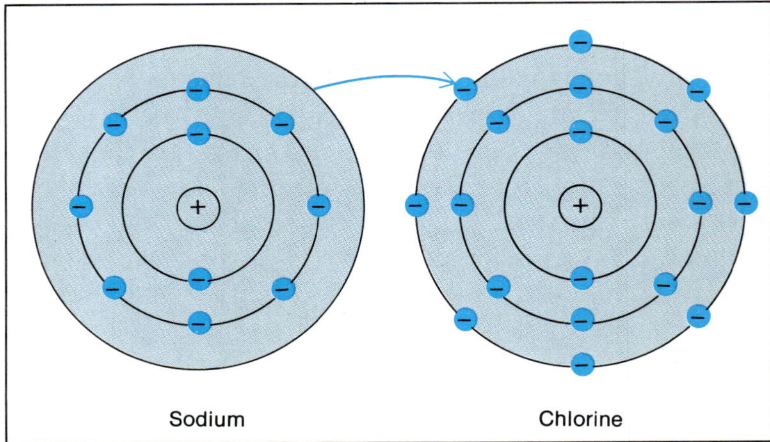

Fig. 17–5 Sodium transfers one electron to chlorine to form an ionic bond.

gains an electron and becomes a negative ion, Cl^-. The two oppositely charged ions are then attracted to each other. A chemical bond now holds the sodium and chlorine ions together. Bonds that are formed between atoms as a result of a *transfer* of electrons are called **ionic bonds.** Sodium and chlorine form an *ionic bond* to become sodium chloride, which is common table salt.

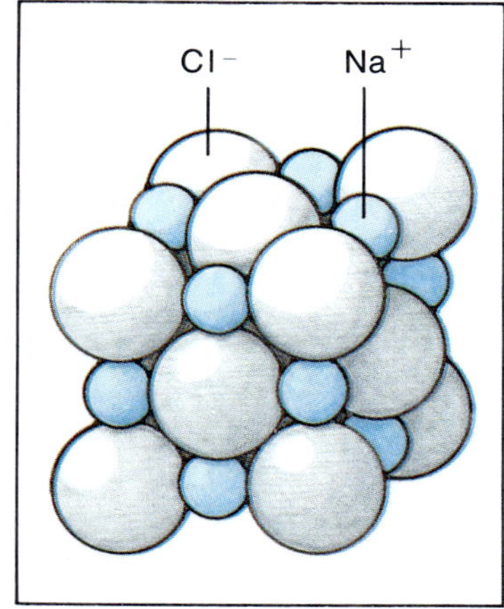

Fig. 17–6 The diagram shows the arrangement of sodium ions (Na^+) and chloride ions (Cl^-) in a crystal of sodium chloride (NaCl).

If you look at salt crystals through a magnifier, you will see that many of the salt crystals are small cubes. Each salt crystal is made up of sodium ions and chloride ions. These ions are held together by their opposite electrical charges. Each positive sodium ion is surrounded by negative chloride ions. Each chloride ion is surrounded by sodium ions. See Fig. 17–6. As a result, the ions form a crystal of sodium chloride with the shape of a cube. Notice that a salt crystal is not made up of separate molecules that are packed together. Instead, each crystal is made up of one sodium ion for each chloride ion. Substances that are held together by ionic bonds are alike in two ways. First, they melt at a higher temperature than compounds held together by covalent bonds. Second, when dissolved in water, these substances conduct an electric current while covalent compounds do not.

Ionic bond A chemical bond formed when atoms transfer electrons from one to another.

PREDICTING HOW ATOMS WILL COMBINE

You have seen that an atom's outer electrons determine much of the atom's chemical behavior. For example, the outer electrons determine how atoms will join other atoms. If you know the outer electron arrangement of an atom, you can predict how the atom will form chemical bonds. **Oxidation number** describes the number of electrons an atom gains, loses, or shares to form chemical bonds. An atom that loses electrons is said to have a *positive oxidation number.* An atom that gains electrons has a *negative oxidation number.* See Table 17–1.

Oxidation number The number of electrons gained, lost, or shared by an atom when it forms chemical bonds.

Look at the atoms in the second row of Fig. 17–3. The first atom, lithium, has one outer electron that it will lose. Thus the oxidation number of lithium is $1+$ because a lithium atom will lose one electron to form a bond. Now skip down the second row to oxygen. Oxygen has six outer electrons. Thus oxygen has an oxidation number of $2-$ since an oxygen atom gains two electrons in a bond.

OXIDATION NUMBERS OF SOME COMMON ELEMENTS		
Name	Symbol	Oxidation Number
Aluminum	Al	3+
Calcium	Ca	2+
Zinc	Zn	2+
Magnesium	Mg	2+
Hydrogen	H	1+
Potassium	K	1+
Silver	Ag	1+
Sodium	Na	1+
Bromine	Br	1−
Chlorine	Cl	1−
Fluorine	F	1−
Iodine	I	1−
Oxygen	O	2−
Sulfur	S	2−

Table 17–1

Valence electrons Electrons in the outer energy level of an atom that take part in a chemical bond.

Word study: Valence from *valens* (L.), to be strong.

The outer electrons in an atom are called **valence electrons.** Lithium has one *valence electron* and oxygen has six. This number of outer electrons determines the oxidation number of an atom. Notice that some elements, such as carbon, with four valence electrons, have a half-filled outer level. This means that carbon can either lose or gain electrons. Carbon can have an oxidation number of either 4+ or 4−, depending on the other atoms with which it combines.

USING OXIDATION NUMBER

Oxidation number can be used to predict how atoms will form molecules. For example, find the oxidation numbers of hydrogen and oxygen in Table 17–1. The oxidation number of hydrogen is 1+. The oxidation number of oxygen is 2−. You can now predict how hydrogen and oxygen will combine to form a water molecule. When they form bonds, hydrogen loses one electron and oxygen gains two electrons. Thus two hydrogen atoms must combine with one oxygen atom to make a stable molecule. In other words, *the total number of positive and negative oxidation numbers of the atoms in a simple compound must add up to zero.*

To predict how two kinds of atoms will combine, first write the symbols of the atoms. For example, if hydrogen combines with chlorine, you would write H Cl. Then write the correct oxidation numbers at the upper right of each symbol. The oxidation number of hydrogen is 1+ and of chlorine is 1−: $H^{1+}Cl^{1-}$. These oxidation numbers add up to zero: (1+) + (1−) = 0. Therefore one atom of hydrogen will combine with one atom of chlorine.

Skill: Students must use good problem-solving techniques in order to write the correct formulas for chemical compounds.

To predict how magnesium will combine with chlorine, first write: Mg Cl. The oxidation number of magnesium is 2+ and of chlorine is 1−: $Mg^{2+}Cl^{1-}$. These oxidation numbers do not add up to zero. A magnesium atom tends to lose two electrons but a chlorine atom can gain only one. Thus *two* atoms of chlorine are needed to gain the electrons lost by one atom of magnesium. This means that one atom of magnesium will combine with two atoms of chlorine. Magnesium chloride, the compound formed when magnesium and chlorine combine, will contain two atoms of chlorine for each atom of magnesium. In this way, oxidation numbers can help you to predict how atoms will form chemical compounds.

SUMMARY

Atoms join together by forming either covalent or ionic bonds. Atoms that form bonds by transferring electrons become ions. You can predict how atoms will combine by determining the number of electrons that are shared or transferred.

QUESTIONS

Use complete sentences to write your answers.

1. Explain what is meant by a covalent bond between atoms.
2. How does a covalent bond differ from an ionic bond?
3. Use electron dot models to show how hydrogen and oxygen atoms combine to form a water molecule.
4. What is the difference between a negative and a positive oxidation number? What are valence electrons?
5. What is the oxidation number of calcium? What is the oxidation number of chlorine? How many atoms of each element will combine to form ionic molecules of calcium chloride? Explain.

1. A covalent bond is a chemical bond formed when atoms share two or more electrons.
2. A covalent bond involves sharing a pair of electrons. An ionic bond involves the transfer of an electron from one atom to another.
3. H· + H· + :Ȯ: = H :Ö:
H
4. A positive oxidation number means that the atom has a tendency to lose electrons. A negative oxidation number means that the atom has a tendency to gain electrons. Valence electrons are the electrons in an atom's outer energy level.
5. Calcium has an oxidation number of 2+ and chlorine has an oxidation number of 1−. Two atoms of chlorine will combine with one atom of calcium to form an ionic molecule of calcium chloride since each chlorine atom will lose one electron to calcium, which needs two.

SKILL-BUILDING ACTIVITY

See teacher's commentary for teaching hints, safety, and answers to questions.

IONIC AND COVALENT BONDS

PURPOSE: You will compare and contrast the characteristics of ionic and covalent bonds.

MATERIALS:

3 test tubes	sugar
salt	baking soda
test-tube holder	250 mL beaker
Bunsen burner	distilled water
matches	2 flashlight batteries
container of water for burned matches	3 wires
	flashlight bulb and socket

CAUTION: Always wear goggles when heating something over a burner. Be sure to tie back long hair or loose clothing.

PROCEDURE:

A. Put about 2 grams of salt in a test tube. Label the tube.

B. Use the test-tube holder to hold the tube 10 cm above the flame of a Bunsen burner. Record your observations. See Fig. 17–7 (a).

C. Repeat steps A and B with sugar and with baking soda.

1. Which substance melted at the lowest temperature?
2. Which substance is held together by covalent bonds?

D. In the beaker, dissolve about 2 to 3 grams of sugar in 200 mL of distilled water. Test to see if this solution conducts electricity. See Fig. 17–7 (b).

3. Does the solution conduct electricity?

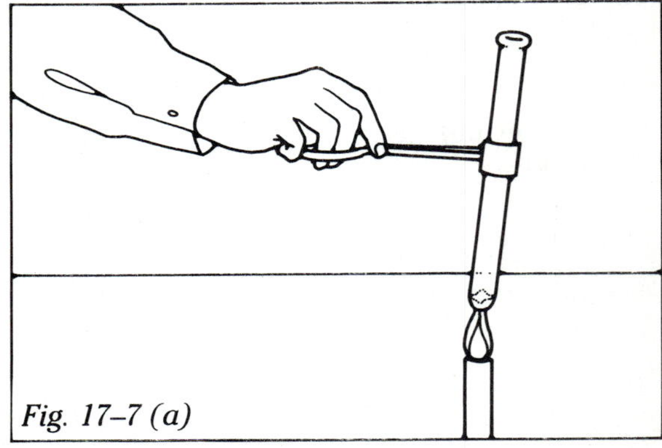
Fig. 17–7 (a)

E. Repeat step D using salt and then baking soda.

4. Does the salt and water solution conduct electricity?
5. Does the baking soda solution conduct electricity?
6. Do your answers to questions 3, 4, and 5 verify your answer to question 2? Explain why or why not.

CONCLUSIONS:

1. Is baking soda an ionic or a covalent substance?
2. Describe two tests used to determine if a substance is held together by ionic bonds or covalent bonds.

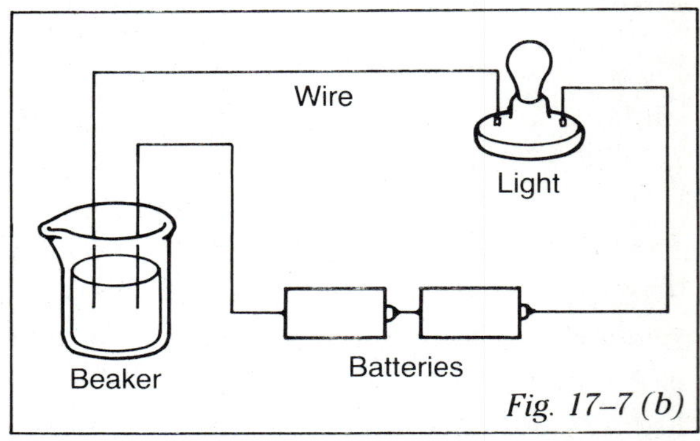

Fig. 17–7 (b)

17-3. Chemical Formulas

At the end of this section you will be able to:

- ☐ Explain the meaning of a *chemical formula.*
- ☐ Use oxidation numbers to write and name chemical formulas.
- ☐ Explain what is meant by a radical.

When you mix lemonade, you may make it too sweet by adding too much sugar or too sour by adding too much lemon juice. Like all mixtures, the composition of a solution is not always the same. However, chemical compounds are always made up of the same elements in the same proportions. A pure compound, such as water or sodium chloride, will always be exactly the same. See Fig. 17–8.

Fig. 17–8 When you make a mixture, you can add the components in different proportions. The elements in a compound, however, always combine in the same ratio.

DESCRIBING A CHEMICAL COMPOUND

A chemical compound such as water always contains the same kinds and numbers of atoms. Every atom can be represented by its symbol. Thus a compound can be described by using the symbols for the atoms in the compound. For example, water contains hydrogen and oxygen atoms. The symbols H for hydrogen and O for oxygen can be used to describe water. However, you have seen that a certain number of hydrogen and oxygen atoms combine to make water molecules. Because of the number of valence electrons, two hydrogen atoms combine with each oxygen atom. These numbers must be included in a correct description of water. Thus the symbol for a molecule of water is H_2O. The number 2 written below the symbol for hydrogen is called a *subscript.* This indicates that there are two atoms of hydrogen in each molecule of water. A description of a chemical compound using symbols and numbers is called a **chemical formula.** Every chemical compound can be described by a *chemical formula.*

Chemical formula A way of describing compounds by using atomic symbols and subscript numbers.

The subscript number 1 is never used as part of a chemical formula. If no subscript number is given after the symbol of an atom, it means that the molecule contains one atom of that element. For example, the correct formula for common table salt is NaCl. This formula says that salt always contains one atom of sodium for each atom of chlorine.

Diatomic molecule A molecule made up of two atoms of the same element.

Formulas can also be used to describe the molecules formed when the same atoms form bonds with each other. Remember that two chlorine atoms can form a molecule by sharing electrons. The formula for a chlorine molecule is Cl_2. A molecule consisting of only two atoms of the same kind is called a **diatomic** (die-uh-**tom**-ik) **molecule.** Chlorine gas consists of *diatomic* molecules. Oxygen gas, O_2, is also made up of diatomic molecules. Many elements actually exist as diatomic molecules rather than as single atoms. Other diatomic molecules include hydrogen, nitrogen, fluorine, bromine, and iodine.

WRITING CHEMICAL FORMULAS

The valence electrons of atoms determine how they will combine. For example, a calcium atom has two outer electrons. Calcium tends to lose two electrons to become stable, giving it an oxidation number of 2+. Suppose a calcium atom forms an ionic bond with chlorine atoms. Each chlorine atom has seven outer electrons. It can gain only one electron, giving it an oxidation number of 1−. Thus two chlorine atoms will combine with one calcium atom as follows:

$$\cdot Ca \cdot + :\ddot{\underset{\cdot\cdot}{Cl}}\cdot + :\ddot{\underset{\cdot\cdot}{Cl}}\cdot = Ca^{2+} + 2Cl^{1-}$$

The compound formed when calcium and chlorine combine will contain two chlorine atoms for each calcium atom. The formula for the compound is written as $CaCl_2$.

Oxidation numbers can also be used to predict correct chemical formulas. For example, this is how to write the correct formula for the compound formed from calcium and chlorine.

Skill: *Problem solving.* Outline the steps in writing chemical formulas on the board and give individual help where needed.

1. Write the atomic symbols and their oxidation numbers: $Ca^{2+}Cl^{1-}$.

2. If the oxidation numbers do not add up to zero, write the oxidation number of each atom as a subscript of the opposite symbol. The oxidation number of calcium is 2+. Therefore, write the number 2 as a subscript of Cl. Since the oxidation number of chlorine is 1−, do not write a subscript for Ca: $Ca^{2+}Cl_2{}^{1-}$.

3. The formula for calcium chloride is thus $CaCl_2$.

Follow these three steps to write the correct formula for the compound formed from aluminum and oxygen. The oxidation number of aluminum is 3+. The oxidation number of oxygen is 2−.

1. First write the atomic symbols and their oxidation numbers: $Al^{3+}O^{2-}$.

2. Then write the oxidation numbers as subscripts: Al_2^{3+} O_3^{2-}.

3. The correct formula is thus Al_2O_3.

Notice that the symbol of the atom with the positive oxidation number is written first in the formula.

GROUPS OF ATOMS

Experiments show that there are certain groups of atoms that remain together in chemical changes. Such a group of atoms is called a **radical.** The sulfate *radical* is made up of one sulfur atom joined to four oxygen atoms. Chemically, this group of atoms acts like a single atom. It has a single oxidation number of 2−. The names and oxidation numbers of some other common radicals are given in Table 17–2.

Radical A group of atoms that remain together in a chemical change and behave as if they were a single atom with a single oxidation number.

OXIDATION NUMBERS OF SOME COMMON RADICALS	
Name of Radical	Oxidation Number
Nitrate (NO_3)	1−
Hydroxide (OH)	1−
Carbonate (CO_3)	2−
Sulfate (SO_4)	2−
Phosphate (PO_4)	3−
Ammonium (NH_4)	2+

Table 17–2

Follow the same steps in writing formulas using radicals that you learned for formulas using single atoms. If a molecule contains more than one radical, write the symbols in the radical inside parentheses. Write the correct subscript after the parentheses. For example, the formula for the compound formed from a calcium atom and two hydroxide radicals can be written as follows:

1. Ca^{2+} OH^{1-}
2. Ca^{2+} $(OH)_2^{1-}$
3. $Ca(OH)_2$

The formula for calcium hydroxide is thus $Ca(OH)_2$.

NAMES OF COMPOUNDS

The names of most chemical compounds come from their formulas. The formulas of many compounds contain only two elements. These compounds are named for the first element followed by the second element ending in *-ide*. For example, NaCl is sodium chlor*ide*, $CaCl_2$ is calcium chlor*ide*, and Al_2O_3 is aluminum *oxide*. Compounds, such as aluminum oxide, that are composed of only two elements are called *binary compounds*. Compounds containing radicals are named in the same way as binary compounds. If the formula contains a radical, the name of the compound includes the name of that radical. For example, NaOH is sodium hydroxide and NH_4Cl is ammonium chloride.

SUMMARY

A chemical compound is always made up of the same atoms in the same proportions. A chemical formula describes one molecule of a compound using symbols and subscript numbers. Oxidation numbers of atoms and radicals can be used to help write correct chemical formulas.

QUESTIONS

Use complete sentences to write your answers.

1. What do the symbols and numbers in a chemical formula stand for?
2. How many atoms of each element does a molecule made up of carbon and chlorine contain? Write the chemical formula for this molecule.
3. How many atoms of fluorine will combine with one atom of aluminum in a compound? Write the chemical formula and name of this compound.
4. How many atoms of oxygen will combine with two atoms of aluminum? Write the chemical formula and name of this compound.
5. What is the oxidation number of aluminum? What is the oxidation number of sulfur? What is the chemical formula for a compound of aluminum and sulfur?
6. What is a radical? Write the formula of a compound of sodium atoms and sulfate radicals.

1. In a chemical formula the symbols stand for the elements involved and the numbers tell how many atoms of the elements are involved.
2. One carbon atom and four chlorine atoms: CCl_4.
3. Three atoms of fluorine will combine with one atom of aluminum in a compound: AlF_3 aluminum fluoride.
4. Three atoms of oxygen will combine with two atoms of aluminum in a compound: Al_2O_3.
5. The oxidation number of aluminum is 3+ and of sulfur is 2−. The most likely compound to form is Al_2S_3.
6. A radical is a group of atoms that remain together during chemical changes. Na_2SO_4.

CAREERS IN SCIENCE

SPACE CHEMIST

Chemists research, evaluate, test, and help develop space vehicles, which must be able to sustain the stress of launching, space travel, and re-entry while remaining light enough to conserve fuel and glide to a landing. Finding safe fuel systems powerful enough to launch spacecraft is one of the major research challenges for chemists in the space program. Chemists also design some of the research programs to be done in spacelabs.

Some chemists also work as astronauts for the space program. These mission specialists design, conduct, and develop their own experiments to be performed in flight. Most of these experiments are sponsored by NASA, the Department of Defense, and government agencies. But an increasing number are being sponsored by private companies and being carried out by their personnel on board the spacecraft.

For further information, contact: Lewis Research Center, NASA, 21000 Brookpark Road, Cleveland, OH 44135.

SCIENTIFIC ILLUSTRATOR

Scientific illustrators create sketches, diagrams, paintings, drawings, and three-dimensional representations of scientific concepts, formulas, equipment, and study objects. Since it is easier to explain and understand things that can be seen, scientific illustration is used a great deal in teaching. Drawings enable students to visualize difficult concepts like chemical bonding or nuclear fusion. Illustrators are also used to help demonstrate technical products and equipment, to catch the eye of the reader in sales brochures and advertisements, and to clarify concepts in scientific journals.

Firms hiring scientific illustrators usually require a minimum of a bachelor's degree in graphics, illustration, or fine arts. But an impressive portfolio (a representative sampling of an artist's work) is sometimes enough to get a good job or to begin work as a freelance artist.

For further information, contact: Art Student's League of New York, 215 W. 57th Street, New York, NY 10019.

CHAPTER REVIEW

See teacher's commentary for answers.

VOCABULARY

On a separate piece of paper, match each term with the number of the statement that best explains it. Use each term only once.

chemical bond, diatomic molecule, radical, ionic bond, chemical formula, electron dot model, oxidation number, valence electrons, covalent bond

1. A force that joins atoms together.
2. A way of picturing the outer electrons of an atom.
3. The number of electrons that are gained, lost, or shared by an atom in bonding.
4. Outer electrons that take part in a chemical bond.
5. A group of atoms that acts like a single atom.
6. A bond in which atoms share two or more electrons.
7. A bond in which atoms transfer electrons from one atom to another.
8. A molecule consisting of only two atoms of the same element.
9. A way of describing a compound using symbols and subscript numbers.

QUESTIONS

Give brief but complete answers to each of the following questions. Unless otherwise indicated, use complete sentences to write your answers.

1. Why will only two hydrogen atoms bond together to form a molecule?
2. How does the bonding of two neon atoms differ from the bonding of two hydrogen atoms? What determines the difference?
3. Write the electron dot model for two fluorine atoms bonded to each other.
4. Why is the number of an atom's outer electrons important to its chemical behavior? What are these electrons called?
5. Compare and contrast covalent bonding and ionic bonding.
6. What are the oxidation numbers of aluminum, calcium, magnesium, and sodium? Show the steps in the formation of a compound of each of these elements with sulfur.
7. Two hydrogen atoms form a bond with one sulfate radical. What is the oxidation number of the sulfate radical? Explain your answer.
8. Explain why silicon can have an oxidation number of either $4+$ or $4-$.
9. Copy the following table. In each blank space, write the chemical formula for

the compound formed from the element or radical at the top of each column and the element at the left of each row.

Oxidation → Number ↓		1−	2−	3−	1−	2−
	Element → ↓	F	S	N	OH	CO_3
1+	Na					
2+	Be					
3+	B					

APPLYING SCIENCE

1. How does the size of particles affect the rate at which a substance dissolves? Place a large crystal of copper (II) sulfate in a beaker of water. Place an equal mass of small crystals of copper (II) sulfate in a second beaker of water. Cover and label both beakers. Let them stand for several days. Observe both beakers and record your observations and conclusions. CAUTION: Copper (II) sulfate is poisonous. Do not touch copper (II) sulfate crystals directly. Use tongs. Rinse any spills immediately with water. Wear goggles.
2. Make a display of models of different compounds using Styrofoam spheres to represent atoms. Find out the relative size of atoms of various elements to make the models more realistic.
3. Carefully melt about 100 grams of paraffin. CAUTION: Wear goggles. When melted, remove the paraffin from the heat. Place a thermometer in the melted wax and record the temperature every minute until the wax solidifies. Draw a graph of temperature versus time. Follow the same procedure using stearic acid. Compare the two graphs.

BIBLIOGRAPHY

Chester, M. *Particles: An Introduction to Particle Physics.* New York: Macmillan, 1978.

Hansen, J. "The Delicate Architecture of Cement." *Science 82,* December 1982.

Weiss, M. E. *Why Glass Breaks, Rubber Bends and Glue Sticks.* New York: Harcourt, 1979.

CHAPTER

18

Natural and synthetic fibers are made of organic molecules. There are two kinds of synthetic fibers: those made of cellulose from wood pulp and those made of molecules called polymers.

ORGANIC CHEMISTRY

CHAPTER GOALS

1. Describe how carbon atoms form bonds with each other and with other atoms.
2. Explain what is meant by an organic compound and give general examples.
3. Name some examples of hydrocarbons and draw their structural formulas.
4. Explain the importance of carbohydrates, fats, and proteins to living things.

18-1. Carbon and Its Compounds

At the end of this section you will be able to:

- ☐ Show two ways in which carbon atoms form bonds with each other.
- ☐ Give examples to show how carbon forms bonds with other atoms.
- ☐ Explain what is meant by an *organic compound.*

Coal has always been important as a fuel. Diamonds are very valuable for a different reason. They are beautiful gems. Yet both diamonds and coal are made up of carbon atoms. Pencil lead is also made of carbon.

TWO FORMS OF CARBON

Look at the periodic chart on pages 414 and 415. Carbon may be found in the upper right section of the periodic table. Fig. 18–1 shows the electron arrangement of a carbon atom. As you can see, a carbon atom has four valence electrons. Carbon forms covalent bonds by sharing these four electrons. For example, one carbon atom forms covalent bonds with four other carbon atoms. Fig. 18–2 shows how each carbon atom may link to four others so that each atom has four equally close neighbors. Carbon atoms bonded together in this way form diamond. A diamond crystal is made up of pure carbon. The properties of diamond result from the strong covalent bonds joining each carbon atom equally to all its neighbors.

Enrichment: Graphite in various forms, such as coal, is far more common than diamond. Pure graphite is a good electrical conductor because the bonding electron between the layers is held loosely. Diamond, in which all bonding electrons are held tightly, is a nonconductor.

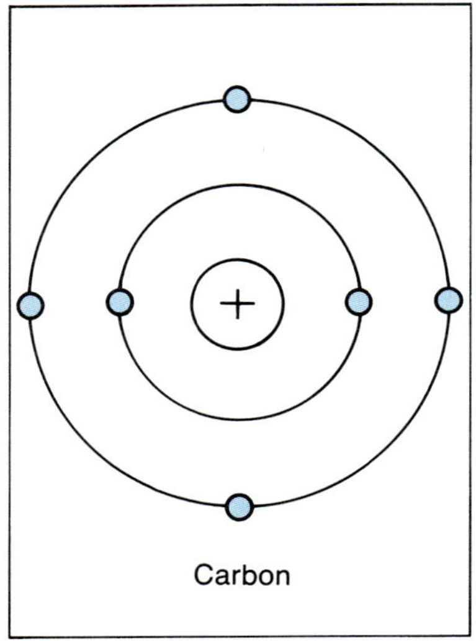

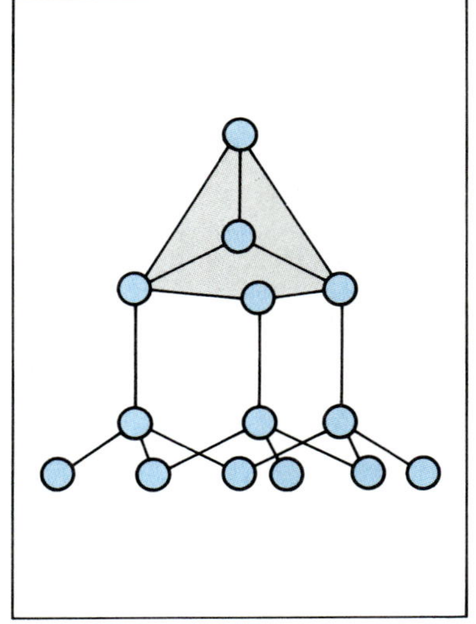

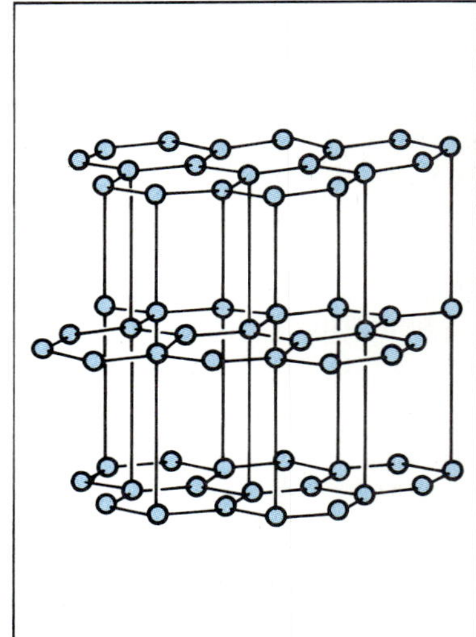

Fig. 18–1 A carbon atom has four valence electrons.

Fig. 18–2 In diamond, the carbon atoms bond as shown.

Fig. 18–3 In coal and other forms of graphite, the carbon atoms are in layers.

Carbon atoms may also join to each other in a different way. See Fig. 18–3. Three of the four bonds between the carbon atoms are strong covalent bonds, as in diamond. But the fourth bond is a weaker bond. As a result, the layers of carbon atoms can split off from each other. This form of carbon is called *graphite.* The "lead" in pencils is really graphite. You can write with a pencil because flakes of graphite rub off as you move the pencil over the paper. Thus, both diamond and pencil lead are different forms of pure carbon. The difference is in the way the carbon atoms bond to each other.

Word study: Graphite from *graphein* (Gr.), to write.

CARBON COMBINES WITH OXYGEN

Carbon forms bonds easily with other kinds of atoms. For example, when carbon in the form of coal burns, it combines with oxygen:

$$C + O_2 = CO_2 \text{ (carbon dioxide)}$$

$$\cdot C \cdot + :O::O: = :O::C::O:$$

In carbon dioxide, the carbon and oxygen atoms are joined by two **double bonds.** Four electrons instead of two are shared in a *double bond.* Carbon atoms often form double bonds with other atoms. Carbon and oxygen can also react to form carbon monoxide (CO): $2C + O_2 = 2CO$. When carbon burns in a good supply of oxygen, only CO_2 is produced. However, when carbon fuels burn without enough oxygen, as in an automobile engine, CO is produced. Carbon dioxide and carbon monoxide have very different effects on the body. As

Double bond The bond formed when atoms are joined together by sharing two pairs of electrons.

Fig. 18–4 Carbon monoxide is a poisonous gas that is found in automobile exhausts.

long as CO_2 is mixed with enough O_2 gas, it is harmless to breathe. Unlike CO_2, carbon monoxide is poisonous even in small amounts. Carbon monoxide interferes with the substance in the blood that carries O_2. The CO in car exhaust fumes adds to air pollution. Many cars are now being built with special filters which help to reduce the amount of CO they emit. See Fig. 18–4.

Common fuels such as coal, petroleum, and natural gas contain carbon compounds. When these fuels burn, large amounts of carbon dioxide are released into the atmosphere. Some scientists think that this buildup of CO_2 in the atmosphere may cause the earth's climate to change. This might result from the *greenhouse effect.* Carbon dioxide can trap the sun's heat in the atmosphere in the same way that glass traps heat in a greenhouse. Thus, the release of large amounts of CO_2 into the atmosphere might cause temperatures all over the earth to rise. No one can be sure how this would change the earth's climate. Some scientists have predicted that an increase of only 5°C in the average temperature of the earth would be enough to cause a large part of the polar icecaps to melt. The water added to the oceans would cause the sea level to rise and would flood many coastal cities.

ORGANIC COMPOUNDS

A carbon atom, with its four valence electrons, can have an oxidation number of $4+$ or $4-$. Thus carbon forms chemical bonds with many other kinds of atoms as well as with other carbon atoms. Scientists have found more than two million compounds that contain carbon. Many of these carbon compounds are found in living things. Scientists once thought that these compounds could only be made by living things. For this reason, compounds containing carbon came to be called *organic* compounds. Organic means "coming from life." However, chemists can now make organic compounds in the laboratory. But almost all carbon compounds, except simple ones such as carbon dioxide, are still called organic compounds. The branch of science that deals with carbon and its compounds is called **organic chemistry.**

Organic chemistry The chemistry of carbon compounds.

Organic compounds are found in food, clothing, automobiles, and the paper these words are printed on. Your body is made up of a huge number of different organic compounds. When organic compounds are heated, they burn or melt. A black residue of carbon remains. This property can be used as a test for carbon compounds. In the following sections, you will learn more about these important compounds.

SUMMARY

Carbon atoms have four outer electrons. They can take part in many kinds of chemical bonds. Diamond and graphite are examples of carbon atoms bonded in two different ways. Carbon can also combine with oxygen to make two compounds with very different properties. The study of carbon compounds is called organic chemistry.

QUESTIONS

Use complete sentences to write your answers.

1. Give an example of two ways carbon atoms form bonds with each other. Why is pencil lead so soft and diamond so hard?
2. Use an electron-dot model to show how carbon bonds to oxygen to form carbon dioxide. What kind of bond forms between the carbon atom and each oxygen atom?
3. What does the word "organic" mean? Where are organic compounds found?
4. How many valence electrons does carbon have? What is the oxidation number of carbon? Why is this important?

1. Carbon atoms may bond equally with four other carbon atoms, each of which is also bonded equally to four other carbons as in diamond. Carbon atoms may bond with three other carbon atoms. In this case, the fourth bond is weaker as in graphite.
2. :Ọ̇::C::Ọ̇:
The carbon-oxygen bond is a double bond.
3. "Organic" means "coming from life." Organic compounds are those that contain carbon atoms. They are found in people, other animals, paper, wood, food, etc.
4. Carbon has four valence electrons. Its oxidation number is 4+ or 4−. This allows carbon to bond to a large number of other elements to produce organic compounds.

INVESTIGATION

See teacher's commentary for teaching hints, safety, and answers to questions.

PROPERTIES OF CARBON COMPOUNDS

PURPOSE: You will test several substances to determine if they contain carbon.

MATERIALS:

samples of white bread, sugar, salt
3 test tubes
Bunsen burner
matches
can of water for burned matches
test-tube holder
test-tube rack

PROCEDURE:

A. Place a small amount of white bread in one test tube. Place 2 g of sugar in another test tube. Place 3 g of salt in a third test tube. Label each tube.

B. Light and adjust the Bunsen burner. CAUTION: Wear goggles.

C. Using a test-tube holder, hold the tube with the bread sample over the burner. The peak of the light blue flame should be 5 cm below the tube. See Fig. 18–5 (a). Hold the tube in this position for 2 to 3 minutes.

1. What happened to the bread?

D. After 2 to 3 minutes, remove the tube from the flame and place it in the test-tube rack to cool for several minutes.

E. Repeat step C using the tube of sugar. Hold it in the flame for 2 to 3 minutes.

2. What happened to the sugar?

F. After heating the sugar, remove the test tube from the heat and let it cool as in step D.

G. Heat the salt sample as in step C for 2 to 3 minutes.

3. What happened to the salt?

H. Place the test tube in the rack to cool. See Fig. 18–5 (b).

CONCLUSION:

1. Examine your samples. Which samples contain carbon? Which do not? Explain.

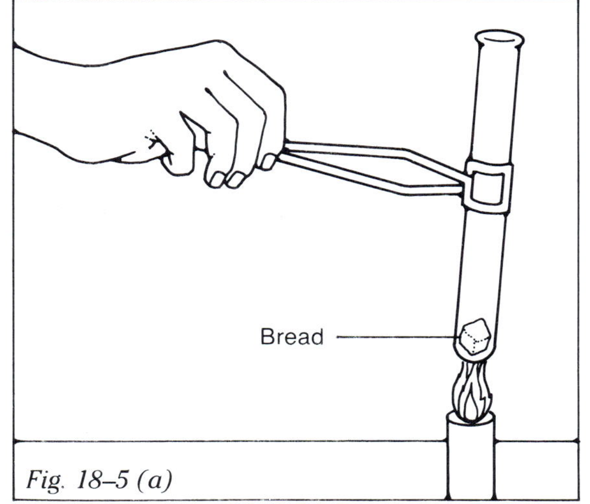

Fig. 18–5 (a)

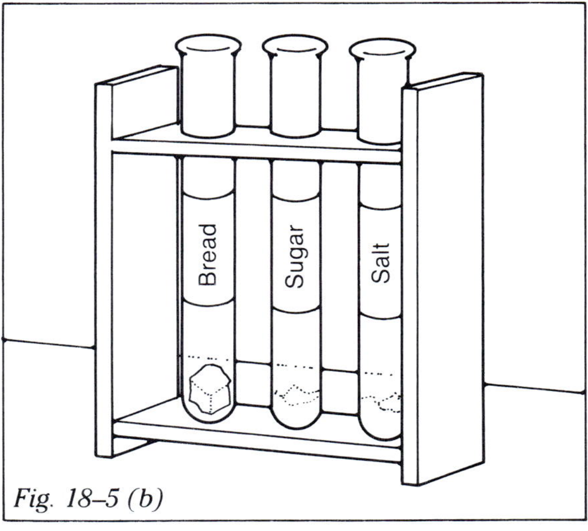

Fig. 18–5 (b)

18-2. Hydrocarbons

At the end of this section you will be able to:

- ☐ Name five compounds that are *hydrocarbons.*
- ☐ Show how structural formulas are used to describe hydrocarbon molecules.
- ☐ Describe four groups of hydrocarbons.

Fig. 18–6 Like items in a supermarket, carbon compounds are classified into groups.

A large grocery store has thousands of different items. Can you imagine shopping in a store where the items were arranged at random? Could you find the canned corn if it was with the milk? Grocery stores arrange the items they sell in groups. Similar items, such as frozen foods, are all in the same place. See Fig. 18–6. Organic compounds can also be put into groups.

CARBON AND HYDROGEN

Hydrocarbon A compound containing only carbon and hydrogen.

Each of the millions of organic compounds that exists is made up of different kinds of molecules. However, all these molecules have some things in common. Therefore, they can be put into general groups. For example, one large group of organic compounds is the **hydrocarbons.** *Hydrocarbon* molecules contain only carbon and hydrogen atoms which are bonded together.

You have seen how hydrogen atoms form a single bond with other atoms. Carbon forms one bond with each of the four electrons in its outer shell for a total of four bonds. Thus the simplest hydrocarbon molecule has one carbon atom and four hydrogen atoms. It is called *methane*, CH_4. In a methane molecule, one carbon atom is bonded to four hydrogen atoms. Methane is often called *marsh gas*. It is formed when plants decay. Natural gas fuel is mostly methane. See Fig. 18–7.

Fig. 18–7 Natural gas, which is mostly methane, is shipped in tank cars for use as a fuel.

A simple way to represent a methane molecule is by a **structural formula.** A *structural formula* is a diagram of a molecule. The lines on this diagram represent the covalent bonds between atoms. The electron model and the structural formula for methane are:

Structural formula A diagram of a molecule showing the bonds between atoms.

```
     H              H
     ..             |
   H : C : H     H—C—H
     ..             |
     H              H
electron dot    structural
   model          formula
```

Ethane is a hydrocarbon molecule with two carbon atoms. The formula for ethane is C_2H_6. The structural formula for ethane is:

```
    H   H
    |   |
 H—C—C—H
    |   |
    H   H
```

Fig. 18–8 Propane is another hydrocarbon that is used as a fuel. It is often used in outdoor barbecue grills.

Ethane is also usually found in natural gas. Adding one more carbon atom to an ethane molecule produces *propane*, C_3H_8:

```
    H   H   H
    |   |   |
H — C — C — C — H
    |   |   |
    H   H   H
```

Propane is also found in natural gas and is used as a fuel. See Fig. 18–8. Can you see a pattern in the way the hydrocarbon molecules are formed? In each new hydrocarbon molecule, another carbon atom and two more hydrogen atoms are added to build a chain. In the next hydrocarbon molecule, *butane*, more carbon and hydrogen atoms are added. The formula for butane is C_4H_{10}:

```
    H   H   H   H
    |   |   |   |
H — C — C — C — C — H
    |   |   |   |
    H   H   H   H
```

Do you see any other way in which this molecule could be put together? The structural formula for butane can also be shown as:

```
    H   H   H
    |   |   |
H — C — C — C — H
    |   |   |
    H   |   H
    H — C — H
        |
        H
```

Name	Formula	Two dimensional	Three dimensional
Methane	CH_4		
Ethane	C_2H_6		
Propane	C_3H_8		
Butane	C_4H_{10}		
Pentane	C_5H_{12}		

Fig. 18–9 This diagram shows the structures of the first five hydrocarbons: methane, ethane, propane, butane, and pentane.

The formula for this molecule is also C_4H_{10}. It is still a molecule of butane. This molecule is an **isomer** (**ie**-suh-mer) of butane. *Isomers* contain the same atoms arranged differently. This isomer of butane is called isobutane. Some organic molecules have many isomers. For example, the hydrocarbon with five carbon atoms is called *pentane.* Pentane has three isomers. The formation of isomers is one of the reasons why there are so many organic compounds.

Isomers Two or more molecules with the same chemical formulas but with different arrangements of their atoms.

Word study: Isomer from *isomers* (Gr.), having equal parts.

Fig. 18–9 shows the arrangement of the atoms in the first five hydrocarbon molecules. These molecules are part of a very large group. In this group, the atoms are joined by a single covalent bond. The members of this group of hydrocarbons

Alkanes A group of hydrocarbons in which the carbon atoms are joined by only single bonds.

are called **alkanes.** The simplest *alkane* is methane. The other molecules in the group are built up by adding one carbon atom and two hydrogen atoms to make the next molecule. The names of all hydrocarbons start with a root that tells how many carbon atoms are present. See Table 18–1. The ending identifies the group to which the hydrocarbon belongs. For example, all alkane hydrocarbons have names which end with the suffix *-ane.*

Root of Name	Number of Carbon Atoms	Example
meth-	1	methane
eth-	2	ethane
prop-	3	propane
but-	4	butane
pent-	5	pentane
hex-	6	hexane
hept-	7	heptane
oct-	8	octane
non-	9	nonane
dec-	10	decane

Table 18–1

OTHER KINDS OF HYDROCARBONS

Word study: Saturated from *saturare* (L.), to fill full.

In the hydrocarbons you just read about, the carbon atoms are joined by single bonds. Organic compounds with carbon atoms joined by single bonds are called *saturated.* Many organic molecules contain carbon atoms joined by double or triple bonds. These compounds are called *unsaturated.* The following structural formula is an example of an unsaturated hydrocarbon:

```
H       H
 \     /
  C===C
 /     \
H       H
```

This molecule is called *ethylene,* C_2H_4. Ethylene is the first member of another group of hydrocarbon molecules. This group is called the **alkenes.** In the *alkenes,* one pair of carbon atoms in each molecule is joined by a double bond. All members of the alkene group have names ending with *-ene*.

Alkenes A group of hydrocarbons in which each molecule has one pair of carbon atoms joined by a double bond.

Fig. 18–10 These robots are using oxyacetylene torches to cut sheets of metal.

Carbon atoms can also form triple bonds. In a triple bond, three pairs of electrons are shared by two atoms. The simplest hydrocarbon molecule with a triple bond is *ethyne*. It is commonly called *acetylene*, C_2H_2:

$$H{-}C{\equiv}C{-}H$$

Acetylene burns with a very hot flame when it is mixed with oxygen. Welding torches burn a mixture of acetylene and oxygen. They produce a flame that is hot enough to melt most metals. See Fig. 18–10. Acetylene is the first member of a group of hydrocarbons called **alkynes** (al-*kines*). In *alkynes*, each molecule has one pair of carbon atoms joined by a triple bond. All alkyne hydrocarbons have names that end with *-yne*.

Alkynes A group of hydrocarbons in which each molecule has one pair of carbon atoms joined by a triple bond.

You have seen that carbon atoms can form either long chains or branching molecules. Six carbon atoms can also join in a ring to form *benzene*, C_6H_6:

```
        H
        |
        C
      /   \\
 H—C        C—H
   ||       |
 H—C        C—H
      \   //
        C
        |
        H
```

Enrichment: Six single-bonded carbons in a ring with two hydrogens bonded to each carbon is called *cyclohexane.*

1. methane, CH_4; ethane, C_2H_6; propane, C_3H_8; butane, C_4H_{10}.
2.

```
    H            H  H
    |            |  |
H—C—H        H—C—C—H
    |            |  |
    H            H  H
 methane        ethane

  H  H  H          H  H  H  H
  |  |  |          |  |  |  |
H—C—C—C—H        H—C—C—C—C—H
  |  |  |          |  |  |  |
  H  H  H          H  H  H  H
  propane            butane
```

Aromatics Hydrocarbons containing carbon atoms arranged in a ring structure.

At ordinary temperatures, benzene is a clear liquid that has a strong odor. It is used as a raw material for making other organic compounds. It is also used as a solvent to dissolve other organic substances. For example, rubber cement is a glue that is made by dissolving rubber in benzene. However, benzene should be used with care. It is dangerous to breathe the vapor given off by benzene. Exposure to benzene can destroy your body's ability to make blood cells and may also cause leukemia. Benzene vapors are also very flammable.

Another large group of hydrocarbon molecules also have ring structures as in benzene. These hydrocarbons are often called **aromatics** because they usually have a strong odor. All *aromatics* contain carbon atoms joined in a ring.

There are thousands of different compounds made up of only carbon and hydrogen. These different molecules exist because carbon atoms form bonds with other carbon atoms. Thus molecules with long chains, chains with branches, or rings of carbon atoms can be formed. All of these hydrocarbons can be put into a few large groups.

3. An isomer of a molecule contains the same atoms but they are arranged differently.

```
                            H  H  H
                            |  |  |
                          H—C—C—C—H
  H  H  H  H                |  |  |
  |  |  |  |                H  |  H
H—C—C—C—C—H                  H—C—H
  |  |  |  |                   |
  H  H  H  H                   H
    butane                 isobutane
```

4. Alkanes have only a single bond between carbons. Alkenes have a double bond between one pair of carbons. Alkynes have a triple bond between one pair of carbons. Aromatics have carbons arranged in a ring structure.
5. Ethylene has a double bond between the carbon atoms while ethane has only a single bond. Ethane has two more hydrogen atoms than ethylene.

```
H       H          H  H
 \     /           |  |
  C = C          H—C—C—H
 /     \           |  |
H       H          H  H
```

SUMMARY

Carbon and hydrogen can bond together in different ways to produce a great number of hydrocarbons. Each hydrocarbon can be put in a group with other hydrocarbons that are similar in structure. Large hydrocarbon molecules with the same number and kind of atoms can have different structures.

QUESTIONS

Use complete sentences to write your answers.

1. Give the names and chemical formulas of four hydrocarbon molecules with single bonds between the carbon atoms.
2. Draw the structural formulas for the molecules you named in question 1.
3. How is an isomer different from a basic hydrocarbon molecule? Draw a structural formula to illustrate a molecule and its isomer.
4. Name and describe the four groups of hydrocarbons.
5. How is ethylene different from ethane? Draw the structural formula for each.

INVESTIGATION

See teacher's commentary for teaching hints, safety, and answers to questions.

HYDROCARBON MOLECULE MODELS

PURPOSE: You will build models of hydrocarbon molecules and study their structure.

MATERIALS:
hydrocarbon molecular model kit

PROCEDURE:

A. Look carefully at the kit you are using. The instructions will tell you which balls represent carbon, hydrogen, oxygen, nitrogen, and other atoms. The sticks are used to join the balls to one another. They represent the electron pairs in a bond. See Fig. 18–11.

B. Build a methane molecule (CH_4) by joining one carbon atom to four hydrogen atoms, using the sticks for bonds.

C. Construct an ethane molecule (C_2H_6) by joining two carbon atoms. Fill the remaining holes with sticks joined to hydrogen atoms. See Fig. 18–12.

D. Build models of the hydrocarbon molecules with three, four, and five carbon atoms.

CONCLUSIONS:

1. How many bonds can hydrogen atoms form?
2. How many bonds can carbon atoms form?
3. What are the names of the hydrocarbon molecules with three, four, and five carbons?
4. How many isomers are there for the hydrocarbon molecules with three, four, and five carbons?
5. Where are the bonds in a carbon atom located?

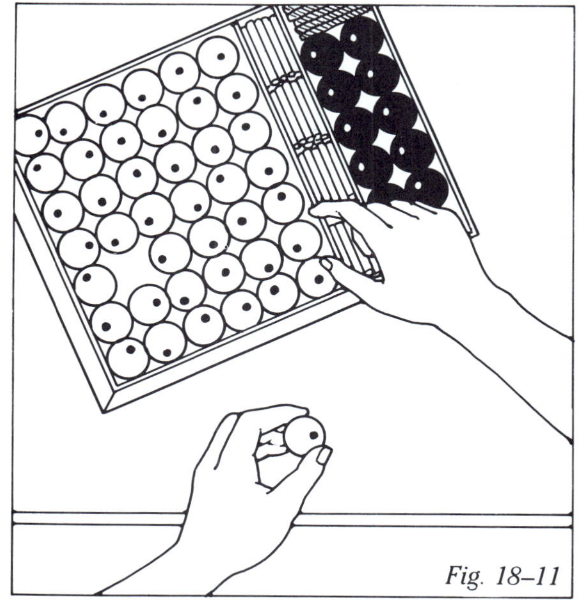

Fig. 18–11

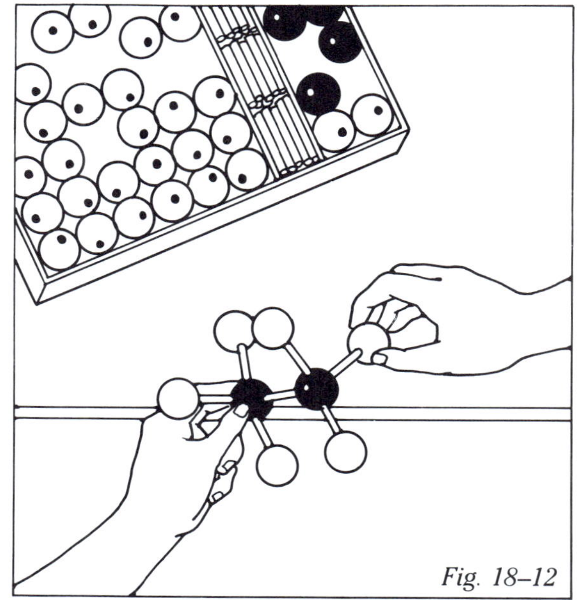

Fig. 18–12

18-3. Substituted Hydrocarbons

At the end of this section you will be able to:

- Describe two ways in which hydrocarbon molecules can be changed into different molecules.
- Give three examples to show how organic molecules can become substituted hydrocarbons.
- Predict the result of combining an organic acid with an alcohol.

One player often substitutes for another during a football game. This player enters the game for a special purpose. For example, a field goal is usually kicked by a player who is sent in for only that one play. See Fig. 18–13.

Fig. 18–13 Like a field-goal kicker, substituted hydrocarbon molecules are used for special purposes.

SUBSTITUTING ATOMS

Football and other sports have players who substitute for the regular players in special situations. A similar thing happens in organic chemistry. There is a huge variety of hydrocarbon molecules. These molecules are built around a skeleton of carbon atoms. Hydrocarbons such as methane contain only hydrogen and carbon atoms:

$$
\begin{array}{ccc}
 & H & \\
 & | & \\
H - & C & - H \\
 & | & \\
 & H &
\end{array}
$$

Could a methane molecule be changed into another molecule? Suppose three of the hydrogen atoms in methane were replaced by three chlorine atoms:

```
        Cl
        |
  H ——— C ——— Cl
        |
        Cl
```

The molecule now has the formula $CHCl_3$. It is called *chloroform.* The substitution of chlorine atoms makes chloroform a totally different compound from methane. Chloroform is a liquid that evaporates easily. In the days before better drugs were available, chloroform was used to put people to sleep during surgery. Other halogen atoms such as fluorine, bromine, and iodine can also be substituted for some of the hydrogen atoms in methane. The gas once used as a propellant in spray cans contains both chlorine and fluorine:

```
        H
        |
  Cl ——— C ——— F
        |
        Cl
```

This compound is called *freon.* Freon is also used in the cooling coils of refrigerators. Freon is no longer used in spray cans because it harms the ozone layer of the atmosphere. A decrease in the ozone layer may allow more harmful ultraviolet rays from the sun to reach the earth.

Enrichment: Freon is a general name for various fluorochloromethanes, also called fluorocarbons. These compounds react in the upper atmosphere and reduce the ozone concentration of the air. Since ozone filters out much of the sun's harmful ultraviolet rays, scientists are concerned about the long-term effects of the release of freon compounds into the atmosphere. An increase in the amount of ultraviolet rays reaching the earth could cause an increase in the incidence of skin cancer.

Now you have seen another reason why there are so many different kinds of organic compounds. Carbon does not only form bonds with other carbon atoms and with hydrogen atoms. It also can form bonds with other kinds of atoms such as chlorine and fluorine. This means that another atom can substitute for one or more of the hydrogen atoms in a hydrocarbon molecule. A new compound is formed that still has the skeleton of a hydrocarbon molecule. For example, chloroform and freon are built on the skeleton of a methane molecule. However, the new compounds have different properties. Chloroform and freon are very different from methane.

ALCOHOLS

Radicals as well as single atoms can also substitute for hydrogen atoms. For example, the OH or hydroxide radical can substitute for one or more hydrogen atoms. When a hydroxide radical substitutes for one hydrogen atom in methane, the new molecule has the following structure:

```
        H
        |
  H ——  C —— OH
        |
        H
```

The formula for this compound is CH_3OH. Because it is built on a methane skeleton, the compound is called *methanol.* Methanol is an **alcohol.** Any organic molecule in which OH radicals replace hydrogen atoms is an *alcohol.* All alcohols have names with the ending *-ol* added to the root name of the hydrocarbon skeleton. Methanol is also known as *wood alcohol.* It is used as a solvent in some kinds of paints. Methanol or wood alcohol is poisonous. You should avoid breathing methanol vapors.

Alcohol A kind of organic molecule having at least one OH group.

Methanol is not the alcohol in alcoholic beverages. The alcohol in wine, beer, and other alcoholic beverages is *ethanol.* It is so named because it is built on the basic ethane structure (C_2H_6). The formula for ethanol is C_2H_5OH:

```
        H     H
        |     |
  H ——  C  —— C —— OH
        |     |
        H     H
```

Ethanol is also called *grain alcohol* because it can be made from grain or fruit juices mixed with yeast. Doctors use ethanol on your skin to kill germs before giving you an injection. A mixture of about 10 percent ethanol and 90 percent gasoline, called *gasohol,* is used as a fuel for cars.

There are many kinds of alcohols. Some alcohols have more than one OH radical. See Fig. 18–14. Ethylene glycol is an alcohol with two OH groups: $C_2H_4(OH_2)$. Glycerol, or glycerin, has three OH groups: $C_3H_5(OH)_3$.

Fig. 18–14 Ethylene glycol is used as an antifreeze in car radiators because it lowers the freezing temperature of water.

ORGANIC ACIDS

Enrichment: Ants use formic acid to make ant trails. Ants can follow the scent of formic acid. An interruption of the trail will sometimes cause confusion until it is reestablished.

Another group that identifies an important kind of organic compound is the COOH group. For example, a COOH group is found in the following molecule:

$$\mathrm{H-\overset{\overset{\displaystyle O}{\|}}{C}-OH}$$

The compound shown above is an example of an **organic acid.** All organic acids have names ending with *-oic.* Methanoic acid has the skeleton of a methane molecule. Methanoic acid is also called *formic acid.* The pain from an ant bite is caused by formic acid produced by the ant.

Organic acid A kind of organic molecule having at least one COOH group.

Another organic acid is made by substituting a COOH group for one hydrogen atom in an ethane molecule:

$$\mathrm{H-\underset{\underset{\displaystyle H}{|}}{\overset{\overset{\displaystyle H}{|}}{C}}-\overset{\overset{\displaystyle O}{\|}}{C}-OH}$$

This is *ethanoic acid.* It has the formula CH_3COOH. It is also commonly called *acetic acid.* You are familiar with acetic acid in the form of vinegar. Acetic acid gives vinegar its sour taste. Ordinary vinegar contains about 5 percent acetic acid. See Fig. 18–15.

Fig. 18–15 Vinegar contains acetic acid. The pH of vinegar is about 2.8.

Citric acid gives a sour taste to fruits such as lemons, limes, and oranges. It is also an organic acid.

Amino acid A kind of organic molecule having both NH_2 and COOH groups.

Organic acids that are necessary for life are called **amino acids.** *Amino acids* contain both the COOH group and the *amino* group, NH_2:

$$\begin{array}{ccccccccc} & & H & & H & & O & & \\ & & | & & | & & \| & & \\ H & - & N & - & C & - & C & - & OH \\ & & & & | & & & & \\ & & & & H & & & & \end{array}$$

This compound is called *glycine.* All amino acids have names that end with *-ine.* Amino acids are examples of organic compounds in which more than one radical is substituted for hydrogen atoms in a hydrocarbon. Every amino acid has at least one NH_2 group and one COOH group in the molecule.

ESTERS

Ester A kind of molecule formed by combining an organic acid and an alcohol.

An organic acid can combine with an alcohol. For example, acetic acid can combine with methanol. These two molecules join to form an **ester** as shown below:

$$\underset{\text{acetic acid}}{\begin{array}{ccccccccc} & & H & & O & & & & \\ & & | & & \| & & & & \\ H & - & C & - & C & - & O & - & H \\ & & | & & & & & & \\ & & H & & & & & & \end{array}} + \underset{\text{methanol}}{\begin{array}{ccccc} & & H & & \\ & & | & & \\ HO & - & C & - & H \\ & & | & & \\ & & H & & \end{array}} =$$

$$\underset{\text{ester}}{\begin{array}{ccccccccccc} & & H & & O & & & & H & & \\ & & | & & \| & & & & | & & \\ H & - & C & - & C & - & O & - & C & - & H \\ & & | & & & & & & | & & \\ & & H & & & & & & H & & \end{array}} + \underset{\text{water}}{H_2O}$$

As you can see, the *ester* is made of the skeletons of the acid molecule and the alcohol molecule. An H atom from the acid and the OH group from the alcohol make up a water molecule (H_2O). The formation of an ester shows how organic compounds can combine to make new compounds with larger molecules.

Different kinds of esters are common in foods. For example, natural esters in fresh fruits such as strawberries give the fruits their sweet odor.

POLYMERS

Organic molecules can join together to form long chains. For example, the hydrocarbon ethylene, C_2H_4, can form a chain-like molecule as shown below.

Word study: Polymer from *poly* (Gr.), many and *meros* (Gr.), parts.

```
H  H      H  H      H  H   ethylene molecules
|  |      |  |      |  |
C==C      C==C      C==C
|  |      |  |      |  |
H  H      H  H      H  H

   H  H  H  H  H  H
   |  |  |  |  |  |
 --C--C--C--C--C--C--
   |  |  |  |  |  |
   H  H  H  H  H  H          polymer
```

The very long molecule is called a **polymer.** The *polymer* made from ethylene is called *polyethylene.* You probably use articles made of polyethylene every day. Polyethylene is a common plastic. It is used in such things as trash bags. Other kinds of organic molecules also can form polymers. They make other plastics such as nylon. Many natural substances are also made up of polymers. Cotton, wool, and rubber are examples of natural polymers.

Polymer A long chain-like molecule.

SUMMARY

Organic molecules can be made from hydrocarbons by substituting other atoms or radicals for hydrogen atoms. These compounds have different properties and can be thought of as substituted hydrocarbons. Polymers can be formed by combining different kinds of organic molecules.

QUESTIONS

Use complete sentences to write your answers.

1. Why is chloroform called a substituted hydrocarbon?
2. Name three organic compounds that are substituted hydrocarbons. How is each one used?
3. How does freon differ from methane?
4. Name three fruits that contain an organic acid. What is the acid?
5. What is an ester? Where can you find esters?

1. Chloroform is called a substituted hydrocarbon because it has the structure of a methane molecule with three chlorine atoms substituted for three of the hydrogen atoms.
2. Answers will vary. For example: chloroform, puts people to sleep; freon, coolant in refrigerators; methanol, used as a solvent; ethanol, used in gasohol.
3. Freon has the same skeleton as methane with two chlorine atoms and one fluorine atom substituted for three hydrogen atoms.
4. Oranges, lemons, limes, and grapefruit contain the organic acid citric acid.
5. An ester is made from the skeleton of an organic acid molecule and an alcohol molecule. The sweet smell of fruits is caused by esters.

INVESTIGATION

See teacher's commentary for teaching hints, safety, and answers to questions.

SUBSTITUTED HYDROCARBON MODELS

PURPOSE: You will build and compare models made of several substituted hydrocarbon molecules.

MATERIALS:
hydrocarbon molecular model kit

PROCEDURE:

A. Use the balls that represent hydrogen and oxygen to form three OH groups with a single bond between the oxygen atom and the hydrogen atom. See Fig. 18–16.

B. Use the balls for carbon and hydrogen to form a methane (CH_4) molecule. Remove one of the hydrogen atoms and substitute the OH group for it.

1. What is the name of this molecule?

C. Build an ethanol molecule in the same way. Keep the OH group together.

2. In how many different ways can you build an ethanol molecule?

D. Make a propanol molecule.

3. In how many different ways can you build a propanol molecule?

E. Make a butanol molecule.

4. In how many different ways can you make a butanol molecule with the carbon atoms in a single chain?

F. Make a pentanol molecule.

5. In how many different ways can you make a pentanol molecule with the carbon atoms in a single chain?

CONCLUSIONS:

1. Explain what is meant by a substituted hydrocarbon molecule.
2. What is meant by an isomer of a substituted hydrocarbon?
3. Name and compare three substituted hydrocarbon molecules.

Fig. 18–16

18-4. Molecules Needed for Life

At the end of this section you will be able to:

- ☐ Explain how living things get their energy from *carbohydrates.*
- ☐ Describe a fat molecule.
- ☐ Describe the structure of a *protein* molecule and explain why a huge number of proteins exist.

Some chemicals such as carbon monoxide and methanol are bad for you. Other chemicals are good for you. Some are even necessary for your survival. Food is made up of chemical compounds. To have a good diet, you must eat certain amounts of the foods containing the molecules needed for life. See Fig. 18–17.

Fig. 18–17 A well-balanced meal should contain all the carbohydrates, fats, proteins, vitamins, and minerals needed by the body.

CARBOHYDRATES

Carbohydrates, fats, proteins, and vitamins should be familiar names to you. All of these substances must be in your diet if you want to stay healthy. Except for vitamins, all of these substances are groups of organic compounds. We cannot possibly describe all the compounds necessary for life in a book this size. There are simply too many of them. However, you have already learned that different organic compounds can be put into general groups. In this section, you will study the structures of the three most important groups of molecules needed for life: carbohydrates, fats, and proteins. These organic compounds must be dissolved in water before your body can use them. Some organic compounds are more soluble than others.

Carbohydrates Compounds of carbon, hydrogen, and oxygen whose molecules contain two atoms of hydrogen for every atom of oxygen.

Word study: Glucose from *glykys* (Gr.), sweet.

Carbohydrates (kahr-bo-**hie**-drates) are compounds of carbon, hydrogen, and oxygen. The simplest *carbohydrate* is called *glucose*. The formula for glucose is $C_6H_{12}O_6$. The structure of a glucose molecule is shown below:

```
         OH
         |
     H—C————————┐
         |      |
     H—C—OH     |
         |      |
   HO—C—H       O
         |      |
     H—C—OH     |
         |      |
     H—C————————┘
         |
        CH2OH
```

Word study: Fructose from *fructus* (L.), fruit.

Glucose is found in many fruits. It is an example of a *simple sugar*. Another simple sugar is called *fructose*. Fructose is found in some fruits and in honey. See Fig. 18–18. Glucose and fructose are both ring-shaped molecules. All carbohydrates are made by joining glucose and other simple sugar molecules. For example, a glucose ring and a fructose ring can be joined to form a double-ring sugar molecule:

```
                      O
    H—C——————————┐ /     \
      |          |          CH2OH
    H—C—OH       |            |
      |          |            C————————┐
  HO—C—H         O            |        |
      |          |       HO—C—H        |
    H—C—OH       |            |        |
      |          |         H—C—OH      O
    H—C——————————┘            |        |
      |                    H—C—————————┘
     CH2OH                    |
                             CH2OH
```

Word study: Sucrose from *sucre* (Fr.), sugar.

The double sugar formed from glucose and fructose is called *sucrose*. The formula for sucrose is $C_{12}H_{22}O_{11}$. You use sucrose every day as common table sugar. Sucrose is also known as cane sugar because we obtain most of our supply of it from the sugar cane plant. Both simple and double sugars give food

Fig. 18–18 Fruits and honey contain the simple sugars glucose and fructose.

a sweet taste. There are many kinds of simple and double sugars in the food we eat.

The ring-shaped molecules of glucose can also join together to make a polymer. This long polymer made of many glucose molecules is the carbohydrate called *starch*. Each starch molecule has from several hundred to thousands of joined glucose rings as shown below:

```
 ──────┐             O──────────┐              O──────────┐              O──────── etc.
  H─C──────┐         │          C──────┐       │      H─C──────┐         │
    │      │         │          │      │       │        │      │         │
  H─C─OH   │         │        H─C─OH   │       │      H─C─OH   │         │
    │      │         │          │      │       │        │      │         │
 HO─C─H    O         │       HO─C─H    O       │     HO─C─H    O         │
    │      │         │          │      │       │        │      │         │
  H─C──────┼─────────┘        H─C──────┼───────┘      H─C──────┼─────────┘
    │      │                    │      │                │      │
  H─C──────┘                  H─C──────┘              H─C──────┘
    │                           │                       │
   CH2OH                       CH2OH                   CH2OH
```

Plants use starch to store food. You eat starch in bread, cereal, potatoes, and rice. See Fig. 18–19.

Carbohydrates are the body's main source of energy. The starch and double sugars in a bowl of cereal are broken down in your body into simple sugars. The simple sugars then combine with oxygen to release energy as follows:

$$C_6H_{12}O_6 + 6O_2 = 6CO_2 + 6H_2O + \text{energy}$$

Any sugar that is not used right away for energy is stored in the body as a starch called *glycogen* or as body fat.

Fig. 18–19 Starches are found in bread, cereal, and pasta.

FATS

Fats Esters formed by combining three organic acids and glycerol.

Enrichment: Saturated fats are always solid at room temperature; unsaturated fats are always liquid at room temperature.

An organic acid and an alcohol combine to form an ester. A **fat** molecule is a type of ester. A *fat* molecule is formed from an organic acid with a long chain of carbon atoms. Three of these organic acids combine with one molecule of an alcohol called *glycerol* to make a fat molecule. The organic acid that makes a molecule of fat may have only single bonds between its carbon atoms. Such an acid produces a *saturated fat.* People who eat large amounts of saturated fats may develop diseases of the blood vessels and heart. Saturated fats are found mainly in foods that come from animals, such as meat and milk products. Fats that come from plants, such as vegetable oil, usually have one or more double bonds. These are *unsaturated fats.* Your diet probably includes both saturated and unsaturated fats from foods such as milk, butter, margarine, fatty meats, and vegetable oils. See Fig. 18–20.

Fats store energy. In your body, fats are broken down into organic acids and glycerol. These compounds then release energy as they are slowly changed into carbon dioxide and water. Like the carbohydrates, most of the fat you eat is used to supply energy. However, if you eat too much fatty food, the fat is stored in your body. If you eat too much butter, ice cream, candy, or french fries, you will quickly become aware of your own fat layer! An efficient diet is based on the fact that both carbohydrates and fats can be broken down to release energy. Fats are broken down more slowly than carbohydrates. Some fats are needed in the diet. But a high-fat diet may increase the risk of heart disease and cancer.

Fig. 18–20 Fats are found in milk, butter, eggs, and nuts.

PROTEINS

When you look at yourself in a mirror, most of what you see is made of **proteins** (**proe**-teenz). Your skin, muscles, hair, and nails are mostly made of *proteins.* Proteins do more different things than any other group of molecules in your body. They make up a large part of the substance that carries oxygen in the blood. Many of your body processes are also controlled by proteins. For example, when you are angry or frightened, proteins are suddenly released into your blood. In addition, proteins build, repair, and maintain the body. Each gram of protein supplies about four Calories of energy. However, most people eat twice as much protein as they need.

Proteins Very large molecules that are formed when many amino acids join together.

Protein molecules are formed when amino acid molecules join together. For example, molecules of the amino acid *glycine* can join together as shown below:

glycine molecules

$$\begin{array}{cccccccccccccccccccccccc}
 & & H & & H & & O & & & & & & & & H & & H & & O & & & & & \\
 & & | & & | & & \| & & & & & & & & | & & | & & \| & & & & & \\
H & — & N & — & C & — & C & — & O & — & H & + & H & — & N & — & C & — & C & — & O & — & H & = \\
 & & & & | & & & & & & & & & & & & | & & & & & & & \\
 & & & & H & & & & & & & & & & & & H & & & & & & &
\end{array}$$

$$\begin{array}{ccccccccccccccccccccc}
 & & H & & H & & O & & H & & H & & O & & & & & & & & \\
 & & | & & | & & \| & & | & & | & & \| & & & & & & & & \\
H & — & N & — & C & — & C & — & N & — & C & — & C & — & O & — & H & + & O & — & H \\
 & & & & | & & & & & & | & & & & & & & & | & & \\
 & & & & H & & & & & & H & & & & & & & & H & &
\end{array}$$

Skill: This is an opportunity for students to review *problem solving* skills.

There are about 23 different amino acids that combine to make proteins. A single protein molecule is a long chain of amino acids joined together. Most proteins are made of hundreds of different arrangements of amino acids. Protein molecules perform many different functions. Thus there are a large number of different proteins in your body. Also, the proteins in your body are different from the proteins in any other living person! How can only 23 amino acids form so many different proteins?

There is a simple mathematical way to find the possible combinations. You must know the length of the protein chain and the number of amino acids involved. For example, suppose you want to arrange two amino acids in a chain three units long. The number of possible arrangements is represented by 2^3. This means that 2 is multiplied by itself 3 times: $2 \times 2 \times 2 = 8$. Thus eight arrangements are possible.

Most proteins are hundreds of amino acids long. Try to think of the different ways in which 23 amino acids could be arranged in a chain made up of hundreds of acids. If only 10 amino acids were included in a chain 100 units long, the number of possible combinations would be 10^{100} or 10,000,000,000,000,000,000,000,000,000,000,000,000,000,000,-000,000,000,000,000,000,000,000,000,000,000,000,000,000,-000,000,000,000,000.

Your body builds the proteins it needs from such foods as meat, fish, milk, and eggs. See Fig. 18–21. The proteins you eat in these foods are broken down into amino acids. These amino acids are then used to make the proteins you need. The body can make some amino acids. Others, called *essential amino acids,* are provided by the food you eat.

Fig. 18–21 Proteins are found in cheese, meat, and fish.

VITAMINS AND MINERALS

A balanced diet is mostly made up of carbohydrates, fats, and proteins. In addition, you need small amounts of other substances. For example, you need small quantities of the compounds known as *vitamins.* If vitamins are not present, many essential chemical changes cannot take place in your body. The compounds called vitamins do not belong to a single group of organic compounds. They include different kinds of molecules with long chemical names. For this reason, the vitamins are known by letters such as A, B, C, D, and E. A well-balanced diet can supply all of the vitamins needed for good health. Taking large amounts of vitamins can be harmful. Foods such as eggs, milk, liver, green vegetables, and citrus fruits supply all of the essential vitamins.

In addition to the organic compounds in food, you also need a small amount of nonorganic materials. These are called *minerals.* The minerals you need include sodium, calcium, potassium, chloride, and iron ions. Very small amounts of other elements such as zinc and copper are also needed. These minerals are found in many different foods. A balanced diet can easily supply all the minerals you need.

SUMMARY

The foods you eat contain the three basic molecules needed for life: carbohydrates, fats, and proteins. To maintain a healthy body and get the energy you need, you should eat a proper balance of all three at every meal. A well-balanced diet will also include the necessary vitamins and minerals.

QUESTIONS

Use complete sentences to write your answers.

1. List three sources of carbohydrates in your diet. Name the carbohydrate in each source.
2. How does your body use carbohydrates to make energy?
3. How is a fat molecule formed?
4. Describe a protein molecule. Why are there so many different proteins?
5. What would happen if your body did not get the proper amino acids from your diet?

1. Fruits provide fructose, sugar cane provides sucrose, bread and cereals provide starch. Other answers are also acceptable.
2. The following chemical equation shows how energy is obtained from a simple sugar:

$C_6H_{12}O_6 + 6O_2 =$
$6CO_2 + 6H_2O +$ energy.

3. A fat is a kind of ester. A fat molecule is formed when an organic acid with a long chain of carbon atoms joins with an alcohol molecule.
4. A single protein molecule is a long chain of amino acids joined together. There are 23 amino acids. A single protein molecule may have hundreds of different combinations of amino acids.
5. If your body did not receive a proper supply of amino acids from your diet, it would not be able to make the necessary proteins.

¡COMPUTE!

SCIENCE INPUT

Organic chemistry is the branch of science which studies carbon and the compounds made with carbon. This element is extremely important to human life on earth. In combination with other elements, it forms compounds which are part of our atmosphere, our food supply, and our fuel. Understanding these different forms of carbon is essential. As we have already seen, learning the formulas and facts of science takes time and effort. Learning new definitions takes the same discipline, yet knowing the proper definition of a compound or process is essential to sharing scientific communications. Scientists are very specific in their research and statements. Therefore, when you are learning scientific definitions you should make every attempt to be as accurate as possible.

COMPUTER INPUT

Here again, the computer will be put to use as a learning tool, but this time in a game format. You may already have played a pencil-and-paper version of this game with your friends. You choose a word and then draw a number of dashes to represent each letter. The other players try to guess the word by filling in the dashes with letters. In Program Letter Game, the computer will be programmed to print definitions of concepts or terms in organic chemistry on the screen. Then you will be asked to guess what concept or term is being defined by guessing one letter at a time. By filling in the letters, the concept or term will appear on the screen.

WHAT TO DO

Program Letter Game was written to contain ten data statements. From your text, choose 10 concepts or terms relating to organic chemistry. On a separate piece of paper, make a data chart similar to the one on this page, defining each term briefly and accurately.

Before entering data statements in lines 301 to 310, check the correctness of your definitions. Remember the computer will only be as accurate as your input. A sample data chart follows.

Data Chart

Term or Concept	Definition
organic	coming from life
diamond	has tightly bonded carbon atoms
carbon dioxide	a poisonous gas
graphite	the carbon in lead pencils
hydrocarbon	compound of carbon & hydrogen
methane	marsh gas—a hydrocarbon
structural formula	diagram of a molecule

ORGANIC DEFINITIONS: PROGRAM LETTER GAME

GLOSSARY

byte — a number, letter, or symbol stored in a computer's memory

ROM — READ ONLY MEMORY

RAM — RANDOM ACCESS MEMORY (see Bits of Information)

PROGRAM

```
100 REM LETTER GAME
110 FOR X = 1 TO 20: PRINT: NEXT
115 REM READING WORDS IN DATA
120 READ W$,H$: IF W$ = "0" THEN
    END
130 T$ = "  ": Q = 0
140 FOR X = 1 TO LEN(W$): T $ = T$ +
    "-": NEXT
145 REM INPUT OF GUESS
150 PRINT: PRINT: PRINT: PRINT
    H$"- "T$: PRINT: INPUT "GUESS A
    LETTER ——→ ";L$
160 G$ = T$: T$ = "": Q = Q + 1:
    Q1 = 0
165 REM BEGIN CHECK FOR CORRECT
    LETTER
170 FOR X = 1 TO LEN(W$)
180 IF MID$(W$,X,1) = L$ AND Q1 = 0
    THEN Q = Q - 1: Q1 = 1
190 IF MID$(W$,X,1) = L$ THEN T$ =
    T$ + L$: GOTO 210
200 T$ = T$ + MID$(G$,X,1)
210 NEXT
220 FOR X = 1 TO LEN(W$)
230 IF MID$(T$,X,1) = "-" THEN GOTO
    150
240 NEXT
245 REM RESPONSE SHOWING WRONG
    CHOICE
250 PRINT W$;"- ";Q;" WRONG
    GUESS(ES)": PRINT: PRINT
260 FOR X = 1 TO 15: PRINT: NEXT:
    GOTO 120
300 REM GUESS WORD AND CLUE
301 DATA ORGANIC, COMING FROM
    LIFE
400 DATA 0,0
```

PROGRAM NOTES

A more interesting way to play this game is to guess terms for which you have not written the definition. If it is possible, enter the program several times using different people's definitions. (Give each program a separate name.) Run the program guessing the terms and concepts written by someone else. This can also give you a better chance to understand what makes a clear and accurate definition.

BITS OF INFORMATION

When buying a computer, you need to know how much memory it has. Computer memory is described in terms of bytes of information. The more bytes in a computer's memory, the greater its capacity. A 16K memory (K = 1,024) means there are 16,384 bytes of memory storage available. Some of this is RAM, a section of the memory that the user can work in, erase, and reuse. When the power is turned off the data in RAM disappears, unless it has been saved on a disk or cassette. Another part of the computer's memory is ROM, which cannot be changed. When you buy a computer game and play it, it is stored in the READ ONLY MEMORY. ROM data is permanently fixed in the computer. The data can be read but not erased.

INVESTIGATION

See teacher's commentary for teaching hints, safety, and answers to questions.

SOLUBILITY OF ORGANIC COMPOUNDS

PURPOSE: You will test the solubility of five organic compounds.

MATERIALS:

5 test tubes
test-tube rack
samples of sugar, starch, MSG, gelatin, vegetable oil
water
beaker
ring stand
Bunsen burner
matches
container of water for burned matches
test-tube holder

PROCEDURE:

A. Copy the table below in your notebook.

Test tube	Organic Compound	Dissolves in Cold Water		Dissolves in Hot Water	
		Yes	No	Yes	No
A	glucose (sugar)	X			
B	starch		X	X	
C	MSG (amino acid)	X			
D	gelatin (protein)		X	X	
E	vegetable oil (fat)		X		X

B. Label five clean test tubes A, B, C, D, and E. Place the test tubes in order in the test-tube rack.

C. Place a small amount of each compound in the test tubes as shown in the table. Label each tube with the name of the compound.

D. Add water to each test tube until it is about one-fourth full.

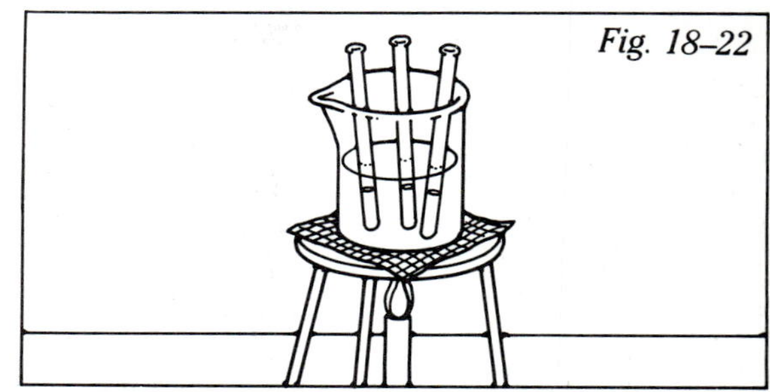
Fig. 18–22

E. Shake each test tube back and forth. Place a check mark in the "yes" column of the table if the compound dissolved in cold water. Check the "no" column if it did not.

F. Fill a beaker one-half full of water. Place it on a ring stand over a Bunsen burner.

G. Put the test tubes containing the compounds that did not dissolve into the beaker. See Fig. 18–22. Heat the beaker over the burner until the water begins to boil. Then turn off the Bunsen burner. CAUTION: Wear goggles when heating the beaker.

H. Leave the test tubes in the beaker for 4 to 5 min. Remove the test tubes one at a time and shake them. Record your observations in your data table.

CONCLUSIONS:

1. Which organic compounds dissolve in cold water?
2. Which organic compounds dissolve in hot water?
3. Which compound is more soluble, a protein or an amino acid?
4. Why are proteins broken down into amino acids in your body?

CAREERS IN SCIENCE

COSMETICS CHEMICAL TECHNICIAN

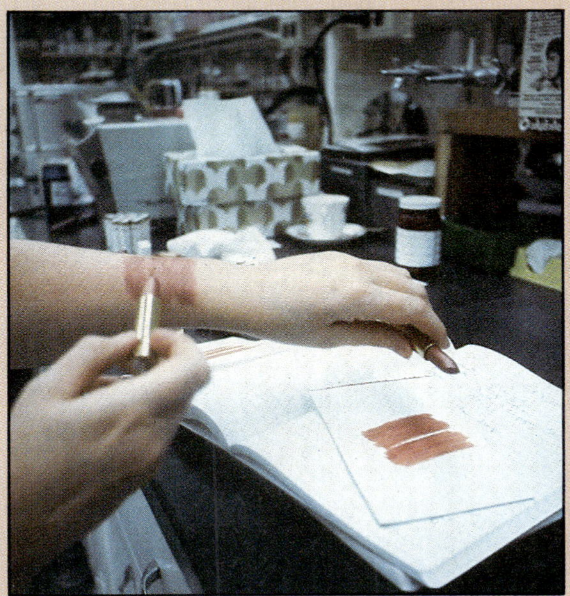

Chemical technicians do the practical rather than the theoretical work of chemical research. Technicians actually conduct the tests, record the information, compile the results, and assist in quality control of the procedures. Cosmetics technicians assist in the development and production of cosmetic products or the ingredients that make up these products. They weigh and measure the components of shampoos or shaving lotions. They monitor the mixing machines or heated kettles used to prepare ointments, creams, or powders, adding ingredients according to designated formulas. Some technicians work combining fragrances for perfumes and oils.

Many companies now offer on-the-job training to cosmetics technicians. Training is also available at vocational schools, community colleges, and at some four-year colleges.

For further information, contact: American Chemical Society, Career Services, 1155 16 Street NW, Washington, DC 20036.

PETROLEUM CHEMICAL TECHNICIAN

Working from a chemist's research design and instruction, petroleum chemical technicians test samples of crude oil and petroleum products to determine their characteristics. During the processing of these substances, they test continually to ensure that products meet quality control standards. They analyze the contents of these products to determine the presence of gases after processing. Some petroleum technicians test air and water samples for the presence of industrial pollutants. These technicians work with extremely complicated equipment such as hydrometers, fractionators, and mass spectrometers.

Most petroleum chemical technicians have at least an associate degree in applied sciences. Many firms now offer training programs for prospective technicians that concentrate on the special needs of the company.

For further information, contact: American Chemical Society, Career Services, 1155 16 Street NW, Washington, DC 20036.

CHAPTER REVIEW

See teacher's commentary for answers.

VOCABULARY

On a separate piece of paper, match each term with the number of the statement that best explains it. Use each term only once.

alcohol	fats	structural formula	ester
alkenes	organic chemistry	double bond	organic acid
alkynes	hydrocarbon	alkanes	proteins
amino acid	isomers	aromatics	polymer
carbohydrates			

1. Compounds with a double bond between one pair of carbons.
2. Two or more molecules with the same formulas but different arrangements of their atoms.
3. An organic molecule having both NH_2 and COOH groups.
4. A diagram of a molecule.
5. An ester formed by combining three organic acids and glycerol.
6. Compounds of carbon, hydrogen, and oxygen whose molecules contain two atoms of hydrogen for every one of oxygen.
7. A kind of organic molecule having at least one OH group.
8. A compound containing only carbon and hydrogen.
9. A kind of organic molecule with at least one COOH group.
10. A very large molecule formed when many amino acids join together.
11. Compounds with a triple bond between one pair of carbons.
12. A kind of molecule formed by combining an organic acid and an alcohol.
13. Hydrocarbons containing carbon atoms arranged in a ring structure.
14. Bond formed when atoms are joined by sharing two pairs of electrons.
15. A long, chain-like molecule.
16. A group of hydrocarbons in which the carbon atoms are joined by single bonds.
17. The chemistry of carbon atoms.

QUESTIONS

Give brief but complete answers to each of the following questions. Unless otherwise indicated, use complete sentences to write your answers.

1. Explain what is meant by an organic compound. Name four common organic compounds.
2. Draw a diagram showing the energy levels, electron arrangement, number of protons, and number of neutrons in a carbon atom.
3. List the characteristics of a hydrocarbon molecule.

4. Give a use for each of the following: methane, ethane, propane, and butane.
5. Name three kinds of substituted hydrocarbon molecules. What chemical radicals are used to identify them?
6. Describe how glucose, fructose, sucrose, and starch are related.
7. Explain how your body obtains energy from starch and simple sugars.
8. Distinguish between saturated and unsaturated fats. Where are they found in your diet?
9. Compare and contrast diamond and graphite.
10. Draw the structural formulas for the three isomers of pentane.
11. Name the alcohol that has three carbon atoms and the one that has four carbon atoms. Draw their structural formulas.
12. Alanine is the name of the amino acid with a skeleton of an ethane molecule. Draw the structural formula for alanine.
13. What is polyethylene? What is it used for?

APPLYING SCIENCE

1. Compare the labels on several kinds of mouthwash. How many contain alcohol? What are the percentages of alcohol listed? Determine the relative strengths of the mouthwashes based on the alcohol content of each solution.
2. Chloroform was one of the first substances used as an anesthetic. Find out who first used chloroform for this purpose. Why can it be used as an anesthetic? Why is it not often used today? Also explain why chloroform is considered a hazard in some municipal water supplies. Ether is another substance used as an anesthetic. Find out how it was discovered. What is the chemical formula of the ether used as an anesthetic? Draw its structural formula.

BIBLIOGRAPHY

Bernard, Harold. *The Greenhouse Effect.* Cambridge, MA: Ballinger, 1980.

Bershad, Carol and Deborah Bernick. *Bodyworks: The Kids' Guide to Food and Physical Fitness.* New York: Random House, 1981.

Burt, O. W. *Black Sunshine: The Story of Coal.* New York: Messner, 1977.

Kraft, B. H. *Oil and Natural Gas.* New York: Watts, 1978.

Nourse, Alan E. *Vitamins.* New York: Watts, 1977.

Shephard, Roy J. *Carbon Monoxide: The Silent Killer.* Springfield, IL: C. C. Thomas, 1983.

UNIT

6

REACTIONS OF MATTER

CHAPTER

19

You may think that chemical reactions take place only in a laboratory. However, chemical reactions are all around you. In fact, chemical reactions are taking place in your body right now.

CHEMICAL REACTIONS

CHAPTER GOALS

1. Describe a chemical reaction using a chemical equation.
2. Give examples of different kinds of chemical reactions.
3. List the conditions that can change the speed of a chemical reaction.
4. Describe two types of chemical reactions that absorb or release energy.

19-1. Types of Reactions

At the end of this section you will be able to:

- Give some examples of a *chemical reaction.*
- Explain how a *chemical equation* describes a chemical reaction.
- Describe four types of chemical reactions.

In an earlier chapter, you learned that a chemical change is different from a physical change. For example, chopping wood is a physical change. Burning the wood in a fireplace is a chemical change. In a chemical change, the molecules of one substance are changed into another substance. This chapter will give examples of other kinds of chemical change.

DESCRIBING A CHEMICAL CHANGE

How would you describe charcoal burning in a barbecue grill? Burning charcoal, or any other material, produces a chemical change. When a chemical change takes place, the substances that are present before the change are called *reactants.* The reactants are the substances that react or change. The new substances formed as a result of the chemical change are called *products.* Thus a general description of a chemical change could be written as: reactants yield products. For example, charcoal is made up of carbon atoms. When charcoal burns, it combines with oxygen to form carbon dioxide. Carbon and oxygen are the reactants and carbon dioxide is the product. The burning of charcoal can be described as follows:

carbon plus oxygen yields carbon dioxide

Chemical reaction A process in which a chemical change takes place.

When charcoal burns, the carbon atoms combine with oxygen. The combination of an element such as carbon with oxygen is called *oxidation.* Oxidation is an example of a **chemical reaction.** A *chemical reaction* is the result of a chemical change. Burning charcoal is a chemical reaction because the carbon and oxygen are chemically changed into the compound carbon dioxide.

You can usually observe some evidence that a chemical reaction has taken place. For example, many chemical reactions result in an increase or a decrease in the temperature of the reactants. This change in temperature is the result of heat energy being released or used up as the reaction takes place. You will learn more about these types of reaction in a later section of this chapter.

CHEMICAL EQUATIONS

Another way of writing the reaction of carbon with oxygen is with the formulas for carbon and oxygen:

$$C + O_2 \longrightarrow CO_2$$

Chemical equation A description of a chemical reaction using chemical formulas for the reactants and products.

This description of a chemical reaction is called a **chemical equation** (ih-**kway**-zhun). The *chemical equation* for the burning of charcoal says that one atom of carbon reacts with one molecule of oxygen to form one molecule of carbon dioxide.

In a chemical equation, the formulas for all reactants are written on the left side. Each reactant is separated from the others by a plus (+) sign. The formulas for the products are written on the right. Reactants and products are separated by an arrow that means "produces" or "yields."

The following chemical equation shows the reaction of hydrogen and oxygen to form water:

$$\text{hydrogen} + \text{oxygen} \longrightarrow \text{water}$$

Using formulas, the equation is:

$$H_2 + O_2 \longrightarrow H_2O$$

However, this equation is not complete. Look at the number of oxygen atoms on each side of the equation. There are two oxygen atoms on the left of the arrow but only one oxygen atom on the right. One oxygen atom seems to have disappeared. Scientists have shown that atoms do not disappear during chemical reactions. The *law of conservation of matter* explains what happens during a chemical reaction. This law says that *the same number of atoms exists after a chemical reaction as before the reaction.* To correct the above equation you must *balance* it. Since there are two oxygen atoms on the left of the arrow, there must also be two on the right:

$$H_2 + O_2 \longrightarrow 2H_2O$$

Now the oxygen atoms are balanced but the hydrogen atoms are not. There are four hydrogen atoms on the right but there are only two hydrogen atoms on the left. The problem must not be solved by changing the formulas H_2, O_2, or H_2O. Each of these formulas correctly describes a molecule of hydrogen, oxygen, and water. The problem can be solved by placing a 2 in front of H_2. A number written in front of a formula is called a *coefficient* (koe-uh-**fish**-unt). A coefficient tells how many molecules are used. With the coefficient added, the equation now reads:

$$2H_2 + O_2 \longrightarrow 2H_2O$$

The equation now says that two molecules of H_2 react with one molecule of O_2 to yield two molecules of H_2O. Now there are four hydrogen atoms and two oxygen atoms on the left. Four hydrogen atoms and two oxygen atoms are also on the right. This equation is now correctly balanced. A balanced equation shows that atoms are not created or destroyed in the reaction.

In summary, a correctly balanced chemical equation shows the following information about a chemical reaction:

1. The formulas of the molecules that are reacting (reactants) are shown on the left of the arrow.
2. The formulas of the molecules that are produced by the reaction (products) are shown on the right of the arrow.
3. The total number of atoms of each reactant equals the number of those same atoms in the products. No atoms are created or lost during the reaction.

WRITING CHEMICAL EQUATIONS

You can write a balanced chemical equation describing a reaction by following three steps. For example, natural gas contains the hydrocarbon called methane, CH_4. When methane burns, it yields carbon dioxide and water. In order to write a chemical equation showing the burning of methane, follow these steps:

1. Describe the chemical reaction in words: Methane combines with oxygen to yield carbon dioxide and water.

2. Write the correct formulas for the reactants on the left and the products on the right with an arrow in between. Separate the reactants and the products with plus signs:

$$CH_4 + O_2 \longrightarrow CO_2 + H_2O$$

3. Write coefficient numbers in front of the formulas as needed to balance the equation:

CH_4	+	$2O_2$	$\longrightarrow$	CO_2	+	$2H_2O$
1 atom C	+	4 atoms O	$\longrightarrow$	1 atom C	+	4 atoms H
4 atoms H				2 atoms O		2 atoms O

KINDS OF CHEMICAL REACTIONS

There are many kinds of chemical reactions. When a nail rusts, or milk turns sour, or bread bakes, a chemical reaction is taking place. Each of these reactions can be described by one or more chemical equations. Most reactions can be put into one of four general groups. In each group, the atoms are arranged into different combinations as a result of the reaction. The four kinds of chemical reactions are:

Fig. 19–1 The rusting of metal is a synthesis reaction in which iron combines with oxygen:

$$4Fe + 3O_2 \rightarrow 2Fe_2O_3$$

1. Synthesis. Synthesis (**sin**-thuh-sus) means "to combine." When a synthesis reaction occurs, two substances combine to form a different kind of molecule. See Fig. 19–1. You have seen examples of this when carbon reacts with oxygen to form carbon dioxide, or hydrogen combines with oxygen to make water. Another example of a synthesis reaction is the reaction between iron and sulfur. If these elements are heated in a test tube over a Bunsen burner, the compound iron sulfide is formed. Heat and light are given off during this reaction. A new substance with different properties is formed in a synthesis reaction. The rust formed when iron combines with oxygen gas has different properties than either iron or oxygen.

2. Decomposition. A molecule breaks down into different molecules in a decomposition reaction. See Fig. 19–2. This kind of reaction is the opposite of a synthesis reaction. For example, water can be broken down into hydrogen and oxygen as shown by the following chemical equation:

$$2H_2O \longrightarrow 2H_2 + O_2$$

The compound potassium chlorate can be broken down by heating into two new substances:

$$2KClO_3 \longrightarrow 2KCl + 3O_2$$

This is another example of a decomposition reaction.

Fig. 19–2 Many compounds can be decomposed by heat. Decomposition is the opposite of synthesis.

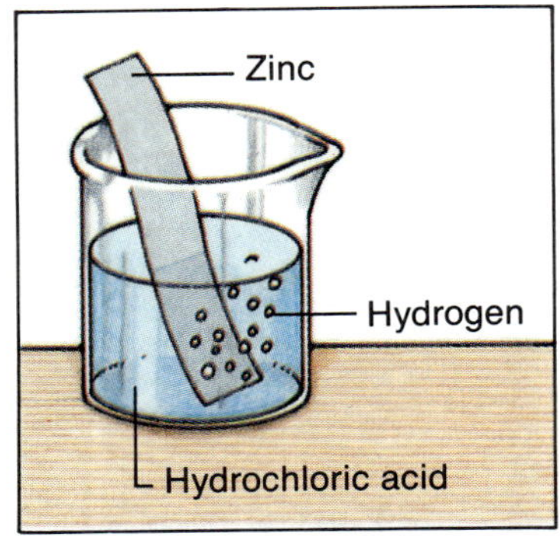

Fig. 19–3 The reaction between zinc and hydrochloric acid is a single replacement reaction. Zinc replaces hydrogen to form zinc chloride.

3. Single replacement. In a single replacement reaction, one kind of atom trades places with another. For example, when zinc metal is put into hydrochloric acid (HCl), hydrogen gas and zinc chloride (ZnCl) are produced. See Fig. 19–3. The equation for this reaction is:

$$Zn + 2HCl \longrightarrow H_2 + ZnCl_2$$

Zinc atoms have replaced hydrogen atoms in the hydrochloric acid.

4. Double replacement. In a double replacement reaction, atoms of two different compounds trade places. For example, when solutions containing silver nitrate ($AgNO_3$) and sodium chloride (NaCl) are mixed, the following reaction occurs:

$$AgNO_3 + NaCl \longrightarrow AgCl + NaNO_3$$

Two new compounds (silver chloride and sodium nitrate) have been formed as a result of silver atoms and sodium atoms replacing each other.

SUMMARY

A chemical equation is a useful form of shorthand to describe a chemical reaction. A balanced equation tells you what substances are reacting and what products are formed in the reaction. Atoms are not created or destroyed in a chemical reaction. There are four general kinds of chemical reactions.

QUESTIONS

Use complete sentences to write your answers.

1. Give two examples of chemical reactions.
2. What information do the following two chemical equations give you?

$$\text{(a) } 2H_2 + O_2 \longrightarrow 2H_2O$$

$$\text{(b) } 2Na + Cl_2 \longrightarrow 2NaCl$$

3. Write and balance chemical equations that show (a) hydrogen plus oxygen produces water; (b) carbon plus oxygen produces carbon dioxide; (c) hydrogen plus chlorine produces hydrogen chloride.
4. Name four types of chemical reactions. Give an example of each reaction.

1. Answers will vary. Any two chemical reactions are acceptable.
2. (a) Two hydrogen molecules react with one oxygen molecule to produce two water molecules. (b) Two sodium atoms react with one chlorine molecule to produce two sodium chloride particles.
3. (a) $2H_2 + O_2 \longrightarrow 2H_2O$
(b) $C + O_2 \longrightarrow CO_2$
(c) $H_2 + Cl_2 \longrightarrow 2HCl$
4. In a synthesis reaction, two substances combine to form a different kind of molecule. In a decomposition reaction, one kind of molecule is broken down into two different molecules. In a single replacement reaction, one kind of atom trades places with another kind of atom. In a double replacement reaction, atoms in two different compounds trade places.

INVESTIGATION

See teacher's commentary for teaching hints, safety, and answers to questions.

TEMPERATURE CHANGES IN A CHEMICAL REACTION

PURPOSE: You will observe evidence that a chemical reaction has taken place.

MATERIALS:

plaster of paris | water
small paper cup | stirring rod

PROCEDURE:

A. CAUTION: Wear goggles. Place about 20 g of plaster of paris in a small paper cup. See Fig. 19–4. The chemical formula for plaster of paris is $(CaSO_4)_2 \cdot H_2O$. This formula indicates that there is a water molecule (H_2O) attached to the calcium sulfate molecules, $(CaSO_4)_2$.

B. Stir in small amounts of water until you have a thick paste. The plaster of paris will get hard within a few minutes.

Fig. 19–4

C. As the plaster of paris hardens, feel the cup from time to time.

1. Do you observe any change in the temperature of the cup?

D. The chemical reaction between plaster of paris and water can be described by a chemical equation. Copy the following equation. Use your observations in step C to complete the equation.

$$(CaSO_4)_2 \cdot H_2O + 3H_2O \longrightarrow$$
$$2\ CaSO_4 \cdot 2H_2O + \underline{\qquad\qquad}$$

CONCLUSION:

1. In your own words, describe one kind of change you can observe when a chemical reaction takes place.

EXTENSION: You will find out if mass is gained or lost in a chemical reaction.

MATERIALS:

balance | flash bulb
camera with flash holder

PROCEDURE:

A. Use the balance to find the mass of the flash bulb.

1. What is the mass of the bulb?

B. Put the bulb into the flash holder of a camera and flash it.

2. How do you know a chemical reaction has taken place?

C. Allow the bulb to cool and place it on the balance.

3. Was mass gained or lost in this chemical reaction?

19-2. Speed of Reactions

At the end of this section you will be able to:

- ☐ Explain what is meant by the *collision theory.*
- ☐ Describe four ways to change the speed of a chemical reaction.

Food spoils as a result of chemical reactions. In this section you will learn how a refrigerator helps control those reactions. See Fig. 19–5.

COLLIDING MOLECULES

Collision theory The theory that molecules must collide in order to react with each other.

If you want to cause a chemical reaction between two substances, you must mix them together. The molecules, atoms, or ions in the substances must come in contact. No new chemical bonds will form until there are collisions between the particles. This principle is called the **collision theory.** According to the *collision theory,* chemical reactions are the result of molecular collisions. See Fig. 19–6. Anything that makes the molecules collide more often will speed up a reaction. Similarly, anything that causes molecules to collide less often will slow down a reaction.

Fig. 19–5 The chemical reactions that cause food to spoil are slowed down when the temperature is lowered.

CONTROLLING REACTION SPEED

There are four conditions that can cause the speed of a chemical reaction to change. These conditions are:

1. Concentration. **Concentration** (kon-sun-**tray**-shun) describes how many molecules are found in a given space. One way to make molecules collide more often is to crowd more of them together. For example, you can speed up the burning reaction by blowing air on the fire. More oxygen molecules combine with the fuel and the burning reaction speeds up. See Fig. 19–7. Similarly, cutting off the oxygen supply is one way to put out a fire. Generally, an increase in the *concentration* of reactants speeds up a reaction and a decrease in concentration slows down a reaction. However, the effect of concentration on the speed of a specific reaction must be found by experiment.

2. Increasing surface area. When one of the reactants is a solid, the reaction speed can be increased by breaking the solid into smaller pieces. This increases the *surface area* and permits more of the solid to touch the other reactants. The surface area of a piece of wood is greatly increased if the wood is made into sawdust. Sawdust burns dangerously fast. Explosions can occur in grain elevators, coal mines, and flour mills

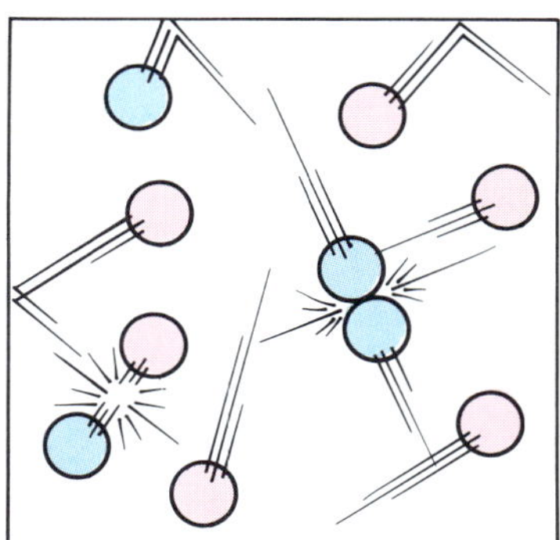

Fig. 19–6 Molecules are always in motion. Reactions occur when molecules collide.

Concentration A description of the number of molecules found in a given space.

Fig. 19–7 When wood burns, it combines chemically with oxygen. Increasing the concentration of oxygen speeds up the reaction.

Fig. 19–8 A source of heat is needed before the charcoal will begin to burn.

where the air becomes filled with dust. A small spark can cause the dust particles to begin burning rapidly. The sudden release of heat causes an explosion. Another example is ordinary sugar. It dissolves faster than a sugar cube because more surface area of the sugar is exposed to water.

Enrichment: A piece of old yellow newspaper and a piece of burned newspaper have both undergone the same chemical reaction. Burning is faster.

3. Temperature. Molecules must do more than just touch each other in order to react. They must collide. The force of the collision must be great enough to break the chemical bonds and allow new ones to form. This means that molecules cannot react unless they have enough energy to collide with a certain force. A chemical reaction will not start unless its reactants have the needed energy. The amount of energy needed to start a chemical reaction is called *threshold energy.* The threshold energy needed to start the chemical reactions in a match head is not large. The friction of rubbing the match against a rough surface is enough. On the other hand, the carbon in charcoal has a large threshold energy. A match or some other source of heat is needed before the charcoal begins to burn. See Fig. 19–8.

Cooking usually causes chemical changes in food. A good cook controls the speed of these changes by controlling the temperature. Chemical reactions generally speed up if the temperature goes up. Lower temperatures usually slow down a reaction. The reactions that cause food to spoil can be slowed by cooling or freezing the food. In a home refrigerator, the temperature is usually between 2°C and 5°C. At these low temperatures, the chemical reactions are slowed but not completely stopped. Most food can be kept refrigerated safely for only a few days. However, in a freezer the temperature stays below 0°C. Food can remain at this temperature for several months without spoiling. Some food such as meats can be frozen for years. If a frozen food is heated at ordinary temperatures until it thaws, the chemical reactions causing it to spoil will begin again. Once it is thawed, food should not be frozen again, since it will not be as fresh as it was before freezing.

As a general rule, the speed of a reaction doubles for every 10°C rise in temperature. The number of collisions increases as the molecules move faster at the higher temperature.

4. Catalysts. The speed of a reaction can also be changed by adding a **catalyst** (**kat**-l-ust). The *catalyst* remains unchanged after the reaction. For example, you can buy hydrogen peroxide (H_2O_2) at a drugstore to use as an antiseptic. Hydrogen peroxide cannot be kept forever because it slowly breaks down into water and oxygen:

$$2H_2O_2 \longrightarrow O_2 + 2H_2O$$

This reaction is ordinarily slow. However, if a piece of steel wool is dropped into the hydrogen peroxide, bubbles of oxygen gas will form. The steel wool greatly speeds up the normally slow reaction. When the reaction stops, the steel wool is unchanged. The steel wool acts as a catalyst. A catalyst changes the speed of a reaction but is not changed itself by the reaction. Most catalysts speed up a reaction by lowering the threshold energy needed for the reaction to start. More molecules can collide and react without raising the temperature. Catalysts play an important part in many chemical reactions in living things. Without the right catalyst, many of the chemical reactions needed to carry on life processes could not take place quickly enough. Catalysts that control chemical reactions in living things are called *enzymes*. Your body contains thousands of enzymes. Each one controls the speed of a certain chemical reaction. For example, an enzyme called *insulin* controls the way in which your body uses sugars and starches in your diet. A serious disease called *diabetes* results when a person's body does not make enough insulin. Most people with severe diabetes control the disease by taking insulin and limiting the sugars and starches in their diets.

Catalyst A substance that changes the speed of a chemical reaction but that remains the same after the reaction.

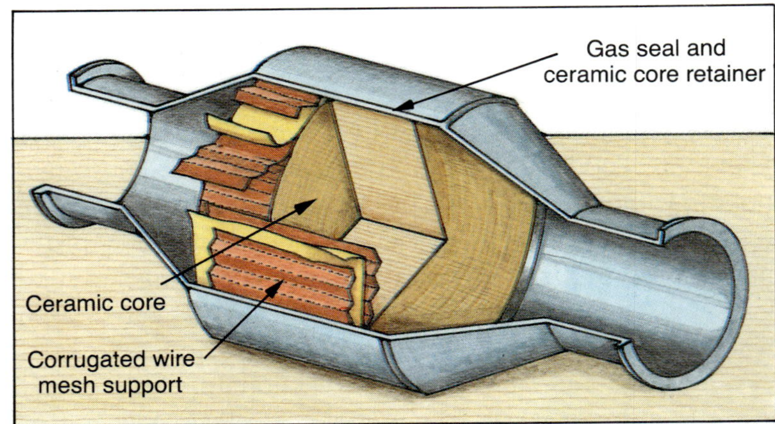

Fig. 19–9 This diagram shows a catalytic converter that, in a car, changes harmful pollutants into carbon dioxide and water.

Catalysts are also part of a car's exhaust system. The exhaust gases pass through a *catalytic converter.* See Fig. 19–9. There gases such as hydrocarbons and carbon monoxide that cause air pollution combine with oxygen to form carbon dioxide and water. The catalyst in the converter speeds up the reaction as the gases pass through.

Enrichment: Catalysts can also slow down reactions. For example, tetraethyl lead is added to gasoline in order to slow down the rate at which gasoline burns. This prevents the knocking caused by premature explosion of the fuel-air mixture. A catalyst that slows down a reaction can be called an inhibitor.

Just as catalysts speed up reactions, *inhibitors* slow them down. Preservatives added to food are inhibitors. For example, sodium nitrate and sodium nitrite are added to hot dogs, bacon, and ham. Preservatives prevent the growth of harmful bacteria and molds. Without preservatives, foods would have to be refrigerated constantly.

SUMMARY

Chemical reactions take place as a result of molecular collisions. Some chemical reactions happen very rapidly. Other reactions take place slowly. The speed at which a reaction takes place can be controlled by changing the concentration, the surface area, or the temperature, or by using a catalyst.

QUESTIONS

Use complete sentences to write your answers.

1. How will crowding molecules closer together make them react with each other more often?
2. What effect does temperature have on chemical reactions?
3. What part does a catalyst play in a chemical reaction?
4. Why is sawdust in a sawmill dangerous?

1. Crowding molecules more closely together causes them to collide more often and therefore react more often with each other.
2. In order to react, the collision must be hard enough to break bonds. Increasing the temperature causes the molecules to move faster and therefore to collide harder. The rate of the reaction will increase.
3. A catalyst causes a chemical reaction to take place faster or at a lower temperature.
4. Sawdust has a large surface area. It will burn explosively if it is accidentally ignited by a spark.

INVESTIGATION

See teacher's commentary for teaching hints, safety, and answers to questions.

CATALYSTS IN A CHEMICAL REACTION

PURPOSE: You will test the effect of a catalyst on a chemical reaction.

MATERIALS:

4 test tubes and rack
hydrogen peroxide
small piece of meat
salt
manganese dioxide

PROCEDURE:

A. Copy the table below in your notebook.

Test Tube	Gas Given Off		Rate	
	Yes	No	Slow	Fast
1. Meat + H_2O_2	X		X	
2. Salt + H_2O_2		X		
3. MnO_2 + H_2O_2	X			X
4. H_2O_2		X		

B. Fill four test tubes one-third full of hydrogen peroxide. Label each tube and put them in the test-tube rack.

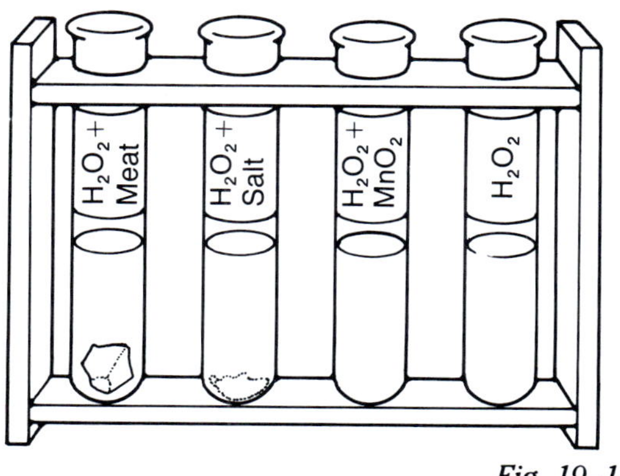

Fig. 19–10

C. Place about 2 g of meat in the first tube. Add this to the label.

D. Place 0.5 g of salt in the second tube. Add this to the label.

E. Place a pinch of manganese dioxide in the third tube. Add this to the label.

F. Do not add anything to the fourth tube. This is your control.

G. Observe the test tubes for about 5 min. Look for bubbles of oxygen gas to form. See Fig. 19–10. Record the rate as *slow* or *fast* in your table.

1. Did you see oxygen gas bubble out of the tube containing only the hydrogen peroxide?
2. In which tube was the rate fastest?

CONCLUSIONS:

1. Which substances acted as catalysts?
2. Which acted as the best catalyst?

EXTENSION: You will find out which foods use inhibitors to slow down decay.

A. Copy the table below in your notebook.

Preservatives	Foods
propylene glycol	
sodium nitrite	
sodium proprionate	
calcium proprionate	
potassium sorbate	

B. Read the labels on packages of food. List the foods in which each of the preservatives is found.

19-3. Endothermic and Exothermic Reactions

At the end of this section you will be able to:

- Explain how energy is released in chemical reactions.
- Distinguish between an *endothermic* and an *exothermic* reaction.
- Give examples of some *fuels*.

The explosion of fireworks is caused when chemical reactions rapidly release energy. See Fig. 19–11. All explosions are the result of this kind of reaction. Many chemicals are dangerous because they release energy rapidly when they react.

Fig. 19–11 When fireworks explode, chemical energy is released rapidly. Fireworks are dangerous and should be handled only by experienced people.

REACTIONS THAT RELEASE ENERGY

Chemical energy may be given off when atoms form bonds with each other. An atom that does not have a stable number of electrons can release energy and become more stable by forming a chemical bond. The energy released is chemical energy.

Chemical energy is usually released in the form of heat. The heat given off in a chemical reaction is often included in a chemical equation. For example, the complete equation for the burning of carbon is:

$$C + O_2 \longrightarrow CO_2 + \text{heat}$$

Chemical reactions that give off heat are called **exothermic** (ek-soe-**thur**-mik) reactions. All burning reactions are *exothermic*. Many other kinds of reaction that do not involve burning are also exothermic. When sodium metal combines with chlorine gas, for example, heat is produced.

Exothermic reaction A chemical reaction that gives off energy in the form of heat.

$$2Na + Cl_2 \longrightarrow 2NaCl + \text{heat}$$

One way to measure the amount of heat produced is by means of a *calorimeter*. You saw an example of a calorimeter in Chapter 5. Using a calorimeter, you will find that burning a lump of carbon with a mass of 12 g will produce about 94,000 calories. Heat is also measured in joules. One calorie is equal to about 4.18 joules.

The energy content of food can also be measured with a calorimeter. A small sample of the food is dried and then combined with oxygen in the calorimeter. The heat released is measured in calories. The number of calories represents the energy released by the food in our bodies. Because most foods produce large amounts of energy, heat content is given in a unit that is 1,000 times the value of an ordinary calorie. A food Calorie is equal to 1,000 calories or 1 kilocalorie (kcal). Food Calories are also called large Calories and are always spelled with a capital C. See Table 19–1.

CALORIES USED IN VARIOUS ACTIVITIES					
Activity	Weight in Pounds				
	100	120	140	160	180
Bicycling	112	134	157	179	202
Dancing	352	423	493	564	643
Dishwashing	45	54	63	72	81
Driving	40	48	56	64	72
Eating	18	22	25	29	32
Playing piano	63	75	88	100	113
Running	314	376	439	502	564
Skating	157	188	220	251	282
Tennis	218	261	305	348	392
Walking	372	446	521	596	669
Writing	18	22	25	29	32

Table 19–1

REACTIONS THAT ABSORB ENERGY

Endothermic reaction A chemical reaction that absorbs energy.

Not all chemical reactions are exothermic. Some reactions take place only if energy is added. No energy is given off. A chemical reaction that absorbs energy is called **endothermic** (en-doe-**thur**-mik). The breakdown of water to form hydrogen and oxygen is an example of an *endothermic* reaction. Water will only form hydrogen and oxygen if a large amount of heat or electric energy is added:

$$\text{energy} + 2H_2O \longrightarrow 2H_2 + O_2$$

An important kind of endothermic reaction takes place in green plants. The plants absorb light energy from the sun. This energy causes carbon dioxide in the plants to react with water to produce *glucose*. Glucose is a sugar with the formula $C_6H_{12}O_6$. The equation below shows how plants produce sugar and oxygen by an endothermic reaction:

$$6CO_2 + 6H_2O + \text{energy} \longrightarrow C_6H_{12}O_6 + O_2$$

This reaction is part of the process of *photosynthesis* by which green plants produce food using energy from the sun.

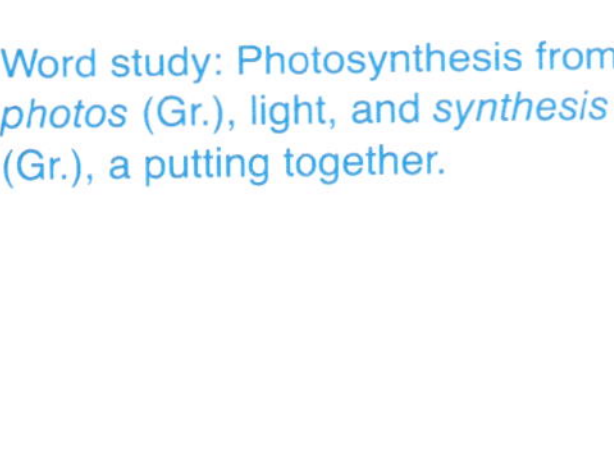

Word study: Photosynthesis from *photos* (Gr.), light, and *synthesis* (Gr.), a putting together.

Fig. 19–12 Most of the earth's supply of coal was formed during the Carboniferous period.

Fig. 19–13 In a refinery, petroleum is made into many other useful products.

FUELS

Exothermic reactions are important to us because they are the source of chemical energy. Any substance used as a source of chemical energy is called a **fuel.** Carbon and some of its compounds are important *fuels.* Carbon fuels are the remains of plants and animals that died millions of years ago. These fuels are called *fossil fuels.* Fossils are the remains of ancient plants and animals that died about 250 million years ago. The fossil fuels are made up of the carbon compounds that were once part of living things. See Fig. 19–12. These compounds were changed by heat and pressure when they became trapped in the earth. Fossil fuels are found in three forms:

Fuel A substance used as a source of chemical energy.

1. Liquid fuels. The source of almost all liquid fuels is **petroleum.** *Petroleum* is a mixture of compounds of carbon and hydrogen found deep in the earth. Petroleum can be separated into simpler compounds such as gasoline, kerosene, lubricating oil, petroleum jelly, paraffin, and asphalt. This is done by heating the liquid petroleum (also called *crude oil*). The various liquids that make up the petroleum mixture boil at different temperatures. As each kind of liquid boils, its vapor is carried away. The vapor cools and changes back to a liquid. These different parts of the petroleum mixture are called *fractions*. The process of separating liquids with different boiling temperatures is called *distillation.* Thus crude oil is separated into its parts by the process called *fractional distillation.* See Fig. 19–13.

Petroleum A natural mixture of compounds of carbon and hydrogen.

Word study: Petroleum from *petra* (L.), rock, and *oleum* (L.), oil.

Word study: Distillation from *distillare* (L.), to drop down.

Fig. 19–14 There are four forms of coal: peat, lignite, bituminous, and anthracite. Bituminous is the most important as well as the most plentiful form of coal.

2. Gas fuels. Natural gas is often found with petroleum. Natural gas also consists of compounds of carbon and hydrogen. The main compound in natural gas is *methane.* Methane has the formula CH_4. *Butane* and *propane* are also carbon-hydrogen compounds obtained from petroleum. They are often used as fuels in places where natural gas is not available. Some gas fuels are artificial. The most common artificial gas is *water gas.* Water gas is a mixture of carbon monoxide and hydrogen. Steam passed over hot carbon forms water gas:

$$\underset{\text{steam}}{H_2O} + \underset{\text{hot carbon}}{C} \longrightarrow \underset{\text{carbon monoxide}}{CO} + \underset{\text{hydrogen}}{H_2}$$

Hydrogen gas by itself may be a common fuel in the near future.

3. Solid fuels. *Coal* is the most common solid fuel. See Fig. 19–14. Coke is a solid fuel made from coal. Coke is made by heating coal without air. This reaction produces almost pure carbon. Most coke is used as a fuel by the iron and steel industries. Several useful byproducts are also produced in the manufacture of coke. These byproducts are used to make fertilizers, dyes, perfumes, and medicines.

As the earth's population has grown, the need for energy has also increased. See Fig. 19–15. We have already used up much of the earth's supply of carbon fuels. All carbon fuels will probably be gone within a few hundred years. New sources and methods must be found to satisfy the great energy needs of the earth's people. Solar energy, geothermal energy, nuclear energy, tidal energy, and wind energy may all be used to supply our energy needs in the future.

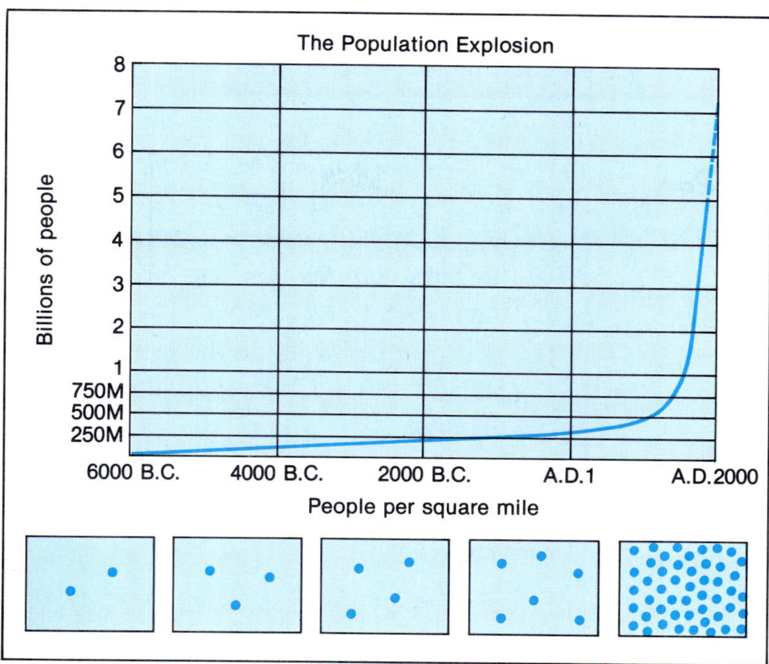

Fig. 19–15 As the earth's population continues to grow, we will need ever-increasing supplies of energy.

SUMMARY

Most of the energy we use every day comes from chemical reactions. Atoms produce chemical energy when they become more stable by forming bonds with other atoms. Chemical reactions are either endothermic or exothermic. Liquid, gaseous, and solid fuels also yield chemical energy. Carbon fuels are the remains of ancient living things. These carbon fuels will be used up in the near future.

QUESTIONS

Use complete sentences to write your answers.

1. In what form is chemical energy usually released in a chemical reaction?
2. Explain why energy is released in a chemical reaction.
3. Write a chemical equation for a reaction in which energy is released.
4. How do exothermic and endothermic reactions differ?
5. Name three forms of fossil fuel. Why does the use of fossil fuels present a problem for the future? What are some alternatives to fossil fuels?

1. Chemical energy is usually released in the form of heat.
2. In a chemical reaction, the atoms release energy in order to become more stable.
3. Answers may vary. For example, $C + O_2 \longrightarrow CO_2$ + heat or $2Na + Cl_2 \longrightarrow 2NaCl$ + heat.
4. An exothermic reaction releases heat; an endothermic reaction absorbs heat.
5. Fossil fuels include liquid, gaseous, and solid forms. In the future it is likely that these forms of fuel will be used up. Alternatives to fossil fuels include solar energy, geothermal energy, tidal energy, and wind energy.

SKILL-BUILDING ACTIVITY

See teacher's commentary for teaching hints, safety, and answers to questions.

COMPARING AND CONTRASTING EXOTHERMIC AND ENDOTHERMIC REACTIONS

PURPOSE: You will observe an exothermic and an endothermic reaction and compare them.

MATERIALS

2 400 mL beakers
hypo (sodium thiosulphate)
stirring rod
thermometer
water
washing soda (sodium carbonate)

PROCEDURE:

A. Copy the data table below.

Beaker	T_i (°C)	T_f (°C)	$\Delta T = T_f - T_i$ (°C)	Exothermic		Endothermic	
				Yes	No	Yes	No
1. Hypo							
2. Washing soda							

B. Place 20 g of hypo in a beaker. Label the beaker. Stir the dry hypo with a glass stirring rod.

C. Insert a thermometer and record the initial temperature (T_i) in the data table. See Fig. 19–16.

D. Add 15 mL of water to the hypo. Stir carefully with the rod. Record the final temperature (T_f).

1. Is this an exothermic or an endothermic reaction?

E. Rinse the rod and the thermometer with water and dry them.

F. Place 20 g of washing soda in the second beaker. Label the beaker.

G. Stir the washing soda with the rod. Record the temperature of the dry soda (T_i) in the data table.

H. Add 15 mL of water to the washing soda. Stir with the rod and record the final temperature (T_f).

2. Is this an exothermic or an endothermic reaction?

CONCLUSIONS:

1. What is meant by an exothermic reaction? Give an example of an exothermic reaction.
2. What is meant by an endothermic reaction? Give an example of an endothermic reaction.

Fig. 19–16

TECHNOLOGY

HYDROGEN: UNLIMITED ENERGY SOURCE?

Hydrogen could be the ultimate source of energy. There are already working models of buses with engines that could use hydrogen as fuel and one U. S. utility company already uses hydrogen in one of its forms as an energy source.

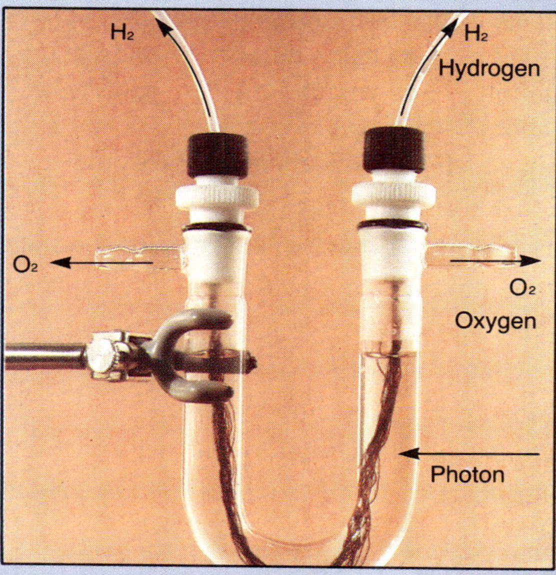

Until now, hydrogen could only be separated from water by electrolysis. This method, however, is tremendously expensive. At least one new way of producing hydrogen has now been developed. Hydrogen can now be produced by means of an artificial "chloroplast," a device which imitates the way in which green plants function to produce hydrogen.

Natural chloroplasts, found in the cells of green plants, produce glucose (sugar) during photosynthesis. In this process, sunlight separates the hydrogen from the water within the plant cell. The hydrogen then combines with carbon dioxide from the air to form carbohydrates, and oxygen is given off into the atmosphere. An artificial chloroplast is designed to release the hydrogen in the form of a gas. It prevents its combination with the carbon dioxide in the atmosphere.

The artificial chloroplast is the invention of Dr. Melvin Calvin, who won a Nobel prize in 1961 for his work on photosynthesis. The exact reactions and the sequence of events in photosynthesis were not understood, but enough was learned by the 1970's to isolate chloroplasts from spinach and cause hydrogen to escape as a gas. Spinach chloroplasts were not the answer. They were not very efficient producers of hydrogen. Calvin felt that artificial chloroplasts could be more efficient. Dr. Calvin has created a U-shaped tube device made of hollow fibers, similar to those used in an artificial kidney, which separates molecules of water into hydrogen and oxygen, releasing these gases (see photo).

In water, hydrogen exists in its lowest energy state combined with oxygen. Sunlight (solar energy) acting upon the molecule of water causes the hydrogen and oxygen to separate. The energy of the hydrogen is raised in the separation. When the hydrogen combines with the oxygen, the added energy is released as heat. This heat is the energy that can be used to power engines and furnaces. It is now possible to generate and collect these gases. The main problem for future development is one of cost. The first application of the artificial chloroplast may be to produce oxygen. The artifical chloroplast generates a form of oxygen (O) that is used in the manufacture of fibers, foams, and other substances. Industries that require oxygen may be the first to build synthetic chlorophyll factories. An inexpensive supply of hydrogen gas would be the by-product of these factories. At least one scientist has predicted that we will be using hydrogen commercially by the year 2000 as a substitute for all the energy purposes now served by fossil fuels.

CHAPTER REVIEW

See teacher's commentary for answers.

VOCABULARY

On a separate piece of paper, match each term with the number of the statement that best explains it. Use each term only once.

catalyst	collision theory	endothermic reaction	fuel
chemical equation	concentration	exothermic reaction	petroleum
chemical reaction			

1. A process in which a chemical change takes place.
2. A reaction that absorbs energy.
3. Changes the speed of a reaction but remains the same afterward.
4. Describes the number of molecules in a given space.
5. A reaction that releases energy.
6. A source of chemical energy.
7. A natural mixture of carbon and hydrogen.
8. Molecules must collide in order to react with each other.
9. Chemical formulas used to describe a chemical reaction.

QUESTIONS

Give brief but complete answers to each of the following questions. Unless otherwise indicated, use complete sentences to write your answers.

1. Write a complete chemical equation to show that hydrogen and oxygen combine to form water.
2. Explain the following chemical equation: $4Al + 3O_2 \longrightarrow 2Al_2O_3$
3. How does a correctly written chemical equation demonstrate the law of conservation of matter?
4. Name four kinds of chemical reaction and write a chemical equation for each kind.
5. Explain how to balance a chemical equation.
6. Give an example to show how surface area affects the rate of a chemical reaction.
7. How does temperature affect chemical reactions? Why? What is meant by threshold energy?
8. What is the purpose of the catalytic converter on an automobile?
9. Explain what happens in a chemical reaction to produce energy. In what form is the energy produced?

10. Write a chemical equation that shows a release of energy. What is this kind of reaction called?
11. Write a chemical equation that shows energy being absorbed. What is this kind of reaction called? Why is heat needed?
12. Name three forms of fossil fuel and give an example of each. Why is there a need to conserve fossil fuels? What are some of the alternative fuels we might use in the future?

APPLYING SCIENCE

1. Exothermic reactions are a source of energy for immediate use, while endothermic reactions can be used to store energy for later use. Place 20 g of sodium thiosulfate (photographer's hypo) in a test tube or other Pyrex container. Place the test tube in a beaker of boiling water and heat the hypo until it turns to a liquid. CAUTION: Wear goggles. (This can be done in a Pyrex beaker over a Bunsen burner, using a low flame.) Allow the hypo to cool slowly. It will remain liquid. After it has cooled to room temperature, add several crystals of solid hypo to the liquid. Describe what happens. Feel the test tube from time to time to see if energy is being released or absorbed. Is this an exothermic or an endothermic reaction? If you were heating your home with solar energy, how could this reaction be used?
2. The Solvay process was developed by a Belgian chemist named Ernest Solvay. It is a classic example of efficiency in chemical production. Go to the library and write a report on this process. What are the final products? Draw a diagram showing each step in the process and the chemical reactions that take place.
3. Report on the process of fractional distillation. Use a diagram to explain how different products are produced from crude oil by this process.

BIBLIOGRAPHY

Epstein, I. R. et al. "Oscillating Chemical Reactions," *Scientific American,* March 1983.

Kaplan and Lebowitz. *The Student Scientist Explores Energy and Fuels.* New York: Rosen Group, 1981.

Kraft, B. H. *Oil and Natural Gas.* New York: Watts, 1978.

Rice, Dale. *Energy from Fossil Fuels.* Milwaukee, WI: Raintree, 1983.

CHAPTER

20

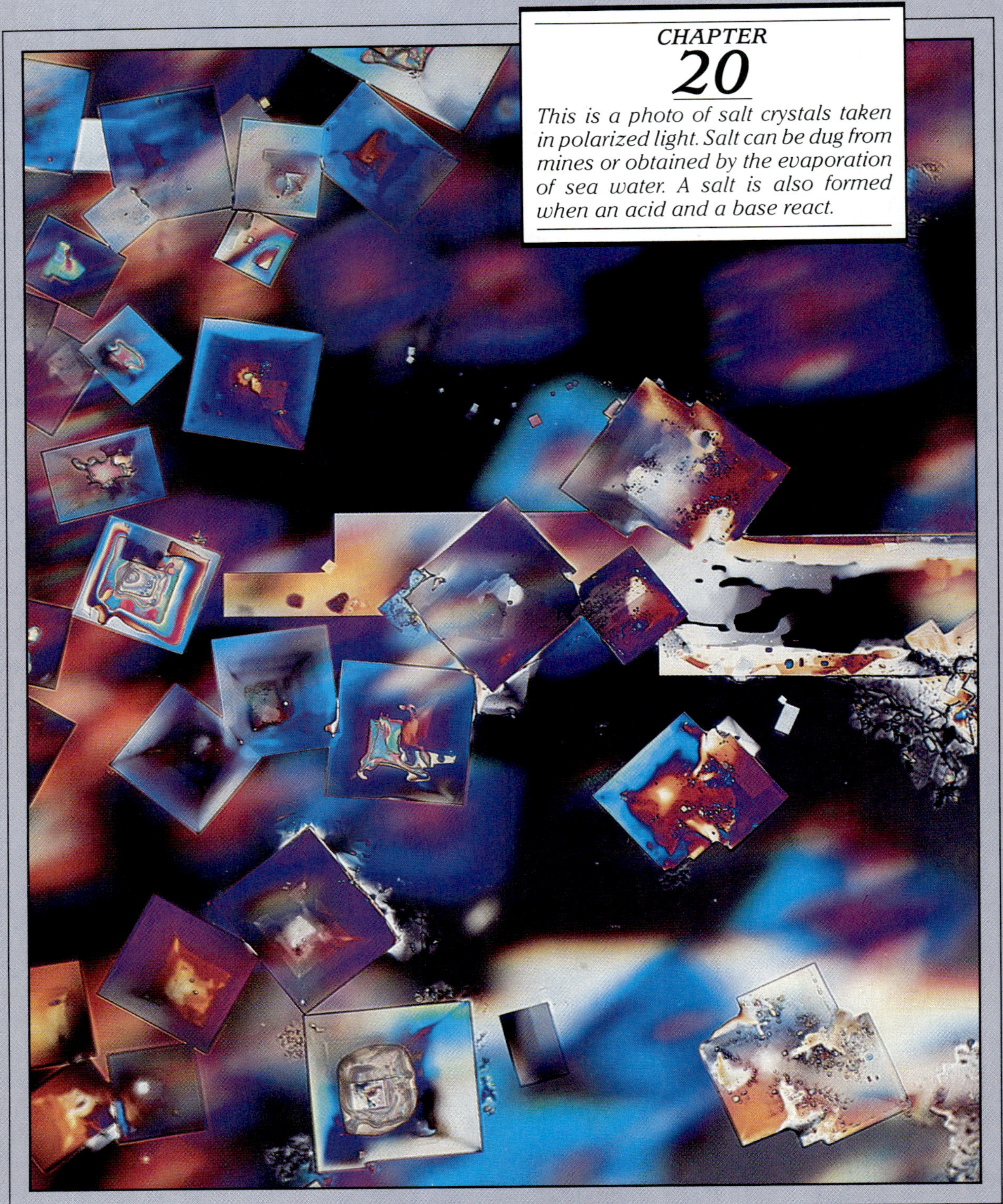

This is a photo of salt crystals taken in polarized light. Salt can be dug from mines or obtained by the evaporation of sea water. A salt is also formed when an acid and a base react.

ACIDS, BASES, AND SALTS

CHAPTER GOALS

1. Predict the result of dissolving a substance such as sodium chloride in water.
2. Describe the properties of solutions that contain ions.
3. Identify the characteristics of an acid.
4. Compare an acid with a base.
5. Describe the results of mixing an acidic solution with a basic solution.

20-1. Water

At the end of this section you will be able to:

- Relate the shape of a water molecule to its ability to act as a solvent.
- Describe how water supplies can become polluted.
- Explain why some solutions conduct electric currents.

You could live about five weeks without eating a bite of food. However, you could live only about five days without drinking any water. Water makes up about 65 percent of the total volume of your body. The loss of only 15 percent of your normal body water can be fatal. We share this need for water with all other living things. One of the reasons water is so important for living things is that it can dissolve many different materials. Substances must first dissolve in water in order to react. In this section you will learn why water is such a good solvent.

WHY IS WATER A GOOD SOLVENT?

The shape of a molecule is determined by the way the atoms making up the molecule are joined. For example, the electron-dot symbol for water is:

$$\begin{array}{c} H : \ddot{\underset{\cdot\cdot}{O}} : \\ \quad\; H \end{array}$$

Each hydrogen atom shares its electron with the oxygen atom. The two hydrogen atoms are joined to the oxygen atom by covalent bonds. The "bent" shape of the water molecule is shown in Fig. 20–1.

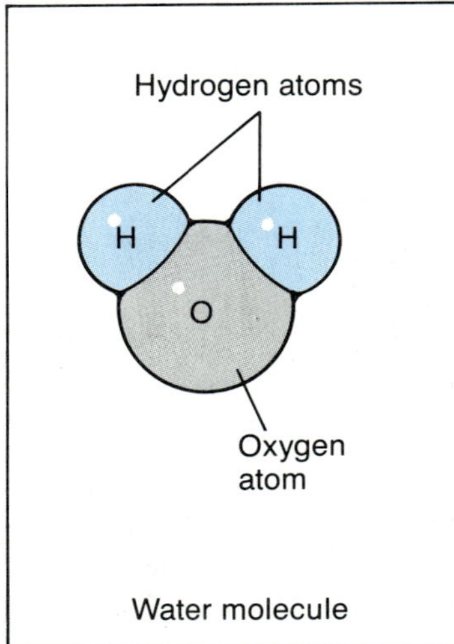

Fig. 20–1 In a water molecule, the two hydrogen atoms are slightly positive and the oxygen atom is slightly negative.

Fig. 20–2 Polar water molecules form hydrogen bonds with each other. Water forms drops because of this attraction between the molecules.

Polar molecule A molecule that carries small electric charges on opposite ends.

Word study: Polar from *polus* (L.), the pole.

Because of the way electrons are shared in the hydrogen-oxygen bonds, the two hydrogen atoms in a water molecule are slightly positive. The oxygen atom is slightly negative. Because the water molecule has positive and negative parts, water is a **polar molecule.** In a *polar molecule,* one part of the molecule carries a positive electrical charge while another part carries a negative electrical charge. As a result of their oppositely charged parts, water molecules attract each other. See Fig. 20–2. Each polar water molecule is also attracted to other substances that have an electric charge. For example, common salt is made up of positive sodium ions and negative chloride ions. The ions are held together by the attraction of the opposite charges. If salt crystals are dropped into water, the polar water molecules are attracted to the sodium and chloride ions. The attraction of the water molecules pulls the ions out of the salt crystals. The ions are then surrounded by the water molecules. See Fig. 20–3. Once that happens, the salt is dissolved. The Na^+ ions and the Cl^- ions are separated and spread throughout the solution. Water can dissolve salt because the water molecules are polar. Because polar water molecules can dissolve so many different things, water is a good solvent.

A slightly positive hydrogen atom may also be weakly attracted to a slightly negative oxygen atom in a second water molecule. This is an example of a hydrogen bond. In liquid water, molecules form groups joined by hydrogen bonds.

POLLUTION

Since polar water molecules can dissolve many substances, water is important in our lives. The water in your body contains dissolved substances that are necessary to life. For example, your blood contains ions such as Na^+, K^+, and Cl^-. However, the ability to dissolve many substances can also cause water to become **polluted.** Water that is chemically *polluted* contains harmful dissolved substances.

Most water pollution is caused by human activities. Sewers, for example, carry two kinds of pollution into lakes, streams, and oceans. See Fig. 20–4. The various waste materials in sewage contain harmful bacteria and viruses that can cause disease. In addition, sewage contains harmful chemicals. The chemicals called phosphates and nitrates are particularly harmful. These substances encourage the growth of tiny algae and other water plants. When the plants die and decay, they use up the oxygen dissolved in the water. Streams and lakes can usually clean themselves naturally if their water is rich in dissolved oxygen. Too much sewage can destroy the ability of a body of water to purify itself.

Sewage may also contain chemicals from industrial and agricultural wastes. In time, many of these chemicals decay and become harmless. But others remain unchanged and slowly build up in the water supplies. Over a period of years, these chemicals can be a threat to the health of people drinking the water.

Water supplies can be protected from pollution if the sewage is treated to remove harmful organisms before it is released.

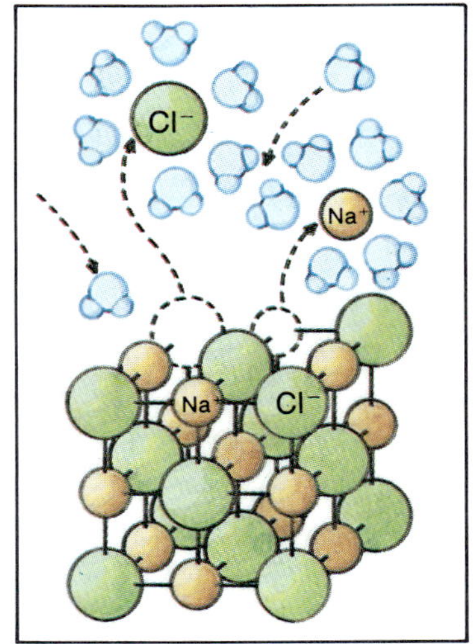

Fig. 20–3 The positive and negative ions in a salt crystal are attracted to the polar water molecules and the crystal dissolves.

Polluted A description of water that contains harmful substances.

Enrichment: Biodegradable materials are those that can be broken down into simpler compounds by the processes of nature, including bacterial and chemical action. In some detergents, phosphates have been reduced in quantity or eliminated by the manufacturer in order to make them biodegradable.

Fig. 20–4 Chemical pollutants can dissolve in water and spread from one place to another.

Removing dissolved chemicals, including phosphates and nitrates, is difficult and expensive. Most cities provide sewage treatment to remove dissolved chemicals.

Not all water pollution comes from substances added to the water. *Thermal pollution* is a result of heating rivers and lakes. The heat comes from power plants. All types of electric generating plants produce excess heat. Water from streams, lakes, or oceans pumped through the plant removes this excess heat. Heated water loses some of its dissolved oxygen. This may cause a change in the way plants and animals grow in the water. In some cases, these changes harm the natural environment where the heated water is discharged. Many power plants cool the water before returning it to its source.

Although water is very common, only a small part of the total amount on earth is available for use. Most of the earth's water is in the oceans, in ice at the poles, or deep beneath the surface of the earth. Our need for a steady supply of clean water is met by less than 1 percent of the earth's water. This limited supply of water must be protected from all forms of pollution.

HARD WATER

Some parts of the world have another water problem. In these places, the water is *hard*. Hard water is caused by the presence of dissolved minerals such as calcium, magnesium, or iron. The word "hard" in this case means that it is hard to make soapsuds in this water. Detergents, which are chemically different from soap, are not affected by hard water. Hard water is sometimes treated to remove the dissolved minerals. One way to remove the minerals from hard water is to boil it. The steam is then condensed to liquid water. This process produces distilled or *soft* water.

Enrichment: The electrolyte used in electroplating is a salt of the metal that is being plated. Thus ions of the metal are already in solution. The electrodes consist of the object being plated and a piece of the metal that is to supply the plate. Other chemicals are also used in the electrolyte to help give a uniform plate. The amount of current is also critical if a uniform and nonporous plate is to be obtained.

SOLUTIONS THAT CONDUCT ELECTRICITY

A simple experiment will show you an important difference between dissolved substances. When salt dissolves in water, it separates into sodium ions (Na^+) and chloride ions (Cl^-). If you test this salt solution, you will find that it conducts an electric current. See Fig. 20–5. You can try the same test on a sugar solution. A sugar solution does not conduct an electric current. Salt is an example of an **electrolyte** (ih-**lek**-truh-lite).

Electrolyte A substance that forms a conducting solution when dissolved in water.

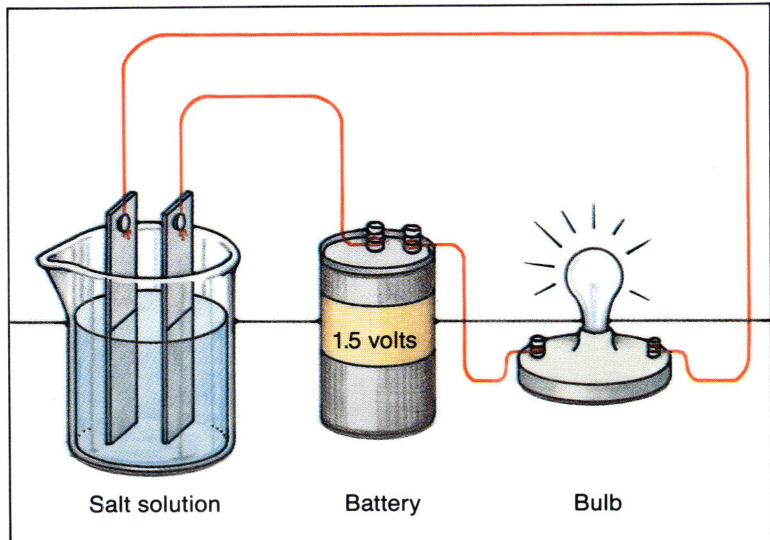

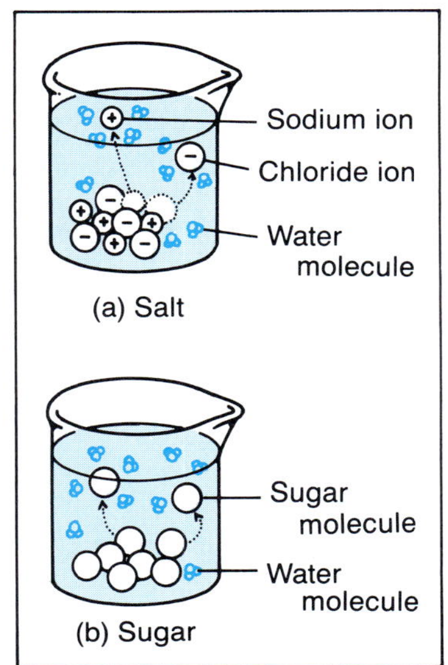

Fig. 20–5 Because a salt solution contains charged ions, it will conduct an electric current.

Fig. 20–6 Unlike salt, sugar does not break down into charged ions when it dissolves in water.

When an *electrolyte* dissolves in water, the resulting solution conducts an electric current. A salt solution conducts electricity because the solution contains ions. Each ion carries either a positive or a negative electric charge. The charged ions are free to move about in the solution. When a metal conducts an electric current, moving electrons carry the current. In a solution, moving ions allow the current to flow.

Some substances do not produce conducting solutions when they dissolve in water. Sugar is an example. When sugar dissolves, the sugar molecules separate and spread out in the water. The sugar molecules do not carry electric charges. Thus, there are no electrically charged ions in a sugar solution to carry a current. See Fig. 20–6. Substances like sugar are called **nonelectrolytes.** A *nonelectrolyte* does not conduct an electric current.

Nonelectrolyte A substance that forms a nonconducting solution when dissolved in water.

DISSOLVED SUBSTANCES CAN REACT

Many chemical reactions will take place only when the reactants are dissolved in water. For example, recipes for some breads and cakes include baking powder as one of the ingredients. If you add a little water to this powder, you will see a rapid reaction. As the baking powder dissolves, bubbles of gas appear. This gas is carbon dioxide. Baking powder is used in some kinds of bread because it releases carbon dioxide gas when water is added. The carbon dioxide bubbles make

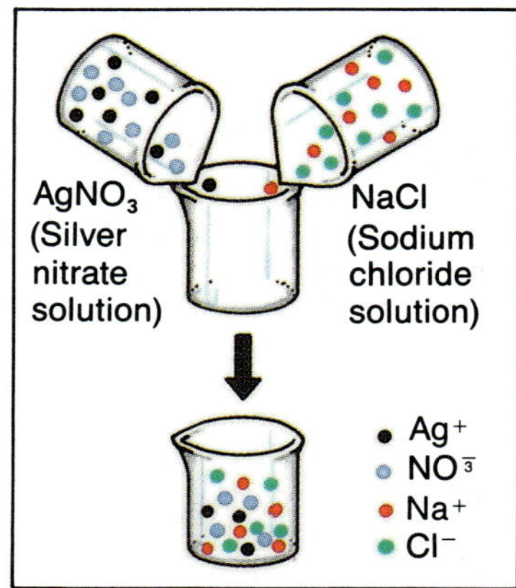

Fig. 20–7 When solutions of silver nitrate and sodium chloride are mixed, four types of ions are present: Ag^+, Na^+, NO_3^-, and Cl^-.

Precipitate A solid substance that separates from a solution.

Soluble Describes a substance that can be dissolved.

Word study: Soluble from *solvere* (L.), to melt.

*AgCl is a precipitate.

the dough expand. The dough is then lighter and the bread will not be heavy. Dry baking powder does not release carbon dioxide. This reaction illustrates an important requirement for many chemical reactions: Water is needed to cause a reaction to take place. Why do many chemical reactions only take place when the reactants are dissolved in water? Study the behavior of the ions released when electrolytes dissolve.

Suppose you mix solid sodium chloride, NaCl, with solid silver nitrate, $AgNO_3$. Like NaCl, the compound $AgNO_3$ is an electrolyte. When $AgNO_3$ dissolves in water, it produces two kinds of ions, as shown by the following equation:

$$AgNO_3 \longrightarrow Ag^+ + NO_3^-$$

If solid NaCl is mixed with solid $AgNO_3$, there is no reaction. The ions from both compounds are locked in solid crystals and cannot move. But if colorless solutions of NaCl and $AgNO_3$ are mixed together, a white solid forms. A solid substance that separates from a solution is called a **precipitate** (prih-**sip**-uh-tate). If a *precipitate* forms when two solutions are mixed, it means that a chemical reaction has taken place. The chemical reaction forming the precipitate is caused by the ions in solutions of NaCl and $AgNO_3$.

A mixture of NaCl and $AgNO_3$ solutions contains four kinds of ions as shown below:

$$NaCl + AgNO_3 \longrightarrow Na^+ + Cl^- + Ag^+ + NO_3^-$$

See Fig. 20–7. These ions are all free to move in the solution. As you know, oppositely charged ions attract each other. Therefore, Na^+ will attract NO_3^- and Ag^+ will attract Cl^-. Sometimes oppositely charged ions form a substance that remains dissolved in water. This type of substance is said to be **soluble** in water.

Look at Table 20–1. This table lists some common ions. By looking at this table, you can tell whether a particular combination of ions forms a *soluble* compound (S) or a precipitate (P). You can identify the precipitate that forms when NaCl and $AgNO_3$ solutions are mixed. Is the precipitate $NaNO_3$ or AgCl?*

In some chemical reactions, the ions form a gas when they combine. For example, baking powder forms carbon dioxide gas when it dissolves in water. The ions in solutions determine what chemical reactions take place when substances dissolve.

SOLUBILITIES OF SOME IONS IN WATER SOLUTION (P = PRECIPITATE; S = SOLUBLE)						
	Nitrate (NO_3)	Chloride (Cl^-)	Acetate ($C_2H_3O_2^-$)	Carbonate (CO_3^{2-})	Tetraborate ($B_4O_7^{2-}$)	Sulfate (SO_4^{2-})
Silver (Ag^+)	S	P	P	P	S	P
Sodium (Na^-)	S	S	S	S	S	S
Hydrogen (H^+)	S	S	S	—	S	S
Ammonium (NH_4^+)	S	S	S	S	S	S
Calcium (Ca^{2-})	S	S	S	P	P	P
Zinc (Zn^{2+})	S	S	S	P	P	S
Magnesium (Mg^{2+})	S	S	S	P	S	S

Table 20–1

SUMMARY

Because of the shape of water molecules, water can dissolve many substances. Some of the substances dissolved in water supplies are harmful. Some substances produce solutions that conduct an electric current. When these substances are dissolved in water, their ions are free to react. Many chemical reactions take place only between ions in solution.

QUESTIONS

Use complete sentences to write your answers.

1. What property of water makes it possible for water to dissolve many other substances?
2. What is water pollution? Why is it a serious problem? How do our water supplies become polluted?
3. Why can some solutions conduct an electric current while others cannot?
4. What happens when silver ions (Ag^+) and chloride ions (Cl^-) are in solution together?
5. Using Table 20–1, determine which of the following compounds are precipitates: $NaNO_3$, AgCl, $CaCO_3$.

1. Water will dissolve many other substances because water is a polar molecule.
2. Water pollution exists when water contains harmful substances. It is a problem because water is necessary for life. Only a small portion of the water on earth can be used to support life. Pollution reduces the amount of clean water available. Pollution is the result of human activities. Chemical wastes accumulate in our water systems.
3. Solutions that contain ions will conduct an electric current while solutions without ions will not.
4. When silver ions and chloride ions are present in a solution together, a white precipitate forms.
5. AgCl and $CaCO_3$ are precipitates.

INVESTIGATION

See teacher's commentary for teaching hints, safety, and answers to questions.

SOLUBILITY

PURPOSE: You will test the possible combinations of four solutions for the formation of precipitates. You will also identify an unknown solution.

MATERIALS:

waxed paper
set of solutions labeled A, B, C, D
medicine dropper
unknown solution

PROCEDURE:

A. Copy the table below. Place a piece of waxed paper over the page. Your tests will be done on this waxed paper. The squares in the table represent all the possible combinations of ions in the four solutions. See Fig. 20–8.

	A $ZnCl_2$	B Na_2CO_3	C $MgSO_4$	D $Na_2B_4O_7$
B Na_2CO_3				
C $MgSO_4$				
D $Na_2B_4O_7$				
Unknown				

B. Place one drop of solution A in each square of column A on the waxed paper, one drop of solution B in each square of column B, and one drop of solution C in each square of column C. Rinse out the medicine dropper each time.

C. Now add one drop of solution B to each square of row B, one drop of solution C to each square of row C, and one drop of solution D to each square of row D.

D. Carefully remove the waxed paper from the table. Write a "P" in the squares in which a precipitate formed.

E. Obtain an unknown solution from your teacher. Place a clean piece of waxed paper over the table. Place a drop of your unknown solution in each square of the row labeled "unknown." Add one drop of the solutions A,B,C, and D to the proper squares.

F. Compare the results with the precipitates formed in step C.

CONCLUSIONS:

1. Identify your unknown as either solution A, B, C, or D.
2. Write chemical equations for each of the three reactions that took place. Circle the precipitates that formed.

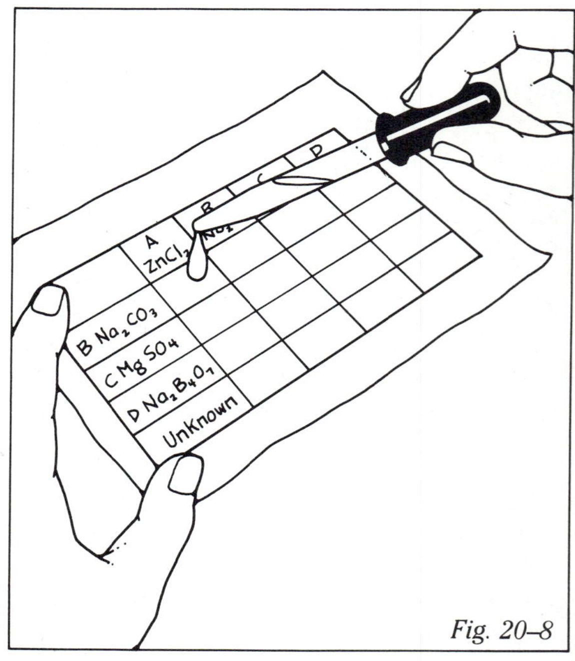

Fig. 20–8

20-2. *Acids and Bases*

At the end of this section you will be able to:

- Distinguish between an *acidic* and a *basic* solution.
- Give examples of the chemical properties of an acidic solution and a basic solution.
- Name several common substances that are acids and several that are bases.

Diet soft drinks taste sweet although they contain no sugar. Chemical compounds that are nothing like sugar can produce a sweet taste. However all compounds that produce a sour taste, such as vinegar, are alike. In this section you will learn why all acids have a sour taste.

ACIDIC SOLUTIONS

You can begin this section by comparing two solutions. One is a salt solution. A salt solution contains sodium ions, Na^{+}, and chloride ions, Cl^{-}.

The second solution is made by dissolving molecules of the electrolyte hydrogen chloride, HCl, in water. This solution of hydrogen chloride contains hydrogen ions, H^{+}, and chloride ions, Cl^{-}. Thus both solutions contain Cl^{-} ions.

The NaCl and HCl solutions are alike in several ways. Both solutions are colorless, both contain Cl^{-} ions, and both can conduct an electric current. But the solutions are different in some ways. For example, a piece of eggshell dropped into the HCl solution dissolves. Bubbles of carbon dioxide gas are given off as the eggshell dissolves. A piece of zinc metal put into the HCl solution also dissolves. Hydrogen gas is given off as the zinc dissolves. However, neither the eggshell nor the zinc dissolves in the NaCl solution. See Fig. 20–9. Think about the results of this experiment. Are the H^{+} ions in the HCl solution the cause of this behavior? Other experiments show that any substance containing H^{+} ions can form a solution that dissolves both eggshell and zinc.

The presence of H^{+} ions in a solution gives that solution special properties. Such a solution is called an *acidic solution.* To make an acidic solution, a material is dissolved in water. The resulting solution has more H^{+} ions than plain water. A

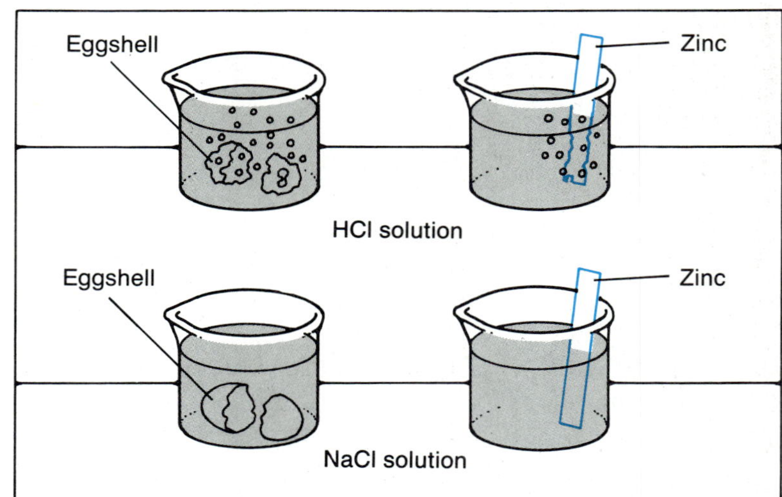

Fig. 20–9 Both eggshell (calcium) and zinc metal will dissolve in a solution of HCl. They do not react with an NaCl solution.

compound such as HCl, which produces H^+ ions when dissolved in water, is called an **acid.** A solution of HCl is commonly called *hydrochloric acid.*

Acid A compound that forms a solution containing more H^+ ions than pure water.

Word study: Acid from *acidus* (L.), sour.

Enrichment: The H^+ ion is chemically very reactive. Because a typical hydrogen nucleus contains only a single proton, the H^+ ion is often referred to as a proton. Acids are sometimes referred to as proton donors in chemical reactions.

You can recognize an acid by the unusual properties caused by H^+ ions. For example, acidic solutions always taste sour. Food and drinks containing acids always have a sour taste. For example, lemon juice contains citric acid. However, it is not safe to taste all kinds of acids. Some acids cause painful chemical burns. Other acids are poisonous.

TESTING FOR ACIDS

A safe way to test for acidic solutions is to use a substance that changes color in an acidic solution. Any substance that changes color in an acidic solution is called an **indicator.** One commonly used *indicator* is *litmus.* Litmus paper turns from blue to red in an acidic solution. See Fig 20–10. Some foods contain substances that are indicators. For example, the substance that causes the color of red cabbage will usually turn blue when cooked unless an acid such as vinegar is added.

Indicator A substance that changes color when put into an acid solution.

Enrichment: The H^+ ion in water solutions combines with a water molecule as follows: $H^+ + H_2O \longrightarrow H_3O^+$. The H_3O^+ ion is called a hydronium ion. This ion gives acidic solutions their characteristic properties.

Word study: Indicator from *indicare,* (L.), to point out.

If you test vinegar with litmus paper or some other indicator, you will find that it is an acidic solution. You also know that vinegar has the sour taste common to all acids. Vinegar is also an electrolyte since it forms a conducting solution. However, a vinegar solution is a poor conductor of electricity. This means that vinegar cannot produce a large number of ions in

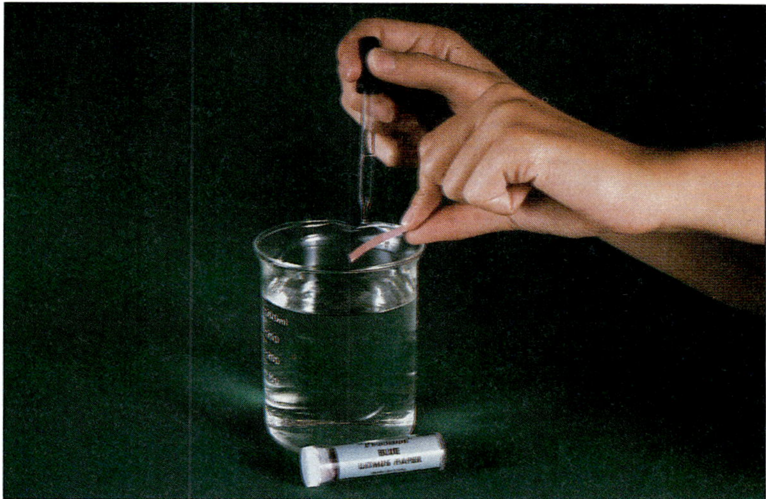

Fig. 20–10 Blue litmus paper turns red in an acid.

solution. In other words, vinegar is a weak electrolyte. Acids like vinegar, which are weak electrolytes, are said to be *weak acids.* Other weak acids are lemon juice and vitamin C. Hydrochloric acid, on the other hand, is a strong electrolyte. It is also a *strong acid.*

Another strong acid is found in automobile batteries. This acid is sulfuric acid, H_2SO_4. Sulfuric acid has other important uses. It is used in manufacturing such products as steel and fertilizers. Nitric acid, HNO_3, is another strong acid. Nitric acid is also an important acid used in manufacturing. For example, it is used in the production of plastics and explosives.

Enrichment: A common weak acid is produced when CO_2 dissolves in water. The equation for this reaction is:
$CO_2 + H_2O \longrightarrow H_2CO_3$
H_2CO_3 is carbonic acid. It is partly responsible for the taste of carbonated drinks.

Enrichment: Sulfur dioxide reacts with water to produce sulfurous acid, H_2SO_3, as follows:
$SO_2 + H_2O \longrightarrow H_2SO_3$

BASIC SOLUTIONS

An acidic solution is one that contains an excess of H^+ ions. The H^+ ions give acidic solutions a sour taste. Have you ever had soapsuds in your mouth by accident? If you have, then you know that soap tastes bitter. This bitter taste is caused by hydroxide ions, OH^-. Consider the compound sodium hydroxide, NaOH. When NaOH dissolves in water, it separates into sodium ions, Na^+, and hydroxide ions, OH^-. A solution of NaOH in water thus has more OH^- ions than pure water. A compound such as NaOH that increases the number of OH^- ions when it dissolves in water is called a **base.** All *basic solutions* have a bitter taste. It is just as dangerous to taste a *base* as it is to taste an acid. Some basic solutions can cause severe burns and some are poisonous.

Base A compound that forms a solution with more OH^- ions than pure water.

Fig. 20–11 Red litmus paper turns blue in a base.

STRONG AND WEAK BASES

Sodium hydroxide is a *strong base.* This means that NaOH is also a strong electrolyte. Bases can dissolve grease and some other materials, such as hair. For this reason, the strong base NaOH is used to make drain cleaners. However, you should remember that strong bases are very dangerous to touch. Drain cleaners containing sodium hydroxide, and other strong bases, must be handled carefully and stored in a safe place away from small children. Never taste household products such as drain cleaners. In addition to its use as a drain cleaner, sodium hydroxide is used in petroleum refining and in producing certain plastics.

Many common bases are *weak.* An example of a weak base is magnesia laxatives. Calcium hydroxide, $Ca(OH)_2$, is a weak base often called *lime.* It is used to make plastic and mortar, to soften hard water, and to make soil less acidic.

Household ammonia is a common weak base. It is useful as a cleaner because its basic properties allow it to dissolve greasy dirt. Ammonia solutions are made by dissolving ammonia gas, NH_3, in water. The resulting solution is a base because some of the dissolved ammonia molecules react with water to produce OH^- ions. This reaction is shown by the following chemical equation:

$$NH_3 + H_2O \longrightarrow NH_4^+ + OH^-$$

You can test for the presence of a base by using an indicator such as litmus. An acid turns blue litmus paper red. A base does just the opposite. Red litmus paper turns blue in the presence of a base. See Fig. 20–11.

NEUTRAL SOLUTIONS

Neutral A solution or substance that is neither an acid nor a base.

Neutralization A chemical reaction that occurs when an acid and a base are mixed.

If a substance does not react with either red or blue litmus paper, it is neither an acid nor a base. A solution that is neither an acid nor a base is **neutral.** When the H^+ ions from an acid react with the OH^- ions from a base, water is formed:

$$H^+ + OH^- \longrightarrow H_2O \text{ (or HOH)}$$

This reaction is called **neutralization** (noo-truh-luh-**zay**-shun). A *neutralization* reaction occurs when an acid and a base are mixed, forming water, which is neutral.

MEASURING THE STRENGTH OF ACIDIC AND BASIC SOLUTIONS

As you learned in Chapter 1, scientists often find it necessary to measure the strength of an acid or a base. This is done by using a special scale called the *pH scale*. The pH scale describes how acidic or basic a solution is. The scale goes from 0 to 14. A pH number between 0 and 7 describes an acidic solution. A number between 7 and 14 indicates a basic solution. A pH number of 7 means that the solution is neutral. A change of one pH number means a change in acidic or basic strength of 10 times. That is, a solution of pH 9 is 10 times stronger in basic strength than a solution of pH 8. Table 20–2 shows the pH of some common liquids.

There are several ways to find the pH value of a solution. For example, a pH meter gives an accurate measurement of pH. Also, a good indicator such as phenolphthalein or methyl violet changes color over a narrow pH range. Methyl orange changes from red at pH 3.1 to yellow at pH 4.4.

pH OF SOME COMMON LIQUIDS	
Liquid	pH
Digestive juices of stomach	1.6
Lemon juice	2.3
Vinegar	2.8
Soft drink	3.0
Orange juice	3.5
Milk	6.5
Pure water	7.0
Human blood	7.4
Sea water	8.5
Milk of magnesia	10.5

Table 20–2

SUMMARY

A solution containing a large number of H^+ ions is an acidic solution. A solution containing more OH^- ions than plain water is a basic solution. When an acidic solution and a basic solution are mixed, the H^+ ions and OH^- ions combine to form water. The strength of acidic and basic solutions is measured on the pH scale.

QUESTIONS

Use complete sentences to write your answers.

1. Compare and contrast with water (a) an acidic solution, and (b) a basic solution.
2. Describe a safe test for acids and a safe test for bases.
3. Name two common substances that are acids and two that are bases. What are the bases used for?
4. How do you know that the H^+ ions in an acid cause an eggshell to dissolve?
5. Write an equation showing a neutralization reaction. What happens in a neutralization reaction?

1. An acidic solution is one that contains more H^+ ions than pure water. A basic solution is one that has more OH^- ions than pure water.
2. A safe test for acids is to use blue litmus paper which turns red in an acid. A safe test for bases is to use red litmus paper which turns blue in a base.
3. Answers may vary. Lemon juice, vitamin C, and vinegar are possible choices for acids. Bases include ammonia, helps dissolve greasy dirt; baking soda, used in cooking; sodium hydroxide, used in soaps.
4. If eggshell is placed in NaCl solution it does not dissolve. In HCl solution it does dissolve. Since Cl^- ions are present in both solutions, it must be the H^+ ions that cause the shell to dissolve.
5. $H^+ + OH^- \longrightarrow H_2O$. The H^+ ions in acid react with the OH^- ions from a base to form water, which is neutral.

INVESTIGATION

See teacher's commentary for teaching hints, safety, and answers to questions.

ACID REACTIONS

PURPOSE: You will determine which ion causes the characteristic properties of an acid.

MATERIALS:

- 6 test tubes
- hydrogen chloride solution
- sodium chloride solution
- test-tube rack
- baking soda
- aluminum foil
- purple cabbage leaf

PROCEDURE:

A. CAUTION: Be careful not to spill any acid. Wear goggles. Label three test tubes Al, A2, and A3.

B. Fill these test tubes 1/3-full of HCl solution. Add HCl to the labels.

C. Label three other test tubes B1, B2, and B3. See Fig. 20–12.

D. Fill these test tubes 1/3-full of NaCl solution. Add NaCl to the labels.

E. Place the six test tubes in a test-tube rack as shown in the diagram.

F. Copy the table below.

Test Material	Reaction with HCl	Reaction with NaCl
Baking soda		
Aluminum foil		
Purple cabbage leaf		

G. Drop a pinch of baking soda into tube A1. Record the result.

H. Drop a piece of aluminum foil into tube A2. Record the result.

I. Drop a piece of purple cabbage leaf into tube A3. Record the result.

J. Now repeat steps G, H, and I, with tubes B1, B2, and B3.

CONCLUSIONS:

1. Which solution reacted with all three test materials, HCl or NaCl?
2. Which ion is responsible for the reactions you observed, H^+, Na^+, or Cl^-? Explain.

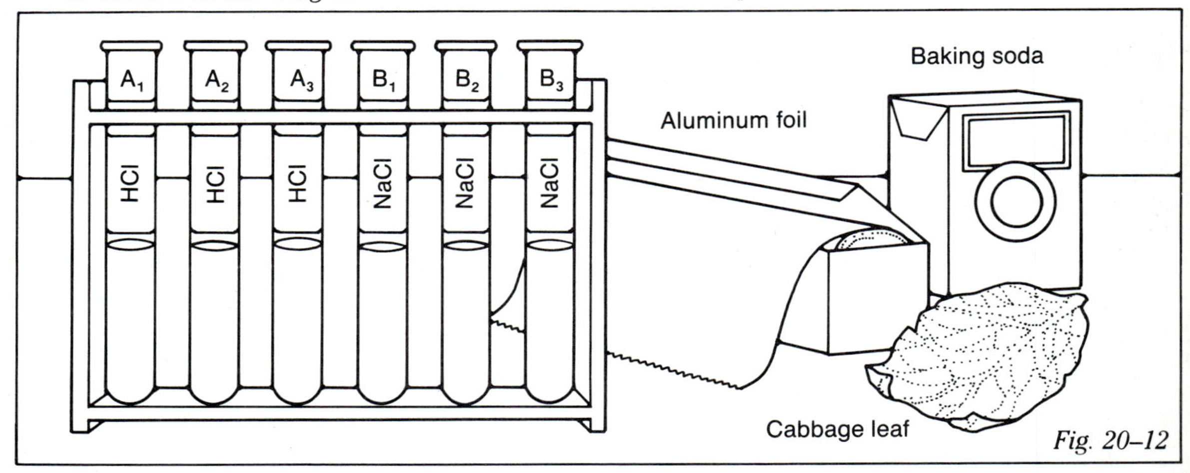

Fig. 20–12

SKILL-BUILDING ACTIVITY

See teacher's commentary for teaching hints, safety, and answers to questions.

CLASSIFYING ACIDS AND BASES

PURPOSE: You will use litmus paper to classify several substances as acidic, basic, or neutral.

MATERIALS:

red and blue litmus paper
distilled water
vitamin C (powdered)
lemon juice
household ammonia
sugar
plastic spoon
medicine dropper
vinegar
table salt (sodium chloride)
baking soda (sodium bicarbonate)

PROCEDURE:

A. Copy the data table below in your notebook. Use this table to record the results of your tests.

Substance Tested	Acid	Base	Neutral
Lemon juice	X		
Household ammonia		X	
Table salt			X
Baking soda		X	
Vitamin C	X		
Sugar			X
Vinegar	X		

B. CAUTION: Wash off any spilled acids or bases thoroughly with water. To test solids, wet a piece of litmus paper with a drop of water. Add a pinch of the solid to it. If the red litmus paper turns blue, place an X in the base column. If the blue litmus paper turns red, place an X in the acid column. If a substance has no effect on either litmus paper, place an X in the neutral column. See Fig. 20–13 (a).

C. Liquid substances, such as vinegar, are already in solution. To test a liquid, simply place one or two drops on the litmus paper. See Fig. 20–13 (b).

D. Now test all the substances available and record the results.

CONCLUSIONS:

1. Which substances are bases?
2. Which substances are acids?
3. Which substances had no effect on either the blue or red litmus paper?

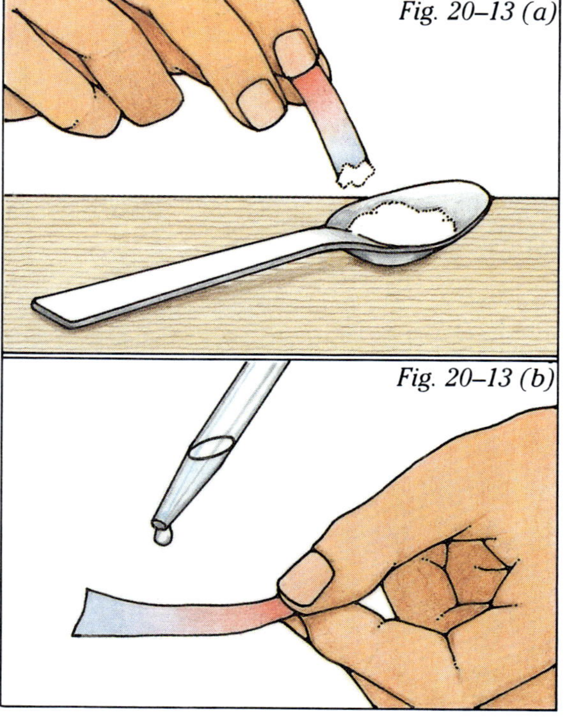

Fig. 20–13 (a)

Fig. 20–13 (b)

20-3. Salts

At the end of this section you will be able to:

- Describe how an acid and a base react to form a salt.
- Predict the results of neutralization reactions.

Would you take a job that paid your wages in common salt? In many parts of the ancient world, salt was a valuable substance. Two thousand years ago, Roman soldiers were often paid in salt. The Latin word for salt is *sal* and our word "salary" comes from this ancient Roman custom. Salt is still a valuable raw material used to manufacture many chemicals, such as hydrochloric acid and baking soda. Salt is also a vital part of our diet. To a chemist, salt is not only sodium chloride, it is also the name of a large group of compounds.

AN ACID + A BASE

An acid and a base are chemical opposites. One way to show this is to mix equal amounts of an acid such as HCl with a base such as NaOH. The mixture is neutral. This is because the H^+ ions from the acid combine with the OH^- ions from the base. The result is water, as shown by the following equation:

$$H^+ + OH^- \longrightarrow H_2O$$

Heat is also produced in addition to water. Look at the equation below. This equation shows the reaction between sodium hydroxide, NaOH, and hydrochloric acid, HCl.

$$NaOH + HCl \longrightarrow H_2O + NaCl + \text{heat}$$

The H^+ ion from HCl and OH^- ion from NaOH join to form water. In addition, the Na^+ ion from NaOH and the Cl^- ion from HCl form NaCl. Sodium chloride is common table salt. This reaction is an example of a neutralization reaction. When an acid and a base are combined, a neutralization reaction always takes place.

When exactly the right amount of an acid reacts with a base, the properties of both the acid and the base disappear. Chemists can detect the point at which the acid and the base are neutralized. For example, the indicator *phenolphthalein* (fee-noe-**thal**-een) turns from colorless in an acid to pink in a base. You can add a few drops of phenolphthalein indicator to the

Fig. 20–14 Phenolphthalein is an indicator that turns pink as a base is added to an acid.

acid you want to neutralize. Then add a base until the solution takes on a slightly pink color. See Fig. 20–14. The point at which an indicator shows the first sign of color change is called the *end point.*

MAKING SALTS

When neutralization reactions take place between acids and bases, one of the products, in addition to water and heat, is always a **salt.** Neutralization reactions produce *salts* when the positive ion from a base joins with the negative ion from an acid. A general equation that shows how a salt is formed by a neutralization reaction is:

Salt A compound that is made up of the positive ion from a base and the negative ion from an acid.

$$\text{an acid} + \text{a base} \longrightarrow \text{a salt} + \text{water} + \text{heat}$$

A typical neutralization reaction is:

KOH	+	HNO_3	$\longrightarrow$	H_2O	+	KNO_3	+	heat
potassium hydroxide (base)		nitric acid (acid)		water		potassium nitrate (a salt)		

Salts can be made from many different positive and negative ions. Thus all salts do not have common properties like acids and bases. Not all salts have a salty taste. Although NaCl is an important part of our diet, many salts are poisonous. Many salts are white in color as is sodium chloride. However, many others are colored. Some salts are soluble in water while

Fig. 20–15 Salt is an important part of our diet. It is also used in many industrial processes. Lye, chlorine, hydrochloric acid, and baking soda are some of the chemicals that are made from sodium chloride.

others are not. Salts do have one thing in common. All salts are made by combining positive and negative ions. As a result, all solid salts are compounds that are held together by ionic bonds.

Salts can also be produced by reactions other than neutralization. For example, zinc metal reacts with hydrochloric acid as shown by the equation:

$$Zn + HCl \longrightarrow ZnCl_2 + H_2$$

Zinc chloride, $ZnCl_2$, is a salt.

Table salt, sodium chloride, is a common chemical compound in the earth's crust. Solid sodium chloride is found in large underground deposits in the form of gray crystals called rock salt. These deposits of rock salt can be mined. See Fig. 20–15. Salt can also be obtained by the evaporation of sea water. The oceans contain a huge amount of sodium chloride dissolved in sea water. The oceans contain about 50 million tons of dissolved salts. There are 35 g of dissolved salts in 1 kg of sea water. This means that if you boiled away 1 kg of sea water, 35 g of solid salts would remain. Not all of this solid material is sodium chloride. Sea water contains many kinds of dissolved ions. See Table 20–3. Thus a mixture of different kinds of salts is left behind when sea water evaporates. Sodium

DISSOLVED SUBSTANCES IN SEA WATER	
Ions	Percentage of Total Dissolved Solids (by weight)
Chloride (Cl^-)	55.04
Sodium (Na^+)	30.61
Sulfate (SO_4^{2-})	7.68
Magnesium (Mg^{2-})	3.69
Calcium (Ca^{2-})	1.16
Potassium (K^+)	1.10
Bicarbonate (HCO_3^-)	0.41
Bromide (Br^-)	0.19
Borate ($H_2BO_3^-$)	0.07
Strontium (Sr^{2+})	0.04

Table 20–3

chloride is the most abundant salt in the mixture. Salt obtained from sea water is sold as *sea salt.*

SUMMARY

When an acid and a base are combined, a neutralization reaction takes place. The products of neutralization are water, a salt, and heat. Many different kinds of salts are produced when different acids and bases react. Salts can also be made by other reactions.

QUESTIONS

Use complete sentences to write your answers.

1. Write an equation that shows what happens when the base NaOH and the acid HCl are mixed.
2. What is the name of the reaction that occurs when a base and an acid are mixed? What is the product called?
3. What ions are present in HCl, HBr, and HI? What ions are present in KOH, LiOH, and $Mg(OH)_2$?
4. What are the chemical formulas for the products of the following reactions: (a) HCl + NaOH, (b) HCl + LiOH?
5. Compare the use of phenolphthalein with the use of red litmus paper.

1. $Na^+ + OH^- + H^+ + Cl^- \longrightarrow HOH + NaCl$.
2. When an acid and a base are mixed, a neutralization reaction occurs. The product is called a salt.
3. H^+, Cl^-, H^+, Br^-, H^+, I^-, K^+, OH^-, Li^+, OH^-, Mg^{2+}, OH^-
4. (a) H_2O + NaCl; (b) H_2O + LiCl.
5. Phenolphthalein indicates the end point of the neutralization of an acid when it turns pink. Red litmus paper turns blue when it is put in a basic solution.

INVESTIGATION

See teacher's commentary for teaching hints, safety, and answers to questions.

THE END POINT IN A NEUTRALIZATION REACTION

PURPOSE: You will test the neutralization of an acid using an indicator.

MATERIALS:

- test tubes
- hydrochloric acid solution
- phenolphthalein solution
- medicine dropper
- sodium hydroxide solution
- acid samples
- test-tube holder

PROCEDURE:

A. Copy the table below and record your data in it. CAUTION: Wear goggles.

Acid	Number of drops of NaOH
HCl	
Others	

B. Fill a test tube about 1/3-full of HCl solution. Label the tube. See Fig. 20–16.

C. Add one or two drops of phenolphthalein solution to the acid in the test tube. Shake the test tube to mix the indicator with the acid. CAUTION: Use care not to splash the acid. Immediately rinse off any acid that gets on your skin.

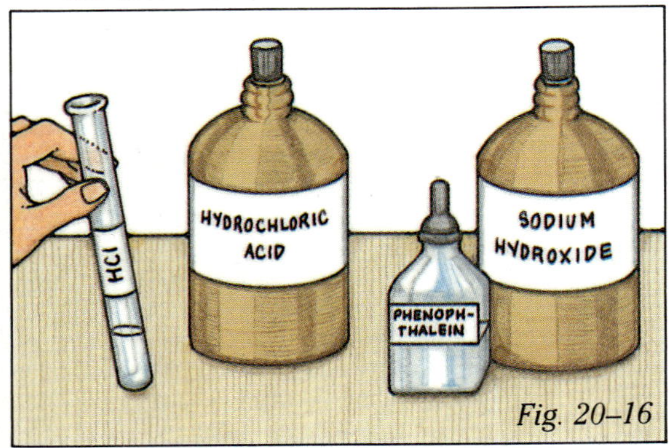

Fig. 20–16

D. Using a medicine dropper, add NaOH solution to the test tube one drop at a time. Shake the test tube each time you add a drop of NaOH. Keep a record of the number of drops of NaOH you add. When the light pink color remains, even after shaking the test tube, you have reached the end point. See Fig. 20–17.

E. Add several more drops of NaOH to go past the end point.

1. What happened to the color of the pink solution?

F. In the same manner, neutralize at least two more acidic solutions. Record your results in the data table.

CONCLUSIONS:

1. Explain how to neutralize an acid.
2. How do you know when the end point has been reached?
3. Write a complete chemical equation for the reaction between HCl and NaOH.

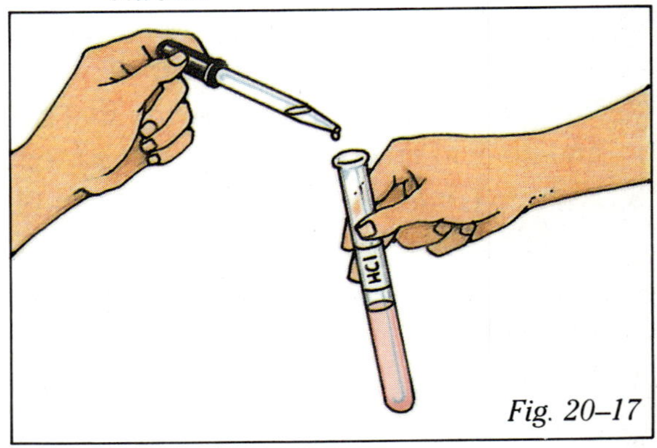

Fig. 20–17

CAREERS IN SCIENCE

ENVIRONMENTAL CHEMIST

Solving the problems surrounding the polluted air or water of a single city requires an extraordinary amount of information. The environmental chemist has to know exactly what is polluting the air or water, how it got there, how the irritant or pollutant interacts with the air or water, and what these interactions mean not just to human life, but to every kind of animal and vegetable life as well.

Beginning workers in industry and government usually have a bachelor's degree in chemistry and then join on-the-job training programs in order to advance.

Chemists with advanced degrees work in industry, for the federal government in such agencies as the Environmental Protection Agency, or in basic research, teaching, or administration at a college or university.

For further information, contact: American Chemical Society, 1155 16th Street NW, Washington, DC 20026.

SOIL TECHNICIAN

Soil technicians examine the physical, chemical, and biological properties of soils, both in the field and in laboratories. They then grade them according to a national classification system based on things such as the ability to produce crops or usefulness as engineering materials. Soil technicians also prepare maps plotting soil, water, vegetation, structures, and topographical features of an area. With this information they can prepare cost surveys to help local landowners or farmers. They can also advise developers on appropriate land use.

Most soil technicians are employed by federal, state, and local governments. A Bachelor of Science degree in agronomy or soil conservation, with a strong concentration of study in chemistry, biology, mapmaking, and engineering, is usually required of soil technicians.

For further information, contact: Soil Conservation Society of America, 7515 Northeast Ankeny Road, Ankeny, IA 50021.

¡COMPUTE!

SCIENCE INPUT

Many ordinary foods and common household substances are acids, bases, or salts. Knowing which they are can help you to achieve the desired results in cooking, and also to maintain safety with cleaning and gardening materials. For example, when you make buttermilk pancakes, you add baking soda to the mixture; when you make pancakes with regular milk you use baking powder. Do you know why? Do you know what happens in each case? When canning fruits and vegetables at home, care must be taken that the bacteria that cause botulism are not present. This is less of a worry when canning tomatoes than when canning stringbeans. Do you know why? Ammonia is a cleaning agent; so is bleach. But don't mix the two for double cleaning effect because together they produce a poisonous gas! Household chemistry is important to know. Distinguishing betwen acids, bases, and salts may not only make your meals tastier, it could prevent a fatal accident!

COMPUTER INPUT

Computer learning takes many forms. In this instance the computer has been programmed to give feedback of different kinds to help you learn the characteristics of acids, bases, and salts. The computer will ask a question, provide a hint when you're wrong, and review the information if you keep answering incorrectly. The advantage in using a computer for this type of learning is that the computer does not get frustrated by repeating the questions or hints. In Program Litmus the computer has not been programmed as a game, nor will it give any final score. In other words, there is no judgment of your performance. For many people, this kind of tutoring reduces the anxiety of learning.

WHAT TO DO

In order to program the computer you will need to collect data about some common foods and household substances. Test with litmus paper to find out whether they are acids or bases. (Consult your textbook to learn how to conduct these tests. Reference books, including your text, can help you identify salts.) Make a data chart similar to the one shown as an example.

Enter Program Litmus into your computer. Enter the information you recorded in your chart in data statements 290 thru 330. Be sure to follow the format given in the program.

The computer will bring up data on the screen for you to study. It will then ask you whether a given substance is an acid, base, or salt. If you do not give the correct answer, it will offer a hint. If you keep giving incorrect answers, Program Litmus will print a review on your screen. Then you can start over again.

Data Chart

Household Item	Classification		
	(1) Acid	(2) Base	(3) Salt
1. orange juice 2. lye 3. vinegar 4. ammonia 5. sodium chloride 6. potash 7. etc.			

HOUSEHOLD CHEMISTRY: PROGRAM LITMUS

GLOSSARY

FEEDBACK	a response to input from the user that corrects wrong answers, or encourages correct answers, or comments on the nature of the input.
PRINT	a command to the computer in BASIC to print out certain statements on the screen. Different from the instruction that directs the computer to start the printer and make a paper copy.

PROGRAM

```
100  REM LITMUS
110  DIM F$(30),H$(3,3),S$(30)
120  FOR X = 1 TO 3: READ I$(X): FOR Y
     = 1 TO 3: READ H$(X,Y): NEXT :
     NEXT
130  FOR X = 1 TO 30: READ S$(X),C(X):
     IF C(X) = 0 THEN M=X - 1: GOTO
     150
140  NEXT :M = 30
150  FOR X = 1 TO 8: PRINT : NEXT
160  PRINT "STUDY THIS
     INFORMATION:"
170  FOR X = 1 TO 3: PRINT : PRINT
     I$(X): FOR Y = 1 TO 3: PRINT
     "      ";Y; " ";H$(X,Y): NEXT :
     NEXT
180  PRINT : INPUT "CONTINUE (Y)? ";
     Y$: IF Y$ <> "Y" THEN END
190  FOR X = 1 TO 25: PRINT : NEXT
200  R = INT ( RND (1) * M) + 1:H = 0
210  PRINT "TYPE 1 FOR ACID, 2 FOR
     BASE, 3 FOR SALT"
220  PRINT S$(R);: INPUT " IS A ——→ ";
     A$:A = VAL (A$)
230  IF A = C(R) THEN PRINT
     "CORRECT": FOR T = 1 TO 2000:
     NEXT : GOTO 190
240  IF H = 3 THEN PRINT "STUDY":
     GOTO 150
250  H = H + 1: PRINT : PRINT "HINT - ";
     H$(C(R),H): GOTO 210
260  DATA ACID, TURNS LITMUS RED,
     CONTAINS HYDROGEN ION, SOUR
     TASTE
270  DATA BASE, TURNS LITMUS BLUE,
     BITTER TASTE, CONTAINS
     HYDROXIDE ION
280  DATA SALT, NO CHANGE IN
     LITMUS, CONTAINS METAL &
     NONMETAL IONS
290  DATA ORANGE, 1
300  DATA LYE, 2
330  DATA 0,0
```

PROGRAM NOTES

Statements 260, 270, and 280 are data statements that list the characteristics of acids, bases, and salts. If you would prefer other descriptions to help you identify these substances, change the statements accordingly.

BITS OF INFORMATION

The concept of "feedback" owes a great deal to Norbert Wiener, one of the early pioneers in the computer field. Wiener defined feedback as the process through which both humans and machines could examine the effects of their action and change their behavior.

CHAPTER REVIEW

See teacher's commentary for answers.

VOCABULARY

On a separate piece of paper, match each term with the number of the statement that best explains it. Use each term only once.

acid	neutral	polluted	indicator
base	neutralization	precipitate	polar molecule
electrolyte	nonelectrolyte	salt	soluble

1. Carries small electric charges on opposite ends.
2. A description of water that contains harmful substances.
3. Forms a conducting solution when dissolved in water.
4. Forms a nonconducting solution when dissolved in water.
5. A solid that separates from a solution.
6. A description of a substance that can be dissolved.
7. Forms a solution with more H^+ ions than pure water.
8. Changes color when put in an acid solution.
9. Forms a solution with more OH^- ions than pure water.
10. Neither an acid nor a base.
11. A chemical reaction that occurs when an acid and a base are mixed.
12. Made up of the positive ion from a base and the negative ion from an acid.

QUESTIONS

Give brief but complete answers to each of the following questions. Unless otherwise indicated, use complete sentences to write your answers.

1. Why is water pollution such a serious problem?
2. Why do some dissolved substances form solutions that can conduct electricity?
3. When the following pairs of ions are in solution, which will form a precipitate: (a) Ag^+ and Cl^-, (b) Zn^{2+} and Cl^-, (c) Mg^{2+} and $CO_3{}^{2-}$?
4. The following ions are all in a solution: Ag^+, $B_4O_7{}^{2-}$, Zn^{2+}, and Cl^-. Write the chemical formulas for any precipitates that will form.
5. Describe what is meant by an acidic solution. Write the chemical formula of the acids in two acidic solutions.
6. Give two examples of the chemical actions of an acidic solution.
7. Describe what is meant by a basic solution. Write the chemical formulas of the bases in two basic solutions.
8. What is a pH scale?
9. What is produced when an acid and a base are mixed? Write a chemical equation that shows such a reaction.

10. Which of the following substances will form a salt with HCl: HBr, KOH, HI, LiOH, H_2O, or $Ca(OH)_2$?
11. Write the chemical formulas for all the possible products if each of the following acids is mixed with each of the following bases:

    acids—HCl, HBr, and HF; bases—KOH, $Ca(OH)_2$, and LiOH.
12. List the steps you would take to safely identify a white powder as either an acid or a base.
13. Using Table 20–1, complete the following chemical equation:

$$ZnCl_2 + Na_2B_4O_7 \longrightarrow ______ + ______ + ______$$

APPLYING SCIENCE

1. Shampoo advertisements claim that their products have balanced pH, contain no detergents, are nonalkaline, or do not cause tears. Test several shampoos with red litmus paper. Test the same shampoos with blue litmus paper. Report your observations to the class. Which shampoo do you suggest using? Why?
2. Test several antacids and compare their effectiveness in neutralizing acid. Dissolve each antacid in a standard amount of water. Add this solution to an acid until its pH is 7.0. The antacid that neutralizes the acid with the least amount of solution is the most effective.
3. As you learned in Chapter 1, certain gases called oxides form acids when they dissolve in rain water. The acid rain that results can be harmful to the environment. Write a report about current research into the causes and effects of acid rain. Use a map to show the areas of the country that are affected.

BIBLIOGRAPHY

Arnov, Boris. *Water: Experiments to Understand It.* New York: Lothrop, 1980.

Gay, Katherine. *Acid Rain.* New York: Watts, 1983.

Gilfond, Henry. *Water: A Scarce Resource.* New York: Watts, 1978.

Goldin, Augusta. *Water: Too Much, Too Little, Too Polluted.* New York: Harcourt, Brace, Jovanovich, 1983.

Jensen, W. B. *The Lewis Acid-Base Concepts: An Overview.* New York: Wiley, 1980.

Multhauf, R.P. *Neptune's Gift: A History of Common Salt.* Baltimore: Johns Hopkins, 1978.

CHAPTER

21

This device is the target chamber of an experimental fusion reactor. The reactor uses laser beams to implode a tiny fuel pellet. The high temperature and pressure cause a fusion reaction.

THE NUCLEUS

CHAPTER GOALS

1. Explain how an atomic nucleus produces radioactivity.
2. Use the term half-life to describe how radioactivity changes over a period of time.
3. Compare nuclear fission and fusion reactions.
4. Describe how nuclear reactions can be used as a source of energy.

21-1. Radioactivity

At the end of this section you will be able to:

- Explain why some atoms are *radioactive.*
- Name and describe three types of natural radioactivity.
- Describe three ways to detect radioactivity.

Many watches have dials that glow in the dark. If you look at such a watch closely in a dark room, you will see tiny flashes of light from the glowing dial. Each of these flashes is caused by a single atom.

UNSTABLE ATOMIC NUCLEI

Try to picture the nucleus of an atom. Suppose, for example, that the nucleus of a typical atom were the size of the period at the end of this sentence. The electron cloud around that nucleus would fill the space of your classroom!

Reinforcement: Review the structure of the atom. This chapter deals with changes in the nucleus.

The tiny nucleus contains all of the atom's protons and neutrons. The protons and neutrons are crowded together in a small amount of space. Remember that all neutrons are neutral. But each proton carries the same positive charge as its neighbors. Thus the protons in a nucleus repel each other. A force is needed to hold the protons together in the nucleus. This force is supplied by the **binding energy** of the nucleus. *Binding energy* holds the atomic nucleus together.

Binding energy The energy that holds the nucleus of an atom together.

Different kinds of atoms have different numbers of protons and neutrons in their nuclei. For example, a typical carbon atom has six protons and six neutrons; most oxygen atoms have eight protons and eight neutrons.

Fig. 21–1 In 1903, Marie and Pierre Curie shared a Nobel Prize in physics with Antoine Henri Becquerel for their research on natural radioactivity. In 1911, Marie Curie received a Nobel Prize in chemistry for the discovery of radium and polonium. She was the first person to win two Nobel Prizes in science.

Each kind of nucleus requires a different amount of binding energy to hold it together. Some nuclei have a small supply of binding energy. The protons and neutrons in these nuclei are not tightly bound. Such nuclei are unstable. Just as an atom with an unstable electron arrangement may change, an unstable nucleus may change to become more stable. An atom whose unstable nucleus changes to become more stable is **radioactive** (raid-ee-oh-**ak**-tiv). *Radioactivity* was discovered by the French scientist Antoine Henri Becquerel in 1896. Becquerel observed that substances containing uranium gave off rays that could pass through paper and affect photographic film. Marie Sklodowska Curie and her husband Pierre became interested in the strange new rays discovered by Becquerel. See Fig. 21–1. After several years of work, they found two previously unknown *radioactive* elements. They named these elements radium and polonium. Following the pioneering work of Becquerel and the Curies, other radioactive elements were found. Radioactive elements are made up of atoms with unstable nuclei.

Radioactive An atom is radioactive when its nucleus decays in order to become more stable.

RADIOACTIVE DECAY

An unstable atomic nucleus can become more stable in many ways. For example, rays or particles can be emitted by the nucleus. These rays and particles from unstable atomic nuclei cause radioactivity. Any change in a nucleus that causes radioactivity is called *decay.* The following are the most common examples of radioactive decay.

Alpha decay A radioactive change in which a nucleus emits an alpha particle made up of two protons and two neutrons.

1. Alpha decay. **Alpha decay** takes place when a nucleus emits a particle made up of two protons and two neutrons. This particle is called an *alpha particle.* Alpha particles are thrown out of a nucleus at high speed, but they slow down as they collide with surrounding atoms. An alpha particle is the same as the nucleus of a helium atom ($^{4}_{2}He$). Each alpha particle can gain two electrons to become a helium atom.

A radium atom decays by emitting an alpha particle. See Fig. 21–2. The atom that remains has two less protons and two less neutrons than radium, and is now an atom of a different element. This atom is now an atom of the element radon. Radioactive decay can be represented by equations similar to chemical equations. For example, the alpha decay of radium is shown by: $^{226}_{88}Ra \longrightarrow ^{222}_{86}Rn + ^{4}_{2}He$

Enrichment: Becquerel's discovery can be partly duplicated using Polaroid sheet film. Place two keys on the exposure side of a Polaroid sheet film packet. Place a piece of radioactive material on one key. Leave it overnight. Develop the film with a roller. The outline of the key caused by radiation will be visible. The second key produces no outline and is used as a control.

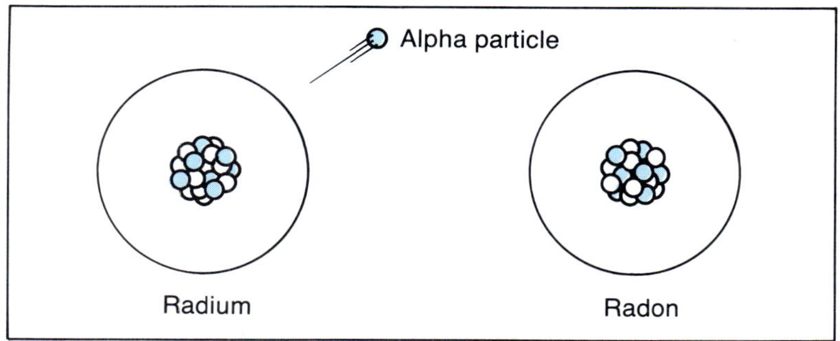

Fig. 21–2 A radium atom emits an alpha particle ($^{4}_{2}He$) and changes into a radon atom.

The atomic nuclei are represented by the chemical symbol with the atomic number at the lower left and the mass number at the upper left.

2. Beta decay. **Beta decay** causes an electron to be shot out of the nucleus at high speed. This rapidly moving electron is called a *beta particle.* How did an electron get into the nucleus? A beta particle is formed when a neutron in the nucleus changes into a proton. When this happens, the neutron loses an electron. This electron leaves the nucleus as a beta particle. When a nucleus gives off a beta particle, it is left with an extra proton. This extra proton changes the atom into an atom of a different element. For example, a radioactive form of carbon, called carbon-14, changes into nitrogen by beta decay. See Fig. 21–3. Beta decay of carbon-14 is represented by:

Beta decay A radioactive change in which an electron (beta particle) is emitted from a nucleus.

$$^{14}_{6}C \longrightarrow ^{14}_{7}N + ^{0}_{-1}e$$

3. Gamma decay. When alpha or beta decay takes place, **gamma rays** are also usually given off. *Gamma rays* are a kind of electromagnetic energy similar to X-rays. Gamma rays have a higher frequency than X-rays. Unlike alpha and beta decay, emission of gamma rays does not cause an atom to

Gamma rays Rays, similar to X-rays, that are emitted when a radioactive atom undergoes gamma decay.

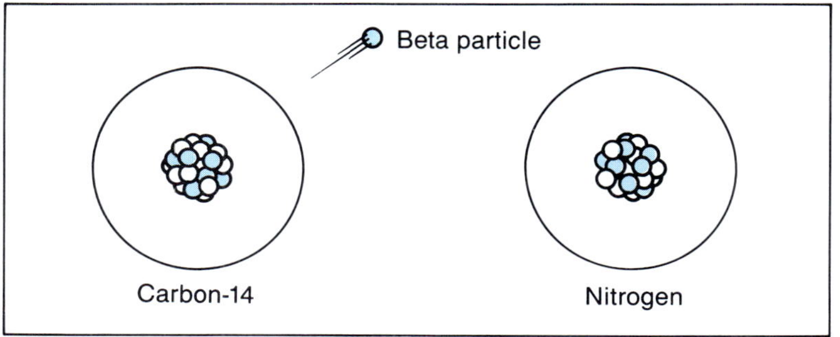

Fig. 21–3 A carbon-14 atom emits a beta particle (an electron) and changes into a nitrogen atom.

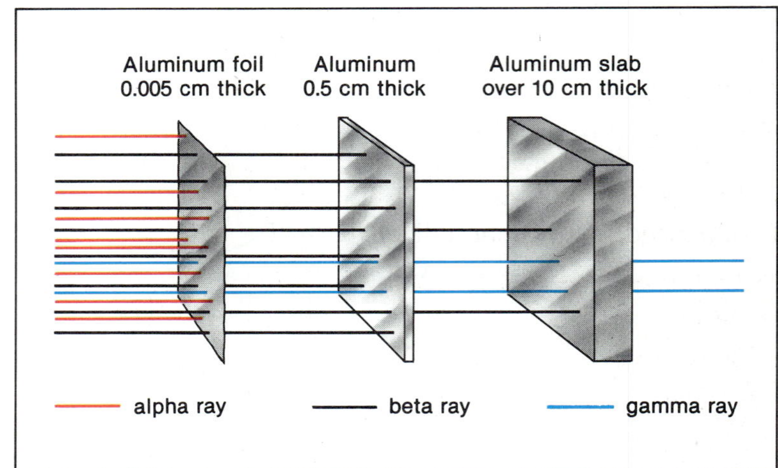

Fig. 21–4 Gamma rays will pass right through most solid materials. In comparison, alpha and beta radiation are easily blocked.

change into another kind of atom. Gamma rays are not atomic particles like alpha and beta particles. Gamma rays can penetrate most materials easily. Figure 21–4 shows that it is easier to shield against alpha and beta particles than against gamma radiation.

Suggestion: Use a Geiger counter to demonstrate the presence of background radiation.

MEASURING RADIOACTIVITY

The face of a watch or clock that glows in the dark contains a small amount of radioactive material. The paint used gives off a small amount of light when it is exposed to radioactivity. Each small burst of light is the result of the radioactive decay of one atom. This light is the only way you can tell that radioactivity is coming from the watch. You cannot see or feel radioactivity directly. Radioactivity is always observed and measured by special instruments.

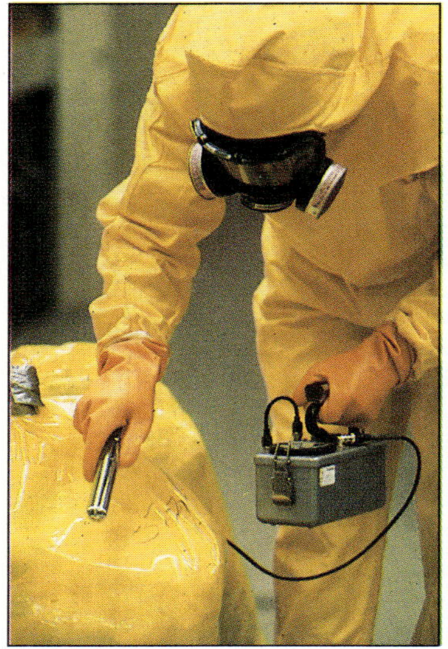

Fig. 21–5 The Geiger counter was invented in 1928 by Hans Geiger, who worked as one of Rutherford's assistants.

One of the instruments used to detect radioactivity is called a *Geiger counter.* See Fig. 21–5. Radioactivity passing through the detector causes an electric current to flow. The electric current is amplified and it causes a meter to register the amount of radioactivity. A Geiger counter will show that a small amount of radioactivity is coming from a watch dial that glows in the dark.

The flashes of light that radioactivity produces in some materials can also be used in electronic devices that measure radioactivity. Photographic film is affected by radioactivity. When the film is developed, small dark streaks are present where radioactive particles and rays passed through the film.

These streaks can be seen with a microscope. Thus photographic film can be used to detect and measure radioactivity. Radioactivity also leaves tracks in a *cloud chamber*. The air in a cloud chamber is saturated with the vapor from a liquid such as alcohol. Radioactivity causes the vapor to condense. This leaves a visible trail just as a high-flying jet leaves a trail of condensed water vapor in the sky. See Fig. 21–6.

Enrichment: Inexpensive cloud chambers are available from science supply houses. Use one to show alpha particle tracks. Be very careful in handling dry ice. Always use heavy gloves. Students should not touch the dry ice.

1. Some atoms are radioactive because they have unstable nuclei that decay to become more stable.

Fig. 21–6 The cloud chamber was invented by C.T.R. Wilson. He shared the 1927 Nobel Prize in physics for his discovery. Each of the tracks in this photo was made by a charged particle.

SUMMARY

Every nucleus requires a certain amount of binding energy to hold it together. A nucleus with too little binding energy is unstable. An unstable nucleus may become more stable by radioactive decay. Radioactivity is the result of nuclear decay that can produce alpha particles, beta particles, and gamma radiation.

QUESTIONS

Use complete sentences to write your answers.

1. What makes an atom radioactive?
2. Compare and contrast alpha, beta, and gamma decay.
3. Explain how each of the following devices can be used to detect radioactivity: (a) Geiger counter, (b) photographic film, (c) cloud chamber.
4. What happens to an atom after it emits an alpha particle?
5. What happens to an atom after it emits a beta particle?

2. Alpha decay is a form of radioactivity in which particles consisting of two protons and two neutrons are ejected from the nucleus. Beta decay is a form of radioactivity in which a neutron changes to a proton and an electron and the electron is ejected from the nucleus. Gamma rays are electromagnetic waves that accompany alpha or beta decay.
3. (a) A Geiger counter uses amplified electric currents to detect radioactivity. (b) The flashes of light produced by radioactivity are recorded on photographic film. (c) Radioactive particles leave visible trails in the vapor of a cloud chamber.
4. When an atom emits an alpha particle, it is left with two less protons and neutrons. It becomes an atom of a different element.
5. When an atom emits a beta particle, it is left with one extra proton. It then becomes an atom of a different element.

21-2. Radioactive Atoms

At the end of this section you will be able to:

- Explain what makes an atom radioactive.
- Define *half-life.*
- Use examples to show how a radioactive *tracer* is used.

The photograph in Fig. 21–7 was made by using instruments that detect small amounts of radioactive atoms inside the body. Radioactive atoms can be traced as they move through the body. Doctors often use radioactive substances in this way to help them find the cause of an illness.

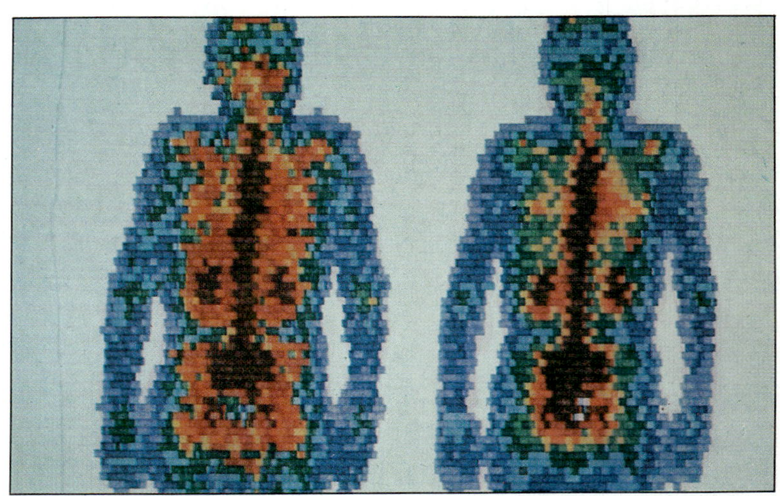

Fig. 21–7 This is a computerized image showing how a radioactive tracer is absorbed by the body.

NATURAL AND ARTIFICIAL RADIOACTIVE ATOMS

A stable atomic nucleus can be made radioactive by hitting it with neutrons or other atomic particles. For example, iodine is not naturally radioactive. However, scientists can make radioactive iodine by shooting neutrons at the nuclei of ordinary iodine atoms. The radioactive form of iodine is called iodine-131 or I-131. When an atom is made radioactive by adding neutrons or protons to its nucleus, the radioactive atom is called a *radioisotope.* Many kinds of radioisotopes can be made. These radioisotopes can be used for many purposes. They can be used to treat cancer, to sterilize food and drugs, or to follow chemical and biological reactions.

Scientists can also increase the size of atomic nuclei to make heavy atoms that do not occur naturally. The largest naturally occurring atom is uranium. Uranium has an atomic number of 92. Elements with atomic numbers larger than 92 have been made by adding protons and neutrons to atoms such as uranium. These atoms are known as *synthetic* or artificial elements. Fig. 21–8 shows where the naturally radioactive and synthetic elements are found on the periodic chart of the elements.

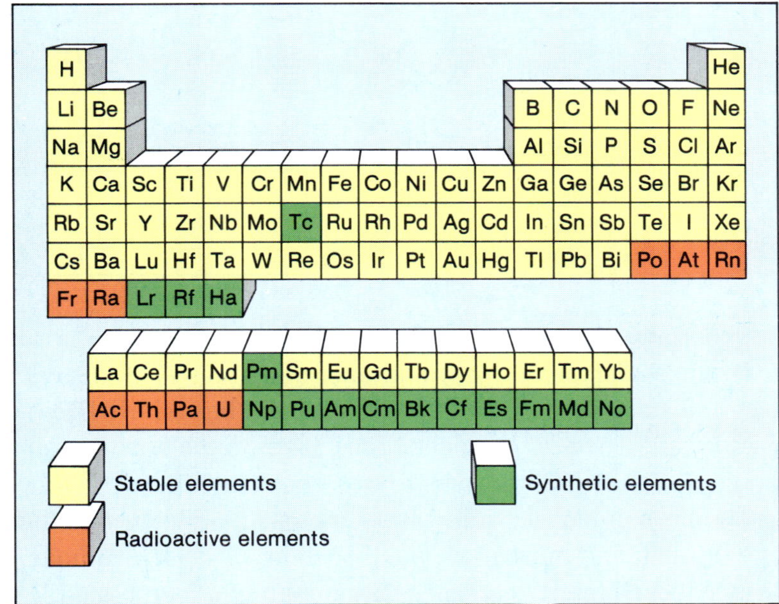

Fig. 21–8 Naturally radioactive and synthetic elements are shown in different colors on this periodic chart.

HALF-LIFE

Carbon has a naturally radioactive isotope. This isotope is called carbon-14. It has six protons and eight neutrons in its nucleus. The common form of carbon, carbon-12, has six protons and six neutrons. Carbon-14 takes part in life processes just as ordinary carbon-12 does. All living things contain a few atoms of carbon-14. The percentage of radioactive carbon-14 in living things remains the same as long as they are alive. However, after a living thing dies, the amount of radioactive carbon-14 slowly decreases. The unstable carbon atoms begin to change into more stable atoms. A piece of wood from an old house, for example, is less radioactive than wood from a freshly cut tree.

Reinforcement: If students do not do the Skill-Building Activity following this section, you can demonstrate a model of half-life. Place 100 coins in a box with a lid. Shake the box. Remove any coins that are face up. Record the number removed and the number remaining. Shake the box two more times, each time removing the coins that are face up and recording the numbers. Plot a graph of the number of coins remaining vs. the number of shakes. This graph duplicates a radioactive decay curve. The "half-life" of the coins is one shake.

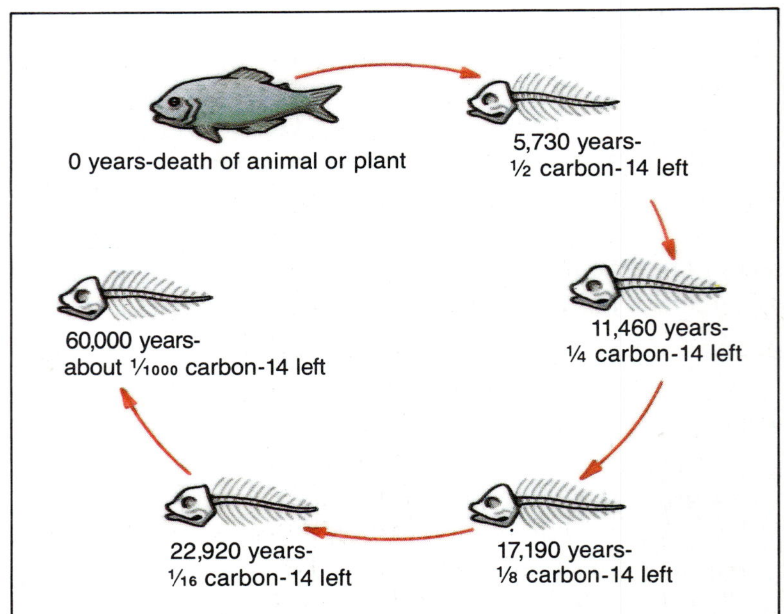

Fig. 21–9 The technique of carbon dating depends on the decay of radioactive carbon-14 atoms.

Half-life The length of time necessary for one half of a given number of atoms to change into new atoms.

Experiments have shown that carbon-14 becomes stable at a certain rate. Half of a given number of carbon-14 atoms will become stable after 5,730 years. Carbon-14 has a **half-life** of 5,730 years. The *half-life* is the time it takes for half of a certain number of radioactive atoms to become stable. Because they know the half-life of carbon-14, scientists can determine the age of plant and animal remains. See Fig. 21–9. The radioactivity of an element decreases by one-half after each half-life. Wood that contains one-fourth (25 percent) of the carbon-14 it had when it was living is two half-lives or approximately 11,500 years old.

Each radioactive element has its own half-life. Some radioactive elements have a very long half-life. For example, uranium has a half-life of about 4.5 billion years. Other radioactive elements have short half-lives, lasting only several days, minutes, or even fractions of a second. Radioactive iodine has a half-life of eight days. At the end of each half-life, half of the radioactive atoms will have changed into stable atoms. For example, radium has a half-life of 1,622 years. Radium becomes stable by changing into lead. If you started with a block of radium, half of the block would be lead after 1,622 years. After two half-lives (3,244 years) had passed, only one-fourth

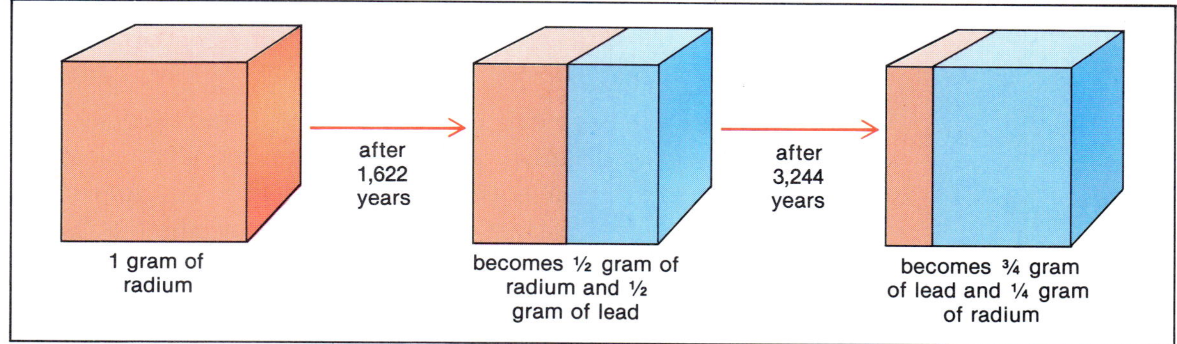

Fig. 21–10 After one half-life (1,622 years), one gram of radium will have become 0.5 g radium and 0.5 g lead.

of the original radium would remain. See Fig. 21–10. Scientists use this technique to study the remains of ancient cultures and people. The Dead Sea Scrolls are a group of religious writings from the Old Testament. They were discovered in 1947 in a cave near the Dead Sea between Israel and Jordan. By using carbon-14 dating, scientists found that the Scrolls are about 2,000 years old. This technique was also used to find the age of moon rocks. Moon rocks as old as 4.5 billion years have been dated. This is close to the age of the solar system itself.

RADIOACTIVITY AND LIFE

Scientists can follow radioactive atoms through chemical reactions by using instruments that detect radioactivity. Radioactive atoms that can be followed through the steps of a chemical reaction are called **tracers.** Agricultural scientists use *tracers* to study plant growth. Tracers can help show the effect of fertilizers and other chemicals on crops. Knowledge of the way plants use the chemicals in fertilizers can help to produce more crops. Scientists hope to use this information to help solve the problem of feeding the world's increasing population.

Tracers Radioactive elements that are used to follow atoms through different chemical reactions.

Tracers can also be used to help find the cause of disease. For example, a person can be given a solution containing radioactive iodine-131. The iodine collects in the small thyroid gland, near the larynx. The thyroid gland normally takes iodine from the blood and makes it into a substance needed by the body. By measuring how fast radioactive iodine is taken in by the gland, a doctor can tell if the gland is doing its job properly. If the thyroid gland is working too slowly, the doctor can prescribe a medicine to correct the problem. Since iodine-131 has a very short half-life of eight days, it quickly disappears from the body.

Some kinds of cancer are treated with radioactivity. The radioactivity destroys only the cancer without harming any other part of the patient's body. There is still no cure for cancer. Radioactivity is just one weapon in the fight against this deadly disease.

Large amounts of radioactivity are harmful to living things. When radioactive particles and rays pass through living cells, some of the molecules within the cells are changed. Alpha and beta particles, for example, may collide with molecules in a cell and break the bonds holding the molecules together. When cells are damaged in this way, they may die. The death of large numbers of cells by exposure to radioactivity can seriously harm or kill a living thing. Radioactivity can also cause *mutations*. As a result of mutations, offspring that are different from the parents are produced. If one or both parents are exposed to too much radioactivity, mutations can result in serious birth defects.

SUMMARY

Some radioactive atoms occur naturally. Others can be made by artificially increasing the size of a stable nucleus. All radioactive elements have a certain half-life. Tracers such as radioactive iodine can be used to detect diseases. Radioactivity can also help fight diseases such as cancer.

QUESTIONS

Use complete sentences to write your answers.

1. How can a stable atom be made radioactive? What are the radioactive forms of stable atoms called?
2. What is meant by the half-life of a radioactive element?
3. Name two radioactive elements. Give their atomic masses and half-lives.
4. What are radioactive tracers? How are they used?
5. Thorium-234 has a half-life of 24 days. After 48 days, how many atoms will *not* have become stable if 1,000,000,000 were present initially?

1. Adding extra neutrons to the nucleus of a stable atom makes the nucleus unstable (radioactive). It is then called a radioisotope.
2. The half-life of an element is the time it takes for half of a given number of radioactive atoms of that element to decay into stable atoms.
3. Carbon-14 has a half-life of 5,720 years. Radium-226 has a half-life of 1,522 years.
4. Radioactive tracers are used by scientists to study the time and the path that the element takes in going through the plants or animals. The effect of fertilizers on plants and drugs on animals can be studied.
5. The number of atoms that would not have decayed after 48 days is 250,000,000.

SKILL-BUILDING ACTIVITY

See teacher's commentary for teaching hints, safety, and answers to questions.

HALF-LIFE

PURPOSE: You will use a model of radioactive decay to measure half-life.

MATERIALS:

100 marked cubes
box with lid
graph paper
pencil
paper

PROCEDURE:

A. Copy the data table below.

Number of Shakes	Number of Cubes Remaining
0	
1	
2	
3	
4	

B. Place the cubes in the box. Cover the box and shake it.

C. Remove the cubes that have the marked side up. These cubes represent the atoms that have decayed. See Fig. 21–11.

D. Count the number of cubes remaining in the box and record it in the data table. These cubes represent the radioactive atoms remaining.

E. Repeat steps B through D four times.

F. Predict the number of cubes that will remain after you shake the box once more.

1. What is your prediction?

G. Shake the box.

2. Was your prediction correct?

H. Plot a graph of the number of cubes remaining. See Fig. 21–12.

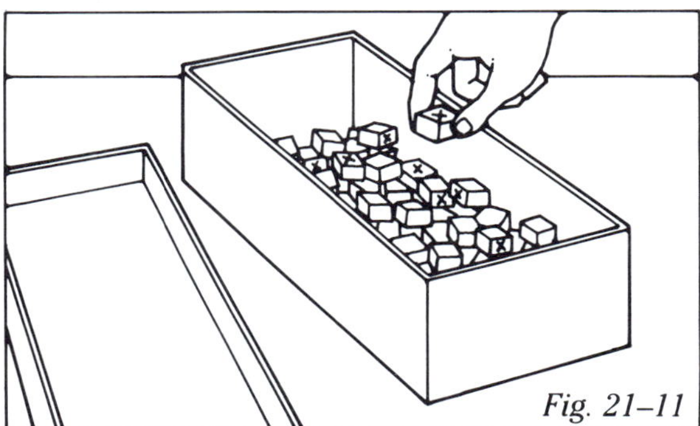

Fig. 21–11

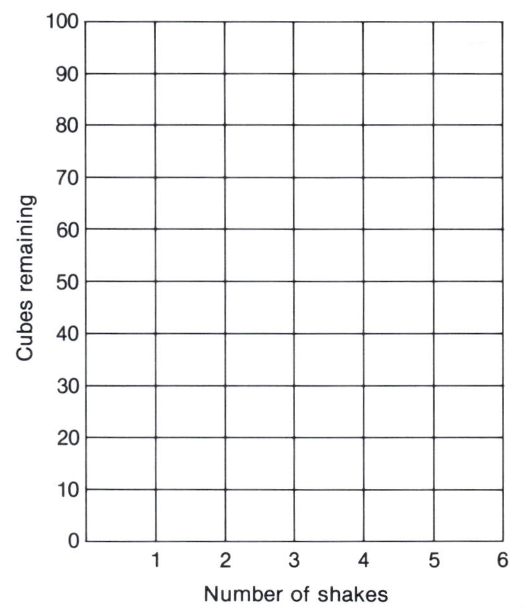

Fig. 21–12

CONCLUSIONS:

1. After how many shakes did one-half of the cubes "decay"?
2. What is the half-life of the cubes?

21-3. Fission and Fusion

At the end of this section you will be able to:

- Explain how energy can be released by splitting a large atomic nucleus.
- Describe a chain reaction.
- Distinguish between *fission* reactions and *fusion* reactions.

Just before dawn on July 16, 1945, the world's first atomic bomb exploded in the New Mexico desert. See Fig. 21–13. For the first time, human beings had released part of the energy trapped inside atoms. Scientists had known that a small portion of this atomic energy was released as radioactivity. The explosion of the atomic bomb proved that the energy in the nucleus could be released in other ways.

Fig. 21–13 An uncontrolled fission reaction results in a nuclear explosion.

NUCLEAR TARGET SHOOTING

Scientists can study atomic nuclei by shooting particles at them. For example, suppose that an alpha particle collides with the nucleus of an atom. The alpha particle can combine with the target nucleus. The collision of an alpha particle with a nitrogen nucleus produces an oxygen nucleus. The following nuclear equation describes this reaction:

$$^{14}_{7}\text{N} + ^{4}_{2}\text{He} \longrightarrow ^{17}_{8}\text{O} + ^{1}_{1}\text{H}$$

Fig. 21–14 Electrons can be accelerated to 99% of the speed of light in a linear accelerator. The first particle accelerator was built by Ernest O. Lawrence in 1930.

However, it is difficult to make an alpha particle collide with a nucleus. Both the nucleus and the alpha particle carry positive charges. Therefore, they repel each other. To overcome this repulsion, machines are used to speed up the particles. The particles then smash into the target atoms with enough energy to change them into different atoms. The machines used to speed up atomic particles are called *accelerators*. The accelerator shown in Fig. 21–14 is called a *linear accelerator*. Accelerators produce beams of different kinds of particles that help scientists study the nuclear reactions that result when the particles hit target atoms.

One result of scientific experiments with nuclear reactions has been the discovery of ways to make synthetic atoms. The largest natural atom is uranium, with atomic number 92. Heavier atoms, up to atomic number 105 and beyond, have been made by different kinds of nuclear reactions. Only very tiny amounts of most of these synthetic elements have been made. Some of these elements have been found to be useful and all of them have added to our knowledge of atoms.

Fig. 21–15 Enrico Fermi (1901–1954) was one of the major physicists of this century. The Fermi National Accelerator Laboratory (Fermilab) in Batavia, Illinois is named after him.

Neutrons are commonly used in nuclear experiments. Since they carry no charge, neutrons can easily enter the target nucleus. One of the first people to use neutrons in this way was Enrico Fermi, an Italian scientist. See Fig. 21–15. In 1938, Fermi was part of a scientific team that made a surprising discovery. They found that the nucleus of a uranium isotope splits when it is hit by a neutron.

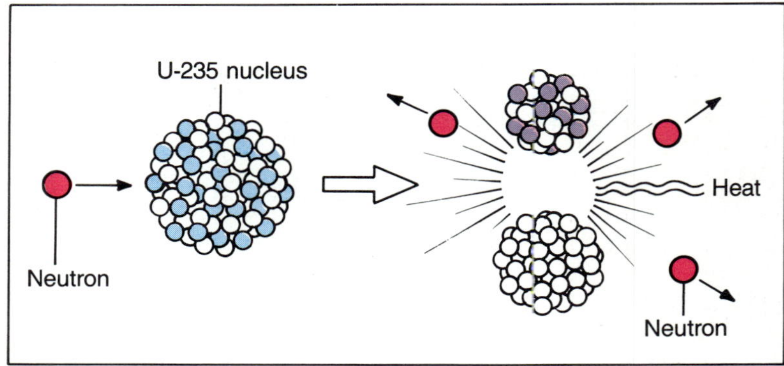

Fig. 21–16 When a neutron strikes a U-235 nucleus, the nucleus splits. In addition, more neutrons are released.

NUCLEAR FISSION

Fig. 21–16 shows what happens when a neutron hits a uranium atom. This uranium atom has a mass of 235 and is called U-235. The more common form of uranium has a mass of 238 and is called U-238. In nature, U-235 atoms are found thinly scattered among U-238 atoms. The U-235 nucleus becomes so unstable after being struck by a neutron that it splits in two. The splitting of an unstable nucleus into two smaller nuclei is called **fission.**

Fission A nuclear reaction in which a large unstable nucleus splits into smaller nuclei.

Word study: Fission from *findere* (L.), to split.

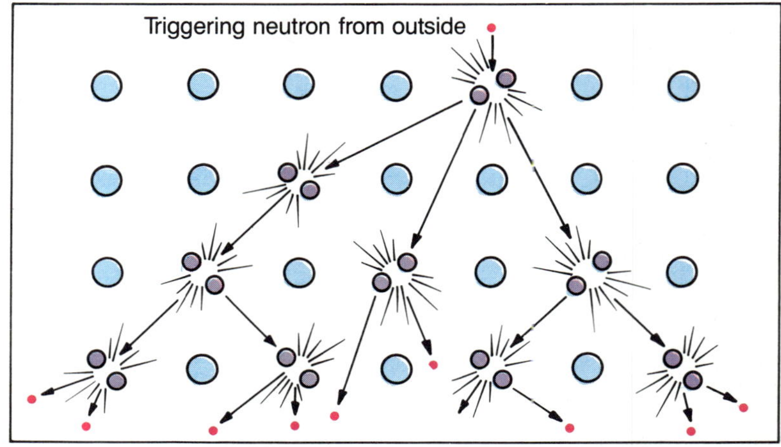

Fig. 21–17 The neutrons released when a U-235 nucleus splits strike other U-235 nuclei, releasing even more neutrons. The result is a chain reaction.

When *fission* occurs, a small amount of energy is released. The amount of energy released by the splitting of a single U-235 nucleus is not large. The huge amount of energy released in an atomic bomb is the result of the fission of *many* U-235 nuclei. When a U-235 nucleus splits, it produces neutrons. These neutrons strike other U-235 nuclei, causing them to undergo fission. As a result, more neutrons are produced. If there are enough U-235 atoms present, the result is a **chain reaction.** See Fig. 21–17.

Uranium-238 is not fissionable. Naturally occurring uranium must be "enriched" with U-235 before it can be used to build an atomic bomb. An atomic bomb consists of pure U-235, or a similar fissionable material. Neutrons act as the trigger to set off a *chain reaction*. An uncontrolled chain reaction results in an explosion.

Enrichment: The minimum amount of fissionable material needed to support a chain reaction is called the *critical mass*. In a nuclear bomb, the critical mass is divided into small portions. The explosion is set off when the portions of the critical mass are suddenly brought together.

Chain reaction A process in which each step causes the same reaction as the previous step.

NUCLEAR FUSION

In addition to fission, there is another type of energy-producing nuclear reaction. This type of reaction occurs when two atomic nuclei collide. Normally, when two atoms approach each other, their negative electrons and positive nuclei repel each other. However, if the temperature is raised to several million degrees, the two atoms move extremely fast. At this temperature, the atoms collide violently. The collision between these atoms brings their nuclei close together. The two nuclei then join to form a single, larger nucleus. This type of reaction is called a **fusion** reaction. Two kinds of *fusion* reaction are shown in Fig. 21–18.

Fusion A nuclear reaction in which small nuclei join to form a larger nucleus.

Word study: Fusion from *fundere* (L.), to melt.

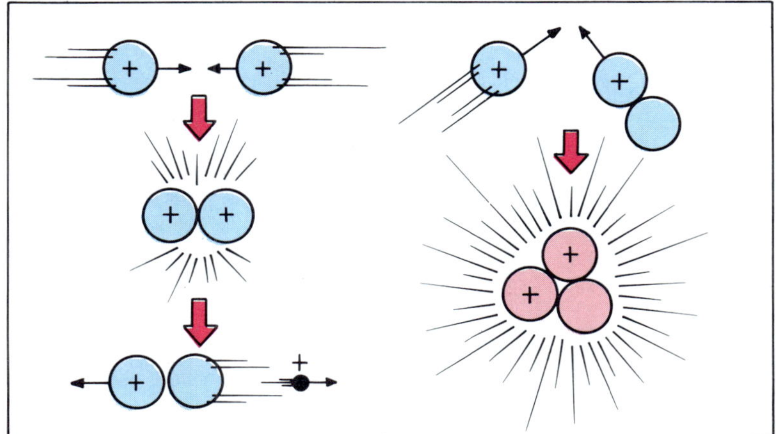

Fig. 21–18 On the left, two hydrogen-2 nuclei fuse to form a nucleus of hydrogen-3 and a proton: $^{2}_{1}H + ^{2}_{1}H \rightarrow ^{3}_{1}H + ^{1}_{1}H$. *On the right, a hydrogen-2 nucleus and a hydrogen-3 nucleus fuse to form a helium nucleus and a neutron:* $^{2}_{1}H + ^{3}_{1}H \rightarrow ^{4}_{2}He + ^{1}_{0}n$.

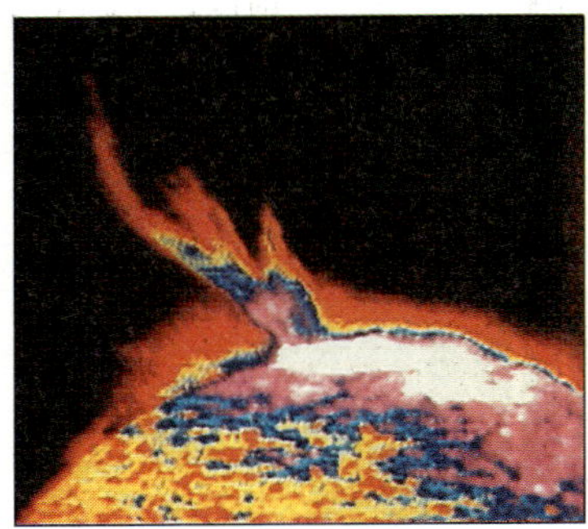

Fig. 21–19 The fusion of four protons to form a helium nucleus is the main source of the energy of the sun.

Fusion reactions happen naturally inside the sun and other stars. Here the temperatures are high enough for the reactions to take place. See Fig. 21–19. The temperature near the center of the sun is probably about 15 million degrees Kelvin. Such high temperatures can be found on earth only in an atomic explosion. The first atomic bomb exploded in New Mexico was a fission bomb. The high temperatures caused by fission reactions can be used to make a fusion bomb.

Making nuclear fusion take place slowly in a controlled way is much more difficult than causing an uncontrolled explosion. The heat given off by fusion reactions creates very high temperatures. Any materials used to contain the reaction would be vaporized by the great amount of heat released. One solution to this problem is to contain the fusion reaction in a magnetic field or so-called *magnetic bottle*. Another machine uses powerful laser beams to create the high temperatures needed. See Fig. 21–20. Both of these ideas are now being tested. Scientists are working hard to find a way to use nuclear fusion as a source of energy. We already use controlled fission reactions as an energy source, as you will see in the next section.

Fig. 21–20 These lasers are part of an experimental fusion device at Lawrence Livermore Laboratory. Temperatures as high as 10^8 °K are needed in order for fusion to take place.

MATTER INTO ENERGY

The release of energy by nuclear reactions was predicted by a theory developed by Albert Einstein in 1905. Einstein's theory states that matter and energy are different forms of the same thing. This idea is expressed in the famous equation $E = mc^2$. This equation shows that matter or mass (m) can be converted into energy (E). In the equation, c is the velocity of light. The velocity of light is about 3×10^8 m/s. Thus the equation says that a small amount of matter can be changed into a large amount of energy. For example, suppose 1 kg of sand could be completely converted into energy. This amount of energy could meet the electric power needs of the entire United States for about two weeks. With this energy, you could also drive an automobile around the world about 400,000 times. In nuclear reactions, small amounts of matter disappear. This small loss of mass produces the huge amount of energy released by fission and fusion reactions. Einstein's equation says that matter is a form of energy. In other words, a given mass is equal to a specific amount of energy.

SUMMARY

A tremendous supply of energy is packed into the nucleus of an atom. Some of that energy can be released by two different kinds of nuclear reactions. A fission reaction takes place when large nuclei split into smaller nuclei. A fusion reaction takes place when small nuclei join to become a larger nucleus.

QUESTIONS

Use complete sentences to write your answers.

1. How does splitting a large nucleus result in a release of energy?
2. Draw a diagram to explain what happens in a nuclear chain reaction.
3. Compare and contrast fission and fusion reactions.
4. Suppose that the fission of each atom in a chain reaction causes two additional atoms to undergo fission. See Fig. 21–17. How many atoms will undergo fission in the twenty-first step of the reaction?

1. When a large nucleus is split into smaller nuclei, the energy holding the nucleus together is released.
2. See Fig. 21–17.
3. Nuclear fission is the splitting of a large nucleus into smaller nuclei. Nuclear fusion is the joining of small nuclei to make a larger nucleus.
4. In the twenty-first step, 1,048,576 atoms will undergo fission.

21-4. Nuclear Energy

At the end of this section you will be able to:

- Explain how a nuclear *reactor* controls a nuclear fission reaction.
- Describe two types of nuclear reactors that may be used as energy sources.
- Identify some of the problems caused by the use of nuclear fission to produce energy.

You are already familiar with many kinds of fuels. Gasoline, coal, and wood are all common examples of fuels. Fig. 21–21 shows a different kind of fuel.

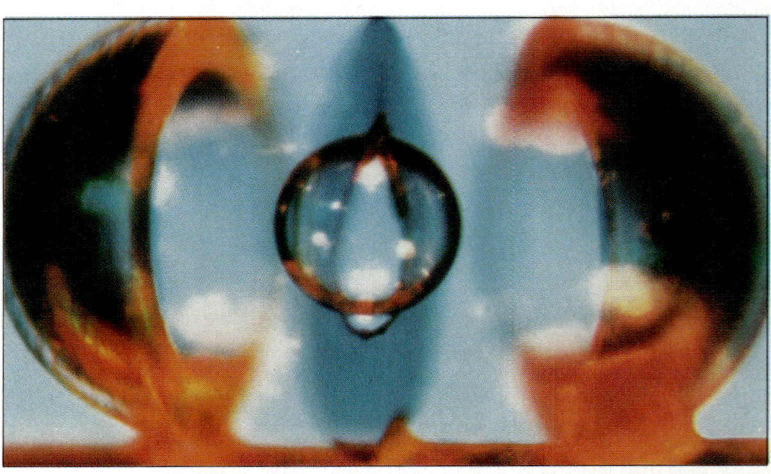

Fig. 21–21 This double-shell target is used in laser fusion research. (See page 524 and Fig. 21–20.) The inner sphere has a diameter of 150 microns (0.15 mm). It contains 15 nanograms of gaseous deuterium-tritium fuel ($^2_1H/^3_1H$). When the target is struck by laser beams, its density is increased from 10 mg/cm^3 to 20,000 mg/cm^3.

USEFUL ENERGY FROM THE ATOM

Nuclear reactor A machine used to produce a controlled nuclear chain reaction.

A controlled nuclear chain reaction takes place in a **nuclear reactor.** Uranium is used as fuel in a *nuclear reactor.* In the reactor, the unstable uranium atoms are bombarded with neutrons. The unstable atoms then split. This fission reaction produces heat and more neutrons. The neutrons hit more uranium atoms, producing a chain reaction. The speed of the chain reaction is controlled by rods made of an element such as boron, which absorbs neutrons. When the rods are pushed partway into the reactor, the boron absorbs neutrons. Fewer neutrons are then available to strike uranium atoms and the reaction slows down. The reaction speeds up again as the rods are pulled partway out of the reactor.

A working nuclear reactor releases heat. This heat can be used in the same way as the heat produced by burning carbon fuels. The heat produced by a nuclear reactor can be used to make steam. The steam drives generators to make electricity. See Fig. 21–22. The fission of one gram of uranium produces as much heat as burning three tons of coal. A piece of uranium the size of a golf ball could run a nuclear-powered car for 100 years. You can see that nuclear power plants can produce large amounts of energy.

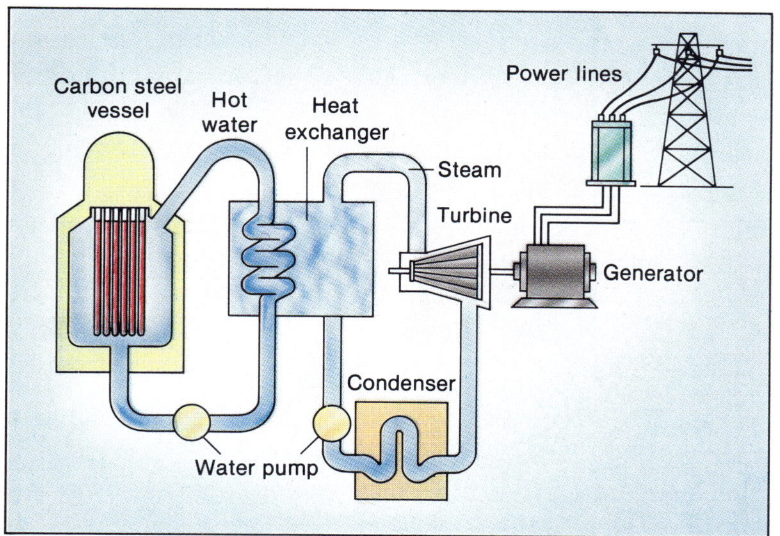

Fig. 21–22 This diagram shows how a nuclear reactor produces electricity. A uranium fuel pellet only 1.25 cm long produces as much energy as 800 kg of coal, 615 L of fuel oil, or 650 L of gasoline. Eight such pellets could supply all of your home energy needs for one year.

Unfortunately, making energy from nuclear fission also creates some serious problems. All nuclear reactors produce radioactive wastes. Since radioactivity is harmful, no radioactivity can be allowed to escape from the reactor. The reactor must be surrounded by a heavy lead and concrete shield.

RADIOACTIVE WASTES

Many nuclear power plants are already in operation. In the same way that a kitchen produces garbage, an operating nuclear power plant produces dangerous wastes. These wastes are radioactive and will be dangerous for hundreds of years. Most radioactive wastes are now sealed in underground tanks. Some sealed containers of wastes are sunk in deep ocean water. However, in both cases containers may corrode or rupture and release the waste materials. If more nuclear power plants are built, more radioactive waste will be produced. We must find a safe and inexpensive way to get rid of this nuclear garbage.

In addition to radioactive waste, there is another problem involved in using nuclear power plants. Most plants now in operation use uranium as fuel. However, the supply of uranium is limited. A possible solution to this problem would be to use nuclear *fusion reactors.* Fusion reactors could also produce large amounts of energy. The fuel used in fusion reactors is hydrogen. Unlike uranium, hydrogen is available on earth in great amounts. Another great advantage of fusion reactors is that they would produce less radioactive waste. At present, scientists have not yet been able to produce and control the extremely high temperatures needed to cause fusion. Research is still being done on this form of nuclear energy. At some time in the future, the almost limitless energy of the sun and stars may be available for our use. Reliable estimates indicate that obtaining energy from fusion will not become practical for at least 50 years.

SUMMARY

Nuclear fission can produce useful energy when nuclear fuels such as uranium release energy in a controlled reaction. A nuclear reactor produces useful energy from these nuclear reactions. Nuclear fission reactors produce dangerous radioactive wastes. If scientists learn to control nuclear fusion, nuclear fusion reactors may someday provide a cleaner, safer source of energy.

QUESTIONS

Use complete sentences to write your answers.

1. How is the chain reaction in a nuclear reactor controlled?
2. What natural fusion reaction have people always used as a source of energy?
3. What are two problems caused by the use of fission to produce energy?
4. What are two advantages of using fusion reactors to produce energy?
5. Describe how electricity is generated by a nuclear fission reactor.

1. The chain reaction in a nuclear reactor is controlled by rods made of a substance that absorbs neutrons.
2. The sun uses fusion reactions as the source of its energy. The sun is the ultimate source of all our energy.
3. Two problems caused by the use of fission reactors to produce energy are waste disposal and limited uranium fuel supplies.
4. Two advantages of using a fusion reactor are that it produces less radioactive waste and that the hydrogen fuel supply is almost unlimited.
5. The reactor heats water to make steam. The steam turns a turbine that turns a generator, which produces electricity.

FUSION POWER: REACHING FOR THE STARS

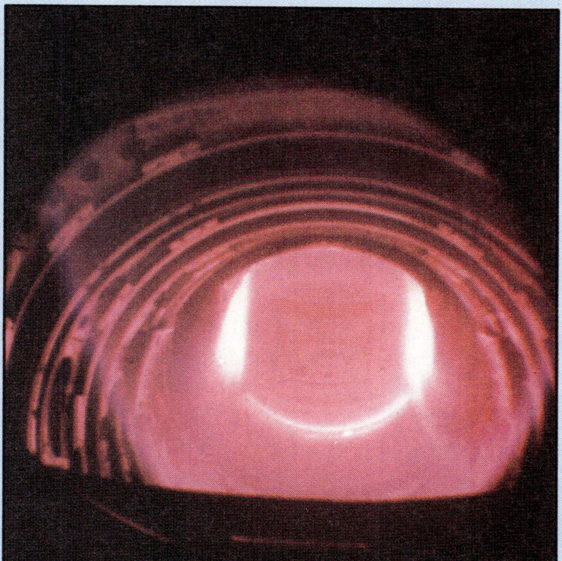

We don't have an endless amount of fossil fuel to meet our energy needs, and changing international situations often prevent us from obtaining fuel from other countries. Being able to use the energy of nuclear fusion instead of fossil fuels to generate electrical power has been a goal of scientists for years. To reach this goal the U.S. has built an experimental machine, called a tokamak fusion reactor, at the Plasma Physics Laboratory in Princeton, New Jersey (see photo).

The tokamak uses two isotopes of hydrogen as fuel, deuterium and tritium. However, extremely high temperatures are necessary to start the fusion reaction between the isotopes. Fusion occurs naturally within the stars where the temperatures are about five million degrees Kelvin. Reaching these temperatures on earth is very difficult. But once the temperature is approached, other problems arise. When the isotopes of hydrogen, a gas, are reaching fusion temperature, the molecules bounce off one another so vigorously they form electrically charged ions. These ions give the gas the ability to conduct electricity. A gas that can conduct electricity is called a plasma. Most substances give up their heat to anything they touch. Fusion will not occur if plasma gives up its heat before the nuclei of the isotopes fuse. Since energy is not released until fusion succeeds, the problem is to hold the plasma together until fusion occurs. In a tokamak reactor this is done by creating magnetic fields which act upon the electrically charged particles. These "magnetic bottles," created by immense and multishaped magnets, hold in the plasma and, at the same time, increase its temperature so that fusion can occur. Unfortunately, the amount of energy required to power the reactor is still many times greater than the amount of energy generated. It cannot, at this time, replace any currently used energy source. The engineering problems in building a fusion reactor with commercial possibilities are also awesome. The amount of heat generated requires very large pieces of machinery and some of these pieces would have to be rebuilt every ten years.

Fusion energy may be achieved in another way, through the use of laser technology, a process already being tried. With the use of lasers, small amounts of matter can be heated to intensely high temperatures very quickly. Only small amounts of energy are lost in the process.

After a great deal of research and experimentation, advances have been made, research continues, and hopes are still high. The basic question, however, is still unanswered: How can fusion become a practical and economical source of energy?

¡COMPUTE!

SCIENCE INPUT

Half-life refers to the period of time required for one-half of the atoms in a radioactive substance to change. This process takes place at a constant rate. In each half-life, one-half of whatever is remaining changes. For example, your textbook tells you that the half-life of radioactive iodine is 8 days. Therefore, if you have 10 grams of radioactive iodine, 5 grams will be stable in 8 days; 2.5 more grams will have stabilized in the next 8 days; 1.25 additional grams will stabilize in 8 more days and so forth. Radioactive half-life is used to determine the age of some rocks and minerals and of some organic substances. Therefore, it can be useful for dating certain kinds of fossil finds. Half-life calculations are also important in dealing with issues surrounding the disposal of radioactive waste.

COMPUTER INPUT

The methods used to determine the exact age of a substance by the half-life dating method are complex and time-consuming. However, by programming the computer to repeat a mathematical calculation, it can produce a great deal of data in a short time. In Program Half-Life the computer calculates half-life years and what percentage of radioactive material remains after each half-life for ten half-lives of a substance. This information can be very useful for dating certain kinds of fossil finds.

Check your own calculation time against that of the computer. The half-life for carbon-14 is 5,730 years. If one-half of the substance becomes stable in one half-life, what percentage remains in 3 half-lives and how many years will that take? (Check it with the computer.)

WHAT TO DO

Make a list of half-lives of some substances. A few possibilities are: radium (1,622 years); lead-210 (24.1 years); strontium-90 (28 years). On a separate piece of paper prepare a chart similar to the one below to record the data printed by the computer.

Enter Program Half-Life When you run it, the program will ask you to input the half-life of a substance. It will then generate data telling you the percentage of remaining radioactive materials and also the number of years that have passed with each half-life. In order to give yourself a visual idea of what is occurring, plot the data on a graph.

If you found a substance which you could identify and analyze for radioactivity, could you figure out how old it is? For example, if you analyzed a tree trunk found buried in the sand and discovered that it contained 25% carbon-14, what would be the age of the wood?

Data Chart

Substance	Half-Lives	Total Years	Remaining Radioactive Material
Carbon-14	0		100%
(5,730 yrs)	1		
	2		

THE NUCLEUS: PROGRAM HALF-LIFE

GLOSSARY

DISK DRIVES — the section of the hardware that "reads" the program stored on a disk. If software is in cassette form, not on disk, then a drive is not necessary.

PIXEL — a picture element—a pixel is a point or tiny box on the screen. The screen is composed of vertical and horizontal pixels.

RESOLUTION — the number of pixels on a TV screen or monitor. High resolution means there are a large number of pixels. Low resolution means there are fewer. The higher the resolution, the sharper the image or display.

PROGRAM

```
100  REM HALF-LIFE
110  A = 100
120  PRINT: INPUT "SUBSTANCE'S HALF-
     LIFE (1-100000)? ";HL$: HL =
     VAL(HL$)
130  IF HL < 1 OR HL > 100000 THEN
     GOTO 120
140  PRINT: PRINT "HALF-LIVES";
     TAB(15) "YEARS"; TAB(25)
     "REMAINING"
150  FOR X = 0 TO 10
160  IF X = 0 THEN GOTO 180
170  A = A * .5
180  PRINT X; TAB(15) X * HL; TAB(25)
     INT(A * 100 + .5) / 100; " %"
190  NEXT
200  GOTO 110
```

PROGRAM NOTES

Although this program does calculations only, there is a great deal of software which plots graphs and draws charts and tables. In fact, it would be possible to rewrite Program Half-Life to include a graph in the screen display. Such illustrations are especially useful in business, for financial analysis, and for mathematical problem-solving. Most personal computers can use software that will produce these kinds of graphics.

BITS OF INFORMATION

Archaeologists—social scientists who study social history through artifacts, paleontologists—scientists who study fossils, and geologists have started to use electronic sensors and computers to do the complicated calculations needed to date ancient finds. Many of our ideas about early civilizations are being changed because of the application of electronic and computer technology to the study of ancient and prehistoric times.

Computers are also being used to analyze rock samples for information about the present. There is, for example, a computer program called "Prospector," which can analyze geological field data and identify different kinds of deposits. In 1982 Prospector, through the analysis of information provided by geologists, identified a $100 thousand mineral deposit in an area that had been mined for years with little success. Prospector's program was designed to imitate the thought processes of 20 highly respected geologists.

CHAPTER REVIEW

See teacher's commentary for answers.

VOCABULARY

On a separate piece of paper, match each term with the number of the statement that best explains it. Use each term only once.

alpha decay	fission	nuclear reactor	chain reaction
beta decay	fusion	radioactive	half-life
binding energy	gamma ray	tracer	

1. A process in which each step causes the same reaction as the previous step.
2. A nuclear change in which an electron is released from the nucleus.
3. Two nuclei join to form a larger one.
4. Electromagnetic radiation given off by a decaying nucleus.
5. An atom whose nucleus is becoming more stable.
6. A nucleus releases particles made up of two protons and two neutrons.
7. The time taken for half of a given number of radioactive atoms to decay.
8. A large unstable nucleus splits into smaller nuclei.
9. A radioactive element used to follow atoms in chemical reactions.
10. A machine used to produce a controlled nuclear chain reaction.
11. A force that holds the nucleus together.

QUESTIONS

Give brief but complete answers to each of the following questions. Unless otherwise indicated, use complete sentences to write your answers.

1. Explain why some atoms are radioactive while others are not.
2. Name two radioactive atoms. Give the atomic mass and tell what kind of decay they undergo.
3. Name and describe three types of natural radioactive decay.
4. If the half-life of a radioactive element is 2,000 years, how long will it be before three-fourths of the atoms in a given sample will have decayed?
5. How is radioactivity used to determine the age of plant and animal remains?
6. Use an example to show how energy is released by fission of a large atomic nucleus. Where does the energy come from?
7. Compare a fission reaction with a fusion reaction.
8. Discuss the advantages of using fusion reactors to produce energy.
9. Describe how a nuclear reactor can be used to control a fission reaction.
10. Describe some problems arising from the use of nuclear fission to produce energy.

11. Describe two ways in which radioactivity can be harmful to living things.
12. What are radioisotopes? How are they made? List three uses of radioisotopes.
13. What are radioactive tracers? How are they used?
14. Identify the major problems that must be overcome before we can use nuclear fusion for energy. What are some possible solutions?

APPLYING SCIENCE

1. Write a report on the experiments that led to the discovery of some of the particles that scientists currently believe exist in the nuclei of atoms.
2. What is the current status of controlled fusion research? Are the arguments for and against the use of fusion power the same as those for fission power? Describe some of the experimental fusion reactors being tested.
3. Borrow a Geiger counter from your school, fire department, or local college. Measure the amount of radioactivity around you all day. Which things are most radioactive?
4. Organize your class into opposing teams to debate the use of nuclear power.

BIBLIOGRAPHY

Asimov, Isaac. *How Did We Find Out about Nuclear Power?* New York: Walker, 1976.

Bickel, Lennard. *The Deadly Element: The Story of Uranium.* New York: Stein and Day, 1980.

Chester, M. *Particles: An Introduction to Particle Physics.* New York: Macmillan, 1978.

Dank, Milton. *Albert Einstein.* New York: Watts, 1983.

Epstein, S.S. and Carl Pope. *Hazardous Waste in America.* San Francisco: Sierra, 1982.

Fermi, Laura. *The Story of Atomic Energy.* New York: Random House, 1961.

Gold, M. "To Breed or Not To Breed." *Science '82,* May 1982.

Grey, J. *Beachheads in Space.* New York: Macmillan, 1983.

Lightman, A. "Weighing the Odds." *Science '83,* December 1983.

Pringle, Laurence. *Nuclear Power: From Physics to Politics.* New York: Macmillan, 1979.

Roberts, L. "Reactors in Orbit." *Science '83,* December 1983.

GLOSSARY

A

Absolute zero. The temperature (−273°C) at which particles of matter stop moving.

Acceleration. A change in the velocity (speed or direction) of a moving object.

Acid. A compound that forms a solution containing more H^+ ions than pure water.

Acid rain. Rain containing acids formed from gases given off by power plants and industrial boilers. Acid rain has a pH below 5.6.

Alcohol. A kind of organic molecule having at least one OH group.

Alkali metals. A group of elements whose atoms all have one electron more than the stable number.

Alkanes. A group of hydrocarbons in which the carbon atoms are joined by only single bonds.

Alkenes. A group of hydrocarbons in which each molecule has one pair of carbon atoms joined by a double bond.

Alkynes. A group of hydrocarbons in which each molecule has one pair of carbon atoms joined by a triple bond.

Alloy. A mixture of two or more metals.

Alpha decay. A radioactive change in which a nucleus emits an alpha particle made up of two protons and two neutrons.

Alternating current. An electric current that constantly changes its direction of flow.

Amino acid. A kind of organic molecule having both NH_2 and COOH groups.

Ampere. A measure of the amount of current moving past a given point in an electric circuit in one second. One ampere is equal to one volt per ohm of resistance.

Amplitude. The distance a wave rises or falls from a normal rest position.

Aromatics. Hydrocarbons containing carbon atoms arranged in a ring structure.

Atom. The smallest particle of an element that can be identified as that element.

Atomic mass. The average of all the masses of the isotopes of a particular element.

Atomic mass unit. A unit used to express the masses of atomic particles and atoms; $1\ u = 1.660 \times 10^{-27}$ kg.

Atomic number. The number of protons in the nucleus of an atom.

Atomic particles. The basic building blocks of all atoms.

Aurora. The northern or southern lights.

Average speed. The total distance traveled divided by the total time.

B

Base. A compound that forms a solution with more OH^- ions than pure water.

Beta decay. A radioactive change in which an electron (beta particle) is emitted from a nucleus.

Binding energy. The energy that holds the nucleus of an atom together.

Boiling point. The temperature (at ordinary air pressure) at which the molecules of a liquid have enough energy to become a gas.

C

Calorie. The amount of heat needed to raise the temperature of one gram of water one degree Celsius.

Carbohydrates. Compounds of carbon, hydrogen, and oxygen whose molecules contain two atoms of hydrogen for every atom of oxygen.

Catalyst. A substance that changes the speed of a chemical reaction but that remains the same after the reaction.

Celsius (C). The commonly used temperature scale in science.

Chain reaction. A process in which each step causes the same reaction as the previous step.

Chemical activity. Describes the way in which an atom reacts with other kinds of atoms.

Chemical bond. A force that holds two atoms in a molecule together.

Chemical change. A change in matter in which one kind of molecule is changed into another kind.

Chemical equation. A description of a chemical reaction using chemical formulas for the reactants and products.

Chemical family. A group of elements that are very similar in their chemical behavior.

Chemical formula. A way of describing compounds by using atomic symbols and subscript numbers.

Chemical property. A description of how one kind of matter behaves in the presence of another kind of matter.

Chemical reaction. A process in which a chemical change takes place.

Circuit breaker. A switch that turns off if too much current flows in a circuit.

Collision theory. The theory that molecules must collide in order to react with each other.

Complementary colors. A pair of colors of light that combine to produce white.

Compound. A substance that can only be broken down into simpler parts by a chemical change. A compound contains only one kind of molecule.

Concave lens. A lens in which the curved surface curves inward and the edges are thicker than the middle.
Concave mirror. A curved mirror whose surface curves inward.
Concentrated. Describes a solution made by dissolving a large amount of solute in a solvent.
Concentration. A description of the number of molecules found in a given space.
Conduction. Transfer of heat by direct contact.
Conductor. A material that can carry an electric current because electrons can move through it easily.
Convection. Transfer of heat by movement of a heated gas or liquid.
Convex lens. A lens with at least one curved surface that curves outward.
Convex mirror. A curved mirror whose surface curves outward.
Corrosion. The eating away of the surface of a metal by chemical action.
Covalent bond. A chemical bond formed when atoms share two or more electrons.
Crystal. A solid whose orderly arrangement of particles gives it a regular shape.

D

Data. Recorded observations.
Diatomic molecule. A molecule made up of two atoms of the same element.
Dilute. Describes a solution made by dissolving a small amount of solute in a large amount of solvent.
Direct current. An electric current that flows in one direction in an electric circuit.
Doppler effect. An apparent change in the frequency of waves caused by the motion of either the observer or the source of the waves.
Double bond. The bond formed when atoms are joined by sharing two pairs of electrons.

E

Efficiency. Percentage found by comparing the work output of a machine with its work input.
Electric circuit. A complete path through which an electric current flows.
Electric current. The result of electrons moving from one place to another.
Electric field. The region of space around an electrically charged object in which an electric force is noticeable.
Electric force. The force that causes two like-charged objects to repel each other or two unlike-charged objects to attract each other.
Electrolyte. A substance that forms a conducting solution when dissolved in water.
Electromagnet. A temporary magnet made when an electric current flows through a coil of wire wrapped around a piece of iron.
Electromagnetic spectrum. All of the electromagnetic waves.
Electromagnetic induction. Production of an electric current by motion of a conductor in a magnetic field.
Electromagnetic wave. A form of energy that moves through empty space at a speed of 3.0×10^8 m/s.
Electron. A negatively charged particle of matter that is so small it is invisible.
Electron dot model. A way of picturing the outer electrons of an atom by placing dots representing the outer electrons around the atomic symbol.
Electronic device. A device that uses electric circuits in which part of the current flows through a semiconductor, a vacuum, or a gas.
Element. The simplest form of matter.
Endothermic reaction. A chemical reaction that absorbs energy.
Energy. The ability to do work. Energy is commonly expressed in joules.
Energy level. A region around an atomic nucleus in which electrons move.
Engineer. A person who uses technology to make new products or to solve practical problems.
Ester. A kind of molecule formed by combining an organic acid and an alcohol.
Excited electron. An electron that has absorbed energy and has moved farther away from the atomic nucleus.
Exothermic reaction. A chemical reaction that gives off energy in the form of heat.
Experiment. An activity that is designed to test a hypothesis.

F

Fats. Esters formed by combining three organic acids and glycerol.
Fission. A nuclear reaction in which a large unstable nucleus splits into smaller nuclei.
Focal point. The point at which parallel light rays meet after being refracted by a convex lens.
Focus. A point at which light rays come together.
Force. Any push or pull that causes an object to move, or to change its speed or direction of motion.
Frequency. The number of complete waves that pass a given point each second.
Friction. A force that opposes motion.
Fuel. A substance that is used as a source of chemical energy.
Fuse. A part of an electric circuit that prevents too much current from flowing in the circuit.
Fusion. A nuclear reaction in which small nuclei join to form a larger nucleus.

G

Gamma rays. Rays, similar to X-rays, that are emitted when a radioactive atom undergoes gamma decay.

Gravity. The force that tends to pull all objects toward the center of the earth.

H

Half-life. The length of time necessary for one half of a given number of atoms to change into new atoms.

Halogens. A group of elements whose atoms all have one electron less than the stable number.

Heat engine. A machine that changes heat energy into mechanical energy.

Heat of fusion. The amount of heat required to change one gram of a solid to a liquid at the same temperature.

Heat of vaporization. The amount of heat required to change one gram of a liquid to a gas at the same temperature.

Hertz. A unit used to measure the frequency of waves. A frequency of 1 Hz means that one complete wave passes a given point each second (1 wave/s).

Hydrocarbon. A compound containing only carbon and hydrogen.

Hypothesis. A statement that explains a group of related observations.

I

Incandescent. Giving off visible light as a result of being heated.

Indicator. A substance that changes color when put into an acid solution.

Inert. A description of an atom that does not react in nature with other atoms.

Inertia. The resistance of objects to any change in their motion.

Insulator. A material that does not allow electrons to flow through it easily.

Interference. The effect two or more waves have on each other if they overlap.

Interference colors. Colors produced when reflected light waves combine to strengthen or cancel each other.

Ion. An atom or molecule with an electric charge.

Ionic bond. A chemical bond formed when atoms transfer electrons from one to another.

Isomers. Two or more molecules with the same chemical formulas but with different arrangements of their atoms.

Isotopes. Atoms whose nuclei contain the same number of protons but a different number of neutrons, for example, carbon-12 and carbon-14.

K

Kelvin temperature scale. A scale of temperature on which zero is equal to absolute zero.

Kilogram (kg). The basic unit of mass in the metric system.

Kilowatt hour. The amount of energy supplied in one hour by one kilowatt of power. It is used to measure how much electric energy is consumed.

Kinetic energy. Energy that moving things have as a result of their motion.

Kinetic theory of matter. All matter is made of particles whose motion determines whether the matter is solid, liquid, or gas.

L

Laser. A device that produces an intense beam of light of nearly a single frequency.

Law of conservation of energy. Energy cannot be created or destroyed but may be changed from one form to another.

Law of gravitation. The gravitational force between two objects is directly proportional to the product of their masses and inversely proportional to the square of the distance between them.

Lens. A piece of transparent material, often with at least one curved surface, that refracts light passing through it.

Liter (L). A commonly used unit of volume in the metric system.

M

Magnetic field. A region of space around a magnet in which magnetic forces are noticeable.

Magnetic pole. The part of a magnet where the magnetic forces are strongest.

Magnetic variation. The error in a compass caused by the difference in location of the earth's magnetic and geographic poles.

Mass. The amount of matter in an object.

Mass number. The sum of the protons and neutrons in the nucleus of a particular kind of atom.

Measurement. An observation made by comparing something to a standard.

Mechanical advantage. The relationship of the output force of a machine to its input force.

Melting point. The temperature at which a solid becomes a liquid.

Metalloid. An element with some properties of both metals and nonmetals.

Meter (m). The basic unit of length or distance in the metric system.

Mixture. Any matter that contains more than one kind

of molecule and that can be separated by a physical change.

Molecule. The smallest particle of a substance, such as water, that is still that substance.

Motion. A change in position of an object when compared to a reference point.

N

Negative charge. The electric charge given to a hard rubber rod when it is rubbed with fur. An object has a negative charge after it gains electrons.

Neutral (chemistry). A solution or substance that is neither an acid nor a base.

Neutral (electricity). The term describing an object that has equal amounts of positive and negative electric charge.

Neutralization. A chemical reaction that occurs when an acid and a base are mixed.

Noble gases. The six elements whose atoms have completely filled energy levels.

Nonelectrolyte. A substance that forms a nonconducting solution when dissolved in water.

Nuclear reactor. A machine used to produce a controlled nuclear chain reaction.

Nucleus. The small central core of an atom where most of the mass of the atom is located. This core is made up of protons and neutrons.

O

Observation. Any information that we gather by using our senses.

Ohm. A measure of the amount of resistance in an electric circuit. One ohm is equal to a potential difference of one volt per ampere of current flow.

Organic acid. A kind of organic molecule having at least one COOH group.

Organic chemistry. The chemistry of carbon and its compounds.

Oxidation number. The number of electrons gained, lost, or shared by an atom when it forms chemical bonds.

Oxide. Compound formed from oxygen and usually one other material.

P

pH scale. A scale used to measure acidity on which each number lower than the preceding number represents ten times the acidity. For example, a reading of pH 5.0 is 10 times as acidic as a reading of pH 6.0.

Parallel circuit. An electric circuit in which all the parts are in separate branches.

Periodic chart. An arrangement of all the elements, showing the chemical families.

Petroleum. A natural mixture of compounds of carbon and hydrogen.

Physical change. A change in matter in which the individual molecules are not changed.

Physical property. A characteristic of matter that can be observed by using our senses.

Pitch. A property that describes the highness or lowness of a sound; it is determined mainly by the frequency of the sound waves.

Polar molecule. A molecule that carries small electric charges on opposite ends.

Polluted. A description of water or air that contains harmful substances.

Polymer. A long chain-like molecule.

Positive charge. The electric charge given to a glass rod when it is rubbed with a silk cloth. An object has a positive charge after it loses electrons.

Potential energy. Energy stored in an object as a result of a change in its position.

Power. The rate at which work is being done. Power = work/time. It is expressed in joules per second (J/s).

Precipitate. A solid substance that separates from a solution.

Pressure. The amount of force applied to a unit of area.

Primary colors (of light). Red, green, and blue light. These colors of light can be added together to produce any other color.

Prism. A specially shaped piece of glass that can divide white light into its separate colors.

Proteins. Very large molecules formed when many amino acids join together.

Proton. A very small particle of matter with a positive electric charge.

R

Radiation. Transfer of heat through space by infrared waves.

Radical. A group of atoms that remain together in a chemical change and behave as if they were a single atom with a single oxidation number.

Radioactive. An atom is radioactive when its nucleus decays in order to become more stable.

Rays. Straight lines showing the path followed by light.

Reflection. The process in which a wave is thrown back after striking a barrier that does not absorb its energy.

Refraction. The process in which a wave changes direction because its speed changes.

Resistance. Any condition that limits the flow of

electrons in an electric circuit, for example, a light bulb in a circuit.

Resonance. The ability of objects to respond to sounds of certain frequencies.

S

Salt. A compound that is made up of the positive ion from a base and the negative ion from an acid.

Saturated. Describes a solution that has all the solute that it can hold without changing the conditions.

Scientific method. The set of skills used to solve problems in an orderly way.

Scientific model. A kind of mental picture used by scientists to describe something that cannot be seen.

Series circuit. An electric circuit in which all the parts are connected one after another.

Simple machine. A device that can be used to change the direction and size of forces.

Solubility. The amount of solute that can dissolve in a given solvent under a given set of conditions.

Soluble. Describes a substance that can be dissolved in a solvent.

Solute. The part of a solution that is dissolved.

Solution. A mixture that is formed when one kind of molecule fills the spaces between another kind of molecule.

Solvent. The part of a solution that does the dissolving of a solute.

Sound wave. A longitudinal wave moving through air or some other medium.

Specific heat capacity. The amount of heat needed to raise the temperature of one gram of a substance one degree Celsius.

Speed. The distance covered by a moving object per unit of time.

Stable electron arrangement. An arrangement in which all of an atom's energy levels are filled.

Structural formula. A diagram of a molecule showing the bonds between atoms.

Symbol. One or two letters used to represent an atom of a particular element.

T

Technology. The application of scientific knowledge to solve practical problems.

Temperature. Measurement of the average motion of the particles of matter.

Theory. A general statement based on hypotheses that have been tested many times.

Tracers. Radioactive elements that are used to follow atoms through chemical reactions.

Transformer. A part of an electric circuit that changes the voltage of an alternating current.

U

Ultrasonic. Sound waves with frequencies above 20,000 Hz.

V

Valence electrons. Electrons in the outer energy level of an atom that take part in a chemical bond.

Variable. Any factor in an experiment that affects the results of the experiment.

Velocity. The speed and direction of a moving object.

Visible spectrum. The band of colors produced when white light is divided into its separate colors.

Volt. A measure of the electrical potential for doing work in an electric circuit. One volt is equal to one ampere flowing with a resistance of one ohm.

W

Watt. The SI unit of power. It is equal to one joule per second (1 W = 1 J/s).

Wave. A disturbance caused by the movement of energy through a medium.

Wavelength. The distance between two neighboring crests or troughs of a wave.

Weight. A measurement of the gravitational force on an object.

Work. The work done by a force is equal to the size of the force multiplied by the distance through which the force acts.

APPENDIX A: METRIC UNITS (INTERNATIONAL SYSTEM OF UNITS)

BASIC SI UNITS OF MEASUREMENT		
Type of Measurement	Unit	Symbol
length	meter (or metre)	m
mass	kilogram	kg
time	second	s
electric current	ampere	A
thermodynamic temperature	kelvin	K

SI PREFIXES		
Prefix	Symbol	Factor
tera	T	10^{12} (1,000,000,000,000)
giga	G	10^{9} (1,000,000,000)
mega	M	10^{6} (1,000,000)
kilo	k	10^{3} (1,000)
hecto	h	10^{2} (100)
deca	dk	10^{1} (10)
deci	d	10^{-1} (0.1)
centi	c	10^{-2} (0.01)
milli	m	10^{-3} (0.001)
micro	μ	10^{-6} (0.000 000 1)
nano	n	10^{-9} (0. 000 000 000 1)
pico	p	10^{-12} (0. 000 000 000 000 1)

DERIVED UNITS		
Quantity	Unit	Symbol
density	none	kg/m^3
electric potential	volt	V = W/A
electric resistance	ohm	Ω = V/A
energy	joule	J = N·m
force	newton	$N = kg \cdot m/s^2$
frequency	hertz	Hz = 1/s
power	watt	W = J/s

COMMONLY USED METRIC UNITS	
Length 1 kilometer (kg) = 1,000 meters (m) 1 centimeter (cm) = 0.01 m 1 meter (m) = 100 cm 1 millimeter (mm) = 0.001 m 1 meter (m) = 1,000 mm **Mass** 1 kilogram (kg) = 1,000 grams (g) 1 milligram (mg) = 0.001 g 1 gram (g) = 1,000 mg	**Volume** 1 milliliter (mL) = 0.001 liter (L) 1 liter (L) = 1,000 mL **Time** 1 minute (min) = 60 seconds (s) 1 hour (h) = 60 min 1 day (d) = 24 h

APPENDIX B: USING DECIMAL NUMBERS

1. Addition When adding numbers, always line up the decimal points correctly.

a. 153.6 + 6.2 + 12.4

```
 153.6
   6.2
+ 12.4
 172.2
```

b. 31.24 + 5.9 + 6.15

```
 31.24
  5.9
+ 6.15
 43.29
```

2. Subtraction When subtracting numbers, always line up the decimal points correctly.

a. 346.15 − 26.21

```
  346.15
−  26.21
  319.94
```

b. 49.20 − 15.43

```
  49.20
− 15.43
  33.77
```

3. Multiplication When multiplying numbers, it is not necessary to line up decimal points. The number of decimal positions (numbers to the right of the decimal point) in the product is the sum of the number of decimal positions in the numbers being multiplied (factors).

a. 31.46 × 2.3

```
  31.46 (2 decimals)
  ×2.3  (1 decimal)
  9438
 6292
 72.358 (3 decimals)
```

b. 415.10 × 0.156

```
   415.10 (2 decimals)
 × 0.156  (3 decimals)
  249060
 207550
41510
64.75560 (5 decimals)
```

4. Division Division expresses how many times one number goes into another number. Division may be shown as

4.05 ÷ 0.5, as $\frac{4.05}{0.5}$, or as 0.5)4.05

When dividing numbers, only whole numbers can be used as divisors. This means that 0.5 must be multiplied by 10 to make it a whole number. In order not to change the value, 4.05 must also be multiplied by 10. Thus the division is

```
            8.1 (quotient)
(divisor) 5)40.5 (dividend)
           40.0
              5
              5
```

Notice that the decimal in the quotient is located directly over the decimal in the dividend.

a. 32.4 ÷ 0.40

```
          81
0.40.)32.40.
      32 0
         40
         40
```

b. $\frac{4.4748}{3.6}$

```
       1.243
3.6.)4.4.748
     3 6
       8 7
       7 2
       1 54
       1 44
         108
         108
```

5. Finding An Average To average several numbers, find their sum and then divide by the number of values that were added to give the sum. For example, find the average of the four measurements 2.3 cm, 1.8 cm, 2.1 cm, and 2.2 cm. First add:

```
2.3 cm
1.8 cm
2.1 cm
2.2 cm
8.4 cm
```

Then divide by 4:

```
  2.1 cm
4)8.4 cm
  8.0
    4
    4
```

The average of the four measurements is 2.1 cm.

6. Metric Conversions One of the advantages of using metric units is the ease of converting one unit of measurement to another. For example, suppose a measurement is 2.5 cm. You can easily convert this measurement to meters. Since 1 cm = 0.01 m, 2.5 cm = 0.025 m. The calculation is as follows:

$$2.5\ \cancel{\text{cm}} \times \frac{0.01\ \text{m}}{1\ \cancel{\text{cm}}} = 0.025\ \text{m}$$

All conversions in the metric system result in multiplying by a decimal fraction or a multiple of 10. Remember, every measurement must consist of a number and a metric unit. The original unit disappears, leaving the unit to which you are converting.

INDEX

Note: Page numbers in **boldface** type refer to illustrations and those in *italic* type refer to definitions.

A

B

C

D

E

F

G

H

I

J

K

L

M

N

O

P

T

U

V

W

X

PHOTO CREDITS

HRW Photos by Charles Biasiny-Rivera appear on pages: 270 (l), 484
HRW Photos by Bruce Buck appear on pages: 60 (br), 64, 66 (all), 68 (r), 70, 85, 165, 185, 200, 483
HRW Photos by Russell Dian appear on pages: 62, 67, 109, 246, 271, 431, 435 (b), 444, 462, 463, 464
HRW Photo by Louis Fernandez appears on page 69
HRW Photos by Richard Haynes appear on pages: 5 (r), 44, 46 (l), 68 (l), 73, 99 (r), 120, 135 (b), 178, 211 (r), 234, 249, 269 (l), (r), 270 (b), 272 (t), (b), 273, 286, 294 (b), 295, 300, 308, 323, 328, 339, 340, 361 (l), 461, 481, 494
HRW Photos by Ken Karp appear on pages: 299, 350, 351, 354, 379, 414 (all), 479
HRW Photos by Yoav Levy/Phototake appear on pages: 60 (t), 94 (l), 135 (t), (c), 425, 455 (b), 459, 482
HRW Photos by Carol Lynch Michel appear on pages: 60 (bl), 197 (t), (b), 446, 455 (t)
HRW Photo by David Spindel appears on page 29(t)

Chapter 1 p. xii James E. Stoots, Jr./Lawrence Livermore Laboratory; p. 2 Ted Spiegel/Black Star 1982; p. 3 George Hall/Woodfin Camp; p. 4 Joe Azzara/The Image Bank; p. 5(l) Jeff Simon/Wheeler Pictures; p. 6 Jet Propulsion Laboratories; p. 8(t) Joe McNally/Wheeler Pictures; p. 8(b) NASA; p. 10 Michael Melford/Wheeler Pictures: p. 25(c) Howard Sochurek.

UNIT 1 p. 28–29 James Balog **Chapter 2** p. 30 "1984" by Thomas Porter, based on research by Robert Cook. © 1984, Lucasfilm, Ltd.; p. 36 Pat Rogers/The Image Bank; p. 42 Wm.Conway/N.Y. Zoolog. Soc.; p. 43 Eunice Harris/Photo Researchers; p. 45 NASA; p. 55 © John McGrail/Wheeler Pictures **Chapter 3** p. 58 © Mike Mitchell/ Photo Unique; p. 74–75 NASA; p. 79 Roger Ressmeyer/Wheeler Pictures **Chapter 4** p. 82 David Mitchell/Photo Unique; p. 84 Sharon Greer/The Stock Market; p. 87 Thomas Braise/The Stock Market; p. 92 Adam Woolfit/Woodfin Camp; p. 93 A. Howarth/Int. Stock Photo.; p. 94(r) © Frank Grant/Int. Stock Photo; p. 96(t) © Robert Perron; p. 96(b) Greg Davis/Black Star; p. 97 © James Balst; p. 98 Allan Weitz/ Black Star; p. 99(l) © Will Stanton/Int. Stock Photo **Chapter 5** p. 102 © Vanscan/Thermagram Daedelius Enterprises, Inc., Courtesy of National Geographic Magazine; p. 105 Richard Choy/Peter Arnold; p. 111(t) Bettmann Archive; (r) Al Assid/The Stock Market; p. 113(t) NASA; (b) Dennis Brack/Black Star; p. 114(t) Dennis Brack/Black Star; (b) © Van Scan/Daedelius Ent.; p. 115(t) Thomas Braise/The Stock Market; (b) Doug Kirkland/Woodfin Camp; p. 116(t) Allan Weitz/Black Star; (b) Doug Kirkland/Woodfin Camp; p. 118 Dudley Foster/Woods Hole Oceanographic Inst.; p. 127 © Dan McCoy.

UNIT 2 p. 130–131 Douglas Faulkner/Photo Researchers **Chapter 6** p. 132 © Gregory Heisler/Wheeler Pictures; p. 134 M. Dohrn/Science Photo Lib.; p. 143 © Robert Perron; p. 147(l) Michal Heron/Woodfin Camp; p. 147(r) © Jim Balog **Chapter 7** p. 150 Dr. Karl A. Stetson; p. 158 Bill Pierce/Rainbow; p. 160(t) Lou Jones/The Image Bank; (b) Leroy Woodson/Wheeler Pictures; p. 161 Fred Ward/Black Star; p. 163 Sepp Setz/Woodfin Camp; p. 169(l) © R.C.A.; (r) © Alexander Tsiaris/ Photo Researchers **Chapter 8** p. 172 © Burt Glinn/Magnum; p. 174 Marion Patterson/Photo Researchers; p. 185 Ted Spiegel/Black Star; p. 186 Michaud Grapes/Photo Researchers; p. 182 NASA; p. 186 Courtesy of Time/Life Books Life Science Library; p. 188 Fred Ward/Black Star; p. 189 Jack Couffer/Bruce Coleman; p. 201 © Hank Morgan/Photo Researchers **Chapter 9** p. 206 © Erich Hartmann/Magnum; p. 208(t) Bausch and Lomb; (b) Akuma Takagami/Int. Stock Photo; p. 209 Harold Sund/The Image Bank; p. 210 Sepp Seitz/Woodfin Camp; p. 211(l) Gary Cralle/The Image Bank; p. 212 Chuck O'Rear/Woodfin Camp; p. 213 Alexander Tsiaris/Photo Researchers; p. 215 Chuck O'Rear/West Light/Woodfin Camp; p. 220 Prism Photography/Woodfin Camp; p. 221 Bill Strode/Woodfin Camp; p. 224 Russ Kinne/Photo Researchers; p. 227 © Thomas Poerett/Photo Researchers

UNIT 3 p. 230–231 © Hank Brandli **Chapter 10** p. 232 Craig Aurness/ West Light; p. 235 Courtesy of Ontario Science Center; p. 236 Granger Collection; p. 244 Thomas Ives/Black Star; p. 251 Jack Dermid/Bruce Coleman; p. 256 Andy Levin/Black Star; p. 259(l) © James Broderick/ Int. Stock Photo.; (r) © Tom Tracy **Chapter 11** p. 262 A.T. and T., Bell Labs; p. 268 Ted Cowell/Black Star; p. 276 Chuck O'Rear/Woodfin Camp; p. 277 Bettmann Archive; p. 279 Chuck O'Rear/Woodfin Camp; p. 285 James Balog/Black Star; p. 287 © Jim Balog **Chapter 12** p. 292 L.A. Frank/University of Iowa; p. 304 Larry Imperiale/Black Star; p. 306 © Tom Tracy; p. 315 R.C.A.

UNIT 4 p. 318–319 © Roger Sliva **Chapter 13** p. 320 Dr. Robert Mark; p. 322 NASA; p. 325(l) David Pollack/The Stock Market; (r) © Robin Lehman/The Stock Market; p. 336(t)(b) Smithsonian Institution; p. 337(t) © Robert Frerck; (b) Carl Zeiss/Bruce Coleman; p. 338 L.S. Stfanowicz/Bruce Coleman; p. 345(l) © Erich Hartmann/Magnum; (r) © Dan McCoy/Rainbow **Chapter 14** p. 348 © Michael Melford/ Wheeler Pictures; p. 356(l+r) Antonio Cusmao/Black Star; p. 358(t) © Vince Streano/The Stock Market; (b) Willie Rivelli/The Image Bank; p. 361(r) © Tom Tracy **Chapter 15** p. 364 Dr. Albert V. Crewe/ University of Chicago; p. 366(l) Bettmann Archive; p. 370(t) Dan McCoy/Rainbow; (b) Bettmann Archive; p. 374 Courtesy of A/P Neils Bohr Library; p. 383 © Malcom Kirk/Peter Arnold

UNIT 5 p. 386–387 © Michael Melford/Wheeler Pictures **Chapter 16** p. 388 © Manfred Kage/Peter Arnold p. 390 Jawitz/The Image Bank; p. 391 Sargent Welch Scientific; p. 393 Dan McCoy/Rainbow; p. 398 © Shelley Katz/Black Star; p. 399 Wide World; p. 402 University of New Hampshire/Marine Program; p. 404 New York Public Library; p. 410 Brad Hess/Black Star; p. 417 NASA **Chapter 17** p. 420 Dr. Crewe/University of Chicago; p. 435(t) Dan McCoy/Rainbow **Chapter 18** p. 438 © Gabriel Covian/The Image Bank; p. 441 Melchoir Di Giacomo/The Image Bank; p. 445 H. Wendler/The Image Bank; p. 449 © John McGrail/Wheeler Pictures; p. 452 Focus on Sports; p. 469(r) © Paolo Koch/Photo Researchers; (l) © R.S. Uzzell/Woodfin Camp.

UNIT 6 p. 472–473 © 1983 Hiroyuki Matsumoto/Black Star **Chapter 19** p. 474 Chuck O'Rear/Woodfin Camp; p. 478 © Michael Melford/ Wheeler Pictures; p. 488 Hiroyuki Matsumoto/Black Star; p. 490 American Museum of Natural History; p. 491 James Siegal/Black Star; p. 492 © Michael Melford/Wheeler Pictures; p. 495 Lawrence Berkley Laboratory **Chapter 20** p. 498 © Manfred Kage/Peter Arnold; p. 500 G.M. Smith/The Image Bank; p. 501 © Michael Melford/Wheeler Pictures; p. 516 © H. Wendler/The Image Bank; p. 519(l) © James Broderick/Int. Stock Photo; (r) Ted Spiegel/Black Star **Chapter 21** p. 524 Lawrence Livermore Laboratory; p. 526 The Bettmann Archive; p. 528 © William Rivelli/The Image Bank; p. 529 © Dan McCoy/ Rainbow; p. 530 Science Photo Library, London; p. 536 Los Alamos National Laboratory; p. 537(t) Hank Morgan/Photo Researchers; (b) A/P Niels Bohr Library; p. 540(t) NASA; (b) Lawrence Livermore Laboratory; p. 542 Lawrence Livermore Laboratory; p. 545 Princeton Plasma Physics Laboratory